Time Out

Berlin

timeout.com/berlin

Penguin Books

PENGUIN BOOKS

Published by the Penguin Group
Penguin Books Ltd, 80 Strand, London WC2R ORL, England
Penguin Books USA Inc., 375 Hudson Street, New York, New York 10014, USA
Penguin Books Australia Ltd, 250 Camberwell Road, Camberwell, Victoria 3124, Australia
Penguin Books Canada Ltd, 10 Alcorn Avenue, Toronto, Ontario, Canada M4V 3B2
Penguin Books (NZ) Ltd, cnr Rosedale and Airborne Roads, Albany, Auckland, New Zealand

Penguin Books Ltd, Registered Offices: Harmondsworth, Middlesex, England

First published 1993
Second edition 1995
Third edition 1998
Fourth edition 2000
Fifth edition 2002
10 9 8 7 6 5 4 3 2 1

Colour reprographics by Icon, Crown House, 56-58 Southwark Street, London SE1
and Precise Litho, 34-35 Great Sutton Street, London EC1
Printed and bound by Cayfosa-Quebecor, Ctra. de Caldes, Km 3 08 130 Sta, Perpètua de Mogoda, Barcelona, Spain

Edited and designed by
Time Out Guides Limited
Universal House
251 Tottenham Court Road
London W1T 7AB
Tel + 44 (0)20 7813 3000
Fax + 44 (0)20 7813 6001
Email guides@timeout.com
www.timeout.com

Editorial

Editor Jonathan Cox
Deputy Editor Ismay Atkins
Listings Researchers Michael Bennett, Jens Meyer, Gregor Ohlerich
Proofreader Tamsin Shelton
Indexer Selena Cox

Editorial Director Peter Fiennes
Series Editor Ruth Jarvis
Deputy Series Editor Jonathan Cox

Design

Group Art Director John Oakey
Art Director Mandy Martin
Art Editor Scott Moore
Designers Benjamin de Lotz, Lucy Grant
Scanning/Imaging Dan Conway
Ad Make-up Glen Impey
Picture Editor Kerri Littlefield
Deputy Picture Editor Kit Burnet
Picture Librarian Sarah Roberts

Advertising

Group Commercial Director Lesley Gill
Sales Director Mark Phillips
International Sales Co-ordinator Ross Canadé
Advertisement Sales (Berlin) WAS Werbe- und Anzeigenservice GmbH
Advertising Assistant Sabrina Ancilleri

Administration

Publisher Tony Elliott
Managing Director Mike Hardwick
Group Financial Director Kevin Ellis
Marketing Director Christine Cort
Marketing Manager Mandy Martinez
US Publicity & Marketing Associate Rosella Albanese
Group General Manager Nichola Coulthard
Production Manager Mark Lamond
Production Controller Samantha Furniss
Accountant Sarah Bostock

Features in this guide were written and researched by:
Introduction Kevin Cote. **History** Frederick Studemann (*von Humboldts, Schinkel & JFK* Jonathan Cox). **Berlin Today** Natalie Gravenor (*Modern Jewish life* Miriam Singer). **Architecture** Francesca Rogier, Ulf Meyer (*Embassy row* Sophie Lovell). **Accommodation** Sophie Lovell. **Sightseeing** Kevin Cote, Jonathan Cox, Dave Rimmer, Ed Ward (*America's post-Cold War plot* Kevin Cote; *Moses Mendelssohn* Miriam Singer; *Palace for the workers* Martin Kaluza; *The time machine* Kevin Cote; *The Jewish Museum* Jonathan Cox; *Käthe Kollwitz* Ismay Atkins; *A walk on the wild side* Natalie Gravenor). **Restaurants** JJ Gordon, April Lamm, Dave Rimmer, Ed Ward (*Fat chance* Ed Ward). **Cafés, Bars & Pubs** Harry Acton, Jonathan Gainer, Natalie Gravenor, Martin Kaluza, April Lamm, Dave Rimmer, Paul Threlby, Ed Ward (*The breakfast club* Miriam Singer). **Shops & Services** Julie Wedow (*From Berlin Wall to Berlin mall* Natalie Gravenor). **By Season** Lisa Ellis, Ed Meza (*Slaves to love* Ed Meza, Mark Reeder). **Children** Rudi Teichmann. **Film** Andrew Horn. **Galleries** Sophie Lovell. **Gay & Lesbian** Jens Friedrich. **Music: Rock, World & Jazz** Natalie Gravenor. **Nightlife** Natalie Gravenor, Martin Kaluza. **Cabaret** Ingrid Beerbaum. **Performing Arts** *Music: Classical & Opera* Rick Perera. **Theatre** Ingrid Beerbaum. **Dance** Julie Wedow. **Sport & Fitness** Natalie Gravenor, Constance Hanna (*Union keep the red flag flying* Peterjon Cresswell). **Trips Out of Town** Jonathan Cox, Martin Kaluza, Miriam Singer, Ed Ward. **Directory** Chris Bohn, Kevin Cote, Jonathan Cox, John Fitzsimons, Natalie Gravenor, Biba Kopf, Dave Rimmer, Frederick Studemann, Ed Ward (*Going Bezirk* Natalie Gravenor).

The Editor would like to thank:
Kevin Cote, Jan Fuscoe, Natalie Gravenor, Sophie Lovell, Gregor Ohlerich, Mark Reeder.

Maps by JS Graphics, 17 Beadles Lane, Old Oxted, Surrey RH8 9JG.

Photography by Alys Tomlinson except: pages 7, 10, 11, 12, 13, 18, 21, 23, 26, 111, 195 AKG London; page 8 Hulton Archive; page 43 Peter Cook/View Pictures; page 187 Jeurgen Stumpe; pages 98, 212, 260, 261, 262, 266 Jonathan Cox; pages 100, 215, 243 Hadley Kincade; page 224 Hadley Hudson; page 247 Clive Brunskill/Allsport; page 249 Connie Hanna.

The following images were supplied by the featured establishments: pages 127, 185, 198, 237, 238.

Contents

Introduction

Here you are, just hopped off the S-Bahn at Hackescher Markt, in Berlin's central Mitte district. A brand new park is full of young people sitting in the shade chatting, resting, laughing with each other. Tables from cafés under the train arches spill out on to the pavements. The streets to the north have the city's highest concentration of restaurants with a buzz, bars with a design, businesses with an internet angle, art galleries with an attitude and boutiques with an agenda.

Further up Rosenthaler Strasse, the quirky stuff in the shop windows, the mix of people emerging from hidden courtyards, the club flyers littering the pavements and the posters for video festivals on construction barriers... you've suddenly discovered a part of Berlin with human dimensions. A hood you can identify with. The part of town that is going to deliver the inspiration, the adventure or whatever else lured you here in the first place.

But here's the strange thing: appealing as it is, this is the one neighbourhood that real Berliners loathe. Go to rabble-rousing Kreuzberg just to the south, and you'll see reasonable folk wearing 'Mitte Sucks' T-shirts.

Why this is so is one of the most essential things to understand when choosing to visit Berlin over a decade after the excision of the Berlin Wall, and a handful of years after the arrival of the government from Bonn.

Shortly after reunification, there was all kinds of speculation. Among the early predictions: Berlin's combined population would soar from 3.5 to five million by the year 2000. They got it wrong, and by a long shot. Bad enough that the 1.5 million new taxpayers never materialised, but by 2001, the population had actually shrunk by a few hundred thousand.

Now the demographers are saying something more sensible, and much more startling. By 2010, Berlin's population should remain at current levels. But over a quarter of the city's populace will have replaced itself. That means if you visit now, you'll witness nearly a million burned out Berliners heading for the exit, nearly a million enthusiastic new Berliners heading for... Berlin Mitte!

Well, that's the way it seems sometimes. At least that's why defiant Kreuzbergers wear those T-shirts. Most aren't quite this in-your-face about it, but one way or another, every Berliner's life is being touched by the unprecedented demographic upheaval that is tucking and pulling at the fabric of the entire city today.

To prevail, this city can't afford a simple one-to-one exchange of residents. Those one million new Berliners will have to bring something to the game. Jobs. Taxes. Higher disposable incomes. Ideas. Call it urban Darwinism: Berlin evolving in uncontrolled fits and spurts to attract the population mix it needs to survive.

This explains what you see when you come to Berlin today. Architects, performers, entrepreneurs, lots of people pushing established limits in the search of new audiences. A dramatic contrast among even similar neighbourhoods, like Mitte and Kreuzberg. Extraordinary variety in restaurants and nightlife. An expansive urban infrastructure, including public transport and cultural institutions, that is relatively cheap and user-friendly.

As Berlin grapples with the forces of urban Darwinism, sure, there is a lot of dumbing down. But also plenty of wising-up. The opportunity to be swept up in this upheaval, and along with the Berliners, pass judgement on it, will be a compelling reason to visit Europe's youngest capital city for years to come.

ABOUT THE TIME OUT CITY GUIDES

The *Time Out Berlin Guide* is one of an expanding series of Time Out City Guides, now numbering over 35, produced by the people behind London and New York's successful listings magazines. Our guides are all written and updated by resident experts who have striven to provide you with all the most up-to-date information you'll need to explore the city or read up on its background, whether you're a local or a first-time visitor.

THE LOWDOWN ON THE LISTINGS

Above all, we've tried to make this guide as useful as possible. Addresses, telephone numbers, websites, transport information, opening times, admission prices and credit card details are all included in our listings. And, as far as possible, we've given details of facilities, services and events, all checked and correct as we went to press. However, owners and managers can change their arrangements at any time. Before you go out of your way,

we'd advise you whenever possible to phone and check opening times, ticket prices and other particulars.

While every effort has been made to ensure the accuracy of the information contained in this guide, the publishers cannot accept responsibility for any errors it may contain.

PRICES AND PAYMENT

The prices we've supplied were correct at the time of going to press, but should be treated as guidelines, not gospel. If prices vary wildly from those we've quoted, please write and let us know. We aim to give the best and most up-to-date advice, so we always want to know if you've been badly treated or overcharged.

We have noted where shops, restaurants, hotels and so on accept the following credit cards: American Express (**AmEx**), Diners Club (**DC**), MasterCard (**MC**) and Visa (**V**). Be aware that credit cards are not as widely accepted in Berlin (particularly in bars and cafés) as in many major European and US cities. Some shops, restaurants and attractions take travellers' cheques.

THE LIE OF THE LAND

Berlin is a big, sprawling city. For ease of use, we've split many chapters in this guide into districts. The first page of each sightseeing chapter contains a small locator map, by which you can see how each area relates to those around it, and there are also detailed street maps at the back of this guide. Wherever possible, a map reference is provided for every venue listed, indicating the page and grid reference at which it can be found on the street maps. The most convenient public transport options are also listed.

There is an online version of this guide, as well as weekly events listings for 35 international cities, at www.timeout.com.

TELEPHONE NUMBERS

The code for Berlin is 030, which should be dialled before the relevant number when calling the city from within Germany. From abroad, you need to dial the international access code followed by 49 for Germany, 30 for Berlin and then the number. For more information on telephones and codes, *see p283*.

ESSENTIAL INFORMATION

For all the practical information you might need for visiting Berlin, including emergency phone numbers, visa and customs information, advice on facilities for the disabled, useful websites and details of local transport, turn to the **Directory** chapter at the back of the guide. It starts on page 270.

LANGUAGE

Many Berliners, particularly younger people, speak at least some English, and a fair number speak the language extremely well, but you cannot assume that you will be understood. A few basic phrases in German can go a long way, and it's particularly useful having a dictionary handy in restaurants – outside the main tourist areas, many places only have menus in German.

MAPS

The map section at the back of this book starts with an overview of the greater Berlin area, and follows with eight pages of detailed street maps of the central districts (with a street index following). The back page contains a close-up map of Mitte, the area within which many visitors spend the majority of their time. There is also a map of the U- and S-Bahn network. The maps start on page 298.

LET US KNOW WHAT YOU THINK

We hope you enjoy the *Time Out Berlin Guide*, and we'd like to know what you think of it. We welcome tips for places that you consider we should include in future editions and take note of your criticism of our choices. There's a reader's reply card at the back of this book for your feedback, or you can email us at berlinguide@timeout.com.

Advertisers

We would like to stress that no venue or establishment has been included in this guide because it has advertised in any of our publications and no payment of any kind has influenced any review. The opinions given in this book are those of *Time Out* writers and entirely independent.

In Context

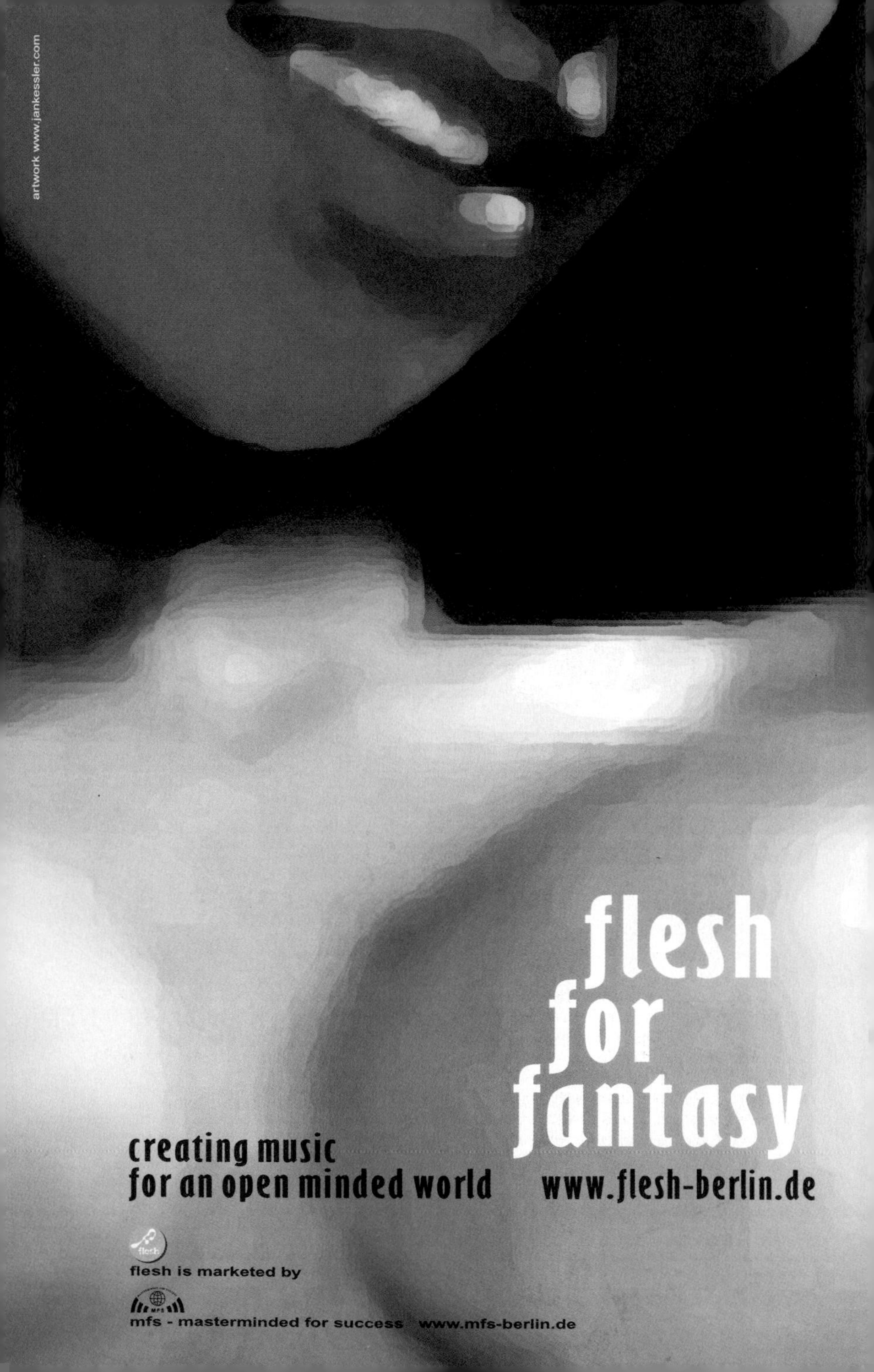
artwork www.jankessler.com
flesh
for
fantasy
creating music
for an open minded world
www.flesh-berlin.de
flesh is marketed by
mfs - masterminded for success www.mfs-berlin.de

History

From twin trading town to reunited capital city, via wars, revolutions and totalitarianism – Berlin's seen it all.

Berlin's origins are neither remarkable nor auspicious. A settlement emerged sometime in the 12th century on unpromising swamplands that pioneering German knights had wrested from the Slavs. The name Berlin is believed to be derived from the Slav word *birl*, meaning swamp.

Facing off across the Spree river, Berlin and its twin settlement Cölln (on what is now the Museumsinsel) were founded as trading posts halfway between the older fortress towns of Spandau and Köpenick. Today the borough of Mitte embraces Cölln and old Berlin, and Spandau and Köpenick are outlying suburbs. The town's existence was first recorded in 1237, when Cölln was mentioned in a church document, and in the same century construction began on the Marienkirche and Nikolaikirche churches, both of which still stand.

The Ascanian family, who held the title of Margraves of Brandenburg, ruled over the twin towns and the surrounding region. Eager to encourage trade, they granted special rights to merchants with the result that Berlin and Cölln emerged as prosperous trading centres linking east and west Europe. In 1307 the two towns were officially united.

Early years of prosperity came to an end in 1319 with the death of the last Ascanian ruler. This opened the way for robber barons from the outlying regions, eager to take control of Berlin. But, despite political upheaval and the threat of invasion, Berlin's merchants did manage to continue business. In 1359 the city joined the Hanseatic League of free-trading northern European cities.

THE HOHENZOLLERNS ARRIVE

But the threat of invasion remained. Towards the end of the 14th century two powerful families, the Dukes of Pomerania and the brutal von Quitzow brothers, began to vie for control of the city.

Salvation came with Friedrich of Hohenzollern, a nobleman from southern Germany sent by the Holy Roman Emperor in 1411 to bring peace to the region. Initially,

Friedrich was well received. The bells of the Marienkirche were melted down to be made into weapons for the fight against the aggressors. (In an echo of history, the Marienkirche bells were again transformed into tools of war in 1917, in the reign of Kaiser Wilhelm II, the last of the Hohenzollerns to rule.)

Having defeated the von Quitzow brothers, Friedrich officially became Margrave. In 1416 he took the further title of Elector of Brandenburg, denoting his right to vote in the election of the Holy Roman Emperor – titular head of the German-speaking states.

Gradually, Berlin was transformed from an outlying trading post to a small-sized capital (in 1450 the population was 6,000). In 1442 foundations were laid for Berlin Castle and a royal court was established.

With peace and stability came the loss of independent traditions as Friedrich consolidated power. Disputes rose between the patrician classes (representing trade) and the guilds (representing crafts). Rising social friction culminated in the 'Berlin Indignation' of 1447-8 when the population rose up in rebellion. Friedrich's son, Friedrich II, and his courtiers were locked out of the city and the foundations of the castle were flooded, but within months the uprising collapsed and the Hohenzollerns returned triumphant. Merchants were shouldered with new restrictions, while courtiers were exempted from communal jurisdiction, and the city began to lose economic impetus.

REFORMATION AND DEBAUCHERY

The Reformation arrived in Berlin and Brandenburg under the reign of Joachim I Nestor (1535-71), the first Elector to embrace Protestantism. Joachim strove to improve the cultural standing of Berlin by inviting artists, architects and theologians to work in the city. In 1538 Caspar Theyss and Konrad Krebbs, two master-builders from Saxony, began work on a Renaissance-style palace. The building took a hundred years to complete, and evolved into the bombastic Stadtschloss (*pictured p 7*), which stood on what is now Museuminsel in the Spree until the East German government demolished it in 1950.

> ## "The people are good, but rough and unpolished; they prefer stuffing themselves to good science."

Joachim's studious nature was not reflected in the behaviour of his subjects. In a foretaste of Berlin's later reputation for

Anti-Semitic pamphlet against Berlin Jews.

debauchery and decadence, self-indulgence characterised much of life in the late 16th-century city. Repeated attempts to clamp down on excessive drinking, rampant gambling and loose morals had little effect. Visiting the city, Abbot Trittenheim remarked that 'the people are good, but rough and unpolished; they prefer stuffing themselves to good science'.

After stuffing itself with another 6,000 people, Berlin left the 16th century with a population of 12,000 – double that of a hundred years earlier.

WAR AND RECONSTRUCTION

The outbreak of the Thirty Years War in 1618 dragged Berlin on to the wider political stage. Although initially unaffected by the conflict between Catholic forces loyal to the Holy Roman Empire and the Swedish-backed Protestant armies, Berlin was eventually caught up in the war, which was to leave the German-speaking states ravaged, divided and weakened for over two centuries.

In 1626 imperial troops occupied Berlin and plundered the city. In the following years Berlin was repeatedly sacked and forced to pay special taxes to the occupying forces. Trade collapsed and its hinterland was laid waste. To top it all, there were four serious epidemics between 1626 and 1631 that claimed thousands of lives. By the time the war ended in 1648, Berlin had lost a third of its housing stock, the population had fallen to less than 6,000 and the municipal coffers were greatly depleted.

THE GREAT ELECTOR

Painstaking reconstruction was carried out under Friedrich Wilhelm, known as the Great Elector. He succeeded his father in 1640, but chose to see out the war in exile. Influenced by Dutch ideas on town planning and architecture (he was married to a Princess of Orange), Friedrich Wilhelm embarked on a policy that linked urban regeneration, economic expansion and solid defence.

New fortifications were built around the city, and a garrison of 2,000 soldiers established as Friedrich expanded his 'Residenzstadt'. In the centre of town, the Lustgarten was laid out opposite the palace. Running west from the palace, the first Lindenallee ('Avenue of Lime Trees' or Unter den Linden) was created.

To revive the economy, housing and property taxes were abolished in favour of a modern-style sales tax. With the money that was raised, three new towns – Friedrichswerder, Dorotheenstadt and Friedrichstadt – were built. (Together with Berlin and Cölln, today these make up the district of Mitte.) In the late 1660s a canal was constructed linking the Spree and Oder rivers, confirming Berlin's position as an east–west trading centre.

But Friedrich Wilhelm's most inspired policy was to encourage refugees to settle in the city. First to arrive were over 50 Jewish families from Vienna. In 1672 Huguenot settlers arrived from France. The influence of the arrivals was pronounced, bringing new skills and industries to Berlin.

The growing cosmopolitan mix laid the foundations for a flowering of intellectual and artistic life. By the time the Great Elector's son Friedrich III took the throne in 1688, one in five Berliners spoke French. This legacy can be seen in the many French words that still pepper Berlin dialect, such as boulette ('hamburger') and étage ('floor').

In 1695 work commenced on Schloss Charlottenburg to the west of Berlin. A year later the Academy of Arts was founded, and, in 1700, intellectual life was further stimulated by the founding of the Academy of Sciences under Gottfried Leibniz. The building of the German and French cathedrals at Gendarmenmarkt in 1701 gave Berlin one of its loveliest squares. Five years later the Zeughaus ('Armoury'), now housing the Deutsches Historisches Museum, was completed on Unter den Linden.

In 1701 Elector Friedrich III took a step up the hierarchy of European nobility when he had himself crowned Prussian King Friedrich I (not to be confused with the earlier Elector). In little more than half a century, Berlin had progressed from a devastated town to a thriving commercial centre with a population of nearly 30,000.

THE PRUSSIANS ARE COMING

The common association of Prussia with militarism can broadly be traced back to the 18th century and the efforts of two men in particular: King Friedrich Wilhelm I and his son Friedrich II (also known as Frederick the Great). Although father and son hated each other, and had very different sensibilities (Friedrich Wilhelm was boorish and mean, Friedrich II sensitive and philosophical), together they launched Prussia as a major military power, and, in the process, gave Berlin the character of a garrison city.

> ## 'With a king much more interested in keeping the books than reading them, intellectual life suffered.'

King Friedrich Wilhelm I (1713-40) made parsimony and militarism state policy – and almost succeeded in driving Berlin's economy into the ground. The only thing that grew was the army, which by 1740 numbered 80,000 troops. Many of these were deployed in Berlin and billeted in the houses of ordinary citizens.

With a king much more interested in keeping the books than reading them, intellectual life suffered. Friedrich Wilhelm had no use for art, so he closed down the Academy of Arts; instead he collected soldiers, and swapped a rare collection of oriental vases for one of the King of Saxony's regiments. The Tsar received a small gold ship in exchange for 150 Russian giants.

But the obsession with all things military did have some positive effects. The King needed competent soldiers, so he made school compulsory; the army needed doctors, so he set up medical institutes. Eventually Berlin's economy also picked up on the back of demand from the military. City administration was reformed. Skilled immigrants (this time mostly from Saxony) met the increased demand. The result was a population boom (from 60,000 in 1713 to 90,000 in 1740) and a growth in trade and manufacturing.

FREDERICK THE GREAT

While his father collected soldiers, Frederick the Great (Friedrich II) deployed them – in a series of wars with Austria and Russia (from 1740-42, 1744-5 and 1756-63; the latter known as the Seven Years War) in a bid to win territory in Silesia in the east. Initially, the wars proved disastrous. The Austrians occupied Berlin city in 1757, the Russians in 1760. However, thanks to a mixture of good fortune and military genius, Frederick finally emerged victorious from the Seven Years War.

When not fighting, the King devoted his time to forging a modern state apparatus (he liked to call himself 'first servant of the state'; Berliners simply called him 'Old Fritz') and transforming Berlin and Potsdam. This was achieved partly through conviction – the King was friends with Voltaire and brought him to live at Potsdam, and Old Fritz saw himself very much as an aesthetically minded figure of the Enlightenment – but it was also a political necessity. He needed to convince enemies and subjects that even in times of national crisis he was able to afford grand projects.

So Unter den Linden was transformed into a grand boulevard. At the palace end, the Forum Fredericianum, designed and constructed by the architect von Knobelsdorff, comprised the Staatsoper, St Hedwigskathedrale, Prince Heinrich Palace (now housing Humboldt-Universität) and the Staatsbibliotek. Although it was never fully completed, the Forum remains one of Berlin's main attractions today.

To the west of Berlin, the Tiergarten was landscaped and a new palace, Schloss Bellevue (now the Berlin residence of the German president), was built. Frederick also decided

Francophone **Frederick the Great**. *See p9.*

to replace a set of barracks at Gendarmenmarkt with a theatre, now called the Konzerthaus.

To encourage manufacturing and industry (particularly textiles), advantageous excise laws were introduced. Businesses such as the KPM (Königliche Porzellan-Manufaktur) porcelain works were nationalised and turned into prestigious and lucrative enterprises.

Legal and administrative reforms also characterised Frederick's reign. Religious freedom was enshrined in law, torture was abolished and Berlin became a centre of the Enlightenment. Cultural and intellectual life blossomed around figures such as philosopher Moses Mendelssohn (*see p82* **Ich bin Berliner: Moses Mendelssohn**) and poet Gottfried Lessing.

By the time Friedrich died in 1786, Berlin had a population of 150,000 and was the capital of one of Europe's grand powers.

ENLIGHTENMENT'S END

The death of Frederick the Great also marked the end of the Enlightenment in Prussia. His successor, Friedrich Wilhelm II, was more interested in spending money on architecture than wasting his time with political philosophy. Censorship was stepped up and the King's extravagance plunged the state into an economic and financial crisis. By 1788 over 14,000 people in the city were dependent on state and church aid. The state apparatus began to crumble under the weight of incompetent and greedy administrators. When he died in 1797 Friedrich Wilhelm II left his son with huge debts.

> **'Towards the turn of the century, Berlin became a centre of German Romanticism.'**

However, the old King's expensive love of classicism left Berlin with its most famous monument: the Brandenburger Tor (Brandenburg Gate). It was built by Karl Gottfried Langhans in 1789, the year of the French Revolution, and modelled on the Propylaea in Athens. Two years later, Johann Schadow added the Quadriga, a sculpture of a bare-chested Victoria riding a chariot drawn by four horses. Originally one of 14 gates marking Berlin's boundaries, the Brandenburger Tor is now the geographical and symbolic centre of the city.

If the King did not care for intellect, then the emerging bourgeoisie did. Towards the turn of the century, Berlin became a centre of German Romanticism. Literary salons

Wir sind Berliner the von Humboldts

As you stroll along Unter den Linden, stop for a moment to contemplate the two statues flanking the gate of the **Humboldt-Universität**. They represent two remarkable, multi-talented brothers: **Wilhelm von Humboldt** (1767-1834; *pictured*) and **Alexander von Humboldt** (1769-1859). Wilhelm was born in Potsdam, Alexander in Berlin; both grew up at the family house at Tegel in what is now the north-west of the city, and were educated at universities in Frankfurt-am-Oder and Göttingen. At this point their lives diverged.

Wilhelm went on to a life of statesmanship and scholarship. From 1802 to 1808 he represented Prussia at the Holy See in Rome, and from 1810 to 1819 in Vienna and London. After his retirement from state service, he produced a range of highly influential writings on linguistics. His most far-reaching achievements, however, were in the field of education, founding Berlin's oldest university in 1809 (subsequently renamed in his honour) on the principle of 'akademische Freiheit' (academic freedom). This system, based on a humanist model, insisted on the independence of universities, the freedom for students to move from one university to another during their studies and allowed better access to education for all social classes. It was fundamental to the modernisation of Prussia, and is still the basis of higher education in Germany today.

Meanwhile, his brother Alexander was enjoying an equally significant life. He developed an early interest in the natural sciences and, after a period in government service as a mines inspector, the death of his mother left him with a substantial income and the freedom to pursue his interests. The following year he met the botanist Aimé Bonpland, and together, from 1799 to 1804, they explored South and Central America, in the process laying down the foundations of the sciences of meteorology and physical geography. The rest of his life was devoted to further trips, lecturing, scientific writings and state service. In many ways, Alexander's ideas and practices were a key link between the Englightenment ideals of the 18th century and the scientific rigour of the 19th. Despite its often bewildering complexity, he believed in the fundamental unity of nature. Charles Darwin described him as 'the greatest scientific traveller who ever lived'.

flourished, and remained a feature of Berlin's cultural life into the middle of the 19th century.

Despite censorship, Berlin still had a platform for liberal expression. The city's newspapers welcomed the French Revolution so enthusiastically that in the southern German states Jacobins were referred to as 'Berliners'.

THE NAPOLEONIC WARS

In 1806 Berlin came face to face with the effects of revolution in France: following the defeat of the Prussian forces in the battles of Jena and Auerstadt on 14 October, Napoleon's army headed for Berlin. The King and Queen fled to Königsberg and the garrison was removed from the city. On 27 October Napoleon and his army marched through the Brandenburger Tor. Once again Berlin was an occupied city.

Napoleon set about changing the political and administrative structure. He called together 2,000 prominent citizens and told them to elect a new administration (called the Comité Administratif). This body oversaw the city's day-to-day administration until the French troops left in 1808.

Napoleon decreed that property belonging to the state, the Hohenzollerns and many aristocratic families be expropriated. Priceless works of art were removed from palaces in Berlin and Potsdam and sent to France; even the Quadriga was taken from the Brandenburg Gate and shipped to Paris. The city also suffered financially. With nearly 30,000 French troops in the city, Berliners had no choice but to supply them with food and lodging. On top of this came crippling war reparations.

When the French left, a group of energetic, reform-minded aristocrats, grouped around Baron vom Stein, seized the opportunity to introduce a series of wide-ranging reforms in a bid to modernise the moribund Prussian state. One key aspect was the clear separation of state and civic responsibility, which gave Berlin independence to manage its own affairs. A new

Ich bin Berliner KF Schinkel

No architect has had a greater impact on Berlin than the man described by Adolf Loos as 'the last great architect'. Born in 1781, Karl Friedrich Schinkel moved to Berlin with his widowed mother and family in 1794. At the age of 16 he was so enraptured by an exhibition of project drawings by Friedrich Gilly, that he decided on architecture as a career. He studied at the newly formed Bauakademie with the Gillys (father and son) – another distinguished student was Carl Gottfried Langhans, designer of the Brandenburger Tor. After completing his studies, Schinkel made the-then *de rigueur* trip to Italy to worship at the altar of classical culture.

Yet the dislocation caused by the Napoleonic Wars and the occupation of Prussia by France meant that it was not until a decade later that he could seriously start his career as an architect. In the meantime he achieved some success as a designer of stage sets, and as a painter of panoramas and romantic landscapes.

Much of Schinkel's talent lay in his slick synthesis of the best of ancient, Medieval and Renaissance architecture, although most of his surviving buildings are essentially neoclassical. The **Neue Wache** (1816; *see p75*) on Unter den Linden, the **Schauspielhaus** (1819-23; now the Konzerthaus; *see p78*) on Gendarmenmarkt and the **Altes Museum** (1823-30; *see p77*) on Museuminsel are all characterised by his free and expressive use of the classical idiom. The latter's stunning loggia, fronted by 18 Ionic columns, is particularly notable.

The brick **Friedrich-Werdersche-Kirche** (1824-30; *see p76*), in contrast, is unmistakably Gothic. Nearby stood Schinkel's

most revolutionary building, the now sadly lost **Bauakademie** (1832-6), which, with its polychrome brick and terracotta reliefs, was a supremely confident display of eclecticism.

Schinkel was fascinated by new industrial methods and materials (though his career came too early to take advantage of Germany's industrialisation). His romantic **Palmhouse** on Pfaueninsel (1930) is the only example of his use of cast iron as a primary building material.

When Schinkel arrived in Berlin it was a small, insignificant town and an architectural backwater. By the time he died in 1841 he had provided it with buildings of a scale and quality appropriate to what was to become the capital of Germany. And his masterly marrying of technological innovation and historical continuity have made him a model to architects up to the present day.

---

council was elected, based loosely on the Comité Administratif (though only property owners and the wealthy were entitled to vote). In 1810 the philosopher Wilhelm von Humboldt (*see p11* **Wir sind Berliner: the von Humboldts**) founded the university. All remaining restrictions on the city's Jewish population were removed.

Other reforms included the introduction of a new and simplified sales tax. A newly created 'trade police' was established to monitor trading standards. Generals Scharnhorst and Gneisenau completely overhauled the army.

Although the French occupied Berlin again in 1812 on their way home from the disastrous

Russian campaign, this time they were met with stiff resistance. A year later the Prussian King finally joined the anti-Napoleon coalition and thousands of Berliners signed up to fight. When Napoleon tried to capture the city once more, he was defeated at nearby Grossbeeren. This, together with a subsequent defeat for the French in the Battle of Leipzig, marked the end of Napoleonic rule in Germany.

In August 1814 General Blücher brought the Quadriga back to Berlin, and restored it to its place on the Brandenburger Tor. One symbolic addition was made to the statue: an Iron Cross and Prussian eagle were added to the staff in Victoria's hand.

BIEDERMEIER AND BORSIG

The burst of reform initiated in 1810 was short-lived. Following the Congress of Vienna (1814-15), which established a new order for post-Napoleonic Europe, King Friedrich Wilhelm III reneged on promises of constitutional reform. Instead of a greater unity among the German states, a loose alliance came into being; dominated by Austria, the German Confederation was distinctly anti-liberal.

In Prussia itself state power increased. Alongside the normal police, a secret service and vice squad were set up. The police president had the power to issue directives to the city council. Book and newspaper censorship increased. The authorities sacked von Humboldt from the university he had created.

With their hopes for lasting change frustrated, the bourgeoisie withdrew into their salons. It is one of the ironies of this time that, although political opposition was quashed, a vibrant cultural movement flourished. Academics like Hegel and Ranke lectured at the university and enhanced Berlin's reputation as an intellectual centre. The period became known as Biedermeier, after a fictional character embodying bourgeois taste, created by Swabian comic writer Ludwig Eichrodt.

Another legacy of this period is the range of neo-classical buildings designed by Schinkel (*see p12* **Ich bin Berliner: KF Schinkel**), such as his Altes Museum and the Neue Wache on Unter den Linden.

For the majority, however, the post-Napoleonic era was a period of frustrated hopes and bitter poverty. Industrialisation swelled the ranks of the working class. Between 1810 and 1840, the city's population doubled to around 400,000, making Berlin the fourth largest city in Europe. But most of the newcomers lived in conditions that would later lead to riot and revolution.

INDUSTRIAL REVOLUTION

Prussia was ideally equipped for the industrial age. By the 19th century it had grown dramatically and boasted one of the greatest abundances of raw materials in Europe.

It was the founding of the Borsig Werke on Chausseestrasse in 1837 that established Berlin as the workshop of continental Europe. August Borsig was Berlin's first big industrialist. His factories turned out locomotives for the new railway network, which had started with the opening of the Berlin to Potsdam line in 1838. Borsig also left his mark through the establishment of a suburb (Borsigwalde) that still carries his name.

The other great pioneering industrialist, Werner Siemens, set up his electrical engineering firm in a house by Anhalter Bahnhof. The first European to produce telegraph equipment, Siemens personified the German industrial ideal, with his mix of technical genius and business savvy.

The Siemens company also left a permanent imprint on Berlin through the building of a new suburb (Siemensstadt) to house its workers. With the growth of companies like these, Berlin became continental Europe's largest industrial city.

1848 AND ALL THAT

Friedrich Wilhelm IV's accession to the throne in 1840 raised hopes of an end to repression; and, initially, he did appear to want real change. He declared an amnesty for political prisoners, relaxed censorship, sacked the hated justice minister and granted asylum to political refugees.

Political debate thrived in coffee houses and wine bars. The university was another focal point for discussion. In the late 1830s Karl Marx spent a term there, just missing fellow alumnus Otto von Bismarck. In the early 1840s Friedrich Engels came to Berlin in order to do his military service.

'Rapid industrialisation had also brought sweatshops, 17-hour days and child labour.'

The thaw didn't last long. It soon became clear that Friedrich Wilhelm IV shared his father's opposition to constitutional reform. Living and working conditions for the majority of Berliners worsened. Rapid

Street battles in Berlin in 1848.

industrialisation had also brought the horrors of sweatshops, 17-hour days and child labour.

These poor conditions were compounded in 1844 by harvest failure, which drove up prices for potatoes and wheat. Food riots broke out on Gendarmenmarkt, when a crowd stormed the market stalls. It took the army three days to restore order.

Things came to a head in 1848, the year of revolutions. Berliners seized the moment. Political meetings were held in beer gardens and in the Tiergarten, and demands made for internal reform and a unification of German-speaking states. At the end of one demonstration in the Tiergarten, there was a running battle between police and demonstrators on Unter den Linden.

On 18 March the King finally conceded to allowing a new parliament, and made vague promises about other reforms. Later that day, the crowd of 10,000 that gathered to celebrate the victory were set upon by soldiers. Shots were fired and the revolution began. Barricades went up throughout central Berlin and demonstrators fought with police for 14 hours. Finally the King backed down (again). In exchange for the dismantling of barricades, the king ordered his troops out of Berlin. Days later, he took part in the funeral service for the 'March Dead' – the 183 revolutionaries who had been killed – and also promised more freedoms.

Berlin was now ostensibly in the hands of the revolutionaries. A Civil Guard patrolled the city, the King rode through the streets wearing the revolutionary colours (black, red and gold), seeming to embrace the causes of liberalism and nationalism. Prussia, he said, should 'merge into Germany'.

But the revolution proved short-lived. When pressed on unification, the King merely suggested that the other German states send representatives to the Prussian National Assembly. Needless to say, this offer was rebuffed.

Leading liberals instead convened a German National Assembly in Frankfurt in May 1848. At the same time, a new Prussian Assembly met in what is now the Konzerthaus on Gendarmenmarkt to debate a new constitution. Towards the end of 1848 reforming fervour took over Berlin.

THE BACKLASH

The onset of winter, however, brought a change of mood to the city. Using continuing street violence as the pretext, the King ordered the National Assembly to be moved to Brandenburg. In early November, he brought troops back into the city and declared a state of siege. Press freedom was once again restricted. The Civil Guard and National Assembly were dissolved. On 5 December the King delivered his final blow to the liberals by unveiling a new constitution fashioned to his own particular tastes.

Throughout the winter of 1848-9 thousands of liberals were arrested or expelled. A new city constitution, drawn up in 1850, reduced the number of eligible voters to five per cent of the population, or around 21,000 people. Increased police powers meant that the position of police president was more important than that of mayor.

By 1857 the increasingly senile Friedrich Wilhelm had gone quite literally mad. His brother Wilhelm acted as regent until becoming king on Friedrich's death in 1861.

Once again, the people's hopes were raised: the new monarch began his reign by appointing liberals to the cabinet. The building of the Rotes Rathaus ('Red Town Hall') gave the city council a headquarters to match the size of the royal palace. Built between 1861 and 1869, the Rathaus was named for the colour of its bricks, and not (yet) the political persuasion of its members.

But by 1861 the King found himself in dispute with parliament over proposed army reforms. He wanted to strengthen his direct control of the armed forces. Parliament wouldn't accept this, so the King went over its members' heads and appointed a new prime minister: Otto von Bismarck.

THE IRON CHANCELLOR

An arrogant genius who began his career as a diplomat, Bismarck was well able to deal with unruly parliamentarians. Using a constitutional loophole to rule against the majority, he quickly pushed through the army reforms. Extra-parliamentary opposition was dealt with in the usual manner: oppression and censorship. Dissension thus suppressed, Bismarck turned his mind to German unification.

Unlike the bourgeois revolutionaries of 1848, who desired a Germany united by popular will and endowed with political reforms, Bismarck strove to bring the states together under the authoritarian dominance of Prussia. His methods involved astute foreign policy and outright aggression.

Wars against Denmark (1864) and Austria (1866) brought post-Napoleonic order to an abrupt end. Prussia was no longer the smallest of the Great Powers, but an aspiring initiator of geopolitical change. Austria's defeat confirmed the primacy of Prussia among German-speaking states.

Victory on the battlefield boosted Bismarck's popularity across Prussia – but not in Berlin itself. He was defeated in his Berlin constituency in the 1867 election to the newly created North German League. This was a Prussian-dominated body linking the northern states as a stepping stone towards Germany's overall unification.

Bismarck's third war – against France in 1870 – revealed his scope for intrigue and opportunism. He exploited a dispute over the succession to the Spanish throne to provoke France into declaring war on Prussia. Citing the North German League and treaties signed with the southern German states, Bismarck brought together a united German army under Prussian leadership.

'In just nine years, Bismarck had united Germany, forging an empire that dominated central Europe.'

Following the defeat of the French army on 2 September, Bismarck moved quickly to turn a unified military campaign into the basis for a unified nation. The Prussian king would be German emperor: beneath him would be four kings, 18 grand-dukes and assorted princes from the German states, which would retain some regional powers. (This arrangement formed the basis for the modern federal system of regional *Länder*.)

On 18 January 1871 King Wilhelm was proclaimed German Kaiser ('Emperor') in the Hall of Mirrors in Versailles.

In just nine years, Bismarck had united Germany, forging an empire that dominated central Europe. The political, economic and social centre of this new creation was Berlin.

IMPERIAL BERLIN

The coming of empire threw Berlin into one of its greatest periods of expansion and change. The economic boom (helped by five billion gold francs extracted from France as war reparations) led to a wave of speculation. Farmers in Wilmersdorf and Schöneberg became millionaires overnight as they sold off their fields to developers.

During the decades following German unification, Berlin emerged as Europe's most modern metropolis. This period was later dubbed the *Gründerzeit* ('Foundation Years').

The *Gründerzeit* were marked by a move away from traditional Prussian values of thrift and modesty, towards the gaudy and bombastic. In Berlin, the change of mood manifested itself in numerous monuments and buildings. Of these the Reichstag, the Siegessäule ('Victory Column'),

the Berliner Dom and the Kaiser-Wilhelm-Gedächtniskirche are the most prominent.

Superficially, the Reichstag (designed by Paul Wallot, and completed in 1894) represented a weighty commitment to parliamentary democracy, but, in reality, Germany was still in the grip of conservative, backward-looking forces. The authoritarian power of the Kaiser remained intact, as was demonstrated by the decision of Wilhelm II to sack Bismarck in 1890 following disagreements over policy.

BERLIN BOOMS

When Bismarck began his premiership in 1861 his offices on Wilhemstrasse overlooked potato fields. By the time he lost his job in 1890 they were in the centre of Europe's newest and most congested city. Economic boom and growing political and social importance attracted hundreds of thousands of new inhabitants to the city. At the time of unification in 1871 820,000 people lived in Berlin; by 1890 this number had nearly doubled.

The growing numbers of the working class were shoved into hastily built *Mietskasernen* tenements (literally, 'rental barracks') that mushroomed across the city – particularly in Kreuzberg, Wedding and Prenzlauer Berg. Poorly ventilated and hopelessly overcrowded, the *Mietskasernen* (many of which still stand) are characterised by a series of interlinked courtyards. They became both a symbol of Berlin and a breeding ground for further social unrest.

The Social Democratic Party (SPD), founded in 1869, quickly became the voice for the city's have-nots. In the 1877 general election it won more than 40 per cent of the Berlin vote. Here was born the left-wing reputation of Rotes Berlin ('Red Berlin') that has followed the city to the present day.

In 1878 two assassination attempts on the Kaiser gave Bismarck an excuse to classify socialists as enemies of the state. He introduced restrictive laws to curb the 'red menace', and outlawed the SPD and two other progressive parties.

The ban existed until 1890   the year of Bismarck's sacking – but did little to stem support for the SPD. In the general election held that year, the SPD dominated the vote in Berlin. And in 1912 it won more than 70 per cent of the Berlin vote to become the largest party in the Reichstag.

KAISER BILL

Famed for his ridiculous moustache, Kaiser Wilhelm II came to the throne in 1888, and soon became the personification of the new Germany: bombastic, awkward and unpredictable. Like his grandmother Queen Victoria, he gave his name to an era. Wilhelm's epoch is associated with showy militarism and foreign policy bungles leading to a world war that cost the Kaiser his throne and Germany its stability.

The Wilhelmine years were also characterised by further explosive growth in Berlin (the population rose to two million by 1910, and by 1914 had doubled again) and a blossoming of the city's cultural and intellectual life. The Bode Museum was built in 1904, and in 1912 work began next door on the Pergamon Museum. In 1912 a new Opera House was unveiled in Charlottenburg (later to be destroyed by wartime bombing; the Deutsche Oper now stands on the same site). Expressionism took off in 1910 and the Kurfürstendamm became the location for many new art galleries. Although Paris still remained ahead of Berlin in the arts, the German city was fast catching up.

By the time of his abdication in 1918 Wilhelm's reign had also seen the emergence of Berlin as a centre of scientific and intellectual development. Six Berlin scientists (including Albert Einstein and Max Planck) were awarded Nobel Prizes.

In the years immediately preceding World War I Berlin appeared to be loosening its stiff collar of pomposity. Tangoing became all the rage in new clubs around Friedrichstrasse – though the Kaiser promptly banned officers in uniform from joining in the fun. Yet, despite the progressive changes, growing militarism and international tension overshadowed the period.

Germany was not alone in its preparedness for war. By 1914 Europe was well and truly armed and almost waiting to tear itself apart. In June 1914 the assassination of Archduke Franz Ferdinand provided the excuse. On 1 August war was declared on Russia, and the Kaiser appeared on a balcony of the royal palace to tell a jubilant crowd that from that moment onwards, he would not recognise any parties, only Germans. At the Reichstag the deputies, who had virtually unanimously voted in support of the war, agreed.

WORLD WAR I AND REVOLUTION

No one was prepared for the disaster of World War I. After Bismarck, the Germans had come to expect quick, sweeping victories. The armies on the Western Front settled into their trenches for a war of attrition that would cost over a million German lives. Meanwhile, the civilian population began to adapt to austerity and shortages. After the 1917 harvest failed there were outbreaks of famine. Dog and cat meat started to appear on the menus in the capital's restaurants.

The SPD's initial enthusiasm for war evaporated, and in 1916 the party refused to pass the Berlin budget. A year later, members of the party's radical wing broke away to form the Spartacus League. Anti-war feeling was voiced in mass strikes in April 1917 and January 1918. These were brutally suppressed, but, when the Imperial Marines in Kiel mutinied on 2 November 1918, the authorities were no longer able to stop the force of the anti-war movement.

'"The old and the rotten have broken down. Long live the new! Long live the German Republic!"'

The mutiny spread to Berlin where members of the Guards Regiment came out against the war. On 9 November the Kaiser was forced into abdication and subsequent exile. This date is weirdly layered with significance in German history; it's the anniversary of the establishment of the Weimar Republic (1918), Kristallnacht (1938) and the fall of the Wall (1989).

It was on this day that Philip Scheidemann, a leading SPD member of parliament and key proponent of republicanism, broke off his lunch in the second-floor restaurant of the Reichstag. He walked over to a window overlooking Königsplatz (now Platz der Republik) where a crowd had massed and declared to them: 'The old and the rotten have broken down. Long live the new! Long live the German Republic!'

At the other end of Unter den Linden, Karl Liebknecht, who, together with Rosa Luxemburg, headed the Spartacus League, declared Germany a socialist republic from a balcony of the occupied royal palace. (The balcony was the same one the Kaiser used when he spoke to Berliners on the eve of the war, and has been preserved as part of the *Staatsratsgebäude* ('State Council building') of the East German government.)

Liebknecht and the Spartacists wanted a radical Communist Germany similar to Soviet Russia; Scheidemann and the SPD favoured a parliamentary democracy. Between them stood those still loyal to the vanished monarchy. All were prepared to fight their respective corners. Barricades were erected in the city centre and street battles ensued.

It was in this climate of turmoil and violence that Germany's first attempt at republican democracy – the Weimar Republic – was born.

TERROR AND INSTABILITY

The revolution in Berlin may have brought peace to the Western Front, where hostilities were ended on 11 November, but in Germany it unleashed a wave of political terror and instability. The new masters in Berlin, the SPD under the leadership of Friedrich Ebert, ordered renegade battalions of soldiers returning from the front (known as the Freikorps) to quash the Spartacists, who launched a concerted bid for power in January 1919.

Within days, the uprising had been bloodily suppressed, and Liebknecht and Luxemburg went into hiding. On 15 January Freikorps officers traced them to a house in Wilmersdorf and arrested them. They were then taken to a hotel near Bahnhof Zoo for interrogation. Between the hotel and Moabit Prison, the officers murdered them, and dumped Luxemburg's body over the Liechtenstein Bridge into the Landwehr Canal. Today a plaque marks the spot.

Four days later, the national elections returned the SPD as the largest party: the Social Democrats' victory over the extreme left was complete. Berlin was deemed too dangerous for parliamentary business, so the government swiftly decamped to the quaint provincial town of Weimar, from which the first German republic took its name.

Germany's new constitution ended up being full of good liberal intentions, but riddled with technical flaws, and this left the country wide open to weak coalition government and quasi-dictatorial presidential rule.

Another crippling blow to the new republic was the Versailles Treaty, which set the terms of peace. Reparation payments (set to run until 1988) blew a hole in a fragile economy already weakened by war. Support for the right-wing nationalist lobby was fuelled by the loss of territories in both east and west. And restrictions placed on the German military led some right-wingers to claim that Germany's soldiers had been 'stabbed in the back' by Jews and left-wingers at home.

In March 1920 a right-wing coup was staged in Berlin under the leadership of Wolfgang Kapp, a civil servant from east Prussia. The recently returned government once again fled the city. For four days Berlin was besieged by roaming Freikorps. Some of them had taken to adorning their helmets with a new symbol: the *Hakenkreuz* or swastika.

Ultimately, a general strike and the refusal of the army (the Reichswehr) to join Kapp brought an end to the putsch. But the political and economic chaos in the city remained. Political assassinations were commonplace. Food shortages lead to bouts of famine. Inflation started to escalate.

There were two main reasons for the precipitate devaluation of the Reichsmark. To pay for the war, the increasingly desperate imperial government had resorted simply to printing more money, a policy continued by the new republican rulers. The burden of reparations also lead to an outflow of foreign currency. In 1914 one dollar bought just over four Reichmarks; by 1922 it was worth over 7,000. And one hyperinflationary year later, a dollar was worth 4.2 billion marks. Workers needed suitcases to carry the near-worthless bundles of notes that made up their salaries. Wheelbarrows replaced wallets as almost overnight the savings of millions were wiped out.

In the same year, 1923, the French government sent troops into the Ruhr industrial region to take by force reparation goods that the German government said it could no longer afford to pay. The Communists planned an uprising in Berlin for October, but lost their nerve.

'Hitler's first attempt at power came to nothing. Instead of marching on Berlin, he went to prison.'

In November, a young ex-corporal called Adolf Hitler, who led the tiny National Socialist Party (NSDAP or Nazi Party), launched an attempted coup from a beer-hall in Munich. His programme called for armed resistance against the French, an end to the 'dictatorship of Versailles' and punishment for all those – especially the Jews – who had 'betrayed' Germany at the end of the war.

Hitler's first attempt at power came to nothing. Instead of marching on Berlin, he went to prison. Inflation was finally brought down with the introduction of a new currency (one new mark was worth one trillion old ones).

But the overall decline of moral and social values that had taken place in the five years since 1918 was not so easy to restore.

THE GOLDEN TWENTIES

Joseph Goebbels came to Berlin in 1926 to take charge of the local Nazi Party organisation. On arriving, he observed: 'This city is a melting pot of everything that is evil – prostitution, drinking houses, cinemas, Marxism, Jews, strippers, negroes dancing and all the offshoots of modern art.'

Omitting the word 'evil', Goebbels' description of 1920s Berlin was not far wrong. During that decade the city overtook Paris as continental Europe's arts and entertainment

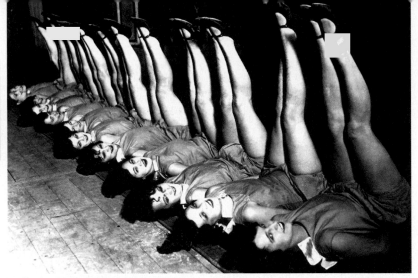

Lie back and think of Deutschland: the 'Scala Girls' practise their high kicks in 1928.

capital, and in the process added its own decadent twist. 'We used to have a first-class army,' mused Klaus Mann, the author of *Mephisto*; 'now we have first-class perversions.'

By 1927 Berlin boasted more than 70 cabarets and nightclubs. At the Theater des Westens, near Bahnhof Zoo, cabaret artist Josephine Baker danced to a packed house. She also danced naked at parties thrown by playwright Karl Volmoeller in his flat on Pariser Platz. 'Berlin was mad! A triumph!' she later recalled.

While Brecht's Dreigroschenoper played at the Theater am Schiffbauerdamm, Berlin's Dadaists were gathered at the Romanisches Café on Tauentzienstrasse (later destroyed by bombing – the Europa-Center now stands on the site). There was a proliferation of avant-garde magazines reflecting new ideas in art and literature.

But the flipside of all the frenetic enjoyment was an underbelly of raw poverty and glaring social tension, reflected in the works of painters like George Grosz and Otto Dix. In the music halls, Brecht and Weill used a popular medium to ram home points about social injustices.

In architecture and design, the revolutionary ideas emanating from the Bauhaus school in Dessau (it briefly moved to Berlin in 1932, but was closed down by the Nazis a year later) were taking concrete form in building projects such as the Shell House building on the Landwehr Canal, the Siemenstadt new town, and the model housing project Hufeisensiedlung ('Horse Shoe Estate') in Britz. Furniture, ceramics, sculptures and sketches, created in the Bauhaus workshop from 1919 until 1933, are kept in the Bauhaus Archiv-Museum für Gestaltung.

STREET-FIGHTING YEARS

The stock market crash on Wall Street and the onset of global depression in 1929 ushered in the brutal end of the Weimar Republic.

The fractious coalition governments that had just managed to hold on to power in the brief years of prosperity in the late 1920s were no match for rocketing unemployment and a surge in support for extremist parties.

By the end of 1929 nearly one in four Berliners were out of work. The city's streets became a battleground for clashes between Nazis, Communists and social democrats. Increasingly, the police relied on water cannons, armoured vehicles and guns to quell street fighting across the city. One May Day demonstration left 30 dead and several hundred wounded. At Bülowplatz (now Rosa-Luxemburg-Platz) where the Communist Party, the KPD, had its headquarters, there were regular battles between Communists, the police and Nazi stormtroopers (the SA). In August 1931, two police officers were murdered on Bülowplatz. One of the men accused of the murders (and later found guilty, albeit by a Nazi court) was Erich Mielke, a young Communist, later to become the head of East Germany's secret police, the Stasi.

In 1932 the violence in Berlin reached crisis level. In just six weeks over the summer, 300 street battles left 70 people dead. In the general election in July the Nazis took 40 per cent of the vote and became the largest party in the Reichstag. Hermann Göring, one of Hitler's earliest followers, and a wounded veteran of the beer-hall putsch, was appointed Reichstag president.

The prize of government, however, still eluded the Nazis. At the elections held in November, the Nazis lost two million votes across Germany and 37,000 in Berlin, where the Communists emerged as the strongest party. (In 'Red' Wedding, over 60 per cent voted for the KPD.)

The election had been held against the backdrop of a strike by 20,000 transport employees, who were protesting against planned wage cuts. The strike had been called by the Communists and the Nazis, who vied with each other to capture the mass vote and bring the Weimar Republic to an end. Under orders from Moscow, the KPD shunned all co-operation with the SPD, ending any possibility of a broad left-wing front.

As Berlin headed into another winter of depression, almost every third person was out of work. A city survey recorded that almost half of Berlin's inhabitants were living four to a room, and that a large proportion of the city's housing stock was unfit for human habitation. Berlin topped the European table of suicides.

The new government of General Kurt von Schleicher ruled by presidential decree. Schleicher had promised President von Hindenburg he could tame the Nazis into a coalition. When he failed, his rival Franz von Papen successfully overcame Hindenburg's innate dislike for Hitler and manoeuvred the Nazi leader into power. On 30 January 1933 Adolf Hitler was named Chancellor and moved from his headquarters in the Hotel Kaiserhof in Glinkastrasse (it was central and his favourite band played there) to the Chancellery two streets away in Wilhelmstrasse.

That evening, the SA staged a torchlight parade through the Brandenburger Tor and along to the Chancellery. Looking out from the window of his house next to the Gate, the artist Max Liebermann remarked to his dinner guests: 'I cannot eat as much as I'd like to puke.'

THE NAZIS TAKE CONTROL

The government Hitler now led was a coalition of Nazis and German nationalists, led by the media magnate Alfred Hugenberg. Together their votes fell just short of a parliamentary majority, so another election was called for March. In the meantime Hitler continued to rule by decree.

The last relatively free election of the Republic was also the most violent. Open persecution of Communists began. The Nazis banned meetings of the KPD, shut down Communist newspapers and broke up SPD election rallies.

On 27 February a fire broke out in the Reichstag. It was almost certainly started by the Nazis, who used it as an excuse to step up the persecution of opponents. Over 12,000 Communists were arrested. Spelling it out in a speech at the Sportspalast two days before the election, Goebbels said: 'It's not my job to practise justice, instead I have to destroy and exterminate – nothing else.'

The Nazis still didn't achieve an absolute majority (in Berlin they polled 34 per cent), but that no longer mattered. With the support of his allies in the coalition, Hitler pushed through an Enabling Law giving him dictatorial powers. By summer Germany had been declared a one-party state.

> ## 'Goebbels said: "It's not my job to practise justice, instead I have to destroy and exterminate – nothing else."'

Already ad hoc concentration camps – known as brown houses after the colour of the SA uniforms – had sprung up around the city. The SS established itself in Prinz Albrecht Palais where it was later joined by the secret police, the Gestapo. Just to the north of Berlin near Oranienburg, a concentration camp, Sachsenhausen, was set up.

Along the Kurfürstendamm squads of SA stormtroopers would go 'Jew baiting', and on 1 April 1933 the first boycott of Jewish shops began. A month later Goebbels, who became Minister for Propaganda, organised a book-burning, which took place in the courtyard of the university on Unter den Linden. Books by Jews or writers deemed degenerate or traitors were thrown on to a huge bonfire.

Berlin's unemployment problem was tackled through a series of public works programmes, growing militarisation, which drew new recruits to the army, and the 'encouragement' of women to leave the workplace.

Following the policy of *Gleichschaltung* (co-ordination), the Nazis began to bring all aspects of public life under their control. With a few exceptions, party membership became obligatory for doctors, lawyers, professors and journalists.

During the Night of the Long Knives in July 1934, Hitler settled some old scores with opponents within the SA and Nazi Party. At Lichterfelde barracks, officers of the SS shot and killed over 150 SA members. Hitler's predecessor as Chancellor, General von Schleicher, was shot together with his wife at their home in Wannsee.

After the death of President Hindenburg in August 1934 Hitler had himself named

Führer ('Leader') and made the armed forces swear a personal oath of allegiance to him. Within less than two years, the Nazis had subjugated Germany.

THE VITAL AND THE DEGENERATE

A brief respite came with the Olympic Games in August 1936. In a bid to persuade foreign participants and spectators that all was well in the Reich, Goebbels ordered the removal of anti-Semitic slogans from shops. 'Undesirables' were also moved out of the city, and the pavement display cases that held copies of the racist Nazi newspaper *Der Stürmer* ('The Stormtrooper') were dismantled.

The Games, mainly held at the newly built Olympiastadion in Charlottenburg, were not such a success for the Nazis. Instead of blond Aryan giants sweeping the field, Hitler had to watch the African-American Jesse Owens clock up medals and records.

The Games did work, however, as a public relations exercise. Foreign observers left glowing with reports about a strident and healthy nation. But had any of the foreign visitors stayed, they would have seen the reality of Hitler's policy of co-ordinating all facets of life in Berlin within the Nazi doctrine.

As part of a nationwide campaign to remove what the Nazis considered to be *Entartete Kunst* ('Degenerate Art') from German cultural life, works of modern art were collected and brought together in a touring exhibition designed to show the depth of depravity in contemporary ('Jewish-dominated') culture. But Nazi hopes that these 'degenerate' works would repulse the German people fell flat. When the exhibition arrived at Berlin's Zeughaus in early 1938 thousands queued for admission. The people loved the paintings.

After the exhibition, the paintings were sent to auction in Switzerland. Those that remained unsold were burnt in the fire station in Köpenicker Strasse. More than 1,000 oil paintings and 4,000 watercolours were destroyed.

TOTALITARIAN TOWN PLANNING

Shortly after taking power, Hitler ordered that the lime trees on Unter den Linden be chopped down to give Berlin's boulevard a cleaner, more sanitised form. This was just the first step in Nazi urban planning.

Hitler's plans for the redesign of Berlin reflected the hatred the Nazis felt for the city. Hitler entrusted young architect Albert Speer with the job of recreating Berlin as a metropolis to 'out-trump Paris and Vienna'. The heart of old Berlin was to be demolished, and its small streets replaced by two highways stretching 37 kilometres (23 miles) from north to south and 50 kilometres (30 miles) from east to west. Each axis would be 90 metres (295 feet) wide. Crowning the northern axis would be a huge Volkshalle ('People's Hall') nearly 300 metres (1,000 feet) high with space for over 150,000 people. Speer and Hitler also had grand plans for a triumphal arch three times the size of the Arc de Triomphe, and a Führer's Palace 150 times bigger than the one occupied by Bismarck. The new city was to be called Germania.

The onset of war meant that Speer only built a fraction of what was intended. Hitler's new Chancellery, completed in early 1939, was constructed in under a year. (It was demolished after the war.) On the proposed east–west axis, a small section around the Siegessäule was widened for Hitler's 50th birthday in April 1939.

PERSECUTION

Of the half-a-million Jews living in Germany in 1933 over a third lived in Berlin. The Jewish community had played an important role in Berlin's development, and its influence was especially prevalent in the financial, artistic and intellectual circles of the city.

'Berlin business institutions that had been owned by Jews... were "Aryanised".'

The Nazis wiped out these centuries-old traditions in 12 years of persecution and murder. Arrests soon followed the initial boycotts and acts of intimidation. From 1933 to 1934 many of Berlin's Jews fled to exile abroad. Those who stayed were to be subjected to legislation (the Nuremberg Laws of 1935) that banned Jews from public office, forbade them to marry Aryan Germans and stripped them of citizenship. Jewish cemeteries were desecrated and the names of Jews chipped off war memorials.

Berlin business institutions that had been owned by Jews – such as the Ullstein newspaper group and the Tietz and Wertheim department stores on Alexanderplatz and Leipziger Strasse – were 'Aryanised'. The Nazis either expropriated them from the owners or forced them to sell at ridiculously low prices.

On 9 November 1938 'Kristallnacht' (named after the broken glass), a wave of 'spontaneous' acts of vandalism and violence against Jews and their property, began in response to the assassination of a German diplomat in Paris

Berlin on its knees: the Reichstag in ruins in 1945.

by a young Jewish émigré. Jewish businesses and houses across Berlin were stoned, looted and set ablaze. A total of 24 synagogues were set on fire. The Nazis rounded up 12,000 Jews and took them to Sachsenhausen concentration camp.

WORLD WAR II

Since 1935 Berliners had been taking part in practice air-raid drills, but it was not until the Sudeten crisis of 1938 that the possibility of war became real. At that juncture Hitler was able to get his way and persuade France and Britain to let him take over the German-speaking areas of northern Czechoslovakia.

But a year later, his plans to repeat the exercise in Poland were met with resistance in London and Paris. Following Germany's invasion of Poland on 1 September 1939 Britain and France declared war on the Reich.

Despite the propaganda and spectacular early victories, most Berliners were horrified by the war. The first air raids came with the RAF bombing of Pankow and Lichtenberg in early 1940.

> ## 'They joked and drank brandy as they sat around discussing mass murder.'

In 1941, following the German invasion of the Soviet Union, the 75,000 Jews remaining in Berlin were required to wear a yellow Star of David and the first large-scale and systematic deportations to concentration camps began. By the end of the war only 5,000 Jews remained in Berlin.

Notorious assembly points for the deportations were Putlitzstrasse in Wedding, Grosse Hamburger Strasse and Rosenstrasse in Mitte. On 20 January 1942 a meeting of the leaders of the various Nazi security organisations in the suburb of Wannsee agreed on a 'final solution' to the Jewish question. They joked and drank brandy as they sat around discussing mass murder.

The turning point in the war came with the surrender at Stalingrad on 31 January 1943. In a bid to grab some advantage from this crushing defeat, Goebbels held a rally in the Sportpalast where he announced that Germany had now moved into a state of 'total war'. By summer women and children were being evacuated from Berlin and schools were shut down. By the end of 1943 over 700,000 people had fled Berlin.

The Battle of Berlin, which the RAF launched in November 1943, began to reduce much of the city centre to rubble. Between then and February 1944 more than 10,000 tonnes of bombs were dropped on the city. Nearly 5,000 people were killed and something like a quarter of a million were made homeless.

THE JULY PLOT

On 20 July 1944 a group of officers, civil servants and former trades unionists launched a last-ditch attempt to assassinate Hitler and bring an end to the war. But Hitler survived the explosion of a bomb placed at his eastern command post in East Prussia by Colonel Count von Stauffenberg.

That evening Stauffenberg was killed by firing squad in the courtyard of army headquarters in Bendlerstrasse, now Stauffenbergstrasse. The other members of the plot were rounded up and put on trial at the People's Court near Kleistpark and subsequently executed at Plötzensee Prison.

In early January 1945 the Red Army launched a major offensive that carried it on to German soil. On 12 February the heaviest bombing raid yet on Berlin killed over 23,000 people in little more than an hour.

As the Red Army moved into Berlin's suburbs Hitler celebrated his last birthday on 20 April in his bunker behind Wilhelmstrasse. Three days later Neukölln and Tempelhof fell. By 28 April Alexanderplatz and Hallesches Tor were in the hands of the Red Army.

The next day Hitler called his last war conference. He then married his long-time companion Eva Braun and committed suicide with her the day after. As their bodies were being burnt by loyal SS officers, a few streets away a red flag was raised over the Reichstag. The city officially surrendered on 2 May. Germany's unconditional surrender was signed on 8 May at the Red Army command centre in Karlshorst.

DEVASTATION AND DIVISION

When the playwright Bertolt Brecht returned to Berlin in 1948 he encountered 'a pile of rubble next to Potsdam'. Nearly a quarter of all buildings in the city had been destroyed. The human cost of the war was equally startling – around 80,000 Berliners had been killed, not including the thousands of Jews who would not return from the concentration camps.

There was no gas or electricity and only the suburbs had running water. Public transport had all but completely broken down. In the first weeks following capitulation, Red Army soldiers went on a rampage of random killings and rapes. Thousands of men were rounded up and transported to labour camps in the Soviet Union. Food supplies were used up and later the harvest in the war-scarred land around the city failed. Come winter, the few remaining trees in the Tiergarten and other city parks were chopped down for firewood.

Clearing the rubble was to take years of dull, painstaking work. The *Trümmerfrauen* ('rubble women') cleared the streets and created mountains of brick and junk – such as the Teufelsberg, one of seven such hills that still exist today.

The Soviets stripped factories across the city as part of a programme to dismantle German industry and carry it back to the Soviet Union. As reparation, whole factories were moved to Russia.

Under the terms of the Yalta Agreement, which divided Germany into four zones of Allied control, Berlin was also split into four sectors, with the Soviets in the east and the Americans, British and French in the west. A Kommandatura, made up of each army's commander and based in the building of the People's Court in Elssholzstrasse, dealt with the administration of the city.

Initially, the administration worked well in getting basics, like the transport network, back to some form of running order. But tensions between the Soviets and the Western Allies began to rise as civilian government of

city affairs returned. In the eastern sector a merger of the Communist and Social Democratic parties (which had both been refounded in summer 1945) was pushed through to form the Socialist Unity Party (SED). In the western sector, however, the SPD continued as a separate party.

Events came to a head after elections for a new city government in 1946. The SED failed to get more than 20 per cent of the vote, while the SPD won nearly 50 per cent of all votes cast across the city. The Soviets vetoed the appointment to office of the SPD's mayoral candidate, Ernst Reuter, who was a committed anti-Communist.

THE BERLIN AIRLIFT

The situation worsened in spring 1948. In response to the decision by the Western Allies to merge their respective zones in western Germany into one administrative and financial entity and introduce a new currency, the Soviets walked out of the Kommandatura. In late June all transport links to west Berlin were cut off and the blockade of the city by Soviet forces began. Three 'air-corridors' linking west Berlin with western Germany became lifelines as Allied aircraft transported thousands of tonnes of food, coal and industrial components to the beleaguered city.

> ## 'Having failed to starve west Berlin into submission, the Soviets called off the blockade after 11 months.'

Within Berlin the future division of the city began to take permanent shape as city councillors from the west were drummed out of the town hall. They moved to Rathaus Schöneberg in the west. Fresh elections in the western sector returned Reuter as mayor. The Freie Universität was set up in response to Communist dominance of the Humboldt University in the east.

Having failed to starve west Berlin into submission, the Soviets called off the blockade after 11 months. The blockade also convinced the Western Allies that they should maintain a presence in Berlin and that their sectors of the city should be linked with the Federal Republic, which had been founded in May 1949. The response from the East was the founding of the German Democratic Republic on 7 October. With the birth of the 'first Workers' and Peasants' State on German soil', the formal division of Germany into two states was complete.

Ich bin *ein* Berliner JFK

In the early 1960s the Cold War plunged to its chilliest. In 1961 the East German authorities erected the Wall to prevent its own citizens escaping to the West; the 13 days of the Cuban Missile Crisis in October 1962 brought the world to the brink of nuclear war. In June 1963 US President John F Kennedy set off on a goodwill visit to five European Allied nations – and his first stop was Germany. From Bonn, Cologne and Frankfurt, he moved on to Berlin to deliver one of the most famous speeches of the 20th century.

Outside Rathaus Schöneberg a massive crowd gathered to see Kennedy and hear him speak of his solidarity with the people of the city:

'I know of no town, no city, that has been besieged for 18 years that still lives with the vitality and the force, and the hope and the determination of the city of West Berlin.'

The President then went on to deliver his celebrated conclusion:

'Freedom is indivisible, and when one man is enslaved, all are not free. When all are free, then we can look forward to that day when this city will be joined as one and this country and this great continent of Europe in a peaceful and hopeful globe. When that day finally comes, as it will, the people of West Berlin can take sober satisfaction in the fact that they were in the front line for almost two decades.

'All free men, wherever they may live, are citizens of Berlin and, therefore, as a free man, I take pride in the words "Ich bin ein Berliner".'

A moving piece of rhetoric. Yet today, what most people recall about this speech is that Kennedy, instead of saying 'I am a Berliner', actually said 'I am a doughnut'.

Normally, Germans don't use articles when referring to professions or national origins – so 'Ich bin Berliner' would have been technically correct. 'Ein Berliner' is, in fact, a type of jam doughnut. Yet, there was no ambiguity in Kennedy's speech, and his use of the phrase raised no laughs among his audience. In fact, many Germans consider that his use of 'ein' was perfectly OK, in that it acted as both emphasis, and to reflect that Kennedy was not saying that he was, literally, a citizen of Berlin, but rather a figurative Berliner. So quit the giggling at the back...

THE COLD WAR

During the Cold War, Berlin was the focal point for stand-offs between the United States and the Soviet Union. Far from having any control over its own affairs, the city was wholly at the mercy of geopolitical developments. Throughout the 1950s the 'Berlin Question' remained prominent on the international agenda.

Technically, the city was still under Four-Power control, but since the Soviet departure from the Kommandatura, and the setting up of the German Democratic Republic with its capital in East Berlin (a breach of the wartime agreement on the future of the city), this counted for little in practice.

In principle, the Western Allies adhered to these agreements by retaining ultimate authority in West Berlin, while allowing the city to be integrated as far as possible into the West German system. (There were notable exceptions, such as the exemption of West Berliners from conscription, and the barring of city MPs from voting in the West German parliament.)

Throughout the 1950s the two halves of Berlin began to develop separately as the political systems in East and West evolved. In the East, Communist leader Walter Ulbricht set about creating Moscow's most hardline ally in eastern Europe. Work began on a Moscow-style boulevard – called Stalinallee – running east from Alexanderplatz. Industry was nationalised and subjected to rigid central planning. Opposition was kept in check by the newly formed Ministry for State Security: the Stasi.

West Berlin landed the role of 'Last Outpost of the Free World' and, as such, was developed into a showcase for capitalism. As well as the Marshall Plan, which paid for much of the reconstruction of West Germany, the

Americans poured millions of dollars into West Berlin to maintain it as a counterpoint to Communism. The West German government, which at the time refused to recognise East Germany as a legitimate state, demonstrated its commitment to seeing Berlin reinstated as German capital by holding occasional parliamentary sessions in the city. The prominence accorded West Berlin was later reflected in the high profile of its politicians (Willy Brandt, for example) who were received abroad by prime ministers and presidents – unusual for mere mayors.

Yet despite the emerging divisions the two halves of the city continued to co-exist in some abnormal fashion. City planners on both sides of the sectoral boundaries initially drew up plans with the whole city in mind. The transport system crossed between East and West, with the underground network being controlled by the West and the S-Bahn by the East.

Movement between the sectors (despite 'border' checks) was relatively normal, as Westerners went East to watch a Brecht play or buy cheap books. Easterners travelled West to work, shop or see the latest Hollywood films.

The secret services of both sides kept a high presence in the city, and there were frequent acts of sabotage on either side. Berlin became espionage capital of the world.

RECONSTRUCTION AND REFUGEES

As the effects of American money and the West German 'economic miracle' took hold, West Berlin began to recover. A municipal housing programme meant that by 1963 200,000 new flats had been built. Unemployment dropped from over 30 per cent in 1950 to virtually zero by 1961. The labour force also included some 50,000 East Berliners who commuted over the inter-sector borders.

In the East reconstruction was slower. Until the mid 1950s East Germany paid reparations to the Soviet Union. And to begin with there seemed to be more acts of wilful destruction than positive construction. The old palace, which had been only slightly damaged by bombing, was blown up in 1950 to make way for a parade ground, which later evolved into a car park.

In 1952 the East Germans sealed off the border with West Germany. The only way out of the 'zone' was through West Berlin and the number of refugees from the East rose dramatically from 50,000 in 1950 to over 300,000 in 1953. Over the decade, one million refugees from the East came through West Berlin.

THE 1953 UPRISING

In June 1953, partly in response to the rapid loss of skilled manpower, the East German government announced a ten per cent increase in working 'norms' – the number of hours and volume of output that workers were required to fulfil each day. In protest, building workers on Stalinallee (now Karl-Marx-Allee) downed tools on 16 June and marched towards the government offices on Leipziger Strasse. The government refused to relent, and, by the next day, strikes had broken out across the city. Communist Party offices were stormed and red flags torn from public buildings. By midday the government had lost control of the city and it was left to the Red Army to restore order. Soviet tanks rolled into the centre of East Berlin, where they were met by stones thrown by demonstrators.

By nightfall the uprising was crushed. According to official figures 23 people died, though other estimates put the figure at over 200. There followed a wave of arrests across East Berlin, with more than four thousand people detained. The majority went on to receive stiff prison sentences.

The 17 June uprising only furthered the wave of emigration. By the end of the 1950s it was almost possible to calculate the moment when East Germany would cease to function as an industrial state through the loss of skilled labour. Estimates put the loss to the East German economy through emigration at some DM100 billion. Ulbricht increased his demands on Moscow to take action.

In 1958 the Soviet leader Nikita Khrushchev tried to bully the Allies into relinquishing West Berlin with an ultimatum calling for an end to the military occupation of the city and a 'normalisation of the situation in the capital of the GDR', by which he meant Berlin as a whole. The ultimatum was rejected and the Allies made clear their commitment to West Berlin. Unwilling to provoke a world war, but needing to prop up his ally, Khrushchev backed down and sanctioned Ulbricht's alternative plan for a solution to the Berlin question.

THE WALL

During the early summer of 1961 rumours spread in town that Ulbricht intended to seal off West Berlin with some form of barrier or reinforced border. Emigration had reached a highpoint as 1,500 East Germans fled to the West each day and it became clear that events had reached a crisis point.

However, when in the early hours of 13 August units of the People's Police (assisted by 'Working Class Combat Groups') began to drag bales of barbed wire across Potsdamer Platz, Berlin and the world were caught by surprise.

In a finely planned and executed operation (overseen by Erich Honecker, then Politburo member in charge of security affairs), West Berlin was sealed off within 24 hours. As well as a fence of barbed wire, trenches were dug, the windows in houses lining or straddling the new border were bricked up, and tram and railway lines were interrupted: all this under the watchful eyes of armed guards. Anyone trying to flee West risked being shot, and in the 29 years the Wall stood, nearly 80 people died trying to escape. Justifying their actions, the East Germans later claimed they had erected an 'Anti-Fascist Protection Rampart' to prevent a world war.

> **'In a finely planned and executed operation, West Berlin was sealed off within 24 hours.'**

Days later the construction of a wall began. When it was completed, the concrete part of the 160-kilometre (100-mile) fortification ran to 112 kilometres (70 miles); 37 kilometres (23 miles) of the Wall ran through the city centre. Previously innocuous streets like Bernauer Strasse (where houses on one side were in the East, those on the other in the West) suddenly became the location for one of the world's most sophisticated and deadly border fortifications.

The initial stunned disbelief of Berliners turned into despair as it became clear that (as with the 17 June uprising) the Western Allies could do little more than make a show of strength. President Kennedy dispatched American reinforcements to Berlin, and, for a few tense weeks, American and Soviet tanks squared off at Checkpoint Charlie.

Moral support from the Americans came with the visit of Vice-President Lyndon Johnson a week after the Wall was built. And two years later Kennedy himself arrived and spoke to a crowd of half-a-million people in front of Rathaus Schöneberg. His speech linked the fate of West Berlin with that of the free world and ended with the now famous statement 'Ich bin ein Berliner!' (Literally, alas, 'I am a doughnut' – or maybe not… *see p23* **Ich bin *ein* Berliner: JFK.**)

In its early years the Wall became the scene of many daring escape attempts (all documented in the Museum Haus Am Checkpoint Charlie) as people abseiled off buildings, swam across the Spree river, waded through ancient sewers or simply tried to climb over the Wall.

But as the fortifications along the Wall were improved with mines, searchlights and guard dogs, and as the guards were given orders to shoot, escape became nearly impossible. By the time the Wall fell in November 1989 it had been 'updated' four times to incorporate every conceivable deterrent.

In 1971 the Four Powers met and signed the Quadrapartite Agreement, which formally recognised the city's divided status. Border posts (such as the infamous Checkpoint Charlie) were introduced and designated to particular categories of visitors – one for foreigners, another for West Germans, and so on.

A TALE OF TWO CITIES

During the 1960s, with the Wall as infamous and ugly backdrop, the cityscape of modern Berlin (both East and West) began to take shape. On Tauentzienstrasse in the West the Europa-Center was built, and the bomb-damaged Kaiser-Wilhelm-Gedächtniskirche was given a partner – a new church made up of a glass-clad tower and squat bunker.

Hans Scharoun laid out the Kulturforum in Tiergarten as West Berlin's answer to the Museuminsel complex in the East. The first building to go up was Scharoun's Philharmonie, completed in 1963. Mies van der Rohe's Neue Nationalgalerie (which he had originally designed as a Bacardi factory in Havana) was finished in 1968.

In the suburbs work began on concrete mini-towns, Gropiusstadt and Märkisches Viertel. Conceived as modern solutions to housing shortages, they would develop into alienating ghettos.

Alexanderplatz in the East was rebuilt along totalitarian lines and the Fernsehturm ('Television Tower') was finished. The historic core of Berlin was mostly cleared to make way for parks (such as the Marx-Engels Forum) or new office and housing developments. On the eastern outskirts of the city in Marzahn and Hohenschönhausen work began on mass-scale housing projects.

In 1965 the first sit-down was staged on the Kurfürstendamm by students protesting low grants and expensive accommodation. This was followed by political demonstrations as students took to the streets to protest against the state in general and the Vietnam war in particular. The first communes were set up in Kreuzberg, thereby sowing the seeds of a counter-culture that was to make the district famous.

The student protest movement came into increasingly violent confrontation with the police in 1967 and 1968. One student, Benno Ohnesorg, was shot dead by police at a demonstration against the Shah of Iran, who visited the city in June 1967. A year later the students' leader, Rudi Dutschke, was shot by a right-winger. Demonstrations were held outside the offices of the newspaper group Springer, whose papers were blamed for inciting the shooting. It was out of this movement that the Red Army Faction (also known as the Baader-Meinhof gang) was to emerge. It was often to make headlines in the 1970s, not least through a series of kidnappings of high-profile city officials.

NORMALISING ABNORMALITY

The signing of the Quadrapartite Agreement confirmed West Berlin's abnormal status and ushered in an era of decline, as the frisson of Cold War excitement and 1960s rebellion petered out. More than ever West Berlin depended on huge subsidies from West Germany to keep it going.

Development schemes and tax-release programmes were introduced to encourage businesses to move to the city (to keep the population in the city, Berliners also paid less income tax), but still the economy and the population declined.

> **'The late 1970s and early 1980s saw the rise of the squatter movement, which brought violent political protest back on to the streets.'**

At the same time there was growth in the number of *Gastarbeiter* ('guest workers') who arrived from southern Europe and particularly Turkey, to take on the menial jobs that most Germans shunned. Today there are over 120,000 Turks in the city, largely concentrated in Kreuzberg.

By the late 1970s Berlin was mired in the depths of decline. In the West, the city government was discredited by an increasing number of scandals, mostly connected with property deals. In East Berlin Erich Honecker's regime (he succeeded Ulbricht in 1971), which had begun in a mood of reform and change, became increasingly repressive. Some of East Germany's best writers and artists, who had previously been willing to support socialism, left the country. The Communists were glad to be rid of them. From its headquarters in Normannenstrasse (a building that now incorporates the Stasi Museum), the Stasi directed its policy of mass observation, and increasingly succeeded in permeating every part of East German society. Between East and West there were squalid exchanges of political prisoners for hard currency.

The late 1970s and early 1980s saw the rise of the squatter movement (centred in Kreuzberg), which brought violent political protest back on to the streets. The problem was only diffused after the Senate caved in and gave squatters rent contracts.

In 1987 Berlin celebrated its 750th birthday twice, as East and West vied to outdo each other with exhibitions and festivities. In the East, the Nikolaiviertel was restored in time for the celebrations, and Honecker began a programme to do the same for the few remaining historical sites that had survived both wartime bombing and post-war planning. The statue of Frederick the Great riding his horse was returned to Unter den Linden.

THE FALL OF THE WALL

But restored monuments were not enough to stem the growing dissatisfaction of East Berliners. The development of perestroika in the Soviet Union had been ignored by Honecker,

The Wall goes up in 1961... and 28 years later, down it comes.

who stuck hard to his Stalinist instincts. Protest was increasingly vocal and only initially beaten back by the police.

By the spring of 1989 the East German state was no longer able to withstand the pressure of a population fed up with Communism. Throughout the summer thousands fled the city and the country via Hungary, which had opened its borders to the West. Those who stayed began demonstrating for reforms.

By the time Honecker was hosting the celebrations in the Volkskammer ('People's Chamber') to mark the 40th anniversary of the GDR on 7 October 1989 crowds were demonstrating outside, chanting 'Gorby! Gorby!' to register their opposition. Honecker was ousted days later. His successor, Egon Krenz, could do little to stem the tide of opposition. In a desperate bid to defend through attack, he decided to grant the concession East Germans wanted most – freedom to travel. On 9 November 1989 the Berlin Wall was opened, just over 29 years after it had been built. As thousands of East Berliners raced through to the sound of popping corks, the end of East Germany and the unification of Berlin and Germany had begun.

REUNIFYING BERLIN

With the Wall down Berlin was once again the centre stage of history. Just as the division of the city defined the split of Europe so the freedom to move again between east and west marked the dawn of the post-Cold War era.

Unsurprisingly, such an auspicious moment went to Berlin's head, and for more than a year the city was in a state of euphoria. Between November 1989 and October 1990 the city witnessed the collapse of Communism and the first free elections (March 1990) in the east for more than 50 years; economic unification with the swapping of the tinny Ostmark for the Deutschmark (July 1990); and the political merger of east into west with formal political unification on 3 October 1990. (It was also the year West Germany picked up its third World Cup trophy. The team may have come from the west, but in a year characterised by outbursts of popular celebration, easterners cheered too.)

But Unification also brought problems, especially for Berlin, where the two halves had to be made into one whole. While western infrastructure in the form of roads, telephones and other amenities was in decent working order, in the east it was falling apart or non-existent. Challenges also came from the collapse of a command economy where jobs were provided regardless of cost or productivity. The Deutschmark put hard currency into the wallets of easterners, but it also exposed the true state of their economy. Within months thousands of companies cut jobs or closed down altogether.

The restructuring of eastern industry was placed with the Treuhandanstalt, a huge state agency that, for a while, was the world's largest industrial holding company. Housed in Goering's old air ministry on the corner of Leipziger Strasse and Wilhelmstrasse (now the Finance Ministry building), the Treuhand gave high-paid employment to thousands of western yuppies and put hundreds of thousands of easterners on the dole.

Understandably, easterners soon turned on the Treuhand, which was widely vilified as the main agent of a brutal takeover by the west. Few easterners, however, were prepared to go as far as some extremists – most probably members of the Red Army Faction, a left-wing terrorist group dating back to the 1960s – who, in spring 1991, assassinated the head of the Treuhand, Detlev Karsten Rohwedder.

The killing of another state employee, Hanno Klein, drew attention to another dramatic change in Berlin brought about by Unification: a property boom. The biggest boost to the market ironically came from Bonn, the old federal capital, where in 1991 parliament voted to shift the seat of national government back to Berlin. The decision heralded a wave of speculative private investment and helped turn Berlin into one big building site.

Klein, who was responsible for drawing up a controversial master plan for the development of the new/old city centre where the Wall once stood, and where the glossy new corporate developments of Potsdamer Platz now stand, sought to control the wilder demands of the construction community. Who killed him remains unknown.

DRIFTING TO NORMALITY

The giddy excitement of the post-Unification years soon gave way to a period of disappointment. The sheer amount of construction work, the scrapping of federal subsidies and tax breaks to west Berlin, rising unemployment and a delay in the arrival of the government from Bonn all contributed to dampening spirits. In 1994 the last Russian, US, British and French troops left the city. With them went Berlin's unique Cold War status, and also the added internationalism that came with occupation. After decades of being different, Berlin was on its way to becoming like any other big European capital. City politics were no longer dominated by the big issues of geopolitics, but more by the details of how to cope with empty coffers and spending cuts.

The 1990s were characterised by the regeneration of the east. In the course of the decade the city's centre of gravity shifted towards Mitte. The government and commercial districts were revitalised. On their fringes, especially around Oranienburger Strasse, the Hackesche Höfe and into Prenzlauer Berg, a sprawl of trendy bars, restaurants, galleries and boutiques seemingly sprouted overnight in streets that under Communism had been grey and crumbling.

The fast-track gentrification in the east was matched by the decline of west Berlin. The proprietors of up-market boutiques and bars began to desert Charlottenburg and Schöneberg in favour of the east, or at least to open a branch there. Kreuzberg, once the inelegantly wasted symbol of a defiant west Berlin, degenerated to almost slum-like conditions, while a new bohemia developed across the Spree in Friedrichshain.

Westerners did, however, benefit from the reopening of the Berlin hinterland. Tens of thousands took the opportunity to leave the city and move to greener suburbs and satellite towns in the state of Brandenburg. An attempt by the political leaders of Brandenburg and Berlin to merge the two was voted down in a 1996 referendum. Brandenburgers' resentment of the big city, and antipathy for the east among some west Berliners, conspired to kill the issue.

THE BERLIN REPUBLIC

Having spent the best part of a decade doing what it had done so often in the past – regenerating itself out of the wreckage left by history – Berlin exited the 20th century with a flourish. In spring 1999 the new Reichstag, remodelled by British architect Norman Foster, was unveiled, and within months most of the government and its accompanying baggage of lobbyists and journalists had moved to the city. From Chancellor Gerhard Schroeder down, public figures and commentators sought to mark the transition as the beginning of the 'Berlin republic' – for which read a peaceful, democratic and, above all, self-confident Germany, as opposed to the chaos of the Weimar years or the self-conscious timidity of the Bonn era.

Schroeder himself had to wait two years before getting his full taste of the new Berlin, when, in spring 2001, the purpose-built Chancellery was opened. The building is a subject of some critical dispute, with many observers comparing it to a giant washing machine that bears the bombastic hallmarks of its original patron, Schroeder's predecessor Helmut Kohl. Schroeder himself let it be known that he preferred his slightly tatty temporary offices in the old East German State Council

building, while his wife Doris grumbled about the prospect of life in a high-security enclave. It must have been a short-lived feeling of discomfort, though, as Schroeder soon seemed to delight in showing off his new abode – especially when it came to having his photograph taken on one of the building's balconies where the backdrop of the Reichstag was most dramatic.

The move to a grander scale appeared to reflect Germany's increasing international role. The Kosovo crisis (1999) and the response to the terrorist attacks on the World Trade Centre and the Pentagon in September 2001 saw Germany called upon to play a more active role abroad, including for the first time the deployment of combat troops outside the NATO arena.

But, while new buildings provided tangible evidence of the sweeping changes brought on by the events of 1989, one area of city life – the crusty and crony-ridden local political system – seemed determined to carry on regardless. The grand coalition of Christian Democrats and Social Democrats that had governed the city since 1990 was, in many ways, caught in a (West Berlin) time-warp – mentally still committed to a life of subsidies from central government, desperate to hang on to old privileges and perks and unwilling to face up to tough choices brought on by near-empty coffers and the collapse of traditional industries.

The final collapse came in the summer of 2001 when yet another crisis at Bankgesellschaft Berlin, a bank largely owned by the city, brought down the senate. The crisis that made the city's parlous financial state even worse had its origins in a raft of dud and corrupt real estate loans – perhaps unsurprising given the prominence of the building sector in recent Berlin history. Eberhard Diepgen, the boy from Wedding who made governing mayor even before the Wall fell, was replaced after early elections by Klaus Wowereit, a Social Democrat. The elections highlighted lingering divisions, as the PDS, successors to the East German Communist Party, grabbed almost half of the vote in the east of the city. Despite such a strong showing, Wowereit and the Social Democrats decided against breaking the taboo of no deals with the PDS, and opted for the trusted route of a coalition with the Greens and liberals.

In another area, however, the new mayor was more than willing to smash old taboos. Before going to the polls Wowereit proudly declared his homosexuality. The voters were unmoved, and one of the first cases of a gay being elected to high office passed off barely unnoticed. But then with Berlin, what else did people expect?

Key events

1237 Town of Cölln first mentioned in a church document.
1307 The towns of Berlin and Cölln officially united under the rule of the Ascanian family.
1319 Last of the Ascanians dies.
1359 Berlin joins the Hanseatic League.
1411 Friedrich of Hohenzollern is sent by the Holy Roman Emperor to bring peace to the region.
1447-8 The 'Berlin Indignation'. The citizens rebel and lock Friedrich II out of the city.
1535 Accession of Joachim I Nestor, the first protestant Elector. The Reformation arrives in Berlin.
1538 Work begins on the Stadtschloss.
1618-48 Berlin and Brandenburg are ravaged by the Thirty Years War; the population halves.
1640-88 Reign of Friedrich Wilhelm, the Great Elector.
1662-8 Construction of the Oder–Spree canal.
1672 Jewish and Huguenot refugees arrive in Berlin.
1695 Work begins on Schloss Charlottenburg.
1701 Elector Friedrich III, son of the Great Elector, has himself crowned Friedrich I, King of Prussia. Work begins on the German and French cathedrals at the Gendarmenmarkt.
1713-40 Reign of King Friedrich Wilhelm I, who expands the army; Berlin becomes a garrison city.
1740-86 Reign of Frederick the Great (Friedrich II) – a time of military expansion and administrative reform.
1756-63 Seven Years War ends triumphantly for Prussia.
1788-91 Construction of Brandenburger Tor.
1806 Napoleon marches into Berlin. Two years of French occupation. The Quadriga taken to Paris.
1809 Wilhelm von Humboldt founds the university.
1813 Napoleon defeated at Grossbeeren and Leipzig.
1814 General Blücher brings the Quadriga back to Berlin and restores it on the Brandenburg Gate.
1837 Foundation of the Borsig Werke marks the beginning of Berlin's expansion towards becoming Continental Europe's largest industrial city.
1838 First railway line in Germany, from Berlin to Potsdam.
1840 Friedrich Wilhelm IV accedes to the throne. With a population of around 400,000, Berlin is the fourth largest city in Europe.
1848 The 'March Revolution' breaks out. Berlin briefly in the hands of the revolutionaries.
1861 Accession of King Wilhelm I.

1862 Appointment of Otto von Bismarck as Prime Minister of Prussia.
1871 Following victory in the Franco-Prussian war, King Wilhelm I is proclaimed German Emperor (Kaiser) and Berlin becomes the Imperial capital.
1879 Electric lighting comes to Berlin, which also boasts the world's first electric railway. Three years later telephone services are introduced. The city emerges as Europe's most modern metropolis.
1888 Kaiser Wilhelm II comes to the throne.
1890 Wilhelm II sacks Bismarck.
1894 Completion of the Reichstag.
1902 First underground line is opened.
1914-18 World War I.
1918 9 Nov: the Kaiser abdicates, Philip Scheidemann proclaims Germany a republic and Karl Liebknecht declares Germany a socialist republic. Chaos ensues.
1919 Spartacist uprising suppressed.
1923 Hyperinflation – at one point $1 is worth 4.2 billion marks.
1926 Josef Goebbels comes to Berlin to take charge of the local Nazi Party organisation.
1927 Berlin boasts more than 70 cabarets.
1933 Hitler takes power.
1936 11th Olympic Games held in Berlin.
1938 Kristallnacht, 9 Nov Jewish homes, businesses and synagogues in Berlin are stoned, looted and set ablaze.
1939 Outbreak of World War II, during which Berlin suffers appalling devastation.
1944 A group around Colonel Count von Stauffenberg attempts to assassinate Hitler.
1945 Germany signs unconditional surrender.
1948-9 The Berlin Blockade. The Soviets cut off all transport links to west Berlin. For 11 months the city is supplied by the Allied Airlift.
1949 Foundation of Federal Republic in May and German Democratic Republic in October.
1953 17 June uprising in East Berlin is suppressed.
1961 The Wall goes up on 13 August.
1968 Student leader Rudi Dutschke is shot.
1971 Erich Honecker succeeds Walter Ulbricht as GDR head of state. The Quadrapartite Agreement formalises Berlin's divided status.
1980-81 'Hot Winter': violent squatter protests.
1987 Berlin's 750th birthday.
1989 9 Nov: the Wall comes down.
1990 3 Oct: formal German Reunification.
1994 Last of the Allied military leave Berlin.
1999 The German government moves from Bonn and the 'Berlin Republic' is born.
2001 Financial crisis brings down the senate; openly gay Klaus Wowereit elected mayor; opening of the Jüdisches Museum.

Berlin Today

New political alliances, empty coffers and a disparate population – Berlin is facing an identity crisis.

During the decade since the fall of the Wall, Berlin has been one huge construction site. Old buildings were remodelled or torn down and new ones erected to accommodate private investors and the Federal government, which moved to Berlin in 1999. The building boom also engendered the dodgy real estate deals and bribery that bankrupted the city and eventually felled the grand coalition of Christian Democrats (CDU) and Social Democrats (SPD) that had governed since 1991. The CDU was held largely responsible for the disaster, and an interregnum of SPD and Greens under Mayor Klaus Wowereit generated hope and goodwill. (Wowereit's gay self-outing '*und das ist gut so*' – and that's OK – became a catchphrase.) After new elections, the Social Democrats entered a partnership with the Party of Democratic Socialism (PDS), which grew out of East Germany's former ruling Socialist Unity Party (SED), to govern the financially beleaguered city-state.

BERLIN™

In three CDU-dominated grand coalitions, the city government (Senat) met post-1989 challenges with marketing strategies. Massive events such as the Love Parade or the Christo Wrapping of the Reichstag were supported, or, if nothing else, capitalised on. The most brilliant marketing coup, however, was to make the city and its perpetual 'becoming' the biggest event of all. Construction sites, hitherto downplayed, were celebrated as key events with guided tours and cultural programmes. The development of the new urban centre at Potsdamer Platz and the Federal government's move from Bonn, encapsulated by Sir Norman Foster's glass doming of the Reichstag, were hyped for years in advance. 'Berlin – the event' reinforced Berlin's brand identity – beacon of the 'Berlin Republic', ever-evolving manifest-ation of modern urbanity and hotbed of cutting-edge youth culture.

Significantly, the official city logo was no longer simply the word Berlin in an unadorned typeface, but now accompanied by a stylised Brandenburg Gate as trademark. Tourists and investors happily bought into the brand, supplying the city with much-needed revenue, even if the average Berliner was a touch more cynical.

Few denied the necessity of attracting new businesses, especially in the service sector, the entertainment industry and new economy, to compensate for the 300,000 industrial jobs lost as a result of the collapse of the planned economy, loss of subsidies and a general trend towards de-industrialisation. Nevertheless, lenient zoning regulations and generous subsidies for developers had some questionable effects. Urban renewal projects seemed to centre around shopping malls or other commercial facilities (*see p158* **From Berlin Wall to Berlin mall**), not always organically integrating themselves into the cityscape, and creating primarily low-security McJobs. In fact, the unemployment rate has increased; it was approximately 16 per cent in early 2002.

MULTICULTURAL FABRIC HANGING BY A THREAD

While the population has in fact marginally decreased over the past five years and hovers around 3,400,000 inhabitants, Berlin still attracts workers, artists, students, scholars, business-people and diplomats from all over the world. The lion's share of post-Wall migrants comes from Poland, Russia, the Ukraine and other CIS countries, many of which are so-called *Aussiedler* (ethnic Germans or their descendants who had settled in the former Soviet Union) or Jewish émigrés. Refugees from war-torn Bosnia and Kosovo have also found a temporary home in Berlin. With a community of approximately 130,000, Turks constitute the largest ethnic group in Berlin. Recruited as 'guest workers' 40 years ago, the Turkish population has shaped the face of many (west) Berlin neighbourhoods, especially in Kreuzberg, Neukölln and Wedding, with their restaurants, grocery stores and other small businesses. As the city's longest-standing immigrant group, Turks have become the most integrated into the mainstream of German society, despite considerable religious and cultural differences. (Natives of NATO member Turkey have been subject to less post-September 11 suspicion than those of other Islamic countries.)

While West Berlin had a higher non-German population – guest workers from the former Yugoslavia figuring prominently alongside the Turks – East Berlin also hosted Vietnamese and Angolan guest workers in addition to migrants from eastern European and other 'socialist brother nations'. Inhabitants from 190 countries make Berlin their home, contributing to its unique multicultural mix, which, in turn, attracts further newcomers.

The city's multicultural fabric threatens to be unravelled by the tenuous economic situation, often a root of racial tension. Although the 2001 municipal elections saw the three right-wing extremist parties shut out of both the city-state parliament and borough assemblies, this development is less a reflection of waning neo-fascist sentiment than of a loosening of party allegiance in general. A group of 600 neo-Nazis marched through the Brandenburg Gate in protest at the planned Holocaust memorial nearby and hundreds demonstrated against an exhibition of World War II German army war crimes.

'The Berlin Wall may be a hazy memory... but the proverbial "wall in people's heads" is still erect.'

Many not adhering to the white/Aryan/hetero norm still feel unsafe, especially in east Berlin districts like Hohenschönhausen and Marzahn. On a hopeful note, six-figure crowds turn out for anti-racist marches, so perhaps these one-off shows of support will eventually spill over into day-to-day attitudes and conduct.

EAST IS EAST

Decade Two after reunification finds Berlin not yet a truly united city. Granted, homogenisation of everything from street signs to museum collections has been accomplished. Former CDU (and West Berlin apologist) mayor Eberhard Diepgen somewhat surprisingly spoke out in favour of finally raising eastern wages and salaries to western levels after eastern costs of living had long approached those in the west; in Berlin, the east–west gap in standards of living is narrower than elsewhere. But while the architectural structure of the Berlin Wall may be a hazy memory apart from the tourist attraction East Side Gallery and the more sombre Wall Memorial at Bernauer Strasse, the proverbial 'wall in people's heads' is still erect. *Ossi–Wessi* (easterner–westerner) interaction is still marked by prejudices and misunderstandings, fuelled by controversy over everything from the seemingly indiscriminate eradication of GDR architecture – the demolition of the Ahornblatt and Palast Hotel and the uncertain fate of the Palast der Republik – to a perceived double standard in the handling of Stasi files of Eastern and

Modern Jewish life

The character of today's Berlin Jewish community bares only a faint resemblance to that which flourished before Auschwitz. Still, Jewish life is bouncing back – offering more than just the gleaming, golden dome of the Neue Synagoge.

When Hitler came to power around 170,000 Jews lived in Berlin. By 1939 nearly half had emigrated. Almost all who stayed perished in the Holocaust. Most of the 7,000 German Jews left in Berlin in 1945 survived because they were married to non-Jews. At the same time, tens of thousands of east European Jews flooded into Germany, fleeing anti-Semitism. Most continued on to Palestine and the United States; but by the early 1950s over 10,000 east European Jews had settled in Germany. It was these east European Jews and the surviving German Jews who ounded the post-war *Gemeinde* (community organisation) in Berlin.

The division of Berlin also split the city's Jewish population. The West Berlin *Gemeinde* tentatively settled with the construction of a Community House (Fasanenstrasse), which is still the administrative heart of the *Gemeinde* today. As West Germany stabilised, German Jews gradually returned from abroad. But it was still immigration from eastern Europe and the Soviet Union that kept the *Gemeinde* alive.

In East Germany, Soviet policy influenced the course of Jewish life. German Jews who returned to build a socialist state, were removed from positions of power in Stalin's anti-Semitic purges. East Germany switched tracks in the years of détente, financing the renovation of the Neue Synagoge in 1988. The East Berlin *Gemeinde* membership

dwindled to about 200 in the 1980s, as a result of ageing and mixed marriages, while its Western counterpart was 7,000-strong. German reunification saw the East and West *Gemeinden* merge, but there are still latent east–west divisions in Jewish activities today.

The huge influx of immigrants from the former Soviet Union since German reunification has doubled Berlin's Jewish *Gemeinde* to 11,000 affiliated members, although the total number of Jews in the city is estimated at between 18,000 and 20,000. This numerical boost comes hand in hand with major challenges for the *Gemeinde*: next to language problems, many immigrants arrive with scant religious or cultural Jewish awareness, because Jewish practice was difficult in Communist countries. Some have also been accused of an unwillingness to adapt, while established German Jews (many of whom are themselves descended from immigrants) have been criticised for their arrogance. Another concern is that many immigrants faked their Jewish identity papers to get into Germany.

The fall of communism also let the tourism industry give east Berlin's historical landmarks a makeover. A clutch of Jewish-style non-kosher restaurants sprang up in the Scheunenviertel – the former Jewish quarter. In a bizarre way Jewishness has attained a certain level of ethnic chic. **Café Oren** (*see p128*) focuses on Israeli cuisine; **Am Wasserturm** (Knaackstrasse 22; 442 8807) offers a poor imitation of Ashkenazi classics; kosher eating is limited to **Arche Noah** (Fasanenstrasse 79-80; 882 6138) and **Café Beth** (*see p144*). Berlin's only kosher butcher is the **Kosher Deli** (Goethestrasse

Western dignitaries. 'Ostalgia' for cultural artefacts such as the rock band Puhdys, the children's puppet show Sandmännchen, Cabinet cigarettes and the East Berlin traffic light man are defiant assertions of identity. ('*Wessi*' young professional or creative types setting up shop in abandoned *Plattenbauten*, typical slab high-rises, embrace many of the same things in the name of GDR retro chic.)

The primary benefactor of this climate is the PDS, which presents itself as the mouthpiece for disillusioned and disenfranchised *Ossis*. Since 1990 the PDS went from less than ten per cent city-wide to nearly 23 per cent in the 2001

elections, barely losing second place to the CDU, now something of a pariah; nearly 48 per cent of east Berliners voted PDS, and the party got a respectable six per cent in the western boroughs. But it wasn't until negotiations for a Chancellor Schröder-endorsed three-party alliance (the Greens on one end of the spectrum and the laissez-faire FDP on the other) collapsed that the SPD and PDS joined forces.

STRANGE BEDFELLOWS

The two parties hammered out a coalition rather quickly, but not without controversy. GDR civil rights activists deplored the SPD abetting the former 'cadres' regaining power. The Federal

61; 3150 9243), while **Kolbo** (Auguststrasse 77-8; 281 3135) sells kosher groceries. The Scheunenviertel doesn't match up to the Jewish restaurant and shopping districts in London, Paris or New York. This will only improve if genuine demand, rather than the whim of tourism, grows.

Jewish culture too has returned to the spotlight. Klezmer concerts are put on at the **Hackesches Hof Theater** (Rosenthaler Strasse 40/41; 283 2587) most nights, catering for tourists on the Jewish nostalgia trail. Meanwhile, community groups organise annual events for a wider audience, such as the highly regarded **Jewish Culture Days** (November), the **Jewish Film Festival** (June) and the boisterous **Jewish Street Festival** (June). A recent addition to the cultural scene is the Jewish theatre **Bamah** (Hohenzollerndamm 177; 251 1096).

The most obvious symbol of the Scheunenviertel – the **Neue Synagoge** (*pictured*) on Oranienburger Strasse – is literally just a façade. The site of the original synagogue is wasteland – deliberately left as a memorial to what was damaged by Nazi flames, and finished off by wartime bombs. Today, the building contains a museum and offices; one small room functions as a synagogue. Although it's the most prominent Jewish landmark, it is not representative of the religious tendency in Berlin. It's the only synagogue that offers Reform services, attracting a mix of *Ossis*, *Wessis* and expats from Europe and America.

Of the seven synagogues in Berlin (there were 80 before the Nazi era), three survived the pogroms and bombs: Pestalozzistrasse 14-15 (Liberal) was not fully razed to the

ground because fire-fighters feared that neighbouring buildings would catch fire; Fraenkelufer 10-16 (Conservative) is the surviving wing of a neo-classical synagogue; Rykestrasse 53 (Conservative) was tucked away in an east Berlin courtyard and is now Germany's largest synagogue.

In terms of the day-to-day religious, social and educational activities within the community, which are less obvious to the visitor, Berlin is back on a par with other Jewish communities around the world. But the legacy of destruction and division, and the challenges of growth and integration make Jewish Berlin a unique place.

government was wary of the alliance due to PDS opposition to German military support of the coalition against terrorism.

With Berlin's financial situation as a sombre backdrop, considerable scepticism greeted the announcement that attorney and media darling Gregor Gysi, a PDS politician with little economic policy experience, was designated Economics and Employment Senator and, therefore, chief investment canvasser. However, the business community refrained from outright panic, and Gysi appointed a former Chamber of Commerce official as his under-secretary.

With a debt of €40 billion, this Senat's highest priority will be saving the city from insolvency. The ambitious coalition agreement, which includes a preamble in which the PDS condemns and distances itself from the Berlin Wall, the brutal repression of the 17 June 1953 uprising and general injustices committed by the GDR, effectively boils down to one sentence – all policy measures are subject to their affordability. That doesn't leave much leeway for cultivating Berlin's strengths – diverse and vibrant cultural scenes and excellence in scientific and scholarly research, for example – or to deal

Remember to forget

Of all the debates about the intersection of history, architecture and the shape of Berlin's post-Wall cityscape, few have lumbered on so long or conjured up as much controversy as the memorial to Holocaust victims – **Das Denkmal für die ermordeten Juden Europas** – proposed for a 20,000-square metre (215,000-square foot) site south of Pariser Platz. Since the mid 1990s, every deadline for any kind of decision has led to yet more indecision, mired as the project is in political disagreements about the nature of historical memory and responsibility, both individual and collective.

The idea of some kind of central memorial has been around since the late 1980s, but the fall of the Wall opened up the possibility of it becoming a reality. The winning design in a competition held in 1995 was submitted by Berlin artist Christine Jackob-Marks. It proposed a huge, slanted concrete tablet – about the size of two football fields – bearing the names of all 4.2 million identified Holocaust victims. Then Chancellor Kohl rejected the design, distressed at its very immensity.

But it also found disfavour with left-wing opponents of traditional '19th-century-style monuments' that present history as a completed process rather than encouraging public debate and engagement. Many of those same people wanted no central monument at all, and especially not at a site with no particular links to the Holocaust. Why not just preserve the concentration camps? Why fall prey to the cliché of matching the enormity of the crime with the vastness of the memorial? One argument in favour of the monument's central location was the prominent space it would occupy in the new cityscape and, thus, in the consciousness of natives and tourists alike.

A second competition was held in 1998. From four finalists, the design by Peter Eisenmann and Richard Serra was chosen: 4,000 concrete columns of varying heights. Eisenmann, who had by then parted ways with Serra, had to modify his design, plagued by questions such as: should it include an information centre or could the field of columns speak for itself? The groundbreaking ceremony for the memorial, now scaled down to 1,500 columns, was held in February 2000 amid sizeable protest. A controversial fundraising campaign featuring a poster provocatively parroting Holocaust denial sentiments drew the ire of Jewish community leaders and was discontinued.

Debates about remembrance, and compensation, of other Nazi regime victims also ensued. Roma representatives argued that the extermination of their people should not be separated from that of the Jews. They were promised their own memorial, although there were disagreements about the location – near the central memorial or at the suburban location of a former Gypsy prison camp. Roma leaders in turn refused to share their memorial with homosexuals or Communists, arguing that these groups had not been victimised on racial grounds. Was Berlin to become a landscape of segregated victims' memorials? What would be the most appropriate way to pay tribute to all the victims?

Debate about Third Reich atrocities also continues to be fed by neo-Nazi groups. In late 2001 the NPD party demonstrated against a revised photo exhibition that documented crimes committed by the Wehrmacht, which the demonstrators considered exempt of Nazi guilt. In protest at this latest incident of Holocaust denial, Berliners, including Mayor Wowereit, pointedly visited the exhibition on the day of the Nazi demo. Perhaps the ongoing controversy is the true Holocaust memorial.

with acute problems such as unemployment, social inequality, an education system in desperate need of reform and growing racism and xenophobia.

The coalition's first headlines were budget cuts – notably €1 billion payroll cuts, no Olympic Games campaign, the closing of 12 public swimming pools and three theatres.

The budgetary situation will certainly have profound effects, but whether that merely entails an overall diminishment in the quality of life or whether it will also provide opportunities for creativity will depend on the coalition's resourcefulness and stamina.

Before taking office, Gysi suggested a broad discussion of what Berlin means to itself, as capital and to the country at large. Perhaps the changing of the guard and material necessity will enable Berlin to find an identity and follow a path that a majority feels 'und das ist gut so'.

Architecture

The vicissitudes of history have left
Berlin with a unique urban landscape.

Berlin may be one of Europe's younger capital
cities, but Berliners can boast a distinguished
tradition of architectural experimentation.
During the 1910s and 1920s, the city was home
to some of the century's greatest architects and
designers: Peter Behrens, Bruno Taut, Ludwig
Mies van der Rohe and Walter Gropius, to
name just a few. But the path to modernism
was launched, on the heels of the Napoleonic
occupation, by Karl Friedrich Schinkel (*see p12*
Ich bin Berliner: KF Schinkel), who many
still consider the city's greatest builder. In
addition, fine specimens of nearly every style
since the baroque age can be found here, from
neo-Renaissance to neo-Rationalism.

Though the Berlin we see today was largely
shaped by the rise of the modern era, just about
every political and economic transformation of
the city, before and since, has also been accompanied by a new set of architectural and planning
principles. Another factor is that Berlin has
been a military post of one kind or another for
centuries, not least during the Cold War.

But it wasn't until the late 19th century
that Berlin as a whole was finally able to
hold its own with grander European capitals,
thanks to a construction boom known as the
Gründerzeit, which was triggered by the rapid
progress in industry and technology following
German unification in 1871. From then on, the
city quickly acquired a massive scale, while
spreading out into the countryside, with wide
streets and large blocks. These followed a
rudimentary geometry set out by an 1862
plan by James Hobrecht and were filled in with
five-storey *Mietskaserne* (translates literally
as 'rental barracks') with minimal courtyards.
Thankfully, the monotony – and the smoke
and noise of nearby factories – was partially
relieved by a handful of large public parks,
while later apartment houses gradually became
more humane and rather splendid. During the
1920s, this method of development was rejected
in favour of Bauhaus-influenced slabs and
towers, which were used to fill out the
peripheral zones at the edge of the forests.

The post-war years saw even more radical departures from the earlier tradition in all sectors of the city.

Today, as the cranes finally give way to a new layer of post-Wall architecture, the question becomes: how much of 'new Berlin' meets the cultural, technical and urban design challenges posed by Reunification? On the whole, it is a mixture of contemporary design and historic emulation, some of it implementing new environmental strategies, much of it attempting to restore a sense of continuity to an urban fabric ruptured by division and heavy-handed reconstruction. Inevitably, many of the older architectural landmarks of today's Berlin are more important as markers of these cycles of history than as masterpieces. Many significant works were lost to the war, including Messel's Wertheim department store at Leipziger Platz and Mendelsohn's Columbushaus at Potsdamer Platz. The new buildings in these areas have been reworked with these losses in mind.

> **'The Nikolaiviertel... is the only substantial part of central Berlin to give an idea of how the medieval city might have felt – except it's a fake.'**

The spirit of historic revival has even taken in the city's most famous landmark, the Wall, which was dismantled with breathtaking speed within a year or two after 1989. It is now being commemorated in public art, from the Gedenkstätte Berliner Mauer at Bernauer Strasse to Frank Thiel's portraits of the last Allied soldiers, suspended above former checkpoints in the city centre. With so much new architecture by architects from all over the globe, however, the memory of the Wall is rapidly fading away.

THE FIRST 500 YEARS
Berlin's long journey to world city status began in two tiny fishing and trading settlements on the Spree named Berlin and Cölln, originally Wendish/Slavic towns that were colonised by Germans around 1237. Among their oldest surviving buildings are the parish churches **Marienkirche** and **Nikolaikirche**. The latter was rebuilt in the district known as the **Nikolaiviertel**, along with other landmarks, such as the 1571 pub Zum Nussbaum and the baroque **Ephraim-Palais**. The Nikolaiviertel, between Alexanderplatz and the Spree, is the only

The **Alte Nationalgalerie**. *See p38.*

substantial part of central Berlin to give an idea of how the medieval city might have felt – except it's a fake, rebuilt by the East Germans in time for the city's 750th anniversary in 1987, a few decades after they had levelled the district.

Thanks also to the GDR's subtractive planning ideology, little survives of the massive **Stadtschloss** ('City Palace', 1538-1950), other than recently excavated foundations in front of the Palast der Republik, dating to the reign of Elector Joachim II. The **Schlossbrücke** crossing to Unter den Linden, adorned with figures by Christian Daniel Rauch, and the **Neptunbrunnen** ('Neptune Fountain', now relocated south of Marienkirche), modelled on Bernini's Roman fountains, were designed to embellish the palace.

In 1647 the Great Elector Friedrich Wilhelm II (1640-88) hired Dutch engineers to transform the route to the Tiergarten, the royal hunting forest, into the tree-lined boulevard of **Unter den Linden**. It led west toward **Schloss Charlottenburg**, built in 1695 as a summer retreat for Queen Sophie-Charlotte. Over the next century, the Elector's 'Residenzstadt' expanded to include Berlin-Cölln and the extension of Friedrichswerder to the south-west. Traces of the old stone **Stadtmauer** ('city wall') that enclosed them can still be seen on Waisenstrasse in Mitte. Two further districts, Dorotheenstadt (begun 1673, named after the Great Elector's Dutch queen) and Friedrichstadt (begun 1688), expanded the street grid north and south of Unter den Linden. All were united under one civic administration in 1709.

Andreas Schlüter built new palace wings for Elector Friedrich Wilhelm III (1688-1713, crowned King Friedrich I of Prussia in 1701) and supervised the building of the Zeughaus ('Arsenal'; Nering and de Bodt, 1695-1706; now the Deutsches Historisches Museum), the bellicose ornamentation of which embodies the Prussian love of militarism. In the courtyard, Schlüter depicted the gruesome results of this love in 22 masks of dying warriors.

City life changed when Wilhelm I, the Soldier King (1713-40), imposed conscription and subjugated the town magistrate to the court and military elite. The economy now catered to an army comprising 20 per cent of the population (a fairly constant percentage until 1918). To spur growth in gridded Friedrichstadt – and to quarter his soldiers cheaply – the King forced people to build new houses, which were mostly in a stripped-down classical style. He permitted one open square, **Gendarmenmarkt**, where twin churches were built in 1701, one of which now houses the Hugenotten Museum.

After the population reached 60,000 in 1710, a new customs wall enclosed four new districts – the Spandauer Vorstadt, Königstadt, Stralauer Vorstadt and Köpenicker Vorstadt; all now parts of Mitte. Built in 1737, the 14-kilometre (nine-mile) border remained the city limits until 1860.

Geometric squares later marked three of the 14 city gates in Friedrichstadt. At the square-shaped **Pariser Platz**, axial gateway to the Tiergarten, Langhans built the **Brandenburger Tor** (Brandenburg Gate) in 1789, a triumphal arch later topped by Schadow's **Quadriga** statue. The stately buildings around the square were levelled after the war, but have now largely been reconstructed or replaced, including the **Adlon Hotel** (Patzschke, Klotz, 1997), on an expanded version of its original site, and the twin buildings flanking the gate, Haus Sommer and Haus Liebermann (Kleihues, 1998).

SCHINKEL AND HIS DISCIPLES

Even with the army, Berlin's population did not reach 100,000 until well into the reign of Frederick the Great (1740-86), fan of Enlightenment ideas and absolutist politics. Military success inspired the French-speaking 'philosopher king' to embellish Berlin and Potsdam; many of the monuments along Unter

den Linden stem from his vision of a 'Forum Fredericianum'. Though never completed, the unique ensemble of neo-classical, baroque and rococo monuments includes the vine-covered **Humboldt-Universität** (Knobelsdorff/Boumann, 1748-53, palace of Frederick's brother Prince Heinrich until 1810); the **Staatsoper** (Knobelsdorff, Langhans, 1741-3); the **Prinzessinnenpalais** (1733, now the Operncafé) and the **Kronprinzenpalais** (Unter den Linden 3; 1663, expanded 1732). Set back from the Linden on Bebelplatz are the **Alte Bibliothek**, reminiscent of the curvy Vienna Hofburg (Unger, 1775-81, part of Humboldt-Universität) and the pantheon-like **St Hedwigs-Kathedrale**, a gift to Berlin's Catholics (Legeay and Knobelsdorff, 1747-73).

'Schinkel's... inspired urban visions served the cultural aspirations of an ascendant German state.'

Not long after the Napoleonic occupation, the prolific Karl Friedrich Schinkel (*see p12* **Ich bin Berliner: KF Schinkel**) became Berlin's most revered architect under Prince Friedrich Wilhelm IV. Drawing on early classical and Italian precedents, his early stage-sets experimented with perspective, while his inspired urban visions served the cultural aspirations of an ascendant German state. His work includes the colonnaded **Altes Museum** (1828), regarded by most architects as his finest work, and the **Neue Wache** (Royal Guardhouse, 1818), next to the Zeughaus, whose Roman solidity lent itself well to Tessenow's 1931 conversion into a memorial to the dead of World War I.

Other Schinkel masterpieces include the **Schauspielhaus**, a theatre to replace one lost to fire at Gendarmenmarkt (1817-21, now the Konzerthaus); the neo-Gothic brick **Friedrichwerdersche Kirche** (1830, now the Schinkel-Museum); and the cubic **Schinkel-Pavillon** (1825) at Schloss Charlottenburg. Among his many collaborations with garden architect Peter Joseph Lenné is the picturesque ensemble of classical follies at **Schloss Glienecke**, overlooking the Havel near the Glieneckebrücke, which connects Berlin with Potsdam.

After Schinkel's death in 1841, his many disciples propagated his architectural lessons in brick and stone. Friedrich August Stüler most notably satisfied the King's desire to complement the Altes Museum with the **Neues Museum** (1841-59, Bodestrasse 1-3, Mitte). Originally home of the Egyptian collection, it mixed new wrought-iron technology with classical architecture, terracotta ceiling coffers and elaborate murals. By 1910, Museumsinsel comprised the neo-classical **Alte National-galerie** (also Stüler, 1864; Bodestrasse, Mitte) with an open stairway framing an equestrian statue of the King; the triangular **Bode Museum** (von Ihne, 1904; Am Kupfergraben/ Monbijoubrücke); and the sombre grey **Pergamonmuseum** (Messel and Hoffmann, 1906-9). These are a stark contrast to the neo-Renaissance polychromy of the **Martin-Gropius-Bau** across town (Gropius and Schmieden, 1881).

HISTORICISM AND ECLECTICISM

As the population boomed after 1865, doubling to 1.5 million by 1890, the city began swallowing up neighbouring towns and villages. Factory complexes and worker housing gradually moved to the outskirts. Many of the new market halls and railway stations used a vernacular brick style with iron trusses, such as **Arminiu-shalle** in Moabit (Blankenstein, 1892; Bremer Strasse 9) and Franz Schwechten's Romanesque **Anhalter Bahnhof** (1876-80, now a ruin; Askanischer Platz). Brick was also used for civic buildings, like the neo-Gothic **Rotes Rathaus** (1861-9), while the orientalism of the gold-roofed **Neue Synagoge** on Oranienburger Strasse (Knoblauch, Stüler, 1859-66) made use of colourful masonry and mosaics.

Restrained historicism gave way to wild eclecticism as the 19th century marched on, in public buildings as well as apartment houses with plain interiors, dark courtyards and overcrowded flats behind decorative façades. Eclecticism was also rampant among lavish *Gründerzeit* villas in the fashionable suburbs to the south-west, especially Dahlem and Grunewald. In these areas the modest yellow-brick vernacular of Brandenburg was rejected in favour of elaborately modelled plaster and stone.

The **Kurfürstendamm**, a tree-lined shopping boulevard built up in the 1880s, soon helped the 'new west' rival the finery of Leipziger Strasse. Further out, in Nikolassee and Wannsee, private homes hit new heights of scale and splendour. Many were inspired by the English country house, such as **Haus Freudenberg** in Zehlendorf (Muthesius, 1908; Potsdamer Chaussee 48).

THE NEW METROPOLIS

In anticipation of a new age of rationality and mechanisation, an attempt at greater stylistic clarity was made after 1900, in spite of the bombast of works such as the new **Berliner Dom** (Raschdorff, 1905) and the **Reichstag** (Wallot, 1894). The Wilhelmine era's paradoxical mix of reformism and conservatism yielded an architecture of *Sachlichkeit* ('objectivity') in commercial and public buildings. In some cases, like Kaufmann's **Hebbel-Theater** (1908), or the **Hackesche Höfe** (Berndt and Endell, 1906-7; Rosenthaler Strasse 40-41, Mitte), *Sachlichkeit* meant a calmer form of art nouveau (or Jugendstil); elsewhere it was more sombre, with heavy, compact forms, vertical ribbing, and low-hanging mansard roofs. One of the most severe examples is the stripped-down classicism of Alfred Messel's **Pergamonmuseum**; even Bruno Schmitz's food automat at Friedrichstrasse 167 (1905), with its three central bays, is pretty dry.

The style goes well with Prussian bureaucracy in the civic architecture of Ludwig Hoffmann, city architect from 1896 to 1924. Though he sometimes used other styles for his many schools, courthouses and city halls, his towered **Altes Stadthaus** in Mitte (1919; Jüdenstrasse) and the **Rudolf-Virchow-Krankenhaus** in Wedding (1906; Augusten-burger Platz 1), then innovative for its pavilion system, epitomise Wilhelmine architecture.

In housing after 1900, *Sachlichkeit* led to early modernism to serve the masses of the metropolis, now totalling three million. Messel became architect to some of the first successful housing co-ops, designing with a country-house flair (Sickingenstrasse 7-8, Moabit, 1895; and Stargarder Strasse 30, Prenzlauer Berg, 1900). Paul Mebes launched his long career in housing, beginning with a double row of apartments with enclosed balconies (Fritschweg, Steglitz, 1907-8). He and others moved on to larger ensembles, forerunners of the Weimar-era housing estates. Schmitthenner explored a vernacular style with gabled brick terraces arranged like a medieval village in Staaken, built near Spandau for World War I munitions workers (1917). Taut and Tessenow substituted coloured stucco for ornament in the terraced housing of Gartenstadt Falkenberg in Altglienicke (1915), part of an unbuilt larger town plan.

Prior to the incorporation of metropolitan Berlin in 1920, many suburbs had been given full city charters and sported their own town halls, such as the massive **Rathaus Charlottenburg** (1905; Otto-Suhr-Allee 100) and **Rathaus Neukölln** (1909; Karl-Marx-Strasse 83-5). Neukölln's Reinhold Kiehl also built the Karl-Marx-Strasse Passage (1910, now home of the Neuköllner Oper), and the **Stadtbad Neukölln** (1914; Ganghofer Strasse 3-5), whose niches and mosaics evoke a Roman atmosphere. Special care was also given to new suburban rail stations of the period, such as the S-Bahnhof Mexikoplatz in Zehlendorf, set on a lovely garden square with shops and restaurants (Hart and Lesser, 1905), and the U-Bahnhof Dahlem-Dorf, whose half-timbered style goes a step further to capture a countrified look.

RADICAL WEIMAR REFORM

The work of many pioneers brought modern architecture to life in Berlin. One of the most important was Peter Behrens, who reinterpreted the factory with a new monumental language in the façade of the **Turbinenhalle** at Huttenstrasse in Moabit (1909) and several other buildings for the AEG, for whom he also designed lamps and fittings. After 1918, the turbulent birth of the Weimar Republic offered a chance for a final aesthetic break with the Wilhelmine compromise.

A radical new architecture gave formal expression to long-awaited social and political reforms. The *Neues Bauen* ('new buildings') began to exploit the new technologies of glass, steel and concrete, inspired by the early work of Tessenow and Behrens, Dutch modernism, cubism, Russian constructivism, civil engineering and even a bit of Japanese design.

> **'A radical new architecture gave formal expression to long-awaited social and political reforms.'**

Berlin architects could explore the new functionalism to their hearts' content, using clean lines and a machine aesthetic bare of ornament. This was thanks to the post-war housing demand, and a new social democrat administration that brought about the incorporation of the city in 1920 and put planner Martin Wagner at the helm after 1925. The city became the builder of a new form of social housing, and, in spite of rampant inflation, several hundred thousand units were

completed. The Siedlung ('housing estate') was developed within the framework of a 'building exhibition' of experimental prototypes – often collaborations among architects, such as Luckhardt, Gropius, Häring, Salvisberg and the brothers Taut. Standardised sizes kept costs down and amenities like tenant gardens, schools, public transport and shopping areas were offered when at all possible.

Among the best known 1920s estates are Bruno Taut's **Hufeisen-Siedlung** (Bruno-Taut-Ring, Britz, 1927), arranged in horseshoe shape around a communal garden, and **Onkel-Toms-Hütte** (Haring, Taut, 1928-9; Argentinische Allee, Zehlendorf), with Salvisberg's linear U-Bahn station at its heart. Most *Siedlungen* were housing only, such as the **Ringsiedlung** (Goebelstrasse, Charlottenburg) or **Siemensstadt** (Scharoun and others, 1929-32). Traditional-looking 'counter-proposals' with pitched roofs were made by more conservative designers at **Am Fischtal** (Tessenow, Mebes, Emmerich, Schmitthenner et al, 1929; Zehlendorf).

Larger infrastructure projects and public works were also built by avant-garde architects under Wagner's direction. Among the more interesting are the rounded U-Bahn station at Krumme Lanke (Grenander, 1929), the totally rational **Stadtbad Mitte** (1930; Gartenstrasse 5-6), the **Messegelände** (Poelzig, Wagner, 1928; Charlottenburg), the ceramic-tiled Haus **des Rundfunks** (Poelzig, 1930; Masurenallee 10, Charlottenburg), and twin office buildings on the southern corner of Alexanderplatz (Behrens, 1932).

Beginning with his expressionist **Einsteinturm** in Babelsberg, Erich Mendelsohn distilled his own brand of modernism, character-ised by the rounded forms of the **Universum Cinema** (1928; now the Schaubühne theatre) and the elegant corner solution of the **IG Metall building** (1930; Alte Jacobstrasse 148, Kreuzberg). Before emigrating – as did so many other architects, Jewish and non-Jewish – Mendelsohn was able to build a few private homes, including his own at Am Rupenhorn 6 in Charlottenburg (1929).

GRAND DESIGNS AND DEMOLITION

In the effort to remake liberal Berlin in their image, the Nazis undertook a form of spatial re-education. This included banning modernist trademarks such as flat roofs and slender columns in favour of traditional architecture, and shutting down the Bauhaus school shortly after it was banished from Dessau. Modern architects fled Berlin as Hitler dreamt of refashioning it into the mega-capital 'Germania', designed by Albert Speer. The crowning glory

The **Olympiastadion**. *See p40.*

was to be a grand axis lined with the embassies of newly subjugated countries, with a railway station at its foot and a massive copper dome at its head, some 16 times the size of St Peter's in Rome. Work was halted by the war, but not before demolition was begun in parts of Tiergarten and Schöneberg.

Hitler and Speer's fantasy was that Germania would someday leave picturesque ruins à la ancient Rome. But ruins came sooner than expected. Up to 90 per cent of inner city districts were destroyed by Allied bombing. Mountains of rubble cleared by women survivors rose at the city's edge, such as the Teufelsberg in the west and Friedrichshain in the east. Duringthe reconstruction period, the ornate plaster decoration of many apartment buildings was never replaced; others never recovered from the three weeks of street combat prior to capitulation.

'Fascism left an invisible legacy of a bunker and tunnel landscape.'

Fascism left an invisible legacy of a bunker and tunnel landscape, much of which was re-used as listening stations by the East Germans. The more visible fascist architecture can be recognised by its stripped-down, abstracted classicism, typically in travertine: in the west, **Flughafen Tempelhof** (Sagebiel, 1941) and the **Olympiastadion** (March, 1936); in the east, the marble-halled **Reichsluftfahrt-ministerium** (Sagebiel, 1936; Leipziger Strasse 5-7, Mitte), which served the GDR administration refurbished with socialist murals, while the downright scary **Reichsbank** (Wolff, 1938; Werderscher Markt, Mitte), a design personally chosen by Hitler, became home to the central committee of the Communist Party.

THE TWO BERLINS

The **Berlin Wall**, put up in a single night in 1961, introduced a new and cruel reality that rapidly acquired a sense of permanence. The city's centre of gravity shifted as the Wall cut off the historic centre from the west, suspending the Brandenburger Tor and Potsdamer Platz in no man's land, while the outer edge followed the 1920 city limits.

Post-war architecture is a mixed bag, ranging from the crisp linear brass of 1950s storefronts to concrete 1970s mega-complexes. Early joint planning efforts led by Scharoun were scrapped, and radical interventions cleared out vast spaces. Among the architectural casualties in the East were Schinkel's Bauakademie and much of Fischerinsel, clearing a sequence of wide spaces

from Marx-Engels-Platz to Alexanderplatz. In West Berlin, Anhalter Bahnhof was left to stand in ruins but Schloss Charlottenburg narrowly escaped demolition.

Though architects from East and West shared the same modernist education, their work became the tool of opposing ideologies, and housing was the first battlefield. The GDR adapted Russian socialist realism to Prussian culture in projects built with great effort and amazing speed as a national undertaking. First and foremost was **Stalinallee** (1951-4; now **Karl-Marx-Allee**, Friedrichshain; *see p90* **Palaces for the workers**). The Frankfurter Tor segment of its monumental axis was designed by Herman Henselmann, a Bauhaus modernist who briefly agreed to switch styles. In response, West Berlin called on leading International Style architects such as Gropius, Niemeyer, Aalto and Jacobsen to build the **Hansaviertel**. A loose arrangement of inventive slabs and pavilions at the edge of the Tiergarten, it was part of the 1957 Interbau Exhibition for the 'city of tomorrow' (which included Le Corbusier's Unité d'Habitation in Charlottenburg). Oddly enough, today both the Hansaviertel and Karl-Marx-Allee contain highly sought-after housing.

East and West stylistic differences diminished in the 1960s and 1970s, as new *Siedlungen* were built to even greater dimensions. The **Gropiusstadt** in Britz and **Märkisches Viertel** in Reinickendorf (1963-74) were mirrored in the East by equally massive (if shoddier) prefab housing estates in Marzahn and Hellersdorf.

To replace the cultural institutions then cut off from the West, Dahlem became the site of various museums and of the new **Freie Universität**, with its daring rusted-steel exterior (Candilis Woods Schiedhelm, 1967-79). Scharoun conceived a '**Kulturforum**' on the site cleared for Germania, designing two masterful pieces: the **Philharmonie** (1963) and the **Staatsbibliothek** (1976). Other additions were Mies van der Rohe's slick **Neue Nationalgalerie** (1968) and the **Gemäldegalerie** (Hilmer & Satler, 1992-8; Matthäikirchplatz, Tiergarten). In its incomplete state, the Kulturforum has instigated years of debate.

The US presented Berlin with Hugh Stubbin's **Kongresshalle** in the Tiergarten (1967, now the **Haus der Kulturen der Welt**), an entertainingly futuristic work, which rather embarrassingly required seven years of repair after its roof collapsed in 1980. East German architects brewed their own version of futuristic modernism in the enlarged, vacuous **Alexanderplatz** with its **Fernsehturm** (TV

Tower, 1969), the nearby **Haus des Lehrers** (Henselmann, 1961-4), and the enjoyable cinemas, **Kino International** (Kaiser, 1964) and **Kosmos** (Kaiser, 1960-62; Karl-Marx-Allee 131, Friedrichshain).

POSTMODERN PRESERVATION

Modernist urban renewal gradually gave way to historic preservation after 1970. In the West, largely in response to the squatting movement, the city launched a public-private enterprise, the Internationale Bauausstellung (IBA), to conduct a 'careful renewal' of the *Mietskaserne* and 'critical reconstruction' with infill projects to close up the gaps left in areas along the Wall. A few schools and recreation centres were also built, such as Langhof's **Spreewaldbad** (1988).

Within the huge catalogue of IBA architects are many brands of postmodernism, both local and foreign, from Ungers, Sawade and Behnisch, to Krier, Moore and Hertzberger; many had never built anywhere. It is a truly eclectic collection: the irreverent organicism of the prolific Ballers (Fraenkelufer, Kreuzberg, 1982-4) contrasts sharply with the neo-rationalist work of Eisenman (Kochstrasse 62-63, Kreuzberg, 1988) and Rossi (Wilhelmstrasse 36-8, Kreuzberg, 1988); a series of projects was also placed along Friedrichstrasse. IBA thus became a proving-ground that created a new panorama of contemporary architectural theories about the city and its many layers of history.

In the East, urban renewal slowed to a halt when funds for the construction of new housing ran dry; and towards the end of the 1970s, inner-city areas became again politically and economically attractive. Unlike the Nikolaiviertel, where the medieval core was replicated after total clearance, most East-bloc preservation focused on run-down 19th-century buildings on a few streets and squares in Prenzlauer Berg. Some infill buildings were also added on Friedrichstrasse in manipulated grids and pastel colours, so that the postmodern theme set up by Abraham and other IBA architects on the street south of Checkpoint Charlie was taken over the Wall. But progress was slow, and in 1989 many sites still stood half-finished.

NEW CRITICAL RECONSTRUCTION

The task of joining east and west was the challenge of the century, requiring new work of all kinds, from massive new infrastructure to daycare centres. But the first impulse of the city fathers (and former West Berliners) was to erase evidence of four decades of division, mainly by restoring as much of the pre-war past as possible. They thus created the notion of 'Berlinische Architektur' – a homogenised historicism imposing limits on height and materials in Friedrichstadt. Its pilot project

was the **Friedrichstadt Passagen**, three blocks of urban shopping malls now housing **Galeries Lafayette** and **Quartiers 205** and **206** (Ungers, Cobb/Fried/Pei, Nouvel, 1993-6), which were followed by several other exercises in punched-window façades nearby. Pariser Platz features Frank Gehry's **DG Bank** (1998), the **Akademie der Künste** (Behnisch, 2000) and the **French** and **British embassies** (Wilford, 2000; Portzamparc 2002).

A more modern interpretation of 'critical reconstruction' was attempted at the **American Business Center on Checkpoint Charlie** (Philip Johnson, SOM, Lauber + Wöhr, 1996-8; Friedrichstrasse 200, Mitte) to fill in the open space left behind by Checkpoint Charlie. But it only half succeeded; not all buildings could be financed. Hans Kollhoff's glitzy Internet-age concoction for a smaller Alexanderplatz (multiplying the Rockefeller Center by 12) does more to eradicate GDR memory; nine of his towers (out of 13 in the original plan) have been approved so far. Meanwhile, the fate of the bronze-tinted **Palast der Republik** (Graffunder, 1976; Schlossplatz, Mitte), the world's only parliament with a bowling alley, is contingent on its asbestos being removed and on a campaign to rebuild the Kaiser's Stadtschloss in its place. Interestingly, the new stone and glass **Foreign Ministry** (Mueller Reimann, 2000), built in front of the old Reichsbank on the Friedrichswerder, is oddly compatible with the Palast.

The largest commercial post-Wall project to be completed is the $4.8 billion makeover of **Potsdamer Platz**. This has been a considerable feat of engineering, from the use of scuba divers to pour foundations in water-filled sites to the special 'logistics centre' monitoring the removal of millions of tons of soil (and the delivery of enough truckloads of sand to have circled the globe several times), and the north–south tunnel for road and rail, which passes under the project. As the new shopping mall, cinemas, hotel and office towers gradually become a fixture in Berlin life, the memory of its origins in a notorious pre-Unification land deal between the SPD and Daimler-Benz recedes.

Larger than many downtowns, it is a denser and higher rendition of the thriving centre silenced by the war. An array of local and international stars (Piano, Rogers, Isozaki, Moneo) joined to create a 'European city' in architecture that somewhat paradoxically could have been found just about anywhere, as if its motto was 'dare to be mediocre'. On an urban level, it has yet to meet its goal of suturing east and west. In fact, if anything, it actually creates barriers on almost every edge, and even lacks internal gateways. These barriers include the water-filled moat at the tunnel entrance off the Landwehrkanal, awkwardly located building entrances and sculpture, and the way Scharoun's Staatsbibliothek next door is blocked off by its pushy new neighbours. At least Potsdamer Platz did achieve its principle goal: to bring a new commercial centre to Berlin, nothing more and nothing less.

SONY, SO FAR

The question of authenticity recurs in many of the new projects. Embedded somewhere within the triangular mega-block of the **Sony Center** (intended as an 'urban entertainment centre; Murphy, Jahn, 1996-2000; *pictured p35*) is one of the last real pieces of Wilhelmine Berlin: the grand old Kaisersaal Café from the Esplanade Hotel, a listed building which was

Embassy row

Almost every international architectural firm of note has built at least one building in the new German capital over the last 12 years. But those heading for a place in the annals of architectural history are more likely to be the designers of one of Berlin's myriad new embassies than those of grandiose shopping arcades or weighty bank buildings. 'International Bland' à la Potsdamer Platz, no matter how big the names behind it, remains, well, just bland, no matter how much you hype it: no new German vernacular, no risky experiments, no big surprises.

Of the 150 odd countries with diplomatic representations in Germany, over 100 have acquired new, or adapted existing, embassy buildings in the new capital in recent years. And with this flurry of building, a new kind of diplomatic building is emerging. The architecture of, for example, Rem Koolhaas' new **Dutch Embassy** (Klosterstrasse/Rolandufer, 2002) and Michael Wilford's **British Embassy** (Wilhelmstrasse 70-71; 2001) speaks volumes about how these countries feel about themselves and their relationship with their neighbours and the rest of the world. It is these new embassies that are proving to be the most fascinating products of Berlin's *Bauboom*.

The key words in today's modern embassy are openness and accessibility. With a few notable exceptions, the days of secretive, barricaded buildings with high walls housing some old duffer behind his desk and his minions are more or less gone.

Excellent, or at least interesting, architecture can go a long way to raising the profile of a particular embassy, and, therefore, the profile of the relevant nation. Two of Berlin's most delightful new examples: the unashamedly modern and fabulous **Mexican Embassy** (Serrano & González de León, 2001; Klingelhöferstrasse 3/ Rauchstrasse 27) and the symbolic,

stylish **Scandinavian Embassies** complex (Berger & Parkkinen, 2000; Rauchstrasse 1) are cases in point.

The recently occupied **Swiss Embassy** (Diener & Diener, 2001; Otto-von-Bismarck-Allee 4) balances the interesting combination of traditional Palladian villa and new brutalist concrete architecture rather well and it has a very 'Berlin' history. Thanks to a combination of amazing good fortune and studied neutrality, the Swiss Embassy was the only building from an entire city district to survive both Hitler and Albert Speer's megalomanic urban development plans and the war. It now stands bizarrely alone, encircled by a curve of the River Spree and two huge government buildings – a chipper little piece of Switzerland right in the physical heart of a foreign government. A fitting metaphor for the country's own European status that rarely fails to raise a smile from passers-by.

The **Japanese Embassy** (Tiergartenstrasse 24-27/Hiroshimastrasse) has been far less successful in leaving its past behind. This is due almost entirely to an apparent underestimation of the uncanny ability some buildings have of wearing their past like last season's skirt lengths. Built as phase one of the Nazi capital 'Germania', in the 'Diplomaten Viertel' (diplomatic quarter) in the 1930s, alongside the embassies of Italy, Spain and other Axis partners, the Japanese Embassy was about as 'Nazi' a building as you could get. Despite considerable rebuilding and modern extensions, the original architecture has not been tampered with significantly enough. Therefore, critical reception after the reopening was somewhat reserved; it was felt in some quarters that a more symbolical break with the past would have been more appropriate.

Nazi history is not the only history that embassy occupiers are keen to distance themselves from in Berlin. Both the **Hungarian Embassy** and the **Polish Embassy** moved 75 metres (246 feet) to fit into the new layered complex of eight buildings into the apartment complex on Bellevuestrasse.

The focus of this media and film centre (with numerous shops, restaurants, cinemas, an IMAX theatre and luxury apartments) is a large public 'forum', covered by a dynamic, permeable structure 12 storeys up. Made with an off-centre ring-beam supported by spokes

and cables like an erratic bicycle wheel and draped with strips of translucent fabric, it allows natural light and provides a stage for media events. Framed with high-tech elements, and forming its own system of open spaces, the spatial logic of the complex is a direct challenge to the narrow streets and flattened public spaces of its neighbours in Potsdamer Platz. This translates in architecture to a

The **British Embassy.**

buildings (rare and listed examples of 1960s GDR International Style architecture on Unter den Linden; Nos.76 and 72, respectively) were not considered suitable for a new, post-Communist, national image. The old Hungarian Embassy has just been replaced with a new neo-traditionalist one. The Polish building too is earmarked for demolition, despite its architectural importance. The designs for the new building currently resemble nothing more than one of the world's uglier Hiltons – a style that the new **Chinese Embassy** (Märkisches Ufer 54) also appears to adhere to, by the way. Most post-Communist architecture is turning out to be just as bad as most democratic architecture – who would have thought it?

Many nations, however, have found themselves looking for alternatives to laying out large amounts of cash for prestige projects. Alongside new openness, new prudence is an equally recognisable trend in contemporary diplomacy. The canny Brits have made full use of 'Third Way' principles and got a private consortium of German businesses to finance the entire building of their new embassy and then leased it back for 30 years. This is the first time ever that a new embassy building has been built and then leased, and, as such, represents a new economic model for the financing of public buildings. Whether it really does work out cheaper in the long run is questionable, though.

For some countries, a diplomatic presence in Berlin is not even an option right now, and its not for lack of desire. There may well be 111 new diplomatic representations in Berlin, but there are another 37 still left out in ghost-town Bonn, a full five hours' train ride away from all the action. These are the embassies that got left behind because they can't afford the move. They are the representations of developing countries, mainly African, who most desperately need a lobbying presence in Berlin. The fact that the German government considerately left the ministry for development aid behind in Bonn as well is small consolation.

With all this 'new openness', security had been visibly low-key, or even absent, in many of Berlin's new embassy buildings until September 2001. Nowadays, there are a few more police around the front gates of certain 'sensitive' buildings and extended 'no parking' zones but that's about all (with a couple of notable exceptions at both extremes). The **Brazilian Embassy** (Pysall, Stahrenberg & Partner, 1998-2000; Wallstrasse 59), for example, has no security at all because, as the ambassador happily points out, 'we have no enemies'. It's probably not strictly true of course, but it's a powerful statement to make nonetheless.

The USA on the other hand has not even started building its new embassy because of an extended wrangle with the Berlin authorities over security that has been dragging on for the last eight years (*see p72* **America's post-Cold War plot**). Until recently many might have accused the US of being somewhat petty and self-important. Now it looks perhaps like they had a far better grasp of their unpopularity in certain quarters than the Europeans gave them credit for. It's going to be a while yet before everyone sleeps as soundly in their beds as the Brazilian ambassador to Berlin.

stand-off between the late modernist aesthetic of Helmut Jahn's glazed, semicircular 103-metre (338-foot) office tower, and the neo-traditional throwback of the punched windows and brick cladding of Hans Kollhoff's 88-metre (289-foot) office tower (1996-2000). Together they form a gateway to Potsdamer Strasse, where the old Potsdamer Tor once stood.

Still to follow will be the new **Beisheim Center** on the Lenné Dreieck to the north of the Sony Center, and the completion of **Leipziger Platz**, dotted with assorted commercial buildings. The northern half of the octagonal square will accommodate a headquarters for the Deutsches Reisebüro and the Canadian Embassy. The **Mosse Palais**, built on the former site of publisher Rudolf Mosse's residence, has already been completed for the Berlin office of the American Jewish Committee (HDS & Gallagher, Boston, 1995-7). The site of the former Wertheim department store (Alfred Messel, 1896; demolished 1958), under which passes the U2 U-Bahn line, will be broken up into smaller parcels for redevelopment.

In short, there is already more than enough new work for visitors to take in, and a whole lot more to come. Only time will tell if the real estate market, which collapsed after the Bonn government delayed acting on its 1990 decision to move here, has recovered enough to support all this new office and commercial space.

Also still to come is the **Denkmal für die ermordeten Juden Europas** ('Memorial to the Murdered European Jews') on a large site south of Pariser Platz. Quite what shape this will take has been mired in controversy for over a decade (*see p34* **Remember to forget**), but the city went ahead with a design by Peter Eisenman involving 1,500 rectangular concrete columns, each up to four metres (13 feet) high, forming a dense labyrinth of stelae.

ABSTRACTIONS OF FATE

Ironically, the two most important new architectural works of the post-Unification period were designed before 1989: Daniel Libeskind's **Jüdisches Museum** (Jewish Museum, Lindenstrasse 14, Kreuzberg) and the **Reichstag** (orig. Wallot, 1884-94) in the Spreebogen. Libeskind has created a masterful and well-built deconstructivist provocation, a silvery abstraction of fate. Since the completed museum and exhibition opened in autumn 2001, the expected contradiction between structure and contents has proved non-existent. Meanwhile, after its two-week wrap by Christo, the space where Hitler came to power was stripped, retrofitted, and brilliantly domed by Sir Norman Foster, winner of the Pritzker Architecture Prize in 1999. With a double helix

of ramps spiralling to the top, the light-filled dome is set on a generous roof terrace and has clean, elegant details.

The Reichstag is neighbour to a second large-scale project, now all but complete: the **Band des Bundes**, designed by Axel Schultes, who built the Federal Chancellery. Together with the maze of offices for the MPs, the Spreebogen ensemble joins east and west and overwhelms the Reichstag in its expression of Germany's regained unity. It is linked to historic Friedrich-Wilhelm-Stadt by an elegant new bridge by Santiago Calatrava. Adjacent to the Spreebogen are new buildings for political and media parties such as the ARD studios (Ortner & Ortner, 1999); a group of new buildings to house delegations from the German *Länder* (regional governments) is located between Pariser Platz and Potsdamer Platz.

All this adds up to a new city within the city – which will be complemented by the new railway station at Lehrter Bahnhof (by von Gerkan Marg and partner), flanked by even more office space. Since Berlin has never really had a central station, this is arguably as historically significant as the reconstruction of lost monuments. Built on the site of the original Lehrter Bahnhof, which was destroyed in World War II, the new station will function as a major junction for regional and international rail routes as well as for the local U- and S-Bahn systems. The glass upper hall will be covered with 3,500 square metres (37,672 square feet) of solar panels. Construction began in 1996 and should be completed by 2005.

More daring work may be found outside the old core, in Nicholas Grimshaw's skeletal whale of a Stock Exchange, known as **Ludwig-Erhard Haus** (1998; Fasanenstrasse 83-4), the silver disk of the **Velodrom** in Prenzlauer Berg (Dominique Perrault, 1998), or among the scores of new embassies scattered from Mitte to Tiergarten (*see p42-3* **Embassy row**). Of the latter, one of the most innovative is the complex housing the **Scandinavian Embassies** (Berger & Parkkinen, 1999; Rauchstrasse 1, Tiergarten), a collection of irregularly shaped buildings, each designed by a different architect from the relevant country, but united by a green copper wall that encircles the compound.

Further chances for good new architecture by younger architects lie in housing, infrastructure and parks on the periphery. Some is directly sponsored by the city, like the **Adlershof Science and Business City**, where the **Photonic Center** by Sauerbruch/Hutton is outstanding. Like the new Lehrter Bahnhof, this new ring of suburban development is the final confirmation that Berlin is on its way (back) to becoming a modern metropolis.

Accommodation

Accommodation

As more and more hotels are built, the choice is no longer only
between bland international luxury chains and grotty two-stars.

Berlin's hotel industry has undergone dramatic
changes in the last decade. The steadily
increasing number of visitors (there were
8.5 million overnight guests in 2001) has
encouraged heavy investment in the market.
The number of hotel beds in Berlin has more
than doubled since 1991 – there are now around
63,000 – and every major international hotel
chain has built a new hotel in the city, or is in
the process of doing so.

This boom is, however, decidedly top-heavy,
being primarily in the four- and five-star
category, and it remains unclear whether the
city will attract enough visitors willing to fork
out for luxury accommodation. There's still a
shortage of quality cheaper hotels.

Don't be lulled into a false sense of security,
though. A new hotel doesn't necessarily mean
a good hotel and the best have a tendency to
fill early. Try and book well ahead, especially
at times when there are major holidays,
conventions and festivals, such as the Berlin
Marathon in September or the Love Parade
in July. Prices tend also to go up in most
places at these times.

Most hotels now have websites, which are
worth checking for information about facilities
and special deals. Some, for example, offer
cheaper rates at weekends. The concept of bed
and breakfast is beginning to take hold here.
Berlin Tourismus Marketing (*see p47*) can
book private rooms.

LOCATION, LOCATION, LOCATION

Hotels are mainly concentrated in Mitte, and
around the Zoo and Savignyplatz (the former
focal point of West Berlin). The selection of
cheaper options on the east side of the city
has improved considerably in the last couple
of years. We have listed hotels by area, and
included a short introduction to each, giving
the pros and cons of staying in that district.

While location is important, it's worth
remembering that the Berlin public transport
system is excellent. Unless you really are out in
the suburbs, you're rarely more than half an hour
away from anywhere you might want to be.

PRICES

The good news for visitors is that the average
price of a hotel room in Berlin is €103, still
considerably lower than most other cities in

Maritim proArte Hotel Berlin. *See p51.*

Europe. You will pay more, on average, in
Prague (€106), Paris (€185) and Amsterdam
(€146), and almost double in London (€199),
according to figures for 2000.

Our price categories work as follows: a
Deluxe hotel is one in which the cheapest
double room costs **€175 or more** per night;
in an **Expensive** hotel it costs **€115 to €174**;
Moderate is **€65 to €114**; and a double in a
Budget hotel or hostel costs **under €65**. All
prices given are room prices, unless specified.
Note that hotel rates tend to drop at weekends.

Remember to add the cost of breakfast to
your room price if it is not included. Most hotels
offer breakfast as a buffet, which can be as
simple as coffee and rolls (called *Schrippen*
in Berlin) with cheese and salami, or the full
works (smoked meats, smoked salmon, muesli
with fresh fruit and yoghurt, and even a glass
of sparkling wine).

For accommodation catering to a primarily
gay clientele, *see p210*.

INFORMATION

The two organisations below can help find accommodation for visitors.

Berlin Tourismus Marketing

Europa-Center, Budapester Strasse, Charlottenburg, 10787 (reservations 250 025/information 0190 754 040/information when calling from outside Germany +49 1805 75 40 40/fax 2500 2424/www.berlin.de). **S3, S5, S7, S9, S75, U2, U9, U12** *Zoologischer Garten.* **Open** 8am-10pm Mon-Sat; 9am-9pm Sun. **Map** p305 D4.

The privatised official tourist organisation can sort out hotel reservations for you and provides a free hotel listings booklet (but bear in mind that the hotels listed have paid to be included). It also has a list of campsites and youth hostels (€1) and another of private apartments and holiday homes (€1.20). The website is reasonably comprehensive but bug-ridden, difficult to navigate, not updated frequently enough and contains no phone numbers. Allow yourself plenty of time when visiting the centre, as staff are not always particularly speedy or helpful. Warning: calling the information number costs an outrageous €1.20 per minute and you can expect to spend at least ten minutes on hold listening to bad music. Normal rates apply when calling from abroad. The reservations number is free, however.

Branches: Brandenburger Tor, Tiergarten; Tegel Airport; KaDeWe, Tauentzienstrasse 21-4, Charlottenburg.

Berlin Information Group

Oderberger Strasse 20, Prenzlauer Berg, 10435 (282 4883/fax 2809 6995/www.berlinfo.com). **S4, S8, U2** *Schönhauser Allee.* **Map** p303 G2.

This small English-language information service is pretty helpful all round. It doesn't have a big office with counters and hordes of staff and you can't reserve accommodation by telephone, but it does have a very useful website from where you can book hotels. Look under the 'traveltime' section for a selected hotel listing and reservation service that is considerably more user-friendly than many others of its kind.

Mitte

It's been over ten years since re-unification and Mitte is still undergoing rapid change; new hotels, shops and buildings are popping up at such a speed that it's hard to keep up. As a result, the variety of accommodation available in the area is steadily improving, primarily at the top end of the market and at the budget end with backpacker hotels. Just about every place listed in this category is new or newly renovated. You won't find much of the historic pension charm of, say, Charlottenburg here but it is without doubt the most exciting part of Berlin to be in.

The best Hotels

For stylish luxury

The **Royal Dorint AM Gendarmenmarkt**: cool, impeccable taste. *See p48.*

For prime location at low prices

A whisker away from Unter den Linden at bargain rates: **Hotel Garni Gendarm**. *See p51.*

For backpackers

The best in town, with the most helpful staff: **Circus – The Hostel**. *See p53.*

For affordable charm

The **Honigmond Garden Hotel** offers character aplenty and great value for money. *See p51.*

For apartment living

A great location in the heart of Prenzlauer Berg and fine flats at **Pension Acksel Haus**. *See p55.*

For intimacy and style

The loveliest, chicest small hotel in town – **Hotel Art Nouveau**. *See p62.*

For echoes of old Berlin

The **Hotel Garni Askanischer Hof** is packed with old-style atmosphere and dodgy taste. *See p61.*

For sheer craziness

Welcome to the weird world of Lars Strochen's **Propeller Island City Lodge**. *See p54 and p65.*

Deluxe

Adlon Hotel Kempinski Berlin

Unter den Linden 77, 10117 (22610/fax 2261 2222/www.hotel-adlon.de). **S1, S2, S25, S26** *Unter den Linden.* **Rates** €220-€295 single; €255-€330 double; €295 suite; €28 breakfast buffet. **Credit** AmEx, DC, MC, V. **Map** p316/p302 F3.

The original Hotel Adlon, world renowned for its luxurious interiors and discreet atmosphere, opened in 1907 but burned down shortly after World War II. The new Adlon, rebuilt by the Kempinski group on the original site, opened in 1997 with the aim of picking up where its predecessor left off, ostentatiously listing previous guests, such as Albert Einstein, Theodore Roosevelt and Marlene Dietrich, as though they only checked out last week. Right by the Brandenburger Tor, and handy for Berlin's diplomatic quarter, it immediately became a first-stop choice for heads of state and the like, but, if you're not a Kennedy or McCartney, expect to be peering up nostrils here. The frostiness of the staff is a notable feature. There are 337 rooms, including 81 suites, six rooms for allergy sufferers, two for travellers with disabilities and two bullet-proof presidential suites. There are also marble and black granite bathrooms, hairdressers, 12 boutiques and wardrobes in each room with hanging rails that light up.

Hotel services *Bar (lobby). Boutiques. Business & press centre. Conference & banqueting rooms. Fitness spa. Garage. Restaurants (3). Swimming pool.* **Room services** *Air-conditioning. CD player. Fax. ISDN. PC outlet. Telephones (2). TV.*

Art'otel Ermelerhaus Berlin

Wallstrasse 70-73, 10179 (240 620/fax 2406 2222/www.artotel.de). U2 Märkisches Museum. **Rates** (incl breakfast buffet) €153 single; €183 double; €183-€223 suite/apartment. **Credit** AmEx, DC, MC, V. **Map** p316/p307 G4.

On the banks of the Spree, this is a delightful fusion of old and new. The Ermelerhaus building houses immaculately restored rococo dining rooms and an ultra-modern residential section designed by architects Nalbach & Nalbach. The entire hotel is dedicated to the work of artist Georg Baselitz and all the rooms and corridors contain originals of his work, as well as other pieces by AR Penck and Andy Warhol. Besides the art, every detail of the decor has been meticulously attended to, from Philippe Starck bathrooms to the Marcel Breuer chairs in the conference rooms. Service is friendly, the views from the top suites across Mitte are stunning and the food in both restaurants is imaginative, yet traditional. In the summer months an old barge moored by the towpath in front of the hotel becomes a terrace with charmingly picturesque views. Recommended.

Hotel services *Babysitting. Bar. Business services. Conference facilities. Garage. Internet terminal (foyer). Laundry. Restaurant. Ticket reservations.* **Room services** *Hairdryer. Internet access. Radio. TV: pay movies. Telephone.*

Four Seasons Hotel

Charlottenstrasse 49, 10117 (20338/fax 2033 6166/www.fourseasons.com). S1, S2, S3, S5, S7, S9, S75, U6 Friedrichstrasse. **Rates** €195-€295 single; €230-€280 double; €320-€2,500 suite; €20 breakfast. **Credit** AmEx, DC, MC, V. **Map** p316/p302 F3.

This is what five-star luxury is all about: marble bathrooms, huge soft towels and gowns, vast beds with pure wool blankets and highly trained and elegant staff who know what you need before you do. The decor is English/French country house style. Wood panelling, a hell of a lot of marble, open fireplaces, oil paintings of flowers and Scottish landscapes and porcelain vases. The whole effect is one of having been invited up to a country estate for the weekend. Hard to believe it only opened in 1996. If you are a famous film star and don't want everyone to know that you're in town, then stay here. Marvellously discreet.

Hotel services *Bar. Business services (24hrs). Conference rooms. Disabled facilities. Fitness club. No-smoking rooms. Laundry. Parking. Restaurant. Sightseeing trips. Ticket reservations.* **Room Services** *Air-conditioning. Fax. Hairdryer. Minibar. PC/modem connection. Telephone. TV: cable.*

Royal Dorint AM Gendarmenmarkt

Charlottenstrasse 50, 10117 (203 750/fax 203 75100/www.dorint.de/berlin-gendarmenmarkt). U2, U6 Stadtmitte. **Rates** €197-€280 single; €218-€295 double; €255-€510 suites; €22.50 breakfast. **Credit** AmEx, DC, MC, V. **Map** p316/p306 F4.

It's not easy to get a room here, and for good reason. From the calming colour scheme to the excellent lighting and intimate atmosphere, a great deal of attention has been paid to detail. The health spa area is a delight, with plunge pools and views across the picturesque Gendarmenmarkt. Each room is beautifully styled and the bathrooms have to be among the best in Berlin. Conference rooms are also superb. Highly recommended.

Hotel services *Bar. Conference facilities. Fitness centre. Laundry. Massage. Parking. Plunge pools. Restaurants (2). Sauna. Solarium.* **Room services** *Hairdryer. Minibar. Room service. Safe. Telephone. TV.*

Westin Grand

Friedrichstrasse 158-64, 10117 (20270/fax 2027 3362/www.westin-grand.com). U6 Französische Strasse. **Rates** €255-€300 single; €280-€325 double; €445-€1,900 suite; €18 breakfast buffet. **Credit** AmEx, DC, V. **Map** p316/p302 F3.

Just around the corner from Unter den Linden, providing five-star international poshness in a top location. Gratifyingly elegant in style, the hotel manages to live up to its name rather well, despite its prefabricated East German construction. Its 35 suites are individually furnished with period decor according to their name (try the Schinkel or Lessing suites), and its 358 rooms exude traditional taste, design and comfort. There's a hotel garden with a sun patio and atrium as well as bars, two restaurants, a pool and a non-smoking floor. The staircase and foyer are especially bombastic. On the downside, the corridors are kilometres long and a little claustrophobic.

Hotel services *Bar. Business services. Conference facilities. Hairdresser. Health spa. Laundry. Massage. Restaurant. Sauna. Shops & boutiques. Solarium. Swimming pool.* **Room services** *Air-conditioning. Minibar. Nintendo. Safe. Telephone (2 lines). TV/Internet: cable/pay movies. Voicemail.*

Expensive

Hotel-Restaurant Albrechtshof

Albrechtstrasse 8, 10117 (308 860/fax 308 86100/www.hotel-albrechtshof.de). S1, S2, S3, S5, S7, S9, S25, S26, S75, U6 Friedrichstrasse. **Rates** (incl breakfast) €110-€175 single; €140-€205 double; €225-€275 suite. **Credit** AmEx, DC, MC, V. **Map** p316/p302 F3.

Hotel Hackescher Markt – an elegant townhouse hotel in a prime location. *See p51.*

Although it doesn't make a song and dance about it, this place is a member of the Verband Christlicher Hotels (Christian Hotels Association) and has its own chapel. There is a quite pleasant *Hof* garden for breakfast in the summer and a restaurant specialising in local dishes. The staff are kind and the hotel is situated in the new government quarter, remarkably close to Friedrichstrasse station and several theatres. The decor is universal Posh Hotel Style.

Hotel services *Chapel. Conference rooms. Disabled: adapted rooms (3). Parking. Restaurants. Safe. Ticket reservations.* **Room services** *Fax. Minibar. PC/modem connection. Radio. Telephone. TV.*

Alexander Plaza Berlin

Rosenstrasse 1, 10178 (240 010/fax 2400 1777/ www.alexanderplaza.com). S3, S5, S7, S9, S75 Hackescher Markt. **Rates** €117.50-€182.50 single; €127.50-€192.50 double; €177.50-€277.50 suite; €12.50 breakfast buffet. **Credit** AmEx, DC, MC, V. **Map** p316/p303 G3.

Well situated between Alexanderplatz, Museuminsel and Hackescher Markt, this handsome, renovated building houses a comfortable modern hotel. Despite the proximity of a dozen building sites and the frisky Mitte nightlife district, the hotel stands in an oasis of tranquillity not far from the river. The staff are polite and the decor is tasteful. There are 90 rooms, 30 of which are non-smoking and three have facilities for disabled visitors. The hotel has left the Mercure group of which it was originally a member and prices have increased significantly.

Hotel services *Fitness centre. Function rooms (4). Garage. Hairdresser. Restaurant. Sauna. Solarium.* **Room services** *Hairdryer. Minibar. Modem. Telephone (direct line). TV: pay movies.*

Dietrich-Bonhoeffer-Haus

Ziegelstrasse 30, 10117 (2846 7186/ fax 284 67145/www.hotel-dbh.de). S1, S2, S25, S26 Oranienburger Strasse. **Rates** (incl breakfast) €85-€115 single; €125-€150 double; €155-€190 triple. **Credit** AmEx, MC, V. **Map** p316/p302 F3.

The DBH was built in 1987 as a meeting place for Christians from the east and west and is named after the theologian who was executed by the Nazis for alleged participation in the Hitler assassination attempt of 1944. Today the conference centre and DBH hotel are open to all visitors. The building is in a remarkably quiet side street just behind the Museumsinsel – so very central. A friendly atmosphere prevails, with uncommonly smiley staff. There's a notice in the lift telling you the day's weather forecast, the rooms are enormous and the breakfast is good. If you have anything to do with the Church, then this is a good place to stay, and even if you haven't, it's not a bad option.

Hotel services *Club room. Restaurant (closed evenings). Seminar room.* **Room services** *Telephone.*

Forum Hotel

Alexanderplatz, 10178 (2389 4333/fax 2389 4305/www.forum-berlin.interconti.com). S3, S5, S7, S9, S75, U2, U5, U8 Alexanderplatz. **Rates** €103.50-€159.50 single; €113.50-€196 double; €118.50-€131.50 suite; €22 breakfast. **Credit** AmEx, DC, MC, V. **Map** p316/p303 G3.

It's very hard to be enthusiastic about any of the 1,006 rooms here. They are expensive, grey, cramped and so full of fans, minibars and trouser presses there's scarcely room to swing a suitcase. But oh the view! If you can get an *Eckzimmer* (corner room) facing the Fernsehturm (TV Tower) and Karl-Marx-Allee somewhere above the 16th floor

and wait for sunset, it really is quite something. Or go up for a meal in the Panorama restaurant or to play the tables at the casino at the top, which is open to all Fridays and Saturdays 7pm to 1am. **Hotel services** *Bar. Casino. Conference facilities. Disabled facilities. Fitness centre. Laundry. No-smoking floors. Parking. Restaurants (2). Sauna. Solarium.* **Room services** *Minibar. Telephone. TV.*

Hotel Garni Gendarm

Charlottenstrasse 61, 10117 (206 0660/fax 206 06666/www.hotel-gendarm-berlin.de). U2, U6 Stadtmitte. **Rates** €98-€124 single; €118-€149 double; €164-€250 suites; extra bed €20; breakfast €10. **Credit** AmEx, DC, MC, V. **Map** p316/p306 F4.
If you fancy a five-star location without the prices, then this could be the place for you. Hotel Garni doesn't have a lot of extras, but the rooms are smart and you are right next to the beautiful Gendarmenmarkt and some fine restaurants. The opera is just down the road too, so the Gendarm is well placed for cultural visits. For less than half the price of the nearby Dorint, Four Seasons or the Hilton you can't really go wrong. **Hotel services** *Bar.* **Room services** *Hairdryer. Minibar. Safe. Telephone. TV.*

Hotel Hackescher Markt

Grosse Präsidentenstrasse 8, 10178 (280 030/fax 280 0311/www.hackescher-markt.de). S3, S5, S7, S9, S75 Hackescher Markt. **Rates** €105-€155 single; €140-€190 double; €170-€220 suites. **Credit** AmEx, DC, MC, V. **Map** p316/p303 G3.
An elegant new hotel in a nicely renovated old town-house that solves the noise problem at Hackescher Markt by having most rooms face the tranquil green courtyard. Some rooms have balconies, most have their own bath and the suites are roomy and comfortable. The staff speak good English and are kind, smiling and helpful. Not cheap though. **Hotel services** *Covered parking (€10). No-smoking floor. Restaurant.* **Room services** *Hairdryer. ISDN lines (not all rooms). Minibar. Safe. TV.*

Honigmond Garden Hotel

Invalidenstrasse 122, 10115 (28 100 77/fax 28 100 78/www.honigmond-berlin.de). U6 Oranienburger Tor. **Rates** (breakfast included) €85-€95 single; €112-€125 double. **No credit cards.** **Map** p316/p302 F2.
Why doesn't Berlin have more new hotels like this? The sister to Honigmond Pension (*see p52*), 250m up the road, has charm, flair and character and doesn't cost an arm and a leg. It is just as lovely, if not more so, than the original, with a choice of big rooms facing the street (which can be loud if you need open windows) or smaller ones facing the pretty garden. The staircase is fabulously grand and although the owners say the pieces of furniture are old theatre props, they look pretty genuine. There is a breakfast room and, as they say in the brochure, 'all the sights worth seeing of the centre of East Berlin can be reached by foot from here'. **Room services** *Telephone. TV.*

Hotel Luisenhof

Köpenicker Strasse 92, 10179 (241 5906/fax 279 2983/www.luisenhof.de). U8 Heinrich-Heine-Strasse. **Rates** €110-€145 single; €132.50-€195 double; €175-€225 suite. **Credit** AmEx, DC, V. **Map** p316/p307 G4.
The building housing the Luisenhof dates from the early 19th century and was once the headquarters and stables of a Berlin coaching company. When the Communists held sway, it was home to the party training centre of the SED. It was reopened after renovation in 1993 in an original townhouse style, and is well located in the middle of old Berlin, close to Alexanderplatz and Friedrichstrasse. Though primarily a business hotel, the decor is on the romantic side, but not too frilly. **Hotel services** *Bistro. Conference facilities. Laundry. Restaurant.* **Room services** *Minibar. Safe. Telephone. TV.*

Maritim proArte Hotel Berlin

Friedrichstrasse 151, 10117 (203 35/fax 2033 4209/www.maritim.de). S1, S2, S3, S5, S7, S9, S25, S26, S75, U6 Friedrichstrasse. **Rates** €134.50-€234.50 single; €149-€264 double; €265-€1,800 suites/apartments; €16 breakfast buffet. **Credit** AmEx, DC, MC, V. **Map** p316/p302 F3.
On the former site of the Hotel Metropol, this gleaming edifice calls itself a 'designer hotel' but is due for a revamp – it has been eclipsed in the past couple of years by other luxury hotels in Berlin. Packed with huge paintings and designer furniture, the foyer, three restaurants and bar are fairly luxurious. The 403 rooms, apartments and suites all have marble bathrooms. Staff are polite and helpful, particularly when you're dressed to match the surroundings. The Brandenburger Tor and Reichstag are within walking distance, as are Unter den Linden, the swanky shops of Friedrichstrasse and the bars and galleries of the Scheunenviertel. **Hotel services** *Bar. Boutiques. Conference facilities. Gym. Lifts. Parking. Pool. Restaurants (3). Sauna. Solarium.* **Room services** *Air-conditioning. Fax. Minibar. Modem. Room service. Safe. Telephone. TV: pay movies.*

Moderate

Boardinghouse Mitte

Mulackstrasse 1, 10119 (2838 8488/fax 2838 8489). U8 Weinmeisterstrasse. **Rates** €77.50-€120 single apartment; €105-€135 double apartment; €30 extra person. **Credit** AmEx, MC, V. **Map** p316/p303 G3.
This is the kind of place to stay in for a week or more. Fully kitted out, modern, German designer-style little apartments in the pretty Scheunenviertel. Not cheap, especially as extras can add up, but the room prices get lower the longer you stay. Lots of good cafés and restaurants on the doorstep, and within walking distance from Hackescher Markt. **Hotel services** *Garage (€7.50). Ironing facilities (€7.50). Laundry (€12.50 per load).* **Room services** *Kitchen. Stereo. TV/video.*

Honigmond Pension

Borsigstrasse 28, 10115 (284 4550/fax 281 0077/
www.honigmond-berlin.de). S1, S2 Nordbahnhof.
Rates €45-€55 single; €71-€97 double; €111 4-bed
room. **No credit cards. Map** p316/p302 F2.
Simply and pleasantly decorated with stripped
wooden doorframes and floorboards and white walls.
Of the 14 rooms, six have their own shower and WC.
A good place for a family on a budget. Downstairs
is the café-restaurant Honigmond (*see p123*). Within
walking distance of the Scheunenviertel. Note there
is a €5 surcharge if you only stay one night.
Hotel services *Bar. Restaurant.* **Room services**
Telephone. TV.

Hotel-Pension Kastanienhof

Kastanienallee 65, 10119 (443 050/fax 4430 5111).
U8 Rosenthaler Platz or U2 Senefelderplatz. **Rates**
(incl breakfast) €65 single; €90 double; €105 2-room
apartment. **Credit** MC, V. **Map** p316/p303 G2.
If you can handle the pastel peach and pink decor,
the rooms here are generously proportioned and well
equipped. The hotel is well situated for exploring
Prenzlauer Berg and Mitte.
Hotel services *Bar. Parking (€5 per day). Ticket
reservations.* **Room services** *Hairdryer. Minibar.
Safe. Telephone. TV.*

Hotel Märkischer Hof

Linienstrasse 133, 10115 (282 7155/fax 282 4331).
U6 Oranienburger Tor. **Rates** (incl breakfast)
€47.50-€75 single; €70-€99 double; €105 triple.
Credit V. **Map** p316/p302 F3.

A family-run hotel within walking distance of some
of Berlin's main attractions – the Metropoltheater,
the Berliner Ensemble and the Staatsoper – and
some of the city's most beautiful districts. The hotel
itself is quiet and unremarkable, with comfortable
though drab rooms and a pension atmosphere.
Hotel services *Parking.* **Room services**
Minibar. Telephone.

mitArt Pension

Friedrichstrasse 127, 10117 (2839 0430/
fax 2839 0432/mitart@t-online.de). U6
Oranienburger Tor. **Rates** (incl breakfast)
€45-€75 single; €65-€90 double. **No credit cards.**
Map p316/p302 F3.
Opposite Tacheles (*see p243*), this surprisingly
peaceful and elegant pension is also a gallery. The
friendly owner originally let out three rooms to
visiting artists and then expanded to nine. The
grand proportions of the breakfast room are typical
of a 19th-century Berlin townhouse. A healthy
'naturkost' breakfast is served here each morning.
The best room is the 'mädchenkammer', a set of
wooden steps up to a platform and simple white
unadorned walls where the servant used to sleep.
An excellent place if you are in Berlin to look at art.
Auguststrasse is around the corner and the owner
can give good insider tips. Recommended, and not
to be confused with the Artist Hotel-Pension
Die Loge up the road (*see p53*). Look hard at the
labels on the doorbell and go up the main staircase
to the first floor to find it.
Room services *Telephone.*

Less is more at the excellent **Honigmond Pension**.

Hotel am Scheunenviertel

Oranienburger Strasse 38, 10117
(282 2125/2830 8310/fax 282 1115). S1,
S2, S25, S26 Oranienburger Strasse or U6
Oranienburger Tor. **Rates** (incl breakfast) €60
single; €70 double. **Credit** AmEx, DC, MC, V.
Map p316/p302 F3.

In the historical heart and old Jewish quarter of
Berlin, this 18-room hotel is within striking distance
of the Museuminsel, Friedrichstrasse and Hackesche
Höfe. By night the area comes alive with busy cafés,
bars, clubs and restaurants. Rooms are plain but
clean and comfortable, if a little on the dark side,
each with WC and a good strong shower. The buffet breakfast is included in the room price and the
staff are reasonably friendly and helpful. All in all
a good base from which to explore Berlin, but be
warned it can be a tad noisy especially since the
opening of a new nightclub next door – only
recommended for deep sleepers!
Hotel services *Breakfast room.* **Room services**
Telephone. TV.

Taunus Hotel

Monbijouplatz 1, 10178 (283 5254/fax 283 5255).
S3, S5, S7, S9, S75 Hackescher Markt. **Rates** (incl
breakfast) €75 single; €90 double. **Credit** AmEx,
DC, MC, V. **Map** p316/p302 F3.

A small hotel in a renovated building tucked away
behind Hackescher Markt S-Bahn station. The
interior is plain but clean and the location is excellent – close to the Museuminsel – and an ideal base
for exploring Mitte nightlife, though a little near to
the tram terminus if you like to sleep with the windows open. But there is a superb Italian restaurant
on the corner opposite as compensation and you
are bang in the city centre. Ask for a room with a
view of the cathedral.
Hotel services *Bar. Parking (€10).*
Room services *Telephone. TV.*

Budget

Artist Hotel-Pension Die Loge

Friedrichstrasse 115, 10117 (tel/fax 280 7513/
www.artist-hotels.de). U6 Oranienburger Tor.
Rates €35-€45 single; €50-€70 double;
€110 4-person apartment; €2.50 (before 11am)
breakfast or €5 buffet breakfast. **No credit cards.**
Map p316/p302 F3.

The environs of the Artist Hotel-Pension Die
Loge can get a little noisy, but you are very much
in the thick of it as far as nightlife is concerned.
This small, friendly, young pension has special
reduced rates for artists and musicians and is
perfect for small groups travelling together. WC and
showers are shared. There is a cosy foyer with
comfy sofas and rooms have decorative friezes and
borders painted by the owners themselves. They
have a second hotel next to the river, called
'Riverside', which you could go to if they are full.
But it's nicer here.
Room services *Telephone. TV.*

Circus – The Hostel

Rosa-Luxemburg-Strasse 39-41, 10118
(2839 1433/fax 2839 1484/www.circus-berlin.de).
U2 Rosa-Luxemburg-Platz. **Rates** (per bed per
night) €14 6-7-bed room; €17 for 4-5-bed room;
€20 for 3-bed room; €23 2-bed room; €30 1-bed
room; €65-€120 2-4-bed apartment with balcony;
€2 bed linen (compulsory). **No credit cards.**
Map p316/p303 G3.

The Circus has moved location yet again. This time,
it's a five-minute walk from just about every club
or bar you are ever likely to want to go to. This
friendly hostel with clean and bright rooms is heav-
en for weary travellers on a budget. The owners are
young travellers themselves and have worked hard
to offer good value for money. The hostel is open
24 hours and has single-sex rooms available. The
staff strive to help both with your stay and your
onward journey – everything from reduced-price
tickets for clubs and concerts to travel cards. Best
of all, they do special tours to underground bunkers,
around inaccessible archives and even on to the
Brandenburger Tor. Its motto is 'If you need help
you get it', disproving all you might have heard
about grumpy, unhelpful Berliners. Word of a good
place spreads like wildfire and it is often full, so be
sure to book. If it's full, staff will suggest alternatives. Full wheelchair access. Highly recommended.
Hotel services *Bar (cellar). Bike hire. Breakfast
service. Café. Internet. Laundry (self-service). Locker
room. Safe. Storage. Ticket reservations.*

Clubhouse Hostel

Kalkscheunestrasse 2, 10117 (2809 7979/
fax 2809 7977/www.clubhouse-berlin.de).
S1, S2, S3, S5, S7, S9, S25, S26, S75, U6
Friedrichstrasse. **Rates** (per bed per night) €13.50
dormitory; €16 5-7-bed room; €19 3-bed room;
€22 double; €30 single; €2 bed linen (compulsory);
€3.50 breakfast buffet. **No credit cards.**
Map p316/p302 F3.

Exceedingly central, and housed in a historic,
newly renovated building and culture centre
(the Kalkscheune), this is just behind the famous
Tacheles (*see p243*). The staff are international,
friendly and English-speaking. The rooms smell
slightly of socks but that's budget travelling for
you. This is a nice place with an attractive communal room. Oh, and a free welcome beer on arrival.
No curfew or lockout.
Hostel services *Bike hire. Guided tours. Internet
service. Safe. Storage. Pay phone. Ticket reservations.*

Künstlerheim Luise

Luisenstrasse 19, 10117 (284 480/fax 280 6942/
www.kuenstlerheim-luise.de). U6 Oranienburger Tor.
Rates (incl small breakfast) €37.50-€50 single;
€55-€95 double; €120 suite. **Credit** V, MC.
Map p316/p302 E3.

Reopened in summer 1999 after a complete renovation, the Künstlerheim Luise is a pension with a dif-
ference. Each room is the creation of an individually
commissioned artist. Rooms vary considerably:
rooms on the top floor have basic amenities – bed,

telephone and art, with shared bathroom facilities and communal kitchen/breakfast room – to grander rooms and suites on the *belle étage*, with high ceilings, big windows and a private bathroom. Very cool, very different. The only drawback can be the proximity to the S-Bahn, which affects some rooms. Try the Oliver Jordan suite, Dieter Mammel's room with the huge bed, or Rainer Gross' Shaker room. Look at the website for images of the rooms and see what takes your fancy.

Hotel services *Art shop. Bar. Restaurant/brasserie.* **Room services** *Telephone.*

Mitte's Backpacker Hostel

Chausseestrasse 102, 10115 (2839 0965/fax 2839 0935/www.backpacker.de). U6 Zinnowitzer Strasse. **Rates** (per bed per night) €12.50-€16.50 dormitory; €18 4-bed room; €19 3-bed room; €22 2-bed room; €28 1-bed room; €2.50 bed linen (compulsory); breakfast from €2.50. **No credit cards.** **Map** p316/p302 F2.

Open since 1994, this is the longest-established backpacker hostel in Mitte. The rooms are all individually decorated by past guests with an artistic flair and have been named accordingly. The 'Berlin room' is quite amusing with light fittings in the shape of Berlin's two television towers, and the green multi-

bed poem room is good for insomniacs (the walls are covered in lengthy poems in English). There's a video room with English-language films and a self-catering kitchen. The freshly renovated foyer doesn't detract from the homely, student digs atmosphere. Staff are multilingual and very friendly and helpful. No curfew or lockout.

Hotel services *Bike hire. Billiard table. Cooking facilities. Email service. Table football. Tours/tourist information.*

Prenzlauer Berg

This charming borough of Berlin has a surprising dearth of halfway decent hotels and accommodation. The atmospheric architecture, the lovely bar and cafés and the outdoor-all-day-breakfast culture at weekends come together to make this one of Berlin's most desirable places to live. If you find our recommended places to be fully booked and are intending to stay in Berlin for a while, then try renting a private apartment or room from one of the accommodation agencies (*see p66*) – it can work out much cheaper and give you a real feel for the place.

Fantasy island

At last! After much struggle with the authorities, Berlin's wackiest hotel, **Propeller Island City Lodge** (*see also p65*), is ready to welcome guests in the 30 rooms of the newly completed extension. Since we first came upon this tiny *Alice in Wonderland*-style guesthouse several years ago, its fame has spread, and justly so. The artist and musician owner, Lars Stroschen, has created a wild dream landscape in which each room is a unique artwork, and every square inch of the place is individually handcrafted, often by Lars himself – a feat of endurance akin to the painting of the Sistine Chapel.

Moving from one room to the next, it is quite difficult to stop one's jaw from dropping open. A collection of theatre sets would perhaps be a good way to describe them: the only resemblance to a bedroom being that somewhere, in each of them, there is a bed of some description. Take the Upside-Down Room (No.23), for example. You walk in the door and find yourself standing on the ceiling with a table, chair and lamp upside down on the floor above. 'Where the hell do you sleep?', you ask yourself. Closer inspection reveals a series of strange hatches in the 'ceiling' (that's floor to you), which open up to reveal all the real

furniture. Then there's the Grandma Room (No.27) with walls papered in old newspapers and pics of Lars' own grandmother, and a vast wardrobe tilted at an odd angle that opens, Narnia-style, into the en suite bathroom and WC. Or how about the Flying Bed Room (No.11), with tilted walls and floor and a Biedermeier double bed seemingly suspended in thin air in the middle of it. The walls and ceiling are covered in abstract graphic lettering that slithers across the oddly angled planes. There's also the disorienting Mirror Room for narcissists, a Prison Cell for wannabe Papillons and a Rubber Room for, well, whatever...

Stroschen's imagination stretches well beyond the sleeping rooms; bathrooms lined in slate or sandstone; custom-built sinks made of beer kegs; doors upholstered in sheet copper; walls upholstered in rubber. Nothing is what you think it is. There's none of the usual hotel paraphernalia, like room service, telephones or trouser presses. Instead each room is fitted with a control panel and fine quality stereo sound system where you can choose one of five ambient music pieces ('sonic sculptures') to complement your visual adventure. The music is composed by Lars himself – naturally. Utterly unique.

Expensive

Myer's Hotel

Metzer Strasse 26, 10405 (440 140/fax 440 14104/ www.myershotel.de). S3, S5, S7, S75, U2, U5, U8 Alexanderplatz or U2 Senefelderplatz. **Rates** (incl breakfast) €80-€130 single; €130-€165 double. **Credit** MC, V. **Map** p303 G2.

This renovated, well-located, traditional Berlin townhouse building could have done with a more inspired interior design and a bit more TLC with the details. Not that it's unattractive, just a bit boring and somewhat overpriced. However, lovely Kollwitzplatz is just around the corner to make up for things, and Alexanderplatz is a ten-minute walk away.

Hotel services *Bar (lobby). Roof terrace. Ticket reservations.* **Room services** *Hairdryer. ISDN line. Minibar. Radio. Telephone. TV.*

Moderate

Pension Acksel Haus

Belforter Strasse 21, 10405 (4433 7633/fax 441 6116/acksel@t-online.de). U5 Senefelderplatz. **Rates** €64.50-€99 single; €74.50-€99 double. **No credit cards. Map** p303 G2.

An oasis in Prenzlauer Berg. There are seven stylish self-catering apartments with bedroom, sitting room, bathroom and kitchenette. Each has lovely old wooden floorboards, white walls and antique furniture with a Mediterranean feel. Most apartments have two beds; one larger apartment is suitable for four to five people. There's a delightful back garden for sitting out in the summer. The blue and white 'maritime apartment', with its mahogany furniture and seafaring paintings, is particularly charming. Highly recommended, but be sure to book ahead.

Hotel services *Cleaning service. Fax. Garden.* **Room services** *ISDN line. Kitchen. Telephone (not all rooms). TV.*

Hotel Garni Transit Loft

Greifswalder Strasse 219, 10405 (4849 3773/fax 4405 1074/www.transit-loft.de). Tram 2, 3, 4/bus 100, 142, 340, 348. **Rates** (incl breakfast) €61.50 single; €71.50 double; €92 3-bed room; €122.50 4-bed room; €153 5-bed room. **Credit** AmEx, DC, MC, V. **Map** p303 H2.

Located in a renovated factory, this brand new loft hotel caters specifically for backpackers and groups of young travellers. Especially impressive is that the rooms all have en suite bathrooms. In the

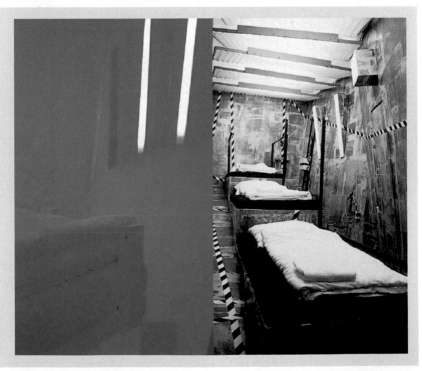

same building are a sauna, fitness studio and billiards salon, all with special rates for guests, and the bar stays open all night long. Excellent wheelchair access too.

Hotel services *Bar. Breakfast area. Cinema (extra charge). Fax. TV lounge.*

Hotel Greifswald
Greifswalder Strasse 211, 10405 (442 78883/fax 442 7898/www.hotel-greifswald.de). Tram 2, 3, 4/ bus 100, 142, 340, 348. **Rates** (incl breakfast) €65-€78 single; €78-€88 double; €102 triple. **Credit** AmEx, DC, MC, V. **Map** p303 H2.

A clean, tidy, no-nonsense hotel in a well-situated part of Prenzlauer Berg, not far from Kollwitzplatz and a short tram hop from Alexanderplatz. The rooms are cheerful, with bright curtains and good-sized beds and the staff are helpful and friendly. There's an interesting collection of signed photographs from various completely unknown bands and musicians in the foyer. Breakfast is in the courtyard in the summer.

Hotel services *Breakfast garden. Fax. Parking (limited).* **Room services** *Telephone. TV.*

Budget

Lette'm Sleep Hostel
Lettestrasse 7, 10437 (4473 3623/fax 4473 3625/ www.backpackers.de). U2 Eberswalder Strasse. **Rates** (per bed per night) €13 6-bed room; €17.50 3-bed room; €22.50 double plus cooking facilities; €2 bed linen (compulsory) . **Credit** MC, V. **Map** p303 G1.

This small Australian-run hostel is in the middle of Prenzlauer Berg's café, club and bar scene. No breakfast is provided, but you can either cook your own in the communal kitchen or get a 10% discount at the café across the road. The hostel is not the prettiest in Berlin and looks a little the worse for wear, but it is functional and has excellent disabled facilities. No curfew or lockout.

Hotel services *Cooking facilities. Internet. Payphone. Ticket reservation. TV.*

Friedrichshain

A former industrial district on the eastern side of Berlin, Friedrichshain is blossoming again as artists, students and creative types colonise the area. There's the domineering Stalinist architecture of Karl-Marx-Allee, the industrial charm of the former docklands area at the Warschauer Brücke, an array of reasonably priced restaurants, bars and cafés scattered around pretty bohemian squares and the East Side Gallery – the longest remaining segment of the Wall covered in colourful and thought-provoking paintings. With its good transport connections, its not-yet-eradicated 'Easty' feel and fantastic café breakfasts, Friedrichshain is a great area to stay in Berlin, especially if you're on a budget.

The **Pension Acksel Haus**. *See p55.*

Moderate

East Side Hotel
Mühlenstrasse 6, 10243 (29 38 33/fax 2938 3555/ www.eastcityhotel.de). S3, S5, S6, S7, S9, S75, U1, U12 Warschauer Strasse. **Rates** (incl breakfast) €67.50 single; €82.50 double. **Credit** AmEx, MC, V. **Map** p307 H4.

Directly opposite the famous East Side Gallery, his modest, simply decorated hotel is great if you want to get some idea of what Berlin was like ten years ago. It's a no-frills establishment, but has good transport connections. Get a room at the back if you have to sleep with an open window, but then you will miss out on a fantastic sunset experience across the old red-brick factory buildings, the Warschauer bridge and the old Wall in all its glory.

Hotel services *Bar. Parking. Restaurant.* **Room services** *Telephone. TV.*

Budget

A&O Backpackers
Boxhagener Strasse 73, 10245 (297 7810/fax 2900 7366/www.aobackpackers.de). S3, S5, S6, S7, S8, S9, S75 Ostkreuz. **Rates** (per bed per night) €10 dormitory; €11-13 6-bed room; €13-23 4-bed room; €19.50-€23.50 double; €40-€45 single; €3 bed linen; €3.50 breakfast. **Credit** MC, V. **Map** p89.

Popular with travelling groups, this place has something of a school camp atmosphere. The rooms – though clean and functional, with basic pine furniture – are not particularly imaginative. The large courtyard area outside with trestle tables and lawn is good in summer, and the huts with pool tables and areas to socialise ensure that all guests are happy

campers. If you really want a taste of the Wild Wild East and to meet young people from all over, this is where you want to be. No curfew or lockout.
Hotel services *Beer garden. Bicycle hire. Cooking facilities. Internet. Laundry. Luggage room. Pool/billiards. Safe. Table tennis. TV.*

Odyssee Globetrotter Hostel
Grünberger Strasse 23, 10243 (2900 0081/ www.hostel-berlin.de) U5 Frankfurter Tor.
Rates (per bed per night) €12 8-bed room; €14 6-bed room; €16 4-bed room; €18 double; €2.50 breakfast buffet. **No credit cards. Map** p89.
Just off Karl-Marx-Allee, this friendly place is in the reasonably priced arty-studenty area of town, with good alternative clubs and bars nearby. The entrance features a pretty, if straggly, courtyard and there's a cosy and interesting style throughout. Super-helpful international staff. Perfect for the 20-something seasoned backpacker. No curfew or lockout.
Hotel services *Bicycle hire. Lockers (free). Luggage room. Pool/table football/table tennis. Safe.*

Kreuzberg

Poor old Kreuzberg: before the Wall came down this was the most alternative place to be in Berlin, if not the whole of Europe. Now everyone seems to overlook its old charms in their rush to see the 'new Mitte'. They are making a mistake though. Kreuzberg has some of Berlin's most picturesque streets, vibrant street markets and charming street cafés, giving it the edge over most of Berlin's newer hip districts.

Expensive

Hotel Riehmer's Hofgarten
Yorckstrasse 83, 10965 (7809 8800/fax 7809 8808/ www.hotel-riehmers-hofgarten.de). U6, U7. Mehringdamm. **Rates** (incl breakfast) €95 single; €120-€135 double. **Credit** AmEx, MC, V. **Map** p316/p306 E5.
Situated in a historic building with one of Berlin's prettiest courtyard complexes, this hotel has exquisite decor, charming staff and airy rooms. Its fine restaurant – the e.t.a. hoffmann – is one of the best in town and revered for its light cuisine and presentation. Excellent quality all round at very reasonable prices. Drawback? The location is a little off the beaten track, but all the sights are easily accessible by public transport.
Hotel services *Bar. Parking (€8). Restaurant.* **Room services** *Minibar. Telephone. TV: satellite.*

Budget

BaxPax Berlin
Skalitzer Strasse 104, 10997 (6951 8322/fax 6951 8372/www.baxpax.de). U1, U12, U15 Görlitzer Bahnhof. **Rates** (per person per room) €13 dormitory; €18 4-bed room; €19 triple; €22 double; €28 single; €2.50 bed linen. **No credit cards. Map** p307 H5.

BaxPax belongs to the same people as the Backpacker Hostel (*see p54*) in Mitte and opened in 2001. It adheres to the usual Berlin backpacker formula, with friendly, English-speaking staff, a youthful, party atmosphere and a self-catering kitchen. There's a good swimming pool nearby, which is perfect in summer after a hard morning's sightseeing, and the girls-only dorms are an option for girls who just want to be girls for once in this very mixed-sex everything city.
Hotel services *Bar (24hrs). Bicycle rental. Billiards. Internet. Kitchen. Laundry. Reception (24hrs). TV/video room.* **Room services** *Safe.*

Die Fabrik
Schlesische Strasse 18, 10997 (611 7116/ fax 618 2974/www.diefabrik.com). U1, U12, U15 Schlesisches Tor. **Rates** €18 dormitory; €36 single; €49 double; €66 triple; €80 4-bed room. **No credit cards. Map** p307 H5.
Fabrik is German for factory and this hostel, like many others in Berlin, is in a former 19th-century factory building. Unlike the other backpacker hostels, Die Fabrik has none of the little extras that make you feel like family: no kitchen, TV room, billiards or bike hire. It's just a bed and a locker; breakfast costs extra in the café next door. There's no charge for bed linen but that may explain why prices are slightly higher than other hostels.
Hotel services *Internet.* **Room services** *Locker.*

Pension Kreuzberg
Grossbeerenstrasse 64, 10963 (251 1362/ fax 251 0638). U6, U7 Mehringdamm. **Rates** (incl breakfast) €22.50 per person 3-5-bed room; €40 single; €52 double. **No credit cards. Map** p306 F5.
A small, friendly 12-room pension in a typical old Berlin building, but not for the unfit as there are four very steep flights of stairs to the reception. Communal bathrooms on each floor, though rooms do have washbasins. Cheap and cheerful. Well worth considering if you are a family travelling on a budget.

Hotel Transit
Hagelbergerstrasse 53-4, 10965 (789 0470/fax 7890 4777/www.hotel-transit.de). U6, U7 Mehringdamm. **Rates** €16.50 dormitory; €130 6-bed room; €110 5-bed room; €90 4-bed room; €70 3-bed room; €45 single; €52.50 double. **Credit** AmEx, MC, V. **Map** p306 F5.
A converted factory houses this unexpectedly bright, airy hotel with 49 rooms. It's nicely located in one of the most beautiful parts of Kreuzberg, handy for Viktoria Park, a host of cafés and restaurants, and a U-Bahn station to head off elsewhere. The rooms are basic but clean, and the €16.50 dormitory bed is good value, but you can't book so you have to take pot luck with what's available. All rooms have showers and the friendly staff speak English. An excellent place to stay, but not so user-friendly as the newer backpacker hostels.
Hotel services *Bar (24hrs). Internet. Laundry. Reception (24hrs). TV (in lobby).* **Room services** *Safe.*

Tiergarten

Just to confuse everyone, Tiergarten, like Wedding, is now officially part of Mitte but nobody seems to pay much attention to this apart from civil servants. The following, mostly five-star, institutions are dotted around the edge of Berlin's huge central park that gives this district its name. Apart from the park, Tiergarten is home to a clutch of embassies and cultural institutions, and, of course, Potsdamer Platz.

Deluxe

Grand Hotel Esplanade

Lützowufer 15, 10785 (254 780/fax 265 1171/ www.esplanade.de). U1, U2, U4, U12, U15 Nollendorfplatz. **Rates** €205-€256 single; €231-€282 double; €507-€1,943 suite; €18 breakfast. **Credit** AmEx, DC, MC, V. **Map** p305 D4.
One of Berlin's better luxury hotels, by the Landwehr Canal and close to the Tiergarten. The entrance is grand, with a huge, gushing wall of water across from the door and hundreds of lights glittering above your head. The lobby is spacious and beautifully decorated, and there are art exhibitions adorning some of the walls on the ground floor. The well-tended rooms are tasteful and gratifyingly non-ornamental. Thirty of them have been set aside for non-smokers. If you decide to stay here, you get the added benefit of being within stumbling-back-to-bed distance from Harry's New York Bar on the ground floor, which fits in with the hotel's distinctly American feel.
Hotel services *Bar. Conference facilities. Laundry. Parking. Restaurant. Sauna. Swimming pool.* **Room services** *Air-conditioning. Minibar. Room service. Telephone. TV: pay movies.*

Grand Hyatt

Marlene-Dietrich-Platz, 10785 (2553 1234/ fax 2553 1235/www.berlin.hyatt.com). S1, S2, S25, S26, U2 Potsdamer Platz. **Rates** €160-€250 single; €180-€270 double; €285-€1,750 suite; €17.50 breakfast buffet. **Credit** AmEx, DC, MC, V. **Map** p306 E4.
The Hyatt, despite the pleasure-seeking Potsdamer-Platz-visiting tourist throng outside, is quite a classy hotel. The lobby is all matt black and wood-panelled slick surfaces, with discreet and minimal art touches – a refreshing break from the usual five-star country mansion/marble look. The rooms are fairly spacious and elegant, with not a floral print in sight. The internet access/TV is handy and the Olympus fitness centre on the roof – one of the best of the big hotel fitness centres in town – has a splendid pool with views across the city as you swim The conference rooms are underwhelming but the lobby restaurant is excellent, with nouveau Italian cuisine and a wine list made in heaven.
Hotel services *Bar. Bistro. Disabled: adapted rooms (2). Fitness club. Meeting/conference rooms.*

Die Fabrik: from factory to hostel. *See p58.*

Restaurant. Parking. Solarium. Sushi bar.
Swimming pool. **Room services** *Air-conditioning.*
Hairdryer. Minibar. Nintendo. PC (with modem
connection). Telephone. TV/internet. Voicemail.

Expensive

Hotel Alt Berlin

Potsdamer Strasse 67, 10785 (260 670/fax 261
4637/www.altberlin.de). U1, U12 Kurfürstenstrasse.
Rates (incl breakfast) €99-€150 single; €130-€150
double; €30.68 extra bed. **Credit** AmEx, DC, MC, V.
Map p306 E5.

This turn of the 20th century-style hotel opened just
a couple of years ago. All room furnishings look retro
but are in fact modern. The restaurant looks a bit like
a cluttered museum and serves up hearty Berlin traditional cooking. Bedrooms are spacious, and the
hotel is within walking distance of Potsdamer Platz.
Hotel services *Bar. Bicycle hire. Parking (€9.20).*
Restaurant. **Room services** *Minibar. Telephone.*

Hotel InterContinental

Budapester Strasse 2, 10787 (26020/fax 2602
2600/www.interconti.com). S3, S5, S7, S9, S75, U2,
U9, U12 Zoologischer Garten. **Rates** €130-€247.50
single; €130-€272.50 double; €232.50-€1,750 suite;
€17.50 breakfast. **Credit** AmEx, DC, MC, V.
Map p305 D4.

If you're on a generous expense account, this isn't a
bad place to stay. Extraordinarily plush and spacious, the Intercontinental exudes luxury. The
rooms are large, tastefully decorated and blessed
with elegant bathrooms. The lobby is huge and airy;
its soft leather chairs are the ideal place to read the
paper or wait for your next appointment. Note that
weekend rates can be very good value.
Hotel services *Bar. Conference facilities. Laundry.*
Parking. Restaurants (2). Sauna. Swimming pool.
Room services *Air-conditioning. Minibar.*
Modem connection. Room service. Safe. Telephone.
TV. Voicemail.

Charlottenburg

You may not find the hippest bars or the
trendiest restaurants in Charlottenburg, but if
you want to be comfortable, central and within
easy reach of everything, you can't do much
better than stay here. You can opt for four- or
five-star luxury in a big hotel or choose
traditional charm in one of the myriad of small
pensions in turn of the 20th-century townhouses
in what is still the smarter end of town.

Deluxe

Hotel Bleibtreu

Bleibtreustrasse 31, 10707 (884 740/fax 8847
4444/www.bleibtreu.com). S3, S5, S7, S9, S75
Savignyplatz or U15 Uhlandstrasse. **Rates** €157-
€207 single; €222-€272 double; €15 breakfast.
Credit AmEx, DC, MC, V. **Map** p305 C4.

The Bleibtreu is a cosy and smart establishment
popular with media and fashion visitors, and is
perfectly located for shopping if you are a Prada
or Gucci fan and prefer a better class of restaurant.
The rooms are perhaps a little on the small side,
but are individually and lovingly decorated with
environmentally friendly materials. A pleasant
change from the posh-bland look of so many
hotels in this category. Expect good service, nice
food and lots of pampering.
Hotel services *Delicatessen. Espresso bar. Fitness*
centre. Florist. Restaurant. **Room services** *Fax.*
Telephone. TV.

Bristol Hotel Kempinski Berlin

Kurfürstendamm 27, 10719 (884 340/fax 883
6075). U9, U15 Kurfürstendamm. **Rates** €197.50-
€272.50 single; €230-€305 double; €360-€1,250
suite; €19 breakfast buffet. **Credit** AmEx, DC, MC,
V. **Map** p305 C4.

Perhaps Berlin's most famous hotel, if not its best,
the Kempinski exudes a faded charm. But even
though the rooms are plush, you never really feel
you're living in the lap of luxury, as you certainly
should for this price. The Bristol Bar on the ground
floor, with its fat leather sofas and lots of old, dark
wood, has a long cocktail list and snooty waiters.
The Kempinski Eck restaurant is nothing special,
and neither is the Kempinski Grill. The pool's nice,
though, and you can take breakfast lounging beside
it in the mornings, which is a boon on a miserable
cold Berlin winter day.
Hotel services *Bar. Beauty salon. Conference*
facilities. Laundry. Massage. Restaurants (3).
Sauna. Solarium. Swimming pool. **Room**
services *Minibar. Room service. Telephone.*
TV: pay movies.

Savoy Hotel Berlin

Fasanenstrasse 9-10, 10623 (311 030/fax 311 03
333/www.hotel-savoy.com). S3, S5, S7, S9, S75, U2,
U9, U12 Zoologischer Garten. **Rates** €142-€192
single; €192-€242 double; €232-€302 suite;
€15 breakfast buffet. **Credit** AmEx, DC, MC, V.
Map p305 C5.

A smart, stylish hotel set back from the hustle and
bustle around Bahnhof Zoo but still very central.
Built in 1929, the Savoy was the hotel of choice
for author Thomas Mann and continues to impress.
The bedrooms are divided into two styles: romantic
and business-like. The restaurant serves South
American-inspired cuisine, and, best of all, there's
the fabulous Savoy Bar downstairs with its
own library and one of the finest collections of
Cuban cigars in Berlin. The Savoy lives up to the
promise of its name both in decor and service and
is well located for business visitors on a tight
schedule who may need to wine and dine with
clients on site.
Hotel services *Babysitting. Cigar bar.*
Flower delivery. Parking. Restaurant. Secretarial
service. Ticket reservations. **Room services**
Hairdryer. Minibar. Room service. Telephone.
TV: cable.

Swissotel Berlin

Am Kurfürstendamm Augsburger Strasse 44, 10789 (220 100/fax 220 102 222/www.swissotel.com). **Rates** €220-€320 single/double; €330-€450 suite; €19 breakfast. **Credit** AmEx, DC, MC, V. **Map** p305 C4.

You know Berlin's being taken seriously when the Raffles chain wants a look in. The styling is exquisite and the foyer on the second floor is an architectural stroke of genius, away from the bustle outside. Rooms look on to the inner courtyard or the Ku'damm. Choose the latter if you are on one of the higher floors for unforgettable sunsets. If your budget stretches to an executive suite on the 9th and 10th floors, then you will find the expense is justified for once. The Anton Mosimann restaurant is so good you may be reluctant to eat elsewhere during your stay. Minus points: the staff seem slightly uniform and there's no swimming pool. But you can have an Ayurveda massage in your room if you feel the urge.
Hotel services *Bar. Beauty salon. Conference facilities. Gym. Laundry. Massage. Restaurant. Sauna. Solarium.* **Room services** *Espresso machine. Hairdryer. Iron & ironing board. ISDN. Minibar. Room service. Telephone. TV.*

Expensive

Hotel Garni Askanischer Hof

Kurfürstendamm 53, 10707 (881 8033/34/fax 881 7206/www.askanischer-hof.de). U15 Uhlandstrasse. **Rates** (incl breakfast) €110 single; €130-€145 double; €205 suite; €25 extra bed. **Credit** AmEx, DC, MC, V. **Map** p305 C4.

One of Berlin's best kept secrets, the Askanischer Hof has been the home from home for a host of visiting actors and literary types since well before the war. The breakfast room doesn't seem to have changed a jot since 1910, and each room is spacious, with its own individual style spanning a century of European interiors: vast chandeliers paired with overstuffed leather Chesterfields, heavy Prussian desks and 1940s wallpaper. This is Berlin of old – plenty of atmosphere, friendly service and dodgy taste.
Hotel services *Bar. Parking.* **Room services** *Telephone. TV.*

Berlin Plaza Hotel

Knesebeckstrasse 62, 10719 (884 130/fax 8841 3754/www.plazahotel.de). U15 Uhlandstrasse. **Rates** (incl breakfast) €78-€144.50 single; €127-€352 double. **Credit** AmEx, DC, MC, V. **Map** p305 C4.

International bland, you-could-be-anywhere styling makes this hotel visually unmemorable. Its 131 rooms decorated in pink, maroon and white are rather small and plain. You can mix your own muesli at the breakfast buffet, the food is freshly made and bread is baked on the premises. German specialities are served in the restaurant and bar. As for the prices – you are paying for its location just off the Ku'damm. Under-16s can stay in their parents' room for free.
Hotel services *Bar. Conference facilities. Laundry. Parking (€10 a day). Restaurant.* **Room services** *Hairdryer. Minibar. Safe. Telephone. TV.*

The view from the breakfast room at the **Holiday Inn Garden Court**. *See p62.*

Concept Hotel

*Grolmanstrasse 41-3, 10623 (884 260/
fax 8842 6500/www.concept-hotel.com).
S3, S5, S7, S9, S75 Savignyplatz.* **Rates** (incl
breakfast) €115-€145 single; €145-€180 double;
€180-€260 suite. **Credit** AmEx, DC, MC, V.
Map p305 C4.

The Concept is generally pretty smart. Ask for a
room in the new wing if you want internet access
and air-conditioning in your room. There's a big roof
terrace for sunbathing (€10) and conference facilities. The hotel is quiet and located in an upmarket
shopping area (as are all the Charlottenburg hotels
listed here) with a good selection of restaurants nearby. Also well situated for quick access to the ICC
congress centre. Boring bar though.
Hotel services *Bar. Conference facilities.
Disabled: adapted rooms (2). Parking (€10.50).
Sauna. Solarium.* **Room services** *Minibar. Safe.
Telephone. TV.*

Hecker's Hotel

*Grolmanstrasse 35, 10623 (88900/fax 889 0260/
www.heckers-hotel.com). U15 Uhlandstrasse.*
Rates €125-€200 single; €150-€230 double;
€350-€485 suite; €15 breakfast; free under-12s.
Credit AmEx, DC, MC, V. **Map** p305 C4.

Unremarkable on the outside, quite pleasant
inside. Although there's not much of a lobby, the
bar/restaurant/breakfast room at Hecker's is a fine
place to sit and wait. Rooms are really spacious and
comfortable, with some nice (and sometimes
surprising) little touches – pencil sharpeners, for
example, and fresh fruit. Bathrooms are clean and
well lit with marble tiling. The walk-in closets are
easily the biggest in Berlin. Quiet and comfortable.
Roof terrace in summer.
Hotel services *Bar (until 10pm). Conference
facilities (capacity 200). No-smoking floors (2).
Parking. Roof terrace.* **Room services** *Fax
(some rooms). Kitchenette. Minibar. Safe.
Telephone. TV.*

Holiday Inn Garden Court

*Bleibtreustrasse 25, 10707 (881 4076/
fax 8809 3939/berlinhigc@aol.com). S3, S5,
S7, S9, S75 Savignyplatz.* **Rates** (incl breakfast)
€102.50 single; €122.50 double; €137.50-€157.50
suite; free under-12s. **Credit** AmEx, DC, MC, V.
Map p305 C4.

Just off the Ku'damm, this hotel is certainly central,
but it won't win any prizes for decor. The 73 rooms
and suites were renovated in 1998, but are pretty
cramped and unremarkable. Still, the bathrooms
are bright and clean. The glass-enclosed breakfast
room on the fifth floor offers a stunning view of
the area. If you stay here in the summer, try and
get a room on the first floor, which has access to a
private courtyard garden. The lobby bar stays open
around the clock.
Hotel services *Bar (24hrs). Conference
facilities. Laundry. Parking.* **Room services** *Air-
conditioning (not all rooms). Hairdryer. Minibar.
Telephone. TV.*

Sorat Art'otel Berlin

*Joachimstaler Strasse 29, 10719 (884 470/
fax 8844 7700/www.sorat-hotels.com).
U9, U15 Kürfurstendamm.* **Rates** €117.50-
€195 single; €137.50-€225 double; €12.50
breakfast buffet. **Credit** AmEx, MC, DC, V.
Map p305 C4.

Just off the Ku'damm in the heart of the west end,
this hotel's theme is the work of artist Wolf Vostell
– his collages and prints adorn the walls. It may
have lost a little of its shine of late, but the rooms
are modern and most are a good size, with fantastic
bathrooms. Ask to see a couple of rooms as they
range from good to great without any apparent
reflection in the price. The *Eckzimmer* (corner
rooms) are the best. The breakfast room is pleasant
with a splendid buffet and it opens out into the
garden in summer.
Hotel services *Bar (24hrs). Conference facilities.
No-smoking floors (2). Parking. Restaurant.*
Room services *Fax/modem connection. Minibar.
Telephone. TV: cable.*

Moderate

Hotel Art Nouveau

*Leibnizstrasse 59, 10629 (327 7440/fax 3277
4440/www.hotelartnouveau.de). U7 Adenauer Platz.*
Rates €95-€140 single; €110-€165 double;
€175-€230 suite. **Credit** AmEx, DC, MC, V.
Map p305 C4.

This has to be just about the loveliest small hotel in
Berlin. The rooms are decorated with flair in a mixture of Conran-modern and antique furniture. The en
suite bathrooms are integrated into the rooms without disrupting the elegantly proportioned townhouse
architecture. Even the TVs are stylish. The breakfast room has a cooking area and a fridge full of goodies should you feel peckish in the wee hours and the
staff are utterly charming. Highly recommended.
Hotel services *Parking (€8).* **Room services**
Internet. Telephone. TV.

Hotel-Pension Columbus

*Meinekestrasse 5, 10719 (tel/fax 881 5061).
U9, U15 Kurfürstendamm or S3, S5, S7, S9, S75,
U2, U9, U12, Zoologischer Garten.* **Rates** €40-€65
single; €65-€85 double. **Credit** AmEx, MC, V.
Map p305 C4.

A higgledy-piggledy, third-floor family hotel right
next to Ku'damm and very good value. The rooms
have extraordinarily eclectic furnishings, and the
breakfast room looks vaguely like a Swiss cuckoo
clock, but the prices are pretty unbeatable for this area
and the owners are kind and friendly. Good beds too.
Room services *Telephone. TV.*

Hotel-Pension Dittberner

*Wielandstrasse 26, 10707 (884 6950/
fax 885 4046). U7 Adenauerplatz or S3,
S5, S7, S9, S75 Savignyplatz.* **Rates** (incl
breakfast) €66.50-€87 single; €87-€107.50 double;
€170 suite; €23 extra bed. **No credit cards.**
Map p305 C4.

Faded, eclectic, grand and full of original artworks, enormous crystal chandeliers and very comfortable rooms furnished with love and care. The owner, Frau Lange, is friendly and helpful and goes to quite some effort to make her guests feel at home. Some of the rooms and suites are truly palatial, with enough space to move in for a month with your extended family. The entrance hall comes complete with mahogany woodwork and gold moiré wallpaper – a real taste of Berlin's glory days.
Room services *Telephone. TV.*

Hotel Gates

Knesebeckstrasse 8-9, 10623 (311 060/fax 312 2060/www.hotel-gates.com). U2, U12 Ernst-Reuter-Platz. **Rates** €85-€155 single; €110-€200 double; €140-€320 apartment; €35 extra bed. **Credit** AmEx, DC, MC, V. **Map** p305 C4.
We are ready to be critical here on the name alone, but to our surprise this turns out to be a pretty good, brand new four-star hotel. Perfect for business travellers, there's a PC in every room, with unlimited internet access – at no extra charge. The superior and deluxe rooms are especially good value with huge bathrooms and plenty of workspace. A good place to stay if you are in town for one of the fairs at the ICC, and if you stroll down the road to Savignyplatz there's a good selection of restaurants for lunch or dinner. Discounts available at weekends.
Hotel services *Bicycle rental. Garage parking (€15). Laundry.* **Room services** *Hairdryer. Internet (free unlimited access). Minibar. Office software. PC with CD ROM. Telephone. TV.*

Pension-Gästezimmer Gudrun

Bleibtreustrasse 17, 10623 (881 6462/fax 883 7476). S3, S5, S7, S9, S75 Savignyplatz. **Rates** €47.50 single; €67.50-€72.50 double. **No credit cards. Map** p305 C4.
This tiny pension has huge rooms and delightful owners who are friendly, helpful and speak English, French, Arabic and German. The rooms have Berlin-style turn of the 20th-century furniture, and for a small group travelling together or a family this are excellent value.
Hotel services *Fridge.* **Room services** *TV.*

Hotel-Pension Imperator

Meinekestrasse 5, 10719 (881 4181/fax 885 1919). U9, U15 Kurfürstendamm. **Rates** €40-€60 single; €75-€95 double; €6-€10 breakfast. **No credit cards. Map** p305 C4.
The building is a huge Berlin townhouse and the Hotel-Pension Imperator occupies the second floor. Its 11 bedrooms are large and well furnished with a mixture of antique and modern furniture. Various jazz musicians and artists have stayed here in the past, Cecil Taylor and John Cage among them. Watch out that you get a room with a new bathroom though – the old cabin showers in some rooms aren't great.
Hotel services *Conference facilities. Laundry. TV room.* **Room services** *Room service.*

Hotel-Pension Modena

Wielandstrasse 26, 10707 (885 7010/fax 8815 294/hotelpensionmodena@hotmail.com). U7 Adenauerplatz or S3, S5, S7, S9, S75 Savignyplatz. **Rates** (incl breakfast) €41-€65 single; €95 double. **Credit** MC, V. **Map** p305 C4.
Not as glamorous as the Hotel-Pension Dittberner (*see p63*) one floor above, but friendly nevertheless and prices are lower. The rooms are freshly decorated, but rather plain and uninspired, and the bathrooms are all spanking new. A good budget option for a small group travelling together who want to be in the heart of the west.
Hotel services *Breakfast/TV room.*
Room services *Telephone.*

Budget

Hotel Bogota

Schlüterstrasse 45, 10707 (881 5001/fax 883 5887/www.hotelbogota.de). S3, S5, S7, S9, S75 Savignyplatz. **Rates** (incl breakfast) €39-€62.50 single; €62.50-€85 double; €15-€20 extra bed. **Credit** AmEx, DC, MC, V. **Map** p305 C4.
The very stylish and attractive foyer of this great value two-star hotel belies its more functional than fancy rooms. That said, this place is terrific value and has a welcoming atmosphere. There's a large variety of rooms available, hence the price range. About half of the double rooms have their own showers and toilets and all have at least a washbasin. If there are four of you on a small budget, you can take a double room and pay an extra €15-€20 per person (including breakfast) for the two extra beds. The cosy sitting rooms on each floor are also a nice touch.
Hotel services *TV room.* **Room services** *Telephone. TV (some rooms).*

Hotel Pension Castell

Wielandstrasse 24, 10707 (882 7181/fax 881 5548/ www.hotel-castell.de). U7 Adenauerplatz or U15 Uhlandstrasse. **Rates** €45-€62.50 single; €55-€80 double. **Credit** AmEx, V. **Map** p305 C4.
Tucked away just off the Ku'damm and near many designer shops, this 30-room pension has friendly staff and clean, good-sized rooms. There's no danger of it gracing the pages of an interiors magazine though, and you need to be quite keen on the colour tangerine to stay here. All rooms have a shower and TV, but not all have their own WC.
Room services *Telephone. TV.*

Hotel Charlot am Kurfürstendamm

Giesebrechtstrasse 17, 10629 (323 4051/fax 327 9666/www.hotel-charlot.de). U7 Adenauerplatz or S3, S5, S6, S7, S9, S75 Charlottenburg. **Rates** €26-€36 single; €31-€59 double. **Credit** AmEx, V. **Map** p304 B4.
This is a moderately priced hotel that would probably go down quite well with your mum. It's in a beautiful residential area full of chic shops and good cafés and there's an English-language cinema opposite. The historical Jugendstil building has been

The Jugendstil **Hotel Charlot am Kurfürstendamm**. *See p63.*

well restored, it has friendly management and the 42 bedrooms are spotlessly clean. Not all have showers and toilets, but the communal ones aren't bad. Note: despite its name, the hotel is actually about five minutes away from the Kurfürstendamm.
Hotel services *Bar. Parking. TV room.*
Room services *Telephone. TV.*

Hotel-Pension Funk

Fasanenstrasse 69, 10719 (882 7193/fax 883 3329). U15 Uhlandstrasse. **Rates** (incl breakfast) €32.50-€60 single; €50-€80 double. **Credit** AmEx, MC, V. **Map** p305 C5.
Opposite Cartier and next door to Gucci, this has to be one of Berlin's most exclusive addresses. In the former apartment of the Danish silent movie star Asta Nielsen, the charming proprietor does his best to maintain the ambience of a graceful pre-war flat. The rooms are furnished with pieces from the 1920s and 1930s, such as satinwood beds and wardrobes. The effect is cosy, and the 14 rooms are comfortable and large. Our only niggle is the variable quality of the showers: some are just fine, others verge on the antique. Some rooms have a WC in the corridor too. A lovely romantic place to lose yourself in nevertheless.

Pension Kettler

Bleibtreustrasse 19, 10623 (883 4949/fax 882 4228). S3, S5, S7, S9, S75 Savignyplatz or U15 Uhlandstrasse. **Rates** (incl breakfast) €50-€72.50 single; €60-€90 double. **No credit cards. Map** p305 C4.
The six quiet and light bedrooms in this grand old building overlook an impressive courtyard. There's a bohemian atmosphere and the Kettler is a favourite abode for thespians. The decor is captivating, with loads of antiques – very Napoleon and Josephine. Most of the double rooms and some of the single rooms (rather small for the price) have showers. The toilets are in the corridor, but this place comes recommended nevertheless.
Room services *Telephone.*

Pension Viola Nova

Kantstrasse 146, 10623 (313 1457/fax 312 3314/www.violanova.de). S3, S5, S7, S9, S75 Savignyplatz. **Rates** €45-€65 single; €60-€80 double; €4.75 breakfast buffet. **No credit cards. Map** p305 C4.
This is a popular tourist area, close to the Ku'damm and Savignyplatz nightlife, and the Viola Nova is one of many similar pensions in the district. Like the others, this is an old, converted Berlin house, but this place is notable for its friendly owners, its pleasant breakfast room and its value for money. It has a wide variety of rooms ranging from good backpacker standard to prettily decorated double rooms with antique furniture. Good for small groups travelling together.
Room services *Telephone. TV.*

Wilmersdorf

Let's face it, Wilmersdorf hasn't got a lot to offer the under-60s. It's green, it's staid, it's quiet, there's a posh bit with villas and there's a not-so-posh bit with language schools and more than its fair share of grotty pensions. However, Wilmersdorf is home to Berlin's ultimate decadently luxurious hotel, its most discreet luxury hotel and – thanks to Propeller Island (*see p65*) – Berlin's most way-out hotel. Can't be that boring then.

Deluxe

Hotel Brandenburger Hof

Eislebener Strasse 14, 10789 (214 050/fax 2140 5100/www.brandenburger-hof.com). U1 Augsburger Strasse. **Rates** (incl breakfast) €165-€245 single; €240-€280 double; €450 suite; €55 extra bed. **Credit** AmEx, DC, MC, V. **Map** p305 D4.

A delightfully discreet hotel tucked away in a quiet side street behind the KaDeWe (Berlin's answer to Harrods; *see p165*). Staff are friendly and surprisingly unsupercilious. There's a very pretty winter garden with a bistro restaurant, and if you duck under the trailing vine to the left and go into the small intimate dining room you will find yourself in the Michelin-starred Quadriga restaurant, which serves some of the best French cuisine in the city. Upstairs, the 82 rooms and suites are decorated with considerable panache and the bed making is an artform in itself. Check for details of the weekend special offers, with visits to the opera, six-course gourmet meals and chauffeur-driven limo sightseeing tours if you fancy an all out binge.

Hotel services *Bar. Bistro. Conference facilities. Garage. Massage/beauty salon. Parking (€18). Restaurant. Sauna.* **Room services** *Fax. Hairdryer. Internet. Minibar. Telephone. TV/VCR.*

Regent Schlosshotel Berlin

Brahmsstrasse 10, 14193 (895 840/fax 8958 4800/www.regenthotels.com). S7 Grunewald. **Rates** €305-€357 single; €325-€375 double; €510-€3,000 suite; €20 breakfast buffet. **Credit** AmEx, DC, MC, V. **Map** p304 A6.

If you aren't the potentate of at least a small country or an industry mogul or in proud possession of the odd title, it is unlikely that you'll feel at home here. This is the sort of luxury that whole countries revolt against. The Schlosshotel, designed down to the smallest detail by Karl Lagerfeld, is situated in a restored 1914 villa on the edge of the Grunewald, about a 15-minute drive from the Ku'damm. It has a pool, two restaurants, a golf course and dining on the beautiful lawn in the summer. There are 12 suites and 54 rooms, a limousine and butler service, marble bathrooms and flocks of staff scuttling around and asking you every two seconds if you need anything. A very beautiful place in a very beautiful setting but, unfortunately, so exclusive that it's somewhat isolated from the rest of Berlin (and the world).

Hotel services *Bars (2). Bistro. Boutiques. Children's playground. Conference facilities. Fitness centre. Golf. Health spa. Jacuzzi. Parking. Restaurants (2). Swimming pool. Tennis.* **Room services** *Air-conditioning. Fax. Hairdryer. Maid service (twice daily). Minibar. Safe. Telephone (2 lines). TV/VCR.*

Moderate

artemisia

Brandenburgische Strasse 18, 10707 (873 8905/ www.frauenhotel-berlin.de). U7 Konstanzer Strasse. **Rates** €59-€79 single; €89-€104 double. **Credit** AmEx, DC, MC, V. **Map** p304 B5.

A shabby elevator brings you to the fourth floor of this art nouveau building not far from the Ku'damm, where Germany's first women-only hotel opened in 1989. The artemisia is comfortable and

bright. Each of the 12 rooms is dedicated to a famous woman from Berlin's history. There are two conference rooms, and the hotel welcomes groups and businesswomen.

Hotel services *Bar. Conference facilities. Roof terrace.*

Hotel-Pension München

Güntzelstrasse 62, 10717 (857 9120/fax 8579 1222/www.hotel-pension-muenchen-in-berlin.de). U9 Güntzelstrasse. **Rates** (incl breakfast) €55-€60 single; €70-€80 double. **Credit** AmEx, MC, V. **Map** p305 C5.

A really charming place. The artist owner has decorated the rooms beautifully and there are original prints all over the clean white walls. All double rooms come with shower and WC. It makes a welcome change from the average pension, as does its helpful and friendly owner. A five-minute walk will get you to the U-Bahn.

Hotel services *Garage (€5).* **Room services** *Telephone. TV: cable.*

Propeller Island City Lodge

Albrecht-Achilles-Strasse 58, 10709 (8am-noon 891 9016/fax 892 8721/ www.propeller-island.com). U7 Adenauerplatz. **Rates** €70-€200 single/double; €8 breakfast. **Credit** MC, V. **Map** p304 B5.

The Propeller Island City Lodge (*see p54* **Fantasy island**) is far out, great fun, reasonably priced and it beats the pants off staying in a pension. It is, however, as much a walk-in work of art as it is a hotel and it differs considerably from the usual reservation experience as well. It is advised to look carefully at all the rooms on the website; you then choose three favourites (it can't be guaranteed that you will definitely get one particular room). Bookings are taken only by fax and your expected time of arrival must be included. There's no reception as such, and the office is only officially open from 8am until noon. Check-in is generally until 11.30am and payment is by cash on arrival (although advance credit card bookings are available). Nothing about this place is ordinary. Don't miss out.

Hotel services *Fax. Telephone.* **Room services** *Stereo. TV (not all rooms).*

Camping

If you want to explore the campsites of Berlin or surrounding Brandenburg, ask for a camping map from the BTM information offices in Berlin (*see p47*) or check its website for details (www.berlin.de). Alternatively, visit the Berlin Information Group's website (www.berlinfo.com) for a list of campsites in Berlin. They are all quite far out of town, so check timetables for last buses if you want to enjoy some nightlife while in town. Prices don't vary much between sites: for tents, expect to pay around €3.75 rent for up to four square metres; for caravans €6.45;

plus €4.95 per person and children aged 6-14 €2.30 per night. Further information can also be obtained from the **Deutscher Camping Club** below:

Landesverband des DCC (Deutscher Camping Club)

Geisbergstrasse 11, Schöneberg, 10777 (218 6071/ 72/213 4416). **Open** 10.30am-6pm Mon; 8am-4pm Wed; 8am-1pm Fri.

Youth hostels

Official youth hostels in Berlin (there are three: **Jugendgästehaus-Berlin, Jugendgästehaus am Wannsee** and **Jugendherberge Ernst Reuter**) are crammed most of the year, so do book ahead. If you book more than two weeks in advance, use the central reservations office on 262 3024. You have to be a member of the YHA to stay in these and they all have single-sex dormitories. To obtain a YHA membership card, if you don't already have one, you need to go to the **Mitgliederservice des DJH Berlin-Brandenburg** (also known as the Jugend-Zentrale) listed below. Remember to take your passport and a passport-sized photo. Individual youth hostels also have a day membership deal where you pay around €3 per day as a temporary member if you don't fancy the whole membership palaver. Check the website address below for further youth hostel info.

Mitgliederservice des DJH Berlin-Brandenburg

Tempelhofer Ufer 32, Kreuzberg, 10963 (264 9520/ fax 262 0437/www.jugendherberge.de/www.djh.de). U2, U7, U12 Möckernbrucke or U1, U2, U12 Gleisdreieck. **Open** 9am-4pm Mon, Wed, Fri; 9am-6pm Tue, Thur. **Map** p306 E5.

Longer stays

For a longer stay, try calling a *Mitwohnagentur* – a flat-seeking agency – to see what they have on offer, but don't forget to ask what the total price will be, including agency fees. The agencies listed below will find you a room in a shared house or a furnished flat for anything from a week to a couple of years. In summer, when Berlin is fairly crowded, they are useful for finding short-term accommodation. Most agencies accept advance bookings and you may want to consider a couple of different offers, so start looking around a month ahead especially at busy holiday times. Don't forget that this is all private accommodation so you will be living in someone's home, often with their books, furniture and belongings. This can be a fantastic way to experience the city and get to know the people who live here, but take your time talking to the owners and looking at the places if you can before you choose to avoid disappointment.

If you're staying for a couple of weeks and manage to find something through a *Mitwohnagentur*, you will probably pay €20-€40 a night. For longer stays, agencies charge different rates. It is always a good idea to ask for the total figure for comparison.

Another alternative is looking for ads in *Zweite Hand, tip, Zitty* and the *Berliner Morgenpost*. Prices vary wildly, but if you look for something 'auf Zeit' (for a limited period) you can often find something quite reasonable. Expect to pay €400-€700 for a two-bedroom flat in the more central districts of Kreuzberg, Prenzlauer Berg and Schöneberg. Mitte can be more pricey because it is so popular, but sometimes you can get lucky.

Agentur Streicher

Immanuelkirchstrasse 8, Prenzlauer Berg, 10405 (441 6622/fax 441 6623/www.housingagency-berlin.com). Tram 1. **Open** 11am-2pm, 3-6pm Mon-Fri. **Credit** V. **Map** p303 G2.

Erste Mitwohnzentrale

Sybelstrasse 53, Charlottenburg, 10629 (324 3031/fax 324 9977/www.mitwohn.com). U7 Adenauerplatz. **Open** 9am-8pm Mon-Fri; 10am-6pm Sat. **No credit cards. Map** p304 B4.

fine + mine Internationale Mitwohnagentur

Neue Schönhauser Strasse 20, Mitte, 10178 (235 5120/fax 2355 1212/www.fineandmine.de). S3, S5, S7, S75 Hackescher Markt or U8 Weinmeisterstrasse. **Open** 10am-6pm Mon-Fri. **Credit** V. **Map** p316/p303 G3.

Freiraum

Wiener Strasse 14, Kreuzberg, 10999 (618 2008/ fax 618 2006/www.freiraum-berlin.com). U1, U15 Görlitzer Bahnhof. **Open** 10am-7pm Mon-Fri; 10am-2pm Sat. **Credit** MC, V. **Map** p307 G5.

HomeCompany

Joachimstalerstrasse 17, Charlottenburg, 10719 (19445/fax 882 6694/www.homecompany.de). U9, U15 Kurfürstendamm. **Open** 9am-6pm Mon-Fri; 11am-2pm Sat. **Credit** AmEx, V. **Map** p305 C4.
Guesthouse also available for up to 35 people from €13 per head per night, plus several apartments rented by the night or for longer periods.

Mitwohnzentrale Mehringdamm

Mehringdamm 66, Kreuzberg, 10961 (786 6002/ fax 785 0614/www.wohnung-berlin.de). U6, U7 Mehringdamm. **Open** 9am-6pm Mon-Fri. **No credit cards. Map** p306 F5.

Sightseeing

Features

Maps

Introduction

It may not have the good looks of a Paris or a Prague,
but Berlin's charms are there for all who care to look.

A relatively young city and never a particularly
beautiful one, Berlin is not a conventional
sightseeing destination in the same way as, say,
Paris or Rome. But this isn't to say that there's
nothing to see. Berlin's turbulent history has
left scars and reminders all over this huge town,
while a new future on the global stage is only
just beginning to take shape following the
transfer of the government from Bonn and a
wave of city-wide building and reconstruction.

Most Berlin sights that could properly
be described as unmissable – either because
you really ought to see them or simply because
you couldn't avoid them – are in and around
the central **Mitte** district. But this is only a
small segment of this enormous, sprawling
city – carved up by rivers and canals,
punctuated by pockets of green and fringed
with lakes and forest.

After Mitte, **Prenzlauer Berg** and
Friedrichshain are the two districts of former
East Berlin that have changed most since
the Wall fell. The former is gentrifying at an
astonishing pace, and, though containing few
specific tourist sites, is one of the most relaxed
and enjoyable areas in town to go out for
a meal or a drink. The latter has a far more
hardcore Communist feel to it, and a lively,
youthful nightlife scene.

Once synonymous with nonconformist
Berlin, **Kreuzberg** may have lost its
monopoly on the arty and the anarchistic, but
it remains fascinatingly diverse. Neighbouring
Schöneberg is largely middle-class and
residential, but contains some great bars
and cafés in its northern reaches, and is
a major hub of the city's gay scene.

Tiergarten is dominated by its huge park
of the same name. Along its southern fringe
are a clutch of fine museums, the zoo and the
reborn Potsdamer Platz.

After Mitte, the district with the most to
occupy visitors is **Charlottenburg**. The
shop-rich area around Bahnhof Zoo and the
Ku'damm was the centre of old West Berlin,
and, to the west, Schloss Charlottenburg and its
surrounding museums is another major draw.

Beyond these central districts' attractions
are spread thinner, but shouldn't be neglected –
from the Dahlem museums complex, the vast
Grunewald woods and the Havel river in the

south-west to the proud town of Spandau in the
north-west to the villagey charms of Köpernick
and the Müggelsee lake in the south-east.

A recent administrative rejig (*see p276*
Going *Bezirk*) has amalgamated many
of Berlin's historic districts, but no resident
of Kreuzberg would say that they live in
'Friedrichshain-Kreuzberg', so in this guide we
use the district names used by Berliners.

For ideas on how to spend your time in the
city, *see p69* **Essential Berlin**.

MUSEUMS AND GALLERIES

If you're planning on doing a lot of sightseeing
and museum visiting, then it may work out
cheaper to invest in one of the various discount
cards that are available. A large number (more
than 50) of Berlin museums and galleries are
administered by the **Staatliche Museen
zu Berlin (SMPK)**, including must-sees like
the Pergamonmuseum, the Gemäldegalerie,
the Ethnologisches Museum and the
Ägyptisches Museum. SMPK offer both
daily and three-day cards, available from
any of its museums. The **one-day card**
costs €6 (€3 concessions), while the **three-
day card** is €8 (€4 concessions). Note that
SMPK museums and galleries are free on
the first Sunday of the month, and most
open late on Thursdays.

Another possibility is the **WelcomeCard**
(€18; valid for one adult and up to three
children under 14), which combines three days
free travel on public transport with reduced-
price or free admission to sightseeing walks,
tours or boat trips, museums, theatres and
attractions – in Berlin and Potsdam. The cards
are available from BTM offices (*see p285*),
S-Bahn offices and many hotels.

Tours

On foot

If you're pushed for time but want a good
overview of the city, go for an **Insider
Tour** (692 3149/www.insidertour.com)
or try **The Original Berlin Walks**
(301 9194/www.berlinwalks.com), whose
three-and-a half tour expertly and accessibly
whips through some 700 years of history.

Essential Berlin

... in one day
The key sights

● Pick a café, any café, for breakfast around the Hackesche Höfe in the Scheunenviertel area of Mitte (*see p143*).

● Get your bearings from the top of the **Fernsehturm** on Alexanderplatz (*see p85*).

● Walk across to Museum-insel and wonder at the riches of the **Pergamonmuseum** (*see p77*).

● Stroll along **Unter den Linden** (*see p71*), detouring to take in the **Gendarmenmarkt** (*see p78*), ending at the **Brandenburger Tor** (*see p73*).

● Ascend the dome of the **Reichstag** (*see p99*; come back in the evening if queues are too terrifying).

● Walk south across **Tiergarten** park (*see p99*) to **Potsdamer Platz** (*see p102*). Grab a snack lunch, and maybe call in at the **Filmmuseum Berlin** (*see p103*).

● Head west, either through Tiergarten, ending up at the **Zoo** and **Aquarium** (*see p104*) or via the Kulturforum complex (lovers of Old Masters should take in the **Gemäldegalerie** – *see p103*; modern art fans head for the **Neue Nationalgalerie** – *see p104*).

● Late afternoon shopping on and around the **Ku'damm** (*see p105*)

● U-Bahn to Kreuzberg to see the extraordinary **Jüdisches Museum** (*see p97*).

● Evening: experience the laid-back bar life of Prenzlauer Berg (*see p147*).

... in two days
Museums, palaces, greenery and a beach

● Head for **Schloss Charlottenburg** (*see p109*). Apart from the palace and its extensive grounds, there are a number of first-rate museums in the area, including the **Ägyptisches Museum** (*see p108*), the **Bröhan-Museum** (*see p108*) and the **Sammlung Berggruen** (*see p109*).

● Then, on a fine day, escape to the wide green spaces of the **Grunewald** (*see p117*) or head for Europe's largest inland beach at **Wannsee** (*see p118*).

● Evening: sample the restaurants and bars of rejuvenated Mitte (*see p143*)

... in three days
Great escapes

● If you've had enough of museums, take a boat trip down the Spree from Mitte through the old East down to the **Müggelsee** (*see p70, p120 and p272*).

● If you want more culture, take the U-Bahn to the museum complex at Dahlem (which includes the brilliant **Ethnologisches Museum**; *see p116*).

● Head on to **Potsdam** and Frederick the Great's Sanssouci park and palace (*see p256*).

● Evening: try the youthful nightlife of Friedrichshain (*see p148*) or the diverse nocturnal attractions of Kreuzberg (*see p150*) or Schöneberg (*see p153*).

... in four days
Wartime and Cold War Berlin

● Get a historical overview at the **Deutsches Historisches Museum** (*see p75*) or the **Story of Berlin** (*see p107*).

● Those interested in Nazi architecture should head out to the **Olympiastadion** (*see p111*) or **Flughafen Tempelhof** (*see p270*). For an insight into the Nazi terror machine, check out the remains of the Gestapo HQ at the **Topographie des Terrors** (*see p96*), the prison memorial site **Gedenkstätte Plötzensee** (*see p110*) and/or the German resistance memorial **Gedenkstätte Deutscher Widerstand** (*see p103*). The most chilling destination, though, is the former concentration camp at **Sachsenhausen** (*see p261*), just outside the city.

● If the Cold War era is of more interest, make for the **Gedenkstätte Berliner Mauer** (*see p112*) to find out more about the Wall and see one of the few remaining stretches of it (another now forms the **East Side Gallery**; *see p89*), or go to the **Haus am Checkpoint Charlie** (*see p96*). The **Stasi Museum** (*see p119*), the **Alliierten Museum** (*see p118*) and the **Museum Berlin-Karlshorst** (*see p120*) also offer fascinating insights into the way both sides operated from 1945 to 1989.

● Evening: return to your favourite bar – you'll certainly have one by now.

The **Berliner Dom** and the **Fernsehturm**.

If, on the other hand, you've got time on your side and the unedited version of Berlin's history appeals, go for **Brewer's Best of Berlin** (www.brewersberlin.com), whose seven-hour walking tour explores the city's history in some depth, with plenty of anecdotes (there is also a tour of Potsdam). **Berlin Sightseeing Tours** (7974 5600/www.berlin-sightseeing-tours.de) have come up with an interactive five-kilometre (three-mile) walking tour that takes in all the major sights, as well as numerous lesser-known ones.

The exemplary **Circus – The Hostel** (*see p53*) can offer help and advice on the above and a broader range of specialist walks.

By bike

Largely flat Berlin is made for getting about by bike. **Berlin Expedition** (4849 5325/www.berlinexpedition.de) organises three- to four-hour tours for groups of five or more, including one along the former border between East and West. **Fahrradstation** (2045 4500/www.fahrradstation.de; *see p273*) offers a range of themed city tours including 'Cold War Berlin' and 'Architecture in Berlin', as well as an appealing Sunday day trip to the countryside; tours are principally in German, but English translation is available. **Insider Tour** (*see p68*) offers four-hour bike excursions covering more or less the same ground as their comprehensive walking tours, though the bike tours can be more rewarding since numbers are lower. Smaller still are the group tours at **Pedal Power** (7899 1939), which organises city tours for two people.

Remember that you may need to leave an official form of ID, such as a passport or credit card, as a deposit if you hire a bike.

For places to hire bikes, *see p273*.

By bus

A cheap and flexible option is **bus 100**, a standard BVG public transport bus running from Zoo in the east to Prenzlauer Berg in the west, which goes past many of the major sights in Tiergarten and Mitte. **Berolina** (8856 8030/www.berolina-berlin.com), on the other hand, offers the works – wraparound windows, a running commentary in a choice of languages and a 'hop on hop off' set-up that allows you to explore the 12 sightseeing stops at your own pace before continuing. **Top Tour Berlin** (2562 4740/hans-peter-neuss@BVG.de) operates on a similarly flexible basis but uses open-top buses. Part of the BVG public transport authority, **Zille Bus** (2562 4740/www.bvg.de/service/citytours05.html) operates tours from Marlene-Dietrich-Platz on old-fashioned open-top buses.

By boat/ship

Spreekrone (349 9595) organises boat tours on the Spree. **Reederei Bruno Winkler** (349 9595) tours ply the Spree, the Wannsee and out west to Brandenburg an Havel. If, on the other hand, you havn't got time for a leisurely cruise then **Historical City Tour** (536 3600) covers a fair few sights in just an hour, including the Reichstag, the Palast der Republik and the Berliner Dom. A nostalgic alternative is the original Amsterdam 'Grachten' boats used in **Berliner Wassertaxi-Stadtrundfahren (BWTS)** (6588 0203).

From Berlin's beautiful southern neighbour, Potsdam (*see p258*), there are numerous opportunities for sightseeing by boat; for instance, **Havel Dampfschiffahrt** (0331 270 6229) organises 90-minute cruises on the Havel river.

See also p272.

Specialist

If you can imagine nothing worse than being herded along the well-beaten track then **City Guide Tour** (614 397) may be able to satisfy any outlandish whims. It specialises in tailor-made tours in Berlin, whereby you can choose not only the theme of your tour but also your preferred method of transport (whether bike, helicopter, steamer, plane or balloon).

Also on the specialist scene is **Susanne Oschmann** (782 1202), who focuses on the musical history of Berlin and **Spielball** (8507 5390) with supervised city tours for children, and **Berlin Starting Point** (3062 721303/www.berlin-starting-point.de), which comes up with customised tours according to the themes in which you are interested.

Mitte

No longer fair to middling, Berlin's historic core has flourished
in the reunited city and is once again at the centre of things.

Unter den Linden.

When the Wall was up, the idea of this part
of town calling itself Mitte – 'middle' – seemed
faintly ludicrous. True, it was the place where
the city was born on the sand islands in the
Spree, and before World War II it had been the
hub of the city. But it was by no means central
to East Berlin, and, despite international-quality
hotels and the International Business Centre
at Friedrichstrasse station, it didn't seem that
important at all. In the reunited city, though,
Mitte has regained its title as centre of the city
in every way possible: culturally, scenically,
administratively. With the historic old
buildings scrubbed until they shine, an influx
of capital promoting new construction, and a
new energy from moneyed settlers (particularly
in the previously ratty north of the area), Mitte
is very much back in the middle again.

Unter den Linden

Map p302 & p316

From before the Hohenzollern dynasty through
the Weimar Republic, and from the Third Reich
to the GDR, the entire history of Berlin can be
found on or close to this celebrated street.

Originally laid out to connect the town
centre with Tiergarten park (*see p99*), **Unter
den Linden**, which runs west–east from the
Brandenburger Tor to Museumsinsel (*see p76*),
got its name from the *Linden* ('lime trees')
that shaded its central walkway. Hitler,
concerned that the trees obscured the view
of his parades, had them felled, but they were
subsequently replanted.

During the 18th and 19th centuries, the
Hohenzollerns erected solid, no-nonsense
baroque and neoclassical buildings along
their capital's showcase street. (Most of these
were rubble by the end of World War II, but
many were subsequently restored.) The side
streets were laid out in a grid by the Great
Elector Friedrich Wilhelm for his Friedrichstadt
(*see p9*), which he hoped would provide the
model for Berlin's continued growth.

▶ For more on accommodation,
restaurants, cafés/bars, shops and
clubs in **Mitte**, see p47, p123, p143,
p176 and p225 respectively.

America's post-Cold War plot

If the Americans hadn't pulled off some truly unselfish stunts in the immediate post-war period for the Berliners, then generously gone on to be among the very first to support their bid for unification in the heady winter of 1989, it could almost be a joke.

But instead, the tale behind the empty plot in the southern corner of Pariser Platz – where the original US Embassy building stood before being taken out in the war – is an epic of hubris, bad accounting, international terrorism and colliding diplomatic priorities.

The Brandenburg Gate may be the symbol of united Berlin. But the verdant site of the unbuilt US embassy, only a few steps away, is a metaphor for how the Americans are having a tough time adjusting to the new local topography.

On a freezing day in January 1993, the then US Ambassador to Germany Robert Kimmitt gave a pretentious little speech on the barren terrain just south of the Brandenburg Gate. He said that though the role of America was changing in the city (the troops would pull out a year later), the US was as committed to Berlin and Germany as ever. As a sign, he said, he was unveiling a marker to symbolise that America was the first nation to return to its pre-war embassy site in united Berlin.

Ahem. Eight years later, the stunning British Embassy is already doing business around the corner from the Adlon Hotel, the French Embassy across the street is nearly complete, and the Americans... well, they now say the Stars and Stripes may be flying over Pariser Platz in 2006.

Turns out the Americans had originally planned to finance a new embassy building with the sale of property their forces had occupied throughout the Cold War period. So nobody bothered to submit a budget request to the US Congress.

But by the time lawyers sorted out exactly which property belonged to whom, the State Department bean counters came up short. And suddenly there was no money for a new embassy. (The US currently occupies its old embassy building to the GDR on Neustädtische Kirchstrasse.)

Eventually, the money came through. There was an architectural competition, and a design was approved. But then, in the late '90s, the State Department issued strict security requirements for all new embassy buildings, following the bloody terrorist attacks on US embassies in Kenya and Tanzania. They included a minimum 30-metre (98-foot) security zone between the structures and adjoining streets.

Well, with the new embassy already designed, approved and budgeted, the only way that could be arranged at the narrow Berlin site would be to move the roads. And that's just what the Americans expected to happen.

Re-route traffic patterns around the Brandenburg Gate; cut into the Tiergarten park. In the good old, bad days of the occupation, that would have been done. But hey, in the new Berlin, it's the Berlin Senate who has sovereignty over planning issues. So there was a stand-off. For years. Rumours circulated that the Americans were so snubbed, they were going to sell the prestigious plot.

At one point in 1999, at the gala opening of Germany's 1,000th McDonald's, in the Berlin district of Treptow, Berlin's then governing mayor Eberhard Diepgen spied US Ambassador to Germany John Kornblum among the hamburger-munching dignitaries. 'I see the American Ambassador is here,' ad-libbed Diepgen from the podium. 'Maybe he should build a McDonald's on Pariser Platz instead of an embassy.'

The *New York Times* ran the cheeky story. It appeared on the front page of sister publication the *International Herald Tribune*, sparking such a diplomatic row that German Chancellor Gerhard Schröder paused from a trip to China with an offer to personally mediate a solution.

By the spring of 2001, Diepgen travelled to Washington and came back with a compromise. The security zone will be reduced to only 25 metres (82 feet), seven of them on the embassy site itself. The building will be narrower and higher, and only Behrenstrasse will have to be moved, and that only a metre south. The Americans are footing two-thirds of the re-roading costs. After all the arguing and to-ing and fro-ing it looks like building will finally commence by the end of 2002.

With its Wall long down and sparkling new buildings up everywhere, Berlin likes to pose as the city of the future. So far, official America is still not part of it.

Brandenburger Tor & Pariser Platz

The focal point of Unter den Linden's western end is the **Brandenburger Tor** (Brandenburg Gate). Constructed in 1791, and designed by Carl Gotthard Langhans after the Propylaea gateway into ancient Athens, the Gate was built as a triumphal arch celebrating Prussia's capital city. It was initially called the Friedenstor ('Gate of Peace') and is the only remaining city gate left from Berlin's original 18. (Today, a handful of U-Bahn stations are named after some of the other city gates, such as Hallesches Tor and Schlesisches Tor.)

The **Quadriga** statue, a four-horse chariot driven by Victory and designed by Johann Gottfried Schadow, sits on top of the gate. It has had a turbulent history. When Napoleon conquered the city in 1806 he took the Quadriga home with him and held it hostage until his defeat in 1814. The Tor was later a favourite place for Nazi rallies, was badly damaged during World War II, and, during its renovation, the GDR removed the Prussian Iron Cross. This was replaced after Reunification and repaired again in 1990. The current Quadriga is a 1958 copy of the 18th-century original. The Tor was the scene of much partying after the Wall came down, having been stranded in no man's land for nearly 30 years. A long-term restoration of the gate should be completed by autumn 2002.

West of the Gate stretches the vast expanse of the **Tiergarten** park (*see p99*), just to the north is the reborn **Reichstag** (*see p100*), while ten minutes' walk south is the even more dramatically reconceived **Potsdamer Platz** complex (*see p102*).

Immediately east of the Brandenburger Tor is **Pariser Platz**, recently lined with embassy and bank buildings, so that the Gate no longer stands in isolation. This was once the city's *Empfangssaal* – reception room. The name commemorates the German occupation of Paris in 1814, and, for 135 years after that, foreign dignitaries would ceremoniously pass through it on their way from Lehrter Bahnhof to visit German tyrants and dictators downtown. (Incidentally, Lehrter Bahnhof, across the Spree to the north-west, is currently being reconstructed in readiness to become Berlin's primary rail terminus in 2006.)

In 1993, plans were drawn up to revive Pariser Platz, with new buildings on the same scale as the old ones, featuring conservative exteriors and contemporary interiors. Some of the old faces are back on the historical sites they occupied before World War II: the reconstructed **Adlon Hotel** (*see p47*) is now

at its old address, as is Michael Wilford's new **British Embassy** (just around the corner at Wilhelmstrasse 70-1; open for visits by appointment 9am-4.30pm; 2045 7254; *see p42*).

While outwardly conforming to the restrictions, inside, many buildings harbour flights of fancy prohibited at street level. In the south-west corner, the new **US Embassy** (when it is eventually constructed; *see p72* **America's post-Cold War plot**) will be a postmodern take on the Blüchersche Palace (in which the embassy was once housed), with a rotunda located behind the façade. Next door stands Frank O Gehry's **DG Bank**, containing a huge, biomorphic interior dome, like something out of *Alien*. The **Dresdner Bank** opposite is virtually hollow (thanks to another atrium at its centre); and, next door, Christian de Portzamparc's **French Embassy** features a space-saving 'vertical garden' on the courtyard wall, and 'french windows' extending over two storeys.

To the south of the US Embassy site will be what is officially, and not very snappily, titled **Denkmal für die ermordeten Juden Europas** – 'Memorial to the Murdered European Jews' – another project enmeshed in controversy over its location (it's not on any particular historical site, and, in some eyes, takes up too much prime real estate), design (American sculptor Richard Serra parted ways with architect Peter Eisenman in 1998), and content (some feel that the memorial should honour all of the victims of the Holocaust, not just the Jewish ones). Work finally got under way in late 2001 and is due to be completed by 2004. The memorial will consist of 2,700 pillars. For more information, look at the website www.holocaustmahnmal.de. *See also p34* **Remember to forget**.

New buildings, soon to be occupied by many of Germany's regional *Länder* governments, have been constructed just south of here.

East along Unter den Linden

Heading east along Unter den Linden, passing the 1950s monolithic, Stalinist wedding cake-style **Russian Embassy** on your right, and, on the next block, the box office of the **Komische Oper** (the theatre entrance is around the corner on Behrenstrasse – the extravagant interior is worth a look; *see p238*), you reach the crossroads with Friedrichstrasse (*see p78*), once a café-strewn focus of Weimar Berlin.

A little further on, on the right, housed in the ground floor of a 1920 building now occupied by Deutsche Bank, is the **Deutsche Guggenheim Berlin** (*see p75*), much more modest in size, scope (and architecture) than

Sightseeing

its big sisters in New York and Bilbao. Facing the art gallery across Unter den Linden stands the grandiose **Staatsbibliotek** (it's open to all, and there's a small café within), usually filled with students from **Humboldt-Universität** next door (see p283). The university's grand old façade has been restored, as have the two statues of the Humboldts (founder Wilhelm and his brother Alexander; see p11 **Wir sind Berliner: the von Humboldts**), between which booksellers set up their tables in good weather.

Across the street is **Bebelplatz**, the site of the huge Nazi book-burning, commemorated by Micha Ullmann's wonderful monument set into the Platz itself. Dominating the square's eastern side is the **Staatsoper Unter den Linden** (see p239), built in neoclassical style by Georg Wenzeslaus von Knobelsdorff in 1741-3. The present building actually dates from 1955, but remains faithful to the original. Established as Frederick the Great's Royal Court Opera, it is now one of Berlin's two major opera houses. The west side of the square is taken up by the late 18th-century **Alte Bibliotek**, commonly known as the 'Kommode', after its resemblance to a curvy piece of baroque furniture.

Alongside it, in the centre of Unter den Linden, stands a restored equestrian statue of Frederick the Great (taken down by the GDR, then suddenly and mysteriously reappearing one night when the Party line on him changed).

Just south of the Staatsoper (and also designed by Knobelsdorff, in 1747) is **Sankt-Hedwigs-Kathedrale** (see p76), a curious circular Roman Catholic church, inspired by the Pantheon in Rome. A minute's walk east of here brings you to another church, **Friedrichs-Werdersche-Kirche**, which now contains the **Schinkel-Museum** (see below), a homage to the building's architect. See also p12 **Ich bin Berliner: KF Schinkel**.

North of here, back on Unter den Linden by the River Spree, is the baroque **Zeughaus**, a former armoury with a deceptively peaceful pink façade, which, after renovation, scheduled to be completed in 2003, will once again house the **Deutsches Historisches Museum** (see below). The new museum will include a new wing, designed by IM Pei (of Louvre glass pyramid fame). Some galleries are likely to open in late 2002.

Just west of the Zeughaus stands the **Neue Wache** (New Guardhouse), constructed by Schinkel in 1816-18, which originally served as a guardhouse for the royal residences in the area. Today, it is a hauntingly plain memorial to the 'victims of war and tyranny', with an enlarged reproduction of a Käthe Kollwitz

sculpture, *Mother with Dead Son*, at its centre. Beneath this are the remains of an unknown soldier and an unknown concentration camp victim, surrounded by earth from World War II battlefields and concentration camps.

Deutsche Guggenheim Berlin

Unter den Linden 13-15 (202 0930/ www.deutsche-guggenheim-berlin.de). S1, S2, S25, S26 Unter den Linden, S1, S2, S3, S5, S7, S9, S25, S26, S75, U6 Friedrichstrasse, U2, U6 Stadtmitte or U6 Französische Strasse. **Open** 11am-8pm Mon-Wed, Fri-Sun; 11am-10pm Thur. **Admission** €3; €2 concessions; free Mon; free under-12s. **Credit** AmEx, DC, MC, V. **Map** p316/p302 F3.

In partnership with the Deutsche Bank (and housed in one of its buildings) this is perhaps the least impressive European branch of the Guggenheim museums. Big bucks, big ads, big boring. Huge, safe, famous name, glossy corporate art that you can safely take your granny to and buy a catalogue afterwards. Warning: the exhibition space is disappointingly small. Recent exhibitions include Rachel Whiteread, Bill Viola and Kara Walker.

Deutsches Historiches Museum

Zeughaus, Unter den Linden 2; Kronprinzenpalais, Unter den Linden 3 (203 040/www.dhm.de). S1, S2, S3, S5, S7, S9, S25, S26, S75, U6 Friedrichstrasse, S3, S5, S7, S9, S75 Hackescher Markt, U2 Hausvogteiplatz or U6 Französische Strasse. **Open** 10am-6pm Mon, Tue, Fri-Sun; 10am-10pm Thur. **Admission** free. **Map** p316/p302 F3.

Housed within the ex-armoury known as the Zeughaus, the revamped Museum of German History is scheduled to be completed in spring 2003 (some galleries should be open by late 2002). The core of the permanent exhibition (extending over three floors) will be the chronological 'period rooms', focusing on crucial times in German history, within the context of European history. There will also be 'topic rooms', dealing with subjects such as 'The Relationship between the Sexes' and 'Changes in Work and Profession'. There will also be temporary exhibitions – the first will be 'Idea Europe – plans for permanent peace'. Until the reopening, temporary exhibitions will be held at the Kronprinzenpalais.

Friedrich-Werdersche-Kirche/ Schinkel-Museum

Werderscher Markt (208 1323). U2 Hausvogteiplatz. **Open** 10am-6pm Tue-Sun. **Admission** €3; €1.50 concessions; free 1st Sun of mth. **No credit cards. Map** p316/p302 F3.

This brick church, designed by Karl Friedrich Schinkel, was completed in 1830. Its war wounds were repaired in the 1980s, and it reopened in 1987 as a homage to its architect. Inside are statues by Schinkel, Schadow and others, bathed in the soft light from the stained-glass windows. Pictures of Schinkel's works that didn't survive the war (like the Prinz-Albert-Schloss) are also displayed. *See also p12 **Ich bin Berliner: KF Schinkel**.

Sightseeing

Sankt-Hedwigs-Kathedrale

*Hinter der katholischen Kirche 3 (203 4810/
www.hedwigs-kathedrale.de). U2 Hausvogteiplatz or
U6 Französische Strasse.* **Open** 10am-5pm Mon,
Tue, Thur-Sun; 10am-3pm, 3.30-5pm Wed.
Admission free. **Map** p316/p302 F3.
Constructed in 1747 for Berlin's Catholic minority,
this circular Knobelsdorff creation was bombed out
during the war and only reconsecrated in 1963. Its
modernised interior contains a split-level double
altar. The crypt contains the remains of Bernhard
Lichtenberg, who preached here against the Nazis,
was arrested and died while being transported to
Dachau in 1943.

Museumsinsel

Map p302 & p316

The eastern end of Unter den Linden abuts
the island in the Spree where Berlin was
born (*see p7*). The northern part, with its
collection of museums and galleries, is
known as **Museumsinsel** (Museum Island),
while the southern half (much enlarged by
landfill), once a neighbourhood for the city's
fishermen (and known as **Fischerinsel**),
is now dominated by a clutch of rather
grim tower blocks.

The five Museumsinsel museums (the
Pergamonmuseum, Altes Museum, Alte
Nationalgalerie, Neues Museum and Bode
Museum) have been undergoing a massive
restoration programme for many years; the
first three are now completed and open, while
much work remains to be done on the latter
two. Such is the importance of the site that
it was added to UNESCO's World Cultural
Heritage list in 2000.

The one must-see is the **Pergamonmuseum**
(*see p77*), a showcase for three huge and
important examples of ancient architecture:
the Hellenistic Pergamon Altar (a Greek temple
complex in what is now western Turkey),
the Babylonian Gate of Ishtar and the Roman
Market Gate of Miletus.

Schinkel's superb **Altes Museum**
(Old Museum; *see p77*), from 1830, has a
small permanent collection and hosts some
excellent temporary exhibitions.

The most recently opened museum is
the **Alte Nationalgalerie** (Old National
Gallery; *see below*), which, since December
2001, has once again become home to a wide-
ranging collection of 19th-century painting
and sculpture.

The **Bode Museum** had a strange
assortment of displays, including the half
a million coins of the **Münzkabinett**
numismatic collection (some of which are
currently on display in the Pergamonmuseum)

and the **Museum für Spätantike und
Byzantinische Kunst** (Museum of Late
Antique and Byzantine Art); it is due to
reopen in 2005.

The **Neues Museum** is finally having its
severe war-time bomb damage repaired – it is
due to reopen by 2010 as the new home for the
Ägyptisches Museum (*see p108*) and the
Museum für Vor- und Frühgeschichte
(*see p108*), both currently in Charlottenburg.

Dominating the Museumsinsel skyline is the
the huge, bombastic **Berliner Dom** (*see p77*).
It's worth climbing up to the cathedral's dome
for fine views over the city. In front of here, and
lined on one side by the Altes Museum, is the
Lustgarten, an elegant green square, forming
a counterbalance at the eastern end of Unter
den Linden to Pariser Platz at the west end.

Across the main road bisecting the
island stands Schlossplatz and the shell of
the **Palast der Republik**. This once-asbestos-
contaminated relic of the GDR has been closed
to the public since 1990. All too obviously built
in the mid 1970s, as the main parliamentary
chamber of the GDR, it also contained discos,
bars and a bowling alley. The Palast replaced
the remains of the war-ravaged **Stadtschloss**,
residence of the Kaisers. Heavily bombed, the
GDR levelled it in 1952, largely for ideological
reasons, leaving only the bit of the façade
from which Karl Liebknecht proclaimed the
German Republic in 1918 (*see p16*). Arguments
continue about whether to rebuild the
Stadtschloss (the original plans are still on
file), totally renovate the existing structure
or grace the site with some new structure.
Further debate revolves around whether
a new Stadtschloss would glorify Prussian
military might, whether the existing Palast
glorifies Communism or just what function
a new structure would have (yet another
shopping mall has been suggested). One
way or another, the communist Palast will
eventually see a change.

Alte Nationalgalerie

*Bodestrasse 1-3 (209 050/www.smb.spk-berlin.de).
S3, S5, S7, S9, S75 Hackescher Markt.* **Open**
10am-6pm Tue, Wed, Fri-Sun; 10am-10pm Thur.
Admission €6; €3 concessions . **No credit cards.**
Map p316/p302 F3.
The Old National Gallery reopened in December
2001 after three years of careful restoration. With
its ceiling and wall paintings, fabric wallpapers
and marble staircase, it provides a sparkling home
to one of the largest collections of 19th-century art
and sculpture in Germany. Among the 440 paintings
and 80 sculptures, which span the period from
Goethe to the beginning of the Modern, German
artists are, unsurprisingly, well represented, including Adolph Menzel, Caspar David Friedrich and

Sightseeing

Schinkel's magnificent neoclassical façade on the **Altes Museum**.

Carl Spitzweg. There are also some first-rank early Impressionist works from the likes of Manet, Monet and Rodin. Although it's well worth the visit, don't come here expecting to see the definitive German national collection. This is a big country and you would have to take in the vast museums of Stuttgart, Weimar, Munich and Hamburg as well to get a true overall view.

Altes Museum

Lustgarten (209 050/266 2987/www.smb.spk-berlin.de). S3, S5, S7, S9, S75 Hackescher Markt. **Open** 10am-6pm Tue-Sun. **Admission** €6; €3 concessions; free 1st Sun of month. **No credit cards. Map** p316/p302 F3.
Opened as the Royal Museum in 1830, the Old Museum originally housed all the art treasures on Museumsinsel. It was designed by Schinkel and is considered one of his finest buildings, with a particularly magnificent entrance rotunda. Like most of the Museumsinsel museums, it is being renovated, slowly, but continues to show a good range of temporary exhibitions; a recent one was dedicated to the Berlin years of architect Ludwig Mies van der Rohe.

Berliner Dom

Lustgarten (2026 9133/guided tours 2026 9119/ www.berliner-dom.de). S3, S5, S7, S9, S75 Hackescher Markt. **Open** *1 Apr-30 Sept* 9am-8pm Mon-Sat; noon-8pm Sun. *1 Oct-31 Mar* 9am-7pm Mon-Sat; noon-7pm Sun. **Admission** €5.10; €3.10 concessions; free under-14s. *Crypt* €4.10; €2.05 concessions. *Crypt & cupola* €5.10; €3.10 concessions. **No credit cards. Map** p316/p302 F3.
The dramatic Berlin Cathedral is now finally healed of its war wounds. Built around the turn of the 20th-century in Italian Renaissance style, it was destroyed during World War II and remained a ruin until 1973, when extensive restoration work began. It has always looked fine from the outside, but now that the internal work is complete, it is fully restored to its former glory. Crammed with Victorian detail, and containing dozens of statues of eminent German Protestants, it is now holding weekly services after several decades of existing in the face of GDR displeasure. Its lush 19th-century interior is hardly the perfect acoustic space for the frequent concerts that are held here, but it's worth a visit to see the crypt containing around 90 sarcophagi of the Hohenzollern dynasty.

Pergamonmuseum

Am Kupfergraben (209 05577/www.smb.spk-berlin.de). S1, S2, S3, S5, S7, S9, S25, S26, S75, U6 Friedrichstrasse. **Open** 10am-6pm Tue, Wed, Fri-Sun; 10am-10pm Thur. **Admission** €6; €3 concessions; free 1st Sun of month. **No credit cards. Map** p316/p302 F3.
One of the world's major archaeological museums, the Pergamon shouldn't be missed. Its treasures are made up of the **Antikensammlung** (Collection of Classical Antiquities) and the **Vorderasiastisches Museum** (Museum of Near Eastern Antiquities) and contain three major draws. The first is the eponymous Hellenistic Pergamon Altar. It dates from 170-159 BC, when Pergamon was one of the major cities of Asia Minor; huge as it is, the museum's partial re-creation represents only one third of its original size. The altar's outstanding feature is the stunning original frieze that once wound 113 metres (371 feet) around the base of the structure. A remarkable proportion of it survives, and depicts the epic battle between the gods and giants with a vividness and vitality that make the frieze one of the greatest artistic legacies of classical antiquity.

In an adjoining room, and even more architecturally impressive, is the towering two-storey Roman Market Gate of Miletus (29 metres/95 feet wide and almost 17 metres/56 feet high), erected in AD 120. This leads through (and back in time) to the third of the big three attractions – the extraordinary blue and ochre tiled Gate of Ishtar and the Babylonian Processional Street, dating from the reign of King Nebuchadnezzar (605-562 BC). There are plenty of other gems to be found in the museum, including some stunning Assyrian reliefs, but, overall, it's an admirably digestible and focused place.

The museum is also now home to the **Museum für Islamische Kunst** (Museum of Islamic Art), which takes up 14 rooms in the southern wing. The collection is wide-ranging, including applied arts, crafts, books and architectural details (the latter are particularly notable) produced by Islamic peoples from the eighth to the 19th century.

An excellent audio guide (included in the price of entrance) gives plenty of interesting, non-patronising background info on the exhibits throughout the museum. The building housing this marvellous museum was constructed in 1909-30.

Sightseeing

South of Unter den Linden

Map p302 & p316

What the Kurfürstendamm tried to be in post-war West Berlin, **Friedrichstrasse** had been and may be again (now it's no longer topped and tailed by the Wall): the city's glitziest shopping street. Like Unter den Linden, the north–south street (starting at Mehringplatz in Kreuzberg and ending at Oranienburger Tor in Mitte) was laid out as part of the baroque late 17th-century expansion of the city.

The liveliest, sleekest stretch of the street is that between Checkpoint Charlie (*see p94*) and Friedrichstrasse station. A huge amount of money has been poured into the redevelopment of this part of the street, with office buildings and upmarket shopping malls galore, though opinions differ as to the effectiveness of the architecture. Look out for the all-glass façade of the modernist-style **Galeries Lafayette** (No.75; *see p163*), the acute angles of the expressionist **Quartier 206** (Nos.71-4; *see p165*) and the monolithic geometric mass of **Quartier 205** (Nos.66-70). Otherwise there are auto showrooms for Rolls Royce, Bentley, Volkswagen, Audi and Mercedes-Benz, boutiques for Mont Blanc, Cartier, DKNY and countless other high class concerns in the Quartiers (as each block is known).

Just to the east of this stretch lies the square of **Gendarmenmarkt**, one of the high points of Frederick the Great's vision for the city. Here, two churches, the **Französischer Dom** ('French Cathedral'; now the **Hugenottenmuseum**; *see below*) and the **Deutscher Dom** (home of the 'Questions on German History' exhibition; *see below*) frame the **Konzerthaus** (*see p238*). This was once a theatre (the Schauspielhaus) and is now home to the Deutsches Symphonie-Orchester Berlin.

Just west of Friedrichstrasse on Leipzigerstrasse is the **Museum für Kommunikation** (*see p79*). There are a number of other interesting sights close by, but just over the Mitte border with Kreuzberg. For these, *see p95*.

Deutscher Dom

Gendarmenmarkt, entrance in Markgrafenstrasse (227 30431/2/3). U2, U6 Stadtmitte or U6 Französische Strasse. **Open** *Sept-May* 10am-6pm Tue-Sun. *June-Aug* 10am-7pm Tue-Sun. **Admission** free. **Map** p316/p302 F3.

Both this church and the Französischer Dom were built in 1780-85 by Carl von Gontard for Frederick the Great, in imitation of Santa Maria in Montesanto and Santa Maria dei Miracoli in Rome. The Deutscher Dom was intended for Berlin's Lutheran community. Its neoclassical tower is topped by a seven-metre (23-foot) gilded statue representing

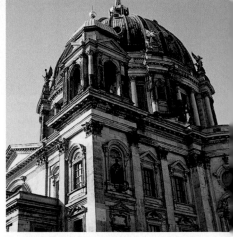

The city's cathedral: **Berliner Dom**. *See p77.*

Virtue. Inside is the 'Questions on German History' exhibition. Guided tours are conducted through parts of the exhibition at 11am and 1pm daily.

Französischer Dom/ Hugenottenmuseum

Gendarmenmarkt (229 1760/tower 2016 6883). U2, U6 Stadtmitte or U6 Französische Strasse. **Open** *Museum* noon-5pm Tue-Sat; 11am-5pm Sun. *Tower* summer 10am-7pm, winter 10am-6pm daily. **Admission** *Museum* €1.60; €0.50 concessions. *Tower* €2; €1.50 concessions. **No credit cards.** **Map** p315/p302 F3.

Built in the early 18th century for Berlin's 6,000-plus-strong French Protestant community (known as Huguenots, who were expelled from France by Louis XIV in 1685), the church was later given a baroque tower, which offers fine views over Mitte. The tower is purely decorative and unconsecrated – and, therefore, not part of the church, which is known as the **Französischen Friedrichstadt Kirche** (2064 9922; noon-5pm Mon-Sat, after service-5pm Sun).

An exhibition on the history of the French Protestants in France and Berlin-Brandenburg is displayed within the building (note: the modest church itself has a separate entrance at the western end). The museum chronicles the religious persecution Calvinists suffered (note the bust of Calvin on the outside of the church) and their subsequent immigration to Berlin after 1685, at the behest of the Hohenzollerns. The development of the Huguenot community is also detailed with paintings, documents and artefacts. One part of the museum is devoted to the church's history, particularly the effects of World War II – it was bombed during a Sunday service in 1944 and remained a ruin until the mid-1980s. Other exports from France can be found in the wine restaurant upstairs.

Museum für Kommunikation

Leipziger Strasse 16 (202 940/
www.museumsstiftung.de/berlin). U2 Mohrenstrasse
or U2, U6 Stadtmitte. **Open** 9am-5pm Tue-Fri;
11am-7pm Sat, Sun. **Admission** free.
Map p316/p306 F4.

Tracing its origins back to the world's first postal
museum (founded in 1872), this once-dispersed collection only reopened in 2000 and covers a lot more
than stamps. It traces the development of telecom-
munications up to the current Internet era, though
philatelists might want to head straight to the basement to check out the 'Blue Mauritius', one of the
world's rarest stamps. The lovely, airy interior of the
museum is worth a look in itself. Three robots
welcome visitors in the main atrium.

North of Unter den Linden

Map p302 & p316

The continuation of Friedrichstrasse north of
Unter den Linden is less appealing and lively
than its southern stretch. Friedrichstrasse
station has been turned into one of Deutsche
Bahn's shopping malls, the formerly grim
building having been totally gutted in
the process. The station interior was once
notable mostly for its ability to confuse,
since its role as the only East–West gateway
for all categories of people (both East and
West German plus foreigners) necessitated
a warren of passageways and interior spaces
to maintain security.

Looming over the nearby plaza is
the **Internationales Handelzentrum**
('International Trade Centre') – built by the
Japanese as a base from which their companies
could trade with the GDR. Its entire front has
recently been replaced by a new structure.

Following the train tracks to the east
along Georgenstrasse, you come upon the
Berliner Antik & Flohmarkt (*see p178*) –
a succession of antique stores, bookshops
and cafés in the Bogen ('arches'), ending
at Museumsinsel.

The building just to the north of the
train station is known as the **Tränenpalast**
('Palace of Tears'), since it was where
departing visitors left their Eastern friends
and relations who could not follow them
back home through the border. Today, this
former checkpoint is a concert and cabaret
venue, and a piece of the Wall can be seen
in its beer garden.

Across Friedrichstrasse stands the
Admiralspalast, originally a luxurious
bathhouse and a survivor of the bombing. In
the 1920s, the **Metropol Theater**, a former
venue for translated Broadway hits and home
to the Distel Cabaret, was opened here.

Crossing the river on the wrought-iron
Weidendammer Brücke, a left turn on
Schiffbauerdamm brings you to the
Berliner Ensemble (*see p241*), with
its bronze statue of Bertolt Brecht, who
directed the company from 1948 to 1956,
surrounded by quotations from his works.
A couple of minutes' walk north-west of here,
on Schumannstrasse, stands the **Deutsches
Theater** (*see p242*), another of the city's
important companies.

Back on Friedrichstrasse stands the
Friedrichstadtpalast, a large cabaret
venue that was one of the entertainment
hotspots during the days of the GDR, since
it took hard currency; it still pulls the crowds
today, albeit mostly grannies from out of
town. Continuing north along the street brings
you to the **Brecht-Weigel-Gedenkstätte**
(*see below*), home to Bertolt Brecht (for the
five years until his death in 1953) and his
wife Helene Weigel. Both are buried in the
Dorotheenstädtische Friedhof (Apr-Sept
8am-7pm, Oct-Mar 8am-4pm, daily) next door,
along with the likes of the architect Schinkel
(*see p12* **Ich bin Berliner: KF Schinkel**),
the auther Heinrich Mann and the
philosopher Georg Hegel.

Two worthwhile museums are five and
ten minutes' walk from here : the **Museum
für Naturkunde** (Natural History Museum;
see p81) and the **Hamburger Bahnhof,
Museum für Gegenwart** (Hamburg Station
Museum of Contemporary Art; *see p81*), which
puts on excellent, varied temporary exhibitions
within the atmospheric confines of a converted
railway station.

Brecht-Weigel-Gedenkstätte

Chausseestrasse 125 (2830 57044). U6
Oranienburger Tor or U6 Zinnowitzer Strasse.
Open *Guided tours* 10am, 10.30am, 11am, 11.30am
Tue, Wed, Fri; 5pm, 5.30pm, 6pm, 6.30pm Thur;
9.30am, 10am, 10.30am, 11am, 11.30am, 12.30pm,
1pm, 1.30pm Sat; every 30mins 11am-6pm Sun.
Admission €3; €1.50 concessions. **No credit
cards. Map** p302 F2.

Brecht's home, from 1948 until his death in 1953,
has been preserved exactly as he left it. Tours of
the house last about half an hour and give interesting insights into the life and reading habits of the
playwright. The window at which he worked
overlooked the grave of Hegel in the neighbouring
cemetery. Brecht's wife, actress Helene Weigel,
continued living here until she died in 1971. The
Brecht archives are kept upstairs. Phone in advance
for a tour in English. The Kellerrestaurant near
the exit serves 'select wines and fine beers and
Viennese cooking in the style of Helene Weigel',
in case you want to extend your Brecht-Weigel
experience. *See p124.*

Sightseeing

coming to Berlin.....

you dont want to miss anything

your guide to Berlin

[030]®

www.berlin030.de

Hamburger Bahnhof, Museum für Gegenwart

Invalidenstrasse 50-51 (397 8340/www.smb.spk-berlin.de). S3, S5, S7, S9, S75 Lehrter Stadtbahnhof. **Open** 10am-6pm Tue, Wed, Fri-Sun; 10am-10pm Thur. **Admission** €6; €3 concessions. **No credit cards. Map** p302 E3.

The Hamburg Station Museum of Contemporary Art Berlin opened with much fanfare in 1997. Housed within a huge and expensive refurbishment of a former railway station, the exterior features a stunning fluorescent light installation by Dan Flavin. The permanent exhibition within comes principally from the bequested Erich Marx Collection, which, despite its distinctly 1980s monolithic, monotone feel, is lightened by a good, varied range of temporary exhibitions and retrospectives. There are wings for works by Andy Warhol and Joseph Beuys, along with pieces by Bruce Nauman, Anselm Kiefer and many others. Upstairs you'll find the sculptures of Rosemarie Trockel and charming pre-pop Warhol drawings from the 1950s. The museum has one of the best art bookshops in Berlin and an *Aktionraum*, hosting various events, such as performances and symposia, plus a video archive of all Joseph Beuys' taped performances. And a café, too.

Museum für Naturkunde

Invalidenstrasse 43 (2093 8591/www.museum.hu-berlin.de). S3, S5, S7, S9, S75 Lehrter Stadtbahnhof or U6 Zinnowitzer Strasse. **Open** 9.30am-5pm Tue-Fri; 10am-6pm Sat, Sun. **Admission** €3.50; €2 concessions; €7 family; free under-6s. **No credit cards. Map** p302 E3.

The Natural History Museum is one of the world's largest and best organised – it's also one of the oldest, and looks it: the core of the collection dates from 1716, and the dull, dusty layout has changed little from GDR days. A tall skeleton of a brachiosaurus greets you in the dinosaur-filled first room, which also contains perhaps the most perfectly preserved skeleton of an archaeopteryx yet unearthed. Another room has a vast display of fossils, from trilobites to lobsters, while other highlights include the skeleton of a giant armadillo. The immense animal collection, assembled in the 1920s, is equally impressive, and the seemingly endless mineral collection is a geologist's playground: row upon row of rocks, set up just as they were when the building first opened in 1889. Don't miss the meteor chunks in the back. Part of Humboldt University, the museum has over 60 million exhibits.

The Scheunenviertel

If the area south of Friedrichstrasse station is the new upmarket face of Mitte, the **Scheunenviertel** (stretching around the north side of the curve of the Spree, running east from Friedrichstrasse to Hackescher Markt) is the face of its moneyed bohemia. This is Berlin's main nightlife district and art quarter, littered with bars and galleries. Once so far out of town that the highly flammable hay barns (Scheunen) were built here, this was also historically the centre of Berlin's immigrant community, including many Jews from eastern Europe. During the 1990s it again began to attract Jewish immigrants, including both young Americans and Orthodox Jews from the former Soviet Union. *See p32* **Modern Jewish life**.

After the fall of the Wall, the Scheunenviertel became a magnet for squatters with access to the list of buildings supposedly wrecked by lazy urban developers, who had checked them off as gone in order to meet quotas – but had actually left them standing. With many other buildings in disrepair, rents were cheap, and the new residents soon learned how to take advantage of city subsidies for opening galleries and other cultural spaces. Result: the Scheunenviertel became Berlin's hot cultural centre.

The first of these art-squats was **Tacheles** (*see p243*) on Oranienburger Strasse, the spine of the Scheunenviertel. Built in 1907, the building originally housed the Friedrichstrasse Passagen, an early attempt at a shopping mall, which in the 1930s was used by various Nazi organisations. It stood vacant for years – at one point the GDR tried to demolish it, but, so the story goes, ran out of dynamite halfway through the job – and was falling apart when it was squatted by artists immediately following the fall of the Wall. It then became a rather arrogant arbiter of hip in the neighbourhood, offering studio space to artists, performance spaces for music, a cinema, and several bars and discos. In 1997, the city presented the squatters with an opportunity to buy it cheaply and was spurned. Recently, Tacheles was taken over by a big Scandinavian investor, and though plans are hazy, art will, apparently, remain a feature of the building's next incarnation.

Across Tucholskystrasse at Oranienburger Strasse 32 is an entrance to the **Heckmann Höfe** (the other is on Auguststrasse), a series of restored courtyards formerly belonging to an engineering firm. The courtyards have been delightfully restored to accommodate shops and restaurants. The free-standing building with the firm's coat of arms in the pavement in front of it was once the stables, as indicated by the sculpture of a horse's head, positioned as if peering out of the building.

A little further down the block stands the **Neue Synagoge** (*see p84*), with its gleaming golden Moorish-style dome. Turning into Grosse Hamburger Strasse, you find yourself surrounded by Jewish history. On the right, on the site of a former old people's home, there is a memorial to the thousands of Berlin Jews who were forced to congregate at this site before being shipped off to concentration camps. Following Jewish tradition, many visitors put a stone on the memorial in remembrance of those who died. Behind the memorial is a park that was once Berlin's oldest Jewish cemetery; the only gravestone left is that of the father of the German Jewish renaissance, Moses Mendelssohn, founder of the city's first Jewish school, next door at No.27 (*see p82* **Ich bin Berliner: Moses Mendelssohn**). That the school has heavy security fencing and a permanent police presence, even today, only adds to the poignancy of this place.

Ich bin Berliner Moses Mendelssohn

Moses Mendelssohn (1729–86) left an indelible mark on the history of Berlin. The Enlightenment philosopher pioneered for Jewish emancipation, and urged orthodox Jews to integrate into secular society. The Torah scribe's son went on to spawn the famous Berlin dynasty that included bankers, literary salon hostesses and the composers Fanny and Felix Mendelssohn-Bartholdy.

Born to a Jewish, Yiddish-speaking family in Dessau, Moses Mendelssohn spent his formative years engaged in Talmudic studies. At the age of 14, he followed his tutor to Berlin, where officials at the city gates granted him a limited residence permit. At that time, only a small number of wealthy Jews were given full residence. Jews were banned from entering many trades; they were subject to ridiculous additional taxes and were only allowed one child per family.

In Berlin, Mendelssohn continued his religious studies, but also immersed himself in modern languages, maths and philosophy. He earned a living managing the books of a silk-making factory. An acquaintance introduced Mendelssohn to up-and-coming figures of the Berlin Enlightenment scene, such as the dramatist Gotthold Lessing and the philosopher Immanuel Kant, who encouraged him to write. Although Mendelssohn's work won acclaim from the prestigious Royal Prussian Academy of Sciences, Kaiser Friedrich II twice blocked the academy's decision to make Mendelssohn a member.

The Age of Reason, which advocated rationality, political maturity and independent thinking, also sparked the growth of a Jewish Enlightenment or Haskalah in central and eastern Europe in the 1770s. Enlightened Jews called on their communities to leave their ghetto lifestyle and integrate in society, by studying secular subjects, and working in skilled crafts, the arts and sciences. Mendelssohn – the movement's torchbearer – realised the goals of the Haskalah with an unprecedented German translation (in Hebrew letters) of the Torah, and established the first Jewish secular school in Berlin in 1778. The Haskalah culminated in the rise of Reform Judaism and the break-up of the Berlin Jewish community.

Mendelssohn did not actively lobby for Jewish emancipation but rather provided the philosophical nourishment. He argued that people must be free to live according to their beliefs, and that the powers of church and state be separated. He demanded equal civil rights for all and an end to restrictions on Jewish life. Mendelssohn called on his co-religionists to abide by the morals and constitution of the country they live in, but strictly keep to the religion of their ancestors. In 1763, Mendelssohn was granted the status of *Schutzjuden* (Jew under Protection), which secured his residence right. But he did not live to see Prussian Jews become legally recognised state citizens (1812).

Mendelssohn personally achieved his ideal of being an observant Jew, who was deeply involved in Berlin life. It's believed that the main character in Lessing's play on religious tolerance *Nathan the Wise* (1779) is based on Mendelssohn himself. Ironically, Mendelssohn's immediate descendants could not live up to that ideal balance. Whether it was out of conviction, social pressure or opportunism, four of his six children converted to Christianity.

A monument to Moses Mendelssohn stands on the site of his grave, in Grosse Hamburgerstrasse in the Scheunenviertel, which was destroyed by the Nazis.

Equally moving, across the street, at Nos. 15-16 is *The Missing House*, an artwork by Christian Boltanski, in which the walls of a bombed-out house have the names and occupations of former residents inscribed on the site of each one's apartment. A little further on, the **Sophienkirche**, from which nearby Sophienstrasse gets its name, is one of the few remaining baroque churches in the city. It is set back from the street behind wrought-iron fences, and, together with its ensemble of surrounding buildings, is one of the prettiest architectural sites in the city. The interior is a little disappointing though.

At the end of Oranienburger Strasse, at the corner of Rosenthaler Strasse, are the famous **Hackesche Höfe**. Built in 1906-7 by some young Jewish idealists, they are a building complex with nine interlinking courtyards in a Jugendstil style with elegant ceramic façades. The Höfe symbolise Berlin's new Mitte: having miraculously survived two wars, the forgotten, crumbling buildings were restored in the mid-1990s using the old plans. Today, they house an upmarket collection of shops, galleries, theatres, cabarets, cafés, restaurants and cinemas and are just about Berlin's top tourist attraction. Try to avoid visiting at the weekend.

A few doors up Rosenthaler Strasse is a tumbledown alley alongside the Central cinema, in which a workshop for the blind was located during World War II. Its owner managed to stock it fully with 'blind' Jews, and helped them escape or avoid the camps. Now it houses alternative galleries and bars. Across the street from the Hackesche Höfe, and under the S-Bahn arches, there is a welter of bars, restaurants and shops as well as the **British Council** building in the Neue Hackesche Höfe, which has a great library and internet lounge with all the latest British newspapers if you need to rest your feet for a while.

There are more fashionable bars and shops along Rosenthaler Strasse and around the corner on Neue Schönhauser Strasse as well as some good sandwich and coffee bars. This area has settled into being Berlin's hip centre with many cool little shops and trendy young pedestrian fashion victims. Most of the original houses have now been renovated and the former gaps left by wartime bombing raids have had some extensive dental treatment in the form of slick new buildings. Even the *Plattenbauten*, the East German prefabs, have been spruced up. Watch out for the pavements though, they still have craters the size of Prada handbags dotted around to snag the unwary.

Leading off Rosenthaler Strasse, **Sophienstrasse** has to be Mitte's most picturesque little side road. Built in the 18th century, it was restored in 1987 for the city's 750th anniversary, with craftworkers' ateliers that have replicas of old merchants' metal signs hanging outside them. This pseudo-historicism has now become part of a more interesting mix of handcraft shops: the excellent woodwind instrument makers, a traditional wooden toy and figurine shop, a whisky and cigar shop, bakers and various galleries. The brick façade of the **Handwerker Verein** at No.18 is particularly impressive. If you wander into the courtyard (as you should with most courtyards if they are not private – only then do you see the really interesting places), you will find the excellent **Asian Art Now** gallery (*see p201*), as well as the **Sophiensaele** (*see p242*), one of Berlin's most interesting theatre and dance spaces, in what was once an old ballroom. The Sophiensaele has a distinguished revolutionary heritage, including being the location of the first HQ of the German Communist Party.

At Nos.20-21 are the **Sophie-Gips Höfe**, which came into being when the wealthy art patrons Erika and Rolf Hoffmann were denied permission to build a gallery in Dresden for their huge collection of contemporary art. Instead, they bought this complex between Sophienstrasse and Gipsstrasse, restored it, and installed the art here, along with their spectacular private residence. Tours of the **Sammlung Hoffmann** (*see p84*) are available on Saturdays, by appointment only. There are also text, earth and light artworks integrated into the building complex itself (which can be seen until 10pm), as well as galleries, cafés and offices.

Running between the west end of Oranienburger Strasse and Rosenthaler Strasse, **Auguststrasse** is the very core of Berlin's eastern gallery district; it was here that the whole Mitte scene originated less than a decade ago, with such important venues as **Eigen + Art** (*see p202*) and **Kunst-Werke** (*see p203*) among many others. This became known as Mitte's 'Art Mile', and the street makes a good afternoon's stroll on any day of the week, although many of the really cutting-edge galleries have moved on to fresh pastures. If you are lucky, you might catch a *Rundgang* or 'walkaround', which are generally held on the first Saturday evening of every other month (check in any of the galleries for details). These gallery crawls are particularly pleasant on summer evenings as galleries open their doors late and occasionally offer wine to visitors.

Sightseeing

Neue Synagoge

Centrum Judaicum, Oranienburger Strasse 28-30
(8802 8316/www.cjudaicum.de). S1, S2, S25, S26
Oranienburger Strasse. **Open** *Sept-Apr* 10am-6pm
Mon-Thur, Sun; 10am-2pm Fri. *May-Aug* 10am-8pm
Mon, Sun; 10am-6pm Tue-Thur; 10am-5pm Fri.
Admission €3; €2 concessions. **No credit cards**.
Map p316/p302 F3.

Built in 1857-66 as the Berlin Jewish community's
showpiece (and inaugurated in the presence of
Bismarck), it was the New Synagogue that was
attacked during Kristallnacht in 1938, but not too
badly damaged – Allied bombs did far more harm
in 1945. The façade remained intact and the Moorish
dome has been rebuilt and given a new gilding.
Inside is an excellent exhibition about Jewish life in
Berlin and a glassed-in area protecting the ruins of
the sanctuary, a reminder for generations to come of
what has been lost.

Sammlung Hoffman

Sophienstrasse 21, Mitte (2849 9121). U8
Weinmeisterstrasse. **Open** by appointment only
11am-4pm Sat. **Admission** call for details.
No credit cards. **Map** p316/p302 F3.

This is Erika and Rolf Hoffmann's private collection
of international contemporary art, including a
charming floor installation work by Swiss video
artist Pippilotti Rist and work by Douglas Gordon,
Felix Gonzalez-Torres and AR Penck. The Hoffmans
offer guided tours through their chic apartment
every Saturday by appointment only – felt slippers
supplied. For some, this kind of ritzy development
signals the beginning of the end of what was good
about Mitte; for others it means the exact opposite.
Both camps are exaggerating.

Alexanderplatz & around

Map p303 & p316

Visitors who have read Alfred Döblin's *Berlin
Alexanderplatz* or seen the multi-part television
series by Fassbinder may arrive here and
wonder what has happened. What happened
was that in the early 1970s Erich Honecker
decided that this historic square should reflect
the glories of socialism, and tore it all down. He
replaced it with a masterpiece of commie kitsch:
wide boulevards; monotonous white buildings
filled with cafés and shops; and, of course, the
impressive golf-ball-on-a-knitting-needle, the
Fernsehturm (Television Tower; *see p85*),
from whose observation deck and revolving
restaurant you can soak in a fantastic view of
the city on a clear day.

At ground level, capitalism's neon icons sit
incongruously on Honecker's erections. A huge
television blares news and adverts at busy
shoppers; the goofy clock topped with the 1950s-
style atom design signals the time in (mostly)
former socialist lands; water cascades from the
Brunnen der Völkerfreundschaft ('Fountain

The atomic clock on **Alexanderplatz**.

of the Friendship of Peoples'); and at the
Markthalle you can sink a beer or bite into a
brand-name burger. There are plans to replace
most of Alexanderplatz with a dozen or so
skyscrapers, among which the Fernsehturm will
likely remain standing, but it's not at all certain
when, or even if, such plans will come to fruition.

Just about the only survivor of pre-war
Alexanderplatz sits incongruously in the shadow
of the Fernsehturm: the **Marienkirche** (*see
p86*), Berlin's oldest parish church, dating from
the 13th century. Later 15th-century (the tower)
and 18th-century (the upper section) additions
enhance the building's harmonious simplicity.

Just south of here stands the extravagant
Neptunbrunnen, an 1891 statue of the trident-
wielding sea god, surrounded by four female
figures representing the most important
German rivers – the Elbe, the Rhine, the Oder
and the Vistula.

Overlooking Neptune from the south-east
is the huge red-brick bulk of the **Berliner
Rathaus** (Berlin Town Hall; *see p85*), while
to the south-west is the open space of **Marx-
Engels Forum**, one of the few remaining
monuments to the old boys – the huge statue
of Karl and Fred begs you to take a seat on
Karl's big lap.

If you yearn to know what this part of
the city might have looked like before Allied
bombers and the GDR did their work, then take
a stroll around the **Nikolaiviertel**, just south

of Alexanderplatz. This is Berlin's oldest quarter, centred around **Nikolaikirche** (dating from 1220; *see p86*). The GDR's reconstruction involved bringing the few undamaged buildings from this period together into what is essentially a fake assemblage of history. There's a couple of historic residences, including the **Knoblauch-Haus** (*see p86*), and the **Ephraim-Palais** (*see p85*), which once belonged to the court jeweller. You'll also find Gottfried Lessing's house, restaurants, cafés (including a reconstruction of Zum Nussbaum, a contender for the oldest bar in Berlin), overpriced shops – and a definite old-time European feeling that's rare in Berlin these days. On the southern edge of the district is the **Henf Museum** (Hemp Museum; *see p86*).

Long before the infamous Wall, Berlin had another one: the medieval **Stadtmauer** (City Wall) of the original 13th-century settlement. There's almost as much left of this wall (a couple of minutes' walk east of the Nikolaiviertel, on Littenstrasse/Waisenstrasse) as there is of the more recent one. Built along the wall is the old (and extremely popular) restaurant Zur Letzten Instanz, which takes its name from the neighbouring law court from which there was no further appeal. There has been a restaurant

The **Fernsehturm**: we have lift off.

on this site since 1525, Napoleon among its customers. The building is one of four old houses that have been reconstructed.

Just over the Spree from here is the church-like red-brick **Märkisches Museum** (*see p86*), which houses a rambling, but not uninteresting, collection tracing the history of the city, and the small neighbouring **Köllnischer Park**. You'll see multi-hued bear statues all over the city, but the park's **bearpit** is home to Schnute, Maxi and Tilo, Berlin's trio of flesh-and-blood brown bears – and official symbols of the city.

Around the corner on Wallstrasse is the **Museum Kindheit und Jugend** (*see p86*), with its not especially thrilling displays of old toys and school life over the last two centuries.

Berliner Rathaus

Rathausstrasse 1 (90260/guided tours 9026 2523 or 9026 2521). S3, S5, S7, S9, S75, U2, U5, U8 Alexanderplatz. **Open** 9am-6pm Mon-Fri. **Admission** free. **Map** p316/p303 G3.
This magnificent building was built of terracotta brick during the 1860s. The history of Berlin up to that point is illustrated in a series of 36 reliefs on the façade. During Communist times, it served as East Berlin's town hall – which made its old nickname, Rotes Rathaus ('Red Town Hall'), after the colour of the façade, especially fitting. West Berlin's city government workers moved here from their town hall, Rathaus Schöneberg, in 1991. For security reasons, admission is restricted to small parts of the building; bring ID with you. Guided tours are organised by appointment.

Ephraim-Palais

Poststrasse 16 (2400 2121/www.stadtmuseum.de). S3, S5, S7, S9, S75, U2, U5, U8 Alexanderplatz or U2 Spittelmarkt. **Open** 10am-6pm Tue-Sun. **Admission** €3; €1.50 concessions; free Wed. *Combined ticket* (with Knoblauch-Haus & Nikolaikirche) €4.50; €2.50 concessions. **No credit cards. Map** p316/p303 G3.
The Ephraim-Palais was built in the 15th century, remodelled in late baroque style in the 18th century, demolished by the Communists, and then rebuilt by them close to its original location for the 750th anniversary of Berlin in 1987. Today, it is home to temporary art exhibitions, a recent one of which was on Berlin fashion from 1820 to 1990. An exhibition on Children's Clothing of the Wilhelmian era (1871-1918) is due to run until 31 October 2002. The Palais's soft, chandelier lighting, parquet floors and spiral staircase add a refined touch to exhibited works without overwhelming them.

Fernsehturm

Panoramastrasse 1A (242 3333/ www.berlinerfernsehturm.de). S3, S5, S7, S9, S75, U2, U5, U8 Alexanderplatz. **Open** *Mar-Oct* 10am-1am daily. *Nov-Feb* 10am-midnight daily. **Admission** €6; €3 concessions; free under-3s; last entry 30mins before closing. **Credit** AmEx, DC, MC, V. **Map** p316/p303 G3.

Built in the late 1960s at a time when relations between East and West Berlin were at their lowest ebb, the 365m (1,198ft) Television Tower – its ball-on-spike shape visible from all over the city – was intended as an assertion of Communist dynamism and modernity. A shame then that such television towers were a West German invention. A shame, too, that they had to get Swedish engineers to build the thing. Communist authorities were also displeased to note a particular phenomenon: when the sun shines on the tower, reflections on the ball form the shape of a cross. Berliners dubbed this stigmata 'the Pope's revenge'. Nevertheless, the authorities were proud enough of the thing to make it one of the central symbols of East Germany's capital; its silhouette even used to form the 'i' in 'Berlin' on all GDR tourist information. It's a great way to orient yourself early on a visit to Berlin, as much of the city is visible from the top. Wend your way through the cheap tourist attractions in the lobby, take the elevator to the observation platform and you'll find a view of Berlin unbeatable by day or night – particularly looking westwards, where you can take in the whole of the Tiergarten and surrounding area. If heights make you hungry, take a twirl in the revolving Telecafé restaurant, which offers an even better view plus a full menu of snacks and meals.

Hanf Museum

Mühlendamm 5 (242 4827/www.hanflobby.de/hanfmuseum). S3, S5, S7, S9, S75, U2, U5, U8 Alexanderplatz or U2 Klosterstrasse. **Open** 10am-8pm Tue-Fri; noon-8pm Sat, Sun. **Admission** €2.50; free under-10s. **No credit cards. Map** p316/p303 G3.
The world's largest hemp museum aims to teach the visitor about the uses of hemp throughout history, as well as touching on the controversy surrounding the herb today. There are a few booklets to leaf through in English. The café (doubling as a video and reading room) has cakes made with and without hemp. Everything, though, is sadly THC-free.

Knoblauch-Haus

Poststrasse 23 (2757 6733/www.stadtmuseum.de). S3, S5, S7, S9, S75, U2, U5, U8 Alexanderplatz or U2 Klosterstrasse or U2 Märkisches Museum. **Open** 10am-6pm Tue-Sun. **Admission** *Combined ticket* (with Ephraim-Palais & Nikolaikirche) €4.50; €2.50 concessions; free Wed. **No credit cards. Map** p316/p303 G3.
This neoclassical mid 18th-century townhouse was home to the influential Knoblauch family and contains an exhibition on some of their more prominent members, but the real draw is the *haute bourgeoise* interior of the house. The building also houses a reconstructed 19th-century wine-restaurant.

Marienkirche

Karl-Liebknecht-Strasse 8 (242 4467). S3, S5, S7, S9, S75, U2, U5, U8 Alexanderplatz or S3, S5, S7, S9, S75 Hackescher Markt. **Open** 10am-4pm Mon-Thur; noon-4pm Sat, Sun. **Admission** free. **Map** p316/p303 G3.

The Marienkirche, begun in 1270, is one of Berlin's few remaining medieval buildings. Just inside the door is a wonderful Berlinish Dance of Death fresco dating from 1485 (though it's in need of restoration). Fans of organ music shouldn't miss a concert on the 18th-century Walther organ here; the instrument is considered this famous builder's masterpiece. Marienkirche hit the headlines in 1989 when the new civil rights movement in East Berlin chose it for one of the first sit-ins in the city, since churches were among the few places large numbers of people could congregate without needing state permission. Guided tours available.

Märkisches Museum

Am Köllnischen Park 5 (308 660). S3, S5, S9, S75 Jannowitzbrücke, U2 Märkisches Museum or U8 Heinrich-Heine-Strasse. **Open** 10am-6pm Tue-Sun. **Admission** €4; €2 concessions; free Wed. **Map** p316/p307 G4.
This extensive, curious and somewhat old-fashioned museum traces the history of Berlin through a wide range of historical artefacts. Different sections examine themes such as Berlin as newspaper city, women in Berlin's history, intellectual Berlin and the military. There are several models of the city at different times, and some good paintings, ranging from early devotional works through to works by members of 'Die Brücke' group, including Kirchner and Pechstein. Some section descriptions are in English.

Museum Kindheit und Jugend

Wallstrasse 32 (275 0383/www.berlin-kindheitundjugend.de). S3, S5, S7, S9, S75 Jannowitzbrücke, U2 Märkisches Museum or U8 Heinrich-Heine-Strasse. **Open** 9am-5pm Tue-Fri. **Admission** €2; €1 concessions; free Wed. **No credit cards. Map** p316/p307 G4.
The Museum of Youth and Childhood is the place to come if you want to show kids how lucky they are to be going to school today and not 50 years ago. Apart from old toys, it displays artefacts from classrooms during the Weimar Republic, the Nazi era and under Communism.

Nikolaikirche

Nikolaikirchplatz (2472 4529/www.stadtmuseum.de). S3, S5, S7, S9, S75, U2, U5, U8 Alexanderplatz, U2 Märkisches Museum or U2 Klosterstrasse. **Open** 10am-6pm Tue-Sun. **Admission** €1.50; free Wed. *Combined ticket* (with Knoblauch-Haus & Ephraim-Palais) €4.50; €2.50 concessions. **No credit cards. Map** p316/p303 G3.
Inside Berlin's oldest congregational church, from which the Nikolaiviertel takes its name, is an interesting historical collection chronicling Berlin's development from its founding (c1230) until 1648. Old tiles, tapestries, stone and wood carvings – even old weapons and punishment devices – are on display. The collection includes photographs of the extensive wartime damage, plus examples of how the stones melted together in the heat of bombardment. Reconstruction was completed in 1987, in time to celebrate Berlin's 750th anniversary.

Prenzlauer Berg & Friedrichshain

Witness the continuing rise of the old East.

Abutting Mitte to the north-east and south-east respectively, the districts of Prenzlauer Berg and Friedrichshain present very different faces of the old East Berlin. The former is rapidly gentrifying, its pleasant bar- and restaurant-studded streets evoking the atmosphere of the pre-war city, while the latter – stretching out from the great Stalinist spine of Karl-Marx-Allee – has a harsher, more blatantly Communist-era feel, though it too has a lively bar and club scene. Conventional tourist attractions are rare in both districts.

Prenzlauer Berg

Map p303

If the fall of the Wall has precipitated a renaissance in any neighbourhood in Berlin, it is surely Prenzlauer Berg. Once thought of as a grey, depressing working class district, unrelieved by any sites of historical or touristic interest, Prenz'lberg (as the locals call it) has had its façades renovated, its streets cleaned, and its buildings newly inhabited by everyone from artists to yuppies. Galleries and cafés have sprung up, and hundred-year-old buildings have had central heating, bathrooms and telephones installed for the very first time. Anarchists, squatters and more hardcore alternative types might now have upped sticks and moved out to rawer Friedrichshain, feeling the district has lost its edge, but, for most Berliners (and especially the newcomers), there's no cooler part of the city.

Laid out at the end of the 19th/beginning of the 20th century, Prenzlauer Berg seems to have had more visionary social planners than other neighbourhoods dating from the same period. It has wider streets and pavements, giving the area a distinctive, open look unique in Berlin. Although some buildings still await restoration, looking down a street that's been scrubbed and painted gives the impression of a 19th-century boulevard.

The district's focal point is pretty Kollwitzplatz, named after Käthe Kollwitz, the socially minded artist who lived much of her life in Prenzlauer Berg (*see p111* **Ich bin Berliner: Käthe Kollwitz**). The square is lined with bars, cafés and restaurants, and hosts an organic/wholefoody type market every Thursday. It was here in the Café Westphal (now a Greek restaurant) that the first meetings of East Berlin dissidents were held in the early 1980s, until they got too crowded and had to be moved to the nearby Gethsemane-Kirche (near Schönhauser Allee S- and U-Bahn station).

Pick any street leading into Kollwitzplatz and you'll be spoilt for choice of places to imbibe, dine and shop. Particularly appealing is wide, gracious **Husemannstrasse**, which was picked out by the GDR for restoration to celebrate the 750th birthday of the city in 1987 (though the scaffolding now up to catch falling plaster suggests that the job was botched).

Knaackstrasse, heading south-east from Kollwitzplatz, brings you to one of the district's main landmarks, the **Wasserturm**. This circular water tower, constructed by English architect Henry Gill in 1852-75, provided running water for the first time in Germany.

▶ For more on accommodation, restaurants, cafés/bars, shops and clubs in **Prenzlauer Berg**, *see p54, p129, p147, p176* and *p229* respectively.
▶ For more on accommodation, restaurants, cafés/bars, shops and clubs in **Friedrichshain**, *see p57, p131, p148, p176* and *p229* respectively.

The **East Side Gallery**. See p89.

During the war the Nazis used its basement as a prison and torture chamber. A plaque commemorates their victims. The tower has now been converted into apartments and is surrounded by a park. If you want to know more about the district's history, look in at the **Prenzlauer Berg Museum** (*see below*) on the east side of the park.

The north-west extension of Knaackstrasse from Kollwitzplatz leads to the vast complex of the **Kulturbrauerei**, an old brewery that now houses galleries, artists' studios, a food market, officess and a cinema. Just west of here, the area around Kastanienallee (running south-west from Eberswalder Strasse U-Bahn station) is another of Prenzlauer Berg's hot centres, with plenty of good bars, restaurants and shops.

South-west of Kollwitzplatz is the **Jüdischer Friedhof** (Jewish Cemetery), Berlin's oldest, and fairly gloomy even by local standards, due to its closely packed stones and canopy of trees. Close by on Rykestrasse is the **Synagoge Rykestrasse**, a neo-Romanesque turn-of-the-20th-century structure, badly damaged during Kristallnacht (*see p20*) in 1938, and, after being repaired in 1953, the only working synagogue in old East Berlin.

Heading north on Prenzlauer Allee, you come to **Ernst-Thälman-Park**, named after the leader of the pre-1933 Communist Party in Germany. In its north-west corner stands the **Zeiss-Grossplanetarium** (*see below*), a fantastic GDR interior space that once hymned Soviet cosmonauts and still runs programmes on what's up there in space.

The highest profile museum in Prenzlauer Berg is the recently opened **Vitra Design Museum Berlin** (near Schönhauser Allee U- and S-Bahn station; *see below*), which puts on excellent temporary exhibitions.

Prenzlauer Berg Museum
Prenzlauer Allee 227 (4240 1097). U2 Senefelderplatz. **Open** 11am-5pm Tue, Wed; 1-7pm Thur; 2-6pm Sun. **Admission** free. **Map** p303 G2.
An interesting museum on the history and culture of the district, with occasional temporary exhibitions.

Vitra Design Museum Berlin
Kopenhagener Strasse 58 (473 7770/www.design-museum.de). S4, S8, S85, U2 Schönhauser Allee. **Open** 11am-8pm Tue-Thur, Sat, Sun; 11am-10pm Fri. **Admission** €5.50; €3.50 concessions; free under-12s. **Credit** AmEx, MC, V. **Map** p303 G1.
This, the first satellite museum of the Vitra Design Museum in Weil am Rhein, opened in July 2000 and hosts first-rate temporary exhibitions. Recent examples include shows on the furniture and buildings of Mies van der Rohe, and on Charles and Ray Eames.

Zeiss-Grossplanetarium
Prenzlauer Allee 80 (4218 4512/www.astw.de). S4, S8, S85 Prenzlauer Allee. **Open** 8am-noon, 1-3pm Mon-Fri. **Admission** varies. **No credit cards**. **Map** p303 H1.
This vast planetarium was built in the 1980s. Though the changing exhibitions are only in German, the shows in the auditorium are entertaining for all.

Friedrichshain

Map p89 & p303
As first Prenzlauer Berg, then Mitte became gentrified, Berlin's restless bohemia needed new space, and the neighbouring district of Friedrichshain to the south-east inherited the mantle. It's convenient for the centre and the incoming trains at Ostbahnhof, and it's the next step for an eastward-growing city.

That said, much of Friedrichshain is pretty bleak (certainly when compared to Prenzlauer Berg), dominated as it is by big Communist-era housing blocks – more than half of its buildings were destroyed during World War II. The district, originally known as Stralau, was historically a largely industrial district, with Berlin's central wheat and rye mill and its first city hospital, and Osthaven, its eastern port. Much of its southern portion bordering the Spree contains the remains of industrial buildings.

There are few galleries as yet in Friedrichshain, but a growing agglomeration of bars, clubs, restaurants and natural food stores on Simon-Dach-Strasse and the parallel Gabriel-Max-Strasse near Boxhagener Platz. North of Frankfurter Allee is another concentration of hangouts in the Rigaer Strasse area.

The best way to get a feeling for both Friedrichshain and its place in the life of the GDR is to walk east from Alexanderplatz down Karl-Marx-Allee. The Kino International (No.33) gives hints, but it's only at Lichtenberger Strasse that the street truly turns into a socialist paradise, with row after row of Soviet-style apartment blocks, stretching as far as Proskauer Strasse (*see p90* **Palaces for the workers**). The **Internationales Berliner Bierfestival** (*see p186*) is held on the street every August, and is a good time to visit as the neighbourhood comes out in force.

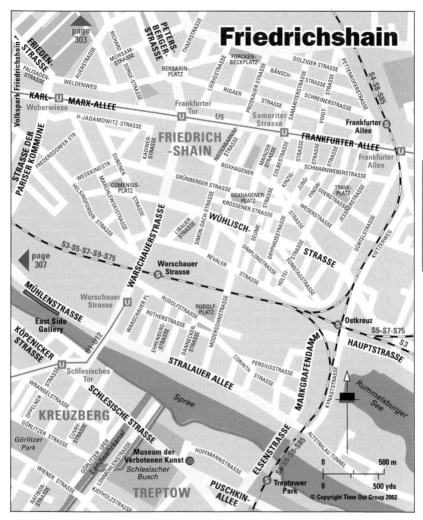

To the south, on Mühlenstrasse (the name means 'Mill Street'; the old mill is at No.8) along the north bank of the Spree is the **East Side Gallery**, a long stretch of former Wall that was given over to international artists. The industrial buildings here have been renovated and rechristened Oberbaum City – they are now home to loft spaces, offices and artists' studios. To set a seal on the area's new hipness, the International Design Zentrum (IDZ) moved here a couple of years ago. Property development is a big thing in this part of town and, particularly if the new international airport is built to the south of the city, the Friedrichshain riverside is set to blossom yet further.

There are no tourist attractions in the district, but green relief can be found in Friedrichshain's north-west corner in the **Volkspark Friedrichshain**. This huge park is scattered with socialist realist art, an open-air stage and a fountain of fairytale characters among lush greenery. The graves of the fighters who fell in March 1848 in the battle for German unity are here. It's also a popular gay cruising zone.

Palaces for the workers

Karl-Marx-Allee – stretching south-east from Alexanderplatz – was made to impress. Simply crossing the street is a 90-metre (295-feet) walk, and one look at the tiled fronts of the massive, Soviet-style buildings gives you the distinct impression of being in Moscow. The street was even called 'Stalinallee' until 1961. Ridiculed in West Germany for its wedding-cake style, Europe's 'only post-war boulevard' was viewed by the GDR as a symbol of its enthusiasm to build a new society. It was along here (the old Frankfurter Allee) that the Red Army had fought its way to the centre of Berlin. After the war, the rubble of the destroyed buildings was used to erect what were to be labelled 'workers' palaces' – Soviet-inspired architecture pointing right at the heart of the German capital.

Although very similar at first glance, the buildings of the Allee were designed by five different architects who were forced into the same formal language, laden with columns, pilasters, window gables and tiled façades. The best known of them, Herman Henselmann, had drawn up plans for a rather sober and modernist design – a style the Party considered faceless, American and 'internationalist'. Reluctantly, Henselmann changed his plans within six days. (Just a few years before his death in 1995 he grunted that not only didn't he like Stalinallee, but that it made him want to throw up.)

However, a change in the party line put an end to this costly era even before the second cupola at Frankfurter Tor was finished. The Party's Central Committee opted for the cheaper box-like design based on prefabricated concrete elements. From now on, the shape of multi-storey apartment buildings was no longer determined by aesthetic considerations, but by the construction cranes' radius – hence the breach in style as you walk further west from Strausberger Platz.

Many of today's Karl-Marx-Allee inhabitants belong to the first generation who moved in (and who had actually worked on the construction in after-work extra shifts). A good part of the now-retired feel that they are worse off after reunification – to them the Allee is a point of identification and pride. To others who had lived in GDR the boulevard is a symbol of the state they hated and by which they were oppressed. Many still believe that it was not ordinary workers but corrupt party members and officials who got their hands on the privileged flats. Both groups are not backwards coming forwards with their views, and if you take a guided tour you're likely to bump into an elderly person eager to explain his way of looking at the street's history, especially the 1953 uprising, which had been started by Stalinallee workers protesting against rising work quotas (*see p24*).

However, time is ridding the boulevard of its ideological implications. A new generation of inhabitants, as well as shop and bar owners, is beginning to take over, oscillating between genuine admiration for the all-listed architectural ensemble and a knowing retro-penchant for Soviet kitsch. Ironically, when the Berlin Chamber of Architecture moved in 1993, it picked a Karl-Marx-Allee wedding-cake block as its new home – abandoning its former base in a 1950s building in western Berlin's Hansaviertel.

The Förderverein Karl-Marx-Allee (Friends of Karl-Marx-Allee) runs Café Sibylle (Karl-Marx-Allee 72; 2935 2203; U5 Weberwiese; 10am-8pm daily; 'Theodoras Literatursalon' is held every 1st and 3rd Monday of the month at 8pm), which, apart from *Kaffee und Kuchen*, has a permanent exhibition about the street and organises English tours on request. It has also installed 39 information posts (in German and English) all along the boulevard. To take the complete, self-guided tour, start at Strausberger Platz.

The Karl-Marx-Buchhandlung (Karl-Marx-Allee 78; 293 3370/www.kmbuch.de; open 10am-7pm Mon-Wed, Fri; 10am-7.30pm Thur; 9am-4pm Sat) just a few doors down the street has a very good selection of books on the workers' palaces. The owner Erich Kundel also invented the game 'Stalinallee', a sort of 1950s socialist Monopoly. Of course you don't buy property – the winner gets to rent one of the sought-after flats.

Sightseeing

Kreuzberg & Schöneberg

The remarkably varied districts south of Mitte and Tiergarten are home to gentility, ethnically mixed neighbourhoods and some of the city's best nightlife.

Bordering Mitte to the south is the district of Kreuzberg. Though it is now administratively joined to its eastern neighbour across the Spree, Friedrichshain, it maintains the independence of spirit that drew so many hippies, punks and other seekers after alternative lifestyle in the 1970s and 1980s. Many (but not all) of these have moved on, and Kreuzberg is now better known for its sizeable immigrant (particularly Turkish) community, and relaxed and varied nightlife. To its west (and south of Tiergarten) lies the wealthier, largely residential district of Schöneberg. Much of Berlin's irrepressible gay life is focused in its northern reaches.

Kreuzberg

Map p306 & p307

Back in November 1994, one of the last Kreuzberg demonstrations attempted to prevent the opening of the Oberbaumbrücke to motor traffic. During the Cold War, this bridge across the Spree and into Friedrichshain was a border post and spy-exchange venue. Only pedestrians, most of them old-age pensioners from the East, could cross. Its renovation by Santiago Calatrava and its opening to the traffic that now surges across it, was effectively the fall of one of the last pieces of the Wall. But it was also the fall of the Kreuzberg of old.

East Kreuzberg

In the 1970s and 1980s, the eastern half of Kreuzberg north of the Landwehrkanal was off at the edge of inner West Berlin. Enclosed

on two sides by the Wall, on a third by the canal, and mostly ignored by the rest of the city, its decaying tenements came to house Berlin's biggest, and most militant, squat community. The area was full of punky left-wing youth on a draft-dodging mission and Turks who came here because the rents were cheap and people (mostly) left them alone. The air was filled with the smell of hashish, the sound of Turkish pop music and the clamour of political activity.

No area of west Berlin has changed quite so much since the Wall came down. This once-isolated pocket found itself recast as desirable real estate in the centre of the unifying city. Much of the alternative art scene shifted north to the Scheunenviertel in Mitte, and even the **May Day Riots** – long an annual Kreuzberg tradition (*see p184*) – began taking place in Prenzlauer Berg.

Oddly enough, gentrification never really took off in this end of Kreuzberg, but it did so in Prenzl'berg, and now the riots have moved back. Though Kreuzberg is no longer a magnet for young bohemia, enough of the anarchistic old guard stayed behind to ensure that the area still has a distinct atmosphere. This half of Kreuzberg is still an earthy kind of place, full of cafés, bars and clubs, dotted with small cinemas, and is an important nexus for the city's gay community. It's just much, much quieter and a lot less radical than it used to be. A certain spark has gone. On some Tuesday nights, the once-teeming Oranienstrasse might as well have tumbleweed blowing down the middle of the road.

One thing hasn't changed. It's still the capital of Turkish Berlin, the world's fifth-largest Turkish city. The scruffy area around Kottbusser Tor, with its kebab shops, Galatasaray supporters' club bars and Anatolian

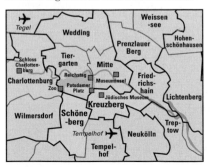

▶ For more on accommodation, restaurants, cafés/bars, shops and clubs in **Kreuzberg**, *see p58, p131, p150, p176* and *p231* respectively.
▶ For more on restaurants, cafés/bars, shops and clubs in **Schöneberg**, *see p135, p153, p177* and *p231* respectively.
▶ For more on gay **Schöneberg**, *see p207*.

East Kreuzberg – the hub of Turkish Berlin.

travel agents, is the heart of Turkish Berlin. The open-air **Türkischer Markt** (*see p178*) stretches along the Maybachufer every Tuesday and Friday. **Görlitzer Park**, once an important train station, turns into one of the world's largest outdoor Turkish barbecues on fine weekends. The area is full of döner takeaways and Turkish grocery stores, while at night Turkish street gangs face off to defend their territories – mostly from other Turkish street gangs.

Oranienstrasse is the area's main drag, and is packed with bars and clubs, and the area to the north and west of here is home to even more places to booze and boogie. The excellent **Babylon** cinema (*see p196*) is here, on Dresdener Strasse. Fans of art deco in the service of commerce are urged to check out the gigantic warehouse on Pfuelstrasse, which runs for a block towards the Spree.

South across Skalitzer Strasse, Oranienstrasse changes into Wiener Strasse, running alongside the old Görlitzer Bahnhof, where more bars and cafés welcome what's left of the old Kreuzberg crowd. A couple of blocks further south lies Paul-Linke-Ufer, the border with Neukölln, lined with canal-bank cafés that provide a favourite spot for weekend brunch.

The U1 line runs overhead through the neighbourhood along the middle of Skalitzer Strasse. The onion-domed Schlesisches Tor U-Bahn station was once the end of the line. These days it continues one more stop across the Spree to Warschauer Brücke. You can also walk across into Friedrichshain and the post-industrial nightlife of Mühlenstrasse (*see p89*). Heading east down Schlesische Strasse leads you over the canal and into the borough of **Treptow**. The waterside **Verein der Visionare** (*see p156*) and the **Arena** concert venue (*see p219*) are just along Puschkinallee, as is the **Museum der Verbotenen Kunst** (Museum of Prohibited Art; *see below*) and **Treptower Park** with its **Sowjetisches Ehrenmal** (Soviet War Memorial), lies beyond.

Museum der Verbotenen Kunst

Puschkinallee/Schlesische Strasse, Treptow (229 1645). U1 Schlesisches Tor. **Open** noon-6pm Wed-Sun. **Admission** free. **Map** p307 H5.
The Museum of Prohibited Art is located in a four-storey former Cold War watchtower constructed in 1963, which stands close to the border between Treptow and Kreuzberg. Entered in a historical monument preservation register in 1992, it's now home to a modest exhibition on the history of the Wall. Photos and documentation illustrate its construction, operation and security measures. There's also a gallery of art with Wall themes.

South-west Kreuzberg

The southern and western part of Kreuzberg contains some of the most picturesque corners of west Berlin, including the 'cross hill' (the literal meaning of 'Kreuzberg') in Viktoriapark after which the borough is named.

Viktoriapark is the natural way to enter the area. It has a cheery, fake waterfall cascading down the Kreuzberg, and paths wind their way to the summit, where Schinkel's 1821 monument commemorates victories in the Napoleonic Wars – most of the streets hereabouts are named after battles and generals of that era. From this commanding view over a mainly flat city, with the former Schultheiss brewery (now being developed as trendy apartments) at your back, the landmarks of both east and west spread out before you: Friedrichstrasse dead ahead, the Europa-Center off to the left, the Potsdamer Platz highrises in between the two, and the Fernsehturm over to the right. The view is better in winter, when the trees are bare, but the waterfall only runs in summer.

Back on ground level, walking along Kreuzbergstrasse over Mehringdamm (where you'll find the **Schwules Museum**; Gay Museum, *see p96*) brings you to **Bergmannstrasse**, the main hub of neighbourhood activity. Bucking the general tendency of anything happening in Berlin to move eastwards, this street of cafés and junk shops, grocery stores and record shops by day does seem livelier than ever, although the area is relatively lacklustre at night . It leads down to Marheinekeplatz, site of one of Berlin's busiest market halls. Zossener Strasse (north from here) also bustles.

Bergmannstrasse continues east to Südstern, past several large cemeteries, and eventually comes to the **Volkspark Hasenheide**, the other of the neighbourhood's large parks, with another good view from atop the Rixdorfer Höhe.

If you've ever seen 'old Berlin' in a movie, chances are it was filmed in the streets just to the south of Bergmannstrasse. Many buildings in this neighbourhood survived the wartime bombing and the area around Chamissoplatz has been immaculately restored. The cobbled streets are lined with houses still sporting their Prussian façades and illuminated by gaslight at night. This is one of the most beautiful parts of this largely unbeautiful city, and contains a number of good bars and restaurants.

The edge of this area is dominated by the hulking presence of the **Columbiahaus**, a red-brick monster that once had a Nazi prison in its basement and is currently used by the police for car registration. Beyond that, just across the border into the borough of the same name, stands the huge **Tempelhof Airport**. Once the central airport for the city, it was begun in the 1920s and later greatly expanded by the Nazis. The largest building in Berlin – and one of the largest in the world – its curving bulk looms with an authoritarian ominousness. Tempelhof

Airport was where main German national carrier Lufthansa started, but its place in the city's affections was cemented during the **Berlin Airlift** of 1948-9, when it served as the base for the 'raisin-bombers', which flew in and out at a rate of one a minute, bringing much needed supplies to the blockaded city and tossing sweets and raisins to kids who were waiting close by as the planes taxied in. The monument forking towards the sky on Platz der Luftbrücke nearby commemorates the pilots and navigators who flew these missions, as does a photo-realist painting stuck over in a corner of the terminal building. After commercial flights to Tempelhof were discontinued in the early 1970s, it became the centre of the US air operation in Berlin. Today, it's once more a civil airport catering to small airlines running small planes on short-hop European routes.

This facility uses only a tiny fraction of the Tempelhof's enormous structure, other parts of which have been converted into entertainment venues, such as **Hangar II**, which occasionally houses a club of the same name, and the **La Vie en Rose** cabaret (*see p233*). Over on the other side of Columbiadamm are the **Columbiahalle** and **ColumbiaFritz** concert venues (for both, *see p220*). The latter was built by the US Airforce as a cinema for use by their airmen, and is a classic example of '50s cinema architecture.

North-west Kreuzberg

The north-west portion of Kreuzberg, bordering Mitte, is where you'll find most of the area's museums and tourist sights. The most prominent is the extraordinary **Jüdisches Museum** (*see p97* **The Jewish Museum**) on Lindenstrasse, a sensory onslaught, a unique example of architecture at its most cerebral and a powerful experience. West of here, close to the Landwehrkanal, is the enjoyable **Deutsches Technikmuseum Berlin** (German Museum of Technology; *see p95*).

Over the canal to the north is the ruin of **Anhalter Bahnhof**, once the city's most important railway station, only a tiny piece of façade remains today, preserved in its bombed state near the S-Bahn station that bears its name. The legendary **Tempodrom** venue (*see p94* **The time machine**) has returned to life at a site here as of December 2001.

Another ruin near the station is a modest section of the 18th-century city wall that was excavated and reconstructed in time for the city's 750th birthday celebrations. The **Grusel Kabinett** (*see p95*), a chamber of horrors, occupies an old air-raid shelter on the Schöneberger Strasse side of the empty space where platforms and tracks once stood.

Sightseeing

On Stresemannstrasse, the Bauhaus-designed **Europahaus** was heavily bombed during World War II, but the lower storeys remain, and the Café Stresemann on the corner is a popular local neighbourhood hangout. Nearby, on the north side of the street, Berlin's parliament, the **Abgeordnetenhaus von Berlin** (Berlin House of Representatives), meets in what was formerly the Prussian parliament. Dating orginally from the 1890s, the building was renovated in the early 1990s.

Opposite stands the **Martin-Gropius-Bau** (*see p95*), which hosts extravagant, well-curated art shows. The building was modelled on London's South Kensington museums – the figures of craftspeople on the external reliefs betray its origins as an applied arts museum.

Next to it is a deserted patch of ground that once held the Prinz Albrecht Palais, which the Gestapo took over as its headquarters. In the basement's 39 cells, political prisoners were held, interrogated and tortured. The land was flattened after the war. In 1985, during an acrimonious debate over the design of a memorial to be placed on the land, a group of citizens cut the wire surrounding it and staged a symbolic 'excavation' of the site. To their surprise, they hit the Gestapo's basement, and immediately plans were made to reclaim the site.

Today, the **Topographie des Terrors** (*see p97*) exhibition here, with an open-air photographic display of the site's history and railings overlooking the cells, is undergoing renovation and a library document centre and new building complex is due to open in 2005. Along the northern boundary of the site stands one of the few remaining stretches of the Berlin Wall, its concrete pitted and threadbare after thousands of souvenir-hunters in 1990 pecked away at it with hammers and chisels.

From here, it's a short walk down Kochstrasse – once Berlin's Fleet Street – to Friedrichstrasse, where the notorious Checkpoint Charlie once stood and where the **Haus am Checkpoint Charlie** (*see p96*) documents the history of the Wall. Most of the space where the border post once stood has been claimed by new buildings, notably the **Philip-Johnson-Haus**, designed by the eminent American architect and now home to the American Business Center on Checkpoint Charlie, although tenants have been slow to come – perhaps deterred by the strangely ugly spherical sculpture that stands outside. The actual site of the borderline itself is memorialised by Frank Thiel's photographic portraits of an American and a Soviet soldier. The small white building that served as the gateway between East and West is now in the

The time machine

From its name you might think it is a nuclear particle accelerator, but it looks like a New Age temple, more suited for the deserts of Nevada than a tiny wood at the edge of Kreuzberg. Towering behind the ruin of the Anhalter Bahnhof, the new **Tempodrom** is Berlin's most enduring alternative performance venue.

Tempodrom debuted in 1980, when a visionary young nurse called Irene Mössinger spent her inheritance to buy a huge circus tent and pitched it right where West Berlin ended and the death strip behind the Wall on Potsdamer Platz started. For the time, the international programme mix was similarly on the edge – San Francisco Mime Troupe, Jérome Savary's Grand Magic Circus, plus diverse rock acts, including East Berliner Nina Hagen, who actually lived for a time in a Tempodrom circus wagon. Much of the entertainment had a subversive political slant, which drew more talent.

'We would rather have played three gigs in the Tempodrom than one in the (bigger)

Deutschlandhalle,' says Far Urlaub, from the now-famous krautrockers Die Ärtzte. 'The atmosphere was so unique.'

By 1985 the Tempodrom was such a happening venue that even the desolation of Potsdamer Platz couldn't contain the noise. The tent then moved to Tiergarten, and the show went on, with a vengeance. More beer was sold here in the summer months than at any other venue in the city. The bizarre Catalan theatre troupe La Fura des Baus began its international career here, and, in 1988, a 'Consciousness Congress' brought the world's New Age allstars, including Timothy Leary and the Dalai Lama.

Tempodrom's legendary, leafy location across from the Reichstag and eclectic line-up of rock, jazz and world music helped it survive the early 1990s, just as a smattering of locations in east Berlin were quickly absorbing a new generation of counter-culture vultures. But when construction began on the new Chancellery in 1998, Tempodrom was forced out of the Tiergarten. Its third move

Alliierten Museum (*see p118*) – the one in the middle of the street is a replica; while what would have been a new control station had the Wall not fallen has now been built into the apartment buildings at Friedrichstrasse 207-8, right next to a Greek restaurant.

Deutsches Technikmuseum Berlin

Trebbiner Strasse 9 (902 540/www.dtmb.de). U1, U7, U12 Möckernbrücke or U1, U2, U12 Gleisdreieck. **Open** 9am-5.30pm Tue-Fri; 10am-6pm Sat, Sun. **Admission** €3; €1.50 concessions. **Map** p306 E5.
Opened in 1983 in the former goods depot of the once-thriving Anhalter Bahnhof, the German Museum of Technology is a quirky collection of industrial objects. The rail exhibits have pride of place, with the station sheds providing an ideal setting for locomotives and rolling stock from 1835 to the present. On view are also exhibitions on the industrial revolution; street, rail, water and air traffic; computer technology and printing technology. Behind the main complex is an open-air section with two functioning windmills and a smithy. Oddities, such as vacuum cleaners from the 1920s, make this a fun place for implement enthusiasts. The Spectrum annex, in an old railway administrative building, houses 200 interactive devices and experiments. A further new wing to house an exhibit on ship, air and space travel should be completed by 2003. One part of the museum, accessible from Möckernstrasse 26, contains a hands-on science exhibits for kids.

Grusel Kabinett

Schöneberger Strasse 23A (2655 5546). S1, S2 Anhalter Bahnhof. **Open** 10am-7pm Mon-Tue, Thur, Sun; 10am-8pm Fri; noon-8pm Sat. **Admission** €7; €5 concessions. **No credit cards. Map** p306 F4.
The 'Chamber of Horrors', or 'Berlin Creepy Show', as it's informally known, is housed in the city's only visitable World War II air-raid shelter. Built in 1943, the five-level bunker was part of an underground network connecting various other bunkers and stations throughout Berlin, and today houses both the Grusel Kabinett and an exhibit on the dark and chilly bunker itself. The latter includes a few personal effects found here after the war, various bunker plans and a video documentary in German only. The actual structure is the most interesting thing. The 'horrors' begin at ground level with an exhibit on medieval medicine (mechanical figures amputate a leg to the sound of canned screaming). Elsewhere there's a patented coffin designed to call attention to your predicament should you happen to be buried alive. Upstairs is scarier: a shadowy, musty labyrinth with a simulated cemetery, strange cloaked figures, lots of spooky sounds and a few surprises. Kids love it, but not those under ten.

Martin-Gropius-Bau

Niederkirchnerstrasse 7 (254 860/ www.martingropiusbau.de). S1, S2 Anhalter Bahnhof. **Open** varies. **Admission** varies. **Credit** AmEx, MC, V. **Map** p306 F4.

was to an abandoned post office complex near the Ostbahnhof, smack in the middle of a growing network of white-hot clubs.

But this move was only ever intended to be temporary. When exodus from the Tiergarten was certain, Mössinger started a campaign to raise funds for a permanent facility. She managed to attract some moneyed benefactors (including the millionaire who aided Christo in securing donations for wrapping the Reichstag) and plenty of political support, and began plans to create a huge complex that would include a permanent, high-tech tent for 3,700 spectators, a bar, outdoor performance arenas, plus a wet area for pools and electronic music that she called the 'Liquidrom'. But the project quickly went over budget. For years it was unclear whether Mössinger would get the funds together, and many started to question whether the Tempodrom was even relevant any more.

Mössinger made compromises, including a concrete roof instead of the trademark tent,

and opening the edgy venue to mainstream shows like *Holiday on Ice*, but the costs were still astronomical. In autumn 2001 the Tempodrom project faced bankruptcy. But at the last minute, a cash-strapped Berlin Senate injected about six million euros, ensuring a grand reopening at the new location behind the ruin of Kreuzberg's Anhalter Bahnhof in December 2001. (The first bands to play, however, have complained about the terrible acoustics.)

Everyone admires the tenacity of Mössinger for keeping her vision alive, but many of the small alternative theatre and art projects that have had their support cut are livid that the Senate bought into the new Tempodrom, and its new, often crassly commercial programme. But Mössinger takes it all in her stride, confident that her favourite acts will still have a place. Says the nurse turned counter-culture impresario:

'The name "Tempodrom" has always stood for speed and change. So what's the big deal about a new building?'

The **Jüdisches Museum**. *See p97.*

Cosying up to where the Wall once ran (you can still see a short and pitted stretch of it running along the south side of nearby Niederkirchnerstrasse), the Martin-Gropius-Bau is named after its architect, uncle of the more famous Walter (the Bauhaus pioneer). Built in 1881, the building has been renovated and serves as a venue for large-scale art exhibitions and major touring shows, for which it is ideal. Recent exhibitions have included Christo and Jeanne Claude: Early Works 1958-69. No permanent exhibition.

Haus am Checkpoint Charlie

Friedrichstrasse 43-5 (253 7250). U6 Kochstrasse. **Open** 9am-10pm daily. **Admission** €7; €4 concessions. **No credit cards.** **Map** p306 F4.

Haus am Checkpoint Charlie is an essential trip for anyone interested in the Wall and the Cold War. The museum opened not long after the GDR erected the Berlin Wall in 1961 with the purpose of documenting the grisly events that were taking place. The exhibition charts the history of the Wall, and gives details of the ingenious and hair-raising ways people escaped from the GDR – as well as exhibiting some of the contraptions that were used, such as suitcases and a weird car with a propeller. There's also a display about non-violent revolutions – including information about Mahatma Gandhi, Lech Walesa and, of course, the peaceful 1989 upheaval in East Germany.

Schwules Museum

Mehringdamm 61 (693 1172/ www.schwulesmuseum.de). U6, U7 Mehringdamm. **Open** 2-6pm Mon, Wed-Sun. *Tours* 5pm Sat. **Admission** €4; €2 concessions. **No credit cards.** **Map** p306 F5.

The Gay Museum, opened in 1985, is the first and still the only one in the world dedicated to the research and public exhibition of homosexual life in all of its forms. The museum, its library and archives are staffed by volunteers and function thanks to private donations, including bequests (such as the archive of GDR sex scientist Rudolf Klimmer). On the ground floor is the actual museum, which (in rather limited space) houses temporary exhibitions that include photography, video, installations, sketches, sculpture, and so forth. More impressive are the library and archives on the third floor. Here can be found around 8,000 books (around 500 in English), 3,000 international periodicals, collections of photos, posters, plus TV, film and audio footage, all available for lending. Information about the whole place is available in English.

Topographie des Terrors

Niederkirchnerstrasse 8 (2548 6703/ www.topographie.de). S1, S2, S25, S26, U2 Potsdamer Platz. **Open** 10am-6pm Tue-Sun. **Admission free. No credit cards. Map** p306 F4.

The Topography of Terror is a piece of waste ground where once stood the Prinz Albrecht Palais, headquarters of the Gestapo. It was from here that the Holocaust was directed, and where the Germanisation of the east was dreamt up. You can walk around – small markers explain what was where – before examining the fascinating exhibit documenting the history of Nazi state terror. This is housed in some former basement cells of the Gestapo complex. The catalogue (available in English) is excellent. A surviving segment of the Berlin Wall runs along the northern boundary of the site. When the new building complex and documentation centre are completed in 2005, the entire 6.2-hectare (15-acre) site will be open to the public and there will be four different exhibition areas.

Schöneberg

Map p305 & p306

Both geographically and in terms of atmosphere, Schöneberg lies between Kreuzberg and Charlottenburg. It's a diverse and vibrant part of town, mostly built in the late 19th century, and these days veering from 'alternative' towards upmarket. Though largely devoid of conventional sights, Schöneberg is rich in intriguing reminders of Berlin's recent history.

Schöneberg means 'beautiful hill' – oddly, because the borough is mostly flat. It does have an 'island', though: the triangular **Schöneberger Insel** (by the Kreuzberg border), carved away from the rest of the city by the two broad railway cuttings that carry S-Bahn line 1 and lines 2, 25 and 26, with an elevated stretch of line S4, 45 and 46 providing the southern boundary. In the

The Jewish Museum

The idea of a Jewish museum in Berlin was first mooted in 1971, the year in which the city's Jewish community commemorated its 300th birthday. (There had, in fact, been such a museum in Berlin before – opened on Oranienburger Strasse just before Hitler's rise to power in 1933, and closed by the Nazis in 1938.) In 1975 an association was formed to start acquiring historical documents, art, artefacts and other materials for eventual display in the museum. As the collection grew, parts of it were displayed in various existing museums and buildings (particularly in the Martin-Gropius-Bau; see p95-6).

The desire to find a permanent home for the exhibits led the Jewish Department of the Berlin Museum to launch an architecture competition for an extension to the Berlin Museum in Kreuzberg. In 1989, competing against 165 other architects, Daniel Libeskind emerged as the winner. The foundation stone was laid in 1992 and the building was completed in 1998. And on 9 September 2001, the permanent exhibition opened.

Libeskind's remarkable building has had a profound effect on the city and on public consciousness around the world. Not since Gehry's Bilbao Guggenheim has a museum's architecture generated so many column inches, and possibly never has such architecture been so symbolically laden.

The ground plan is in part based on an exploded Star of David, in part on lines drawn between the site and former addresses of figures in Berlin's Jewish history – Heinrich von Kleist, Heinrich Heine, Mies van der Rohe, Arnold Schönberg, Walter Benjamin. Its structure points in all directions towards the city and its history. One even enters through history – through the baroque Kollegienhaus next door, formerly the Berlin Museum.

From the outside there seems to be no connection between the Kollegienhaus and the zinc panelled lightning strike next door. That's because the Libeskind building is reached via an underground labyrinth where the geometry is startlingly independent of that of the above-ground building. One passage leads up to the exhibition halls, two others intersect en route respectively to the chilling Holocaust Tower, and outside to the ETA Hoffmann Garden – the Garden of Exile and Emigration – a grid of 49 columns, tilted to disorientate. Elsewhere,

a playground is named after Walter Benjamin, whose *One-Way Street* is (along with Schönberg's *Moses und Aron*) one of the building's chief inspirations. Throughout, diagonals and parallels carve out surprising spaces, while windows slash through the structure and its zinc cladding like the knife-wounds of history.

And then there are the 'voids', cutting through the convoluted layout in straight lines. These negative spaces can be viewed or crossed but not entered, standing for the emptiness left behind by the destruction of German Jewish culture.

The great problem with telling the story of German Jewish history is that we all know only too well what it was all leading up to. What makes the museum so engaging and resonant is its focus on the personal. Taking a broadly chronological approach, it tells the stories of prominent Jews through the years, what they contributed to the development of their community and to the cultural and economic life of Berlin and Germany.

The greatest tragedy of the story is that after the centuries of prejudice and pogroms, the outlook for Germany's Jews seemed to be brightening. Bismarck attended the opening of the Neue Synagoge in Oranienburger Strasse; full civil equality was finally achieved under the Weimar Republic; Jews had never seemed more integrated in German society. And then came the Holocaust. This part of the museum, inevitably, is the most harrowing. The emotional impact of reading countless stories of the eminent and the ordinary (and the fate that almost all of them shared) is hard to convey adequately in print. And what shocks most of all is that the rest of the world was well aware of the sort of persecution Jews started to suffer almost as soon as Hitler came to power, and did nothing about it.

The museum is a must-see, its only drawback being that it is in danger of being a victim of its own success. Expect to queue to get in and crowded internal spaces.

Jüdisches Museum

Lindenstrasse 9-14 (259 933/guided tours 2599 3333/www.jmberlin.de). U1, U6 Hallesches Tor. **Open** 10am-8pm daily. Closed Jewish holidays & Christmas Eve. *Guided tours* phone for details. **Admission** €5; €2.50 concessions. **No credit cards. Map** p306 F4.

Nollendorfplatz in Schöneberg.

1930s it was known as Rote Insel ('Red Island'),
because, approached mostly over bridges
and thus easy to defend, the area was one
of the last to resist the Nazification of Berlin.
There's a fine view of central east Berlin from
Monumentenbrücke, on the east side of the
island going towards Kreuzberg's Viktoriapark.
On the north-west edge of the island is **St
Matthäus-Kirchhof**, a large graveyard
and last resting place of children's storytellers,
the Brothers Grimm.

Continuing west along Langenscheidtstrasse
– named after the dictionary publishers whose
offices stand close by– leads you towards
the Kleistpark. Here Schöneberg's main
street is called Hauptstrasse to the south and
Potsdamer Strasse to the north. Hauptstrasse
leads south-west in the direction of Potsdam.
David Bowie and Iggy Pop once resided at
No.152 – Bowie in a big, first-floor apartment
at the front, Iggy in a more modest *Hinterhof*
flat. **Dominicuskirche** nearby is one of
Berlin's few baroque churches.

Walking north-west from here along
Dominicusstrasse brings you to **Rathaus
Schöneberg**, distinguished only by being
the place outside of which John F Kennedy
declared himself to be a Berliner (*see p23* **Ich
bin *ein* Berliner: JFK**). The square outside
the Rathaus (town hall) now bears Kennedy's
name. This was also the seat of the provisional
government of Berlin during the Cold War, and
the place where Berlin mayor Walter Momper
welcomed East Berliners in 1989. (Chancellor
Kohl was there too, but was practically booed
off stage – unlike Momper's SPD, Kohl's CDU
had kept the GDR at a distance.)

From here, Belziger Strasse leads back
towards **Kleistpark**, once Berlin's first
botanical gardens. The entrance to the park

on Potsdamer Strasse is an 18th-century double
colonnade, which was moved here from near
Alexanderplatz in 1910. The mansion within
the park was formerly a law court (where
the 1944 July bomb plotters were sentenced
to death; *see p21*), and after the war it became
the headquarters for the Allied Control
Council. After the signing of the Ost-Verträge
in 1972, which formalised the separate status
of East and West Germany, the building
stood virtually unused. What it did see were
occasional Allied Council meetings, before
which the Americans, British and French would
observe a ritual pause, as if expecting the Soviet
representative, who had last attended in 1948,
to show up. In 1990 a Soviet finally did wander
in and the Allies held a last meeting here to
formalise their withdrawal from the city in
1994. This may be the place where the Cold
War officially ended.

On the north-west corner of Potsdamer
Strasse's intersection with Pallasstrasse
stood the **Sportpalast**, site of many Nazi
rallies and the scene of Goebbels' famous
'Total War' speech of 18 February 1943.
Leading west along Pallasstrasse from here is
a block of flats straddling the road and resting
on the south side on top of the huge hulk of a
concrete Nazi air-raid shelter planners were
unable to destroy. It, along with some of the
used furniture shops on nearby Goebenstrasse,
featured in Wim Wenders' award-winning film
Wings of Desire (1987).

At the west end of Pallasstrasse stands
St-Matthias-Kirche. South from here,
Goltzstrasse is lined by cafés, bars and pricey
but interesting shops. To the north of the
church is **Winterfeldtplatz**, site of bustling
Wednesday and Saturday morning produce
markets, engendering a particularly lively café
life. Winterfeldtstrasse has many antiquarian
bookshops and at night the area is alive with
bars and restaurants.

Nollendorfplatz, to the north up Maassenstrasse, is the central hub of Schöneberg's
night-time activities. Outside Nollendorfplatz
U-Bahn, the memorial to the homosexuals
killed in concentration camps is a reminder
of the immediate area's history – Christopher
Isherwood chronicled Berlin from his rooming
house at Nollendorfstrasse 17, and currently
Motzstrasse is one of the most conspicuous
centres of Berlin's gay life. Gay Schöneberg
continues around the corner and across Martin-
Luther-Strasse into Fuggerstrasse.

Schöneberg's most famous daughter is
German screen icon Marlene Dietrich, who
is buried just over the district's southern
boundary in the tiny **Friedhof Friedenau**
on Fehlerstrasse (map p305 C6).

Tiergarten

A clutch of cultural attractions, a mega-mall and one huge park.

The huge green swathe of the Tiergarten park dominates (and gives its name to) this district. The Wall once ran along its eastern side, but now Tiergarten once again forms the east–west link between Mitte and Charlottenburg, the park stretching from the Reichstag and the Brandenburg Gate in the north-east to the Zoo in the south-west. Along the park's northern boundary the Spree meanders (above this is the largely residential area of Moabit), while south of the park is a host of cultural, architectural and commercial attractions, including the reborn Potsdamer Platz and the museums and galleries of the Kulturforum.

The park & the Reichstag

Map p301 p302, p305, p306 & p316

A hunting ground for the Prussian electors since the 16th century, **Tiergarten**, the park that stretches west from the Brandenburg Gate was opened up to the public in the 18th century. During the war it was badly damaged, and, in the desperate winter of 1945-6, almost all the trees that were left were cut down for firewood. It wasn't until 1949 that Tiergarten started to recover – towns from all over Germany donated trees (as did Queen Elizabeth II) and are commemorated by an inscribed stone on the Grosser Weg, the large path in the park. Today, Berliners – joggers, nature lovers, gay cruisers, football players, picnickers – pour into the park in fine weather, yet its 167 hectares (412 acres), much of which feels quite wild, rarely seem crowded. There is no nicer place from which to appreciate it all than the gardens of the Café am Neuen See on Lichtensteinallee (*see p155*).

Berlin's central lung: **Tiergarten** park.

All roads entering Tiergarten lead to the park's largest monument, the **Siegessäule** (Victory Column; *see p101*), which celebrates late 19th-century Prussian military victories. The park's main thoroughfare, Strasse des 17.Juni (named after the date of the East Berlin workers' strike of 1953) is one piece of Hitler's plan for 'Germania' – a grand east–west axis linking the Brandenburger Tor to Charlottenburg. Close by stands a huge statue of Bismarck, flanked by those of Prussian generals Moltke and Roon, reminders of the past, which, judging by the graffiti, seem to have a few people worried.

Towards the eastern end of Strasse des 17.Juni's stands the **Sowjetisches Ehrenmal** (Soviet War Memorial). Once the only piece of Soviet property in West Berlin, it was built in 1945-6 from marble that came from the ruins of Hitler's Reich Chancellery. Once, this monument posed quite a political problem: built in the British Zone, it was surrounded by a British military enclosure, which was, in turn, guarded by the Berlin police, and all to protect the monument and the two Soviet soldiers who stood 24-hour guard there. The two tanks flanking this Tiergarten monument are alleged to have been the first two Soviet ones into Berlin, but this is probably just legend.

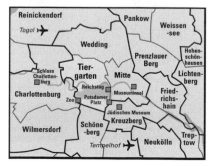

At the north-eastern corner of the park, just north of the Brandenburger Tor (*see p73*), stands the **Reichstag** (*see p101*). Described by Kaiser Wilhelm II as the 'Imperial Monkey House', scene of unseemly Weimar squabblings, left as a burnt-out ruin during the Third Reich, regarded by the Red Army as its main prize, and stranded for forlorn decades beside the Wall that divided the *Deutsches Volk* whose representatives it was intended to house, the Reichstag hasn't exactly had a happy history.

Shortly after reunification, the artist Christo wrapped the Reichstag in aluminium-coated fabric, drawing a somewhat ironic line under all that, and, four years later, Sir Norman Foster's brilliant refitting of the building was unveiled to the public in 1999. His crowning achievement is the new glass cupola – a trip up to the top should be a must-do on any visitor's agenda.

When the decision was made in 1991 to make Berlin the German capital, the area north of the Reichstag was picked as the central location for the new government buildings. Designed by Axel Schultes and Charlotte Frank, the immense Spreebogen complex, also known as the **Band des Bundes**, is built over a serpentine twist in the River Spree (*Bogen* meaning 'bend'). It crosses the river twice, although it is built in a straight line, symbolising the joining of west and east Berlin.

Just south of the western end of the complex's most notable building, the **Bundeskanzleramt** (Federal Chancellery), is the **Haus der Kulturen der Welt** (*see p101*; formerly the Kongresshalle), an impressive piece of modern architecture whose reflecting pool contains a Henry Moore sculpture. The Haus was designed by Hugh Stubbins, its nearby carillon by Bangert, Jansen, Scholz and Schultes. A gift from the Americans, known to the locals as the 'pregnant oyster', it opened in 1957, and its roof collapsed in 1980 – an event that gave the name to one of Berlin's best-known bands, Einstürzende Neubauten ('collapsing new buildings'). Today, it houses exhibits of world culture and hosts musical ensembles and cinema screenings from far-off lands.

Also on the park's northern boundaries, a little further west, stands **Schloss Bellevue**, a minor palace from 1785, and now home to the German President when he's in town (indicated by a flag flying from the roof). His 150 employees work next door in a new elliptical office building, discretely shielded from the street.

Across the river from here, a serpentine 718-apartment residence for Federal employees, appropriately nicknamed '**Die Schlange**' (the Snake), winds its way across land that was formally used as an arsenal and then a rail goods yard.

To the west of Schloss Bellevue is the **Englischer Garten**, the creation of which came about after King Ludwig I of Bavaria decided that the lack of constant revolutions in England was due to the plentiful open green spaces in the cities. The idea caught on, and these gardens became such an integral part of German life that Lenin once commented that revolution in Germany was impossible because it would require people to step on the grass.

Just north of here stands the **Akademie der Künste** (*see below*), which offers an impressively varied programme of arts events. The district between the Akademie and the loop of the Spree is known as the **Hansaviertel**, a post-war housing project whose buildings were designed by a *Who's Who* of architects. Perhaps of most interest to specialists, it draws bus-loads of architecture students from around the world, who see something other than a group of fairly sterile modern buildings.

Akademie der Künste

Hanseatenweg 10 (390 760). S3, S5, S7, S9 Bellevue or U9 Hansaplatz. **Open** 1-7pm Mon; 10am-7pm Tue-Sun. **Admission** *Exhibitions* €4; €2.50 concessions; 1st Sun of mth free. *Performances* €5-€6. **No credit cards. Map** p301 D3.

Founded by the Prussian Prince Friedrich III in 1696, the Akademie der Künste is one of the oldest cultural institutions in Berlin. By 1938, however, the Nazis had forced virtually all of its prominent

The dome of the **Reichstag**. *See p101.*

members into exile. Re-established in 1954, in a fine new building from architect Werner Duttmann, to serve as 'a community of exceptional artists' from the world over, its multifaceted programme now offers a great variety of events, ranging from free jazz concerts and poetry readings to performances and film screenings as well as art exhibitions.

Haus der Kulturen der Welt
John-Foster-Dulles-Allee 10 (397 870). S3, S5, S7, S9, S75 Bellevue. **Open** 9am-9pm Tue-Sun. **Admission** varies. **No credit cards**. **Map** p302 E3.

A unique institution and an important part of Berlin's cultural life. Funded by the Federal government and the Berlin Senate, the 'House of World Cultures' was set up in January 1989 to promote artists from developing countries, mounting spectacular large-scale exhibitions such as contemporary Indian art, Bedouin culture in North Africa and the avant-garde in China. The programme also features film festivals, readings, lectures, panel discussions, concerts and dance performances. Hugh Stubbins' oyster-like Kongresshalle was erected in 1957-8 as America's contribution to Berlin's first international building exhibition.

Reichstag
Platz der Republik (2272 2152). S1, S2, S25, S26 Unter den Linden. **Open** *Dome* 8am-midnight daily; last entry 10pm. **Admission** free. **Map** p316/p302 E3.

The hugely imposing Reichstag was controversial from the very beginning. Architect Paul Wallot struggled to find a style that would symbolise German national identity at a time – 1884-94, shortly after Unification – when no such style (or identity) existed. It was burned on 17 February 1933 – an event the Nazis may or may not have done themselves, but which they blamed on the (mentally ill) Dutchman Marius van der Lubbe, and certainly used as an excuse to clamp down on Communists and suspend basic freedoms. Today, after its celebrated renovation by Sir Norman Foster, the Reichstag is again home to the Bundestag (the German parliament), and open to the public.

Foster conceived his architectural approach as a 'dialogue between old and new'. Graffiti scrawled by Russian soldiers in 1945, for example, has been left in view and there has been no attempt to clean up or even deny the building's turbulent history. No dome appeared on his original competition-winning plans, but the German government insisted upon one. Foster, in turn, insisted that, unlike the structure's original dome (damaged in the war and demolished in the 1950s), the new one should be a public space, open to visitors. A trip to the top of the dome is one of the most worthwhile experiences the 'new Berlin' has to offer (though beware the queues: come first thing or in the evening if possible). A lift whisks you to the roof in seconds, then, from there, a double-helix of ramps lead up to the top, affording fine views of the capital that is taking shape all around.

The best Views

Berliner Dom
Fine prospects of Museuminsel and Unter den Linden from the Cathedral dome. *See p77.*

Fernsehturm
The mother of all city views, from the observation deck of the TV Tower. *See p85.*

Funkturm
See west Berlin laid out at your feet from the top of the Radio Tower. *See p110.*

Kreuzberg
Climb the 'Cross Hill' in Viktoriapark after which the district is named. *See p92.*

Reichstag
Norman Foster's spectacular glass dome offers fine viewing day or night. *See p101.*

Siegesäule
Lord it over Tiergarten from the top of the Victory Column. *See p101.*

Teufelberg
Views over Grunewald and south-west Berlin from this mound of war-time rubble. *See p117.*

At its centre is a funnel of mirrors, angled so as to shed light on the workings of democracy below. They also have an almost funhouse effect: strolling the spiral walkways, the visitor can see his head in this mirror, his legs in that one. Foster has managed to create a space that is open, playful and defiantly democratic.

Siegessäule
Strasse des 17. Juni (391 2961). S3, S5, S7, S9 Bellevue. **Open** *Summer* 9.30am-6.30pm Mon; 9.30am-7pm Tue-Thur, Sat; 9.30am-8pm Fri. *Winter* 9.30am-5.30pm Mon; 9.30am-6pm Tue-Sat. **Admission** €1.20; €0.60 concessions. **No credit cards**. **Map** p301 D3.

Tiergarten's biggest monument is the Siegessäule, built in 1871-3 to commemorate the Prussian campaigns against Denmark (1864), Austria (1866) and France (1870-71). On top of the column is an eight-metre (26-foot) gilded Goddess of Victory by Friedrich Drake; captured French cannons and cannonballs, sawn in half and gilded, provide the decoration of the column proper. Fans of Wim Wenders' *Wings of Desire* can climb the 285-step spiral staircase to the viewing platform at the top for a fine view.

South of the park

Map p305 & p306

At the south-east corner of Tiergarten park is what was for many years following reunification Europe's largest building site: the now reborn **Potsdamer Platz**, intended as the city's new commercial centrepiece. Since this once-bustling intersection was bombed flat and then found itself just on the east side of the Wall, it was a no man's land for many years. Fierce debate ensued over whether the redevelopment should be in keeping with the typical scale of a 'European' city or American-style high-rise or truly avant-garde. In the end the former was the favoured option, with medium-height development except at Potsdamer Platz itself, where high-rises up to 90 metres (295 feet) were allowed.

Opinions are mixed as to the success of the finished article. Despite the presence of many of the world's heavyweight architects, there's little to truly excite in the new structures. Helmut Jahn's soaring **Sony Center**, homogenous in steel and glass, made up of a series of buildings around a plaza under a tent-like roof, contains the Forum, conceived as an urban entertainment complex. In this, at least, the complex has succeeded, containing as it does the **CineStar** and **CinemaxX** multiplexes, the more offbeat **Arsenal** cinema (for all three, *see p196*) and the excellent **Filmmuseum Berlin** (*see p103*). It is also now the main venue for the **Berlin International Film Festival** (*see p198*).

The other major corporate presence at Potsdamer Platz is Daimler-Chrysler, which is responsible for most of the development south of the Sony Center. This includes buildings by Richard Rogers, Renzo Piano and Hans Kollhof. The company's major cultural contribution to the area came with the recent opening of the **Sammlung DaimlerChrysler** (*see p104*), which contains works by a good number of the major names in 20th-century art.

Some of the technological feats involved in the reconstruction of Potsdamer Platz are mind-boggling: one of the two buildings to survive the bombing and subsequent cleansing was the Kaisersaal Café from the old Grand Hotel Esplanade, a listed building. When the plans for the renovation were solidified, the café was found to be in a bad position, so the whole structure, weighing 1,300 tonnes, was moved 75 metres (246 feet) to its present position, where it has been integrated into the apartment complex on Bellevuestrasse.

In anticipation of the increased human traffic through Potsdamer Platz, the Potsdamer Platz Arkaden were grafted on to the U-Bahn and S-Bahn stations, three storeys of what is essentially an American shopping mall.

Just outside the Arkaden, on Alte Potsdamer Strasse, the other survivor of the bombing, Weinhaus Huth, is back selling wine at its old location.

Immediately west of the Potsdamer Platz development is one of the city's major concentrations of museums, galleries and cultural institutions. Collectively known as the **Kulturforum**, this cultural quarter was based on the designs of Hans Scharoun (1946-57). Scharoun himself was responsible for the building of the **Staatsbibliotek** (State Library) and the unmistakeable gold **Philharmonie** (*see p238*), home to the Berlin Philharmonic Orchestra, and famous for offering near-perfect acoustics and near-perfect sightlines from all of its 2,200 seats. Adjacent is the not especially thrilling **Musikinstrumentenmuseum** (Musical Instrument Museum; *see p104*).

Just west of here is a low-rise museum complex. By far the biggest draw here is the wonderful collection of 13th- to 18th-century art of the **Gemäldegalerie** (Picture Gallery; *see p103*). Also worth a peek is the **Kunstgewerbemuseum** (Museum of Applied Art; *see p104*). Here too is the **Kunstbibliotek** (Art Library) and a decent café and shop.

Next door stands the **Matthäuskirche** (Matthias Church) and, on its south side, the bold glass cube of the **Neue Nationalgalerie** (New National Gallery; *see p104*). The gallery hosts major temporary shows (a Warhol retrospective was a recent highlight).

Along much of the south flank of Tiergarten runs Tiergartenstrasse, Berlin's revived diplomatic quarter. Part of Albert Speer's plan for 'Germania', the fantasy Nazi city, the original embassy buildings were designed by German architects as a means of proving German superiority. Damaged by bombing, they were largely abandoned, and Tiergartenstrasse became an eerie walk past decaying grandeur. But with the grounds still the properties of the respective governments, when the move from Bonn came, they were reconstructed, or, in the case of the complex that houses the Nordic countries' embassies, for instance, new buildings were constructed from scratch. Today, many of Berlin's embassies can again be found here. For further information on some of the new buildings in the area, *see p42* **Embassy row**.

Just south of here, the **Gedenkstätte Deutscher Widerstand** (Memorial to the German Resistance; *see p103*) stands on Stauffenbergstrasse, named after the leader of the July 1944 plot to kill Hitler. At the corner of this street and Reichpietschufer is **Shell House**, a curvaceous masterpiece by Emil Fahrenkamp (1932) that survived the war and is now offices for the BEWAG electricity company.

Five minutes' walk west from here along the Landswehrkanal is the gleaming white building housing the **Bauhaus Archiv – Museum für Gestaltung** (Bauhaus Archive – Design Museum; *see below*), while a further ten minutes' walk west brings you to the less high-brow attractions of the **Zoologischer Garten & Aquarium** (*see p104*) and to the hub of former West Berlin around Bahnhof Zoo and the Ku'damm (*see p105*).

Bauhaus Archiv – Museum für Gestaltung
Klingelhöferstrasse 13-14 (254 0020). Bus 100, 129, 187, 341. **Open** 10am-5pm Mon, Wed-Sun. **Admission** €4; €2 concessions. **No credit cards.** **Map** p305 D4.

Walter Gropius, founder of the Bauhaus school, designed this elegant white building, which now contains the Bauhaus Archive – Museum of Design. The absorbing single-floor museum presents furniture, ceramics, prints, scultpures, photographs and sketches created in the Bauhaus workshop between 1919 and 1933 (when the school was closed down by the Nazis). There are first-rate temporary exhibitions too. A computerised introduction in German and English provides a useful context, and there's also a short history of the Bauhaus and translations of the text panels in the permanent exhibition are available.

Filmmuseum Berlin
Potsdamer Strasse 2 (300 9030/www.filmmuseum-berlin.de). S1, S2, S25, S26, U2 Potsdamer Platz. **Open** 10am-6pm Tue, Wed, Fri-Sun; 10am-8pm Thur. **Admission** €6; €4 concessions. **No credit cards.** **Map** p316/p306 E4.

Founded in 1963, the Deutsche Kinemathek (German Cinematheque) has amassed a major collection of films, memorabilia, documentation and apparatus chronicling the history of German cinema, as well as its transposition to Hollywood via the World War II exiles. For years it was a sort of museum without portfolio, but with the Kinemathek's move to Potsdamer Platz the public has now been given access to the collection. With a large exhibition space on two floors of the Filmhaus in the Sony Center, it is not only comprehensive but strikingly visual. The well laid out displays of posters, photos and macquettes are enhanced by an engaging thematic design, particularly in the two-storey-high video wall of disasters from Fritz Lang's adventure films and an exhibition space for 'Films in the Third Reich' that resembles a burnished steel-walled morgue. On a lighter note, highlights include a collection of Dyanimation figures from Ray Harryhausen films such as *The Seven Voyages of Sinbad* and *Jason and the Argonauts* as well as the museum's keynote attraction, the Marlene Dietrich collection, displaying personal effects, home movies, fabulous designer clothes and some revealing (and occasionally bitchy) correspondence. The vertigo inducing-entrance hall is almost worth the admission fee in itself.

The **Kulturforum**. See p102.

Gedenkstätte Deutscher Widerstand
Stauffenbergstrasse 13-14 (2699 5000/www.gdw-berlin.de). U1 Kurfürstenstrasse or S1, S2, S25, S26, U2 Potsdamer Platz. **Open** 9am-6pm Mon-Wed, Fri; 10am-6pm Thur, Sat, Sun. **Admission** free. **Map** p306 E4.

The Memorial of the German Resistance is an exhibition chronicling the German resistance to National Socialism. The building is part of a complex known as the Bendlerblock, which was owned by the German military from its construction in 1911 until 1945. At the back is a memorial to the conspirators killed during their attempt to assassinate Hitler at this site on 20 July 1944.

Gemäldegalerie
Matthäikirchplatz 8 (266 2951). S1, S2, S25, S26, U2 Potsdamer Platz. **Open** 10am-6pm Tue, Wed, Fri-Sun; 10am-8pm Thur. **Admission** €3; €1.50 concessions. **No credit cards.** **Map** p306 E4.

The Picture Gallery's first-rate early European painting collection is arranged chronologically and by region, and features a healthy selection of the biggest names in Western art. Although there are many fine Italian, Spanish and English works on display, the highlights are the Dutch and Flemish pieces. Fans of Rembrandt can indulge themselves with around 20 of the master's paintings – the best of which are the majestic portrait of preacher and merchant Cornelis Claesz Anslo and his wife, a Samson and Delilah radiating tension and an electric Samson confronting his father-in-law. Two of Franz Hals' finest works are here – the wild, fluid, almost impressionistic *Malle Babbe* ('Mad Babette') contrasts with the far more detailed, but no less joyous, portrait of the one-year-old Catharina Hooft and her nurse.

Other highlights include a couple of astonishingly unflinching portraits by Robert Campin (early 15th century), a version of Botticelli's *Venus Rising* (the complete painting is in Florence) and Corregio's brilliant *Leda with the Swan*. Look out also for a pair of (contrasting) Lucas Cranach Venus and Cupid paintings and his *Fountain of Youth*, depicting old, haggard women entering a pool and emerging from the other side young and beautiful again. Pick up the excellent (free) English-language audio guide.

Kunstgewerbemuseum

Kulturforum, Matthäikirchplatz (266 2951). S1, S2, S25, S26, U2 Potsdamer Platz. **Open** 10am-6pm Tue-Fri; 11am-6pm Sat, Sun. **Admission** €3; €1.50 concessions. **No credit cards. Map** p306 E4.

The Museum of Applied Art contains a rather frustrating collection of European arts and crafts, stretching from the Middle Ages, through Renaissance, baroque and rococo to Jugendstil and art deco styles. There are some lovely pieces on display, particularly furniture and porcelain, but the labelling is only in German and the layout and structure of the building is fractured and hard to follow.

Musikinstrumentenmuseum

Tiergartenstrasse 1 (254 810). S1, S2, S25, S26, U2 Potsdamer Platz. **Open** 9am-5pm Tue-Fri; 10am-5pm Sat, Sun. **Admission** €3; €1.50 concessions; free under-12s; free 1st Sun of mth. **No credit cards. Map** p306 E4.

Over 2,200 string, keyboard, wind and percussion instruments dating back to the 1500s are crammed into this small museum next to the Philharmonie. Among them are assorted rococo musical clocks, for which 18th-century princes commissioned jingles from Mozart, Haydn and Beethoven. The place comes alive during tours, when guides play such obsolete instruments as the Kammerflugel. Concerts are held on the first Saturday of the month, and once a month the wonderful Wurlitzer organ is cranked up – it was salvaged from an old-time American movie house, where it once provided sound effects – like thunder storms and car horns – for silent movies.

Neue Nationalgalerie

Potsdamer Strasse 50 (266 2662). S1, S2, S25, S26, U2 Potsdamer Platz. **Open** 10am-6pm Tue, Wed; 10am-10pm Thur; 10am-8pm Fri; 11am-8pm Sat, Sun. **Admission** €3; €1.50 concessions. *Special exhibitions* varies. **No credit cards. Map** p306 E4.

The thoroughly contemporary glass cube building housing the New National Gallery was designed in the 1960s by Mies van der Rohe, and houses German and international paintings from the 20th century. It's strong on German expressionists and surrealists such as Max Beckmann, Otto Mueller, Ernst Ludwig Kirchner, Paul Klee and Max Ernst. The *Neue Sachlichkeit* is also well represented by George Grosz and Otto Dix. Many major non-German 20th-century artists are also featured, Picasso, de Chirico, Léger, Munch, Wols and Dali among them. However, the pleasure of the gallery is in discovering lesser-known artists like Ludwig Meidner, whose post-World War I apocalyptic landscapes exert the great, garish power of the most action-packed *Marvel* comic centrefold. Be warned that the permanent collection is sometimes put into storage for the duration of some of the bigger shows; phone to check.

Sammlung DaimlerChrysler

Alte Potsdamer Strasse 5, Tiergarten (2594 1420/ www.sammlung.daimlerchrysler.com). S1, S2, S25, S26, U2 Potsdamer Platz. **Open** 11am-7pm daily. **Admission** free. **Map** p306 E4.

Mies van der Rohe's **Neue Nationalgalerie.**

As you would expect from one of the world's largest car manufacturers the Daimler-Chrysler collection has some seriously big names. It has sensibly stuck to one particular area with its collection, namely 20th century abstract, constructivist, conceptual or minimal art (it didn't have to be a small area). What you can see here in its quarterly changing exhibitions in the only remaining original house on Potsdamer Platz is as good as anything in the rest of the world's big modern art museums. Among the collection are works by Josef Albers, Max Bill, Walter de Maria, Jeff Koons, Andy Warhol and a few newcomers as well.

Zoologischer Garten & Aquarium

Hardenbergplatz 8 (254 010/www.zoo-berlin.de). S3, S5, S7, S9, S75, U2, U9, U12 Zoologischer Garten. **Open** *Zoo* 9am-5pm daily. *Aquarium* 9am-6pm daily. **Admission** *Zoo* €8; €4-€6.50 concessions. *Aquarium* €8; €4-€6.50 concessions. *Combined admission* €13; €6-€10.50 concessions. **No credit cards. Map** p305 D4.

Germany's oldest zoo was opened in 1841 to designs by Martin Lichtenstein and Peter Joseph Lenné. Containing almost 14,000 creatures, the Zoologischer Garten is today one of the largest and most important zoos in the world, with more endangered species in its collection than any in Europe save Antwerp's. The zoo is huge, and beautifully landscaped, and there are plenty of places to sit down and have a coffee, beer or Bratwurst, and in summer there is sometimes even an oompah band. Some of the enclosures are plainly too small (the polar bear seems far from happy), but the inhabitants of others seem quite content. The building of an impressive new enclosure for the penguins is a recent highlight.

The aquarium can be entered either from within the zoo or from its own entrance on Olof-Palme-Platz by the reconstructed Elephant Gate, and is a good option for a rainy day. It is also one of the world's most varied, comprising more than 500 species, arranged over three floors. On the ground floor are the fish (and some impessive sharks); on the first you'll find the reptiles (the high, light crocodile hall is the highlight, as it were); while insects and amphibians occupy the second. The dark corridors and liquid ambience, with colourful tanks lit up and curious aquarian creatures moving behind thick refracting glass, are as absorbing as many an art exhibit.

Charlottenburg

It may have lost its tourist monopoly, but the heart of the old West beats on.

Before the fall of the Wall, Charlottenburg *was* Berlin to most tourists. This huge swathe of the former West stretches west from Tiergarten to Spandau, from Tegel Airport in the north down to Wilmersdorf to the south. The area has two main focuses – the commercial cauldron centred around Bahnhof Zoo, around the southwest corner of Tiergarten, and extending west along the Kurfürstendamm, and the gaggle of cultural treasures in and around Schloss Charlottenburg to the north.

Bahnhof Zoo & the Ku'damm

Map p305

Hymned by U2 and centrepiece of the film *Christiane F*, **Bahnhof Zoo** (Zoo Station – Bahnhof Zoologischer Garten, to give it its full name) was once a spooky anomaly – slap in the middle of West Berlin but policed by the East, which controlled the intercity rail system – and a seedy hangout for junkies and old soaks. Today, it has a postmodernised interior full of glossy chain stores and self-service food outlets, and now the façades are also being spruced up. The original building was designed in 1882 by Ernst Dircksen; the modern glass sheds were added in 1934.

The surrounding area, with its mixture of sleaze and shopping, huge cinemas and bustling crowds is the gateway to the Kurfürstendamm, the main shopping street of western Berlin. The discos and bars along Joachimstaler Strasse are best avoided – the opening of the **Beate-Uhse Erotik-Museum** (*see p107*) actually added a touch of class to the area – but the rest of this district is worth a wander.

The most notable nearby landmark is the fractured spire of the **Kaiser-Wilhelm-Gedächtniskirche** (Kaiser Wilhelm Memorial Church; *see p107*) in Breitscheidplatz. Close by is the 22-storey **Europa-Center**, whose Mercedes star can be seen from much of the rest of the city. It was built in 1965 and looks like it was. Intended as the anchor for the development of a new western downtown, it was the first of Berlin's genuinely tall buildings, and is now the grande dame of the city's shopping malls. Its exterior looks at its best when neon-lit at night. The strange sculpture in front was erected in 1983. It is officially called *Weltenbrunnen* (Fountain of the Worlds), but, like almost everything else in Berlin, it has a nickname: *Der Wasserklops* (Water Meatball).

Just north of here is the entrance to the enjoyable **Zoologischer Garten** (Zoo) and **Aquarium** (for both, *see p104*).

Running along the south of the Europa-Center, **Tauentzienstrasse** is the westernmost piece of the *Generalzug*, a sequence of streets laid out by Peter Joseph Lenné to link the west end with Kreuzberg and points east. Constructed around 1860 they are all named after Prussian generals from the wars against Napoleon: Tauentzien; Kleist; Bülow; Yorck; and Gneisenau. The tubular steel sculpture in the central reservation east along Tauentzienstrasse was commissioned for the city's 750th anniversary in 1987 and represents the then divided city in that the two halves twine around each other but never meet.

The street continues past **KaDeWe** (*see p165*), Berlin's most prestigious department store, and the largest in continental Europe. Its full title is Das Kaufhaus des Westens (Department Store of the West), and it was founded in 1907 by Adolf Jandorf, acquired by Herman Tietz in 1926 and later 'aryanised' and expropriated by the Nazis. KaDeWe is the only one of Berlin's famous turn-of-the-century department stores to survive the war intact, and has been extensively modernised over the last decade. Its most famous feature is the sixth-floor food hall, and rightly so.

> ► For more on accommodation, restaurants, cafés/bars, shops and clubs in **Charlottenburg**, see p60, p138, p155, p177 and p232 respectively.

The shock of the new, the shell of the old: **Kaiser-Wilhelm-Gedächtniskirche.** *See p107.*

Tauentzienstrasse ends at **Wittenburgplatz.** The 1911 neoclassical U-Bahn station here (by Alfred Grenander) is a listed building and has been wonderfully restored with wooden kiosks and old ads on the walls. Outside stands a memorial to those who died in concentration camps, looking eerily like a departure board in a train station.

A block further is the huge steel sculpture at An der Urania with its grim monument to children killed in traffic by Berlin's drivers. This marks the end, or the beginning, of the western 'downtown'.

Leading south-west from the Kaiser-Wilhelm-Gedächtniskirche, the **Kurfürstendamm** (or Ku'damm, as it's universally known), west Berlin's tree-lined shopping boulevard is named after the Prussian Kurfürst ('Elector') – and for centuries it was nothing but a track leading from the Elector's residence to the royal hunting palace in the Grunewald. In 1881 Bismarck insisted it be widened to 5.3 metres (17 feet). To the south of the street, many villas were put up, and, though few survive today, one sizeable exception contains the **Käthe-Kollwitz-Museum** (*see p107*), the Villa Griesbach auction house and the Literaturhaus Berlin with its Wintergarten am Literaturhaus café on Fasanenstrasse. The villas were soon replaced by upmarket tenement buildings with enormous apartments – sometimes upwards of ten rooms and as large as 500 square metres (5,400 square feet). About half of the original buildings were destroyed in the war and replaced by functional office buildings, but there remain many bombastic old structures.

The ground-level Ku'damm soon developed into an elegant shopping boulevard. It remains so today with cinemas (mostly showing dubbed Hollywood fare), restaurants (from the classy to assorted burger joints) and upmarket fashion shops – the Ku'damm is a street dedicated to separating you from your cash. When you tire of spending, pop into the **Story of Berlin** (*see p107*) for an entertaining trip through the history of the city.

The side streets to the south are a bit quieter, albeit even more upmarket, and Bleibtreustrasse to the north has more shops and some of the most outrageous examples of 19th-century *Gründerzeit* architecture in Berlin (*see p35*).

The **Ku'damm-Eck** on the south-east corner of the intersection of Ku'damm and Joachimstaler Strasse was formerly West Berlin's rather weak answer to Piccadilly Circus, with a giant video screen and neon adverts. The old building was torn down in 1999 to make way for a new complex with a hotel, department store and gallery. Diagonally across from it is the **Neues Kranzler-Eck**, a Helmut Jahn-designed ensemble built around the famous old Café Kranzler, with a 16-storey tower and pedestrian courtyards including a habitat for various exotic birds.

Other notable new architecture in the area includes Josef Paul Kleihues' **Kant-Dreieck** (on the corner of Fasanenstrasse and Kantstrasse), with its large metal 'sail', and British high-tech architect Nicholas Grimshaw's **Ludwig-Erhard-Haus** for the Chamber of Commerce and Stock Exchange at Fasanenstrasse 83-4.

Just north of here on Hardenburgstrasse is the grand turn-of-the-20th-century neo-baroque HQ of the **Universität der Künste** (University of the Arts; *see p107*), while back towards the Ku'damm end of Fasanenstrasse is the **Jüdisches Gemeindehaus** (Jewish Community House) and, opposite, the **Zille-Hof** flea market (*see p178*).

Kantstrasse runs more or less parallel to the Ku'damm at its northern end, and contains the grandiloquently eclectic **Theater des Westens** and more shops in which to browse. Since the opening of the **stilwerk** design centre (see *p166*), the stretch around Fasanenstrasse and beyond Savignyplatz has become a centre for designer homeware stores. The environs of leafy Savignyplatz are dotted with numerous chic restaurants, cafés and shops, particularly on Grolmanstrasse and in the Savignypassage. Nearby Knesebeckstrasse is the place to come for bookshops, including many antiquarian dealers on the northern stretch.

Beate-Uhse Erotik-Museum

Joachimstaler Strasse 4 (886 0666). S3, S5, S7, S9, S75, U2, U9, U12 Zoologischer Garten. **Open** 9am-midnight daily. **Admission** €5; €4 concessions. **Credit** AmEx, MC, V. **Map** p305 C4.
The three floors of this collection (above a flagship Beate-Uhse retail outlet offering the usual videos and sex toys) contain oriental prints, some stupid showroom-dummy tableaux, and glass cases containing such delights as early Japanese dildos, Andean penis flutes, Javanese erotic dagger hilts, 17th-century chastity belts, a giant coconut that looks like an arse and a vase used in the film *Caligula*. A small exhibit on pioneering sex researcher Magnus Hirschfeld sadly comprises nothing more than a few boards of dry documentary material, worthily considering the history of his Institut für Sexualwissenschaft, which was opened in Berlin in 1919 and eventually closed down by the Nazis. The only other things with any connection to Berlin are an inadequate item on Heinrich Zille and a corner documenting the career of Frau Uhse herself, who went from being a Luftwaffe pilot and post-war potato-picker to annual sex-aid sales of €50 million (the pictures of her frolicking with dolphins and playing golf, 'her new hobby', seem positively bizarre). Oddly respectable, given its subject.

Kaiser-Wilhelm-Gedächtniskirche

Breitscheidplatz (218 5023/www.gedaechtniskirche. com). S3, S5, S7, S9, S75, U2, U9, U12 Zoologischer Garten. **Open** 9am-7pm daily. *Guided tours* 1pm, 2pm, 3pm Mon-Sat. **Admission** free. **Map** p305 D4.
The Kaiser Wilhelm Memorial Church is one of Berlin's best-known sights, and one of its most dramatic at night. The neo-Romanesque church was built in 1891-5 by Franz Schwechten in honour of – you guessed it – Kaiser Wilhelm I. Much of the building was destroyed during an Allied air raid in 1943. These days the church serves as a stark reminder of the damage done by the war, although some might argue that the bombing has improved what was originally a profoundly ugly structure. Inside the rump of the church is a glittering art nouveau-style ceiling mosaic depicting members of the House of Hohenzollern going on pilgrimage towards the cross (the free-thinking Frederick the Great is conspicuous

by his absence). Here, you'll also find a cross made from the nails from the destroyed cathedral at Coventry, and photos of the church before and after the war. The ruin of the tower is flanked by ugly modern concrete extensions, yet inside the chapel the wraparound blue stained glass in the windows is quite stunning – at night the windows glow eerily.

Käthe-Kollwitz-Museum

Fasanenstrasse 24, Wilmersdorf (882 5210). U15 Uhlandstrasse or U9, U15 Kurfürstendamm. **Open** 11am-6pm Mon, Wed-Sun. **Admission** €5; €2.50 concessions. **No credit cards**. **Map** p305 C4.
Käthe Kollwitz lived the majority of her life (1867-1945) in the now trendy district of Prenzlauer Berg. Her powerful, deeply empathetic work embraces the full spectrum of life, from the joy of motherhood to the pain of death (with rather more emphasis on the latter than the former). Charcoal sketches, woodcuts (a medium that was particularly well suited to her style) and sculptures are displayed to good effect over the four floors of this grand villa just south of the Ku'damm. Harrowing and moving. Some labelling is in English. *See p111* **Ich bin Berliner: Käthe Kollwitz**.

Story of Berlin

Kurfürstendamm 207-8 (01805 992 010/ www.story-of-berlin.de). U15 Uhlandstrasse. **Open** 10am-8pm daily; last entry 6pm. **Admission** €9.30; €7.50 concessions. **No credit cards**. **Map** p305 C4.
If you're interested in the city's history, the Story of Berlin should not be missed. The huge floor space is filled with superbly designed rooms and multimedia exhibits created by renowned authors, designers and film and stage specialists, telling Berlin's story from its founding in 1237 to the present day. Equipped with a strange headset (you cannot but feel self-conscious), visitors are taken through a series of 20 historically themed rooms, recalling with sound and narration various stages in the city's history: from Frederick the Great's world of war to the Golden Twenties; from the Nazi era to daily life in East Berlin. The English language version of the headset doesn't work in all rooms, but it doesn't really matter as everything is extensively labelled in German and English. Underneath all this is a massive nuclear shelter. Built by the Allies in the 1970s, this low-ceilinged, oppressive bunker is still a fully functional shelter and can hold up to 3,500 people. Guided tours are given several times a day.

Universität der Künste

Hardenbergstrasse 33 (31850/www.udk-berlin.de). U2 Ernst-Reuter-Platz or S3, S5, S7, S9, S75, U2, U9, U12 Zoologischer Garten. **Open** 9am-8pm daily. **Admission** varies. **No credit cards**. **Map** p305 C4.
The Universität der Künste isn't a gallery as such, but the city's main art college. Until autumn 2001 this was Berlin's Hochschule der Künste, the HdK (pronounced 'ha day car'), and you may still hear it called by that name. Enter the main lobby and you'll

Sightseeing

usually find a colourful diversity of student displays ranging from traditional painting to video installations and computer graphics. Most of the Junge Wilde painters are in some way connected with the UdK – either as teachers (Karl-Horst Hödicke, Georg Baselitz) or as former students (Salomé, Helmut Middendorf, Rainer Fetting). The school has annual open days and also hosts symposia and other events.

Schloss Charlottenburg & around

Map p300

The palace that gives the district of Charlottenburg its name lies about three kilometres (two miles) north-west of Bahnhof Zoo. In stark contrast to the unabashed commercialism and crush of humanity around the latter, this part of the city is quiet, wealthy and serene. **Schloss Charlottenburg** (*see p109*) was built at the end of the 17th century as a summer palace for Queen Sophie-Charlotte, wife of Friedrich III (later King Friedrich I), and was intended to be Berlin's answer to Versailles. It's not a very convincing answer, but there's plenty of interest to be found in the buildings and grounds of the palace – the apartments of the New Wing and the gardens are the main attractions.

Next to the west wing of the palace is the **Museum für Vor- und Frühgeschichte** (Primeval and Early History Museum; *see below*), while directly in front of the *Schloss* entrance is a trio of first-rate museums – the **Sammlung Berggruen: Picasso und seine Zeit** (Berggruen Collection: Picasso and his Time; *see p109*), the art nouveau and art deco **Bröhan-Museum** (*see below*) and the superb **Ägyptisches Museum** (Egyptian Museum; *see below*).

There are few eating, drinking or shopping opportunities in the immediate vicinity of the palace, but if you head down Schlossstrasse and over Bismarckstrasse, the streets south of here, particularly those named after philosophers (Leibniz, Goethe) have a lot of interesting small shops selling antiques, books, and the fashions that well-to-do residents sport around Charlottenburg's cafés and restaurants.

Ägyptisches Museum

Schlossstrasse 70 (3435 7310/www.smb.spk-berlin.de). U2 Sophie-Charlotte-Platz or U7 Richard-Wagner-Platz. **Open** 10am-6pm Mon-Fri; 11am-6pm Sat, Sun. **Admission** €3; €1.50 concessions; free Sun. **No credit cards. Map** p300 B3.
Just across the street from Schloss Charlottenburg is this deservedly popular museum, destined to move to a new home in the Neues Museum (*see p76*)

on Museumsinsel by the end of the decade. The Egyptian Museum's most celebrated exhibit is the bust of Nefertiti, dating from around 1350 BC. Much of its popularity is down to the fact that its swan-neck delicacy chimes with contemporary ideas of ideal beauty; the bust was, in fact, probably used as a model for sculptors (a supposition supported by the fact that only one eye was painted). The portrayal of the human face is one of the most compelling aspects of the museum (a nearby, damaged bust looks remarkably like a Francis Bacon creation), and there's plenty of evidence to countermand the cliché that all Egyptian art is symbolic rather than realistic. Particularly notable in this respect is a series of characterful model faces, and also the vivid 'Berlin Green Head', which may date from around 500 BC – it looks disconcertingly like a bad-tempered nightclub bouncer. By the time we reach Graeco-Roman Egypt, there are examples of arresting realistic portraits being painted on mummies. Another unique treasure is a piece of papyrus on which is the only known example of Cleopatra's handwriting. Labelling is only in German – it's worth buying the enlightening *Egyptian Art in Berlin* booklet from the shop before wandering around.

Bröhan-Museum

Schlossstrasse 1A (3269 0600/www.broehan-museum.de). U2 Sophie-Charlotte-Platz or U7 Richard-Wagner-Platz. **Open** 10am-6pm Tue-Sun. **Admission** €4; €2 concessions. **No credit cards. Map** p300 B3.
Opposite the Ägyptisches Museum, this quiet, private museum on Schlossstrasse contains three well laid out levels of international art nouveau and art deco pieces that businessman Karl Bröhan began collecting in the 1960s and donated to the cit of Berlin on his 60th birthday. The wide array of paintings, furniture, porcelain, glass, silver and sculptures dates from 1890 to 1939. Hans Baluschek's paintings of social life in the 1920s and 1930s, and Willy Jaeckel's series of portraits of women are the pick of the fine art bunch; the furniture is superb too. Labelling is only in German.

Museum für Vor- und Frühgeschichte

Langhansbau, Schloss Charlottenburg (3267 4811/ www.smb.spk-berlin.de). U2 Sophie-Charlotte-Platz or U7 Richard-Wagner-Platz. **Open** 10am-6pm Tue-Fri; 11am-6pm Sat, Sun. **Admission** €3; €1.50 concessions. **No credit cards. Map** p300 B3.
The Primeval and Early History Museum – spread over six galleries – traces the evolution of Homo sapiens from 1,000,000 BC to the Bronze Age. The highlights are without a doubt the replicas (and some originals) of Heinrich Schliemann's famous treasure of ancient Troy, including works of ceramics and gold, as well as weaponry. Keep an eye out also for the sixth-century BC grave of a girl buried with a gold coin in her mouth. Information is available in English.

Sightseeing

Sammlung Berggruen: Picasso und seine Zeit

Westlicher Stülerbau, Schlossstrasse 1 (3269 5811/ www.smb.spk-berlin.de). U2 Sophie-Charlotte-Platz or U7 Richard-Wagner-Platz. **Open** 10am-6pm Tue-Fri; 11am-6pm Sat. **Admission** €3; €1.50 concessions. **No credit cards. Map** p300 B3.

Heinz Berggruen was an early dealer in Picassos in Paris, and the subtitle of this museum 'Picasso and his Time' sums up this satisfying and important collection. Displayed over an easily digestible three circular floors, it's inevitable that Pablo's works dominate (taking up much of the ground floor, and almost all of the first); his astonishingly prolific and diverse output is well represented. There are also works by Braque, Giacometti, Cézanne and a good slew of Matisses. Most of the second floor is given over to some wonderful paintings by Paul Klee (*City of Dreams* is particularly hallucinogenic). An audio guide is available.

Schloss Charlottenburg

Luisenplatz & Spandauer Damm (320 911/ www.spsg.de/F_chab.html). U2 Sophie-Charlotte-Platz or U7 Richard-Wagner-Platz. **Open** *Old Palace* 9am-5pm Tue-Fri; 10am-7pm Sat, Sun. Last tour 4pm. *New Wing* 10am-6pm Tue-Fri; 11am-6pm Sat, Sun. *New Pavilion* 10am-5pm Tue-Sun. *Mausoleum* Apr-Oct 10am-noon, 1-5pm Tue-Sun. *Belvedere* Apr-Oct 10am-5pm Tue-Sun. Nov-Mar noon-4pm Tue-Fri; noon-5pm Sat, Sun. All sections of the palace closed Mon. **Admission** *Combination tickets* €5-€8; €4-€5 concessions. *Individual sights* call for details. **No credit cards. Map** p300 B3.

Queen Sophie-Charlotte was the impetus behind this sprawling palace and gardens (and gave her name to both the building and the district) – her husband Friedrich III (later King Friedrich I) built it in 1695-9 as a summer home for his queen. Later kings also summered here, tinkering with, and adding to the buildings. It was severely damaged during World War II, but has now been restored, and stands as the largest surviving Hohenzollern palace.

There are a number of parts of the palace to which the public are admitted, though the bafflingly complicated individual opening times and admission prices have many a visitor scratching their heads. The easiest option is to go for the combination ticket that allows entrance to all parts of the palace, with the exception of the state and private apartments of King Friedrich I and Queen Sophie-Charlotte in the **Altes Schloss** (Old Palace), which are only accessible on a guided tour (in German only, though English information is available on request). This tour, through more than 20 rooms, some of staggering baroque opulence, has its highlights (particularly the Porcelain Cabinet), but can be skipped – there's plenty of interest elsewhere in the palace. The upper apartments in the old palace can be visited without a guided tour, but, frankly, they are pretty dull, bear little relation to how they might have looked in the past and are really only of interest to silver and porcelain junkies.

Schloss Charlottenburg.

Sightseeing

The one must-see is the **Neue Flügel** (New Wing). Also known as the Knobeldorff Wing (after its architect), the upper floor of the wing contains the State Apartments of Frederick the Great and the Winter Chambers of his successor King Friedrich Wilhelm II. Don't neglect to pick up the free audio guide as you enter – this really brings the apartments alive. The contrast between the two sections is particularly interesting – Frederick's rooms are all excessive rococo exuberance (the wildly over-the-top, 42m/138ft long Golden Gallery is decorated to make it look like it literally drips gilt), while Friedrich Wilhelm's far more modestly proportioned rooms reflect the more restrained classicism of his time. Frederick the Great was a big collector of 18th-century French painting, and some choice canvases hang from the walls, including Watteau's masterpiece *The Embarkation for Cythera*. Also worth a look are the apartments of Friedrich Wilhelm III on the ground floor of the New Wing.

By the east end of the New Wing stands the **Neue Pavillon** (New Pavilion). Also known as the Schinkel Pavilion, it was built by the eponymous architect (*see p12* **Ich bin Berliner: KF Schinkel**) in 1824 for Friedrich Wilhelm III – the King liked it so much that he chose to live here in preference to the grandeur of the main palace.

The huge gardens at Charlottenburg are one of the palace's main draws. Laid out in 1697, they were originally formally French in style, but were reshaped in a more relaxed English style in the 19th century. Within them you'll find the **Belvedere**, a three-storey structure built in 1788 as a teahouse, and now containing a collection of Berlin porcelain. Also in the gardens is the sombre **Mausoleum**, containing the tombs of Friedrich Wilhelm III, his wife Queen Luise, Kaiser Wilhelm I and his wife – a creepy spot on an overcast day. Look out also for temporary exhibitions in the Orangery. There is a café and restaurant at the front of the palace (and few other refreshment options in the immediate area). Note that the entire palace is closed on Mondays.

The stark Nazi aesthetics of the **Olympiastadion**'s Marathon Gate. *See p111.*

Elsewhere in Charlottenburg

Map p301 & p304

About three kilometres (two miles) north-east of Schloss Charlottenburg, far from any other sights, is a chilling reminder of the all-but-lawless terror inflicted by the Nazi regime on dissidents, criminals and anybody else they deemed undesirable. The **Gedenkstätte Plötzensee** (Plötzensee Memorial; *see below*) preserves the execution shed of the former Plötzensee prison, wherein more than 1,800 people were killed between 1933 and 1945.

A couple of kilometres south-west of Schloss Charlottenburg, at the western end of Neue Kantstrasse, stands the futuristic **International Conference Centre (ICC)**. Built in the 1970s, it is used for pop concerts, political rallies and the like. Next door, the even larger **Messe-und Ausstellungsgelände** (Trade Fair and Exhibition Area), bits of which date back to the late 1920s, plays host to trade fairs ranging from electronics to food to aerospace (the annual International Grüne Woche – *see p188* – is particularly popular). Within the complex, the **Funkturm** (Radio Tower; *see below*) is well worth ascending for the panoramic views of western Berlin it affords. Nearby, Hans Poelzig's **Haus des Rundfunks** (Masurenallee 9-14) is an expressive example of monumental modernism in brick.

Another couple of kilometres north-west of here is Hitler's impressive neoclassical **Olympiastadion** (*see p111*). One of the very few pieces of fascist-era architecture still intact in Berlin, it's actually a surprisingly pleasing and harmonious structure, despite its unpalatable origins. The stadium is undergoing major renovation in preparation for the 2006 World Cup Finals.

Immediately south of Olympiastadion S-Bahn station is a huge apartment block designed by Le Corbusier. The **Corbusierhaus**, with its multicoloured paint job, was constructed for

International Building exhibition of 1957, at which time it was hailed as a model for contemporary urban living. From here, a ten-minute walk along Sensburger Allee brings you to the sculptures of the **Georg-Kolbe-Museum** (*see below*).

Funkturm

Messedamm (3038 1905). U2 Theodor-Heuss-Platz or Kaiserdamm. **Open** 11am-9pm Mon; 10am-11pm Tue-Sun. **Admission** €3.60; €1.80 concessions. **No credit cards. Map** p304 A4.
The 138m (453ft) high Radio Tower was built in 1926 and looks not unlike a smaller version of the Eiffel Tower. The Observation Deck stands at 126m (413ft) so vertigo sufferers should seek solace in the restaurant, which is only 55m (180ft) from the ground.

Gedenkstätte Plötzensee

Hüttigpfad (344 3226). Bus 123.
Open *Mar-Oct* 9am-5pm daily. *Nov-Feb* 9am-4pm daily. **Admission** free. **Map** p301 C2.
The Plötzensee Memorial stands on the site where the Nazis executed over 2,500 (largely political) prisoners. In a single night in 1943, 186 people were hanged in groups of eight. In 1952 it was declared a memorial to the victims of fascism, and a memorial wall was constructed. There is little to see today, apart from the execution area, behind the wall, with its meat hooks from which victims were hanged (many were also guillotined), and a small room with an exhibition on the relevant documentation. Excellent (if depressing) booklets in English are available. The stone urn near the entrance is filled with earth from Nazi concentration camps. Today, the rest of the prison is a juvenile corrective centre.

Georg-Kolbe-Museum

Sensburger Allee 25 (304 2144/www.georg-kolbe-museum.de). S5, S75 Heerstrasse/bus X34, X49, 149. **Open** 10am-5pm Tue-Sun. **Admission** €3; €2 concessions. *Special exhibitions* €5; €3 concessions. **No credit cards.**
Georg Kolbe's former studio in a quiet corner of Charlottenburg has been transformed into a showcase for his work. The Berlin sculptor, regarded as Germany's best in the 1920s, mainly focused on

Ich bin Berliner Käthe Kollwitz

Berlin was home to one of the greatest graphic artists of the last century, whose surviving works stand as powerful testimonies of social conditions in Germany during the late 19th and early 20th century. Drawing on elements of both German Expressionism and Romanticism, Käthe Kollwitz's etchings, lithographs, woodcuts, sculptures and charcoal drawings reveal a deep, dark, unsentimental passion seldom matched by other artists, and an almost obsessive preoccupation with poverty, death and war.

Such melancholic reflection did not develop in a vacuum. Kollwitz's life was punctuated by tumultuous events and harrowing experiences. She lost her youngest son in World War I – and tormented herself thereafter for having encouraged him to fight for his ideals – and her grandson in World War II. Under the Nazis, she was expelled from the Prussian Academy on account of her 'degenerate art' and left-wing political beliefs. Her husband died in 1940, and in 1943 her home was destroyed by an Allied bomb, wiping out scores of works of art and driving her to flee to Moritzburg. And then, just days before the end of the war, she herself died.

Kollwitz didn't employ themes of human suffering solely for the purposes of personal catharsis – she was a strong believer in the possibility of social change, and was more than prepared to get her hands dirty on the political scene. In 1922 she wrote: 'I should like to exert influences in these times when human beings are so perplexed and in need of help.'

She was a radical socialist and pacifist, and provided prints and posters for various Leftist publications. Later she signed an 'Urgent Appeal against Nazism', placing herself at considerable risk of retribution.

Though born into a relatively wealthy liberal family, her 50-year residence in one of Berlin's poorest areas, Prenzlauer Berg (ironically, now one of the city's trendiest districts), where her husband worked as a doctor for factory workers, played a major role in shaping and directing her heartfelt political concerns about social injustice and poverty. Although the **Käthe-Kollwitz-Museum** (housing over 200 of her works; see p107) is in Charlottenburg, there are still traces of Kollwitz in Prenzlauer Berg. A statue of her stands in leafy Kollwitzplatz park, and her sculpture *The Mother* marks the site of her house at Kollwitzstrasse 25 (formerly known as Weissenburgerstrasse), where she lived from 1892 to 1942.

By far the most moving tribute to Kollwitz, though, is the enlarged version of her sculpture *Mother with Dead Son* at the memorial to the 'victims of war and tyranny' within the Neue Wache (see p75) on Unter den Linden in Mitte.

Though scarred by tragedy, Käthe Kollwitz's life was defiantly and, ultimately, triumphantly lived, for she succeeded in achieving the wish expressed in a letter of 1915.

'I do not want to die... until I have faithfully made the most of my talent and cultivated the seed that was placed in me until the last small twig has grown.'

---

naturalistic human figures. The museum features examples of his earlier, graceful pieces, as well as his later sombre and larger-than-life works created in accordance with the ideals of the Nazi regime. One of his most famous pieces, *Figure for Fountain*, is outside in the sculpture garden.

Olympiastadion

Olympischer Platz 3 (3006 3430/tours & museum 301 1100). U2 Olympia-Stadion (Ost) or S5 Olympiastadion. **Open** *Exhibition* 10am-6pm Wed, Sun. **Admission** *Exhibition* €2.50. *Tours* call for details. **No credit cards.**

Designed by Werner March and opened in 1936 for the Olympic Games – an attempt at Aryan propaganda that was gloriously sunk by four-golds Jesse Owens, much to Hitler's chagrin. The 76,000-seat stadium is currently undergoing a major renovation (due to be completed in 2004, in time for the 2006 World Cup) but can still be toured in the meantime (though only by groups of ten or more, with a week's notice; the exhibition is open to all). Home of Hertha BSC (see p248), it also hosts the German Cup Final, plus other sporting events and rock concerts. Its swimming pool (see p256) is popular in summer.

Other Districts

Berlin's outer suburbs encompass a fascinating mix of bourgeois gentility
and industrial grit – plus some fine museums, and greenery in abundance.

Sightseeing

Because Berlin's underlying soil is sandy,
until recently large buildings could not be built
here, which means that the city sprawls for
miles – but the U-Bahn and S-Bahn system
can take you to lesser-known neighbourhoods
(many with easy access to lakes and woods)
in minutes. Here are some suggestions for
further exploration.

North of the centre

To the north, the city eventually gives itself
up to block after block of industrial buildings
and housing for the people employed there;
it's hard to summon up any reasonable kind
of enthusiasm for districts like Wedding and
Reinickendorf. Though anyone with a penchant
for the offbeat might find the area's industrial
legacy interesting (*see p114* **A walk on
the wild side**).

Wedding

Map p302

Following the reorganisation of the *Bezirke*
(city administrative districts; *see p276*), the
solidly working class/industrial district of
Wedding, sitting atop Mitte and Tiergarten
is now officially part of Mitte, but few tourists
venture into its largely grim fastnesses. Apart
from a couple of low-key attractions – the
Anti-Kriegsmuseum (Anti-war Museum;
see below) and the nearby **Zucker Museum**
(Sugar Museum; *see below*), and one of the
few remaining stretches of the Wall at the
Gedenkstätte Berliner Mauer (Berlin Wall
Memorial; *see below*) – the area is chiefly of
interest to those who want to learn more about
Berlin's industrial heritage.

Anti-Kriegsmuseum

*Brüsseler Strasse 21 (4549 0110/tours 402 8691/
www.anti-kriegs-museum.de). U9 Amrumer Strasse.*
Open 4-8pm daily. **Admission** free. **Map** p301 D1.
The original Anti-war Museum was founded in 1925
by Ernst Friedrich, author of the book *War Against
War*. It was destroyed in 1933 by the Nazis, and
Friedrich fled to Brussels. There he had another
museum from 1936 to 1940, at which point German
troops once again showed up and trashed the place.
In 1982 a group of teachers including Tommy
Spree, grandson of Friedrich, re-established the

museum in West Berlin. It now hosts changing
exhibitions (for example, on the work of Gandhi, or
persecution of Kurds in Turkey), as well as a
permanent display including some grim World War
I photos and artefacts from the original museum,
children's war toys, information on German
colonialism in Africa and pieces of anti-Semitic
material from the Nazi era. Information on the museum and copies of *War Against War* are available in
English, but the exhibitions themselves are only in
German. Call ahead to arrange a tour in English with
British director Tommy Spree.

Gedenkstätte Berliner Mauer

*Bernauer Strasse 111 (464 1030/www.berliner-
mauer-dokumentationszentrum.de). S1,
S2 Nordbahnhof or U8 Bernauer Strasse.*
Open *Documentation centre* 10am-5pm Wed-Sun.
Admission free. **Map** p302 F2.
Immediately upon Unification, the city bought this
stretch of the Wall to maintain as a Wall Memorial,
and it was finally dedicated in 1998. Impeccably
restored (graffiti disappears virtually overnight), it
is also as sterile a monument as Berlin boasts, with
a brass plaque decrying the Communist 'reign of
terror', which is regularly defaced. A documentation
centre, featuring displays on the Wall and a data-
base of escapees, is across the street at Bernauer
Strasse 111, and from its roof you can view the
Wall, and the Versöhnungskirche (Chapel of
Reconciliation) – built on the site of a former church
destroyed by the East Germans.

Zucker Museum

*Amrumer Strasse 32 (3142 7574/www.dtmb.de/
Zucker-Museum). U6 Seestrasse or U9 Amrumer
Strasse.* **Open** 9am-4.30pm Mon-Thur; 11am-6pm
Sun. **Admission** €2.30; €1 concessions. **No credit
cards. Map** p301 D1.
Any museum devoted to the chemistry, history and
political importance of sugar would have problems
thrilling the punters. But the Zucker does have a
very unusual collection of sugar paraphernalia.
Most interesting is a slide show on the slave trade,
on which the sugar industry was so dependent.
Something to ponder over a coffee.

West of the centre

The westernmost extent of the city is the once
independent (and still independent in spirit)
settlement of **Spandau**. The district to which
it gives its name stretches from the Tegeler See
in the north to the Havel lake in the south.

The old town in **Spandau**.

Spandau

Berlin's western neighbour and eternal rival, Spandau is a little baroque town that seems to contradict everything about the city of which it is now, reluctantly, a part. Spandauers still talk about 'going into Berlin' when they head off to the rest of the city. Berliners, for their part, basically consider Spandau as part of west Germany, though travelling there is easy on the U7, alighting at either Zitadelle or Altstadt Spandau, depending on which sights you want to visit. None is thrilling, but they make for a low-key escape from the city.

The **Zitadelle** (Citadel; *see p114*) contains within one of its museums Spandau's original town charter, which dates from 1232, a fact that Spandauers have relied on ever since to assert their legitimacy before Cölln and Berlin to be the historical heart of the capital. Founded in the 12th century, the Zitadelle is an interesting if not enthralling place to pass half an hour or so.

The old town centre of Spandau is mostly pedestrianised, with two- and three-storey 18th-century townhouses interspersed with burger joints and department stores. One of the prettiest examples is the former Gasthof zum Stern in Carl-Schurz-Strasse; older still are the houses in Kinkelstrasse (until 1933, Judenstrasse) and Ritterstrasse; but perhaps the best-preserved district is north of Am Juliusturm in the area bounded by Hoher Steinweg, Kolk and Behnitz. Steinweg contains a fragment of the old town wall from the first half of the 14th century; Kolk has the **Alte Marienkirche** (the Catholic garrison church, 1848); and in Behnitz, at No.5, stands the elegant baroque **Heinemannsche Haus**. At Reformationsplatz, the brick nave of the **Nikolaikirche** dates from 1410-50; the west tower was added in 1468, and there were later additions by Schinkel (*see p12* **Ich bin Berliner: KF Schinkel**).

One of the most pleasant times to visit the town is in the run-up to Christmas, when the market square houses a life-size Nativity scene with real sheep and the Christmas market is in full swing (*see p188*). The café and bakery on Reformationsplatz are excellent.

Spandau may have inspired the name of a dodgy 1980s New Romantic band, but for most visitors it is chiefly known for its association with Rudolf Hess. Hitler's deputy was imprisoned in the Allied jail after the Nuremberg trials, where he remained (alone after 1966) until his suicide on 17 August 1987, hanging from a piece of lamp flex at the age of 93. Once he'd gone, the 19th-century brick building at Wilhelmstrasse 21-4 was demolished to make way for a supermarket for the (also now departed) British forces.

Some distance south of Spandau, west of Grunewald and the Havel river, and a long and convoluted journey by public transport, is the **Luftwaffenmuseum** (*see below*).

Luftwaffenmuseum

Gross-Glienicker Weg, Gatow (3687 2601/ www.luftwaffenmuseum.de). S5, S75, U7 Rathaus Spandau, then bus 134 to Alt-Gatow/Gross-Glienicker Weg, then bus 334 to Luftwaffenmuseum (last stop) or bus X34 from Bahnhof Zoo to Aussenweg, then bus 334 to Luftwaffenmuseum (last stop). **Open** 10am-5pm Tue-Sun. **Admission** free.
On the western fringes of the city at one of the airbases integral to the Berlin Airlift, this sizeable museum is still being developed. An old hangar houses much of the exhibition, which includes information on the history of the Luftwaffe as well as fighter and surveillance planes from the beginning of the century through to 1970s NATO equipment. There's a World War I tri-plane, a restored Handley Page Hastings (as used in the Airlift) and an Antonov An-2 from the GDR Air Force. Outside are more recent aircraft, including modern fighter planes and helicopters. As well as more than 150 aircraft, there are uniforms and personal equipment galore. Guided tours in English by prior arrangement.

Spandau's **Zitadelle** – 800 years of history.

Sightseeing

A walk on the wild side

If conventional sightseeing tours bore you, discover more about Berlin's industrial heritage with this two-hour stroll through a little-visited part of the city.

The area in the Reinickendorf district stretching from the south shore of the Tegeler See to the Berlin–Hamburg autobahn is one of Berlin's few still-productive historical industrial centres, along with Siemensstadt in Spandau and, to a lesser degree, Siegfriedstrasse in Lichtenberg.

Getting off at the Holzhauser Strasse U-Bahn station (U6), and turning left, first sight is the **Justizvollzugsanstalt Tegel** (Tegel Penitentiary) across Seidelstrasse. The red-brick prison, modelled after a correction facility in Pennsylvania, was completed in 1898 and gained infamy during the Third Reich, when opposition leaders Count James Moltke, Dietrich Bonhöffer and Bernhard Lichtenberg (a small square nearby bears his name) were incarcerated here prior to their executions.

Taking a left on Flohrstrasse, one passes the head office and production plant of **Otis**, the market leader in elevators and escalators. Original buildings of the Flohr Company (which merged with Otis in 1951) peacefully coexist with modern asphalt-glass. Turning right on Strasse 22, then left on Otisstrasse, one encounters an odd mixture of turn-of-the-century red-brick industrial buildings (the Grundt cargo company at the corner of Flohrstrasse and Strasse 22), functional commercial constructions (the flat white and blue complex housing the Tornado logistics and accounting software firm at Flohrstrasse 1-9) and 1960s housing high-rises on the right-hand side of Otisstrasse.

After turning left on Wittestrasse, the contrast becomes especially striking. The **Gewerbezentrum Wittestrasse 21**, a half-abandoned office complex, is a particularly inhospitable example of '60s futuristic architecture, with fibred concrete and porthole-like windows. Then, a few houses down Wittestrasse, one is startled by the sight of the **Russische Friedhof** (Russian Cemetery) at Wittestrasse 37. Completed in 1894, this balmy oasis lost within an industrial wasteland is the last resting place of composers Alexander Rimsky-Korsakov (grandson of Nicholas) and Mikhail Glinka, known for his folk operas *A Life of the Czar* and *Ruslan and Lyudmila*. The blue onion tower-topped chapel houses a collection of icons open during worship times.

Depending on which way the wind blows, a chocolate scent permeates Borsigwalde (Borsig Woods), as the area is known. The smell originates from the **Sawade** chocolate factory at Wittestrasse 26B. Sawade's owner Confidessa prides itself on its ecologically sound means of production, but unfortunately doesn't open its doors for a factory tour. However, Sawade specialities are available at discerning confectioners around town.

The last leg of Wittestrasse is dominated by the **Top Tegel** commercial complex at No.30, with its distinctive dark blue ribbed plastic entrance. ThyssenKrupp steel, Deutsche Telekom, the Berliner Volksbank and Oracle computer systems have offices here, a mix of old and new economy. The purple postmodern pueblo next door houses only software firms, while the customer service centre of consumer electronics giant Grundig towers over the grounds in a red-brick construction, as if to make the transition to the more traditional industrial architecture around the corner smoother.

Crossing Berliner Strasse where Wittestrasse ends, one passes from Borsigwalde to Borsig land proper. The company founded by August Borsig put steam engine know-how from Britain to profitable use. Borsig first manufactured locomotives in Mitte and branched out into Moabit before his

Zitadelle

Am Juliusturm, Spandau (3549 44212/tours 334 6270). **U7** *Zitadelle.* **Open** 9am-5pm Tue-Fri; 10am-5pm Sat, Sun. **Admission** €2.50; €1.50 concessions. **No credit cards**.

The oldest structure in the citadel (and the oldest secular building in Berlin) is the **Juliusturm**, probably dating back to an Ascanian (*see p7*) water fortress from about 1160. The present tower, with 154 steps and walls measuring up to 3.6m (12ft)

thick, was home until 1919 to the 120-million Goldmark reparations, stored in 1,200 boxes, which the French paid to Germany in 1874 after the Franco-Prussian War. In German financial circles, state reserves are still referred to as *Juliusturm*. The bulk of the Zitadelle was designed in 1560-94, in the style of an Italian fort. Its purpose was to dominate the confluence of the Spree and Havel rivers. Since then it has been used as everything from garrison to prison to laboratory. Today, much of the

Tegel-Borsigwalde

entertainment complex in Berlin besides those at Potsdamer Platz. The street Am Borsigturm passes by the namesake clinker building, completed in 1924 and designed by Eugen Schmohl, architect of the Ullsteinhaus in Tempelhof. Eleven storeys and 65 metres (213 feet) high, the Borsigturm was built to house the Borsig administration and was Berlin's first skyscraper.

Continuing on Am Borsigturm, one passes a recently built Motorola plant on the left, abandoned old warehouses with broken window panes to the right. The imposing all-steel Herlitz headquarters looms in the distance. Possibly more than any other place in Berlin, the Borsig complex visualises the shift from the industrial to the information age and service economy.

grandsons acquired 22 hectares (54 acres) of lakeshore property and moved the company here in 1898. (Borsigwalde was founded as a residential area for Borsig employees). After changing hands with Rheinmetall steel, Babcock and the city of Berlin, a subsidiary of stationery manufacturers Herlitz, bought by realtors RSE, purchased the grounds and developed it. Much of the original plant designed by Fritz Reimer and Konrad Körte is still intact, notably the pointed red-brick entrance gate with bronze statues of medieval craftsmen. The centrepiece of the Borsig factory, the locomotive assembly hall, has been remodelled as a shopping centre, flanked by steel and glass constructions – a multiplex cinema and more retail space. The **Hallen am Borsigturm**, opened in 1999, already boasts seven million visitors and is arguably the most high profile urban

Turning right on Medebacher Weg and left on Veitstrasse leads to Borsig Harbour, offering the pre-industrial pleasures of the Tegeler See, the mosaic harbour arch and the shoreside Greenwichpromenade (complete with red phone box and hydrant in honour of Reinickendorf's partner city). The ambitious 1980s postmodern urban development project in the Tegel Harbour comes into view, and the rustic old village Alt-Tegel and the Schinkel-designed Tegel (or Humboldt) Castle are a stone's throw away. Turning right on to Alt-Tegel leads you to the U-Bahn station of the same name.

huge site is under restoration and archaeological excavation – and not accessible to the public, except for its museums (one tells the story of the citadel, with some good models and maps; the other is a museum of local history and of limited interest – neither have any English labelling), galleries and a restaurant. To reach the Zitadelle from the U-Bahn station, look for the Toyota showroom, walk past it on Am Juliusturm, and the Zitadelle is a few minutes' walk further on.

South-west of the centre

South of Charlottenburg and west of Schöneberg lies **Wilmersdorf**. This is a mostly boring district of smart apartments that has a bit of night-time sparkle and street life in the area around Ludwigkirchplatz.

South of Wilmersdorf, the huge, largely residential district of **Zehlendorf** is chiefly of interest to visitors for the cluster of museums in **Dahlem**, and the bucolic and aquatic attractions of the **Grunewald, Wannsee** and **Glienicke**.

Zehlendorf & the Dahlem museums

South-west Berlin was the American Sector pre-1989, and districts like **Steglitz** and **Zehlendorf** contain some of the city's wealthier residences. The major draw for visitors is the clutch of museums at leafy, villagey **Dahlem** in Zehlendorf. The standout is the **Ethnologisches Museum** (Museum of Ethnology; *see below*), one of the world's finest collections of its type. In the same building are the **Museum für Indische Kunst** (Museum of Indian Art) and the **Museum für Ostasiatisches Kunst** (Museum of East Asian Art; for both, *see below*). Nearby is the **Museum Europäischer Kulturen** (Museum of European Cultures; *see p117*), which hosts thematic exhibitions.

Dahlem is also home to the **Freie Universität**, some of whose departments occupy former villas seized by the Nazis from their Jewish owners. Just north-west of the U-Bahn station, opposite the Friedhof Dahlem-Dorf (cemetery), is the **Domäne Dahlem** working farm (*see below*) – a great place to take kids.

Ten minutes' walk east from Dahlem along Königin-Luise-Strasse brings you to the **Botanischer Garten** and **Botanisches Museum** (Botanical Garden and Museum; *see below*), while taking the same street for a kilometre or so west of Dahlem to the edge of the Grunewald (*see p117*) takes you towards the **Alliierten Museum** (Allied Museum; *see p118*) and the **Brücke-Museum** (*see p118*).

Botanischer Garten & Museum
Königin-Luise-Strasse 6-8 (8385 0100/www.bgbm.fu-berlin.de/BGBM). S1 Botanischer Garten or S1, U9 Rathaus Steglitz. **Open** *Botanischer Garten 9am-dusk daily. Botanisches Museum Oct-Feb 10am-6pm daily.* **Admission** *Combined €4; €2 concessions. Museum only €1; €0.50 concessions.* **No credit cards**.

The Dahlem museums complex.

The Botanical Garden was landscaped at the beginning of the 20th century on a 42-hectare (104-acre) plot of land. Today, it is home to approximately 18,000 species of plants, and includes 16 greenhouses and a museum with special displays on herbs and dioramas of flowers. Its museum is intended to show behind the scenes of the plant kingdom, but there is no information in English, and the museum looks like it was finished around the time the Wall went up and has never been redecorated since, but it's free with a ticket for the gardens. Note that the Garden is a ten to 15-minute walk from the S-Bahn station.

Domäne Dahlem
Königin-Luise-Strasse 49 (832 5000/ www.domaene-dahlem.de). U1 Dahlem-Dorf. **Open** 10am-6pm Mon, Wed-Sun. **Admission** €2; €1 concessions; free under-14s; free to all Wed. **No credit cards**.
On this organic working farm, children can see how life was lived in the 17th century. Craftspeople – including blacksmiths, carpenters, bakers and potters – preserve and teach their skills. It is best to visit during one of several festivals held during the year, when children can ride ponies, tractors and hay-wagons. The admission charge applies to the Museum im Herrenhaus; the farm is accessible at any time free of charge.

Ethnologisches Museum
Lansstrasse 8 (830 1438/www.smb.spk-berlin.de). U1 Dahlem-Dorf. **Open** 10am-6pm Tue-Fri; 11am-6pm Sat, Sun. **Admission** €3; €1.50 concessions. **No credit cards**.
Berlin's Ethnological Museum is a stunner – extensive (over 500,000 exhibits), authoritative and beautifully laid out and lit. It encompasses cultures from Oceania to Central America to Africa to the Far East, and also has an educational department, which includes a junior museum and museum for the blind. Only the heavyweight ethno-fan should attempt to see it all, but no one should miss the Südsee (South Sea) room. Here you'll find New Guinean masks and effigies, and a remarkable collection of original and reconstructed canoes and boats – some huge and elaborate. There's also a fully intact men's clubhouse. The figure of a woman, suspended over the doorway with her legs wide open, just goes to show that boys have always been boys. The African rooms are also particularly impressive – look out for the superb carvings from Benin and the Congo, and the beaded artefacts from Cameroon (including a beautiful throne). An enlightening small exhibit explores the considerable influence of African art on the German expressionists.

Within the same building are the **Museum für Indische Kunst** (Museum of Indian Art) and the **Museum für Ostasiatische Kunst** (Museum of East Asian Art). The former represents more than 3,000 years of Indian culture and is particularly strong in the areas of terracottas, stone sculptures

The lush **Botanischer Garten**. *See p116.*

and bronzes and Central Asian wall paintings and sculptures from mainly Buddhist cave temples along the Silk Route. The latter features archaeological objects and works of fine and applied art from Japan, China and Korea from the early Stone Age to the present. An audio guide in English (included in the entrance price) is available for the Indian and East Asian museums. There's a good little café within the museum.

Museum Europäischer Kulturen

Im Winkel 6-8 (8390 1279/1297/www.smb.spk-berlin.de). U1 Dahlem-Dorf. **Open** 10am-6pm Tue-Fri; 11am-6pm Sat, Sun. **Admission** €3; €1.50 concessions. **No credit cards.**
Located close to the main Dahlem Museum complex (take Archivstrasse, opposite Dahlem-Dorf U-Bahn station, to reach it), the Museum of European Cultures opened in 1999 and aims to 'trace cultural phenomena common to all of Europe and specify their particular ethnic, regional, and national characteristics'. Its first exhibition was entitled 'Cultural Contacts in Europe: the Fascination of Pictures'. An additional exhibition 'Exotic Europe – Journey to the early examples of the Cinema' will run from 12 July 2001 to 28 October 2002.

Grunewald

The western edge of Zehlendorf is formed by the Havel river and the extensive green swathe of the **Grunewald**, largest of Berlin's many forests, and also its most visited. On a fine Sunday afternoon, its lanes and paths are as packed as the Kurfürstendamm, but with walkers, runners, cyclists, horse riders and dog walkers. This is because it's so easily accessible by S-Bahn. There are several restaurants next to Grunewald rail and S-Bahn station, and on the other side of the motorway at Schmetterlingsplatz, open during the season (April to October).

One particularly popular destination is the **Teufelsee**, a tiny lake that is packed with (usually naked) bathers in summer, reached by heading west from the station along Schildhornweg for 15 or so minutes. Close

by is the mound of the **Teufelsberg**, a product of wartime devastation. A railway was laid from Wittenbergplatz, along the Kurfürstendamm, to carry rubble from the city centre for depositing in a great pile at the terminus here. There are great views from the summit. The disused American electronic listening post that stood on the top is being dismantled, to be replaced (to the dismay of environmentalists and local residents) by a hotel and conference centre complex.

In the portion of the Grunewald south of the rail station, at Grunewaldsee, the 16th-century **Jagdschloss Grunewald** (Grunewald Hunting Lodge) is a good example of hundreds of such buildings that once maintained the country life of the landed gentry, the Prussian Junkers. Here, you can find bathing by the lake in the summertime, including a well-signposted nudist section. The Grunewaldsee is also a favourite promenade for chic dogs and their owners, who refresh themselves in the deer-horn-bedecked Forsthaus Paulsborn.

A further kilometre south-east through the forest, you'll find **Chalet Suisse**, an over the top Swiss-themed restaurant popular with families because of its extensive playground and petting zoo. Continuing for a further ten-minute walk takes you to the **Alliierten Museum** (Allied Museum; *see p118*) on Clayallee. A kilometre north of here is the **Brücke-Museum** (*see p118*), housing many of the surviving works by the influential Brücke group (including Kirchner, Heckel and Schmidt-Rottluff), known for their expressionistic views of Berlin.

Further south, **Krumme Lanke** and **Schlachtensee** are pleasant urban lakes along the south-eastern edge of the Grunewald, perfect for picnicking, swimming or rowing – and each with its own eponymous station: U1 for Krumme Lanke, S1 for Schlachtensee. Close to the former station is the **Haus am Waldsee**, which put on pioneering art exhibitions in the couple of decades after World War II, but rarely features anything of great interest today.

On the west side of the Grunewald, halfway up Havelchaussee, close to the Havel river, is the **Grunewaldturm**, a tower built in 1897 in memory of Wilhelm I. It has an observation platform 105 metres (344 feet) above the lake, with views as far as Spandau and Potsdam. There is a restaurant at the base, and another on the other side of the road, both with garden terraces. A short walk south along Havelufer brings you to the ferry to Lindwerder Insel (island), which also has a restaurant.

Sightseeing

Alliierten Museum

*Clayallee 135, corner of Huttenweg (818 1990/
www.alliiertenmuseum.de). U1 Oskar-Helene-
Heim/bus 115.* **Open** 10am-6pm Mon, Tue,
Thur-Sun. **Admission** free.

The Allied forces arrived as conquerors, kept West
Berlin alive during the 1948 Airlift and left many
Berliners with tears in their eyes when they finally
went home again in 1994. Housed in what used to
be a cinema for US Forces personnel, the Allied
Museum is mostly about the period of the Blockade
and the Airlift, documented with photos, tanks,
jeeps, planes, weapons, uniforms, cookbooks and
music. Outside you can find the building that was
once the stop-and-search centrepiece of Checkpoint
Charlie. Guided tours in English are available if
arranged in advance. The museum is ten minutes'
walk north up Clayallee from the U-Bahn station.

Brücke-Museum

*Bussardsteig 9 (831 2029/www.bruecke-museum.de).
U1 Oskar-Helene-Heim, then bus 115 to
Pücklerstrasse.* **Open** 11am-5pm Mon, Wed-Sun.
Admission €4; €2 concessions. **No credit cards.**

This interesting museum is dedicated to the work
of Die Brücke ('The Bridge'), a movement of artists
established in Dresden in 1905 and credited with
introducing expressionism to Germany. On display
are oils, watercolours, drawings and sculptures
by the main members of the movement: Schmidt-
Rottluff; Heckel; Kirchner; Mueller and Pechstein.
Although a little out of the way, the Brücke is
definitely worth seeing: a connoisseur's museum,
small but satisfying and coherently arranged, full
of fascinatingly colourful work.

Wannsee & Pfaueninsel

At the south-west edge of the Grunewald,
you'll find boats and beaches in summer, castles
and forests all through the year on the 'Berlin
Riviera'. **Strandbad Wannsee** is the largest
inland beach in Europe. Between May and
September it is the most popular resort in
Berlin, with service buildings housing showers,
toilets, cafés, shops and kiosks. There are boats
and pedaloes and hooded, two-person wicker
sunchairs for hire, a children's playground and
a separate section for nudists.

The waters of the Havel (the Wannsee
is an inlet of the river) are extensive and in
summer are warm enough to make swimming
comfortable; there is a strong current, so do
not stray beyond the floating markers. The rest
of the open water is in constant use by ferries,
sailing boats, speedboats and water-skiers.

Beyond the Strandbad lie the
Wannseeterrassen, a couple of rustic lanes on
the slopes of the hill, at the bottom of which
private boats and yachts are moored. A small
bridge north of the beach takes you across to
Schwanenwerder, once the exclusive private

island retreat of Goebbels and now home to the
international think-tank, the Aspen Institute.

The town of Wannsee to the south is
clustered around the bay of the Grosser
Wannsee and is dominated by the long stretch
of promenade, Am Grossen Wannsee, which is
scattered with hotels and fish restaurants. On
the west side of the bay is the **Gedenkstätte
Haus der Wannsee-Konferenz** (*see p119*).
At this house, in January 1942, a meeting of
prominent Nazis chaired by Reinhard Heydrich
laid out plans for the extermination of the
Jewish race – the Final Solution. The house, an
elegant *Gründerzeit* mansion, is now a museum.

A short distance from S-Bahn Wannsee along
Bismarckstrasse is a little garden where the
German dramatist Heinrich von Kleist shot
himself in 1811; the beautiful view of the Kleiner
Wannsee was the last thing he wanted to see.

On the other side of the railway tracks
is **Düppler Forst**, a little-explored forest
including a nature reserve at Grosses Fenn
at the south-western end. Travelling on the S-
Bahn three stops to Mexikoplatz and then the
629 bus to Krummes Fenn brings you to the
reconstructed 14th-century village at
Museumsdorf Düppel (*see p119*).

From Wannsee, bus 216 or 316 takes you
through the forest to a ferry pier on the Havel,
from where what must be one of the shortest
ferry journeys in the world brings you to
Pfaueninsel (Peacock Island). This 98-hectare
(242-acre) non-smoking island was inhabited
in prehistoric times, but isn't mentioned in
archives until 1683. Two years later the Grand
Elector presented it to Johann Kunckel von
Löwenstein, a chemist who experimented with
alchemy and instead of gold produced 'ruby
glass', examples of which are on view in the
castle. But it was only at the start of the
Romantic era that the island's windswept
charms began to attract more serious interest.
In 1793 Friedrich Wilhelm II purchased it and
built a *Schloss* for his mistress, but died in 1797
before they had a chance to move in. Its first
residents were the happily married couple
Friedrich Wilhelm III and Queen Luise, who
spent much of their time together on the island,
even setting up a working farm there.

The island was later added to and adorned.
A huge royal menagerie was developed, with
enclosed and free-roaming animals (most of
which were moved to the new Tiergarten Zoo in
1842). Only peacocks, pheasants, parrots, goats
and sheep remain. Surviving buildings include
the **Jakobsbrunnen** (Jacob's Fountain), a
copy of a Roman temple; the **Kavalierhaus**
(Cavalier's House), built in 1803 from an
original design by Schinkel; and the Swiss
cottage, also based on a Schinkel plan. All are

linked to each other by winding, informal paths laid out in the English manner by Peter Joseph Lenné. A walk around the island, with its monumental trees and rough meadows, and views of the waters of the Havel and the mainland beyond, provides one of the most complete sensations of escape from urban living to be had within the borders of Berlin.

Back on the mainland, a short walk south along the bank of the Havel, is the **Blockhaus Nikolskoe**, a re-creation of a huge wooden chalet, built in 1819 by Friedrich Wilhelm II for his daughter Charlotte, and named after her husband, the future Tsar Nicholas of Russia. There is a magnificent view of the Havel from the terrace, where you can also enjoy mid-priced Berlin cuisine, or just coffee and cakes in the afternoon. The nearby church of St Peter and St Paul dates from 1834-7 and has an attractive interior.

Gedenkstätte Haus der Wannsee-Konferenz

Am Grossen Wannsee 56-8 (805 0010/ www.ghwk.de). S1, S7 Wannsee, then bus 114. **Open** 10am-6pm daily. **Admission** free.
On 20 January 1942 a grim collection of prominent Nazis – Heydrich and Eichmann among them – gathered here on the Wannsee to draw up plans for the Final Solution, making jokes and sipping brandy as they sorted out the practicalities of genocide. Today, this infamous villa has been converted into the Wannsee Conference Memorial House, a place of remembrance, with a standing photo exhibition about the conference and its consequences. Call in advance if you want to join an English-language tour (8050 1026), otherwise all information is in German.

Museumsdorf Düppel

Clauertstrasse 11 (802 6671). S1 Mexikoplatz or U1 Krumme Lanke, then bus 211, 629. **Open** *early Apr-late Oct* 3-7pm Thur; 10am-5pm Sun. **Admission** €2; €1 concessions. **No credit cards.**
At this 14th-century village, reconstructed around archeological excavations, workers demonstrate handicrafts, medieval technology and farming techniques. Ox-cart rides for kids. Small snack bar.

Glienicke

West of Wannsee, and only a couple of kilometres from Potsdam, Glienicke was once the south-westernmost tip of West Berlin. The suspension bridge over the Havel here was named '**Brücke der Einheit**' (Bridge of Unity) because it once joined Potsdam with Berlin. The name continued to be used even when, after the building of the Wall, it was painted different shades of olive green on the East and West sides and used only by Allied soldiers and for top-level prisoner and spy exchanges – Anatoly Scharansky was one of the last in 1986.

The main reason to come to Glienicke is for the green space of **Park Glienicke**. The centrepiece of the park is **Schloss Glienicke** (not open to the public), originally a hunting lodge designed by Schinkel (*see p12* **Ich bin Berliner: KF Schinkel**) for Prinz Carl von Preussen, who quickly became notorious for his ban on all women visitors. On at least one occasion, Prinz Carl's wife was turned away at the gate by armed guards. The Prinz adorned the walls of the gardens with ancient relics collected on his holidays around the Mediterranean, and decided to simulate a walk from the Alps to Rome in the densely wooded park, laid out by Pückler in 1824-50. The summerhouses, fountains and follies are all based on original Italian models, and the woods and fields surrounding them make an ideal place for a Sunday picnic, since this park is little visited. At Moorlake, there's a restaurant in a Bavarian-style 1842 hunting lodge, which is good for game dishes or afternoon coffee and cakes.

East & south-east of the centre

Much of the eastern side of the city is often thought of as a wasteland of decaying Communist apartment blocks with few redeeming features – and much of it truly is depressing – but there's still a lot of the flavour of old Berlin in the east. There are a couple of decent museums and parks in **Lichtenberg** and **Treptow**, but for the most rewarding escapism in the east, head for characterful **Köpernick**.

Lichtenberg & Treptow

Many of the neighbourhoods of the old east have little to offer the visitor. Bordering the eastern sides of Prenzlauer Berg and Friedrichshain, **Lichtenberg** isn't very appealing, though it does contain the huge **Tierpark Berlin-Friedrichsfelde** (Berlin-Friedrichsfelde Zoo; *see p120*) and the **Stasi Museum**, otherwise known as the **Forschungs- und Gedenkstätte Normannenstrasse** (*see p120*). A kilometre south of the park is the **Museum Berlin-Karlshorst** (*see p120*), documenting Russian-German relations in the 20th century.

South of Lichtenberg and bordering Neukölln, **Treptow** is chiefly of note for **Treptower Park**, containing the massive **Sowjetisches Ehrenmal** (Soviet War Memorial). From here, several boats leave in the summer for trips along the Spree. The park continues to the south, where it becomes the **Plänterwald** and houses a big amusement park.

Sightseeing

Forschungs- und Gedenkstätte Normannenstrasse (Stasi Museum)

Ruschestrasse 103 (553 6854/www.stasimuseum.de).
U5 Magdalenenstrasse. **Open** 11am-6pm Mon-Fri;
2-6pm Sat, Sun. **Admission** €3; €2 concessions.
No credit cards.
These days you almost need evidence that
Communism ever happened. This museum (the
unwieldy name means Normanstrasse Research and
Memorial Centre), housed in part of what used to be
the gruesome headquarters of the Ministerium für
Staatssicherheit (the Stasi), offers some proof. You
can look round the old offices of secret police chief
Erich Mielke – his old uniform still hangs in his
wardrobe – and view displays of bugging devices
and spy cameras concealed in books, plant pots and
Trabant car doors. There's also a lot of Communist
kitsch: tasteless furniture, tacky medals, banners
and busts of Marx and Lenin. The documentation
is in Germany only. Guided tours in English are
available with advance notice.

Museum Berlin-Karlshorst

Zwieseler Strasse 4, corner Rheinsteinstrasse
(5015 0841/www.museum-karlshorst.de).
S3 Karlshorst. **Open** 10am-6pm Tue-Sun.
Admission free.
Built between 1936 and 1938, this place was used
until 1945 as a German officers' club. After the
Soviets took Berlin, it was commandeered as HQ for
the military administration and it was here, during
the night of 8-9 May 1945, that German commanders
signed the final and unconditional surrender of the
Nazi army, thus ending the war in Europe. It was also
here, five years later, that Soviet General Chuikov
authorised the first Communist government in the
GDR. The museum looks at the German-Soviet relationship over 70 years. Divided into 16 small rooms
including the Allied flag-adorned conference room in
which the Nazis surrendered, it takes us through two
world wars and one cold one, assorted pacts, victories and capitulations, and varying degrees of hatred
and camaraderie. The permanent exhibit includes
lots of photos, memorabilia, documents, campaign
maps, video footage and propaganda posters. Buy a
guide in English; the exhibits are explained in
German and Russian. Interesting enough to warrant
a couple of hours. Guided tours in English are
available with advance notice.

Tierpark Berlin-Friedrichsfelde

Am Tierpark 125 (51531/www.tierpark-berlin.de).
U5 Tierpark. **Open** *Jan, Feb, mid Oct-Dec*
9am-4pm daily. *Mar, mid Sept-mid Oct* 9am-
6pm daily. *Apr-mid Sept* 9am-6pm daily.
Admission €7.50; €4-€6 concessions.
No credit cards.
This is one of the largest zoos in Europe, providing
plenty of roaming space for some animals, though
others are kept in distressingly small cages. Bears,
elephants, big cats, penguins… you name it. In the
north-west corner of the grounds is the baroque
Schloss Friedrichsfelde.

Köpenick

The name **Köpenick** is derived from the
Slavonic *copanic*, meaning 'place on a river'.
The old town, around 15 kilometres (nine miles)
south-east of Mitte, stands at the confluence
of the Spree and Dahme, and, having escaped
bombing, decay and development by the
GDR, still maintains much of its 18th-century
character. Of all the areas of east Berlin,
Köpenick was (and still is) the most sought
after, with handsome and increasingly affluent
shops, cafés and restaurants clustered around
the old centre. With its old buildings and
extensive riverfront, it's a fine place for a
Sunday afternoon wander.

The imposing Rathaus (Town Hall) is a good
example of late Victorian *Wilhelmenisch* civic
architecture. It was here, in 1906, that two years
after the building's completion, that Wilhelm
Voigt, an unemployed cobbler who'd spent half
his life in jail, disguised himself as an army
captain and ordered a detachment of soldiers
to accompany him into the Treasury, where
they confiscated the town coffers. He instantly
entered popular folklore, Carl Zuckmeyer
immortalised him in a play as *Der Hauptmann
von Köpenick* (Captain of Köpenick), and the
Kaiser pardoned him because he had shown
how obedient Prussian soldiers were. His theft
is re-enacted every year during the Köpenicker
summer festival in late June.

Close by on Schlossinsel, **Schloss Köpenick**,
with its medieval drawbridge, Renaissance
gateway and baroque chapel, contains the
Kunstgewerbemuseum (Museum of Applied
Art; 657 2651; an outpost of its namesake in
Tiergarten, *see p104*), which is due to reopen
after refurbishment in 2003. Occasional open-air
concerts are held in the *Schloss* in the summer.

Friedrichshagen & the Müggelsee

A couple of kilometres east of Köpenick, the
village of **Friedrichshagen** has retained a lot
of its independent character. The main street,
Bölschestrasse, leading down from the S-Bahn
station, is lined with steep-roofed Brandenburg
houses, and ends at the shores of the large
lake called the **Grösser Müggelsee**. Worth a
visit on any fair day (though it gets very busy),
Friedrichshagen is particularly enjoyable when
the Berliner Burgerbräu brewery, family-owned
since 1869, throws open its gates for its annual
celebration in the summertime. Booths line
Bölschestrasse, the brewery lays on music, and
people sit on the shores with cold beer and look
out onto the lake. Boat tours are available, and
the restaurant Braustubl, next to the brewery,
serves especially good Berlin cuisine.

Eat, Drink, Shop

Restaurants

Never pig-ignorant, Berliners are now starting to cast
their culinary net wider than the borders of Brandenburg.

No, Berlin could never be described as a haven
of gastronomy, but it's quite possible to dine well
here. And if you're after a hearty hunk of roast
pork, you should relish the prospect. There's no
doubt the city's eating out scene has improved
immeasurably since Reunification, but the
starting point was low. There are many reasons
for this. First, Germany's colonial experience
didn't last very long, so there has been no long-
term link with a foreign cuisine, as with India and
Britain or Indonesia and the Dutch. Second, the
basic building blocks of a great cuisine just aren't
found in Prussian food (*see p124* **Fat chance**).
Third, many locals are highly conservative in
their tastes, and reject foreign influences and
strong flavours out of hand. Fourth, there's no
great ethnic presence here besides the Turks, and
they mostly prefer to eat at home and sell snacks
to the general public. And fifth, there aren't
enclaves of ethnic communities in Berlin. True,
the Turks dominate Kreuzberg, but there's no
Chinatown, no East End, no East LA where
competition can bring about superb dining.

Compared to a decade ago, though, it's a
paradise. For one thing, the opening of the
east meant a lot of cheap real estate that young
restaurateurs found irresistible, so some of the
most adventurous dining in Berlin is now found
in Mitte and Prenzlauer Berg. For another, it's
always the young and affluent who dictate dining
trends, and Berlin's young and affluent have
visited places like London, California and
Tuscany, where they go for work and play, and
have returned with demands for lighter, healthier
and better seasoned eating. They drink red wine
– from Italy, Spain and South Africa – and eat
salads. The Italian influence in particular is felt
everywhere; it's hard to find a restaurant that
doesn't offer *caprese* (tomato, mozzarella and
basil salad), a pasta dish, or something with
rucola (rocket) in it.

No longer is going out to dinner with a
vegetarian in tow a chore: it's now hard to walk
into a decent restaurant here without finding
several vegetarian options on the menu. There's
still plenty missing, though. Chinese food is rare.
Sushi places have erupted in the past couple of
years, but other Japanese food is hard to find.
Indian restaurants too have proliferated, but
the fare is so Germanised that Indians wouldn't
recognise it. Neither would a Mexican recognise

nearly all Berlin's 'Mexican' cuisine. And
Americans are perfectly within their rights to
decry what's sold as American food, right down
to the frozen hockey-pucks universally used in
the hamburgers. Still, they're better off than the
British, whose cuisine doesn't get a look in.

So wake up and get yourself some breakfast:
if your hotel doesn't have it (or if you've overslept
and missed it), head to a café. *See p152* **The
breakfast club**.

Lunch in Berlin tends to be lunch, unlike in
other parts of Germany, where the day's main
meal is served at noon. Bakeries usually offer a
variety of sandwiches, all on fresh *Brötschen*.
If you're after more, try an *Imbiss*, or snack bar.
These come in various varieties and embrace
just about anywhere you get food but not table
service, from stand-up street corner stalls to self-
service snack bars offering all manner of exotic
cuisine. The quality varies wildly, but some
excellent, cheap food can be found. The Turkish
Imbisse will offer the ubiquitous *Kebap*, Turkish
'pizza', half chickens and salads, while German
Imbisse will tempt you with various kinds of
sausage, or a *Boulette* (a spicy hamburger-like
patty described as 'a fight between the butcher
and baker that the baker won').

In the evenings, of course, there's much more
choice. Take heed, though: Berliners like to eat
out, particularly at weekends, and a place empty
on a Tuesday may well be packed when you
decide to go on a Friday. Reservations are a good
idea, especially at more upmarket places.

Whenever you eat, you'll encounter the
legendary Berlin service, legendary because
when you get back home and tell people about it
they won't believe you. 'Why', they'll ask, 'would
anybody go back to a place like that?' The
answer is, because they're all like it. Things
are changing for the better, but the surly, slow,
uninterested waiter is still with us, and heaven
forbid you should have any special requests.

In restaurants, a service charge of 17 per cent
is added to the bill, but unless service has been
awful (not impossible in Berlin, alas), diners
usually round up the bill or, in the classier joints,
add ten per cent. Tips are handed to the server (or
you tell staff how much to take) and never left on
the table, which is considered by some insulting.
When you hand over the cash, never say 'danke'
unless you want staff to keep the change.

Mitte

German

Adlon
Hotel Adlon, Unter den Linden 77 (2261 1555). S1, S2, S25, S26 Unter den Linden. **Open** 6-11pm Tue-Sat. **Main courses** €22-€35. **Credit** AmEx, DC, V. **Map** p316/p302 F3.

Try master chef Karlheinz Hauser's orgasmic lemongrass soup as a starter and be equally astonished by his lobster en gelée. He has also caused a huge sensation in Berlin recently with his duck served in two courses – an astonishing feat of culinary skill. The airy, bright dining area has great views over Unter den Linden and the Brandenburg Gate. A gourmet restaurant named **Lorenz** (after the hotel's original founder, Lorenz Adlon) run by Maestro Hauser opened on the Adlon's first floor in 2000.

Borchardt
Französische Strasse 47 (2038 7110). U6 Französische Strasse. **Open** noon-1am daily. **Main courses** €16-€20. **Credit** V. **Map** p316/p302 F3.

In the late 19th century, Friedrich Wilhelm Borchardt opened a restaurant of this name right next door at No.48. It became the place for politicians and society folk, but was destroyed by bombing in World War II. Since 1991 it has belonged to Roland Mary and Marina Richter, who have reconstructed

Gugelhof. *See p129*

a highly fashionable, Maxim's-inspired bistro serving eminently respectable French food. So why not snorkel down a dozen oysters and tuck into a fillet of pike-perch or beef after an evening at the Komische Oper, the Staatsoper or the Konzerthaus?

Ganymed
Schiffbauerdamm 5 (2859 9046). S1, S2, S3, S5, S7, S9, S25, S26, S75, U6 Friedrichstrasse. **Open** *Summer* 11.30am-1am Mon-Fri; 10am-1am Sat. *Winter* 6pm-1am Mon-Sat; 11.30am-1am Sun. **Main courses** €12-€20. **Credit** AmEx, DC, MC, V. **Map** p316/p302 F3.

Like German wine? The cellar here was reserved for VIPs back when the GDR was in business. Theatre-goers heading to or from the Berliner Ensemble can now enjoy what they did: an anthology of the best, with prize-winners galore. The food doesn't exactly play second fiddle, but does seem to exist for the wine, rather than playing full partner. Still, with wines so fine, you need exceptional food, and the chef does a great job with standard German specialities, only erring when trying to get too modern.

Guy
Jägerstrasse 59-60 (2094 2600). U6 Französische Strasse. **Open** noon-3pm, 6pm-1am Mon-Fri; 6pm-1am Sat. **Main courses** €23-€26. **Credit** AmEx, MC, V. **Map** p316/p306 F4.

The name comes from the Franco-German proprietor, Hartmut Guy. The burgundy velvet, dark wooden interior (shades of Gaultier's designs for Greenaway's *The Cook, the Thief, His Wife and Her Lover*) is so theatrical that it just might distract your attention from what can be stunningly banal food. Witness, for instance, the watery 'wild mushroom risotto', the undercooked Wels (a type of catfish) on tough pasta and the niggardly cheese platter. Service can be poor too. The downstairs bar is hugely popular.

Hackescher Hof
Rosenthaler Strasse 40-41 (283 5293). S3, S5, S7, S9 Hackescher Markt. **Open** 7am-2am daily. **Main courses** €8-€16.50. **No credit cards**. **Map** p316/p302 F3.

It's huge, it's loud, it's almost always full, and the pricey food will never win any prizes for startling originality. So why is it so popular? Location, for one, and long opening hours for another. If you can get a window table, it's not a bad place for watching the crowds over a cup of coffee or a beer.

Honigmond
Borsigstrasse 28 (285 7505). U6 Zinnowitzer Strasse. **Open** 11am-2am daily. **Main courses** €6-€13.50. **No credit cards**. **Map** p302 F2.

This quiet, neighbourhood place serves up traditional German food alongside a bi-weekly menu of innovative dishes ranging from kangaroo to Swiss fondue. Not to be missed are the *Königsberger Klöpse* (east Prussian meatballs in a creamy caper sauce), and the best Caesar salad in town. If the decor is somewhat short of the 1920s nostalgia it tries to evoke, the excellent small wine list and remarkable home-made bread (and butter!) make up for it. Small hotel upstairs too (*see p52*).

Kellerrestaurant im Brecht-Haus

Chausseestrasse 125 (282 3843). U6 Oranienburger Tor. **Open** *Summer* noon-1am Mon-Fri, Sun; 6pm-1am Sat. *Winter* 6pm-1am daily. **Main courses** €9-€15. **Credit** AmEx, MC, V. **Map** p316/p302 F3.
Berthold Brecht got that sleek, well-fed look from the cooking his partner Helene Weigel learned in Vienna and Bohemia. This atmospheric place, crammed with model stage sets and other Brecht memorabilia, serves a number of her specialities (indicated on the menu), including *Fleischlabberln* (spicy meat patties) and a mighty Wiener Schnitzel. In summer, the garden more than doubles the place's capacity.

Langhans

Charlottenstrasse 59 (2094 5070). U2, U6 Stadtmitte. **Open** *Summer* 10am-2am Mon, Tue, Sun; 10am-3am Fri, Sat. *Winter* 11.30am-2am daily. **Main courses** €17-€24. **Credit** AmEx, MC, V. **Map** p316/p306 F3.
Named after the architect of the Brandenburg Gate, Langhans is a great spot for post-Gendarmenmarkt relaxation. Chef Jens Krause is famous for his Japanese-Italian fusion cooking: cannelloni with lobster, or sea-devil fish with fennel, and an odd, but fine risotto with blueberries and mint with smoked rabbit fillet.

Lutter & Wegner

Charlottenstrasse 56 (2029 5410). U2, U6 Stadtmitte. **Open** 11am-2am daily. **Main courses** €15-€22. **Credit** AmEx, DC, MC, V. **Map** p316/p306 F4.
This place has it all: history (one of Berlin's earliest wine merchants, its champagne became known locally as 'Sekt', a word that now includes all sparkling white wine); atmosphere in its airy, elegant rooms with plenty of fresh flowers; great German/Austrian/French cuisine; and excellent service. The wine list is justifiably legendary, and if the prices look high, just head for the bistro, where the same list holds sway along with perfect salads, cheese and ham plates, and excellent desserts, as well as a more informal atmosphere.
Branch: Schlüterstrasse 55, Charlottenburg (881 3440).

Margaux

Unter den Linden 78 (2265 2611). S1, S2, S25, S26 Unter den Linden. **Open** noon-2pm, 7-10.30pm Tue-Sat. **Main courses** €30-€40. **Credit** AmEx, DC, MC, V. **Map** p316/p302 F3.

Eat, Drink, Shop

Fat chance

Great regional cuisines: in California, it's Pacific Rim; in France, Provençal; in Italy, Piemontese; in Germany... Prussian?

Well, no. Classy cooking can be found in many parts of Germany, but Berlin's local specialities have a more earthy appeal – and that's putting it kindly.

If you've eaten at a 'German restaurant' outside the German-speaking world, it's virtually certain you've had Bavarian cuisine. This style of cooking encompasses several kinds of roasted pork, pork pot-roasted as *Sauerbraten*, creative ways with *Sauerkraut*, dumplings, potatoes, and desserts piled high with whipped cream. In fact, Munich's Paulaner brewery owns a highly successful chain of Paulaner restaurants based on just such a concept.

Within Germany, one of the favourite regional cuisines is Swabian, from the south-west. Italian influences abound in this cooking, especially pasta, with which the Swabians have done great things. In Germany's several wine-growing regions – Saxony, the Mosel and Rhine valleys – you'll also discover some fine cooking.

However, Berlin is located in the north-east of the country, and, as the French will tell you, the cuisine is the soil. Berlin's soil – and the soil of much of the surrounding countryside – is very sandy, which makes it very poor for growing crops. Here, besides the ubiquitous pork, little but cabbage and potatoes is successful.

History too plays a part. Frederick the Great, who put Berlin on the map, was a Francophile (a dinner with Parmentier at Versailles caused him to introduce the potato to farmers). This Gallic influence is still felt in Berlin argot, although not on its tables (except in the higher price range). For instance, the hamburger-like patty known in most places as a *Frikadelle* is here called a *Boulette*, as it is in French. Sadly, Berlin's Francophilia helped deter the city from producing an haute cuisine of its own.

To the extent that there is a Berlin cuisine, it is working people's food, so it's cheap. Probably the signature dish of Berlin is *Eisbein*, yet this delicacy – pig's trotter with leathery skin and an overwhelming abundance of fat – is often enough to send people looking elsewhere for nourishment all by itself. However, once you get inside the gelatinous mass of the *Eisbein*, there are morsels of flesh that,

Perhaps the ultimate example of a 'new Berlin' dining temple, this top-flight restaurant features Michael Hoffman's superbly aromatic cuisine. Hoffman is slightly avant-garde in his approach to classic French cooking; try, for instance, the stewed shoulder of venison seasoned with hints of coriander, anise and saffron. The spacious interior is lit by glowing columns of honey-hued onyx, which reflect in the black marble floors. The restaurant is named in deference to its extraordinary wine list, which includes some 30 vintages of Château Margaux. Service is well informed and first-rate.

Maxwell

Bergstrasse 22 (280 7121). U6 Oranienburger Tor. **Open** *Summer* noon-midnight daily. *Winter* 6pm-midnight daily. **Main courses** €16-€24. **Credit** AmEx, DC, V. **Map** p302 F2.

Set in a handsome old brewery, Maxwell is one of the only places in the world where the plates of food imitate the art on the walls. Witness the friendly polka-dotted platter, Duck à la Hirst, created by chef Uwe Popall. The duck's black pepper sauce supposedly brings out the subliminal dark side of Hirst's works. Service is slow, the portions are small, but nobody seems to mind when surrounded by so many 'beautiful people'. The summer courtyard is a bonus.

Seasons

Four Seasons Hotel, Charlottenstrasse 49 (2033 6363). U2, U6 Stadtmitte. **Open** 6.30am-10.30pm daily. **Main courses** €15-€30. **Credit** AmEx, DC, V. **Map** pp316/p306 F4.

Great value for money and fine seasonal cooking can be had here. The room exudes relaxed grandeur, with large tables spaced far apart to allow for considerable discretion. Try the tortellini with mangetout, rocket and cream cheese in a pine nut sauce, and the sublime 'pot au feu' of lobster and sea bass with pepper crostini.

stäV

Schiffbauerdamm 8 (2859 8735) S1, S2, S3, S5, S7, S9, S25, S26, S75, U6 Friedrichstrasse. **Open** 11am-1am daily. **Main courses** €10-€15. **Credit:** MC, V. **Map** p316/p302 F3.

A 'ständige Vertretung' (the term West Germany used for their non-Embassy in the East) on the Rheinland in Berlin, stäV makes good money out of homesick Bonners in what has become a quarter catering to large numbers of them. Both Berliners and Rheinlanders-in-exile can sink their teeth into *Himmel und Ääde* ('heaven and earth': *Blutwurst* with mashed potatoes and apples), raisiny *Rheinish Sauerbraten*, and drink Cologne's

Eat, Drink, Shop

having been cooked with all that fat around them, are delicious and moist. Some people spoon the fat into their mouths, but we wouldn't recommend it. *Eisbein* is either pickled or not, and is served with puréed peas, *Erbsenpuree*.

If you'd rather have more meat than fat, try a *Kasseler*. Invented in Berlin by a butcher called Kassel (and not in the city of the same name) this delicately smoked pork chop or steak can be quite delicious, although it's not often to be found on menus. Another popular main course is liver, onions and apples, a Berlin tradition that's even rarer to find if you're eating out.

A good lunch can be made from the Currywurst, where the meat is treated with curry powder, as is the heated ketchup that's poured over the top. It sounds horrible, but has its charms. The ur-Currywurst can be found at Prenzlauer Berg's Konnopke's Imbiss (*see p130*).

Berlin bread is legendarily bad by German standards (although if this is your first stop in the country, you'll probably love it until you get to your next destination). The city's contribution to the bread basket

is the hard wholemeal roll called *Berliner Schusterjunge*, 'Berlin shoemaker's apprentice', presumably so-called because it was what these unfortunates subsisted on.

The city's beer isn't held in much higher regard; the huge Schultheiss brewery produces a truly lousy product, and its competition at Berliner Kindl isn't much better. Fortunately, the east comes to the rescue with Berliner Pilsner (owned by Schultheiss) and Berliner Bürgerbräu (owned by Kindl). The Braustub'l restaurant next to the Bürgerbräu brewery in remote Friedrichshagen is considered by insiders to be one of the most authentic Berlin home cooking places around. If you're there in the winter, make sure you get one of the brewery's Dunkelbock beers.

In many ways, Berlin cuisine epitomises everything that's wrong with German cooking in general: pig and stodge. No wonder Berliners flock to Italian restaurants. Nevertheless, once you've lived through a winter here and experienced coming out of the snow to a good hearty Berliner feast, you realise there's a time and place for everything. Even the heaviest food is sometimes a comfort.

sneakily powerful beer, Kölsch, while puzzling over the political in-jokes on the wall. Good list of Rhine wines, as might be expected.

Vau

Jägerstrasse 54-5 (202 9730). U6 Französische Strasse. **Open** noon-2.30pm, 7pm-midnight Mon-Sat. **Menus** €75-€100. **Credit** AmEx, DC, MC, V. **Map** p316/p306 F4.

The love of innovation and inspiration from all corners of the globe make chef Kolja Kleeberg's menu one of the best in town. His lobster with mango and black olives with a tapenade, and braised pork belly with grilled scallops are complemented by an extensive wine list (starting at €26). A glass of Banyuls to go with your wine tart with red wine ice-cream is no shabby finish to a fine meal. Downstairs, the fake-library bar is a terrific place to book for special occasions. Booking essential.

Zur Nolle

Georgenstrasse S-Bahn Bogen 203 (208 2655). S1, S2, S3, S5, S7, S9, S25, S26, S75, U6 Friedrichstrasse. **Open** 11am-midnight daily. **Main courses** €6.50-€10. **Credit** AmEx, DC, MC, V. **Map** p316/p302 F3.

Despite a bunch of chain snack bars inside Friedrichstrasse station, there's not much in the way of real food around here. That's why Zur Nolle gets

The best Restaurants

For intellectuals
Berthold's old gaff: **Kellerrestaurant am Brecht-Haus.** *See p124.*

For celebrity watching
Maxwell draws the stars with art on the walls and on the plates. *See p125.*

For spying on diplomats
A gastronome's and oenophile's dream: **Margaux.** *See p125.*

For a romantic evening
Munch on classic Teutonic cuisine at eccentric **Offenbach Stuben.** *See p129.*

For vegetarians
Abendmahl serves up not just great veggie food, but great food, period. *See p134.*

For those on a budget
Carouse with the students at **Tiergarten Quelle.** *See p137.*

For old Berlin atmosphere
Bovril: a classic soup-serving Berlin institution. *See p138.*

customers: people who'd rather tarry over a cup of coffee or a beer in its antique-laden interior or, in good weather, outside on the pavement. Food is basic solid German fare, nothing exciting, but like the real estate boys say: 'location, location, location'.

Americas

Andy's Diner & Bar

Potsdamer Strasse 1 (2300 4990). S1, S2, S25, S26, U2 Potsdamer Platz. **Open** 10am-3.30am daily. **Main courses** €7-€16.50. **Credit** AmEx, MC, V. **Map** p316/p306 E4.

Avert your eyes from the decoration and the sports TVs, avoid the hamburgers and milkshakes (which are presented as 'health food'), and dig into a pretty good steak. Or come for breakfast and enjoy authentic American-style pancakes and eggs.

Las Cucarachas

Oranienburger Strasse 38 (282 2044). S1, S2, S25, S26 Oranienburger Strasse. **Open** noon-late daily. **Main courses** €5-€15. **Credit** AmEx, MC, V. **Map** p316/p302 F3.

Chileans in the kitchen mean a pretty odd take on Mexican food at times, and, between the blaring salsa music and the Margarita-fuelled customers, the noise level can be unbearable, but Las Cucs (named after Villa's revolutionaries, not the literal translation: cockroaches) is one of this strip's most popular hangouts for expats and tourists, as well as locals. The Lone Star emphasises tacos, including fine tacos al pastor, and is altogether more relaxing. **Branch**: Lone Star Taqueria, Bergmannstrasse 11, Kreuzberg (692 7182).

QBA

Oranienburger Strasse 45 (2804 0505). S3, S5, S7, S9, S75 Hackescher Markt or S1, S2, S25, S26 Oranienburger Strasse. **Open** 6pm-late daily. **Main courses** €5-€15. **Credit** AmEx, MC, V. **Map** p316/p302 F3.

You've got to hand it to the decorators here: they took a perfectly normal interior and made it look like a funky, falling-apart Havana bar. Fortunately, the kitchen keeps the illusion alive, with some sterling interpretations of Cuban beef, pork and chicken dishes. Unfortunately, of late the chefs have felt the need to add MSG to some sauces and dressings. Still, stick to the simpler items like baked chicken and you'll be OK, albeit a bit deaf thanks to the high-volume salsa pounding away.

Soul Kitchen

Linienstrasse 136 (280 40362). U8 Rosenthaler Platz. **Open** 5pm-1am daily. **Main courses** €7-€14. **No credit cards. Map** p316/p302 F3.

Leta Davis, a pixie-ish African-American woman, is on a crusade to introduce the food she grew up with to her adopted home town. Mostly, Soul Kitchen is a bar (with a long list of innovative cocktails), but sometimes you get homesick for good fried chicken, and the greens here are to die for. Less successful are the cornbread and hush-puppies, because the cornmeal sold in Germany is too fine, but Ms Davis scores more often than she misses. An oasis from mad, tourist-choked Oranienburger Strasse.

¡Viva México!
Chausseestrasse 36 (280 7865). U6 Zinnowitzer Strasse. **Open** 11am-11pm daily. **Main courses** €8-€25. **No credit cards. Map** p302 E2.
A valuable find: a Mexican woman and her family preparing authentic interior Mexican food in Berlin. Highlights include the own-made refried beans and at least four salsas (three of which are good and spicy) to put on tacos, burritos and tortas, and the decent range of dinner items. This place would be good in Mexico, let alone Germany.

Greek

Skales
Rosenthaler Strasse 12 (283 3006). U8 Weinmeisterstrasse. **Open** 6pm-2am Mon-Thur, Sun; 6pm-3am Fri, Sat. **Main courses** €7-€13. **Credit** AmEx, DC, MC, V. **Map** p316/p302 F3.
To look at this huge, high-ceilinged room, you'd never guess it was once a storage space for uniforms and other paraphernalia of the Freie Deutsche Jugend, the GDR's youth organisation. It has since gone through a severe ideological change: snooty service matches the often snooty customers, but at least the Greek food is well prepared.

Imbiss/fast food

See also p234.

Astor
Oranienburger Strasse 84 (283 6834). S3, S5, S7, S9, S75 Hackescher Markt. **Open** 11am-1am Mon-Thur, Sun; 11am-2am Fri, Sat. **Main courses** €5-€8.50. **No credit cards. Map** p316/p302 F3.
The idea behind the large name of this tiny place was to parody Buckingham Palace. Before the breakout of BSE, this German-owned fish 'n' chippery offered exclusively British cuisine. Hard times called for a 50/50 British/American split. Lunch specials (11am-3pm) fill expats' need for comfort food: chicken wings, spare ribs, chicken tacos, or burgers sans buns. The chips are handcut and fat, and a generous portion of salad makes a healthy bed for the fried fish dieter's demon. Takeaway is available at reduced prices wrapped in yesterday's newspapers.

Marcann's
Invalidenstrasse 112 (2832 6171). U6 Zinnowitzer Strasse. **Open** 7am-6pm Mon-Fri; 8.30am-2pm Sat. **Main courses** €1-€3. **No credit cards. Map** p302 E2.
Marc, Ann and the crew came to Berlin from France to work in Galerie Lafayette's bakery and then quit to open their own place. Hitting this corner just

MONSIEUR VUONG

Soft, strong and very, very **Vuong**. *See p129.*

as a bunch of offices opened nearby, they serve packed lunchtime crowds with panini, home-baked baguettes, and also offer a fine selection of French pastries, soft drinks and even a few bottles of wine. Fillings include home-made pâtés, various French cheeses and tuna Niçoise.

Misuyen Asia-Bistro
Torstrasse 22 (247 7269). U2 Rosa-Luxemburg-Platz. **Open** 11am-9pm Mon-Sat. **Main courses** €2.50-€6. **No credit cards. Map** p303 G2.
Sometimes, if you look behind the surface of one of Berlin's many Asian *Imbisse*, you'll find something unexpected. In Misuyen's case, it's Laotian food, albeit mixed with the usual greatest hits: Thai, Indonesian, Chinese. Lighter and with more fresh vegetables than the usual Asian fare, the Laotian dishes can also be made without MSG if you say the three magic words: '*Ohne Glutamat, bitte*'.

Italian

Cantamaggio
Alte Schönhauser Strasse 4 (283 1895). U8 Rosa-Luxemburg-Platz. **Open** 6pm-midnight daily. **Main courses** €8-€16. **Credit** AmEx, DC, MC, V. **Map** p316/p303 G3.

Eat, Drink, Shop

A quick perusal of Cantamaggio's menu will give you an idea of the wild mix of fancy schmanzy new dishes and old standbys to be had. From the former, what about rose petal pan-fried duck breast with strawberry vinaigrette on lamb's lettuce, or duck liver with yellow chanterelles? Or perhaps you'd rather stick to the classic cannelloni with beef or fettuccine with lamb ragout. Desserts are of the classic variety. This is a well-loved, elegant, if a mite spartan, restaurant; the loud floral arrangements don't help much to absorb the loud chatter of habitués.

Rosmini Pastamanufaktur

Invalidenstrasse 151 (2809 6844). U8 Rosenthaler Platz. **Open** noon-midnight Mon-Fri; 5.30pm-midnight Sat, Sun. **Main courses** €8-€17. **No credit cards. Map** p302 F2.

Appealing, affordable southern Italian food emerges from Rosmini's kitchens, and, yes, pasta is made on the premises. Although the starters and *secondi* here are wonderful, it's obvious that pasta is a passion, and the chefs seem to come up with endless variations; try the asparagus ravioli in the spring. To see what's current, book a seat at the reservation-only pasta party, usually the first Saturday of the month, to enjoy a staggering 16 pasta courses.

Salumeria Culinario

Tucholskystrasse 34 (2809 6767). S1, S2, S25, S26 Oranienburger Strasse. **Open** 10am-11pm Mon-Thur, Sun; 10am-midnight Fri, Sat. **Main courses** €8-€19. **No credit cards. Map** p316/p302 F3.

The daily changing lunch menu here is a great way to recharge your depleted batteries after a morning of shopping and gallery-hopping. Pick up a bottle of wine, cheese, olives and salami, or ponder the many panettones stocked in the Italian import section, or simply grab a plate to go. The size of this small café belies the 18 staff members needed to keep up with the demand for the home-made gnocchi and busy catering service for small parties within the neighbourhood. There is space for 60 at the crowded beer tables on the pavement.

Schwarzenraben

Neue Schönhauser Strasse 13 (2839 1698). U8 Weinmeisterstrasse. **Open** *Café* 10am-2am Mon-Thur, Sun; 10am-4am Fri, Sat. *Restaurant* 6.30pm-2am Mon-Thur, Sat; 6.30pm-4am Fri, Sat. **Main courses** €13-€23. **Credit** AmEx, MC, V. **Map** p316/p303 G3.

Some contend that so many of Berlin's young film and theatre stars eat here because they're non-paying bait to draw other punters to owner Rudolf H Girolo's chicest of Berlin's Italo-Mediterranean joints. Savour, if you can, overpriced, banal Italian food and wine while surrounded by pseudo film stars. Service comes with a snarl. Hugely popular yet hugely overrated, although the downstairs club often features interesting DJs and live acts.

Oriental artistry at **Mao Thai**. *See p130.*

Jewish

Café Oren

Oranienburger Strasse 28 (282 8228). S1, S2, S25, S26 Oranienburger Strasse. **Open** noon-1am Mon-Fri; 10am-1am daily Sat, Sun. **Main courses** €6-€14. **Credit** AmEx, V. **Map** p316/p302 F3.

A Jewish (not kosher) restaurant right next to the Neue Synagoge offering standard fish and vegetarian dishes with Middle Eastern specialities. The garlic cream soup is thick and tasty; the salad fresh and crispy; and the soya cutlet breaded with sesame, in a light curry sauce served with fried banana and rice, is absolutely heavenly. There's an excellent vegetarian borscht and the Orient Express platter (a large choice of meze) is great value. Oren is just as bustling as Oranienburger Strasse outside, so it's best to book. Tables appear in the courtyard every summer. Breakfast is served at weekends.

Oriental

See also p127 **Misuyen Asia-Bistro**.

Good Time

Chausseestrasse 1 (280 46015). U6 Oranienburger Tor. **Open** noon-midnight daily. **Main courses** €8.50-€17. **Credit** MC, V. **Map** p302 F3.

To tell the truth, we've hardly tried the Thai offerings at this Thai/Indonesian restaurant because Indonesian food in Berlin is so rare, and Good Time does it so well. The Indonesian *rijstafel* is excellent, the soup and the *rendang* (a beef dish) being particularly notable. German tastes are catered to with a wide range of noodle dishes. Service is wonderfully friendly. If you get a window seat, there's great people-watching opportunities to be had at this busy corner site.

Pan Asia

Rosenthaler Strasse 38 (279 0811/www.panasia.de).
S3, S5, S7, S9, S75 Hackescher Markt. **Open** 11am-
midnight daily. **Main courses** €5-€10. **No credit**
cards. Map p316/p302 F3.
A designer's dream hidden away in a *hinterhof* right
off busy Rosenthaler Strasse. The tall room at Pan
Asia is furnished with long tables and minimal
decor; video screens are attached in the oddest
places, and the toilets are easily the most avant-
garde in town. Oh, the food? A notch up from the
Asiapfanne at the normal German 'Chinese' greasy
spoon, maybe, but the sushi is rubbery, the noodle
dishes bland, the so-called kim-chi red sauerkraut
and the curries underseasoned. If you've had this
cuisine anywhere else, you'll be decidedly under-
whelmed, but given the location, it's unlikely anyone goes for the food.

Vietnamese

Monsieur Vuong

Alte Schönhauser Strasse 46 (3087 2643/
www.monsieurvuong.de). U2 Rosa-Luxemburg-
Platz. **Open** noon-midnight Mon-Sat; 4pm-midnight
Sun. **Main courses** €5-€9. **No credit cards.**
Map p316/p303 G3.
Given the phenomenal popularity of M Vuong's original tiny orange-painted noodle bar on nearby
Gippsstrasse, it was only a matter of time before larger premises were sought. They duly opened in late
2001. The colour scheme may have shifted to red,
and the dining space increased by a factor of six or
more, but the locals still come in their droves. And
the reason? Astonishingly toothsome, bitingly fresh
Vietnamese soups and noodles, served up with
charm. A couple of daily specials supplement a
handful of regular dishes. Once you've tried the
glass noodle salad, you'll understand why less is
more. Chic, cheap and cheery.

Prenzlauer Berg

German

Gugelhof

Knaackstrasse 37 (442 9229). U2 Senefelderplatz.
Open 10am-1am daily. **Main courses** €12-€18.
Credit AmEx, MC, V. **Map** p303 G2.
Yes, this is the place where Gerhard Schröder
took Bill Clinton. He probably took one look at
Bill and decided the former president would like
something filling, but with a touch of refinement –
and that's just what you get at this Alsatian
restaurant that pretty much pioneered the
Kollwitzplatz scene in the 1990s. The *choucroûte*
contains the best charcuterie in town, and the
backöfe (meat and potatoes with root vegetables)
uses superb riesling subtly to underpin its
simplicity. Reservations a must.

Offenbach-Stuben

Stubbenkammerstrasse 8 (445 8502). S4, S8,
S10 Prenzlauer Allee. **Open** 6pm-2am daily. **Main**
courses €10-€15. **No credit cards. Map** p303 G2.
An eccentric survivor from the old East Berlin, this
was a private (non-state-owned) restaurant catering
largely to the theatre crowd – and it has made the
transition gracefully. There's nothing fancy in the
kitchen, just classic German cuisine prepared with
top-notch ingredients and the sure skill that comes
from long practice. A fine Saxon wine list helps the
food down. The walls are covered with memorabilia relating to the French composer from which the
place takes its name. The waiters can be very odd
indeed, although they won't can-can.

Villa Groterjan

Milastrasse 2 (440 6755). U2, S8, S10 Schönhauser
Allee. **Open** noon-1am daily. **Main courses** €6-
€12. **No credit cards. Map** p303 G1.
The food here isn't really worthy of a rave: it's standard east Berlin fare, made palatable by the
kitchen's use of fresh ingredients. You'll also find
good soups, schnitzel, and of course *Eisbein*, plus
cheap bar snacks and a Thursday buffet. But the
place itself, tucked down a side street off
Schönhauser Allee, is an architectural gem: all Old
German architecture and vaulted ceilings. It was
once a brewery, then a cinema in the 1920s, then a
canteen for the DEFA film studio. Whether you're
in the huge dining hall, the beer garden, or merely
at the astonishing bar, it's a very special place.

Americas

Joy

Sredzkistrasse 30 (442 2578). U2 Eberswalder
Strasse. **Open** 4pm-2am daily. **Main courses** €4-
€9. **No credit cards. Map** p303 G2.
A typical Berlin 'American' restaurant, Joy has
a menu that's half faux-Mexican, its hamburger
patties are the same ones everyone else uses, and
there are the usual college-kid cocktails available.
What's good, though, are the blackboard specials,
the fried catfish, and, each November, an authentic
Thanksgiving dinner.

Chinese

Ostwind

Husemannstrasse 13 (441 5951). U2 Senefelderplatz.
Open 6pm-1am Mon-Sat; 10am-1am Sun. **Main**
courses €8-€18. **No credit cards. Map** p303 G2.
Good Chinese food is rare in Berlin, so Ostwind's
stabs at authenticity are welcome. True, some of it
is pretty bland, but such light dishes as dan-dan noodles sauced with spicy meat and bean sauce, make
a great lunch. Main courses are, by Chinese tradition, keyed to the seasons and change four times a
year. It's not all great, but choose carefully and you'll
be rewarded with superb country cooking.

Eat, Drink, Shop

French

Bistro Chez Maurice

Bötzowstrasse 39 (4280 4723). S4, S8, S10 Greifswalder Strasse. **Open** noon-midnight daily. **Main courses** €10-€16. **No credit cards. Map** p303 H2.

Maurice is gone, and so is the deli next door and the confusing 'menu and supplement' system that made for such chaos once upon a time. But at least the idea of serving solid, working class French fare – a complete rarity in Berlin – is intact. The working class vibe strays over to the wine list (solid but not elite) and, on occasion, to the patrons.

Imbiss/fast food

See also p234.

Konnopke's Imbiss

Under U-Bahn tracks, corner Danziger Strasse/ Schönhauser Allee (no phone). U2 Eberswalder Strasse. **Open** 5am-7pm Mon-Sat. **Main courses** €1.25-€3.50. **No credit cards. Map** p303 G1.

When the BSE scare hit Berlin, Chancellor Gerhardt Schröder headed straight for Konnopke's, ordered one of its justifiably famous Currywursts, and said: 'I eat what I want!' A brilliant political move: not only did he say something savvy, but he went to an east Berlin *Wurstbudde* that has been under the same family management since 1930, and he ordered the same thing as more than half its customers do. A quintessentially Berlin experience.

Safran

Knaackstrasse 14 (no phone). U2 Senefelderplatz. **Open** 11am-1am Mon-Fri, Sun; 11am-3am Sat. **No credit cards. Main courses** €2-€6. **Map** p303 G2.

'The best falafel in east Berlin,' the counterman says, and he's right, but it doesn't stop there: shredded chicken breast with herbs, almonds and pine nuts (also available in a pitta), stewed okra with aromatic rice, fish soup and many other daily specials.

Italian

Trattoria Lappeggi

Kollwitzstrasse 56 (442 6347). U2 Senefelderplatz. **Open** 10am-2am daily. **Main courses** €8-€16. **Credit** AmEx, MC, V. **Map** p303 G2.

It's hard to call somewhere that's only been around for a few years an 'institution', but that's the most accurate term for this eaterie, which has been adopted by locals as the place for meeting and eating. Part of its success, of course, is due to the well-prepared food, especially the pastas and salads. Part of it is down to the staff, who are friendly and welcoming. Part of it is the lovely shaded tables on the pavement in summer – one of Prenzlauer Berg's top people-watching locations. Another bonus is Lappeggi's child-friendliness, which goes down well with all the new parents who are changing the face of this part of town. All in all, a lovely venue.

Trattoria Paparazzi

Husemannstrasse 35 (440 7333). U2 Eberswalder Strasse. **Open** 6pm-1am daily. **Main courses** €8-€15. **No credit cards. Map** p303 G2.

Hiding behind a daft name and a fairly ordinary façade is one of Berlin's best Italian restaurants, with the awards to prove it. Cornerstone dishes are *malfatti* (pasta rolls seasoned with sage) and *strangolapretti* ('priest stranglers' of pasta, cheese and spinach with tiny slivers of ham), but pay attention to daily specials. The southern Italian waiters can seem a bit spaced-out. House wines are excellent, though there are few other choices. Booking essential.

Russian

Pasternak

Knaackstrasse 22-4 (441 3399). U2 Senefelderplatz. **Open** 10am-2am daily. **Main courses** €9-€18. **No credit cards. Map** p303 G2.

Book if you want to dine in this small bar and Russian restaurant on Prenzl'berg's most chic corner. It's usually crammed to the gunnels, which can be irritating as people constantly brush past you looking for places. Try for a table in the small back room. The staff also let buskers in to play, so avoid if you don't want to hear ancient Neil Young songs murdered. But the atmosphere is friendly and the food fine and filling. Kick off with the borscht or the ample fish plate, then broach the *pelmeni* or *vareniki* – Russian ravioli filled with either meat or potatoes – or the hearty beef stroganoff.

Thai

Bangkok

Prenzlauer Allee 46 (443 9405). U2 Eberswalder Strasse/tram 1. **Open** 11am-11pm daily. **Main courses** €4-€5. **No credit cards. Map** p303 G2.

This deservedly popular little Thai restaurant, with a loose beach-hut decor and pleasingly authentic dishes, is a firm local favourite. Informal, friendly and fun. Booking is recommended.

Mao Thai

Wörther Strasse 30 (441 9261). U2 Senefelderplatz. **Open** noon-11.30pm Mon-Thur, Sun; noon-midnight Fri, Sat. **Main courses** €10-€20. **Credit** AmEx, DC, MC, V. **Map** p303 G2.

Its gorgeous interior always packed, Mao Thai is perhaps not the most authentic Thai restaurant in town (it's more southern Chinese, if anything), but it's certainly one of the most popular. So much so that it has spun off two others: **Kamala Siam** is in a cellar on Oranienburger Strasse (a convenient lunchtime location); and **Tuans Hütte** is hidden by the railroad tracks near Alexanderplatz. Chicken served in a coconut is the signature dish, but everything is of a high quality, so look around.
Branches: Kamala Siam Oranienburger Strasse 69, Mitte (283 2797); **Tuans Hütte** Dircksenstrasse 40, Mitte (283 6940).

Friedrichshain

German

Umspannwerk Ost

Palisadenstrasse 48 (4280 9497). U5 Weberwiese.
Open 11am-late daily. **Main courses** €10-€20.
Credit AmEx, DC, MC, V. **No credit cards.**
Map p303 H3.

Formerly a transformer station, this amazing tiled hall built in 1900 proved high enough to have an open gallery for additional seating constructed within it. Instead of conserving the rough industrial charm of the building, the owners turned it into something elegant (dress up if you like, but nobody expects you to). The impressive show-kitchen is not separated from the dining area, so you can peek over to check whether the cook is working on your pasta. The menu is short, but well thought-out; it changes weekly, with a fuzzy focus on Mediterranean cuisine. Portion sizes seem dwarfed by the surroundings, however.

Kreuzberg

German/Austrian

Altes Zollhaus

Carl-Herz-Ufer 30 (692 3300). U1 Prinzenstrasse.
Open 6-11.30pm Tue-Sat. **Menu** €30-€50.
Credit AmEx, DC, MC, V. **Map** p307 G5.

It's hard to believe you aren't ensconced in a quiet, riverside inn when you dine at the Zollhaus – at least until you check the menu, which is rather more up-to-date than that of the average rustic hostelry. Brandenburg's organic farmers stop off here on their way to market. Given the portion sizes, the prices are pretty good. The wine list, highlighting the produce of German vineyards, is well stocked and well chosen. A lovely spot.

Austria

*Bergmannstrasse 30, on Marheineke Platz
(694 4440). U7 Gneisenaustrasse.* **Open** *Sept-May* 6pm-1am daily. *June-Aug* 7pm-1am daily.
Main courses €13.50-€17.50. **Credit** MC, V.
Map p306 F5.

With an awesome collection of deer antlers, and with the crack of old wooden floorboards under foot, this restaurant is the spitting image of an Austrian hunting lodge. The meat is organic, and there's a list of organic wines as well. From the Kapsreiter or Zipfer beer on tap to the famous, over-the-plateful schnitzel – not to forget the *obstler* (fruit brandy) as the finishing touch to a more than hearty meal – this place is well worth a visit. Outdoor seating under a pretty red-striped awning on a tree-lined square makes Austria a pleasant summer venue too. Book at weekends and always in the summer.

Country meets city at **Altes Zollhaus.**

timeout.com

The online guide to the world's greatest cities

Café Restaurant Jolesch

Muskauer Strasse 1 (612 3581). U1, U12
Schlesisches Tor. **Open** 10am-1am daily.
Main courses €5.20-€16. **No credit cards.**
Map p307 H4.

The question we always ask at Café Restaurant Jolesch is whether we really want to dine looking up at a portrait of a bunch of trendy types cutting up what might well be a live pig. But then the food comes and we concentrate on the plate, which, come to think of it, might well contain pig in need of cutting. A fine Austrian sensibility runs through the cuisine (and wine list). Vegetarians are well taken care of, with a couple of interesting choices. A number of lighter dishes also makes Jolesch a wise choice for lunch, as many in the locality have known for years.

Grossbeerenkeller

Grossbeerenstrasse 90 (251 3064). U1, U7,
U12 Möckernbrücke. **Open** 4pm-2am Mon-Fri;
6pm-2am Sat. **Main courses** €7-€16.
No credit cards. **Map** p306 F5.

In business since 1862, Grossbeerenkeller has been keeping Berlin's bar-bands from starvation for the past 30 years – which is what most locals think of when they hear the name. But before the racket starts you can get good home cooking of a solid Berlinisch bent, and the Hoppel-Poppel breakfast is a neighbourhood legend.

Henne

Leuschnerdamm 25 (614 7730). U1, U8
Kottbusser Tor. **Open** 7pm-1am Tue-Sun.
Main courses €7-€14. **No credit cards.**
Map p307 G4.

Only one thing on the menu here: half a roast chicken. What sets Henne apart from other *Imbisse* with chickens rotating in their windows is that its birds are organically raised, milk-roasted and, in short, the Platonic ideal of roast chicken. The only other decisions are whether to have cabbage or potato salad (we'd say cabbage) and which beer to wash it down with (try Bavarian Monchshof). Check the letter from JFK over the bar, regretting missing dinner here.

Markthalle

Pücklerstrasse 34 (617 5502). U1, U12
Görlitzer Bahnhof. **Open** 9am-2am Mon-Thur;
8am-4am Fri, Sat; 10am-2pm Sun.
Main courses €8-€14. **Credit** AmEx,
MC, V. **Map** p307 H4.

This unpretentious restaurant and bar, with chunky tables and wood-panelled walls, has become a Kreuzberg institution over the years. Breakfast is served until 5pm, salads from noon, and, in the evening, a selection of filling and reasonably priced meals – though their quality is nothing to get over-excited about. Afterwards pop into the basement Privat Club or stroll over the road for a drink in the Der Goldene Hahn (*see p151*). Good selection of grappa.

Imbiss/fast food

Fish & Chips

Yorckstrasse 15 (0173 867 0130). U6, U7
Mehringdamm. **Open** noon-1am daily. **Main**
courses €4-€6. **No credit cards.** **Map** p306 E5.

Alarmingly authentic British chippy, serving battered fish – cod, red perch, rock salmon, plaice – with yummy chips doused with Sarson's malt vinegar or a variety of sauces, including the very German Remouladen sauce. Mushy peas, French fish soup and a good selection of bottled Irish beer make this place a funny mix, but prices are low so no one complains. The Union Jack flag painted across the front makes it hard to miss. Seating outside in the summer, and also a great place to pick up a late-night six pack.

Kulinarische Delikatessen

Oppelner Strasse 4 (618 6758). U1, U12 Schlesisches
Tor. **Open** 8am-2am daily. **Main courses** €2-€3.
No credit cards. **Map** p307 H5.

Why do Berliners eat such bad Turkish food? Probably because they know deep in their hearts that some day they'll come upon a place like this, where the same old leaden selections are transmuted into gold. The döners aren't bad, but it's the vegetarian offerings that make the place really special. Try an aubergine-falafel combo kebab, a zucchini kebab or even one of the salads.

Italian

Gorgonzola Club

Dresdener Strasse 121 (615 6473). U1, U8, U12
Kottbusser Tor. **Open** 6pm-midnight Mon-Thur,
Sun; 6pm-2am Fri, Sat. **Main courses** €7-€14.
No credit cards. **Map** p307 G4.

Popular place with a very simple Italian menu. The authentic pizzas are well priced; spaghetti, linguini, gnocchi and ravioli are served with a choice of basic sauces, including, of course, gorgonzola. The walnut-gorgonzola dressing on the salads is excellent. The rush hour between films at the English-language cinema Babylon (*see p196*) down the street gives this trattoria the air of a theatre district restaurant.

Osteria No 1

Kreuzbergstrasse 71 (786 9162). U6, U77
Mehringdamm or U6 Platz der Luftbrücke.
Open noon-1am daily. **Main courses** €12-€20.
Credit AmEx, DC, MC, V. **Map** p306 F5.

Most of Berlin's best Italian chefs paid their dues as waiting staff at this 1977-founded establishment, learning their lessons from a family of restaurateurs from Lecce, Italy's Florence of the south. Osteria is run by Fabio Angilè, the nephew of the owner of Sale e Tabacchi. The daily changing menu surprises even the many regulars who love taking advantage of the three-course lunch menu. In the summer, one of Berlin's loveliest garden courtyards welcomes you. Staff are super-friendly. Booking recommended.

Eat, Drink, Shop

Abendmahl – fine veggie dining. *See p135.*

Ristorante Chamisso
Willibald-Alexis-Strasse 25 (691 5642).
U6 Platz der Luftbrücke. **Open** 6pm-midnight Tue-
Sun. **Main courses** €7-€12. **Credit** DC, MC, V.
Map p306 F5.
This excellent and charming neighbourhood
Italian joint is located by picturesque Chamisso-
platz – a wonderfully quiet and leafy spot to sit
outside in summer – and offers daily menus of
fresh pastas, inventive salads and other authentic
Italian dishes.

Sale e Tabacchi
Kochstrasse 18 (252 1155/2529 5003). U6
Kochstrasse. **Open** 9am-2am Mon-Fri; 10am-2am
Sat, Sun. **Main courses** €7-€13. **Credit** MC, V.
Map p306 F4.
Located close to Checkpoint Charlie, Sale e Tabacchi
serves the best food to be had anywhere in the
vicinity of the recently opened Jewish Museum.
Architects, journalists, politicians (and film
stars during the Berlinale film festival) fill the long
hall and back room with their VIP chatter. The
café up front keeps the quiet lingerers happy too.
The restaurant is well known for fish dishes –
tuna and swordfish carpaccio, *loup de mer* – and
for the very pretty zucchini flowers filled with
ricotta and mint, and, of course, for its large
variety of Italian wines. The interior design is
meant to reflect the time when salt (*sale*) and tobacco (*tabacchi*) were sold exclusively by the state.

In summer, the garden is a wonderful place in which
to enjoy a leisurely lunch or dinner under lemon,
orange and pomegranate trees.

Trattoria da Enzo
Grossbeerenstrasse 60 (785 8372).
U6, U7 Mehringdamm. **Open** 6pm-1am daily.
Main courses €7-€13. **No credit cards.**
Map p306 F5.
A bustling little place that serves up authentic piz-
zas and recommended pasta dishes as well as com-
mendable meat, chicken and a decent antipasti
selection. You can wash it all down with a philan-
thropically priced Salentino.

Sri Lankan

Chandra Kumari
Gneisenaustrasse 4 (694 3056). U6, U7
Mehringdamm. **Open** noon-1am daily. **Main**
courses €6-€45. **No credit cards. Map** p306 F5.
Authentic Sri Lankan food is to be had at both these
restaurants. Dishes include fiery curries, many
involving exotic vegetables such as jackfruit; others
feature organic Neuland meat. Try the hoppers
('string' hoppers – like pasta – and 'milk' hoppers –
similar to crêpes – are served on alternate days of
the week) instead of rice, and cool down afterwards
with an avocado milkshake.
Branch: Suriya Kanthi, Knaackstrasse 4, Prenzlauer
Berg (442 5301).

Thai

Pagoda
Bergmannstrasse 88 (691 2640). U7
Gneisenaustrasse. **Open** noon-midnight daily.
Main courses €11-€18. **No credit cards.**
Map p306 F5.
You can spy a gaggle of Thai ladies whipping up
your meal behind the counter here and see that
everything is fresh and authentic. Red curries and
green curries are sensational and the pad Thai is
heavenly. If the place looks too crowded when you
go in, don't worry: there's extra seating in the basement where you can watch the residents of a huge
fish tank glide by.

Turkish

Hasir
Adalbertstrasse 10 (614 2373/www.hasir.de).
U1, U8 Kottbusser Tor. **Open** 24hrs daily.
Main courses €6-€11. **No credit cards.**
Map p307 G4.
All hail the mother church of the döner kebab! You
thought the Turks had been chewing on this tasty
sandwich-like item for ages? Sorry: it was invented
here in Germany in 1971 by Mehmet Aygun, who
eventually opened this highly successful chain of
Turkish restaurants. While you'll get one of the very
best döners in Berlin here, you owe it to yourself to

check out the rest of the menu, which involves various other skewered meats with sauces, and some agreeably addictive bread rolls. Desserts too are winners, especially the rice pudding.
Branches: Nürnberger Strasse 46, Wilmersdorf (217 7774); Breite Strasse 43, Spandau (353 04792); Maasenstrasse 10, Schöneberg (215 6060); Oranienburger Strasse 4, Mitte (280 41616).

Merhaba
Hasenheide 39 (692 1713). U7 Südstern or U7, U8 Hermannplatz. **Open** noon-1am daily.
Main courses €7-€14. **Credit** AmEx, DC, MC, V.
Map p307 G5.
A Turkish hotspot heavy on authentic wines and good traditional food. Ignore the main courses and share a selection of spicy appetisers instead. Effusive service but uninspiring decor of mirrors and chrome.

Vegetarian

Abendmahl
Muskauer Strasse 9 (612 5170). U1 Görlitzer Bahnhof. **Open** 6pm-1am daily.
Main courses €8-€16. **No credit cards**.
Map p307 H4.
No matter whether you translate the name as 'evening meal', 'last supper' or 'communion', this is Berlin's temple of vegetarian gastronomy (although there's also fish on the menu). Dishes change with the seasons. The weird and wonderful names with which they're christened form part of Abendmahl's offbeat charm: I Shot Andy Warhol for dessert anyone? The Flammendes Inferno (a Thai fish curry) isn't exactly flaming, but there are great things done with *seitan* here, and the creativity is at a very high level throughout. Booking is advisable.

Schöneberg

German/Austrian

Café Einstein
Kurfürstenstrasse 58 (261 5096). U2 Kurfürstenstrasse. **Open** 9am-2am daily.
Main courses €9-€20. **Credit** AmEx, DC, V.
Map p305 D4.
Red leather banquettes, parquet flooring and the crack of wooden chairs all contribute to the old Viennese Café Einstein experience. The other branches in town have less charm than the original (as with most franchises). Fine Austrian cooking is produced alongside several nouveau cuisine specialities. Alternatively, you could simply order *Apfelstrudel* and coffee and soak up the atmosphere of this elegant villa built in 1878. *See also p155.*
Branch: Unter den Linden 42, Mitte (204 3632).

Rockendorfs Restaurant
Passauer Strasse 5-7 (402 3099/www.rockendorfs.de). U1, U2, U12, U15 Wittenbergplatz. **Open** noon-2pm, 7-10pm daily. *Bistro* noon-10pm daily. **Main courses** €9-€17; *bistro* €4-€6. **Credit** AmEx, DC, MC, V.
Map p305 D4.
Siegfried Rockendorf shut up his previous restaurant in Berlin's northern suburbs and reopened here in 2000, but he continues to create the sort of magnificent Franco-German cuisine that has earned him two Michelin stars. With almost 40 years of experience as a chef, there's no more assured hand in a Berlin kitchen today. If you can't stretch to the gourmet restaurant, the bistro next door offers refined versions of Berlin-Brandenburg cuisine – *Königsberger Klopse* (meatballs) and *gefülltes Eisbein* (stuffed pig's trotters) – at slightly less ruinous prices.

Storch.
See p136.

Classy fusion food at **Shima**. *See p137.*

the Odeon cinema, it offers a long menu with many choices for vegetarians. The almond soup is excellent and the malay kofta delicious. There's a cheaper *Imbiss* attached.

Storch

Wartburgstrasse 54 (784 2059). U7 Eisenacher Strasse. **Open** 6pm-1am daily. **Main courses** €8-€15. **Credit** AmEx. **Map** p305 D5.
It's hard to recommend Storch too highly. The Alsatian food – one soup starter, a sausage and sauerkraut platter, plus varying meat and fish dishes from the place where German and French cuisines rub shoulders – is finely prepared and generously proportioned. House speciality is *tarte flambée*: a crispy pastry base cooked in a special oven and topped with either a combination of cheese, onion and bacon or (as a dessert) with apple, cinnamon and flaming Calvados. The cosmopolitan front-of-house staff are among the best and nicest crews in Berlin. Long wooden tables are shared by different parties and the atmosphere nearly always buzzes. Booking essential; no reservations accepted for after 8pm.

Indian

India Haus

Feurigstrasse 38/corner Dominicusstrasse (781 2546). S4, U4 Innsbrucker Platz. **Open** 5pm-midnight Mon-Fri; noon-1am Sat, Sun. **Main courses** €7-€15. **Credit** AmEx, DC, V. **Map** p305 D6.
Though more and more places are opening, Berlin is not a great town for Indian food and most venues seem to have the same menu. India Haus is a cut above. Just off Schöneberg's Hauptstrasse and near

Italian

Café Aroma

Hochkirchstrasse 8 (782 5821). S1, S2, S25, S26, U7 Yorckstrasse. **Open** 6pm-1am Mon-Fri; noon-midnight Sat; 11am-midnight Sun. **Main courses** €12-€15. **No credit cards. Map** p306 E5.
A temple of Tuscanophilia, Café Aroma has informal language classes on Sunday mornings, a wide selection of Italian magazines to read, and, oh yes, some of the best northern Italian food in Berlin. Appetisers and pastas are so good you may never stray over to the *secondi* (where all the meat is organic). The wine list – including a wide variety of wines by the glass – matches the standard set by the food. Aroma fills up quickly, so booking is advised.

Petite Europe

Langenscheidtstrasse 1 (781 2964). U7 Kleistpark. **Open** 5pm-1am daily. **Main courses** €7-€13. **Credit** MC, V. **Map** p306 E5.
You may have to queue for a table in this highly popular, friendly place, but the turnover's fast. The weekly specials are first-rate, as are the fine pasta dishes. None of this is haute cuisine, but it's well made and inexpensive. Salads could be better, but the wine list is very interesting, and so is the crowd.

Trattoria á Muntagnola

Fuggerstrasse 27 (211 6642). U4 Viktoria-Luise-Platz. **Open** 5pm-1am daily. **Main courses** €8-€15. **Credit** AmEx, MC, V. **Map** p305 D5.
This small chain of restaurants is run by Berlin's first family of southern Italian food. Muntagnola is the flagship, **Contadino** the eastern branch and **La Rustica** the pizzeria. All feature huge portions, an authenticity rare in Berlin, own-baked sourdough bread, rustic china and a superb wine list. The two larger places require reservations as they're jammed nightly with diners enjoying perfectly cooked pastas and *secondi*. La Rustica's pizzas may be twice as expensive as those at other pizzerias, but they're twice as good. It also has a blackboard listing a couple of non-pizza choices, and is one of Mitte's best lunch bargains.
Branches: Al Contadino Sotto Le Stelle Auguststrasse 34, Mitte (281 9023); **La Rustica** Kleine Präsidentenstrasse 4, Mitte (218 9179).

Middle Eastern

Habibi

Goltzstrasse 24 (215 3332). U1, U2, U4, U12 Nollendorfplatz. **Open** 11am-3am Mon-Fri, Sun; 11am-5am Sat. **Main courses** €4-€11. **No credit cards. Map** p305 D5.
Freshly made Middle Eastern specialities including falafel, kibbeh, tabouleh and various combination

plates. Wash it down with freshly squeezed orange or carrot juice, and finish up with a complimentary tea and one of the wonderful pastries. The premises are light, bright and well run. Everything is excellently presented and served with a flourish. The Winterfeldtplatz branch can get very full.
Branches: Akazienstrasse 9, Schöneberg (787 4428); Körtestrasse 35, Kreuzberg (692 2401); Oranienstrasse 30, Kreuzberg (6165 8346).

Pacific Rim

Shima
Schwäbische Strasse 5 (211 1990). U7 Eisenacher Strasse. **Open** 6pm-2am daily. **Main courses** €12-€20. **Credit** MC, V. **Map** p305 D5.
An innovative 'Asian fusion' menu originally conceived by the Canadian 'food designer' Gordon W has been drawing diners to this quiet Schöneberg corner since Shima first opened in 1999. Gado gado, dim sum and satay mingle on a menu that also offers chapatis, various noodle dishes and outstanding soups. There's a neat cocktail lounge area to complement a dining space that expands in summer to include pavement tables. Service is cool and efficient, though sometimes the kitchen can take its time.

Turkish

Çardak
Eisenacher Strasse 54 (782 7172). U7 Eisenacher Strasse. **Open** noon-midnight Tue-Thur; 4pm-3am Fri, Sat; 10am-midnight Sun. **Main courses** €4.50-€15. **No credit cards. Map** p305 D5.
After a cheap Monday night English-language film at the Odeon, a bowl of hot and spicy *Linsensuppe* (lentil soup) with fresh baked bread might put the circulation back into your winter-chilled bones. Feta-filled pastry sticks with salad and the *köfte* (meatballs) with a curry mustard sauce are just as good – and cheap. The straw mat ceiling plays off the Turkish name of this small restaurant, whose popularity with successful Turkish 20-somethings more than easily funded a recent renovation and expansion. Live music (9pm-3am Fri-Sat) and youngsters lounging on the divans in the back of the restaurant singing along to Turkish folk tunes make Çardak an oasis of colour and warmth.

Vegetarian

Hakuin
Martin-Luther-Strasse 1 (218 2027). U1, U2, U12, U15 Wittenbergplatz. **Open** 5-11.30pm Tue-Sat; noon-11.30pm Sun. **Main courses** €7.50-€14. **Credit** DC, MC, V. **Map** p305 D5.
Excellent but expensive Buddhist vegetarian food. In the beautiful main room people eat quietly amid a jungle of plants and a large fish pool with a gentle fountain. Fruit curries are often served on bamboo serving plates, in tune with the decor.

Tiergarten

German

Tiergarten Quelle
Stadtbahnbogen 482, Bachstrasse, near Haydnstrasse (392 7615). S3, S5, S7, S9 Tiergarten. **Open** 4pm-midnight Mon-Fri; noon-1am Sat, Sun. **Main courses** €7-€13. **No credit cards. Map** p301 D3.
Students jam this funky bar for huge servings of the food Grandma used to make: pork medallions with tomatoes and melted cheese with *Käsespätzle*; mixed grill with sauerkraut; *Maultaschen* on spinach. To drink, there are stone *steins* of foaming Schultheiss beer. The *Kaiserschmarren* is a meal in itself.

Americas

Café Nola
Dortmunder Strasse 9 (399 6969/www.nola.de). U9 Hansaplatz. **Open** 4pm-1am Mon-Sat; 10am-1am Sun. **Main courses** €4-€13. **Credit** AmEx, MC, V. **Map** p301 D3.
'Californian Cuisine und Cocktail Lounge' the sign says, and that's about three-quarters true. The cocktails are big and extremely popular in this out-of-the-way Moabit institution, but the Californian cooking has been scaled back. The chefs still use exotic fruit and chillies in some dishes (such as their signature chilli mango chicken salad), but the chicken wings and fajitas that most 'American' restaurants feature are getting the upper hand. Many immigrants from Bonn seem to have discovered the place (never a good sign) and the service can be excruciatingly slow. Still, pick your meal and your wine (from an excellent list) wisely, and you can do well here. Magician on Sundays.

Imbiss/fast food

Spätzle
S-Bahnbogen 390, Lüneberger Strasse (no phone). S3, S5, S7, S9 Bellevue. **Open** 9am-8pm Mon-Sat; 11am-8pm Sun. **No credit cards. Map** p301 D3.
A lovely little place serving the pastas of Swabia, including *Spätzle* (with Bratwurst, lentils or meatballs), *Käsespätzle* (with cheese), *Maultaschen* (like giant ravioli) and *Schupfnudeln* (a cross between pasta and chips), accompanied by a dark Berg beer.

Portuguese

Casa Portuguesa
Helmholtzstrasse 15 (393 5506). U9 Turmstrasse. **Open** 6pm-1am daily. **Main courses** €10-€20. **No credit cards. Map** p301 D3.
For years, this is the best place in Berlin for a simple vinho verde, a crisp salad and – above all – a freshly grilled Mediterranean fish, chosen from a list of daily specials and cooked to simple perfection.

Eat, Drink, Shop

Charlottenburg & Wilmersdorf

German/Austrian/Swiss

Alt-Luxemburg
Windscheldstrasse 31 (323 8730). U2 Sophie-Charlotte-Platz. **Open** 5pm-midnight Mon-Sat. **Main courses** €10-€18. **Credit** AmEx, DC, V. **Map** p304 B4.
Karl Wannemacher combines classic French flavours with Asian influences in a wonderfully romantic dining room. Sample such wonders as horseradish terrine with smoked eel, or monkfish with a succulent saffron sauce informed with tomato. But this pretty little restaurant's wine list could do with more moderately priced bottles.

Bamberger Reiter
Regensburger Strasse 7 (218 4282/bistro 213 6733). U4 Viktoria-Luise-Platz. **Open** 6pm-1am Tue-Sun. **Main courses** €15-€18.50. **Credit** *Restaurant* AmEx, DC, V (no credit cards in bistro). **Map** p305 D5.
This romantic and subdued, country-elegant restaurant is run by Franz and Anja Raneburger. Enjoy tender monkfish or flounder, succulent Bresse pigeon or foie gras served with plums in balsamic vinegar and a sprinkling of delicate beans. The cellar does a fine turn in Austrian wines, the cheeseboard is impeccable and the service fresh and youthful. Next door, the bistro serves similar, slightly less polished food at lower prices.

Bovril
Kurfürstendamm 184 (881 8461). U7 Adenauerplatz. **Open** 11am-2am Mon-Sat. **Main courses** €13-€21. **Credit** AmEx, V. **Map** p304 B5.
The ladies who lunch do so here. This venerable Berlin institution is still going strong despite the decline of the Ku'damm, simply because the French-German fusion it pioneered eons ago is still in favour. Three generations of well-heeled Berliners count on it. Book days in advance for lunch, but you might get lucky as a dinnertime walk-in. Whichever meal you choose, start with one of the soups, which have set the standard in a town that loves the stuff.

First Floor
Hotel Palace, Budapester Strasse 38 (2502 1020). S3, S5, S7, S9, S75, U2, U9, U12 Zoologischer Garten. **Open** noon-2.30pm, 6-10.30pm Mon-Fri; 6pm-midnight Sat. **Menus** €66.50-€100. **Credit** AmEx, DC, MC, V. **Map** p305 D4.
Now under the sway of hot young chef Mathias Bucholz, First Floor is the place to come for refined French/European cuisine of the highest order. Try, for example, Bresse pigeon served with chanterelles and a ragout of potatoes, or venison richly stuffed with foie gras – to say nothing of his *loup de mer* and Breton lobster served with saffron and tomato

confit. Three menus are offered daily. The frozen Grand Marnier soufflé is as honourable as the unobtrusive service. Don't let the fact this is a hotel dining room in the unappealing Europa-Center put you off; it's one of Berlin's top tables.

Florian
Grolmanstrasse 52 (313 9184). S3, S5, S7, S9, S75 Savignyplatz. **Open** 6pm-3am daily. **Main courses** €8.50-€15. **No credit cards**. **Map** p305 C4.
Florian has anchored this quietly posh street for a couple of decades now. The two sisters who started the place knew what they were doing: offering fine south German food to the neighbourhood. The fact that the neighbourhood is filled with Berlin's media types, particularly theatre and film people, didn't hurt, of course. The cooking is hearty, the service impeccable. Yes, staff will put you in Siberia if they don't like your looks, but they'll also welcome you back if you're good.

Heinrich
Sophie-Charlotten-Strasse 88 (321 6517). U2 Sophie-Charlotte-Platz. **Open** 4pm-midnight daily. **Main courses** €10-€20. **Credit** AmEx, MC, V. **Map** p304 B4.
Named after satirist and illustrator Heinrich Zille, who used to live at this address, this is the only place in Berlin where you'll find horse ragout on the same menu as buckwheat pancakes. A wide spread of vegetarian options rubs shoulders with traditional German standbys, and original wooden fittings are interspersed with Zille's photos of the area at the turn of the century. Service is courteous and unhurried, the wine list is long, the cheese soup and dandelion salads are particularly good.

Marjellchen
Mommsenstrasse 9 (883 2676). S3, S5, S7, S9, S75 Savignyplatz. **Open** 5pm-midnight Mon-Sat. **Main courses** €11-€20. **Credit** AmEx, DC, MC, V. **Map** p305 C4.
There aren't many places like this any more, serving specialities from East Prussia, Pomerania and Silesia in an atmosphere of old-fashioned *Gemütlichkeit*. There's a beautiful bar, service is great and the larger-than-life owner likes to recite poetry and sings sometimes too.

Americas

Hard Rock Café
Meinekestrasse 21 (884 620). U9, U15 Kurfürstendamm. **Open** noon-1am daily. **Main courses** €10-€20. **Credit** AmEx, MC, V. **Map** p305 C4.
It is with deep regret we announce that Berlin's best hamburger is to be found in this loud, pricey chain, yet it's true. The hamburger may be costly but it's a winner. The rest of the main courses are forgettable, but the onion rings and chicken wings also score for authenticity, and the desserts are a study in American overkill.

Sabu: the *papasan* of Berlin's Japanese restaurants. *See p142.*

Jimmy's Diner

*Pariser Strasse 41 (886 0607). U7
Hohenzollernplatz.* **Open** noon-2am Sun-Thur,
Sun; noon-4am Fri, Sat. **Main courses** €3-€10.
No credit cards. Map p305 C5.
The grand old man of American restaurants in
Berlin, Jimmy's has inspired a raft of inferior copies
with its scrupulously authentic decor, decent
hamburgers and big portions. It's a mecca for late-
night meals, despite the fluorescent lighting, and
can get pretty noisy.

Cambodian

Angkor Wat

*Seelingstrasse 36 (325 5994). U2 Sophie-Charlotte-
Platz.* **Open** 6-11.30pm Mon-Thur, Sun; noon-
11.30pm Fri, Sat. **Main courses** €9.50-€17.
No credit cards. Map p300 B3.
Extraordinarily friendly service and exotic decor
make this a good spot for dinner. Spicy
Cambodian food – think twice before asking for
extra hot. Try the cold ricepaper rolls stuffed
with shrimp or the beef with Asian aubergine and
coconut sauce.

Chinese

Tai Ji

*Uhlandstrasse 194 (313 2881). S3, S5, S7, S9, S75,
U2, U9, U12 Zoologischer Garten.* **Open** noon-
midnight daily. **Main courses** €8-€12.50.
Credit MC, V. **Map** p305 C4.
Chinese food in Berlin is legendarily bad, which is
why this quiet, classy 64-seat place is so welcome.
True, it's not cheap, but the menu, featuring seasonal
cuisine, is absolutely authentic, as is the preparation.

Half the Beijing-Sichuan offerings are vegetarian,
chefs make a point out of not using MSG, and there's
a gourmet selection of teas. Menus change weekly.

French

Paris Bar

*Kantstrasse 152 (313 8052). S3, S5, S7, S9, S75
Savignyplatz.* **Open** noon-2am daily. **Main courses**
€9-€15. **Credit** AmEx, MC, V. **Map** p305 C4.
Owner Michel Wurthle's friendship with Martin
Kippenberger and other artists is obvious by the art
hanging over every available inch of wall and ceiling space here. Paris Bar, with its old-salon appeal,
is one of Berlin's tried and true spots. It attracts a
crowd of rowdy regulars, but newcomers can feel left
out when seated in the rear. The food, to be honest,
isn't nearly as good as the staff pretend. The adjoining Bar du Paris Bar, which opened in May 2001, has
yet to gain that settled-in feel. To experience the often
rude service and pricey food, you'll need to book.

Imbiss/fast food

See also p234.

Fleischerei Bachhuber's bei Witty's

*Wittenbergplatz (no phone). U1, U2, U12, U15
Wittenbergplatz.* **Open** 11am-1am daily. **No credit
cards. Main courses** €2-€3. **Map** p305 D5.
Home to Berlin's best Currywurst? We won't touch
that question, but here are the facts: this friendly
place serves only Neuland organic meat, has stunning french fries with a variety of sauces, and
always has a queue (despite quick service) even
though it's directly across the street from the
KaDeWe and its food halls. You do the sums.

Indian

Surya

Grolmanstrasse 22 (312 9123). S3, S5, S7,
S9, S75 Savignyplatz. **Open** noon-11pm daily.
Main courses €6-€10. **No credit cards.**
Map p305 C4.

You've probably had these dishes before, but not cooked so well – at least, not in Berlin. That's probably why Surya is in its second decade on flashy Grolmanstrasse, while many ritzier places come and go. It's related to both the *Imbiss* across the street and the grocery store way down the block. With a little bit of encouragement, the chef will amp up the spice levels for you. Service is top-drawer.

Italian

Enoteca Il Calice

Walter-Benjamin-Platz 4 (324 2308).
U7 Adenauerplatz. **Open** 11am-1am daily.
Main courses €15-€20. **Credit** AmEx, MC, V.
Map p304 B5.

One for the oenophile – a relaxed place serving mostly Italian food conceived to complement its 40-page list of wines. Many bottles are listed with full and rather fruity descriptions; there's also a selection of rather complicated offers, including seasonal menus with recommended bottles, and the friendly staff will organise a *Weinkarusell* with four wines for your own private tasting. Carpaccio is a speciality.

Understanding the menu

USEFUL PHRASES

I'd like to reserve a table for... people.
Ich möchte eine Tisch für...
Personen reservieren.
Are these places free?
Sind diese Plätze frei?
The menu, please. **Die Speisekarte, bitte.**
I am a vegetarian. **Ich bin Vegetarier.**
I am a diabetic. **Ich bin Diabetiker.**
We'd/I'd like to order.
Wir möchten/Ich möchte bestellen.
We'd/I'd like to pay. **Bezahlen, bitte.**

BASICS

Frühstück breakfast
Mittagessen lunch
Abendessen dinner
Imbiss snack
Vorspeise appetiser
Hauptgericht main course
Nachspeise dessert
Brot/Brötchen bread/rolls
Butter butter
Ei/Eier egg/eggs
Spiegeleier fried eggs
Rühreier scrambled eggs
Käse cheese
Nudeln/Teigwaren noodles/pasta
Sosse sauce
Salz salt
Pfeffer pepper
gekocht boiled
gebraten fried/roasted
paniert breaded/battered

SOUPS (SUPPEN)

Bohnensuppe bean soup
Brühe broth
Erbsensuppe pea soup

Hühnersuppe chicken soup
klare Brühe mit Leberknödeln clear broth
with liver dumplings
Kraftbrühe clear meat broth
Linsensuppe lentil soup

MEAT, POULTRY AND GAME (FLEISCH, GEFLUGEL UND WILD)

Ente duck
Gans goose
Hackfleisch ground meat/mince
Hirsch venison
Huhn/Hühnerfleisch chicken
Hähnchen chicken (when served in
one piece)
Kaninchen rabbit
Kohlrouladen cabbage-rolls stuffed
with pork
Kotelett chop
Lamm lamb
Leber liver
Nieren kidneys
Rindfleisch beef
Sauerbraten marinated roast beef
Schinken ham
Schnitzel thinly pounded piece of meat,
usually breaded and sautéd
Schweinebraten roast pork
Schweinefleisch pork
Speck bacon
Truthahn turkey
Wachtel quail
Wurst sausage

FISH (FISCH)

Aal eel
Forelle trout
Garnelen prawns
Hummer lobster

XII Apostoli

Savigny-Passage, Bleibtreustrasse 49 (312 1433).
S3, S5, S7, S9, S75 Savignyplatz/N49. **Open** 24hrs
daily. **Main courses** €8.20-€17. **No credit cards.**
Map p305 C4.

It's overcrowded, it's cramped, it's pricey, the service varies from rushed to rude, the music is tedious
trad jazz doodling irritatingly at the edge of per-
ception – but the pizzas are excellent and, more to
the point, XII Apostoli is open 24 hours. There's a
superb choice of breakfast pastries too. The same
goes in all respects for the Mitte branch.
Branch: S-Bahnbogen 177-80, Georgenstrasse, Mitte
(201 0222); Frankfurter Allee 108, Friedrichshain
(2966 9123).

Japanese

Kuchi

Kantstrasse 30 (3150 7815/delivery service
3150 7816/www.kuchi.de). S3, S5, S7, S9, S75
Savignyplatz. **Open** noon-midnight Mon-Thur;
12.30pm-1am Fri-Sun. **Main courses** €10-€21.
No credit cards. Map p305 C4.

A new wave sushi bar that's a wild hit with Berlin's
fab crowd. Kuchi isn't for traditionalists, but is ideal
for diners interested in funky takes on Japanese specialities. Sure, you can get standard sashimi and
sushi, miso soup and yakitori (very good yakitori,
we might add). But don't miss such delicacies as 'My
best friend's roll' (an unlikely inside-out roll with

Kabeljau cod
Karpfen carp
Krabbe crab or shrimp
Lachs salmon
Makrele mackerel
Matjes/Hering raw herring
Miesmuscheln mussels
Schellfisch haddock
Scholle plaice
Seezunge sole
Thunfisch tuna
Tintenfisch squid
Venusmuscheln clams
Zander pike-perch

HERBS AND SPICES (KRAUTER UND GEWURZE)
Basilikum basil
Kümmel caraway
Mohn poppyseed
Nelken cloves
Origanum oregano
Petersilie parsley
Thymian thyme
Zimt cinnamon

VEGETABLES (GEMUSE)
Blumenkohl cauliflower
Bohnen beans
Bratkartoffeln fried potatoes
Brechbohnen green beans
Champignons/Pilze mushrooms
Erbsen green peas
Erdnüsse peanuts
grün Zwiebel spring onion
Gurke cucumber
Kartoffel potato
Knoblauch garlic
Knödel dumpling

Kohl cabbage
Kürbis pumpkin
Linsen lentils
Möhren carrots
Paprika peppers
Pommes chips
Rosenkohl Brussels sprouts
Rösti Swiss grated roast potatoes
rote Bete beetroot
Rotkohl red cabbage
Salat lettuce
Salzkartoffeln boiled potatoes
Sauerkraut shredded white cabbage
Spargel asparagus
Tomaten tomatoes
Zwiebeln onions

FRUIT (OBST)
Ananas pineapple
Apfel apple
Apfelsine orange
Birne pear
Erdbeeren strawberries
Heidelbeeren blueberries
Himbeeren raspberries
Kirsch cherry
Limette lime
Zitrone lemon

DRINKS (GETRANKE)
Bier beer
dunkles Bier/helles Bier dark beer/lager
Glühwein mulled wine
Kaffee coffee
Mineralwasser mineral water
Orangensaft orange juice
Saft juice
Tee tea
Wein wine

Eat, Drink, Shop

smoked salmon and vegetable tempura) and the spicy tuna roll, filled with a nicely seasoned toro tartare. Newcomers should try the Imperial plate, which is big enough for two to snack on. The Vietnamese and Chinese owners have fun with sauces too, though some are a bit sweet and sticky. Sit at the bar and watch the fish in the little aquarium. Next door you can pick up a takeaway.

Sabu
Pfalzburger Strasse 20 (863 94173/www.sabu-ro.de).
U1 Hohenzollernplatz. **Open** 5pm-midnight Tue-Sun.
Main courses €11-€21. **Credit** MC. **Map** p305 C5.
The demand for Japanese food isn't great in Berlin, but the quality of what's offered is high. Sabu, in business for over 15 years, is the shogun of the lot. Here you'll find absolutely fresh sushi (other sushi chefs come to sample it on their nights off), great grilled fish, and a fine *tonkatsu* (deep-fried pork cutlet). The little branch, Sabu-Ro, is every bit as good, with a lunchtime selection of bento lunch boxes. Sato-san, the boss, speaks good English.
Branch: Sabu-Ro, Damaschkestrasse 31, Charlottenburg (327 4488).

Sachiko Sushi
Grolmanstrasse 47 (313 2282). S3, S5, S7, S9, S75 Savignyplatz. **Open** noon-midnight daily. **Main courses** €12-€24. **No credit cards.** **Map** p305 C4.
Not just Berlin's best sushi bar, but its first kaiten sushi ('revolving sushi') joint. The scrummy morsels come round on little boats that circumnavigate a chrome and black stone bar. Sachiko is invariably packed with upmarket Charlottenburg 30- and 40-somethings, undoubtedly due to its location in the Savignypassagen.

Middle Eastern

Mesa
Paretzer Strasse 5 (822 5364). U1 Heidelberger Platz. **Open** 4pm-midnight daily. **Main courses** €8-€14. **Credit** AmEx, V. **Map** p305 C6.
A classy yet relaxing venue, Mesa creates neat variations of the Lebanese staples. There are many lamb and chicken dishes, couscous, and plenty for vegetarians – try the vegetable rösti that comes with three dipping sauces, and the spicy lentil soup. Egyptian cigarettes are sold.

Pacific Rim

Woolloomooloo
Röntgenstrasse 7 (3470 2777). U7 Richard-Wagner-Platz. **Open** 5pm-1am daily. **Main courses** €9-€20. **Credit** MC, V. **Map** p301 C3.
Long before BSE brought ostrich and kangaroo into German supermarkets, this Australian restaurant was serving them up as a matter of course, in various Pacific Rim-tinged dishes enhanced with coconut milk and exotic fruits. There's a superb choice of wines from Down Under, too, courtesy of Vineyard, Berlin's top importer from that part of the world.

Thai

Kien-du
Kaiser-Friedrich-Strasse 89 (341 1447).
U2, U7 Bismarckstrasse. **Open** 5pm-1am daily.
Main courses €10-€19. **No credit cards.**
Map p304 B4.
It still doesn't look much – lots of Buddhas and other South-east Asian paraphernalia – but Kien-du serves some of Berlin's best Thai curries. There's a huge variety of them too, and though the selection for vegetarians is fairly small, all the offerings are very good indeed. Try the beef, potatoes and peanuts in hot yellow sauce or the curried pineapple, bamboo and peppers. The staff are extremely flexible here, and happy to prepare things to your specifications.

Mahachai
Schlüterstrasse 30 (313 0879). S3, S5, S7, S9, S75 Savignyplatz. **Open** 5pm-1am Mon-Fri; noon-1am Sat, Sun. **Main courses** €10-€20. **Credit** MC, V. **Map** p305 C4.
This little jewel of a Thai eaterie may be hard on the S-Bahn tracks, but it retains a serenity inside that belies the location. The food is superb, with most of the usual Thai favourites on offer, but cooked with fresher than usual ingredients. Service is equally sterling.

Turkish

Hitit
Corner Danckelmannstrasse/Knobelsdorffstrasse (322 4557). U2 Sophie-Charlotte-Platz. **Open** 5pm-midnight Mon-Thur; 5pm-1am Fri, Sat; 11am-midnight Sun. **Main courses** €10-€15. **Credit** MC, V. **Map** p304 B4.
Completely different from most of the other Turkish restaurants in the city, Hitit serves excellent Anatolian/Turkish food in an elegant setting, complete with Hittite wall-reliefs, stylish high-backed chairs and pale walls. You can choose from more than 150 dishes listed, with plenty of options for vegetarians. The service is extremely friendly and the atmosphere is calm and soothing, embellished by the small waterfall running down the wall at the front of the restaurant.

Istanbul
Knesebeckstrasse 77 (883 2777). S3, S5, S7, S9, S75 Savignyplatz. **Open** 10am-midnight daily.
Main courses €5-€10. **Credit** AmEx, DC, MC, V.
Map p305 C4.
The oldest Turkish restaurant in Berlin serves well-cooked meals at relatively high prices. The menu is extensive, offering a wide selection of starters, meat and fish dishes: vegetarians can opt for a selection of hot and cold meze. From the street you can't see inside: open the door and you could almost be in the Turkish capital. The interior is dark and lavishly decorated with all manner of Islamic and Turkish paraphernalia.

Cafés, Bars & Pubs

Whether you're after brunch, lunch, *steins* or wines, Berlin boasts every conceivable type of snacking and boozing establishment.

Café Bar Morena: famed for breakfasts – just steer clear of the beans. *See p151.*

The pace of city life might be speeding up, but Berliners still find time to malinger over a coffee and savour a slab of cake. The café culture of the German capital is as lively, diverse and entrenched as that of any other central European city. These are the venues for Berlin breakfasts (*see p152* **The breakfast club**), light lunches with friends and colleagues, or spaces to spread out the daily papers – provided free for your perusal in most establishments – and laze around for an hour or two. Afternoon *Kaffee und Kuchen* – coffee and cakes – remains a widely observed ritual that cuts across all social classes, though the American way of coffee is beginning to mount a challenge.

In Berlin it's often a blurry line that separates the café from the bar. You can breakfast, lunch, snack, dine and then get horribly drunk all in the same place. The choice of poison used to be indicative of social stratum or state of mind – beer for the 'proles' and no-nonsense types, wine for the intellectuals, cocktails for the *jeunesse d'orée* and their aged

counterparts. Yet while Berlin still has *Kneipen* (pubs), wine restaurants and cocktail bars catering to those specialised crowds, most places offer a more or less balanced selection of all three. So it's generally possible to order a bottle of Beck's or draught Warsteiner, a glass of Rioja and an ever-popular caipirinha at the same joint – how's that for the dissolution of class boundaries?

Places that are primarily clubs or music venues are listed in the **Nightlife** chapter, *see pp225-34.*

Mitte

Mitte is everything it wants to be and more – just ask anyone who lives there. In the centre of unified Berlin there's no shortage of confidence or ostentation, but commercial utility and wanting it badly have brought more cultural representation than real life to the district.

Squatters in **Oranienburger Strasse** were the first to open cafés and initiate culture programmes after the Wall fell. As a thank you,

Eat, Drink, Shop

the city evicted most of them, often quite violently, and treated the eternal leisure mill that is the Oranienburger Strasse-Rosenthaler Strasse nexus as if it were a *tabula rasa* for their own cultural designs. Planners were so meticulous in their licensing agreements that in quiet moments acute visitors will hear the Oranienburger Strasse whispering stipulations for calming pastel walls and requisite ratios of Italian lamps per square metre of dining space.

That said, many of the cafés and bars look good and do fulfil their mandates of providing contemporary, in-the-know environments. In summer, Oranienburger Strasse proper is about 70 per cent tourists. Things calm down and become more tasteful as you move up **Auguststrasse**. The corner of Auguststrasse and Tucholskystrasse is a bustling area in the evenings.

Like Potsdamer Platz, **Hackescher Markt** promises everything and draws a lot of tourists. The restored buildings across from the S-Bahn station are indeed impressive, but their renovation coincided with the disappearance of the neighbourhood's most intense nightspots. Oxymoron (*see p227*) manages to pack crowds of cosmopolitan aspirants on weekends, as do various other identikit bars in the area.

Friedrichstrasse is the Champs-Élysées without a pulse, and should be avoided by anybody looking for a good time out.

See also p151 **Barcomi's**, *p226* **Bergwerk**, *p227* **Kurvenstar**, *p227* **Oxymoron** and *p229* **Zosch**.

Bar Lounge 808

Oranienburger Strasse 42-3 (2804 6727/ www.barlounge808.de) U6 Oranienburger Tor. **Open** 10am-3am daily. **Credit** AmEx, DC, MC, V. **Map** p316/p302 F3.
Latest venture by former 90° and Café Moskau impresario Bob Young who, like most people now setting up shop in this part of Mitte, seems to be betting on a lot of money flowing into the area and being spent on cocktails. Triangular front bar with gold columns and windows on to the corner with Auguststrasse; roomy back lounge with large aquarium, heavy drapes, chill-out sounds and lots of places to sit and chat.

Broker's Bierbörse

Schiffbauerdamm 8 (3087 2293). S1, S2, S3, S5, S7, S9, S25, S26, S75, U6 Friedrichstrasse. **Open** 8am-3am daily. **Credit** AmEx, MC, V. **Map** p316/p302 F3.
Mad little place where 'market forces' dictate beer prices, which rise and fall throughout the evening. One minute there's a run on Jever, the next everyone gets bullish about Beck's. Tends to get going after the nine-to-fivers come out to play, and can get so full in mid evening that there are queues outside. Breakfasts, snacks and sausages served.

Café Aedes East

Hof II, Hackesche Höfe, Rosenthaler Strasse 40-41 (285 8275). S3, S5, S7, S9, S75 Hackescher Markt. **Open** 10am-2am daily. **Credit** AmEx, MC, V. **Map** p316/p302 F3.
This small and stylish Hackesche Höfe café fills with insiders who know that the food here is better – and better-priced – than the expensive goodies on offer in the larger places in the first Hof. Aedes attracts a mixture of people from the nearby theatres, bars and offices, and thankfully fewer of the young western social climbers who otherwise haunt the Hackesche Höfe establishments.

Café Beth

Tucholskystrasse 40 (281 3135). S1, S2, S25, S26 Oranienburger Strasse. **Open** noon-8pm Mon-Thur, Sun. **No credit cards. Map** p316/p302 F3.
Meeting place for the Jewish community in a bistro atmosphere. American and British Jews may puzzle over what gets delivered when they order familiar kosher favourites, since the knishes and Gefüllte Fisch Amerikaner Art bear scant resemblance to what they get at home, but this café wing of the Congregation Adass Jisroel guarantees kashruth and everything is tasty and well made. Don't be put off by the gun-toting police in front of Berlin's Jewish-oriented businesses: they're friendly. Jazz accompanies Sunday brunches.

The golden glow of **Hackbarth's**. *See p145.*

The best Spots for al fresco imbibing

Café am Neuen See

Nestled lakeside in the Tiergarten park, not far from the zoo, this idyllic café belies its location near bustling Bahnhof Zoo. *See p155.*

Café Schönbrunn

GDR-chic restaurant-cum-lounge with outdoor seating near the Märchenbrunnen (Fairytale Fountain) in the Friedrichshain park. *See p148.*

Café Übersee

Pleasant spot for breakfast and/or afternoon coffee on the Kreuzberg shore of the Landwehrkanal. *See p151.*

Kastanie

Rustic beer garden, around the corner from Charlottenburg Castle (Schlossstrasse 22; 321 5034; U2 Sophie-Charlotte-Platz; noon-2am Mon-Sat, 11am-2am Sun).

Prater

Traditional Berlin beer garden also serving hearty Austro-German cuisine. Convenient place to cap off a theatre evening at the Volksbühne (*see p242*) offshoot or meet before clubbing at Bastard (*see p220*), both on the premises. *See p148.*

Verein der Visionäre

Exotic watering hole at the junction of Landwehrkanal and Spree. Open only in warm weather. *See p148.*

Wintergarten im Literaturhaus

Cultured garden wining and dining on a quiet side street off the fürstendamm. The Literaturhaus hosts readings, lectures and exhibitions, and a museum with sculptures and drawings by Käthe Kollwitz is nearby. *See p156.*

YAAM

Caribbean-style playground for kids and grown-ups alike, offering streetball and footbag for the athletic as well as food stalls, tropical drinks and sound systems blasting reggae, ragga, dancehall and dub. Check website for opening days and times (Eichenstrasse 4; no phone/www.yaam.de; S6, S8, S9, S10 Treptower Park or U1, U12 Schlesisches Tor; summer 2pm-late Sun).

Gorki Park

Weinbergsweg 25 (448 7286). U8 Rosenthaler Platz. **Open** 10am-2am daily. **No credit cards.** **Map** p302 F2.

Tiny Russian-run café with surprisingly tasty and authentic snacks – blini, pierogi and the like. Guests range from students and loafers to the occasional guitar-toting Ukrainian and scenesters having a quiet coffee before heading down to pose at more centrally located bars. Interesting weekend brunch buffet includes a selection of warm dishes.

Hackbarth's

Auguststrasse 49A (282 7706). U8 Weinmeisterstrasse. **Open** 9am-3am daily. *Breakfast* 9am-2pm. **No credit cards.** **Map** p316/p302 F3.

Popular spot for a leisurely breakfast among ex-squatters, art-world scenesters, and other long-time Scheunenviertel residents. By night, it's less a café than a busy local scene bar, where the large intruding V-shaped brass bar gives the place the feel of a landlocked ship. The golden light can be flattering even for the most pale, and facilitates the pick-up tendency of Berlin's late-night seekers of fun.

Ici

Auguststrasse 61 (no phone). U6 Oranienburger Tor. **Open** 3pm-3am daily. **No credit cards.** **Map** p316/p302 F3.

Featuring original painting and sculpture from local artists, a copy of Camus will help you feel at home among the self-consciously literary set that inhabits this quiet café. Good selection of wines by the glass.

Jarman

Bergstrasse 25 (280 473 78). U8 Rosenthaler Platz. **Open** 6pm-late Tue-Sun. **No credit cards.** **Map** p316/p302 F3.

Engaging, cultish bar removed from the passive, be-seen places south of Torstrasse, Jarman is subdued, intimate and unpredictable... as idiosyncratic as its artsy, Vienna-educated proprietor Daniel Jarman (the late film director Derek's cousin). The place is lined with his porcelain teapot and quirky figurine collection, with red glass balls dangling from the ceiling. Jarman stocks a hand-picked selection of tasty Austrian beers and unlabelled bottles of smoky whisky from his native Scotland. Occasional DJs, readings and special events, such as the Persian Buffet or the Robert Burns Night, with haggis on the menu.

Kapelle

Zionskirchplatz 22-4 (4434 1300). U8 Rosenthaler Platz. **Open** 9am-3am daily. **No credit cards.** **Map** p302 F2.

A comfortable, high-ceilinged café-bar across from Zionskirch, Kapelle is named after Die Rote Kapelle, 'The Red Orchestra', a clandestine anti-

Eat, Drink, Shop

Cocktail quaffing at **Schokoladen**.

fascist organisation. In the 1930s and 1940s the Kapelle's basement was a meeting place for the anti-Hitler resistance. The regularly changing menu features organic meat and vegetarian dishes, and proceeds are donated to local charities and social organisations.

Mitte Bar

Oranienburger Strasse 46 (283 3837).
U6 Oranienburger Tor. **Open** noon-late daily.
Admission €2 (Fri, Sat when DJ playing).
No credit cards. Map p316/p302 F3.
During the day locals involved with nightlife or students with a few hours' break will congregate for coffee or the first beer of the day. Later it fills with people just finished gawking at the tourist sights of Oranienburger Strasse. Still, at night the music is sometimes adventurous, the decor dark, and a back room is frequently occupied by a wide spectrum of DJs playing everything from trip hop to 1960s sleaze.

Odessa

Steinstrasse 16 (no phone). U8 Weinmeisterstrasse.
Open 7pm-2am daily. **No credit cards.**
Map p303 G3.
A beautiful minimalist bar that's unusually quiet for this part of town. Wooden tables in the small back room are complemented by a bar out front, behind which can usually be found the well-travelled proprietor from Lichtenstein. No music, nor room for many guests, and only a small but carefully chosen selection of drinks, but this is a welcome antidote to too much fake cool on nearby Rosenthaler Strasse.

Opern Café

Unter den Linden 5 (2026 8433/
www.opernpalais.de). U6 Französische Strasse.
Open 8am-midnight daily. **No credit cards.**
Map p316/p302 F3.
In the elaborately decorated palatial villa right next to the Staatsoper, this is a traditional coffee-stop for Berliners and music-loving visitors. Choose from a huge selection of beautifully displayed cakes. Excellent place to sit outside in summer and watch Unter den Linden go by.

Roberta

Zionskirchstrasse 7 (4405 5580). U8 Bernauer
Strasse. **Open** 6pm-late daily. **No credit cards.**
Map p302 F2.
All the elements seem to be here – high ceilings, apricot walls, civilised drink prices and turntables playing house, bigbeat, easy listening, funk, soul and other musics dear to the pleasantly mixed straight and gay crowd's heart. And yet there's something hip-bar-by-numbers about the place. Something's gotta give before Roberta replaces the older, DJ-less, but infinitely more enjoyable Kapelle (*see p145*) down Zionskirchstrasse in barcrawlers' affections. DJs most nights.

Schokoladen

Ackerstrasse 169-70 (282 6527). U8 Rosenthaler
Platz/bus N8. **Open** 8pm-late daily. **No credit**
cards. Map p302 F2.
This eastern scene stalwart, located in the former ZAR chocolate factory, is still going strong and never fails to amaze with its adventurous mix of theatre, poetry and music off the beaten track, both live and from turntables. Attracts a knowing, but not terminally hip, student and intellectual-artsy crowd with humane drink prices and a playful, yet down-to-earth atmosphere.

Strandbad Mitte

Kleine Hamburger Strasse 16 (283 6877). S1, S2,
S25, S26 Oranienburger Strasse. **Open** 9am-2am Mon-Sat; 10am-2am Sun. **No credit cards.**
Map p302 F3.
'Strandbad' is German for bathing beach, and this café adds a touch of seaside resort to this dead-end street off Auguststrasse. In summer, beach chairs strewn on the pavement in front of the entrance are great to sink in to – if you can get one. If not, try to get a seat on the divan inside to sip your *Milchcafé* or enjoy one of the hearty breakfasts served until 4pm.

Prenzlauer Berg

A centre of pre-war Jewish life and the one genuinely bohemian district in Communist East Berlin, Prenzlauer Berg has always taken its cultural status very seriously. Most of its *fin-de-siècle* buildings have been studiously renovated, and green-inclined yuppies have opened dozens of health-food shops. **Kollwitzplatz** is a delightful green square surrounded by scores of cafés and bars where young professionals court one another over gourmet food and cocktails.

In **Rykestrasse**, the local literati and green strategists discuss perennial political issues. The cafés near Helmholtzplatz (in the so-called 'LSD' neighbourhood, standing for the first letters of Lychener Strasse, Schliemannstrasse and Dunckerstrasse) are a bit further downmarket and somewhat more spontaneous than those in the vicinity of Kollwitzplatz and the Wasserturm, staying lively from 7-8pm until 2-3am. The Prater Biergarten in nearby Kastanienallee is a pleasant place for a Hefeweizen on warm summer evenings, and a fine starting point for interminable drinking tours down Kastanienallee and Oderberger Strasse.

See also p229 **Soda-Club.**

Akba

Sredkistrasse 64 (441 1463). U2 Eberswalder Strasse. **Open** 7pm-late daily. **No credit cards.** **Map** p303 G2.
In front is a quiet, terribly smoky café that can host an eclectic crowd, especially late at night. Through the back is the Akba Lounge, a mini-club devoted to a broad selection of music – featuring everything from cheesy 1960s *Schlager* to hip hop.

Café Anita Wronski

Knaackstrasse 26-8 (442 8483). U2 Senefelderplatz. **Open** 9am-2am Mon-Fri; 10am-2am Sat, Sun. **No credit cards.** **Map** p303 G2.
Friendly café on two levels with scrubbed floors, beige walls, hard-working staff and as many tables crammed into the space as the laws of physics allow. Excellent brunches, and plenty of other cafés on this stretch if there's no room here.

Café Maurer

Templiner Strasse 7 (4404 6077). U2 Senefelderplatz. **Open** noon-midnight Mon; noon-1am Tue-Fri; 10.30am-1am Sat; 10.30am-midnight Sun. **No credit cards.** **Map** p303 G2.
This new café looks a little too posh and unlived-in (big marble tables, high ceilings), but makes up for it with its clever location in a leafy square behind the Pfefferberg, an outgoing staff of anglophone Berliners, and a fantastically gooey selection of cakes and fine Genoese dishes. A growing daytime melting pot for recovering clubbers, people with kids and English-speaking locals and visitors.

Café November

Husemannstrasse 15 (442 8425). *U2 Eberswalder Strasse.* **Open** 10am-2am daily. *Breakfast* 10am-4pm daily. **No credit cards.** **Map** p303 G2.
Café November's a friendly place that's great at any time of the day, but it's especially nice during the day, when light floods into this bright, white café through show windows that also offer views of beautifully restored Husemannstrasse.

Cafe Torpedokäfer

Dunckerstrasse 69 (444 5763). U2 Eberswalder Strasse. **Open** 11am-late daily. **No credit cards.** **Map** p303 G2.
Cafés like this are rare in Prenzlauer Berg these days; not themed, anonymous but minimally stylish – and run by a relaxed collective. Many regulars have roots in the legendary Dunckerstrasse squat, making it a welcome decompression chamber after too much exposure to Prenzlauer Berg's growing gentrification. Drop in for a buffet breakfast on Sundays or after 10pm any night and contribute to the buzz of a café where a still-active political/literary journal has editorial meetings and readings.

Eckstein

Pappelallee 73 (441 9960). U2 Eberswalder Strasse. **Open** 9am-2am Mon-Thur, Sun; 9am-3am Fri, Sat. **No credit cards.** **Map** p303 G1.
This beautiful café, with its broad corner front and deco-ish look, draws one of the most mixed crowds outside of the Hackesche Höfe. But unlike many cafés around the Wasserturm or Rosenthaler Strasse, Eckstein maintains a following among the less-well-scrubbed residents of Prenzlauer Berg, adding a pleasingly old-school bohemian feel to a place otherwise clean enough for you to take your parents.

Hausbar

Rykestrasse 54 (4404 7606). U2 Senefelderplatz. **Open** 7pm-5am daily. **No credit cards.** **Map** p303 G2.
All bright red and gold, with a glorious cherub-filled sky on the ceiling, this small pocket of fabulousness seats about 15 people at a push. Hausbar is much more fun than all the wanky cafés with Russian literary names you'll find around the corner, and it's particularly inviting at three or four in the morning.

Lampion

Knaackstrasse 54 (442 6026). *U2 Eberswalder Strasse.* **Open** 6pm-3am Mon-Thur; 4pm-3am Fri-Sun. **No credit cards.** **Map** p303 G2.
This small and quiet bar has a distinguished bohemian pedigree and dozens of umbrellas hanging from the ceiling. Occasional puppet shows are put on in the small theatre at the back. Locals predominate, though tourists are tolerated if they're respectful.

Luxus

Belforter Strasse 18 (4434 1514). U2 Senefelder Platz. **Open** 8pm-late daily. **No credit cards.** **Map** p303 G2.

Killer cocktails served in a tiny bar a stone's throw from the Wasserturm but mercifully removed from that area's trendy bustle.

Nemo

Oderberger Strasse 46 (no phone). U2 Eberswalder Strasse. **Open** 6pm-3am Mon-Sat; 11am-3am Sun. **No credit cards.** **Map** p303 G2.

When the Wall came down, the owner of this former grocer's emigrated to Costa Rica, and it is his dreams of a warmer clime that inspired the cartoonish beach and cactus murals and the straw matting on the ceiling. A variety of cheap meals and snacks are served until late along with Mexican and Bavarian beers, there's an all-you-can-eat buffet on Sunday, and lots of games machines. If it's too crowded, you'll have no problem finding other cheap eats and drinks on a street now hosting a dozen other bars and restaurants.

Prater

Kastanienallee 7-9 (448 5688). U2 Eberswalder Strasse. **Open** *Summer* 6pm-2am Mon-Fri; 9am-2am Sat, Sun. *Winter* 6pm-2am Mon-Fri; 10am-2am Sat, Sun. **No credit cards.** **Map** p303 G2.

Almost any evening this huge and immaculately restored swing-era bar, across the courtyard from the theatre of the same name, attracts a smart, high-volume crowd – a good place to drag a large gathering and add to the conversational roar, although the Pils-swilling lustiness can make you feel you've been teleported to Munich. In summer the shady beer garden edged by the sweeping concrete forms of an old GDR sports facility makes for more of an all-day buzz. Weekend brunch is available from 10am to 4pm on Saturdays and Sundays.

Wohnzimmer

Lettestrasse 6 (445 5458). U2 Eberswalder Strasse. **Open** 10am-4am daily. **No credit cards.** **Map** p303 G1.

Days are rather slow at this shabbily elegant café. Visitors who make it past the poignantly drunken, would-be anarchists sunning in Helmholtzplatz will find, behind the door to this 'living room', a suspiciously bar-like structure made from an inspired ensemble of kitchen cabinets. Threadworn divans and artsy bargirls make this the perfect place to discuss Dostoevsky with career students over a tepid borscht. Evening light from candelabra reflects on gold-sprayed walls as students and maudlin poets chase brandies with Hefeweizen and bodily fluids.

Friedrichshain

In the downmarket eclecticism of its bars and cafés, Friedrichshain today is much like the Mitte or Prenzlauer Berg of the early 1990s. But working class, underdeveloped and not very central, the neighbourhood has neither Prenzlauer Berg's bohemian history nor Mitte's architectural flair.

The area around **Simon-Dach-Strasse** is full of fun bars, cheap cafés and ethnic restaurants. Recently, its orbit has been expanding towards Ostkreuz S-Bahn station (Sonntagstrasse), a neighbourhood previously dotted with down-at-heel *Kneipen* (pubs). The former socialist showcase boulevard **Karl-Marx-Allee** is also coming into its own as a nightlife hotspot.

Cheap rents have attracted students, and **Rigaer Strasse** and **Mainzer Strasse** were hubs of the squatter scene. Apart from proles, neo-fascists, part-time prostitutes and disgruntled pensioners, Friedrichshain is still home to radicals of many stripes and swaggers. Many of these people are unhappy these days, as modernisation has meant rising rents and crumbling social institutions. Locals may sneer at you if you wear flashy designer clothes or attempt to pay with credit cards.

See also p230 **Astro Bar.**

Café 100Wasser

Simon-Dach-Strasse 39 (2900 1356). U5 Samariterstrasse. **Open** 10am-late daily. **No credit cards.** **Map** p89.

The all-you-can-eat Sunday brunch buffet has a cult following among students and other late-risers. Take your time and don't panic as the buffet gets plundered. Just when the food seems to be finished, out comes loads of new stuff. Pleasant during the week too, but when crowded it can be hard to flag down a waiter.

Café Schönbrunn

Am Schwanenteich, Volkspark Friedrichshain (4202 8191). Bus 200. **Open** 11am-1am Mon-Fri; 10am-2am Sat, Sun. **No credit cards.** **Map** p303 H3.

Not for those afraid to take a walk in the park at night, but for everyone else it's a favoured hangout. A couple of years ago, this place by the lake sold coffee and *Würstchen* to an elderly crowd. With a change of management, the music and food quality improved dramatically. The unspectacular concrete front was left as it was, and the (new) lounge furniture is pure '70s. On a sunny afternoon, 60-plus park-goers take their first afternoon beer out on the terrace side by side with the in-scene crowed having breakfast. On your first visit come during the day – just to make sure you find it.

Conmux

Simon-Dach-Strasse 35 (291 3863). S3, S5, S6, S7, S9, S75, U1, U12 Warschauer Strasse. **Open** 9am-late daily. **No credit cards.** **Map** p89.

For those who love outdoor tables: here, even in winter there are seats outside on Simon-Dach-Strasse, and the waiters will light one of the gas heaters to warm you up. Inside there are sewing-machine tables and pieces of scrap-metal art. The menu offers a huge variety of well-priced light meals. Service is at best monosyllabic, at worst downright indifferent.

Cueva Buena Vista

Andreasstrasse 66 (2408 5951). S3, S5, S7, S9, S75 Ostbahnhof. **Open** 5pm-late Mon-Sat; 2pm-late Sun. **No credit cards. Map** p89.

'Buena vista' (literally meaning 'good view') is probably not a feature you would expect from a cave ('cueva'). Take it as a hint that the place is Cuban-run. The owner claims Ibrahim Ferrer to be some sort of uncle of his, and, indeed, before playing one of his Berlin gigs the old man came down here, grabbed a marker and wrote some greetings on the wall. Upstairs (on the ground level, that is) the cueva is a pub that offers cocktails and reasonably priced Caribbean food. The basement (which, in fact, is quite cave-like) hosts a salsoteca with live music at weekends. But don't expect them to play slowish stuff à la Buena Vista Social Club.

Dachkammer

Simon-Dach-Strasse 39 (296 1673). U5 Samariterstrasse. **Open** *Cocktail bar* 7pm-late daily. *Restaurant* noon-late Mon-Fri; 10am-late Sat, Sun. **No credit cards. Map** p89.

There's a pub/restaurant on the ground floor, but the interesting part is the upper-level cocktail bar. If you buy a beer downstairs staff won't let you take it upstairs, just to keep the atmosphere relaxed and loungey. Sounds odd, but you'll appreciate it as soon as you stretch out on one of the sofas. Youngish, casual crowd.

DeziBel

Scharnweberstrasse 54 (2900 3939). U5 Samariterstrasse. **Open** 4pm-late Mon-Sat; noon-late Sun. **No credit cards. Map** p89.

Co-owned by a South African and positioned away from the bar/nightlife circus that is Simon-Dach-Strasse, this is a pleasantly unspectacular pub that's become a hang-out for local anglophones. Irish beer, indie rock, occasional movies in the back room, plus DJs, open-mic nights and performances by drunk singer-songwriters. Sunday is 'family day', which means it's open from noon and smoking is *verboten*.

Ehrenburg

Karl-Marx-Allee 103 (4210 5810). U5 Weberwiese. **Open** 9am-late daily. **No credit cards. Map** p303 H3.

Named after the Russian-Jewish novelist Ilja Ehrenburg, a committed socialist, this newish café/espresso bar, with its sober, geometric decoration, is one of the few stylish places in the neighbourhood around Weberwiese U-Bahn station. Although the library looks like it's part of the decorative style, you're free to pick up a book and study the works of Ehrenburg, Lenin, Stalin, Engels or Marx as you enjoy a latte macchiato and other capitalist achievements.

Eckstein: a classic café. *See p147.*

Ex

Rigaer Strasse 25 (420 8744). U5 Samariterstrasse. **Open** 5.30pm-late daily. **No credit cards. Map** p89.

The pioneer purveyor of cocktails in the Rigaer Strasse area and still one of the best. Maybe its secret is stripping things down to basics: bare walls and spartan tables make it look like a simple pub rather than a fancy cocktail bar. And, in spite of the variety of drinks on offer, everyone just chooses the two or three frighteningly cheap daily specials.

Intimes

Boxhagener Strasse 107 (2966 6457). U5 Samariterstrasse. **Open** from 10am daily. **No credit cards. Map** p89.

Next door to the cinema of the same name, decorated with painted tiles and offering a good variety of Turkish and vegetarian food as well as breakfast at very reasonable prices. Pleasures can be as simple as fried potatoes with garlic sausage; best deal is the Wednesday special. Friendly service.

Supamolly

Jessnerstrasse 41 (2900 7294). S4, S8, S10, U5 Frankfurter Allee. **Open** 3pm-late daily. **No credit cards. Map** p89.

Having started life in the early 1990s as a semi-legal bolt-hole fronting a lively squat, Supamolly is a miracle of survival. It's still murky, candlelit and Mandela-muralled, still very cheap and still filled with all types and ages of a fuck-the-system persuasion – from dreadlocked commune-dwellers to ageing punks and tidy young eastern activists. In the best Berlin tradition, rebellion goes with an ethos of real tolerance – people are too focused on problems like fighting far-right groups to take much account of surface differences – but that said, leave the Armani coat at home. The bar's back door still gives on to the former squat, now venue for a laudably unfiltered stream of performances, from folk drumming to digital light shows.

Tagung
Wühlischstrasse 29 (292 8756).
U5 Samariterstrasse. **Open** 7pm-late daily.
No credit cards. Map p89.
Small bar decked out in GDR memorabilia and still serving things like Club Cola, the old Eastern brand. The patrons are 20- and 30-somethings and not at all bitter or sad. Instead, the place seems to provide good laughs and drunken nights for all. The Cube Club downstairs is likewise 'ostalgically' decorated and offers mainstream dance music and occasional one-off events and hosts readings by the 'Chaussee der Enthusiasten' literary circle.

Tilsiter Lichtspiele
Richard-Sorge-Strasse 28A (426 8129).
U5 Frankfurter Tor. **Open** 6pm-3am daily.
No credit cards. Map p89.
Situated in a quiet residential area off the well-known pub-mile, Tilsiter Lichtspiele is a relaxed hangout for locals. Beer is not expensive, the staff are friendly and some pub food is available. The vending machine by the entrance (the 'Tilsomat 2000') has a weird selection of things on offer, ranging from chocolate bars to bicycle dynamos and electric pocket fans. In the back room there's a full-size cinema, and, if you're lucky, you might even catch a subtitled English movie. Be quick to get a seat in the row with lots of foot space and tables to put your beer down.

Kreuzberg

West Berlin's former art and anarchy quarter is nowadays very quiet compared to the madness and mayhem of old – the artists have moved to Mitte, the anarchists to Friedrichshain. But enough ageing scenesters and alternative types have hung on to ensure that the atmosphere hasn't completely evaporated.

The **Bergmannstrasse** neighbourhood, though lively and enjoyable by day, is these days pretty somnolent after dark, with Haifisch providing the only really decent late-night option, though there are plenty of fading bars along Bergmannstrasse, and more still on **Gneisenaustrasse** and around **Südstern**.

The area around **Oranienstrasse** and **Wiener Strasse** offers a much better range of opportunities for partying and drinking, and remains one of the city's gay hubs. Even though it's not much more than a shadow of its former chaotic self, it's still possible to have fun in these parts.

Anker-Klause
Kottbusser Brücke/corner Maybachufer, Neukölln (693 5649). **U8** Schönleinstrasse. **Open** 4pm-late Mon; 10am-late Tue-Sun. **No credit cards.**
Map p307 G5.
Although looking over Kreuzberg's Landwehrkanal, the only thing nautical about this 'anchor retreat' is the midriff-tattooed, punk-meets-portside swank of the barstaff. A slammin' jukebox (rock, sleaze, beat),

Welcome to the wacky world of **Nemo**. *See p148.*

a weathery terrace and the best sandwich melts in Berlin offer ample excuse to dock here from afternoon until whenever they decide to close. Convivial during the week, packed at weekends.

Atlantic

Bergmannstrasse 100 (691 9292). U6, U7 Mehringdamm. **Open** 9am-2am daily. **Credit** V. **Map** p306 F5.

After installing both a new ventilation system and a new chef three years ago, things have picked up at this friendly café-restaurant. On the south side of the street, the pavement café thrives in the summer, and a beer as late as 8pm will still have you sitting in a ray of light, if you're lucky enough to get a table. Breakfast (Danish, Swiss, English, Norwegian, etc), including 11 different ways to have your eggs scrambled, is on hand until 5pm. There are daily lunch specials, and dinner is a cheap but decent affair. The waiting staff change every two days, as does the music – sometimes loud, and always of the Air-genre electronic ilk.

Barcomi's

Bergmannstrasse 21 (694 8138). U7 Gneisenaustrasse. **Open** 9am-midnight Mon-Sat; 10am-midnight Sun. **No credit cards**. **Map** p306 F5.

A former dancer who defected from America many years ago has had huge success with her coffee shop and bakery. Barcomi's is a great place for all things Stateside: drink your double cap latte with coffee from Zambia over a quick read of the *Herald Trib* or *New Yorker*. The own-baked bagels and variety of cream cheeses – horseradish-caper-dill or plain ol' sun-dried tomato or a lox bagel – make American expats feel right at home. The cookies, chocolate espresso cheesecake and pecan pie are to die for and can become a dangerous addiction. The fabulous salads will put you back in shape (even if in idea alone). A good wine and beer choice at the Mitte branch makes its hidden courtyard a treat after a round of galleries or a visit to the Sammlung Hoffmann just upstairs (*see p84*).
Branch: Sophienstrasse 21, Sophie-Gips-Höfe, 2 Hof, Mitte (2859 8363).

Café Adler

Friedrichstrasse 206 (251 8965). U6 Kochstrasse. **Open** 8.30am-midnight Mon-Sat; 10am-7pm Sun. **Map** p306 F4.

Next to what used to be Checkpoint Charlie, you could once watch history in the making from this elegant corner café. Today, it's a bustling, businesslike corner and Adler is a well-lit oasis of calm, coffee and decent light meals.

Café Bar Morena

Wiener Strasse 60 (611 4716). U1, U12 Görlitzer Bahnhof. **Open** 9am-5am daily. **No credit cards**. **Map** p307 H5.

Famous breakfasts are served to people who wake up at all hours. Make sure that you avoid the 'English Breakfast', though – it features a kind of

baked beans unknown to culinary science. In the evening the Café Bar Morena bustles, and the service can be rather slow. The music isn't overpowering and the half-tiled walls and parquet flooring give it an art deco feel.

Café Übersee

Paul-Lincke-Ufer 44 (618 8765). U1, U8, U12 Kottbusser Tor. **Open** 10am-2am daily. *Breakfast* 10am-4pm daily. **No credit cards**. **Map** p307 H5.

Vines cover the outside, where summer tables offer a popular spot for breakfast overlooking the Landwehrkanal. Nothing special inside, and if it's full, there are a couple of other places on this stretch.

Fressco

Zossener Strasse 24 (6940 1613). U7 Gneisenaustrasse. **Open** 10am-1am Mon-Fri; 5pm-1am Sat. **No credit cards**. **Map** p306 F5.

Bright and clean new addition to the cafés of the Bergmannstrasse neighbourhood. Good coffee and fresh, tasty food – snacks, light meals, salads, sandwiches and pastries – chosen not from a menu, but from the display case below the bar. Lots for vegetarians. Relaxing and roomy.
Branch: Stresemannstrasse 34, Kreuzberg (2529 9309).

Der Goldene Hahn

Pücklerstrasse 20 (618 8098). U1, U12 Görlitzer Bahnhof. **Open** 7pm-3am daily. **Credit** DC, V. **Map** p307 H4.

A small bar with unpretentious brick walls, old wooden fittings and lots of stuffed chickens, 'The Golden Cock' is relaxed and smart, and the barstaff DJ their own choice of vintage vinyl on a bartop turntable. Menu of light meals. Good spot for an intimate rendezvous.

Haifischbar

Arndtstrasse 25 (691 1352). U6, U7 Mehringdamm. **Open** 8pm-3am Tue-Thur, Sun; 8pm-5am Fri, Sat. **No credit cards**. **Map** p306 F5.

Well-run and friendly bar where the staff are expert cocktail-shakers, the music's always hip and tasteful in a laid-back trancey groove kind of way, and the back room, equipped with a sushi bar, is a good place to chill out at the end of an evening. Certainly the most happening place in the Bergmannstrasse neighbourhood, and with some kind of crowd any night of the week.

Konrad Tönz

Falckensteinstrasse 30 (612 3252). U1, U12 Schlesisches Tor. **Open** 8pm-late daily. **No credit cards**. **Map** p307 H5.

Named after a 1970s true crime show policeman, Konrad Tönz carries the TV detective theme to its logical extreme: beige geometrically patterned wallpaper and DJs spinning easy listening and beat faves on mono turntables. Not much room for dancing and you probably wouldn't want to anyway, lest you be sneered at by the stubbornly cool crowd. DJs from 9pm at weekends.

Eat, Drink, Shop

Madonna

Wiener Strasse 22 (611 6943). U1, U12 Görlitzer Bahnhof. **Open** 11am-3am daily. **No credit cards.** **Map** p307 H5.

With over a hundred whiskies and frescoes detailing a lascivious pageant of falling angels and clerical inebriation, this bar and café offers a friendly vantage on the debauched, counter-culture erudition of Kreuzberg 30-somethings who don't care if or where the government resides. Particularly interesting as neutral ground for subcultures that, until Berlin's modernisation frenzy gave them common cause, had differing opinions on the proper way to burn a car, squat a building or play a guitar.

Milagro

Bergmannstrasse 12 (692 2303). U7 Gneisaustrasse. **Open** 9am-1am Mon-Thur; 9am-2am Fri, Sat; 9am-1am Sun. **No credit cards.** **Map** p306 F5.

Light and friendly café, famous for its breakfasts, which are served until 4pm. There are also cheap but classy, tasty dishes being served until midnight. Disorienting stairs lead to hospital-like toilets. On a winter's afternoon, the front room can be too dim to read your daily paper.

Schnabelbar

Oranienstrasse 31 (615 8534). U1, U8, U12 Kottbusser Tor. **Open** 8pm-late daily. **No credit cards.** **Map** p307 G4.

Once an essential stop on any Oranienstrasse crawl, and still often open throughout the night, this well-known place is recognisable by the metal beak (*Schnabel*) that pokes out over the door. Inside there's a extensive bar and a diminutive dancefloor, over which DJs can be found spinning funk, reggae and rare groove most evenings. It's long past its prime, though.

Wiener Blut

Wiener Strasse 13 (618 9023). U1, U12 Görlitzer Bahnhof. **Open** 6pm-late daily. **No credit cards.** **Map** p307 H5.

This narrow, darkish bar is equipped with lazy booths and a well-abused table football table, Wiener Blut sometimes features DJs who pack the place with wild beats and wild friends and the occasional video show. Otherwise it's just another red bar. Tables out front in the summer are a good alternative to the overcrowded terrace of Morena (*see p151*) up the street.

The breakfast club

Breakfast probably is the most important meal of the day, but Germans take this as a mantra. People invite friends to breakfast, the way other cultures stage dinner parties: with smart crockery and elaborate preparation. Going out for breakfast is also the done thing, and is a handy meeting arrangement if your evenings are full. With its inexhaustible number of cafés, Berlin is the best city to test the mantra out.

Basic breakfasts are available in the week, but the cult kicks into action at the weekend, when you will find unlimited buffet brunches for about €8. These are usually served from 10am until late into the afternoon. If you've been on an all-nighter or are feeling plain lazy, go to **Vienna Art** (Grimmstrasse 1; 691 9178) after 3pm and eat for half the buffet price. Or forget sleeping and head straight for breakfast where it's available 24 hours a day, such as **Schwarzes Café** (*see p156*).

Brunches vary from the standard to the extravagant. All usually include cheeses, cold meats, smoked salmon, bread rolls, scrambled eggs, yoghurt, jam, cereals and fruit salad. A modest buffet for a bargain €3 can be had at **An Einem Sonntag in August** (Kastanienallee 103; 4405 1228).

Mediterranean cuisine is big in Berlin, so olives and mozzarella with pesto have all become common features of the German brunch landscape. Moving up the scale, buffets can include hot dishes, such as pasta and vegetable bakes. So if money's tight, have breakfast, linger around and indulge in some people-watching, then have a hot dinner all for one price. For a sumptuous brunch and excellent service, check out **Maccharoni** (Lychenerstrasse 41; 4473 3508).

Cafés that don't do buffets serve set breakfasts instead. Besides the Fitness-Frühstück – muesli for the health freaks – you can have a platter of various cheeses, or a mix of cheese, meats and an egg. Set breakfasts often take on national themes with no surprises. There are croissants and jam in the French; Parma ham and mozzarella in the Italian; smoked salmon in the Norwegian; and pancakes in the American. For a themed breakfast, try **Atlantic** (*see p151*). Many places have hooked on to the Great British Fry-up. But be warned: Germany is probably the only country where you'll find an English breakfast served with a salad garnish. If that's too bizarre, you'll find something more familiar at one of Berlin's many Irish pubs. Whatever form you choose, breakfast Berlin-style is the way to start the day.

Würgeengel

*Dresdener Strasse 122 (615 5560). U1, U8,
U12 Kottbusser Tor.* **Open** 7pm-late daily.
No credit cards. Map p307 G4.
Red walls and velvet upholstery convey an atmosphere aching for sin, while well-mixed cocktails and a fine wine list served by smartly dressed waiting staff make this a place for the more discerning drinker. The glass-latticed ceiling and a 1920s chandelier elegantly belie the fairly priced drinks and tapas on offer. Daily specials from the adjoining Gorgonzola Club (*see p133*) can also be ordered. Ideal in summer when a canopy of greenery curtains outdoor picnic tables.

Schöneberg

A smart, pleasantly gentrified borough where residents greet one another jovially in the streets and spend long afternoons reading the international papers over *Milchkaffee*. Civilised, tolerant and cosmopolitan, Schöneberg has several street festivals in the summer and loads of comfortable cafés and ethnic restaurants.
Motzstrasse and **Fuggerstrasse** are the hub of gay life in Berlin (*see p211*), with numerous bars for cruising and shops catering to all manner of fetishists. The more conventional **Winterfeldtplatz** is a delightful place for summer carousing and

Multi-purpose **Mutter**. *See p154.*

the bars on nearby Goltzstrasse fill in the evenings with trendy youth, architects and expats of varying ages and nationalities.
Many quirky little bars are nestled in the tree-lined streets around the **Eisenacher Strasse** U-Bahn, offering understated-yet-local colour until the wee hours. Less ostentatious than Mitte's drinkers, and less adventurous than those in Friedrichshain, Schönebergers tend to be monogamous with their bars and cafés, choosing a favourite and then committing.

Bilderbuch

Akazienstrasse 28 (7870 6057). U7 Eisenacher Strasse. **Open** 9am-1am Mon-Fri; 9am-2am Sat; 10am-1am Sun. **No credit cards. Map** p305 D5.
Cavernous book-lined labyrinth whose inner dimensions are a surprise after the modest storefront entrance. Vast spaces between the tables mean considerable room for discretion, though some parts of the café are so far from the kitchen it's a surprise the food isn't cold by the time it reaches your table. Usefully located on one of Schöneberg's more interesting shopping streets.

Café Berio

Maassenstrasse 7 (216 1946). U1, U2, U4, U12 Nollendorfplatz. **Open** 8am-1am daily.
No credit cards. Map p305 D5.
The locals' choice for breakfast, it also has plenty of home-made cakes and excellent ice-cream. Café Berio has been an institution since the 1930s and the tables outside are a prime people-watching spot in summer. *See also p211.*

Caracas

Kurfürstenstrasse 9 (265 2171). U1, U12 Kurfürstenstrasse. **Open** 10pm-late daily.
No credit cards. Map p306 E5.
A wild, wacky Latin American cellar bar decked in pink plastic flowers. A small alcove has tatty sofas to sink into when you've worked your way through the 20 kinds of rum or jigged around to salsa on the tiny dancefloor.

Eisenstein

Viktoria-Luise-Platz 5 (2196 8181). U4 Viktoria-Luise-Platz. **Open** 9am-1am daily. **No credit cards. Map** p305 D5.
This new café is located on a balmy, haute-bourgeois square near the KaDeWe department store. The namesake Soviet director's likeness adorns the wall, flanked by blown-up film stills, and the red and black decor has a constructivist flair. The breakfasts on offer also sport titles of his films, from 'Ivan the Terrible', a not-so-terrible equivalent to the 'kleine Frühstück' (small breakfast) to 'Viva Mexico' with fruit and marinated chicken breast served with pineapple and cheese on toast. Eisenstein also serves a daily lunch special and intriguing snacks, such as mozzarella rolls stuffed with serrano ham or a rocket-red beet salad.

Green Door

Winterfeldtstrasse 50 (215 2515). U1, U2, U4,
U12 Nollendorfplatz. **Open** 6pm-3am daily.
No credit cards. Map p305 D5.

It really does have a green door, and behind it
there's a whole lotta cocktail shaking going on –
the drinks menu is enormous and impressive.
There's also a nice long and curvy bar, perhaps
a few too many yuppies, and a good location just
off Winterfeldtplatz.

Mister Hu

Goltzstrasse 39 (217 2111). U7 Eisenacher Strasse.
Open 5pm-3am daily. **No credit cards.**
Map p305 D5.

Dark and cosy bar decorated in greens and blues
and named after one of its owners, cigar-smoking
Chinese-Indonesian writer Husen Ciawi. Long cocktail list, so at its best during happy hour (5-8pm Mon-
Sat, all day Sun).

Mutter

Hohenstaufenstrasse 4 (216 4990). U1, U2, U4,
U12 Nollendorfplatz. **Open** 9.30am-4am daily.
Credit AmEx, MC, V. **Map** p305 D5.

'Mother' tries to do everything at once: two bars; an
enormous selection of wines, beers and cocktails;
breakfasts from 9am to 4pm; a sushi bar from 6pm,
plus a lot of other snacks on offer throughout the
day. It's a big place, but it can be difficult to find a
seat on weekend nights, when trancey house plays
in the front bar (there are more sedate sounds in the
café area at the back). It's roomy, the decor is heavy
on gold paint and the spectacular corridor to the toilets is worth a visit in itself.

Pinguin Club

Wartburgstrasse 54 (781 3005). U7 Eisenacher
Strasse. **Open** 9pm-4am daily. **No credit cards.**
Map p305 D5.

Though a little past its heyday, this is still one of
Berlin's finest and friendliest institutions. It's decorated with original 1950s Americana and rock 'n' roll
memorabilia, plus assorted kitsch bits and pieces.
Owners and staff are all involved in music, and good
sounds, varying from Dean Martin to David Sylvian
to dub, are a feature. Take your pick from 156 spirits, and don't be surprised if the barman starts doing
card tricks or everyone begins to dance to disco or
sing along to Nick Cave tunes. Occasional weekend
DJs play anything from old soul to punk.

Savarin

Kulmer Strasse 17 (216 3864). S1, S2, U7
Yorckstrasse. **Open** 10am-midnight Mon-Fri; 10am-
9pm Sat, Sun. **No credit cards. Map** p306 E5.

Gorgeously cosy little café with a sophisticated edge,
staff who are glamorous in a worldly kind of way,
and famously excellent cakes and pies. On Sundays
it's not just that you can't find a seat – you can't even
get in the door for all the people queuing to take
away cheesecake slices and apple tarts.

Screwy Club

Frankenstrasse 2 (215 4441). U7 Eisenacher
Strasse. **Open** 8pm-2am Tue-Thur; 8pm-4am Fri,
Sat. **No credit cards. Map** p305 D5.

Small, friendly bar decorated with artwork by Chuck
Jones and Tex Avery. The barstools, for example, are
set on giant Bugs Bunny-style carrots. Specialises
in frozen cocktails.

The **Pinguin Club** – a fun, friendly Berlin bar scene stalwart.

Tim's Canadian Deli

Maassenstrasse 14 (2175 6960). U1, U2, U4, U12 Nollendorfplatz. **Open** 8am-1am Mon-Fri; 9am-2am Sat; 9am-1am Sun. **Credit** AmEx, MC, V. **Map** p305 D5.

Against the odds, this place seems to have conquered the Winterfeldtplatz area, though there's not a café round here that's not full on a market day. Lots of bagels and muffins, egg breakfasts until 4pm, various light meal options, but precious few actual Canadians in evidence.

Zoulou Bar

Hauptstrasse 4 (784 6894). U7 Kleistpark. **Open** 8pm-6am Mon-Thur, Sun; 10pm-9am Fri, Sat. **No credit cards. Map** p306 E5.

Small, atmospheric bar with a funky vibe and occasional DJs. It can get very crowded between 10pm and 2am; after that the crowd thins out and late is maybe the best time for a visit. Usually full of staff from nearby bars until the dawn light gets too bright.

Tiergarten

Bar am Lützowplatz

Lützowplatz 7 (262 6807). U1, U2, U4, U12 Nollendorfplatz. **Open** 5pm-3am Mon-Thur, Sun; 5am-4am Fri, Sat. **No credit cards.** **Map** p305 D4.

Long bar with a drinks list to match, where classy customers in Chanel suits and furs sip expensive, well-made cocktails and spend the evening comparing bank balances.

Café Einstein

Kurfürstenstrasse 58 (261 5096). U1, U2, U4, U12 Nollendorfplatz. **Open** 10am-2am daily. **Credit** AmEx, DC, MC, V. **Map** p305 D4.

A Viennese-style coffee house with hectic waiters in bow ties and waistcoats, international papers and magazines, and a renowned *Apfelstrudel*. In summer you can sit in the garden at the back and enjoy a leisurely breakfast (served all day). *See also p135.* **Branch**: Unter den Linden 42, Mitte (204 3632).

Café am Neuen See

Lichtensteinallee 2 (254 4930). Bus X9, 100, 187, 341. **Open** *Mar-Oct* 10am-11pm, *Nov-Feb* 10am-8pm daily. **Credit** AmEx, V. **Map** p305 D4.

Stretch out at one of the outside tables by a leafy Tiergarten lake and it feels like you've slipped right outside of the city. Coffee, cakes, drinks, light meals and rowing boats for hire nearby.

Kumpelnest 3000

Lützowstrasse 23 (261 6918). U1, U12 Kurfürstenstrasse. **Open** 5pm-late daily. **No credit cards. Map** p306 E4.

This place used to be a brothel, the walls are carpeted and some of the barmen are deaf. Kumpelnest 3000 is at its best at the end of a long Saturday night: crowded, chaotic and with people attempting to dance to disco classics.

Schleusenkrug

Müller-Breslau-Strasse/Unterschleuse (313 9909). S3, S5, S7, S9, S75 Tiergarten. **Open** 10.30am-late daily. **No credit cards. Map** p305 C4.

It has become a familiar story: a location that for decades has catered to old couples is discovered by young hipsters and becomes a cheesy-but-cool lounge for undergroundish events. In this case, the location is a bar and beer garden directly on the canal in the Tiergarten, and the crowds descend on it in droves for easy listening, mod and indie pop nights. During the day the place retains much of its original flavour, hingeing on nautical themes and large glasses of Pils.

Charlottenburg/Wilmersdorf

There are pockets of life around **Savignyplatz** and **Karl-August-Platz**, but Charlottenburg is essentially a place where nothing ever happens. The last happening club checked out of this neighbourhood sometime in the late 1980s and the borough's ageing bars and stiff restaurants are no match for neighbouring Schöneberg, still less for newly redeveloped Mitte. Those establishments here that do business have to cater mostly to tourists, businesspeople and a huge Russian population. Plenty of café life by day, though – as there also is around **Ludwigkirchplatz**, south of the Ku'damm, in Wilmersdorf.

Berlin Bar

Uhlandstrasse 145, Wilmersdorf (2804 5134). U1 Hohenzollernplatz. **Open** 10pm-7am daily. **No credit cards. Map** p305 C5.

Small and narrow (if there's someone standing at the bar, it's hard to squeeze by between them and the wall), this venerable institution goes on serving when all else around here has closed. You pay for the privilege, though. After about 4am it's full of people who've finished working in other places.

Café Aedes West

S-Bahn Bogen, Savignyplatz (3150 9535). S3, S5, S7, S9, S75 Savignyplatz. **Open** 8am-midnight Mon-Fri; 9am-midnight Sat, Sun. *Breakfast* 9am-3pm daily. **No credit cards. Map** p305 C4.

A small, trendy café tucked under the S-Bahn line at Savignyplatz. A steady flow of fashionable yuppie types pop in and out for a cappuccino, a late breakfast, or to look at the other fashionable yuppie types.

Café Hardenberg

Hardenbergstrasse 10 (312 2644). U2 Ernst-Reuter-Platz. **Open** 9am-1am Mon-Thur, Sun; 9am-2am Fri, Sat. **Main courses** €3.50-€7. **No credit cards. Map** p305 C4.

Across from the Technical University, this café is usually packed with students drinking coffee. Simple, decent plates of spaghetti, omelettes, salads and sandwiches are sold at reasonable prices. It's also a good place for cheap vegetarian food.

Eat, Drink, Shop

Café Savigny

Grolmanstrasse 53-4, Charlottenburg (312 8195).
S3, S5, S7, S9, S75 Savignyplatz. **Open** 10am-1am
daily. **No credit cards. Map** p305 C4.

It's hard to find a table at this small and airy café.
Sparsely decorated, painted white with round
arched doorways, the Savigny has a Mediterranean
feel. Good breakfasts, filled baguettes and cakes.
Tables outside in summer, nice bar within.

Crown's

Ludwigkirchplatz 12 (2232 7832).
U1 Hohenzollernplatz. **Open** 9am-1am daily.
No credit cards. Map p305 C5.

Crown's shows another side of British hospitality,
not the blustery pub or fish and chips stall, but how
one imagines Edwardian gentlemen's clubs. In addition to English breakfast and afternoon tea, the
menu also offers dishes influenced by the cuisines
of Britain's former Asian colonies. Don't let the interior and very formal waiter-cum-maître d' intimidate
you – Crown's is just as suitable for a leisurely coffee as it is for a five course lamb in mint sauce dinner (advisable to reserve if that's your intention).
Business lunch served between noon and 3pm.

Diener

Grolmanstrasse 47 (881 5329). S3, S5, S7,
S9, S75 Savignyplatz. **Open** 1pm-late daily.
No credit cards. Map p305 C4.

An old-style Berlin bar, named after a famous
German boxer. There's no music and the walls are
adorned with faded hunting murals and photos of
famous Germans you won't recognise. You could
almost be in 1920s Berlin. Almost.

Elaine's

Schlüterstrasse 69 (313 5038). S3, S5, S7,
S9, S75 Savignyplatz. **Open** 11am-1am Mon-Thur,
Sun; 11am-2am Fri, Sat. **Credit** AmEx, MC, V.
Map p305 C4.

A recently renamed (it used to be called Dralle's)
hangout for an oldish, formerly fashionable crowd,
with a predominantly red decor. Staff are efficient,
drinks are pricey, snacks are also served and the
place feels a bit like an American diner.

Galerie Bremer

Fasanenstrasse 37 (881 4908). U1, U9,
U12 Spichernstrasse. **Open** 8pm-late Tue-Sun.
No credit cards. Map p305 C5.

Hidden in the back room of a tiny gallery in this
quiet, exclusive street, this bar has a nice air of the
well-kept secret. Inside, it's all surprises: the room is
painted in deep, rich colours with a beautiful ship-
like bar designed by Hans Scharoun, architect of the
Philharmonie and Staatsbibliothek. When the per-
sonable assistant barman takes your coat and welcomes you, it's meant to make you feel at home, and
it's also the done thing to make a little conversation
with the majestically bearded owner – he'll remember next time you drop in. Then you can sit back and
feel privileged, and enjoy being nonplussed by the
odd member of parliament entering incognito.

Gasthaus Lenz

Stuttgarter Platz 20 (324 1619). S3, S5, S7, S9, S75
Charlottenburg. **Open** 9am-2am daily. *Breakfast*
10am-11.30am daily. **No credit cards. Map** p304 B4.

An older crowd is drawn to this unpretentious,
spacious café nestled in the cluster of bars on
Stuttgarter Platz. Cigarette-smoking intellectuals
pack the place day and night. If they can find a seat,
Guardian-reading 30-somethings will feel at home
here. No music.

Leysieffer

Kurfürstendamm 218, Wilmersdorf (885 7480).
U15 Uhlandstrasse. **Open** 10am-8pm Mon-Sat;
11am-7pm Sun. **No credit cards. Map** p305 C4.

Indulge yourself in style at this recently refurbished
café housed in what used to be the Chinese
Embassy. Exquisite tortes and fruitcakes are
served upstairs in the high-ceilinged café, which
resembles an art gallery. Tempting mounds of truf-
fles and bonbons, beautifully presented, are sold
downstairs in the shop.

Schwarzes Café

Kantstrasse 148 (313 8038). S3, S5, S7, S9,
S75 Savignyplatz. **Open** 24hrs Mon, Wed-Sun.
No credit cards. Map p305 C4.

Centrally located, and open around the clock for
breakfasts and meals. It used to be all black and
somewhat anarchistically inclined (hence the name)
but these days the decor has been brightened up
and the political crowd moved out of this neighbourhood ages ago. Service can get overstretched
when it's crowded, such as early on a weekend
morning, when clubbers stop by for breakfast on
their way home. *See also p152.*

Wintergarten im Literaturhaus

Fasanenstrasse 23 (882 5414). U15 Uhlandstrasse.
Open 9.30am-1am daily. **No credit cards.**
Map p305 C4.

This is the café of the Literaturhaus, which has
lectures, readings, exhibitions and an excellent
bookshop in the basement. The greenhouse-
like sunny winter garden or salon rooms of the
café are great for ducking into a book or scribbling
out postcards. Breakfast, snacks and desserts
are available.

Other districts

Verein der Visionare

Am Flutgraben 2, Treptow (no phone). S6, S8, S9,
S10 Treptower Park or U1, U12 Schlesisches Tor.
Open varies. **No credit cards.**

On a narrow canal graced by willow trees, this lazy
man's lounge during the day has the air of a
Vietnamese peasant hut gone disco. Open only
when it's warm enough to sit (or dance) outside,
where an old factory makes for an impressive backdrop. The sofas are tattered and torn, but still a
great place to rest your feet after a trip to the
Treptow flea market next door.

Shops & Services

Despite the creeping progress of mall culture, Berlin still has fine independent stores – if you know where to look.

Quartier 206 Department Store. *See p165.*

Shopping in Berlin is much like the city itself, straddling the old world and the new, east and west. Part of it marches upmarket, the other clings to its origins in the offbeat, alternative or underground sub-cultures of a city that was divided for four decades. History is, at least in part, to blame for the fact that many shops, whether one-off independents or international retailers, face a struggle. Apart from spiralling rents and sudden competition from newly arrived malls (*see p158* **From Berlin Wall to Berlin mall**), there is an additional problem inherited from Berlin's past urban development: there is no downtown, no single city centre. Berlin has several, making it hard to decide on a sure-fire location to set up shop. Berliners generally prefer spending their money in their own *Kiez* – or neighbourhood – and most districts have a lively high street that meets the needs of any given day – from Schlossstrasse in Steglitz to Karl-Marx-Strasse in Neukölln and Schönhauser Allee in Prenzlauer Berg.

The arrival of more moneyed consumers with the global corporations, media, cultural organisations and federal institutions that moved to Berlin along with the government fuelled expectations that the city would become Europe's new shopping capital. As world-class architects sculpted a new urban topography, additional shopping drags such as Potsdamer Platz beckoned. Over the past decade, much has appeared to cater to a discerning, globetrotting clientele, from the premises of visionary entrepreneurs in Mitte and Prenzlauer Berg where international trend scouts take the city's pulse, to top-of-the-line designer goods on the western end of the Ku'damm and along Friedrichstrasse.

But there's still enough of old Berlin to delight visitors with a nostalgic bent. Antiquarian booksellers, second-hand clothing warehouses, basements of pre-war furniture, and small *Trödeler* spilling bric-a-brac on to the pavement can be found in most districts. And the capital's vibrant cultural life feeds demand for books, music and art – the latter a roaring trade in Berlin (*see chapter* **Galleries**). So while it can't compete with Paris or London in many ways, the Berlin shopping experience is equally diverse and, in many ways, more rewarding. The treasures are there, you just have to go out and hunt them down.

OPENING HOURS

Shops can sell goods until 8pm on weekdays and 4pm on Saturdays. Retailers in central areas tend to keep these hours, while shops in residential areas begin shutting at 6pm. Most big stores normally open their doors between 8.30am and 9am; newsagents and bakeries as early as 6am; smaller or independent shops tend to open around 10am or later. Many bakeries and are open for a few hours on Sundays.

Antiques

Collectors and browsers with an interest in the 18th and 19th centuries will find many of the better dealers on Keithstrasse and Goltzstrasse in Schöneberg. The streets surrounding Fasanenplatz in Wilmersdorf are worth exploring, as is Suarezstrasse in Charlottenburg. In the east, Kollwitzstrasse and Husemannstrasse in Prenzlauer Berg are home to small, unpretentious *Antiquariaten*. *See also* *p181* **Souvenirs** and *p178* **Flea markets**.

Deco Arts

Motzstrasse 6, Schöneberg (215 8672). U1, U2, U4, U12 Nollendorfplatz. **Open** 3-6.30pm Wed-Fri; 11am-3pm Sat. **No credit cards. Map** p305 D5.
Shell-shaped 1930s sofas and other art deco furniture at fair prices, as well as the odd piece by Marcel Breuer and Carl Jacobs, and treasures from the 1950s and 1960s. If an American bar is too big to take home, pick up a stylish tea set, vase or ashtray.

Emma Emmelie

Schumannstrasse 15A, Mitte (2838 4884). U6 Oranienburger Tor. **Open** 1-7.30pm Mon-Fri. **Credit** MC, V. **Map** p316/p302 F3.
In an area of Mitte that's undergone a major facelift because of its proximity to the seat of government, this little subterranean treasure is refreshingly old Berlin. Antique linens and clothes from the first half of the 20th century, and dolls, jewellery, glasses and china, give this shop all the atmosphere of a lost era.

Fingers

Nollendorfstrasse 35, Schöneberg (215 3441). U1, U2, U4, U12 Nollendorfplatz. **Open** 2.30-6.30pm Tue-Fri; 11am-2.30pm Sat. **No credit cards. Map** p305 D5.
Splendid finds from the 1940s, 1950s and 1960s, including lipstick-shaped cigarette lighters, vintage toasters, weird lighting and eccentric glassware.

Historische Bauelemente

Bärenklauer Weg 2, Marwitz (03304 502 242). Berliner Ring Nord, exit Schwante and follow signs to Henningsdorf & Marwitz. **Open** 2-6pm Tue-Fri; 10am-6pm Sat. **No credit cards.**
In the early 1990s building boom, Olaf Elias began combing the region for construction sites throwing away old doors, window frames, wrought-iron garden fences, tiles and other old building materials. His collection now occupies a massive space in a former pig farm 30 minutes from the city. It includes stunning Jugendstil bathtubs, 1920s sinks, angel sculptures and decorative but practical artefacts from various decades of Berlin-Brandenburg history. You'll need a car to get here, but it's a real treat.

From Berlin Wall to Berlin mall

What a comedown: Potsdamer Platz, Berlin's hyped new centre erected on the no man's land that formerly divided East from West, designed by such star architects as Renzo Piano and Helmut Jahn, is a glorified shopping mall. It's not unusual – urban development projects from Baltimore to Budapest encompass retail and restaurant agglomerations under one roof and one property management. If the mall also has a multiplex, bowling alley, fitness studio or other leisure facilities, it becomes an urban entertainment centre, no less.

Berlin has more than 35 shopping malls. The first was the Europa-Center adjacent to the Kaiser-Wilhelm-Gedächtniskirche near the Ku'damm, completed in 1965. Soon, two other shopping centres, the Ku'damm Eck (demolished in 1999 with Swissôtel now occupying the site) and Ku'damm Karree. All three were pioneer urban entertainment centres, as well, offering cinemas and other

leisure activities; the Europa-Center also housed the legendary Stachelschweine cabaret, while not one but two light comedy theatres are located in the Karree to this day. Interestingly, the mall was not an entirely alien concept to East Berlin, either, as many neighbourhoods had their so-called *Dienstleistungswürfel* (service cubes), uniting several stores under one roof or forerunners of the 'theme-mall' offering 'everything for the modern woman'.

Malls proliferated in the early 1990s, with most new shopping centres opening in the east. The first openings were on the outskirts, but complaints of suburban megamalls siphoning purchasing power away from the inner city led developers to focus on district sub-centres, such as the Ring Center on Frankfurter Allee and Gesundbrunnen Center in Wedding, or on instant urbanity projects like the Potsdamer Platz Arkaden or Friedrichstadt-passagen, three distinct buildings designed by

Lehmanns Colonialwaren

Grolmanstrasse 46, Charlottenburg (883 3942).
S3, S5, S7, S9, S75 Savignyplatz. **Open** 2-6.30pm
Tue-Fri. **No credit cards. Map** p305 C4.
Turn-of-the-20th-century luggage, clothing and
furniture deck out this small shop like a cluttered
Victorian parlour. Much of the eccentric stock
follows a colonial theme, so don't be surprised to
come across a set of snakeskin luggage or a guide
to hunting big game.

Radio Art

Zossener Strasse 2, Kreuzberg (693 9435).
U7 Gneisenaustrasse. **Open** noon-6pm Thur,
Fri; 10am-1pm Sat. **Credit** AmEx, MC, V.
Map p306 F5.
A fine collection of antique transistor radios from
75 years of radio history. From large 1940s wooden-
cased samples for sitting-room display to tiny short
wave receivers in shocking pink, from the likes of
Blaupunkt, RCA and Telefunken.

Wolfgang Haas

Suarezstrasse 3, Charlottenburg (321 4570).
U2 Sophie-Charlotte-Platz/bus 204. **Open** 3-7pm
Tue-Fri; 11am-3pm Sat. **No credit cards.**
Map p304 B4.
Period, lacquered timber furniture, glassware,
ceramics and other small antiques dating from
1800 to 1960. There are classic tables, chairs and
cabinets, as well as some appealing art nouveau
pieces. The selection of German crystal from the
19th and 20th centuries is particularly good; the
paintings are all post-1945.

Antique heaven: **Wolfgang Haas**.

Jean Nouvel, Henry Cobb and Oswald Mathias
Ungers linked by a subterranean passage.

The downtown designer malls and projects like
the refunctioned Borsig locomotive assembly
hall in Tegel arouse aesthetic curiosity, but
most visits to shopping centres, offering largely
the same mix of chain outlets, are motivated by
convenience. Love 'em or loath 'em, an analyst
said, 290 million Europeans visit shopping
malls each year; 70,000 daily trek to the
Potsdamer Platz Arkaden alone. Developers are
taciturn about how visitor frequency translates
into sales volume, and the jury is hung about
whether the mall is the murderer or saviour of
the small neighbourhood shop. Some shopping
centres, like the Schönhauser Allee Arkaden
in Prenzlauer Berg, are said to have revived
the east Berlin shopping street from post-Wall
doldrums. The Gesundbrunnen Center, on the
other hand, which never fulfilled early promise
of housing a large share of small to mid-sized

enterprises in addition to chains, is said
to have sucked business out of the rest of
Badstrasse. As for city officials' favourite
justification for granting yet another mall
building permit, the creation of retail and
service jobs, union functionaries counter that
the chains often transfer personnel from other
outlets instead of hiring new staff. In the past
year, 3,000 more retail jobs have been
destroyed than created, although the
correlation to mall expansion is unproven.

Others see mall expansion as symptomatic
of urban planners' lack of imagination, the
commodification (and eventual loss of) public
space and the elevation of consumption and
brand identity to ersatz culture or even belief
system. On a more ambivalent note, Andy
Warhol predicted that shopping malls would
be the museums of the future. That considered,
maybe Potsdamer Platz is less a comedown
and more an object of study.

Beauty salons

Aveda
Kurfürstendamm 29, Charlottenburg (8855 2757).
U9, U15 Kurfürstendamm. **Open** 10am-8pm
Mon-Fri; 10am-4pm Sat. **Credit** AmEx, DC, V.
Map p305 C4.
Berlin business people frequently extend their
lunch breaks to treat themselves to a Comforting
Eye Treatment or a Himalayan Rejuvenation
Treatment at Aveda. At the back of this cosmetics
shop, the hair and beauty salon offers first-rate
hair styling, cutting and colouring, aromatherapy
massage, manicures, facials and a range of
body treatments, using products based on natural
flower essences.
Branch: Quartier 205, Friedrichstrasse 68, Mitte
(2094 5054).

Hautfit Bio Kosmetik
Goltzstrasse 18, Schöneberg (216 5259).
U1, U2, U4, U12 Nollendorfplatz. **Open** 10am-
6.30pm Mon-Fri; 10am-2pm Sat. **Credit** MC, V.
Map p305 D5.
This salon uses only plant-based products including the brand widely considered to be the purest
of the pure, from the German anthroposophical
company Dr Hauschka. Products used vary according to skin type: treatments include the algae-based
Sea Treatment, the flower essence facial or – if
you're going the whole hog – the two-hour Dr
Hauschka treatment including facial, foot bath
and hand massage. Products are for sale in the
shop, which happens to be a fin-de-siècle butcher's
tiled in Jugendstil ceramics.

Marie France
Fasanenstrasse 42, Charlottenburg (881 6555).
U15 Uhlandstrasse. **Open** 9am-6pm Tue-Wed, Fri;
9am-8pm Thur; 9am-2pm Sat. **Credit** MC, V.
Map p305 C4.
The cosmeticians at Marie France speak reasonable
English (with French accents, of course) and use
luxurious French products at this clean, pleasant
salon, which has been glamming up Berliners
for more than 30 years. Hot-wax depilation is a
speciality, and staff also offer a wide range of
relaxing and beautifying treatments.

Scrub up at **Hautfit Bio Kosmetik**.

Books

Germany is still blessed with a lively
independent bookshop scene, though chain
stores are spreading.

Bücherbogen
*Savignyplatz Bogen 593, Charlottenburg
(3186 9511).* *S3, S5, S7, S9, S75 Savignyplatz.*
Open 10am-8pm Mon-Fri; 10am-4pm Sat.
Credit MC, V. **Map** p305 C4.
This great art-book shop is a prime browsing spot.
This branch stocks books on painting, sculpture,
photography and some architecture; the one at
S-Bahnbogen 585 film; the Kochstrasse branch
architecture, and in Knesebeckstrasse the whole
lot at discount prices.
Branches: S-Bahnbogen 585, Charlottenburg
(312 1932); Kochstrasse 19, Kreuzberg (251 1345);
Knesebeckstrasse 27, Charlottenburg (8868 3695).

Buchhandlung Herschel
Anklamer Strasse 38, Mitte (440 7599).
U8 Bernauer Strasse. **Open** 10am-7pm Mon-Fri;
10am-2pm Sat. **No credit cards.**
Map p316/p302 F2.
Located in the Weiberwirtschaft, this is a small and
personal shop that doesn't stock a huge range but
Frau Herschel goes to great lengths to track down
any German book you're looking for. Interesting
new German writers give readings in the gallery
once or twice a month.

Grober Unfug
Zossener Strasse 32-3, Kreuzberg (6940 1491).
U7 Gneisenaustrasse. **Open** 11am-7pm Mon-Fri;
11am-4pm Sat. **Credit** AmEx, MC, V.
Map p306 F5.
Stockists of comics in all languages, including annu-
als and comic art from *Viz* to French arty stuff. The
new Mitte branch includes a comic gallery.
Branch: Weinmeisterstrasse 9B, Mitte (281 7331).

Kohlhaas & Company
Fasanenstrasse 23, Wilmersdorf (882 5044).
U15 Uhlandstrasse. **Open** 10am-8pm Mon-Fri;
10am-4pm Sat. **Credit** MC, V. **Map** p305 C4.
Elegantly housed beneath the Literaturhaus, this
small, well-run bookshop aims towards the high-
brow. German literature predominates. Service is
friendly and helpful.

Prinz Eisenherz Buchladen
*Bleibtreustrasse 52, Charlottenburg (313 9936/
www.prinz-eisenherz.com).* *S3, S5, S7, S9, S75
Savignyplatz.* **Open** 10am-6pm Mon-Fri; 10am-4pm
Sat. **Credit** MC, V. **Map** p305 C4.
Prinz Eisenherz Buchladen is one of the finest gay
bookshops in Europe, including, among its large
English-language stock, many titles unavailable in
Britain. There's a good art and photography section,
plus magazines, postcards and news of book read-
ings and other events. Small subsidiary at Café
Melitta Sundström (*see p208*).

Hirsute's you, sir: **Another Country**.

yourself to tea and coffee, or borrow books for varying fees. Return them to recoup a deposit, or else hang on to the book. Also stocks antiques. The shop also runs an English club four nights a week, showing English-language films and offering literary and other readings and discussions

Books in Berlin

Goethestrasse 69, Charlottenburg (313 1233).
S3, S5, S7, S9, S75 Savignyplatz. **Open** noon-8pm Mon-Fri; 10am-4pm Sat. **Credit** V. **Map** p305 C4.
Run by a Bostonian, this is a mini-City Lights with a small but solid selection of new and used classical and modern fiction, history and politics, reference and travel books. A lecture series focuses on literary topics and current affairs. US orders for titles not available on Amazon take two to three weeks.

Buchexpress

Unter den Eichen 97, Dahlem (832 8186).
S1 Lichterfelde Ost. **Open** 9am-6pm Mon-Fri; 10am-1pm Sat. **Credit** MC, V.
A reference point for students at the Free University, this is a friendly store with some 6,000 titles of fiction, English and American studies, cross-cultural communication, plus kits for learning German, a section for kids and one for used books, primarily bestsellers.

Fair Exchange

Dieffenbachstrasse 58, Kreuzberg (694 4675).
U8 Schönleinstrasse. **Open** 11am-6.30pm Mon-Fri; 10am-4pm Sat. **No credit cards. Map** p307 G5.
Large selection of second-hand English-language books, with an emphasis on literature.

Hugendubel

Tauentzienstrasse 13, Charlottenburg (214 060).
U1, U2, U12, U15 Wittenbergplatz. **Open** 9.30am-8pm Mon-Fri; 9am-4pm Sat. **No credit cards.**
Map p305 D4.
After Kiepert, Berlin's second largest bookshop. Its four floors house more than 140,000 books, including a big English-language section.
Branch: Friedrichstrasse 83, Mitte (2063 5100).

Kiepert

Hardenbergstrasse 4-5, Charlottenburg (311 880).
U2 Ernst-Reuter-Platz. **Open** 9.30am-8pm Mon-Fri; 9.30am-4pm Sat. **Credit** AmEx, MC, V. **Map** p305 C4.
Berlin's biggest bookshop. Wide selection of fiction and non-fiction, guides, maps and a selection of foreign-language books. Can arrange postal delivery. Other branches have less English-language material.
Branches: Friedrichstrasse 63, Mitte (201 7130); Georgenstrasse 2, Mitte (203 9960).

Le Matou

Reinhardtstrasse 11, Mitte (2809 9601).
U6 Oranienburger Tor. **Open** 10am-7.30pm Mon-Fri. **No credit cards. Map** p316/p302 F3.
International books for children and young people in English, French, Italian, Spanish, Arabic and Russian, as well as bilingual texts. With some 3,000 titles in stock, this shop also has an extensive order catalogue.

Antiquarian & second-hand books

Knesebeckstrasse in Charlottenburg, Winterfeldtstrasse in Schöneberg and Kollwitzstrasse and Husemannstrasse in Prenzlauer Berg all offer rich literary pickings. Most places can provide you with a leaflet listing all the *Antiquariaten* in Berlin.

Antiquariat Senzel

Knesebeckstrasse 13-14, Charlottenburg (312 5887).
U2 Ernst-Reuter-Platz. **Open** noon-6.30pm Mon-Fri; 11am-2pm Sat. **No credit cards. Map** p305 C4.
Most of the books are in German, though odd English and French volumes can be found. Also some beautifully leather-bound tomes and old maps.

Düwal

Schlüterstrasse 17, Charlottenburg (313 3030).
S3, S5, S7, S9, S75 Savignyplatz. **Open** noon-6.30pm Mon-Fri; 11am-2pm Sat. **Credit** DC, MC, V. **Map** p305 C4.
Large store with everything from recent bestsellers to rare first editions. Good selection of foreign titles.

English-language books

Another Country

Riemannstrasse 7, Kreuzberg (6940 1150).
U7 Gneisenaustrasse. **Open** 11am-8pm Mon-Fri; 11am-5pm Sat. **No credit cards. Map** p306 F5.
Spacious premises housing an ambitious bookshop and private library stocked with more than 10,000 English-language titles – around half of them science fiction – from the collection of British owner Alan Raphaeline. A small membership fee allows you to use the reading room downstairs and help

Eat, Drink, Shop

Marga Schoeller Bücherstube

*Knesebeckstrasse 33, Charlottenburg
(881 1112/1122). S3, S5, S7, S9, S75
Savignyplatz.* **Open** 9.30am-7pm Mon-Wed;
9.30am-8pm Thur-Fri; 9.30am-4pm Sat.
Credit MC, V. **Map** p305 C4.
Rated by *Bookseller* as Europe's fourth best
independent literary bookshop, this excellent establishment, founded in 1930, also gets a resounding
thumbs-up from us. It includes a self-contained
English-language section that, though not the
largest selection in town, is certainly the most interesting, with more English titles scattered throughout various specialist sections. Staff are sweet,
helpful, know their stock and will track down anything that's not on their shelves.

Children's clothes & toys

Wooden toys are a German speciality and,
though pricey, are often worth the money.
Puppets from the Dresdener puppet factory
and tiny wooden figures from the Erzgebirge
region are particularly distinctive. Stuffed toys
are another traditional offering: Steiff (which
claims to have invented the teddy bear) and its
competitor Sigikid offer beautifully made and
collectable cuddly animals.

Emma & Co

*Niebuhrstrasse 1, Charlottenburg (882 7373).
S3, S5, S7, S9, S75 Savignyplatz.* **Open** 11am-
6.30pm Mon-Wed; 11am-7.30pm Thur, Fri; 11am-
4pm Sat. **Credit** AmEx, MC, V. **Map** p305 C4.
Melanie Wöltje's charming shop within Bramigk &
Breer (*see p165*) offers well-made but not exorbitant
children's wear, bedding, toys and gift items like
name books and terry-cloth teddies.

Heidi's Spielzeugladen

*Kantstrasse 61, Charlottenburg (323 7556).
U7 Wilmersdorfer Strasse.* **Open** 9.30am-7pm
Mon-Fri; 9.30am-4pm Sat. **Credit** MC, V.
Map p304 B4.
Wooden toys, including cookery utensils and
child-sized kitchens are the attraction here. Heidi's
also stocks a good selection of books, puppets
and wall-hangings.

H&M Kids

*Kurfürstendamm 237, Charlottenburg (884 8760).
U9, U15 Kurfürstendamm.* **Open** 10am-8pm Mon-
Fri; 9am-4pm Sat. **Credit** AmEx, DC, MC, V.
Map p305 C4.
The place for cute, cheap clothes for kids up to 14.
This branch has the largest children's department.

Michas Bahnhof

*Nürnberger Strasse 24A, Schöneberg (218 6611).
U1 Augsburger Strasse.* **Open** 10am-6.30pm Mon-
Fri; 10am-4pm Sat. **Credit** AmEx, DC, MC, V.
Map p305 D4.
Small shop packed with model trains both old and
new, and everything that goes with them.

Tam Tam

*Lietzenburger Strasse 92, Charlottenburg (882
1454). U15 Uhlandstrasse.* **Open** 10am-6.30pm Mon-
Fri; 10am-4pm Sat. **Credit** MC, V. **Map** p305 C4.
A bright, charming shop filled with stuffed animals
and wooden toys, including building blocks, trains,
trucks, dolls' houses, plus child-sized wooden stoves.

v. Kloeden

*Wielandstrasse 24, Charlottenburg (8871 2512).
U15 Uhlandstrasse.* **Open** 9am-7pm Mon-Fri; 10am-
4pm Sat. **Credit** AmEx, DC, MC, V. **Map** p305 C4.
Oldest and friendliest toy store in town, run by a
brother-and-sister team who make it their policy to
help you find the perfect present. The wide selection
includes children's books in English, toys and reading material from the Montessori and Steiner
schools, building blocks by German aeronaut Otto
Lilienthal, handmade Käthe Kruse dolls, Erzgebirge
wooden figures, and all kinds of modern-day fare.

Cosmetics

Belladonna

*Bergmannstrasse 101, Kreuzberg (694 3731). U7
Gneisenaustrasse.* **Open** 10am-7pm Mon-Fri; 10am-
4pm Sat. **Credit** AmEx, MC, V. **Map** p306 F5.

The best toy shop in town: **v. Kloeden**.

The food hall at **KaDeWe**. *See p165.*

Natural and flower-essence products from German firms Logona, Lavera, Dr Hauschka, Weleda and others, plus the entire range of Primavera essential oils and lamps to burn them in. The shop also stocks brushes, make-up and baby clothes.

DK Cosmetics

Kurfürstendamm 56, Charlottenburg (3279 0123). U15 Uhlandstrasse. **Open** 10am-7pm Mon-Fri; 10am-4pm Sat. **Credit** AmEx, DC, MC, V. **Map** p305 C4.
Lotions and potions for pampered globetrotters from cult beauty companies such as Kiehl's, Remde, Eve Lom and Bloom, make-up by Nars, haircare from Bumble & Bumble and jewelled accessories from slides to tiaras. Diptyque scented candles and Sarah Schwartz's shaped or text-bedecked soaps make for more fun in the bath.

Shiseido Beauty Gallery

Bleibtreustrasse 32, Charlottenburg (8867 9840). U15 Uhlandstrasse. **Open** 10am-7pm Mon-Fri; 10am-4pm Sat. **No credit cards. Map** p305 C4.
You can't actually buy anything here, but you'll need an appointment anyway. For 45 minutes, you can try out Shiseido's entire product range with no pressure to purchase. Friendly staff conduct a computer skin analysis, then advise on the right skincare regime and make-up application – all for free! The SBG is unique, boosting Shiseido's Berlin sales in the number of Ku'damm stores stocking the brand nearby.

World of Beauty

Augsburger Strasse 37, Schöneberg (885 4892). U1 Augsburger Strasse. **Open** 9am-7pm Mon-Fri; 9am-4pm Sat. **Credit** MC. **Map** p305 D4.
Afro-American cosmetics plus real and fake hair pieces and extensions in many colours and styles.

Department stores

There is little to distinguish the four main chains, Hertie, Karstadt, Kaufhof and Wertheim. All offer everything you might need in decent quality and at reasonable prices. In an unfortunate development, malls have been mushrooming across the city, threatening small, neighbourhood retailers (*see p158* **From Berlin Wall to Berlin mall**).

Dussmann Das KulturKaufhaus

Friedrichstrasse 90, Mitte (20250). S1, S2, S3, S5, S7, S9, S25, S26, S75, U6 Friedrichstrasse. **Open** 10am-10pm Mon-Sat. **Credit** AmEx, MC, V. **Map** p316/p302 F3.
Set up with the aim of being a 'cultural department store', this is a spacious four-floor retailer mixing books with CDs, videos with magazines, also with internet terminals, an interactive video-viewing room and DVD shop. In the music department there are enough CD players to allow for easy listening.

Galeries Lafayette

Französische Strasse 23, Mitte (209 480). U2, U6 Stadtmitte. **Open** 9.30am-8pm Mon-Fri; 9am-4pm Sat. **Credit** AmEx, DC, MC, V. **Map** p316/p302 F3.
The Jean Nouvel glass block that houses Galeries Lafayette offers state-of-the-art architecture and a refreshing shopping experience. All the merchandise is French, and, though the selection of accessories, cosmetics and clothing is good (highlight is the Agnès B shop-in-shop on the first floor), the best feature is the food floor in the basement, where you'll feel transported to Paris among fresh cheeses, chocolates, wines, breads and condiments.

Karstadt

Wilmersdorfer Strasse 118, Charlottenburg (311 050). U7 Wilmersdorfer Strasse. **Open** 9.30am-8pm Mon-Fri; 9am-4pm Sat. **Credit** AmEx, DC, MC, V. **Map** p304 B4.
You can access this sprawling concrete block directly from the U-Bahn stop, which makes it a good place for one-stop shopping. Recently modernised, this branch has a big selection of household goods, an excellent food department in the basement, and a decent selection of other utilitarian merchandise on the upper floors. It even has a post office.

Eat, Drink, Shop

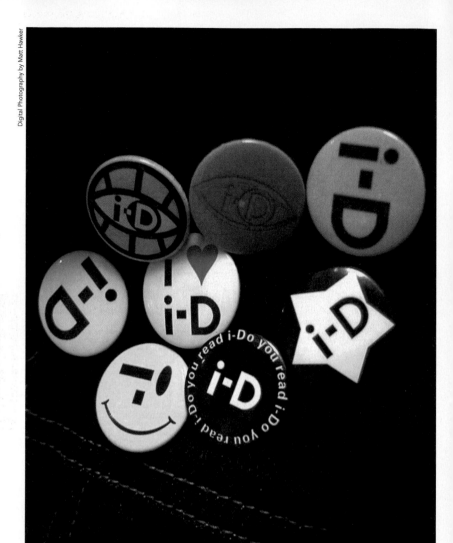

KaDeWe

Tauentzienstrasse 21-4, Schöneberg (21210). U1, U2, U12, U15 Wittenbergplatz. **Open** 9.30am-8pm Mon-Fri; 9am-4pm Sat. **Credit** AmEx, DC, MC, V. **Map** p305 D4.

The KaDeWe is the largest department store in continental Europe and a top tourist attraction. But though it carries name brands in all departments, the presentation is bad and much of the merchandise merely average. The cosmetics department stocks all the big-name brands as well as smaller, hard to find upmarket lines like MAC, La Mer and Erno Laszlo. KaDeWe is famous for its lavish food hall, which takes up the entire sixth floor and features foodstuffs from around the globe. Seafood and *Wurst* lovers will think they've died and gone to heaven. The delicatessen is known for its specialities, the gourmet bars offer everything from oysters to smoked sausage, and special orders for more outré items can be made by phone (213 2455). Some may take a few days to be fulfilled and same-day delivery is possible until 4pm in Berlin and Potsdam.

Kaufhof

Alexanderplatz 9, Mitte (2474 3265). S3, S5, S7, S9, S75, U2, U5, U8 Alexanderplatz. **Open** 9am-8pm Mon-Fri; 9am-4pm Sat. **Credit** AmEx, DC, MC, V. **Map** p316/p303 G3.

The Kaufhof group bought the old East German Centrum stores and dominates the eastern market. Its Alexanderplatz branch façade is so 1970s it's almost hip. This Kaufhof 'Galeria' is structured on the shop-in-shop principle and expat London girls come here to stock up on Oasis. There's also an internet café and kids' cinema.

Naturkaufhaus

Schlossstrasse 101, Steglitz (797 3716). U9 Schlossstrasse. **Open** 10am-8pm Mon-Fri; 10am-4pm Sat. **No credit cards.**

Berlin's first department store for organic goods is located on two floors of the Galleria mall in Steglitz. The selection ranges from the foodstuffs you also find in smaller *Bioläden* to eco-friendly clothes, shoes and cosmetics as well as a selection of wines.

Quartier 206 Department Store

Friedrichstrasse 71, Mitte (2094 6800). U2, U6 Stadtmitte. **Open** 10am-8pm Mon-Fri; 10am-4pm Sat. **Credit** AmEx, DC, MC, V. **Map** p316/p302 F3.

Germans seem to think giving their shop an English name will lend it an international flair. This one needn't have resorted to such tactics. Reminiscent of New York's Takashimaya and designed by that city's Calvin Tsao, it offers not only the most lusted-after designer labels, but those labels' most definitive items. Cult cosmetics and centuries-old perfumes are available on the ground floor along with a fantastic flower department, while the upstairs is devoted to women's and men's fashion, lingerie, jewellery, a Manolo Blahnik shoe department and a home living section stocked with sinfully expensive design trends.

Wertheim

Kurfürstendamm 231, Charlottenburg (880 030). U9, U15 Kurfürstendamm. **Open** 9.30am-8pm Mon-Fri; 9am-4pm Sat. **Credit** AmEx, DC, MC, V. **Map** p305 C4.

Walk in the door and be tempted by several sweet-smelling chocolate and praline counters. This branch has a good perfume and cosmetics department, and is popular among Berliners for no-nonsense accessories, all on the ground floor. Food market in basement.

Design & household goods

For a while it seemed Berlin was so busy rebuilding someone forgot people needed to furnish all this new space. **stilwerk** (*see p166* **Design for life**) came to the rescue, a project that has attracted other retailers to transform this stretch of **Kantstrasse** in Charlottenburg into an oasis for home improvers. The scene in Mitte is big on retro, and the **Alte** and **Neue Schönhauser Strassen** are good places to hunt for neo-cool eastern and western designs from the 1950s to 1970s. The 'ethno' look arrived late in Berlin and is still big here.

Bella Casa

Bergmannstrasse 101, Kreuzberg (694 0784). U6, U7 Mehringdamm. **Open** 11am-7pm Mon-Fri; 10am-4pm Sat. **Credit** MC, V. **Map** p306 F5.

Inexpensive oriental lamps, rugs, pillows, bed throws and ceramics from North Africa and Egypt.

Bramigk & Breer

Niebuhrstrasse 1, Charlottenburg (882 7373). S3, S5, S7, S9, S75 Savignyplatz. **Open** 11am-6.30pm Mon-Wed; 11am-7.30pm Thur, Fri; 11am-4pm Sat. **Credit** MC, V. **Map** p305 C4.

Strikes a balance between Mediterranean and Brandenburg country style with stripped-down furniture, warm lighting and irresistible ornaments. A fine selection of natural linens, hand-blown coloured drinking glasses and realistic silk flowers.

Coldampf's

Uhlandstrasse 54-5, Charlottenburg (883 9191). U1 Hohenzollernplatz. **Open** 10am-8pm Mon-Fri; 10am-4pm Sat. **Credit** MC, V. **Map** p305 C5.

An impressive stock of some 7,000 products to equip any kitchen, from high-tech cooking utensils to sturdy cocktail glasses. You can also hire plates and glasses.

Branch: Wörther Strasse 39, Prenzlauer Berg (4373 5225).

dadriade

Rosenthaler Strasse 40-41, Mitte (2852 8720). S3, S5, S7, S9, S75 Hackescher Markt or U8 Weinmeisterstrasse. **Open** 10am-8pm Mon-Fri; 10am-4pm Sat. **Credit** AmEx, MC, V. **Map** p316/p302 F3.

The pioneering presence of this glossy flagship store was instrumental in establishing Mitte as a hip place

Eat, Drink, Shop

to shop. A mecca for disciples of (mostly Italian) high style, it is filled with breathtaking tableware, cunningly functional kitchens and steel-and-glass furnishings – much of it by Philippe Starck.

Dopo Domani

Kantstrasse 148, Charlottenburg (882 2242). S3, S5, S7, S9, S75 Savignyplatz. **Open** 10.30am-8pm Mon-Fri; 10.30am-4pm Sat. **Credit** AmEx, MC, V. **Map** p305 C4.

A temple for design aficionados installed over three levels of a turn-of-the-20th-century townhouse. Combining an interior design practice with an abundantly stocked shop, the focus is on Italian outfitters and the presentation creates an environment that you'll dream of calling your own.

Formgeber Berlin

Golzstrasse 13B, Schöneberg (2362 4920). U7 Eisenacher Strasse. **Open** 10am-8pm Mon-Fri; 10am-4pm Sat. **Credit** MC, V. **Map** p305 D5.

Pragmatic furniture and accessories for streamlined, style-conscious living with a touch of '70s irony. Appealing ceramics in sleek and inventive shapes.

IKEA

Ruhlebener Strasse 23, Spandau (0180 535 3435/ www.ikea.de). U2 Ruhleben, then bus 145, 235. **Open** 9.30am-8pm Mon-Fri; 8.30am-4pm Sat. **No credit cards.**

All you could want in the way of Scandinavian value-for-money home design.

Branch: Am Rondell 8, Waltersdorf (0180 535 3435).

Design for life

Vaunting buildings by such Bauhaus greats as Walter Gropius and Mies van der Rohe, Berlin is no stranger to good design. Reawakening after the deep sleep of division, design is once again coming into its own here — and **stilwerk** is the centrepiece of an increasingly style-conscious city. A theme centre for high-end products opened in late 1999, it's a 20,000 square-metre (215,000 square-foot) forum for more than 50 retailers offering a huge range of items in modern furnishings, state-of-the-art kitchens, high-tech lighting as well as luxurious bath fittings, hi-fis, fabrics, floor coverings – even grand pianos. From Alessi to Zanotta, you'll find many of the major players in the world of interiors, with large showrooms rented out by the likes of B&B Italia, Rolf Benz, Bulthaup and Cassina. For the city's architects and designers, stilwerk is a reference point, a place to see the items that made the headlines and show clients what they mean when they talk about a €15,000 kitchen. For consumers it's a one-stop shop and for those who can't pay the prices, a glitzy place to browse and experience a stylised world, if only fleetingly.

The best way to approach a tour of stilwerk is to take one of the lifts at the back to the top. There's a fantastic view from the fifth floor, which can be rented out for exhibitions and events. In summer the roof garden is a popular location for parties, some of them open to the (trend-making) public. Then start your descent via the staircase.

Well worth checking out is the Design & Crafts Platform on the fourth floor. It showcases local talents who have shops elsewhere in town – vitrines present such handcrafted goods as jewellery, pottery and unique design accessories, all of which can be purchased, and there are presentations of things you'll have to order, like innovative wall finishes and wrought-iron fences. Get a quick fix on the other end of this floor at the espresso bar, which also sells the most dazzling coffee machinery you'll find anywhere.

Design-related exhibitions are regularly featured in the atrium of the ground floor, as well as evening events such as award ceremonies for national and international design competitions. The muted tones of the restaurant Stil provide a relaxing stop for refreshment.

And if you haven't seen enough design to last you a lifetime, you needn't go as far as the stilwerk developments in Hamburg or Düsseldorf for more — just venture back out on to Kantstrasse. Berlin's stilwerk has acted like a magnet for other retailers of similar ilk and transformed two blocks of this street into a haven for home improvement.

stilwerk

Kantstrasse 17, Charlottenburg (315 150). S3, S5, S7, S9, S75 Savignyplatz. **Open** 10am-8pm Mon-Fri; 10am-4pm Sat. *Viewing only* 2-6pm Sun. **Credit** varies. **Map** p305 C4.

Leinenkontor

Tucholskystrasse 22, Mitte (2839 0277/
www.leinenkontor.de). S1, S2, S25, S26
Oranienburger Strasse. **Open** 10am-6pm Tue-Sat.
Credit MC, V. **Map** p316/p302 F3.
Textile designer Eva Endruweit has a contagious
passion for linen that is likely to infect anyone who
enters her small shop. She has stacks of flaxen materials for the table and bed from her own no-frills
collection, as well as from the exquisite Austrian
company Leitner and Sweden's royal purveyor
Ekelund. Also a collection of shirts, nightdresses
and christening gowns that she makes herself.

Rahaus Wohnen 2001

Am Wittenbergplatz, Schöneberg (218 9393). U2,
U12, U15 Wittenbergplatz. **Open** 10am-8pm Mon-
Fri; 10am-4pm Sat. **No credit cards**. **Map** p305 D5.
Young and fun furniture, lamps and home acces-
sories – often based on designer bestsellers – for
budgets that can't stretch to the real thing.
Branches: Rahaus Country Franklinstrasse 12-
14, Charlottenburg (3999 4834); **Rahaus Loft**
Franklinstrasse 8, Charlottenburg (3999 4870);
Rahaus City Möbel Kurfürstendamm 74,
Charlottenburg (324 3876); **Rahaus Living**
Kanstrasse 151, Charlottenburg (313 2100).

Ruby

Oranienburger Strasse 32, Mitte (2838 6030).
S1, S2, S25, S26 Oranienburger Strasse.
Open 11am-8pm Mon-Fri; 11am-6pm Sat.
Credit AmEx, MC, V. **Map** p316/p302 F3.
Flying the minimalist banner, this small shop in the
beautifully restored courtyard offers Spencer Fung's
architectural furniture, Bowls and Linares lamps,
Henry Dean glass as well as rugs, fabrics, candles
and an alluring selection of ceramics in earth tones.

Schlafwandel

Kantstrasse 21, Charlottenburg (312 6523). S3, S5,
S7, S9, S75 Savignyplatz. **Open** 10am-6.30pm Mon-
Fri; 10am-4pm Sat. **No credit cards**. **Map** p305 C4.
Top brands in towelling and linen for bath and bed,
plus a huge selection of robes and pyjamas.

Schönhauser

Neue Schönhauser Strasse 18, Mitte (281 1704). U8
Weinmeisterstrasse. **Open** noon-8pm Mon-Fri; 11am-
4pm Sat. **No credit cards**. **Map** p316/p303 G3.
All you need to deck out your front room like the
flightdeck of the Starship *Enterprise*, such as bright
plastic swivel chairs, GDR light fixtures, bubble TVs
and other design classics from the 1930s to the 1970s.

Glass & ceramics

Alfar & Sykora

Fasanenstrasse 58, Charlottenburg (881 5922).
U1 Spichernstrasse. **Open** 1-6pm Mon-Fri; 11am-
2pm Sat. **No credit cards**. **Map** p305 C5.
Two potters who aim to take clay where it's not
gone before, with filigree objects that are both works
of art and high design.

Bürgel-Haus

Friedrichstrasse 154, Mitte (204 4519).
U6 Französische Strasse. **Open** 9am-8pm Mon-Sat.
Credit AmEx, MC, V. **Map** p316/p302 F3.
This distinctive blue-and-cream pottery from the
state of Thüringen makes an inexpensive present
for lovers of cosy kitchenware.

Keramikladen am Prenzlauer Berg

Rykestrasse 49, Prenzlauer Berg (441 9109). U2
Senefelderplatz. **Open** 1-6.30pm Tue-Fri; 11am-4pm
Sat. **No credit cards**. **Map** p303 G2.
Bright, inexpensive, humorous household ceramics
from this collective of four potters.

KPM

Wegelystrasse 1, Tiergarten (3900 9215). S3, S5, S7,
S9, S75 Tiergarten. **Open** 10am-7pm Mon-Fri; 9.30am-
4pm Sat. **Credit** AmEx, DC, MC, V. **Map** p305 D4.
Frederick the Great liked porcelain so much that
he bought the company: Königliche Porzellan
Manufaktur. Eat from a king's plate, inexpensively
too if you pick up some seconds at this factory shop.
The full-priced version is at the Kempinski branch.
Branches: Kempinski Hotel Kurfürstendamm 27,
Charlottenburg (886 7210); Unter den Linden 35,
Mitte (206 4150).

Fashion

A quick glance at the average man in the *Strasse*
should tell you that Berlin is a long way from
the cutting edge of style. But this sorry state of
affairs is changing, and recent years have seen
some interesting developments in retail fashion.

One of the most productive places to hunt
for stylish, affordable clothing has sprung up
in the **Scheunenviertel** in Mitte (*see p81*).
The renovated Hackesche Höfe, the Heckmann
Höfe and the surrounding streets are now
home to many of Berlin's designers, their shops
and ateliers. The merchandise on offer may
sometimes seem limited, but the advantage of
having workshops as part of the store is that
styles can be run up quickly in your size and
preferred fabric. Several innovative local labels
have settled on **Kastanienallee** in Prenzlauer
Berg. Many of these shops are on short, cheap
rental contracts, so it's best to call and check
they're still there before setting out. Designers
of a more hefty calibre have moved into the
retail developments on **Friedrichstrasse**,
where new shopfronts are filling with high-
profile, international labels.

But despite all this excitement in the east,
there is still no avoiding the **Ku'damm** and
its affluent offshoots. Here, department stores
and clothing giants (Gap, Esprit, Benetton,
Hallhuber) jostle for space with high-end
fashion boutiques. Most of the designer
merchandise is stuff you'd be able to buy in
any major city, but cross-town competition for

Eat, Drink, Shop

business makes for some lively end-of-season sales (*Schlussverkauf*) and there is usually a lot of merchandise left over. With a favourable exchange rate, you can pick up bargains. The most sophisticated Berlin gets is **Fasanenstrasse**, where you will find the likes of Gucci, Chanel, Tiffany and Bvlgari. Much of the money spent here is Russian, and literal wads of cash change hands.

The following shops are by no means a comprehensive survey of all that Berlin has to offer, but they give a flavour of the more dynamic elements of the city's fledgling fashion culture.

Accessories

Les Dessous

Fasanenstrasse 42, Wilmersdorf (883 3632). U1, U9 Spichernstrasse. **Open** 11am-7pm Mon-Fri; 10am-3pm Sat. **Credit** AmEx, DC, MC, V. **Map** p305 C5.
A beautiful shop featuring luxurious lingerie, silk dressing gowns and striking swimwear by Capucine, Eres, Dior, La Perla and Andres Sarda. **Branch:** Schlüterstrasse 36, Charlottenburg (881 3660).

Fiona Bennett

Grosse Hamburger Strasse 25, Mitte (2809 6330). S3, S5, S7, S9, S75 Hackescher Markt. **Open** noon-6pm Tue-Fri; noon-4pm Sat. **Credit** AmEx, DC, MC, V. **Map** p316/p302 F3.
Fiona's hats are works of art. Redefining traditional shapes, her imagination leaves trends by the wayside to create horned headdresses, feathered fedoras, hats reminiscent of insects or sea urchins, and delicate hairpieces made of a single feather shaped into a curl or shimmering sequins spilling over into a filigree fountain. For all their theatrics, the hats always display their maker's sense for beauty. Plus, the interior of the shop has a remarkable compact design.

Fishbelly

Sophienstrasse 7A, Mitte (2804 5180). U8 Weinmeisterstrasse. **Open** 12.30-7pm Mon-Fri; noon-5pm Sat. **Credit** AmEx, DC, MC, V. **Map** p316/p302 F3.
Often compared to London's Agent Provocateur, this tiny Hackesche Höfe shop is licensed to thrill with extravagant under- and bathing garments by Dolce & Gabbana Intimo, Christian Dior, Capucine Puerari and its own line of imaginative lingerie.

Kaufhaus Schrill

Bleibtreustrasse 46, Charlottenburg (882 4048). S3, S5, S7, S9, S75 Savignyplatz. **Open** 2-8pm Mon-Fri; 11am-4pm Sat. **Credit** AmEx, MC, V. **Map** p305 C4.
Feather boas, sequins, tiaras, pearls, rhinestones, shocking colours, frills and loud, fruity patterns.

Knopf Paul

Zossener Strasse 10, Kreuzberg (692 1212). U7 Gneisenaustrasse. **Open** 9am-6pm Tue, Fri; 2-6pm Wed, Thur. **No credit cards. Map** p306 F4.
A Kreuzberg institution that stocks thousands of buttons in every imaginable shape, colour and material.

Roeckl

Kurfürstendamm 216, Charlottenburg (881 5379). U1, U15 Uhlandstrasse. **Open** 10am-8pm Mon-Fri; 10am-4pm Sat. **Credit** AmEx, DC, MC, V. **Map** p305 C4.
Gloves in all colours and materials, plus scarves, pashminas and shawls by international designers.

Tagebau

Rosenthaler Strasse 19, Mitte (2839 0890). S3, S5, S7, S9, S75 Hackescher Markt or U8 Weinmeisterstrasse. **Open** 11am-8pm Mon-Fri; 11am-6pm Sat. **Credit** MC. **Map** p316/p302 F3.
The six young designers who share this airy, spacious store-cum-workshop specialise in jewellery, fashion, millinery and furniture. Their work also shares a collective sculptural quality that, when it is combined with the Tagebau's generous space and subtle spot-lighting, gives the whole establishment the impression of a gallery.

Costume & formal-wear hire

Graichen

Klosterstrasse 32, Spandau (331 3587). U7 Rathaus Spandau. **Open** 10am-6pm Mon-Fri; 10am-1pm Sat; or by appointment. **Credit** MC.
Tuxedos for men, short and long eveningwear for women. Bridal gowns too.

Theaterkunst

Eisenzahnstrasse 43-4, Wilmersdorf (864 7270). U1, U7 Fehrbelliner Platz. **Open** 8am-4.30pm Mon-Thur; 8am-3.30pm Fri. **No credit cards. Map** p304 B5.

Tagebau: shopping as art.

Three warehouses crammed floor to ceiling with period costumes to kit out any historical fantasy. The choice is immense so allow time to browse and be fitted and go back later to collect. Founded in 1908, the impressive collection was destroyed during the last war and re-established in 1951. Staff know their stuff and give good advice, and there's a free alterations service. Elaborate rococo outfits cost considerably more than costumes from more recent times.

Designer: international

Antonie Setzer
Bleibtreustrasse 19, Charlottenburg (883 1350).
S3, S5, S7, S9, S75 Savignyplatz. **Open** 10am-7pm
Mon-Wed; 10am-8pm Thur-Fri; 10am-4pm Sat.
Credit AmEx, DC, MC, V. **Map** p305 C4.
Fashion for women with an intelligent selection of styles from Capucine, D&G, Miu Miu, Strenesse and the unusual designs of Italian label Gembalies.

Harvey's
Kurfürstendamm 186, Charlottenburg (883 3803).
U15 Uhlandstrasse. **Open** 10.30am-8pm Mon-Fri;
10am-4pm Sat. **Credit** AmEx, MC, V. **Map** p305 C4.
Frieder Böhnisch has held the fort of cutting-edge men's labels for 20 years. Now he stocks clothes and shoes by the Japanese – Yohji Yamamoto and Comme des Garçons – and the Belgians – Bikkembergs and Martin Margiela. His enthusiasm for the designers he sells may persuade you to splurge, but there are no hard feelings if you don't.

Mientus Studio 2002
Wilmersdorfer Strasse 73, Charlottenburg (323 9077). U7 Wilmersdorfstrasse. **Open** 10am-8pm
Mon-Fri; 10am-4pm Sat. **Credit** AmEx, DC, MC, V.
Map p304 B4.
Clean cuts for sharp men from a range of collections including Dsquared, Neil Barrett, Helmut Lang, Miu Miu, Andrew Mackenzie and German rave labels.
Branches: Schlüterstrasse 26, Charlottenburg (323 9077); Kurfürstendamm 52, Charlottenburg (323 9077).

Patrick Hellman
Fasanenstrasse 26, Charlottenburg (8848 7712).
U15 Uhlandstrasse. **Open** 10am-7pm Mon-Fri; 10am-8pm Thur; 10am-4pm Sat. **Credit** AmEx, DC, MC, V.
Map p305 C5.
Prolific Berlin retailer with five stores to his name, specialising in international chic for men and women. A bespoke tailoring service offers men the choice of the Hellman design range in a variety of luxurious fabrics, including some by Italian textile maestro Ermenegildo Zegna.

Sheila
Kurfürstendamm 72, Charlottenburg (324 9808).
U7 Adenauerplatz. **Open** 11am-7pm Mon-Fri; 11am-4pm Sat. **Credit** AmEx, D, MC, V. **Map** p305 C4.
Though it's changed hands three times in the past 30 years, this boutique has remained committed to styles as elegant as they are fun. Stocking names like

Chloë, Alberta Ferretti and the German designer Susanne Bommer, the new owner shows a predilection for luxurious materials and interesting cuts.

Tools & Gallery
Rosenthaler Strasse 34-5, Mitte (2859 9343).
S3, S5, S7, S9, S75 Hackescher Markt or U8
Weinmeisterstrasse. **Open** 10am-8pm Mon-Fri;
10am-4pm Sat. **Credit** MC, V. **Map** p316/p302 F3.
Kai Angladegies is not the first to fuse fashion and fine art, but T&G is a bold and stylish attempt. The interior is camply decked out in rococo splendour, with candelabras and muslin-draped changing cubicles, and the selection of clothing is equally impressive. Menswear is especially strong and often nothing short of outrageous. Names for men and women include Givenchy, Alexander McQueen and Vivienne Westwood. The gallery is accessed via a beautiful 1860 wrought-iron staircase and features exhibitions of fine art, design and haute couture including Balenciaga.

Designer: local

Chiton
Goltzstrasse 12, Schöneberg (216 6013). U7
Eisenacher Strasse. **Open** noon-6.30pm Mon-Fri;
11am-2pm Sat. **Credit** AmEx, MC, V. **Map** p305 D5.
Young husband-and-wife team Robert and Friederike Jorzig are the winning ticket for beautiful bridal and evening gowns. Worked in high-quality fabrics, their striking cuts – from the very simple to designs recalling early Hollywood sophistication – attract many customers from Britain and the US. They also put out summer and winter collections in their signature reductionist style. Allow at least two or three weeks for gowns and men's suits; dresses can be done in three days.

Claudia Skoda Level
Linienstrasse 156, Mitte (280 7211). U6
Oranienburger Tor. **Open** 11am-7pm Mon-Fri.
Credit AmEx, DC, MC, V. **Map** p316/p302 F3.
Berlin's most established womenswear designer has extended her creative energies to include men, and she showcases designs for both in this upper-storey loft space in Mitte. Using high-tech yarns and innovative knitting techniques, the collections bear her signature combination of stretch fabrics and graceful drape effects.
Branch: Second Season, Linienstrasse 154, Mitte (280 7211).

Coration
Kastanienallee 13, Prenzlauer Berg (4404 6090).
U2 Eberswalder Strasse. **Open** 2-8pm Mon, Tue;
noon-8pm Wed-Fri; 11am-6pm Sat. **Credit** AmEx,
MC, V. **Map** p303 G2.
Cora Schwind designs a fresh look for urban men on the move. A hot label among the burgeoning population of DJs and web designers in Prenz'lberg.
Branch: Kopernikusstrasse 18A, Friedrichshain (2904 6626).

Hut Up

Oranienburger Strasse 32, Mitte (2838 6105).
S1, S2, S25, S26 Oranienburger Strasse.
Open 11am-6pm Mon-Sat. **Credit** AmEx, DC,
MC, V. **Map** p316/p302 F3.
Christine Birkle's imaginative felt designs come in
bold colours for a wide variety of uses. Her wares
are handcrafted in one piece shaped from raw wool
using traditional methods. The clothes combine felt
with silk or gauze, and there's a witty range of accessories for the body or home including hats, slippers,
vases, hot-water bottles, mobile phone cases, wine
coolers and egg cosies shaped like dunce hats.

Lisa D

Hackesche Höfe, Rosenthaler Strasse 40-41, Mitte
(282 9061). S3, S5, S7, S9, S75 Hackescher Markt
or U8 Weinmeisterstrasse. **Open** noon-6.30pm Mon-
Sat. **Credit** AmEx, DC, MC, V. **Map** p316/p302 F3.
Long, flowing womenswear in subdued shades from
this avant-garde designer. Austrian-born Lisa D is
a well-known face on the Berlin fashion scene and
was one of the first tenants to move into the renovated Hackesche Höfe.

Molotow

Gneisenaustrasse 112, Kreuzberg (693 0818). U7
Mehringdamm. **Open** 2-8pm Mon-Fri; noon-4pm Sat.
Credit AmEx, DC, MC, V. **Map** p306 F5.
Showcasing local talent, Molotow sells a selection of
fashion and millinery from Berlin designers for men
and women. The clothes are fresh and eye-catching,
ranging from futuristic creations to classical sharp
tailoring. Custom tailoring available.

RespectMen

Neue Schönhauser Strasse 14, Mitte (283 5010). U8
Weinmeisterstrasse. **Open** noon-8pm Mon-Fri; 11am-
4pm Sat. **Credit** AmEx, MC, V. **Map** p316/p303 G3.
When seen on the rail, Dirk Seidel and Karin
Warburg's menswear seems to be traditionally tai-
lored, yet when worn it shows off its contemporary,
body-conscious cut. Suits, trousers, jackets and
coats can be order from the many fabrics on
offer. The inventive cut may not appeal to fashion
conservatives, but this is some of the most interesting menswear you'll find in Berlin. Also stocks
Bikkenbergs and Paul Smith — as obviously,
for the opposite sex, RespectWomen across the street.
Branch: RespectWomen Neue Schönhauser
Strasse 6, Mitte (2804 5666); **RespectLess** Neue
Schönhauser Strasse 19, Mitte (2809 9999).

Yoshiharu Ito

Auguststrasse 19, Mitte (4404 4490). S1,S2, S25,
S26 Oranienburger Strasse. **Open** noon-8pm Mon-
Sat. **Credit** AmEx, DC,MC, V. **Map** p316/p302 F3.
Tokyo-born Ito has been an indispensable part of
the Berlin designer scene for more than ten years.
His Studio Ito label was much-desired in the 1990s
and though unpaid orders bankrupted the small
company, he has made an impressive comeback. His
showroom in Mitte offers his purist collections for
men and women in the tradition of Asian designers

like Yamamoto but with strong European influences. His styles are practical, with great attention
to detail like perfectly worked pockets and seams in
unusual places. With a nod to the avant-garde,
Ito mixes a futuristic style with classic wool or lacquered cotton for fun and wearable clothes.

Dry-cleaning & alterations

Good laundry and dry-cleaning services are in
short supply. Many fashion designers offer an
alterations or made-to-measure service included
in the price, or for a small charge. To get a zip
fixed or a rip mended, alterations shops (many
of them Turkish) will usually provide a next-
day service. Consult the *Gelbe Seiten* (*Yellow
Pages*) under *Änderungsschneidereien*.

Kim Jang Woon

Pestalozzistrasse 69, Charlottenburg (327 5151).
U7 Wilmersdorfer Strasse. **Open** 9am-6pm Mon-Fri;
9am-1pm Sat. **No credit cards.** **Map** p304 B4.
Quick turnaround for all manner of alterations.

Kleenothek

Schönhauser Allee 186, Prenzlauer Berg (449 5833).
U2 Rosa-Luxemburg-Platz. **Open** 7.30am-7.30pm
Mon-Fri; 9am-1pm Sat. **No credit cards.**
Map p303 G2.
Reliable dry-cleaners that will also take in laundry
for service (machine) washing.

Michael Klemm

Wörtherstrasse 31, Prenzlauer Berg (442 4549). U2
Senefelderplatz. **Open** 10am-noon, 1-6pm Mon-Fri.
No credit cards. **Map** p303 G2.
Friendly tailor for all types of alterations. Will also
run up garments on request.

Nantes

Uhlandstrasse 20-25, Charlottenburg (883 5746).
U15 Uhlandstrasse. **Open** 8am-6pm Mon-Fri.
No credit cards. **Map** p305 C4.
Recommended by designer shops, Nantes charges
slightly more than most for dry-cleaning, but
takes up to four days. It's worth the wait for valuable items.

Trendy

Möllendorffstrasse 74, Lichtenberg (9599 73033).
S4, S8, S10, U5 Frankfurter Allee. **Open** noon-6pm
Mon-Fri. **No credit cards.**
Sonja Geier spent seven years working for a major
retailer altering the likes of Armani, Galliano and
Gucci. Her sewing is impeccable and she will pick
up and deliver to your home or hotel.

Fetish

Black Style

Seelower Strasse 5, Prenzlauer Berg (4468 8595/
www.blackstyle.de). S4, S8, U2 Schönhauser Allee.
Open 1-6.30pm Mon-Wed, Fri; 1-8pm Thur; 10am-
2pm Sat. **Credit** AmEx, MC, V. **Map** p303 G1.

From black fashion to butt plugs – if it can be made out of rubber or latex they've got it. High quality, reasonable prices and big variety. Mail order.

Leathers

Schliemannstrasse 38, Prenzlauer Berg (442 7786/www.leathers-berlin.de). U2 Eberswalder Strasse. **Open** noon-7.30pm Tue-Fri; noon-4pm Sat. **Credit** AmEx, MC, V. **Map** p303 G2.
A workshop producing leather and SM articles and furniture of the highest quality. No smut here – just well-presented products and helpful staff.

Mid-range

Essenbeck

Auguststrasse 72, Mitte (2838 8725). U8 Weinmeister Strasse. **Open** noon-8pm Mon-Fri; noon-6pm Sat. **Credit** MC, V. **Map** p316/p302 F3.
Seeking to introduce new names to Germany, owners Sabine Hartung and Dirk Schulte scout around Europe's trendsetting capitals for clothes with an edge. Creativity, quality and cut are their criteria.

Groopie Deluxe

Goltzstrasse 39, Schöneberg (217 2038). U7 Eisenacher Strasse. **Open** 11am-7pm Mon-Fri; 11am-4pm Sat. **Credit** AmEx, MC, V. **Map** p305 D5.
Trendy, sexy gear to party in – lots of bright, skimpy numbers, fake fur, and accessories. On her travels the stewardess owner fills her suitcase with whatever suits her fancy, from Chinese dragonlady dresses to laid-back SoHo chic for boys.

To Die For

Neue Schönhauser Strasse 10, Mitte (2838 6834). U8 Weinmeisterstrasse. **Open** noon-8pm Mon-Fri; 11am-6pm Sat. **Credit** AmEx, DC, MC, V. **Map** p316/p303 G3.
One of the first clothes shops in now thriving Mitte, this shop supplies ready-to-wear collections from the likes of D&G to slip into instant party mode.
Branch: Hotel, Oranienburger Strasse 8, Mitte (2887 9470); Superstore outlet, Alte Schönhauser Strasse 41, Mitte (2463 9643).

Second-hand clothes & shoes

Berlin has a huge market in cheaper clothing, with flea markets, junk shops and second-hand stores offering bargains aplenty. The best hunting grounds are around **Mehringdamm** in Kreuzberg and **Prinzenallee** in Wedding.

Calypso – High Heels For Ever

Münzstrasse 16, Mitte (281 6165). U8 Weinmeisterstrasse. **Open** noon-7pm Mon-Fri; noon-4pm Sat. **No credit cards. Map** p316/p303 G3.
Hundreds of gravity-defying stilettos, wedges and platforms in the vivid shades and exotic shapes of the 1960s and 1970s, almost all in fine condition. Also a selection of stilettoed, thigh-high fetish boots, some in men's sizes.

Checkpoint

Mehringdamm 57, Kreuzberg (694 4344). U6, U7 Mehringdamm. **Open** 10am-6.30pm Mon-Fri; 10am-4pm Sat. **No credit cards. Map** p306 F5.
Huge selection of 1970s gear: Lurex skinny-knit jumpers, printed bellbottoms, leather coats and jackets, and even wedding dresses from the heyday of *Charlie's Angels*.
Branch: Monroe, Kollwitzstrasse 102, Prenzlauer Berg (440 8448).

Colours

1st courtyard, Bergmannstrasse 102, Kreuzberg (694 3348). U7 Gneisenaustrasse. **Open** 11am-7pm Mon-Wed; 11am-8pm Thur, Fri; 10am-4pm Sat. **No credit cards. Map** p306 F5.
Row upon row of jeans, leather jackets and dresses, including party stunners and some fetching Bavarian dirndls. The odd gem from the 1950s and 1960s is thrown in too. Prices depend on condition and vintage.

Falbala

Knaackstrasse 43, Prenzlauer Berg (4405 1082). U2 Senefelderplatz. **Open** 1-6pm Mon-Fri; noon-2pm Sat. **Credit** AmEx, MC, V. **Map** p303 G2.
Right on Kollwitz Platz, this is a treasure trove of vintage clothing — particularly from the 1940s and 1950s. Josefine Edle von Krepl has been collecting for four decades and lets customers take their time to browse through the great quantities of day and evening dresses, blouses, bags, jewellery and hats. Music and decor recreate the era, and she even serves tea.

Garage

Ahornstrasse 2, Schöneberg (211 2760). U1, U2, U4, U12 Nollendorfplatz. **Open** 11am-7pm Mon-Wed; 11am-8pm Thur, Fri; 10am-4pm Sat. **No credit cards. Map** p305 D4.
One of Berlin's cheapest second-hand shops with clothing priced per kilo. Surprisingly well organised, given the barracks-like nature of the place. Good for cheap, last-minute party outfits.

Humana

Karl-Liebknecht-Strasse 30, Mitte (242 3000). S3, S5, S7, S9, S75, U2, U5, U8 Alexanderplatz. **Open** 10am-7.30pm Mon-Wed; 10am-8pm Thur, Fri; 11am-4pm Sat. **No credit cards. Map** p316/p303 G3.
Huge Humana charity megastores are sprouting all over the city, selling acres of cheap second-hand clothing, household textiles, fur and leather. This is the biggest and most central. They usually have a 'trend' section of more fashionable, original numbers and this is worth hunting through for bargains.
Branches across the city.

Made in Berlin

Potsdamer Strasse 106, Tiergarten (262 2431). U1, U12 Kurfürstenstrasse. **Open** 10am-7pm Mon-Wed; 10am-8pm Thur, Fri; 10am-4pm Sat. **No credit cards. Map** p306 E4.
Sister store of Garage (*see above*), where the 'better stuff' supposedly goes. Fear not, it's still pretty cheap though.

Eat, Drink, Shop

Claudia Skoda Level. *See p169.*

Sgt Peppers
Kastanienallee 91-2, Prenzlauer Berg
(448 1121). U2 Eberswalder Strasse.
Open 11am-7pm Mon-Fri; 11am-3pm Sat.
Credit MC, V. **Map** p303 G2.
Bright gear from the 1960s and 1970s, arranged by
size, which is helpful.

Spitze
Weimarer Strasse 19, Charlottenburg
(313 1068). U7 Wilmersdorfer Strasse.
Open 2-6.30pm Mon-Fri; 11am-2pm Sat.
Credit MC, V. **Map** p305 C4.
A goldmine for clothes and accessories from 1860 to
1960, raided by Donna Karan whenever she's in
town. Spitze will rent out some of its nuggets for a
third of the sale price. Evening gloves, handbags,
shoes and other accessories also available.

Sterling Gold
Oranienburger Strasse 32, Mitte (2809 6500).
S1, S2, S25, S26 Oranienburger Strasse.
Open noon- 8pm Mon-Fri; noon-6pm Sat.
Credit MC, V. **Map** p316/p302 F3.
Michael Boenke couldn't believe his luck when
he was offered a warehouse full of 'prom' dresses
during a trip to America. He immediately shipped
them straight to Berlin and has done so well
with them he's opened this second shop – decorated in Cinderella style – in Mitte's Heckmann Höfe.
These wonderful ball- and cocktail gowns, from the
1950s to the 1980s, are in terrific condition and
attract the attention of fashion aficionados from
places as far afield as Hamburg, Cologne and
Düsseldorf. Cocktail dresses in every conceivable
shade and fabric range can be found at Sterling
Gold, plus Boenke's classic vintage silk ballgowns
and elegant wedding dresses.

Waahnsinn
Rosenthaler Strasse 17, Mitte (282 0029). U2,
U8 Weinmeisterstrasse. **Open** noon-8pm Mon-Sat.
Credit MC, V. **Map** p316/p302 F3.
Unashamedly tacky clothes and jewellery from the
1960s and 1970s, chosen to outrage the eye and
complement the plastic egg chairs and lava lamps
also on sale. Not the cheapest second-hand clobber,
but in good nick and on a strong party-girl theme.
Furniture too.

Shoes & leather goods

Bleibgrün
Bleibtreustrasse 29-30, Charlottenburg (882 1689).
S3, S5, S7, S9, S75 Savignyplatz. **Open** 10.30am-
8pm Mon-Fri; 10am-4pm Sat. **Credit** AmEx, DC,
MC, V. **Map** p305 C4.
Berlin's best designer shoe shop, with a nifty selec-
tion from the likes of Lagerfeld, Maud Frizon and
Jan Jansen. Bleibgrün has opened a swanky bou-
tique next door at No.30 that has an equally dis-
criminating choice of cutting-edge womenswear.

Bree
Kurfürstendamm 44, Charlottenburg (883 7462).
U15 Uhlandstrasse. **Open** 10am-7pm Mon-Fri; 10am-
4pm Sat. **Credit** AmEx, MC, V. **Map** p305 C4.
German leather goods company whose practical,
durable and easy-to-organise handbags, briefcases,
rucksacks and suitcases are sported by many a
German professional.

Budapester Schuhe
Kurfürstendamm 43, Charlottenburg (881 1707).
U15 Uhlandstrasse. **Open** 10am-7pm Mon-Wed;
10am-8pm Thur, Fri; 10am-4pm Sat. **Credit** AmEx,
DC, MC, V. **Map** p305 C4.
Impressive selection of designer footwear for
men and women. This is the largest of four Berlin
branches, offering the latest by the like of Prada,
Dolce & Gabbana, Sergio Rossi, JP Tod's and Miu
Miu. Across the street at Kurfürstendamm 199,
you'll find a conservative range for men, including
handmade classics from Austrian Ludwig Reiter.
At the Bleibtrestrasse branch, prices are slashed by
up to 50% for last year's models, remainders and
hard-to-sell sizes.
Branches: Bleibtreustrasse 24, Charlottenburg
(881 7001); Friedrichstrasse 81, Mitte (2038 8110);
Kurfürstendamm 43, Charlottenburg (8862 4206).

Penthesileia
Tucholskystrasse 31, Mitte (282 1152).
U6 Oranienburger Tor. **Open** 10am-7pm
Mon-Fri; 10am-4pm Sat. **Credit** MC, V.
Map p316/p302 F3.
Named after an Amazon queen, this is showroom,
shop and workspace for Sylvia Müller and Anke
Runge, who design and make their highly individ-
ual range of handbags and rucksacks here. Shapes
are novel and organic – sunflowers, cones, shells and
hearts – and crafted from calfskin and nubuck.

Trippen

Hackesche Höfe, Rosenthaler Strasse 40-41,
Mitte (2839 1337). S3, S5, S7, S9, S75 Hackescher
Markt, or U8 Weinmeisterstrasse. **Open** noon-7pm
Mon-Fri; 10am-4pm Sat. **Credit** MC, V.
Map p316/p302 F3.
Not the most reassuring name for a shoe shop
perhaps, but Trippen is home to an idiosyncratic
selection of foot fashion designed by Angela
Spieth and Michael Oehler. Oddly shaped
wooden-soled platforms, heels that shoot out at
right angles and 'horned' toes are just a few of
the surprises here.

Shoemakers

See also p180 **Repairs**.

Breitenbach

Bergmannstrasse 30, Kreuzberg (692 3570).
U7 Gneisenaustrasse. **Open** m8am-6.30pm
Mon-Fri; 10am-2pm Sat. **Credit** AmEx, MC, V.
Map p306 F5.
This respected men's shoe- and bootmaker also
provides a first-class repair service for men's and
women's footwear.

Sports gear

Karstadt Sport

Quartier 205, Friedrichstrasse 67, Mitte
(2094 5000). U2, U6 Stadtmitte. **Open** 10am-8pm
Mon-Fri; 9.30am-4pm Sat. **Credit** AmEx, DC, MC, V.
Map p316/p302 F3.
Three-level megastore with a wide selection of gear
by both name brands and cheaper alternatives. Also
US sportswear and equipment, German football
paraphernalia and children's clothes. Includes
skating area, Alpine ski simulator, internet terminals and sports restaurant.
Branch: Joachimstaler Strasse 5-6, Charlottenburg
(8802 4153).

Niketown

Tauentzienstrasse 7B-7C, Schöneberg (250 70). U1,
U2, U12, U15 Wittenbergplatz. **Open** 10am-8pm
Mon-Fri; 10am-4pm Sat. **Credit** AmEx, DC, MC, V.
Map p305 D4.
Brand retail outlet for the monster US company in
state-of-the art glass and neon design. Training
gear – jerseys, sweatpants, even sunglasses and
watches – embossed with the Nike trademark, if you
like being a walking billboard.

360°

Pariser Strasse 23-4, Wilmersdorf (883 8596).
U7 Adenauerplatz. **Open** 11am-7.30pm Mon-Fri;
10am-4pm Sat. **Credit** AmEx, DC, MC, V.
Map p305 C5.
This is the place to come for designer sportswear
and sundry accessories from Quicksilver, Stüssy,
Sky & High and Vans, plus in-line skates, snow-
boards and windsurfing gear.

Street/clubwear

Eisdieler

Kastanienallee 12, Prenzlauer Berg (285 7351).
U2 Eberswalder Strasse. **Open** noon-7pm Mon-Fri;
11am-6pm Sat. **Credit** MC, V. **Map** p302 F3.
Five young designers pooled their resources to
transform this former ice shop and each manages
a label under the Eisdieler banner – clubwear,
second-hand gear, casualwear and street style.
Till Fuhrmann jewellery in silver and wood is particularly distinctive, and it's his spiky ironwork
adorning the façade.
Branch: Auguststrasse 74, Mitte (2790 8683).

Flex/Melting Point

Neue Schönhauser Strasse 2, Mitte (283 4836/
4844). U8 Weinmeisterstrasse. **Open** noon-8pm
Mon-Fri; noon-4pm Sat. **Credit** AmEx, DC, MC, V.
Map p316/p303 G3.
Clubwear store and dance record shop in one – this
is one of the buzziest stores on the street, especially
in the evening when Mitte's young, bad and beautiful pick out an outfit from German rave labels,
including Sabotage and Thatchers.

Planet

Schlüterstrasse 35, Charlottenburg (885 2717). U15
Uhlandstrasse. **Open** 11am-8pm Mon-Fri; 11am-4pm
Sat. **Credit** AmEx, MC, V. **Map** p305 C4.
Calling themselves Wera Wonder and Mik Moon,
the owners have been supplying Berlin's club
scene with appropriately hip gear since 1985. Their
DJ friends pump out deafening music to put you in
club mode, and the rails and shelves are full of
sparkling spandex shirts, fluffy vests and dance
durable footwear.

Schwarze Mode

Grunewaldstrasse 91, Schöneberg (784 5922). U7
Kleistpark. **Open** noon-7pm Mon-Fri; 10am-4pm Sat.
Credit AmEx, DC, MC, V. **Map** p306 E5.
Leatherette, rubber and vinyl are among the partic-
ular delicacies stocked here for Gummi (rubber)
enthusiasts. As well as the fetish fashions, erotic and
S&M literature in German and English, comics,
videos, CDs and magazines are on offer next door in
Schwarze Medien.

Tenderloin

Alte Schönhauser Strasse 30, Mitte (4201 5785).
U8 Weinmeisterstrasse. **Open** noon-8pm Mon-
Fri; noon-4pm Sat. **Credit** AmEx, MC, V.
Map p316/p303 G3.
Once a purely second-hand store – there are still
flares and flower prints left over from its retro
period – it's the mix of 1960s and 1970s GDR furniture, luminous wigs in rainbow colours and new
clothes that make this shop worth a visit. Berlin label
Stoffrausch draws on the hip hop and techno scene
and each unisex handmade item is an original, so you
can rest assured you won't be caught clubbing in
the same clobber as some beautiful stranger.

Eat, Drink, Shop

Flowers

Blumen 31

Bleibtreustrasse 31, Charlottenburg (8847 4604). U15 Uhlandstrasse. **Open** 9am-8pm Mon-Fri; 9am-6pm Sat. **Credit** AmEx, DC, MC, V. **Map** p305 C4.

This first-rate florest specialises (believe it or not) in roses from Ecuador, creatively combined into bulging bouquets with little more than an array of greens. Delivery service.

Fleurop

713 710. **Open** 7.30am-6.30pm Mon-Fri; 8am-2pm Sat. **Credit** AmEx, DC, MC, V.

Call to have flowers delivered anywhere in the western world. Within Germany, your flowers can arrive within an hour, sent via any one of 7,000 shops nationwide.

Food

There's little joy shopping in Berlin supermarkets. They are small and cramped, generally have uninspiring selections of food, encourage check-out queues, keep idiosyncratic opening hours and never take credit cards. The alternative are specialist shops, from ethno to gourmet, which range from expensive Italian delis to cheap Asian mini-markets. The organic food market is booming, the variety of produce sold in *Bioläden* is huge and subject to strict controls. Several of the major department stores have impressive food halls, most notably **Galeries Lafayette** (*see p163*) and **KaDeWe** (*see p165*).

Aquí España

Kantstrasse 34, Charlottenburg (312 3315). U7 Wilmersdorfer Strasse. **Open** 9am-8pm Mon-Fri; 9am-6pm Sat. **No credit cards**. **Map** p304 B4.

Neighbourhood store stocking Spanish wines and groceries, plus ingredients for Mexican and Latin American dishes, including a full array of dried chillies, flour and corn tortillas and Central American seafood in the freezer.

Broken English

Körtestrasse 10, Kreuzberg (691 1227). U7 Südstern. **Open** 11am-6.30pm Mon-Fri; 10am-4pm Sat. **Credit** MC, V. **Map** p307 G5.

This cosy shop, tucked away in Kreuzberg, is choc-a-bloc with the best of Britain: all UK expats need to keep the homesick blues at bay. There's a massive selection of teas, biscuits, crisps and sweets, as well as important ingredients such as self-raising flour and clotted cream, plus a selection of cheeses and deep frozen pies, and essentials such as Heinz beans, salad cream and Marmite. The gift section includes children's tapes, cookbooks, mugs and malts.

Kolbo

Auguststrasse 77-8, Mitte (no phone). U6 Oranienburger Tor. **Open** 11am-1.45pm, 2.15-7pm, Tue-Thur, Sun; 9am-2pm Fri. **Credit** AmEx, MC, V. **Map** p316/p302 F3.

Small friendly store and bakery in Berlin's old Jewish quarter selling kosher foodstuffs and wines, plus a selection of books (including kosher cookbooks) and ritual objects.

Königsberger Marzipan

Pestalozzistrasse 54A, Charlottenburg (323 8254). S3, S5, S7, S9, S75 Charlottenburg. **Open** 11am-6pm Mon-Wed; 2-6pm Tue, Thur, Fri; 11am-2pm Sat. **No credit cards**. **Map** p304 B4.

Irmgard Wald and her late husband moved from Kaliningrad to Berlin after the war and began again in the confectionery trade. With her smiling American-born granddaughter, Frau Wald still produces fresh, soft, melt-in-your-mouth marzipan. Small boxes of assorted sweets make great gifts.

Leysieffer

Kurfürstendamm 218, Charlottenburg (885 7480). U15 Uhlandstrasse. **Open** 10am-8pm Mon-Sat; 11am-7pm Sun. **Credit** AmEx, DC, MC, V. **Map** p305 C4.

Beautifully packaged confitures, teas and handmade chocolates from this German fine food company make perfect high-calorie gifts. Café upstairs and bakery attached.

Lindenberg

Morsestrasse 2, Charlottenburg (3908 1523). U9 Turmstrasse. **Open** 8am-7pm Mon-Fri; 8am-2pm Sat. **No credit cards**. **Map** p301 D3.

Wholesaler where the city's pro and amateur chefs stock up on live lobster, fresh seafood, New Zealand lamb, local ducks, out-of-season fruit and veg, assorted French cheeses, and wines and spirits. Anyone can walk in but most things are sold only in industrial quantities. Advance orders taken.

LPG

Mehringdamm 51, Kreuzberg (694 7725). U6, U7 Mehringdamm. **Open** 9am-7pm Mon-Fri; 9am-4pm Sat. **No credit cards**. **Map** p306 F5.

If you're shopping a while and are an organic shopper, co-ops are great alternatives to expensive *Bioläden*. For a deposit and a monthly fee of about €17.50, you can save up to 30% on food, wine, juice, cosmetics and household detergents.

Macchina/Caffè

Alte Schönhauser Strasse 26, Mitte (2838 4414). U8 Weinmeisterstrasse. **Open** 11am-8pm Mon-Fri; 11am-4pm Sat. **Credit** AmEx, MC, V. **Map** p316/p303 G3.

Treat your caffeine addiction with a fix from the selection of quality Italian coffee such as Illy and Manresi, and pick up a state-of-the-art espresso machine. Also a wide selection of simple aluminium espresso cans, and a solar-powered milk frother patented by Berlin company SoLait.

Vinh-Loi

Ansbacher Strasse 16, Schöneberg (235 0900).
U1, U2, U12, U15 Wittenbergplatz. **Open** 9am-7pm
Mon-Fri; 9am-4pm Sat. **No credit cards.**
Map p305 D5.
Asian groceries including Thai fruit, veg and herbs
fresh from the airport on Mondays and Thursdays.
Plus woks, rice steamers and Chinese crockery.

Weichardt-Brot

Mehlitzstrasse 7, Wilmersdorf (873 8099). U7,
U9 Berliner Strasse. **Open** 8am-6.30pm Tue-Fri;
7am-1pm Sat. **No credit cards.** Map p305 C5.
The very best bakery in town, Weichardt-Brot grew
out of a Berlin collective from the 1960s. Stone-
ground organic flour and natural leavens make
this a mecca for bread lovers.

General markets

See p178.

Wine & spirits

Getränke Hoffmann

Kleiststrasse 23-6, Schöneberg (2147 3096).
U1, U2, U12, U15 Wittenbergplatz. **Open** 9am-8pm
Mon-Fri; 8am-4pm Sat. **No credit cards.**
Map p305 D4.
Branches offer a wide range of everyday booze at
everyday prices. Call 2147 3096 to make orders for
delivery anywhere in town or check the *Gelbe Seiten*.
Branch: Schönfliesser Strasse 19, Prenzlauer Berg
(444 0682).

Klemke Wein & Spirituosenhandel

Mommsenstrasse 9, Charlottenburg (8855 1260).
S3, S5, S7, S9, S75 Savignyplatz. **Open** 9am-7pm
Mon-Fri; 9am-2.30pm Sat. **No credit cards.**
Map p305 C4.
Respected specialists in French and Italian wines
from the tiniest vineyard to the grandest chateau.
Also digestifs and whiskies. Free delivery in Berlin.

Vendemmia

Akazienstrasse 20, Schöneberg (784 2728).
U7 Eisenacher Strasse. **Open** 10am-6.30pm
Mon-Fri; 10am-2pm Sat. **No credit cards.**
Map p305 D5.
Bulk importers of first-class Italian wines that are
decanted into bottles bearing photocopied labels.
Not the most impressive bottle you can take to a
party, but it's good stuff and very cheap. Several
other good wine and spirits shops on this street, plus
an Italian deli with a good wine selection.

Whisky & Cigars

Sophienstrasse 23, Mitte (282 0376/www.whisky-
cigars.de). S3, S5, S7, S9, S75 Hackescher Markt.
Open noon-7pm Tue-Fri; 11am-4pm Sat.
Credit MC, V. **Map** p316/p302 F3.
Two friends sharing a love of single malts are
behind this shop, which stocks 450 whiskies, and
cigars from Cuba, Jamaica and Honduras. Top of

Winterfeldt Markt. *See p178.*

the range – available on special order – is a bottle of
1919 Springbank at €25,000. They hold regular
whisky tasting and cigar smoking evenings and will
deliver or even ship orders.

Hair salons

Berlin hair stylists' technical skills tend to
outmatch their judgement or taste. And the
state of the average Berlin barnet might
convince you never to trust your crowning
glory to the locals. That said, the city does
boast a few stylists and colourists that can do
a pretty fair job, as well as some international
salons that can cut it with the best of them.

Hanley's Hair Company

Hackesche Höfe, Rosenthaler Strasse 40-41,
Mitte (281 3179). S3, S5, S7, S9, S75 Hackescher
Markt or U8 Weinmeisterstrasse. **Open** 9am-8pm
Mon-Fri; 10am-4pm Sat. **No credit cards.**
Map p316/p302 F3.
Friendly, trendy salon run by Thomas Schweizer
and Deborah Hanley – who does amazing colour
jobs. Full range of styling and treatments, offering
wash, cut and head massage.

Jonnycut

Yorckstrasse 43, Schöneberg (217 0941). S1, S2,
S25, U7 Yorckstrasse. **Open** 11am-7pm Tue-Sat.
No credit cards. **Map** p306 E5.
Known as Berlin's most 'spiritual' hairdresser, Jonny
Pazzo is a versatile stylist who shuttles between
shoots for glossy magazines and record covers to
appointments in his small salon. Decked out with
pictures of angels, Buddhas, reggae musicians
and children, it's frequented by many an established
and rising scene star.

Udo Walz

Kempinski-Plaza, Uhlandstrasse 181-3,
Charlottenburg (882 7457). U15 Uhlandstrasse.
Open 9am-6pm Mon-Fri; 9am-2pm Sat.
Credit AmEx, MC, V. **Map** p305 C4.
Udo Walz is the darling of the Berlin hair brigade,
and likes to have his picture taken with the likes
of Claudia Schiffer. His stylists are well trained,
imaginative and friendly.
Branch: Hohenzollerndamm 92, Wilmersdorf
(826 6108).

Vidal Sassoon

Schlüterstrasse 38-9, Charlottenburg (884 5000).
S3, S5, S7, S9, S75 Savignyplatz. **Open** 9.45am-
6.15pm Tue, Wed; 9.45am-7pm Thur; 9am-7pm
Fri; 8.30am-3pm Sat. **No credit cards.**
Map p305 C4.

An international safe bet. A cut from a top stylist
will cost you €52.50; modelling cuts are €11 to €18.
A cut includes massage, wash, hair treatment, conditioning and styling. Colouring and treatments on offer.

Jewellery

Chic Choc

Holsteinische Strasse 42, Wilmersdorf (861 8191).
U9 Günzelstrasse. **Open** 2-8pm Tue-Fri; 10am-4pm
Sat. **Credit** AmEx, DC, MC, V. **Map** p305 C5.
With mobile vitrines that provide lots of display
space, Chic Choc is a fun shop that has the feel of
an art gallery. Two goldsmiths display both their
own creations and those of others, plus stage exhibitions around topics such as the designs of the
British avant-garde.

Shopping by area

Mitte

Antiques Emma Emmelie *p158*. **Beauty salons**
Aveda *p160*. **Books** Buchhandlung Herschel
p160; Grober Unfug *p160*; Hugendubel *p161*;
Kiepert *p161*; Le Matou *p161*. **Computer
repairs** J.E. *p180*. **Department stores**
Dussman Das KulturKaufhaus *p163*; Galeries
Lafayette *p163*; Kaufhof *p165*; Quartier 206
Department Store *p165*. **Design & household
goods** Bürgel-Haus *p167*; dadriade *p165*;
KPM *p167*; Leinenkontor *p167*; Ruby *p167*;
Schönhauser *p167*. **Fashion: Accessories**
Fiona Bennett *p168*; Fishbelly *p168*; Tagebau
p168. **Fashion: Designer** Claudia Skoda
Level *p169*; Hut Up *p170*; Lisa D *p170*;
RespectMen *p170*; Tools & Gallery *p169*;
Yoshiharu Ito *p170*. **Fashion: Mid-range**
Essenbeck *p171*; To Die For *p171*. **Fashion:
Second-hand clothes & shoes** Calypso –
High Heels For Ever *p171*; Humana *p171*;
Sterling Gold *p172*; Waahnsinn *p172*. **Fashion:
Sports gear** Karstadt Sport *p173*. **Fashion:
Street/clubwear** Eisdieler *p173*; Flex/Melting
Point *p173*; Tenderloin *p173*. **Food** Kolbo
p174; Macchina/Caffè *p174*. **Hair salons**
Hanley's Hair Company *p175*. **Jewellery**
Glanzstücke *p177*. **Markets** Berliner Antik &
Flohmarkt *p178*; Kunst und Nostalgie Markt
p178. **Music: CDs & records** DNS *p179*;
Saturn *p180*. **Opticians** Brille 54 *p180*;
Brilliant *p180*; Fielmann *p180*. **Photography**
PPS *p180*. **Shoes & leather goods** Budapester
Schuhe *p172*; Penthesileia *p172*; Trippen
p173. **Souvenirs** Berlin Story *p181*; Johanna
Petzoldt *p182*; Kunsthandwerk aus dem

Erzgebirge *p182*. **Stationery & art supplies**
J Müller *p182*; RSVP *p182*. **Wine & spirits**
Whisky & Cigars *p175*.

Prenzlauer Berg & Friedrichshain

Design & household goods Coldampf's *p165*;
Keramikladen am P'Berg *p167*. **Dry-cleaning &
alterations** Kleenothek *p170*; Michael Klemm
p170. **Fashion: Designer** Coration *p169*.
Fashion: Fetish Black Style *p170*; Leathers
p171. **Fashion: Second-hand clothes & shoes**
Checkpoint *p171*; Falbala *p171*; Sgt Peppers
p172. **Fashion: Street/clubwear** Eisdieler
p173. **Jewellery** Scuderi *p178*. **Markets**
Kollwitzplatz *p178*. **Music: CDs & records**
D-Fens *p179*. **Photography** Foto Klinke *p180*.
Souvenirs Fanshop *p182*; Mondos Arts *p182*.

Kreuzberg

Antiques Radio Art *p159*. **Books** Another
Country *p161*; Bücherbogen *p160*;
Fair Exchange *p161*; Grober Unfug *p160*.
Cosmetics Belladonna *p162*. **Design &
household goods** Bella Casa *p165*. **Fashion:
Accessories** Knopf Paul *p168*. **Fashion:
Designer** Molotow *p170*. **Fashion: Second-
hand clothes & shoes** Checkpoint *p171*;
Colours *p171*. **Food** Broken English *p174*;
LPG *p174*. **Jewellery** Fritz *p177*. **Music: CDs
& records** Space Hall *p179*. **Photography** Foto
Klinke *p180*. **Shoemakers** Breitenbach *p173*.
Stationery & arts supplies Grüne Papeterie
p182; Propolis *p182*.

Fritz

Dresdener Strasse 20, Kreuzberg (615 1700).
U1, U8, U12 Kottbusser Tor. **Open** 11am-6pm
Tue-Fri; 11am-2pm Sat. **Credit** V. **Map** p307 G4.
Bold designs by this Berliner plus interesting
hand-crafted work in a wide range of materials by
smiths based elsewhere in Germany and Europe.
The selection of rings attracts many brides and
grooms-to-be, with prices ranging from hundreds to
thousands of marks.
Branch: Galerie Fillman, Fasanenstrasse 74,
Wilmersdorf (881 5797).

Glanzstücke

Sophienstrasse 7, Mitte (208 2676).
S3, S5, S7, S9, S75 Hackescher Markt.
Open noon-7pm Mon-Sat. **Credit** AmEx, MC, V.
Map p316/p302 F3.

Original 20th-century costume jewellery with a
strong emphasis on art nouveau and art deco. Owner
Kirstin Pax hunts down dazzling treasures in
rhinestone and glass, and does good trade with US
dealers, who find prices for items in her impressive
Bakelite collection a steal.

Rio

Bleibtreustrasse 52, Charlottenburg (313 3152).
S3, S5, S7, S9, S75 Savignyplatz. **Open** 11am-
6.30pm Mon-Wed; 11am-7pm Thur; 11am-6.30pm
Fri; 10am-4pm Sat. **No credit cards.**
Map p305 C4.
Eye-catching costume jewellery, with a stunning
array of earrings from Vivienne Westwood, Armani
and Herv van der Straeten. Plus Rio's own range of
luminescent frosted-glass necklaces, bracelets and
earrings designed by shop owner Barbara Kranz.

Schöneberg & Tiergarten

Antiques Deco Arts *p158*; Fingers *p158*.
Beauty salons Hautfit Bio Kosmetik *p160*.
Children's clothes & toys Michas Bahnhof
p162. **Cosmetics** World of Beauty *p163*.
Department stores KaDeWe *p165*. **Design
& household goods** Formgeber Berlin *p166*;
KPM *p167*; Rahaus Wohnen 2001 *p167*.
Fashion: Designer Chiton *p169*. **Fashion:
Mid-range** Groopie Deluxe *p171*. **Fashion:
Second-hand clothes & shoes** Garage *p171*;
Made in Berlin *p171*. **Fashion: Sports gear**
Niketown *p173*. **Fashion: Street/clubwear**
Schwarze Mode *p173*. **Food** Vinh-Loi *p175*.
Hair salons Jonnycut *p175*. **Markets** Farmers'
Market *p178*; Strasse des 17.Juni *p178*;
Winterfeldt Markt *p178*. **Music: CDs &
records** Mr Dead & Mrs Free *p179*; WOM
p180. **Photography** Foto Klinke *p180*.
Shoe repairs Picobello *p181*. **Stationery
& art supplies** Ferdinand Braune *p182*.
Wine & spirits Getränke Hoffmann *p175*;
Vendemmia *p175*.

Charlottenburg & Wilmersdorf

Antiques Lehmanns Colonialwaren *p159*;
Wolfgang Haas *p159*. **Beauty salons** Aveda
p160; Marie France *p160*. **Books** Books in
Berlin *p161*; Bücherbogen *p160*; Hugendubel
p161; Kiepert *p161*; Kohlhaas & Company
p160; Marga Schoeller Bücherstube *p162*;
Prinz Eisenherz Buchladen *p160*. **Books:
Antiquarian & second-hand** Antiquariat Senzel

p161; Düwal *p161*. **Children's clothes & toys**
Emma & Co *p162*; Heidi's Spielzeugladen
p162; H&M Kids *p162*; Tam Tam *p162*;
v. Kloeden *p162*. **Cosmetics** DK Cosmetics
p163; Shiseido Beauty Gallery *p163*.
Department stores Karstadt *p163*; Wertheim
p165. **Design & household goods** Alfar &
Sykora *p167*; Bramigk & Breer *p165*;
Coldampf's *p165*; Dopo Domani *p166*; KPM
p167; Rahaus *p167*; Schlafwandel *p167*;
stilwerk *p166*: **Dry-cleaning & alterations**
Kim Jang Woon *p170*; Nantes *p170*. **Fashion:
Accessories** Les Dessous *p168*; Kaufhaus
Schrill *p168*; Roeckl *p168*. **Fashion: Costume
& formal-wear hire** Theaterkunst *p168*.
Fashion: Designer Antonie Setzer *p169*;
Harvey's *p169*; Mientus Studio 2002 *p169*;
Patrick Hellman *p169*; Sheila *p169*. **Fashion:
Second-hand clothes & shoes** Spitze *p172*.
Fashion: Sports gear Karstadt Sport *p173*;
360° *p173*. **Fashion: Street/clubwear** Planet
p173. **Flowers** Blumen 31 *p174*. **Food** Aquí
España *p174*; Königsberger Marzipan *p174*;
Leysieffer *p174*; Lindenberg *p174*; Weichardt-
Brot *p175*. **Hair salons** Udo Walz *p176*; Vidal
Sassoon *p176*. **Jewellery** Chic Choc *p176*;
Fritz *p177*; Rio *p177*; Treykorn *p178*. **Markets**
Zille-Hof *p178*. **Music: CDs & records** Gelbe
Musik *p179*; Hans Riedl Musikalienhandel
p179; ProMarkt *p179*. **Opticians** Brille 54
p180; Brilliant *p180*. **Photography** Fix Foto
p180. **Shoes & leather
goods** Bleibgrün *p172*; Bree *p172*; Budapester
Schuhe *p172*. **Souvenirs** Berliner Zinnfiguren
Kabinett *p182*; J&M Fässler *p182*. **Stationery
& art supplies** Papeterie *p182*. **Wine & spirits**
Klemke Wein & Spirituosenhandel *p175*.

Scuderi

Wörther Strasse 32, Prenzlauer Berg (4737 4240).
U2 Senefelderplatz. **Open** 11am-7pm Mon-Fri;
11am-3pm Sat. **Credit** MC, V. **Map** p303 G2.
The four women who share this space work magic
with gold and silver, pearls, stones and hand-rolled
glass, creating lightweight ornaments that make a
strong statement.

Treykorn

*Passage, Savignyplatz 13, Charlottenburg
(3180 2354). S3, S5, S7, S9, S75 Savignyplatz.*
Open 11am-7pm Mon-Fri; 11am-4pm Sat.
Credit AmEx, DC, MC, V. **Map** p305 C4.
This smart gallery specialises in metal- and stone-
worked jewellery, with styles ranging from the ultra-
modern to contemporary classics. Stock changes
every five weeks and Treykorn also hosts three
major international jewellery design shows a year.

Markets

Flea markets

There's many a treat in store at Berlin's flea
markets, especially for music lovers, collectors
of old books, fans of art deco and those with a
fetish for old GDR knick-knacks. Check *Zitty*
and *tip* for the most up-to-date listings.

Berliner Antik & Flohmarkt

*Bahnhof Friedrichstrasse, S-Bahnbogen 190-203,
Mitte (208 2645). S1, S2, S3, S5, S7, S9, S25, S26,
S75, U6 Friedrichstrasse.* **Open** 11am-6pm Mon,
Wed-Sun. **Map** p316/p302 F3.
More than 60 dealers have taken up residence in the
renovated arches under the S-Bahn tracks, selling
furniture, jewellery, paintings and interesting vin-
tage clothing, some of it from the 1920s and 1930s.

Kunst und Nostalgie Markt

*Museumsinsel, by Zeughaus, Mitte (03341 309
411). S1, S2, S3, S5, S7, S9, S25, S26, S75,
U6 Friedrichstrasse.* **Open** 11am-5pm Sat, Sun.
Map p316/p302 F3.
One of the few places you can still find true GDR
relics, with anything from old signs advertising coal
briquets to framed pictures of Honecker. Also a
section devoted to modern arts and crafts.

Strasse des 17.Juni

*Strasse des 17.Juni, Tiergarten (2655 0096).
U2 Ernst-Reuter-Platz or S3, S5, S7, S9, S75
Tiergarten.* **Open** 10am-5pm Sat, Sun. **Map** p305 C4.
Early 20th-century objects of a high quality with
prices to match, alongside a jumble of vintage and
alternative clothing, second-hand records, CDs and
books. Arts and crafts further along the street. Best
flea market in town, albeit an insanely cramped one.

Zille-Hof

*Fasanenstrasse 14, Charlottenburg (313 4333).
U15 Uhlandstrasse.* **Open** 8am-5.30pm Mon-Fri;
8am-1pm Sat. **Map** p305 C4.

Almost next door to the Kempinski Hotel, a neat and
tidy junk market where you can track down everything from an antique hatpin to a chest of drawers.
You'll find the better bric-a-brac indoors, while the
real bargains lurk in the courtyard outside.

General markets

Berlin's many *Wochenmärkte* offer an
alternative to stores, and usually sell better,
cheaper fresh produce.

Farmers' Market

*Wittenbergplatz, Schöneberg. U1, U2, U12, U15
Wittenbergplatz.* **Open** 8am-2pm Tue-Fri; 10am-
7.30pm Thur. **Map** p305 D4.
Predominantly organic produce, including 'bio'
cheese, bread, fresh pasta and meat stands, plus
fruit and vegetables from farms in the region. You'll
also come across inedible items such as wooden
brushes and sheepskins.

Kollwitzplatz

Kollwitzplatz, Prenzlauer Berg. U2 Senefelderplatz.
Open noon-7pm Thur, Sat. **Map** p303 G2.
Open-air food markets are still rare in the east. This
one is a small and unassuming organic market,
much more lively in summer, though nothing could
be more *gemütlich* in winter than the scene around
the stand serving mugs of steaming punch and fresh
wholegrain cinnamon waffles.

Türkischer Markt

*Maybachufer, Neukölln. U1, U8, U12 Kottbusser
Tor.* **Open** noon-6.30pm Tue, Fri. **Map** p307 G5.
A noisy, crowded market just across the canal from
Kreuzberg, catering for the needs of the neighbour-
hood's Turkish community. Good buys, great tastes.

Winterfeldt Markt

*Winterfeldtplatz, Schöneberg. U1, U2, U4,
U12 Nollendorfplatz.* **Open** 8am-2pm Wed, Sat.
Map p305 D5.
Saturday's multicultural experience. Everybody
shows up to buy their vegetables, cheese, wholegrain breads, *Wurst*, meats, flowers, clothes, pet supplies and toys; or simply to meet over a coffee, beer
or falafel at one of the many cafés off the square.

Music: CDs & records

See also *p173* **Flex/Melting Point** and
p163 **Dussmann Das KulturKaufhaus**.
At www.platten.net there is a complete online
guide to every record shop in Berlin.

DaCapo Records

*Kastanienallee 96, Pankow (448 1771/
www.dacapo-vinyl.de). U2 Eberswalder Strasse.*
Open 11am-7pm Mon-Fri; 11am-4pm Sat.
Credit MC, V. **Map** p303 G2.
Pricey but wide selection of used vinyl, releases
on GDR label Amiga and rare 1950s 10in records.

Eat, Drink, Shop

Minimalist home to minimalist music: **Gelbe Musik**.

D-Fens

Greifswalder Strasse 224, Prenzlauer Berg (4434 2250/www.d-fens-berlin.de). U2 Rosa-Luxemburg-Platz. **Open** noon-7pm Mon-Fri; noon-3pm Sat. **No credit cards.** **Map** p303 G3.

Small DJ shop in a revamped garage, specialising in house (including the Brazilian version), trance, electro, techno and disco. Home base of Berlin labels Formaldahyde and BCC. Owner Ralph Ballschuh, a DJ himself, is happy to turn up the volume on any track you wish. Hard to find so follow the signs for the Knaack Klub.

DNS

Alte Schönhauser Strasse 39-40, Mitte (247 9835). U8 Weinmeisterstrasse. **Open** 11am-8pm Mon-Fri; 11am-4pm Sat. **Credit** AmEx, DC, MC, V. **Map** p316/p303 G3.

Old vinyl, including some rare finds, as well as the latest pressings in the world of techno.

Gelbe Musik

Schaperstrasse 11, Wilmersdorf (211 3962). U1 Augsburger Strasse. **Open** 1-6pm Tue-Fri; 11am-2pm Sat. **Credit** MC, V. **Map** p305 C5.

Arguably Europe's number one outlet for avant-garde music, Gelbe Musik has racks stacked with minimalist, electronic, world, industrial and extreme noise. Rare vinyl and import CDs, music press and sound objects make absorbing browsing, and the store is a hangout for the international and the odd.

Hans Riedl Musikalienhandel

Uhlandstrasse 38, Wilmersdorf (882 7395). U15 Uhlandstrasse. **Open** 8am-6.30pm Mon-Fri; 9am-2pm Sat. **Credit** MC, V. **Map** p306 F4.

Probably the best address for classical music in Berlin, this huge, slightly old-fashioned shop stocks a wide selection of CDs and sheet music, as well as string and brass instruments. Staff are knowledgeable and the shop is patronised by music professionals as well as Berlin's legions of classical music lovers.

Mr Dead & Mrs Free

Bülowstrasse 5, Schöneberg (215 1449). U1, U2, U4, U12 Nollendorfplatz. **Open** 11am-7pm Mon-Wed; 11am-8pm Thur, Fri; 11am-4pm Sat. **Credit** V. **Map** p305 D5.

A strange name, perhaps, but this is Berlin's leading address for independent and underground rock, with bucketloads of British, US and Australian imports, a huge vinyl section, and staff who know and love their music.

Space Hall

Zossenerstrasse 33, Kreuzberg (694 7664). U7 Gneisenaustrasse. **Open** 11am-7pm Mon-Wed; 11am-8pm Thur, Fri; 10am-4pm Sat. **Credit** AmEx, MC, V. **Map** p306 F5.

A spacious shop offering a broad range of new and second-hand CDs at competitive prices and with a huge techno/house vinyl room at the back. There are a couple more good record shops on Zossenerstrasse and a few more round the corner on Bergmannstrasse.

Wagadu

Pannierstrasse 6, Neukölln (6273 2467/ www.wagadu.de). U7, U8 Hermannplatz. **Open** 11am-7.30pm Mon-Fri; 10am-4pm Sat. **Credit** MC, V. **Map** p307 H5.

Large selection of African and Afro-Caribbean CDs and videos.

Chain stores

ProMarkt

Kurfürstendamm 206, Charlottenburg (886 886). U15 Uhlandstrasse. **Open** 10am-8pm Mon-Fri; 10am-6pm Sat. **Credit** AmEx, DC, MC, V. **Map** p305 C4.

The Ku'damm branch of this big chain has friendly service and a decent selection of club sounds. You can also get mainstream English-language videos here.

Branches across the city.

Saturn

Alexanderplatz 8, Mitte (247 516). S3, S5, S7, S9,
S75, U2, U5, U8 Alexanderplatz. **Open** 9am-8pm
Mon-Fri; 9am-4pm Sat. **Credit** AmEx, DC, MC, V.
Map p316/p303 G3.
This chain is one of the cheapest in town, with
plenty of new releases and a good range of back
catalogue. CDs only.

WOM

Augsburger Strasse 36-42, Schöneberg (885 7240).
U1 Augsburger Strasse. **Open** 10am-8pm Mon-Fri;
9am-4pm Sat. **Credit** AmEx, MC, V.
Map p305 D4.
The World of Music chain offers a no-nonsense,
no-frills approach to music retailing, and its
wide selection of CDs includes a good array of
jazz recordings.
Branch: Hertie Wilmersdorfer Strasse 118,
Charlottenburg (315 9170).

Opticians

Brille 54

Friedrichstrasse 71, Mitte (2094 6060). U6
Französische Strasse. **Open** 10am-8pm Mon-Fri;
10am-4pm Sat. **Credit** AmEx, DC, MC, V.
Map p316/p306 F4.
A small but functionally sleek space in Quartier 206
designed by hot young Berlin architects Plajer &
Franz. In stock are Armani, Gucci, Oliver Peoples,
Paul Smith, Prada and Miu Miu. Also handmade,
platinum-coated frames by German designer Lunor,
and the must-haves of the Berlin party scene – aluminium, screwless frames with coloured shades
from IC Berlin.
Branch: Kurfürstendamm 54, Charlottenburg
(882 6696); **B54Sun** Oranienburger Strasse 1, Mitte
(2804 0818).

Brilliant

Schlüterstrasse 53, Charlottenburg (324 1991/
www.brilliant-augenoptik.de). S3, S5, S7, S9, S75
Savignyplatz. **Open** 10am-7pm Mon-Wed; 10am-8pm
Thur, Fri; 10am-4pm Sat. **Credit** AmEx, DC, MC, V.
Map p305 C4.
Sip tea or espresso in the atmosphere of a chic
sitting room while trying out frames designed
by the likes of Vivienne Westwood, Helmut Lang,
Christian Roth, Romeo Gigli, Silhouette, Persol
and legendary German institution Zeiss. The
Mitte branch carries a speciality range of buffalo-
horn rims.
Branch: Reinhardtstrasse 9, Mitte (2790 8991).

Fielmann

Passage, Alexanderplatz, Mitte (242 4507).
S3, S5, S7, S9, S75, U2, U5, U8 Alexanderplatz.
Open 9am-8pm Mon-Fri; 9am-4pm Sat.
Credit AmEx, DC, MC, V. **Map** p316/p303 G3.
Fielmann is Germany's biggest chain of opticians.
Large selection of frames and competitive prices.
Eye-tests in-house.
Branches across the city.

Photography

Fix Foto

Kurfürstendamm 29, Charlottenburg (882 7267).
U15 Uhlandstrasse. **Open** 9am-10pm Mon-Sat;
11am-7pm Sun. **Credit** AmEx, MC, V. **Map** p305 C4.
Half-hour developing from black and white/colour
film or slides, enlargements, CD-Rom and other fast
services at unusually generous opening hours.
Branches across the city.

Foto Klinke

Friedrichstrasse 207-8, Kreuzberg (2529 5530).
U6 Kochstrasse. **Open** 9am-6.30pm Mon-Fri;
9am-2pm Sat. **Credit** MC, V. **Map** p306 F4.
The large processing department can turn around
films in an hour; passport photos arrive in ten minutes. Also a large range of cameras and photo equipment. Branches all over town.
Branches: Schönhauser Allee 105, Prenzlauer
Berg (444 1380); Potsdamer Strasse 141, Schöneberg
(216 3876).

PPS

Alexanderplatz 2, Mitte (726 1090). S3, S5, S7, S9,
S75, U2, U5, U8 Alexanderplatz. **Open** 8am-9pm
Mon-Fri; 2-6pm Sat, Sun. **Credit** AmEx, DC, MC, V.
Map p316/p303 G3.
Professional colour lab offering two-hour developing, digital service, scanning, black-and-white hand-
developed enlargements, large format print and
other services. Also sells cameras, rents out sophisticated equipment and sends off repairs.

Wüstefeld

Grolmanstrasse 36, Charlottenburg (883 7593). S3,
S5, S7, S9, S75 Savignyplatz or U15 Uhlandstrasse.
Open 9.30am-7pm Mon-Fri; 10am-4pm Sat.
Credit MC, V. **Map** p305 C4.
In exchange for a glance at your passport or ID card
and a credit card deposit, you can rent Nikon, Canon,
Hasselblad and Leica cameras and photo equipment
here. Also professional processing service.

Repairs

There are surprisingly few 24-hour emergency
repair services dealing with plumbing,
electricity, heating, locks, cars and carpentry.

Computer repairs

Pabst Computer

Bundesallee 137, Friedenau (859 5200/www.pabst.de).
S4, U9 Bundesplatz. **Open** 10am-8pm Mon-Fri;
10.30am-2pm Sat. **Credit** AmEx, MC, V. **Map** p305 C6.
Mac dealer with its own repair workshop.

J.E.

Poststrasse 12, Mitte (2472 1741/www.je-
computer.de). U2 Klosterstrasse. **Open** 10am-8pm
Mon-Fri; 10am-4pm Sat. **No credit cards.**
Map p316/p303 G3.
PCs repaired, software sold and classes given.

Lock-opening & repairs

For a local locksmith, look in the *Gelbe Seiten* (*Yellow Pages*) under *Schlösser*. **Schlossdienst** (834 2292) offers 24-hour emergency assistance.

Luggage repairs

Kofferhaus Gabriel

Meinekestrasse 25, Wilmersdorf (882 2262). U9, U15 Kurfürstendamm. **Open** 10am-7pm Mon-Fri; 10am-4pm Sat. **Credit** AmEx, MC, V. **Map** p305 C4.
Specialists in Samsonite, Delsey, Airline, Traveller, Rimova and Picard. The staff will be pleased to repair your suitcases within three working days and deliver new ones within the Berlin city limits.

Witt

Hauptstrasse 9, Schöneberg (781 4937). U7 Kleistpark. **Open** 9am-6pm Mon-Fri; 9am-2pm Sat. **Credit** AmEx, DC, MC, V. **Map** p306 E5.
Probably Berlin's most extensive assortment of suitcase spare parts, including patches. Luggage repairs can be completed in a day, and if damage has happened during a flight and you have written airline confirmation of this, the repairs will be billed to the airline. Evening delivery possible.

Shoe repairs

See also p173 **Breitenbach**.

Picobello

KaDeWe, Tauentzienstrasse 21, Schöneberg (2121 2349). U1, U2, U12, U15 Wittenbergplatz. **Open** 9.30am-8pm Mon-Fri; 9am-4pm Sat. **Credit** AmEx, DC, MC, V. **Map** p305 D4.

Staff will heel and sole shoes while you wait, and also engrave and cut keys. There are branches all over Berlin, often to be found in department stores.

Water, gas & heating

In an emergency, try **Ex-Rohr** (6719 8909), **Kempinger** (851 5111) or **Meisterbetrieb** (703 5050).

Souvenirs

As Berlin becomes ever more 'westernised', it's getting increasingly difficult to find relics from its Communist past. You'll find the odd stand selling Commie kitsch such as Party badges, Russian hats or Soviet binoculars plus bits of graffitied plaster, said to be from the Wall, at Checkpoint Charlie and Potsdamer Platz. The **Haus am Checkpoint Charlie** (*see p96*) sells items such as key rings, lighters and mouse pads with a 'You Are Leaving The American Sector' theme. The **Kunst und Nostalgie Markt** and **Strasse des 17.Juni** flea markets (for both, *see p178*) have stalls devoted to artefacts from the old East.

Berlin Story

Unter den Linden 40, Mitte (2016 6139). S1, S2, S25, S26 Unter den Linden. **Open** 10am-8pm daily. **Credit** AmEx, DC, MC, V. **Map** p316/p302 F3.
You won't find a better source of Berlin-related books (in both German and English), with subjects ranging from the history of the Hohenzollerns and the GDR to Prussian architecture and Norman

P-p-p-pick up a Prussian Grenadier at **Berliner Zinnfiguren Kabinett**. *See p182.*

Eat, Drink, Shop

Foster's domed Reichstag. A huge selection of historical city maps, posters, videos, CDs, and souvenirs such as toy Trabbies, mounted wall chunks, and various von Schadow sculptural plaster replicas.

Berliner Zinnfiguren Kabinett

Knesebeckstrasse 88, Charlottenburg (313 0802).
S3, S5, S7, S9, S75 Savignyplatz. **Open** 10am-6pm
Mon-Fri; 10am-3pm Sat. **Credit** AmEx, MC, V.
Map p305 C4.
Armies of tin soldiers line up alongside farm animals and historical characters, all handworked in tin and painted with incredible attention to detail. You could take home an entire battalion of Prussian Grenadiers. Also a fascinating collection of books on Prussian military history.

Fanshop

Grünberger Strasse 38, Friedrichshain (294 7691).
U5 Frankfurter Tor. **Open** 10am-1pm, 2-6pm Mon-
Fri; 10am-12.30pm Sat. **No credit cards.**
Should either of Berlin's major soccer clubs have captured your heart, this is the place to stock up on Hertha or Union caps, shawls and T-shirts.

J&M Fässler

Europa-Center, Charlottenburg (342 7166). S3,
S5, S7, S9, S75, U2, U9, U12 Zoologischer Garten.
Open 10am-6.30pm Mon-Fri; 10am-6pm Sat.
Credit AmEx, DC, MC, V. **Map** p305 D4.
Nasty German ornaments, from Hummel cuckoo clocks to Bavarian beer mugs and musical boxes.

Johanna Petzoldt

Sophienstrasse 9, Mitte (282 6754). S3, S5, S7, S9,
S75 Hackescher Markt or U8 Weinmeisterstrasse.
Open 11am-7pm Mon-Fri; 10am-6pm Sat.
Credit AmEx, MC, V. **Map** p316/p302 F3.
Tiny, charming shop filled with traditional handmade wooden figurines, musical boxes and candlemobiles from the Erzgebirge region. Quirky figures depict rural German life, Christmas figures and military types. Appropriate and appealing souvenirs.

Kunsthandwerk aus dem Erzgebirge

Friedrichstrasse 194-9, Mitte (2045 0977/
www.erzgebirgshaus.de). U2, U6 Stadtmitte.
Open 10am-8pm Mon-Fri; 10am-6pm Sat.
Credit AmEx, MC, V. **Map** p316/p306 F4.
A stone's throw from Checkpoint Charlie, this is another source for wooden handicrafts from the Erzgebirge region, where the woodwork tradition sprang to life in the mid 17th century after the collapse of the mining industry. Nutcrackers, Christmas pyramids that turn like a merry-go-round with the heat from the candles and engravings are all quintessential German gifts.

Mondos Arts

Schreinerstrasse 6, Friedrichshain (4201 0778/
www.mondosarts.de). U5 Samariter Strasse.
Open 10am-7pm Mon-Fri; 11am-4pm Sat.
Credit AmEx, MC, V.

The best of the east, or what's left of it. All types of GDR memorabilia, including flags, posters, clocks, original border signs, CDs of Ost-Rock, videos and various products embossed with the endangered *Ampelmännchen* species — the characterful stop-and-go men on a dwindling number of intersection lights in eastern Berlin.

Stationery & art supplies

Perhaps it is the national predilection for bureaucracy, but Germans love stationery – particularly anything with a whiff of office efficiency about it. Notebooks and files are taken very seriously and designed to last. The quality on offer is high.

Ferdinand Braune

Grunewaldstrasse 87, Schöneberg (7870 3773). U7
Kleistpark. **Open** 10am-6.30pm Mon-Fri; 10am-2pm
Sat. **Credit** MC, V. **Map** p306 E5.
Berlin's painters flock here for Herr Braune's hand-blended oil paints, acrylics, sketchbooks and the finest canvas stretches. Delivery service available.

Grüne Papeterie

Oranienstrasse 196, Kreuzberg (618 5355). U1, U8,
U12 Kottbusser Tor. **Open** 10am-7.30pm Mon-Fri;
10am-4pm Sat. **No credit cards. Map** p307 G4.
Eco-friendly stationery, wrapping paper, wooden fountain pens as well as small gifts and toys.

J Müller

Neue Schönhauser Strasse 16, Mitte (283 2532).
U8 Weinmeisterstrasse. **Open** 8am-6pm Mon-Fri.
No credit cards. Map p316/p303 G3.
Family-run business selling fine stationery and rubber stamps. Also prints signs and business cards.

Papeterie

Uhlandstrasse 28, Charlottenburg (881 6363). U15
Uhlandstrasse. **Open** 9.30am-7pm Mon-Wed; 9.30am-
8pm Thur, Fri; 9.30am-4pm Sat. **Credit** AmEx, DC,
MC, V. **Map** p305 C4.
Upmarket stockists of nicely made notebooks, agendas, diaries, albums and organisers, plus Mont Blanc pens and Count Faber-Castell gilded pencil sets.

Propolis

Oranienstrasse 19A, Kreuzberg (615 2464). U1,
U8, U12 Kottbusser Tor. **Open** 10am-6pm Mon-Fri.
No credit cards. Map p307 G4.
Specialising in pigments, with over 300 to choose from, plus recipes and ingredients for wall finishes. Also available are oil, water and acrylic paints, resins, gold and silver leaf, brushes and canvases.

RSVP

Mulackstrasse 14, Mitte (2809 4644/www.rsvp-
berlin.de). U8 Weinmeister Strasse. **Open** 10am-6pm
Tue-Fri. **Credit** MC, V. **Map** p316/p303 G3.
The aesthete's stationery shop, with a selection of unusual paper for every occasion, plus rubber stamps and Japanese knives.

Arts & Entertainment

Features

By Season

From the abandon of the Love Parade to the refinement of classical music festivals, Berlin's year is packed with events to suit all tastes.

Berlin remains very much alive throughout the year. Springtime is ushered in violently by the traditional May Day Riots, when local anarchists take to the streets for their annual battle with police – an often brutal and fiery signal of warmer days to come. In the summer months, the city hosts parades celebrating everything from hemp and gay life to multiculturalism, sex and techno music. Countless outdoor music festivals attract crowds and cafés and bars spill out on to the street, providing plenty of reason for Berliners to be outside. During quieter periods, like winter, many clubs and cabarets make an effort to stage special events. Cultural venues like the Philharmonie and opera houses are packed for seasonal performances. Christmas markets and ice-skating rinks spring up around the city, giving Berlin a traditional, old-fashioned aura.

For further information on seasonal events, contact the official tourist board **Berlin-Tourismus-Marketing** (*see p285*), or look in the city's listings magazines *tip* and *Zitty*; for climate information, *see p285* **When to go**; for details of public holidays, *see p282* **Public holidays**.

Spring

Zeitfenster – Biennale für alte Musik

Konzerthaus Berlin, Gendarmenmarkt 2, Mitte (203 090). U6 Französische Strasse or U2, U6 Stadtmitte or U2 Hausvogteiplatz. **Tickets** varies. **No credit cards. Map** p316/p306 F4. **Date** 1wk in Apr, every 2yrs (2002, 2004).
The Biennial Festival of Early Music at the impressive Gendarmenmarkt Konzerthaus focuses on 16th- and 17th-century baroque sounds.

May Day Riots

Around Kottbusser Tor, Oranienstrasse, Kreuzberg. **Map** p307 G5. **Date** 1 May.
An annual event since 1987, when anarchist *Autonomen* engaged in violent clashes with police. Its traditions go back to the early 20th century, however, when early Communists and anarchists did the same. The riots are worth checking out only from a safe distance – police have been accused of using brutal methods to disperse crowds, including batons and high-powered water cannons, and some demonstrators lob Molotov cocktails and loot local shops.

Deutschland Pokalendspiele

Olympiastadion, Olympischer Platz 3, Charlottenburg (300 633). S5 Olympiastadion or U2 Olympia-Stadion. Information & tickets: Deutscher Fussball-Bund (678 80/www.dfb.de). **Tickets** varies. **No credit cards. Date** Sat in early May.
The domestic football cup final has been taking place at the Olympic Stadium every year since 1985, when the German FA awarded Berlin permission to host the event on a permanent basis. It regularly attracts some 65,000, often rowdy, football fans.

International Aerospace Exhibition

Flughafen Schönefeld (6091 1620). S9, S45 Flughafen Schönefeld. **Tickets** varies. **No credit cards. Date** 1wk in May, every 2yrs (2002, 2004).
The number of visitors continues to grow at this biennial event held at Schönefeld airport. In 2002, more than 1,000 exhibitors from 40 countries took part, with aircraft of all classes and categories on display, as well as a serious focus on space.

Eurocard Ladies German Open

LTTC Rot-Weiss, Gottfried-von-Cramm-Weg 47-55, Grunewald (ticket hotline 308 785 685/www.german-open-berlin.de). S7 Grunewald. **Tickets** varies. **Credit** AmEx, DC, MC, V. **Date** 2nd wk in May.
The world's fifth largest international women's tennis championship is also a week-long get-together for Germany's rich and famous. After match point, the focus switches to a gala ball and other glitzy social affairs. Tickets are hard to come by.

Theatertreffen Berlin

Various venues. Organisers: Berliner Festspiele, Schaperstrasse 24, Tiergarten (2548 9100/www.berlinerfestspiele.de). **Tickets** varies. **Credit** varies. **Date** 3wks in May.
The 'Berlin Theatre Meeting' presents the best in German-speaking stage productions. A jury chooses ten of the most innovative and controversial new productions from companies in Germany, Austria and Switzerland. The winners come to Berlin to perform their pieces during the festival.

Karneval der Kulturen

Kreuzberg (6097 7022/www.karneval-berlin.de). **Tickets** free. **Date** 4 days in May/June.
Inspired by the Notting Hill Carnival and intended as a celebration of Berlin's ethnic and cultural diversity, the festive long weekend (always seven weeks after Easter) includes a street festival, parties and a 'multi-kulti' parade involving dozens of floats, hundreds of musicians and thousands of spectators. The route changes every year, so phone for details.

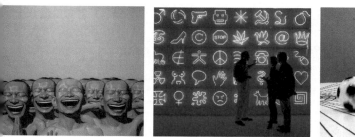

Europe's leading artists rub shoulders at **Art Forum Berlin**. *See p187.*

Summer

Schwul-Lesbisches Strassenfest
Nollendorfplatz, Schöneberg (216 8008). U1, U2,
U4, U12, U15 Nollendorfplatz. **Map** p305 D5.
Tickets free. **Date** 2 days in June.
The traditional summer Gay and Lesbian Street
Party surrounds several blocks in west Berlin's gay
quarter. Participating bars, clubs, food stands, sell-
ers and musical acts make the party a dizzying non-
stop event for gays and straights alike. It is designed
as a primer for the Christopher Street Day Parade
the following week (*see also below*).

Berlin Philharmonie at the Waldbühne
Waldbühne, Glockenturmstrasse, Charlottenburg
(2308 8230). S5 Pichelsburg, then shuttle bus.
Tickets varies. **Credit** AmEx, MC. V.
Date 1 day in June.
The Philharmonie ends its season with a big concert
at the atmospheric outdoor Waldbühne, once used
by Nazi leaders for torchlit political rallies. The
event marks the start of summer for more than
20,000 Berliners, who light up the venue with can-
dlelight once darkness falls.

Fête de la Musique
Various venues (019 058 1058/
www.lafetedelamusique.de). **Tickets** free.
Date 21 June.
A regular summer happening since 1995, this music
extravaganza takes place in nearly every district of
the city and features hundreds of bands and DJs
playing everything from heavy metal and hip hop
to German *Schlager*. *See also p223.*

Christopher Street Day Parade
Route varies (2362 8632/www.csd-berlin.de).
Tickets free. **Date** Sat in mid/late June.
Originally organised to commemorate the 1969 riots
at the Stonewall Bar on Christopher Street in New
York, which marked the beginning of modern gay
liberation, the parade has become one of the summer's most flamboyant street parties for both gays
and straights and an exciting attraction for visitors
to the city. The parade takes place on the Saturday
nearest to 22 June. *See also above.*

Classic Open Air
Gendarmenmarkt, Mitte (Media On-Line 315
7540/www.classicopenair.de). U6 Französische
Strasse, U2, U6 Stadtmitte or U2 Hausvogteiplatz.
Tickets €24-€75. **Credit** AmEx, MC, V. **Map**
p316/p302 F3. **Date** 4-7 days in early July.
Big names usually open this concert series held in
one of Berlin's most beautiful squares. Many local
orchestras take part, as well as soloists from around
Europe. Tickets can be booked online.

Love Parade
Tiergarten (Planetcom 284 620/www.loveparade.de).
Tickets *Parade* free. *Evening parties* varies.
Map p302 E3. **Date** 2nd Sat in July.
Regularly attracting a million visitors from around
Europe, the techno parade includes floats sponsored
by clubs from around the country and beyond. It has
become increasingly controversial in recent years,
however, with many locals opposing the parade's
route through Berlin's Tiergarten park. In 2000,
government officials revoked the event's status as
a political demonstration, forcing organisers to pick
up the cleaning tab. *See p186* **Slaves to love**.

Fuck Parade
069 9435 9090. **Tickets** free. **Date** usually 2nd
Sat in July.
Launched in 1997 as a counter demonstration to the
overly commercial Love Parade, the annual Fuck
Parade has tried to remain both small and underground. The event is meant to represent the edgier,
non-commercial side of electronic music, and has in
the past attracted 2-3,000 ravers and dozens of
floats from techno, drum 'n' bass and gabba clubs
from throughout the country. The route (which
varies), out of earshot of the Love Parade, meanders
through the backstreets of eastern Berlin. The
future of the Fuck Parade is in question, however,
since German courts in 2001 revoked the parade's
status as a political demonstration.

Heimatklänge
Various venues (6128 4235). **Tickets** free.
Date 2wks in July/Aug.
Berlin's biggest world music festival, featuring acts
from around the globe, takes place at various venues
throughout the city. Expect anything from Brazilian

jazz and the rhythmic beats of South African musicians to Patagonian nose flautists and Mongolian chants. *See also p223.*

Deutsch-Französisches Volksfest

Zentraler Festplatz am Kurt-Schumacher-Damm, Kurt-Schumacher-Damm 207-45, Reinickendorf (213 3190/www.berliner-volksfeste.de/seiten/dfv.htm). U6 Kurt-Schumacher-Platz. **Tickets** €1.50. **No credit cards. Date** 4wks in July/Aug.
A hangover from the days when French troops were stationed in the northern district of West Berlin, the month-long annual German-French Festival offers fun-rides, French music and cuisine.

Deutsch-Amerikanisches Volksfest

Truman Plaza, Hüttenweg/Clayallee, Zehlendorf (0172 3900 930/www.deutsch-amerikanisches-volksfest.de). U1 Oskar-Helene-Heim. **Tickets** varies. **No credit cards. Date** 4wks in July/Aug.
Originally established by the US forces stationed in West Berlin, the German-American Festival continues to please adults and kids with a mix of carnival rides, cowboys doing lasso tricks, candy floss, hamburgers, hotdogs and a hell of a lot of real American beer. It has a tacky feel, but Berliners still come en masse.

City Night 10km Run

Kurfürstendamm, Charlottenburg (3012 8810). **Map** p304 B5/p305 C4. **Date** Sat or Sun in early Aug.
The 11th annual evening run along west Berlin's main thoroughfare, the Kurfürstendamm, starts at the Europa-Center shopping mall.

Internationales Berliner Bierfestival

Karl-Marx-Allee, from Strausberger Platz to Frankfurter Tor, Friedrichshain (508 6822). **U5 Frankfurter Tor. Map** p89/p303 G3/H3. **Date** 1 weekend in Aug.
The annual Berlin International Beer Festival showcases over 1,000 beers from more than 60 countries. Beer stalls run along the Stalinist-style Karl-Marx-Allee.

Young Euro Classic

Konzerthaus/Schauspielhaus am Gendarmenmarkt, Am Gendarmenmarkt 2, Mitte (2030 92101/ www.young-euro-classic.de). **Tickets** varies. **No credit cards. Map** p306 F4. **Date** 2wks in Aug.
Young Euro Classic – the annual European summer music programme – brings together youth orchestras from around the continent for a series of recommended concerts.

Slaves to love

Few could have imagined when it was launched in 1989 by 350 devotees that within ten years the **Love Parade** (*see p185*) would pull a million-plus fun-crazed punters into Berlin's Tiergarten park. But today this over-the-top free-for-all has become a mecca for ravers and party-goers from around the continent and beyond, and an undoubted highpoint of Berlin's summer.

Although the parade is usually hot, unbearably crowded, exhausting and extremely loud, it's also a wildly exhilarating experience, even without any artificial stimulants (and there are certainly plenty of those about). If you are well connected, you might be able to get on one of the 50 or so floats organised by clubs, labels and media outlets from Berlin and beyond. Otherwise, you'll be adrift in an ocean of revellers, hopelessly lost in the party zone.

The Love Parade is a paradoxical event: profoundly irritating for some, deeply joyous for others. At night, expect lengthy queues for the toilets, outside every venue, to get back to the dancefloor and for the pleasure of paying exorbitant amounts for a plastic cup of warm beer. It's a unique experience nonetheless, with crowds fired up by DJs

giving their all. There's something primal about the wild abandonment of the event, as participants lose themselves in the frenzy of the dancing masses. The raw energy in the air is almost tangible.

Even public sex during the parade is not something out of the ordinary. Indeed, in the past few years the event has become a favourite location for porn filmmakers to shoot their pictures. And sex is as much an activity as dance on the float organised by the infamous KitKatClub (*see p231*), where people do nothing more than just get it on.

The music has always centred on techno, but the variety of music has been growing and you can hear anything from African drumming to drum 'n' bass or Goa trance. For party-goers who are still raring to go after the parade, it's easy to find out where the evening parties take place as flyers are handed out everywhere.

LOVE ON THE ROCKS?

Originally registered by organisers as a political demonstration 'for love', the parade was stripped of that status in 2001 when courts ruled that it was clearly a commercial event. As a result of the

Lange Nacht der Museen

2839 7444/www.lange-nacht-der-museen.de.
Tickets free. **Date** 1 evening in late Aug.
Twice a year more than 80 museums throughout the
city stay open into the early hours. In addition to
their collections and special exhibitions, the 'Long
Night of the Museums' offers concerts, readings and
stage acts. Visitors can shuttle between venues by
bus, tram or boat for serious museum hopping. Also
takes place in February.

Kreuzberger Festliche Tage

*Viktoria Park, Katzbachstrasse, Kreuzberg
(401 3889). U6, U7 Mehringdamm.* **Tickets** free.
Map p306 E5. **Date** 2wks in late Aug/early Sept.
This annual summer festival in Kreuzberg's charming Viktoria Park offers music, games, beer and food
just before the Autumn kicks in.

Autumn

Hanfparade

*Hallesches Tor to Rotes Rathaus (2472 0233/
www.hanflobby.de/hanfparade).* **Tickets** free.
Date usually 1 Sept.
Celebrating the usefulness of the fibrous weed,
organisers of the Hemp Parade are seeking total

legalisation, though many German states have
already relaxed laws on the use and possession of
cannabis. The route changes occasionally, so check
the local press for details.

Berliner Festwochen

*Various venues. Organisers: Berliner Festspiele,
Schaperstrasse 24, Tiergarten (2548 9218/
www.berlinerfestspiele.de).* **Tickets** varies.
Credit varies. **Date** Sept-Nov.
Summer drifts into Autumn with a couple of months
of events, concerts and performances. Classical
music and international theatre are accompanied by
exhibitions and readings. *See p235.*

Art Forum Berlin

*Messedamm 22, Charlottenburg (30380/
www.art-forum-berlin.de). S4 Witzleben or U2
Kaiserdamm. Information: European Galleries,
Projektgesellschaft (8855 1643).* **Map** p304 A4.
Date 5 days in late Sept.
Since 1996, the Art Forum Berlin has sought to bring
together gallery owners and artists during this five-
day trade fair of contemporary art. The event
attracts many of Europe's leading galleries plus
thousands of lay enthusiasts from around the continent. *See also p205* **Art mart**.

ruling, the organisers (and not the city
government) must now foot the bill for
the costs of the massive clean-up effort
the day after the parade.

It was one of the things that had long
irked local residents, who have become
increasingly critical of the techno
extravaganza. The event, after
all, has turned into a lucrative
venture for the organisers, who
cash in on everything from Love
Parade parties and Love Parade
T-shirts to the official Love
Parade CD. But of all its critics,
environmentalists have been
most vocal in their opposition to
the parade's route through the
beautiful Tiergarten park, which
ends up drenched in urine by
drunken revellers. In 2000, they
made their point by registering
their own conservationist
demonstration on the same day
in a show of solidarity with the
birds, furry creatures and plant-
life that inhabit the area.

Protesters of another sort even formed
the parallel **Fuck Parade** (*see p185*), a more

underground alternative to the now over-
commercialised main event, which meanders
on a different route through the backstreets.

TOP PARADE TIPS

For the past few years the route has remained
fundamentally unchanged, starting at both
the Brandenburger Tor and Ernst-Reuter-Platz,

the two ends of the wide
thoroughfare Strasse des 17.
Juni that runs through Tiergarten.
Things to remember: take
lots of water, snacks and
sunblock too, since there are
few chances to buy them on the
way. Remember that you won't
be able to sit down and rest
whenever you feel like it, so be
sure to pace yourself.

Berlin's public transport
operators BVG issue a special
ticket, often in the form of an
armband, expected to cost
around €5-€10 in 2002, which
allows unlimited travel on public
transport for the whole weekend.
This is the best way to move about – you won't
get a car anywhere near the parade.

Arts & Entertainment

Berlin Marathon

Organisers: Berlin-Marathon, Glockenturmstrasse 23, 14055 (302 5370/fax 3012 8820/www.berlin-marathon.com). **Entrance fee** €40-€60.
Credit call for details. **Date** last Sun in Sept.
The Berlin Marathon – the city's biggest sporting event – takes around 30,000 participants from around the world, including wheelchair racers and in-line skaters, past most of the city's landmarks on its 42-km (26-mile) trek through seven districts. *See also p249.*

JazzFest Berlin

Various venues. Organisers: Berliner Festspiele, Schaperstrasse 24, Tiergarten (2548 9100/ www.berlinerfestspiele.de). **Tickets** varies.
Credit varies. **Date** 4 days late Oct/early Nov.
This festival offers a wide spectrum of jazz from an equally diverse array of internationally renowned artists. A fixture of the local scene since 1964, the JazzFest Berlin is often accompanied by mini-music festivals and exhibitions. *See also p223.*

Winter

Berliner Märchentage

Various venues (282 9140). **Tickets** varies.
Credit varies. **Date** 10 days in mid Nov.
Established in 1989,the Berlin Fairytale Festival celebrates magical tales from around the world with storytelling, music and a carnival atmosphere at 150 locations throughout the city with some 400 events. While 2001's festival theme was inspired by the tales of *The Arabian Nights*, 2002's event, dubbed 'The Treasures of the Czars,' explores the enchanted world of Russian fairytales.

Christmas Markets

Spandauer Altstadt, Marktplatz. U7 Altstadt, Spandau. **Open** 9am-8pm Mon-Sat; 10am-7pm Sun. *Kaiser-Wilhelm-Gedächtniskirche, Breitscheidplatz, Charlottenburg. S3, S5, S7, S9, U2, U9 Zoologischer Garten.* **Open** 11am-9pm Mon-Thur, Sun; 11am-10pm Fri, Sat. **Map** p305 D4. **Date** last wk in Nov-1 Jan.
Traditional Yuletide markets spring up all over Berlin during the Christmas season, offering traditional toys, baked goods, hot spiced wine, gingerbread and many other goodies and gifts besides. While the one at Breitscheidplatz is one of the biggest and Kaiser-Wilhelm-Gedächtniskirche the most central, it's also well worth trekking out to the picturesque market in the old town of Spandau on the western edge of the city.

Berliner Silvesterlauf

Grunewald (302 5370/www.berlin-marathon.com/ events/silvester/anmeldung). S5, S75 Eichkamp.
Tickets free. **Date** 31 Dec.
A local tradition for almost 30 years, the Berlin New Year's Eve Run, which is also known as the 'pancake run', starts in Grunewald at the intersection of Waldschulallee and Harbigstrasse at the foot of Teufelsberg.

Silvester

Date 31 Dec.
With Berliners' enthusiasm for tossing firecrackers and launching rockets from windows, New Year's Eve in the city is always a blast. Thousands of locals celebrate the New Year at the Brandenburger Tor. The claustrophobic are advised to stay away as the crowds can become overwhelming. Thousands more trek up to the Teufelsberg at the northern tip of Grunewald or head up to the Kreuzberg hill in Viktoria Park to watch the fireworks.

Internationale Grüne Woche

Messe Berlin, Messedamm 22, Charlottenburg (30380/www.gruenewoche.com). S4 Witzleben or U2 Kaiserdamm. **Open** 9am-6pm daily. **Tickets** €11.
No credit cards. Date 10 days in Jan.
International Green Week is acutally a ten-day orgy of food and drink from the far corners of Germany and the world.

Lange Nacht der Museen

2839 7444/www.lange-nacht-der-museen.de.
Date 1 evening in Feb.
Late-night museum opening. *See p187.*

Transmediale

Haus der Kulturen der Welt, John-Foster-Dulles-Allee 10, Tiergarten (2472 1907). Bus 100, 248.
Tickets varies. **No credit cards. Map** p302 E3.
Date 5 days in early Feb.
Transmediale is one of the largest international media art festivals in the world, presenting exhibitions from artists working with video, television, computer animation, the Internet and other visual mediums and digital technologies. A forum for communication between artists, experts and media types. Parts of the event may be held at other venues in the city.

Berlin International Film Festival

Potsdamer Platz, Tiergarten & other venues (259 200/www.berlinale.de). S1, S2, S25, S26, U2 Potsdamer Platz. **Tickets** *see p199.*
Credit *see p199.* **Date** 1-2wks in mid Feb.
Now more than 50 years old, this is one of the world's major cinema festivals, featuring over 300 movies from around the world. It is held at the Potsdamer Platz cinemas, and attended by international stars, providing this normally glamour-proof city with a bit of glitz in the dead of winter. *See also p198* **Berlin Film Festival.**

MaerzMusik – Festival für aktuelle Musik

Various venues. Organisers: Berliner Festspiele, Schaperstrasse 24, Tiergarten (2548 9218/ www.berlinfestspiele.de). **Tickets** varies.
Credit varies. **Date** 1-2wks in Mar.
A holdover from the more culture-conscious days of the old East Germany, the former biennial festival is now held annually and highlights trends in contemporary music. The event invites international avant-garde composers and musicians to present their latest works. *See also p235.*

Children

How to plan a fun-filled, stress-free family stay in the city.

Young entrepreneurs set out their stall on **Winterfeldtplatz**. *See p190*.

Berlin isn't exactly made for children and families – it sprawls, isn't too pretty and is loaded towards the heavyweight end of the cultural spectrum. But, with a little priming and planning, the city can still be great fun for kids and, if the metropolis becomes too hectic, it's easy to escape to nearby lakes and woods.

Children are well integrated into daily Berlin life, though it can seem that Berliners like the idea of childhood more than treating children as cogent individuals. But the city is becoming more and more of a multicultural ('multiculti', as a Berliner would say) capital and things are changing for the better. Most locals respond well to children, and you will find it easy to travel in Berlin with children. Using public transport with kids (or with a buggy) is generally not a problem, as main U- and S-Bahn stations have lifts. Buses allow for easy entry with a buggy through the rear doors.

The best way to make sense of Berlin with children is to take a geographical approach to the city. Each of Berlin's districts is distinct, and offers a range of different activities and attractions.

Mitte

In Mitte, the centre of the city, there's no shortage of things to see and do. Most museums are located here, many on **Museumsinsel** (*see p76*), which, with its weekend flea market, is a lovely, lively spot to pass a few hours.

An enjoyable way to orient yourself in Berlin is by a boat tour, many of which operate from in front of the Pergamonmuseum on Museumsinsel. From here you can set out west towards Charlottenburg and the Havel river, the Wannsee (*see p118*) and Potsdam (*see p258*) or head east to the Müggelsee in Köpenick (*see p120*) and the Spreewald forest (*see p262*).

Another way to get the lie of the land is to take in the panorama of the city from the top of Berlin's highest landmark, the **Fernsehturm** (TV Tower; *see p85*) on Alexanderplatz.

Of Mitte's many museums, the superb **Pergamonmuseum** (*see p77*) featuring the offers ancient architecture on a grand scale that will impress most kids and the **Haus am Checkpoint Charlie** (*see p96*) has plenty to interest older children, including the old cars and balloons that people used to attempt to circumvent the Wall. The **Museum Kindheit und Jugend** (Museum of Childhood and Youth; *see p86*) has old toys, and childhood and classroom artefacts from the last century.

If you're looking for entertainment, the **Hackesches Hof Theater** at Rosenthaler Strasse 40-41 (283 2587) puts on an enjoyable Sunday brunch show, with clowns and puppets, from 10am onwards. The **Checkpoint am Spittelmarkt** (Leipziger Strasse 55; 204 4339) offers stage workshops for children. **Milch und Honig** ('milk and honey'; 6162 5761) presents Jewish life in Berlin and offers cultural and other events for parents and children (6162 5761/ www.milch-und-honig.com/kinderseite.htm).

The empty square at **Schlossplatz**, close to the Berliner Dom, is often used for amusement parks, funfairs and circuses.

At Mitte's south-western corner, the gleaming **Potsdamer Platz** complex contains a range of shops, and there are also three multiplex cinemas here, which screen children's and family films (though dubbed into German) each afternoon. If, though, you seek greenery, head for **Monbijou Park** near Oranienburger Strasse, which has cafés and playgrounds.

Many restaurants in Mitte have children's menus, but the area around Hackesche Höfe and Rosenthaler Strasse offers the richest pickings. Try the **Hackescher Hof** at Rosenthaler Strasse 40 (*see p123*), the Asian **GOA** (2859 8451) at Oranienburger Strasse 50, **Der Kartoffelkeller** (282 8548) with regional German food at Albrechtstrasse 14B, the American **Catherine's** (2025 1555) at Friedrichstrasse 90 or international cuisine served at **Boma** (2759 4955) at Neue Schönhauser Strasse 10.

Prenzlauer Berg & Friedrichshain

Prenzlauer Berg is a colourful and lively district, although there are few parks or specific attractions for kids. There are, however, plenty of cafés, restaurants, squares and playgrounds, particularly in the area around **Kollwitzplatz**.

Among the restaurants that offer special children's menus are the Italian **Istoria** (Kollwitzstrasse 64; 4405 0208), **Zander** (No.50; 4405 7678), **Prater** (Kastanienallee 7; *see p148*) with German food; and the Indian **Maharadsha 2** (Schönhauser Allee 142; 448 5172).

Die Schaubude (423 4314) in Greifswalder Strasse 81-4 is a high quality puppet theatre, used by a variety of local and visiting troupes.

The harsh socialist monumentalism of much of Friedrichshain has little charm and there are few, if any, family attractions to enjoy in the area.

Kreuzberg

Together with Prenzlauer Berg, the area between Oberbaumbrücke and Oranienstrasse in Kreuzberg, housing the highest population of Turks outside Turkey and plenty of students and young folk, is certainly the most colourful and sometimes the weirdest district of Berlin. Cheap, good restaurants of all thinkable origins, markets and small shops for everything and nothing create a vibrant and unique feel, which is very friendly to children.

The **Deutsches Technikmuseum Berlin** (*see p95*) in Trebbiner Strasse 9 offers old locomotives and cars to explore, and computers and gadgets to play with. The museum also offers special tours (call 254 840).

Leafy **Viktoriapark**, near Tempelhof Airport, offers all kinds of sports, playgrounds, cafés and the occasional circus or funfair. Nearby are plenty of eating options, such as **Osteria No.1** (*see p133*) at Kreuzbergstrasse 71, **Amun** (Möckernstrasse 73A; 786 4963), one of the best Egyptian restaurants in Berlin, the Latin American **El Chico** (6959 9170) in Baerwaldstrasse 52, the German regional restaurant **Altes Zollhaus** at Carl Hertz Ufer 30 (*see p131*), the vegetarian **Abendmahl** (*see p135*) at Muskauer Strasse 3 and the Italian **Parlamento** (694 7745) at Bergmannstrasse 3.

There is no one major shopping area in Kreuzberg, but a nice spot to visit is the **Marheinicke Halle** at Marheinicke Platz, a huge historic indoor market, which is open Monday to Saturday.

Schöneberg

Schöneberg is a huge, disparate district. The area around **Winterfeldplatz**, around 15 minutes' walk from the Kurfürstendamm, is a pleasant focal point, with an outdoor market each Wednesday and Saturday, lots of cafés and restaurants (good, cheap fast food on Golzstrasse), small parks and lots of playgrounds.

There aren't many specific attractions in the district, though it's worth travelling to the **Planetarium am Insulaner** (Munsterdamm 90; 790 0930), about 20 minutes by S-Bahn (S2, S25, S26 Priesterweg) from the centre of town. Two to four times a week the planetarium offers special programmes for children.

The huge **Volkspark Wilmersdorf**, stretching from the district of Dahlem via Wilmersdorf to Schöneberg, offers myriad slides, playground paraphernalia and a ski lift ride. At the park's eastern end is one of Berlin's best indoor swimming pools (Hauptstrasse). Close by is **Café Milchstrasse**

Museum Kindheit und Jugend. *See p190.*

(Vorbergstrasse 10A; 784 7115), which offers Sunday afternoon entertainment for children, with stage performances, films, and so on.

There's plenty good, child-friendly restaurants all over Schöneberg. Try the old, traditional **Bamberger Reiter** (Regensburger Strasse 7; *see p138*), the newish Japanese **Flying Fish Sushi** (Eisenacher Strasse 67; 782 0663) or the well-established but adventurous Indian/vegetarian **Tuk-Tuk** (Grossgörschen-strasse 2; 781 1588).

At Albrechtstrasse 12 in Steglitz (just south of Schöneberg) there is the new **Indoor Playground 'Kilala'** (7970 2494; open 10am-8pm daily), over three floors packed with just about everything any child could hope for, and with a coffee shop for parents.

Tiergarten

The major draw in Tiergarten is without doubt the park itself. On many spring and summer weekends a pall of smoke hangs over the charming park from the countless family barbecues taking place. Paddle and rowing boats can be hired near the **Café am Neuen See** (*see p155*) in the Tiergarten. Along Strasse des 17.Juni, the main road through the park, an interesting flea market takes place on Saturdays and Sundays.

In the park's south-western corner is Berlin's beautifully landscaped **Zoo** and its sizeable **Aquarium** (for both, *see p104*). The best part of a day can easily be spent here. If your kids fancy a higher level of culture, the excellent **Gemäldegalerie** in Matthäikirchplatz (*see p103*) runs Sunday afternoon tours for children, and the **Haus der Kulturen der Welt** (*see p101*), on the northern edge of the park, offers special programmes for kids.

Kinderfilmfest

For more than 50 years the annual Berlin Film Festival (*see p198* **Berlin International Film Festival**) has been one of the world's major international celebrations of celluloid. Undoubtedly, the section of the festival with the most excited audience is the **Kinderfilmfest**, which began in 1978. Every year around 25 children's films from all around the world compete for the official jury award and the 'Crystal Bear Award' by the children's jury. All films are screened in their original language with English subtitles, three times in three different cinemas. The screenings at the Zoo Palast at Hardenbergstrasse, next door to Bahnhof Zoo, are a stunning event, with its 1,000 seats usually completely sold out. Other cinemas for the Kinderfilmfest are the CinemaxX (*see p196*) at Potsdamer Platz and the Film Theater am Friedrichshain.

The children's jury prize is regarded as the major Kinderfilmfest award. Eleven children, aged between 11 and 14, make up the jury that judges all the films in this tough category to decide on the winner of the 'Crystal Bear'. Recent winners include *Manipulation* (UK, 1991), *Angelothek, Sdelai Radost* (Turkmenistan, 1992), *Wrony* (Poland, 1994), *Belma* (Denmark/Sweden, 1995), *The Whole of the Moon* (New Zealand, 1995), *Where the Elephant Sits* (USA, 1997) and *Rang-e-Khoda* (Iran, 1999).

The February event provides a great backdrop for a winter family visit to the city. Kids can enjoy some first-rate films they otherwise wouldn't have a chance to see. And after each screening, they can talk directly to the director, and very often to the child actors too.

Tickets cost €2 per screening. For further information, see www.berlinale.de.

Charlottenburg

The former focus of West Berlin, around Bahnhof Zoo and the Ku'damm, can seem like a unappealing traffic- and people-infested commercial honeypot. But away from the main thoroughfares the atmosphere is pleasant and intimate, with excellent restaurants, shops and outdoor markets. The Saturday market at Karl-August-Platz, for example, is a gathering point for families, with a central playground, small cafés, and top-notch icecream at **Micha's Eisdiele** (Pestalozzistrasse 85).

Fifteen minutes' walk west of here is the small but beautiful **Lietzenseepark**, with a lake, three playgrounds, two cafés (open between April and October) and two sports areas.

Of more interest to children than the **Schloss Charlottenburg** (*see p109*) is the **Ägyptisches Museum** (*see p108*) opposite – a great place for mummy-mad kids. There are special tours for children above the age of eight (places are limited, call 266 2951 in advance).

There are child-friendly restaurants all over Charlottenburg, particularly in its eastern reaches. The relaxed attitude of Italians to kids is evident at **La Cantina** (Bleibtreustrasse 17; 883 2156) and **Toto** (corner of Bleibtreustrasse and Pestalozzistrasse; 312 5449). Other good family restaurants include the German **Diekmanns** (Meinekestrasse 7; 883 3321) and **Engelbecken** (Witzlebenstrasse 31; 615 2810) at Lake Lietzensee, offering international cuisine. At **Charlottchen** (Droysenstrasse 1; 324 4717) parents eat in the dining room (the food is nothing special) while their children let their hair down in a rumpus room. There are theatre performances for children on Sundays (11.30am).

Other districts

To the south-west of the city, the vast **Grunewald** woods (*see p117*) are great for long walks, and the Kronprinzessinnenweg in its centre is an ideal track for rollerskating and cycling. Bordering the woods, at the **Wannsee** lake (*see p118*), is a small beach area, with boat hire. It's possible to visit **Pfaueninsel** (Peacock Island; *see p118*) with its nature reserve and an eccentric castle built by Friedrich Wilhelm II, or you can take a wonderful boat tour southwards through various small lakes and canals via the Griebnitzsee to Potsdam.

To the east of the Grunewald, **Domäne Dahlem** (*see p116*) is a working farm where life in the 17th century is recreated via demonstrations by blacksmiths, carpenters, bakers and potters. At weekends children can ride ponies, tractors and hay-wagons. Going further back in time, **Museumsdorf Düppel** (*see p119*) is a reconstructed 14th-century village around archaeological excavations near the Düppel forest. Kids can witness craftspeople at work, medieval technology, old farming techniques and ride ox-carts (April to October).

West of the Havel river from the Grunewald in the district of Gatow is the small **British-German Yacht Club** (Kladower Damm 217A; 365 4010), which has an excellent team of sailing teachers for children (Tuesday at 4pm and

It's red hair day at the **Zoo**. *See p104.*

Saturday at 11am, between April and October) and a British pub, where parents can have drink and snack at the waterside, while the youngsters mess about on the water. In the centre of Gatow, children adore jumping in and out of military aircraft at the **Luftwaffenmuseum** (*see p113*).

You can avoid the summer crowds on the Havel and the Wannsee by visiting the **Tegeler See** to the north-west of the city. North-east of here, at the very north end of Quickborner Strasse in the charming old village of Alt Lübars, is **Jugendfarm Lübars**, (S1 to Wittenau, then bus 221; 415 7027; open 9am-5pm Tue-Fri, Sun; free) where children can see farm animals, watch craftspeople at work and eat at the farm's restaurant. Adjacent is a playground and a hill of World War II rubble to climb.

It's a longish drive to **FEZ in der Wuhlheide** (An der Wuhlheide 250; 5307 1257), deep in the woods in Köpenick, south-east of the centre, but FEZ has a lot for children: tricycles, wading ponds, trampolines, forts – its origins go back to GDR days, and it offers a sort of small-scale, less glamorous and cheaper eastern version of Disney World.

Also to the east is the **Tierpark Berlin-Friedrichsfelde** (*see p120*), a huge and nicely landscaped park and zoo. It's good for long walks and views of grassland animals, like giraffes and deer, in open spaces. Playgrounds, a petting zoo and snack stands also feature. Still further east, the **Müggelsee** (*see p120*) is another beautiful sailing and swimming area. A boat tour from Mitte to the Müggelsee and back occupies a full day, but is well worth it in good weather.

Babysitters

There's an excellent online search engine (in German) for babysitters at www.berlinonline.de/service/familie/babysitter/.html/b/b_suchen.htm.

Babysitter Agentur Berlin
01723 070 662. **Prices** around €10 per hr. **No credit cards.**

Babysitter Service Christine Stern
881 1801. **Prices** around €10 per hr. **No credit cards.**

Micys Babsitter Service
568 37 43. **Prices** around €10 per hr. **No credit cards.**

Film

Opportunities aplenty for English-speaking film-lovers.

Every time Berliners flick through their film listings, the number of cinemas seems to have increased. Despite a wave of closings in the east of the city and surrounding areas, since the fall of the Wall the number of screens in Berlin has almost tripled. Unfortunately, as is the case in most major cities, this signals not a widening of variety, but, rather, the overall advance of multiplex culture. Where Berlin was once a little haven of repertory cinema, the choice is becoming increasingly limited to the latest Hollywood fare, with a sprinkling of British and French crossover 'hits'. But mainstream German products do still hold their own, albeit modest, niche.

As a result, the surviving small one-off cinemas have responded by banding together as the Association of Independent Cinemas, which has been retrenching with foreign-language programming, especially European and Asian cinema. The result is that English-language programming, once the speciality of the small and daring, is becoming increasingly the domain of the large, and mainly conservative, multiplex chains. Perhaps the most dramatic expression of this changing emphasis was the shift in 2000 of the **Internationale Filmfestspiele Berlin** (*see p198* **Berlin International Film Festival**) – which, along with Cannes and Venice, is one of the most important international film festivals in the world – to that mighty new shopping mall: Potsdamer Platz.

For those comfortable with the mainstream, you'll feel right at home, be it in the monster multiplex of CinemaxX Potsdamer Platz (usually three of its 19 screens in English) or the more intimate, but no less comfortable, Kurbel (three out of three in English). Even the historically alternative all-English houses, such as Odeon and Babylon, have been veering towards the middle of the road.

But rabid cinéastes should not despair. Variety does survive, most notably in the eclectic programming at the Arsenal, as well as the wildly unpredictable Eiszeit, coming up with a few pleasant surprises here and there.

One typical Berlin phenomenon worth checking out is the city's fascination with silent films, which are very often presented with live musical accompaniment, ranging from simple piano to full symphony orchestra with the occasional hardcore band for variety. Recurrent

The admirable **Arsenal**. *See p196.*

favourites include German historical hits such as *Metropolis, Berlin: Sinfonie einer Grosstadt* ('Berlin: Symphony of a City') and *Das Kabinett des Dr Caligari* ('The Cabinet of Dr Caligari'), though almost anything could show up – for example, a recent series of silent religious spectacles such as *Quo Vadis* and *Ten Commandments*. The most likely venues for silent films are currently Filmkunsthaus Babylon (with a newly installed organ), the Arsenal or any of the outdoor cinemas (*see p196*). The Berlin International Film Festival inevitably has at least one major special event

Another popular German tradition is the outdoor cinema, called *Freiluftkino*, though with Berlin's unpredictable weather, the screen count varies from year to year. It's advisable to check listings and the weather report. Apart from silent films, just about all open-air film shows are in German, but English films do pop up at the Freiluftkino Kreuzberg.

FESTIVALS

A more reliable place to while away summer evenings is the **Fantasy Film Festival** (www.fantasyfilmfest.com), which shows the latest in fantasy, horror and sci-fi films from America, Hong Kong, Japan and Europe, as well as classics from the past. Films are often premières (at least in Europe), with occasional previews, programmed retrospectives and assorted rarities. Aside from the occasional German film, all shows are in English or with English subtitles. The venue changes periodically, but recently the CinemaxX

has hosted the festival. Dates vary too, but it usually takes place over a month between mid July and mid August. The festival also runs in Hamburg, Munich and Cologne.

The most recent addition to the Berlin summer calendar is the week-long **Berlin Beta Festival** (www.berlinbeta.de). It's primarily a conference on new media, but also has a film programme, which has, in previous years, featured a wide variety of films from America, Europe and Asia, ranging from off-Hollywood to Swedish gang films to Malaysian road movies, with an emphasis on the wild and strange. Programmed by the Eiszeit, it takes place at Eiszeit, Central and other venues at the end of August or the beginning of September. All non-German films are in English or with English subtitles.

Berlin's status as a queer-friendly city reflects itself in two winter festivals that spotlight gay and lesbian films. The more elaborate of the two is **Verzaubert: International Queer Film**

Studio boss Goebbels

The myth of the Hollywood Dream Factory rests not only on the stars and directors, but on the studio bosses who, with an iron hand and almost absolute power, hold sway over all aspects of production. In Berlin, at the UFA Studios, things developed slightly differently, with the ultimate power being wielded by early super-directors like Fritz Lang, FW Murnau and Joe May. But the likes of Hollywood's Louis Mayer, Harry Cohen and Jack Warner were soon to meet their dictatorial match when the Nazis nationalised the film industry.

Propaganda Minister Joseph Goebbels (*pictured, right of camera*) – in keeping with his desire for absolute control of all forms of information, media and communication – appointed himself head of the German film industry. With it he became a film mogul to rival any of his Hollywood counterparts, with whom he shared not just a love of control, but also a genuine love of films.

Like his fellow studio bosses, Goebbels immersed himself in every aspect of production, and believed that his films should reflect the national consciousness and offer their own idealised version of 'the good life'. But if you think this meant heavy-handed Nazi propaganda, think again. We are talking about a man whose favourite films were *It Happened One Night* and *Lives of a Bengal Lancer*, and also a Head of Production

whose early attempts at overtly Nazi cinema, such as *Hitlerjunge Quex* and *SA Mann Brand,* were box office hits. And, with an eye towards foreign export, even he realised his home-front tub-thumping was not going to pack them in in Paris, let alone Peoria. Instead he filled the screens with comedies, romances, musicals, adventure stories, family dramas and even a couple of westerns. Interestingly enough, though, he did put the breaks on the supernatural/horror genre.

But while his Hollywood counterparts could make or break careers, Goebbels liked to go one step further – a number of suicides (both spontaneous and organised) and various 'sudden disappearances' (often scheduled so as not to interrupt production) began to form a more sinister part of Berlin's film-land gossip. Not surprisingly, a good proportion of the Berlin film folk opted to get out of town, doing nothing for the talent pool. Those who remained were only rarely ardent Party members – when faced with options of exile, the camps or worse, state-supported stardom didn't look so bad. And so it was that actors such as the Garbo-esque Sybille Schmitz, the Dietrich-esque Zarah Leander and Kristina Söderbaum, known as the *Reichswasserleiche* (the 'National Drowned Corpse') for her propensity for being dredged lifeless from the water at the end of her films, rose to power.

Festival (www.queer-view.com/verzaubert), which is run by the same bunch as the Fantasy Film Festival. It takes place over a week in late November or early December at the Hackesche Höfe, and offers a high profile survey of gay and lesbian cinema from around the world. Like its cousin festival, it runs in Munich, Hamburg and Cologne, and also travels to Prague the following January.

For those with more specific tastes, the week-long **Lesben Film Festival** (www.lesbenfilmfestival.de) happens every October, with a surprisingly wide (though usually more grass-roots) international selection of films and performances concentrating on the various aspects of 'the love that dare not speak its name'. It has now found its home at the Arsenal, within the new mall culture of Potsdamer Platz. Unfortunately for any curious guys around, many events tend to be for women only, though some films could show up later at Arsenal or Xenon.

INFORMATION

The best way to find out what's going on is to check the listings in the city magazines *tip* and *Zitty*, as well as *(030)*, which is available in most bars free of charge. Always check for the notation OV or OF (original version or Originalfassung) or OmU (original with subtitles) or OmE (original with English subtitles, in the case of foreign films). But watch out, OmU could just as easily be a French or Chinese movie with German subtitles. The following list of cinemas are those places most likely to show films in English, but keep your eyes open for showings in other venues.

PRICES

The prices of cinema tickets vary considerably according to the day of the week, and sometimes the time of day. Broadly speaking, tickets are cheaper at the beginning of the week and before 5pm. Call venues for details.

But even their co-operation had its limits, and Goebbels found it almost impossible to fill the necessary positions for his big budget epic, the notorious *Jude Süss*, a historical costume picture based on a popular novel, which was in fact an unusually anti-Semitic opus. He had to apply various means of pressure, including informing his reluctant director, Viet Harlan, that as an employee in the film industry he was considered a soldier who must obey orders without question. When Harlan suggested that as a soldier he would rather be sent to the front, Goebbels replied that if he didn't direct the film he would be shot as a deserter and made this message clear to anyone else at the studio who might be harbouring similar ideas.

Let's face it, light entertainment, National Socialist style, could be pretty dour stuff.

But if Goebbels was failing on the home-front box office, he might, ironically, be considered a significant force in shaping what became the Golden Age of Hollywood. In driving out the cream of Berlin's film talent, a host of writers, producers, directors, actors, composers, cameramen, technicians and even high-powered agents – big names such as Billy Wilder, Douglas Sirk, Fritz Lang, Marlene Dietrich, Conrad Veit, Peter Lorre, Paul Kohner, Friedrich Hollander, Franz Waxman and Gottfried Reinhardt, to name only a few of those who washed up on the shores of La-La Land – Goebbels was indirectly responsible for the creation of a vast array of Hollywood stars and movies – the very type of westerns, comedies, dramas, musicals, romance and adventure stories that he loved so well.

Arts & Entertainment

Cinemas

Arsenal

*Potsdamer Strasse 2, Potsdamer Platz, Tiergarten
(2695 5100/www.fdk-berlin.de/arsenal/arsenal_
index.html). S1, S2, S25, S26, U2 Potsdamer Platz.*
Tickets €5.50; €3-€4 concessions. **No credit
cards. Map** p316/p306 E4.

This is the Berlin Cinematheque in everything but
name. While the Arsenal's brazenly eclectic programming doesn't satisfy all the people all the time,
its diversity is admirable, with everything from
classic Hollywood to contemporary Middle Eastern
cinema, from Russian art films to Italian horror
films, and from documentaries to the ever-popular
silent films with live accompaniment. The Arsenal
shows many English language films, and sometimes foreign films have English subtitles.
Occasionally, filmmakers show up to present their
work. The recent expansion into two state-of-
the-art screening rooms in the Sony Center in
Potsdamer Platz places the Arsenal smack in the
belly of the great Hollywood Beast, which is
probably right where we need it. Like its bigger
neighbours, this is a major venue for the Berlin
International Film Festival (*see p198*).

Babylon A & B

*Dresdener Strasse 126, Kreuzberg (6160 9693/
www.yorck-kino.de/yorck_ie/yorck_kinos/
babylona.php3). U1, U8, U12, U15 Kottbusser Tor.*
Tickets €4-€6.50. **No credit cards. Map** p307 G4.

This twin-screen theatre has a varied programme,
featuring off-Hollywood, indie crossover and UK
films. Once a neighbourhood Turkish cinema, it is
now almost totally English language. Not to be confused with Filmkunsthaus Babylon (*see below*).

Central

*Rosenthaler Strasse 39, Mitte (2859 9973/www.eyz-
kino.de/central/central.html). S3, S5, S7, S9, S75
Hackescher Markt or U8 Weinmeisterstrasse.* **Tickets**
€4-€6. **No credit cards. Map** p316/p302 F3.

On the edge of the busy Hackesche Höfe, this duplex
only occasionally offers its regular programming in
original English, except for frequent special midnight shows (ranging from Pam Grier retros to
Pamela Anderson sex tapes, and a whole lot in
between), its yearly participation in the Berlin Beta
Festival (*see p194*) and other – more unexpected –
special events. And don't miss the fire-breathing
monster installation in the basement.

CinemaxX Potsdamer Platz

*Potsdamer Strasse 5, Potsdamer Platz, Tiergarten
(4431 6316/www.cinemaxx.de). S1, S2, S25,
S26, U2 Potsdamer Platz.* **Tickets** €3.25-€10.
No credit cards. Map p316/p306 E4.

The biggest multiplex in town, with 19 screens (three
of which regularly show films in English). The programming is strictly Hollywood mainstream in mass-
market mall surroundings. This is a main venue for
the Berlin International Film Festival (*see p198*).

CineStar Imax im Sony Center

*Sony Center, Potsdamer Strasse 4, Tiergarten
(2606 6400/recorded info 2606 6260). S1, S2, S25,
S26, U2 Potsdamer Platz.* **Tickets** €11.30-€14.30;
€8.70-€11.80 concessions. **No credit cards.
Map** p316/p306 E4.

The usual big screen nature/history extravaganzas,
with occasional overlaps with Discovery (*see below*).
Mainly in German, with some English. All tickets
are half price on Tuesdays.

CineStar Sony Center

*Potsdamer Strasse 4, Tiergarten (2606 6400/
recorded info 2606 6260/www.cinestar.de). S1, S2,
S25, S26, U2 Potsdamer Platz.* **Tickets** €3.95-
€7.90; €2.40 concessions. **No credit cards.
Map** p316/p306 E4.

Programming is much the same as its Potsdamer
Platz neighbour, CinemaxX (*see above*), but, at the
time of going to press, every screen was showing
films in their original languages, mostly English.

Discovery Channel Imax Theater

*Marlene-Dietrich-Platz 4, Tiergarten (4431 6131/
www.imax-berlin.de). S1, S2, S25, S26, U2
Potsdamer Platz.* **Tickets** €4.75-€7.50.
No credit cards. Map p316/p306 E4.

More of the usual Imax productions. All in German,
but many can be heard in English with headphones.

Eiszeit

*Zeughofstrasse 20, Kreuzberg (611 6016/2431
3030/www.eyz-kino.de/eiszeit/eiszeit.html). U1,
U15 Görlitzer Bahnhof.* **Tickets** €4.25-€5.50;
€3 concessions. **No credit cards. Map** p307 H4.

This is the most energetic cinema in town, established by total film nuts compelled to inflict their
unique tastes upon the world. However, its duplex
renovation, which has brought the prerequisite
plush seats and Dolby Surround, has also resulted
in a more conservative selection of films to pay the
bill. Still, it does mean that you can now sit in
comfort when it chooses to unleash its own special
blend of German underground films, Hong Kong
movies, Japanimation, slash films, gansta films,
US indies and various other oddities. Fewer films
are shown in English than in the past, but it is
still worth checking the place out. Eiszeit is also a
venue for the Berlin Beta Festival (*see p194*) and
various special events.

Filmkunsthaus Babylon

*Rosa-Luxemburg-Strasse 30, Mitte (242 5076).
S3, S5, S7, S75, U2, U5, U8 Alexanderplatz or U2
Rosa-Luxemburg-Platz.* **Tickets** €5.50-€6.50; €5.50
concessions. **No credit cards. Map** p303 G3.

Located in Mitte, and not to be confused with
Babylon in Kreuzberg (*see above*), this was once an
East German première theatre, and remains a land-
mark building (by Hans Poelzig, who designed the
classic German silent film *The Golem*). After years
of renovation, the cinema is finally back to its full
Weimar glory. That alone makes it worth a visit.
Heavy on retrospectives and thematic program-

ming, it shows some interesting Eastern Bloc films, as well as occasional Hollywood movies in English and foreign films with English subtitles. There are also regular series of independent films, and one night a week is usually dedicated to gay films, often in English. The recent addition of programmes curated by the Zeughaus Kino (currently closed for a prolonged renovation but in the meanwhile in exile at the Babylon; *see p196*) has led to an increase in the number of English-language films shown.

Freiluftkino Kreuzberg

Mariannenplatz 2, courtyard of Haus Bethanien, Kreuzberg (2431 3030/www.eyz-kino.de/flk/flk.html). S3, S5, S9, S75 Ostbahnhof or U1, U8 Kottbusser Tor. **Tickets** €6. **No credit cards. Map** p307 G4.
Programmed by the crew at Eiszeit (*see p196*), this big-screen Dolby Stereo outdoor summer cinema offers a mix of past cinema hits, cult films and independent movies. While live events – such as kick boxing demonstrations and Turkish hardcore bands – are not as frequent as they once were, there are now various regular features, such as DJs before and after the films, a wide assortment of freshly prepared food and drink, and a games area featuring basketball and other sports. Some shows in English. Bring a cushion (and an umbrella when necessary). The season runs from the beginning of June to early September.

FSK

Segitzdamm 2, Kreuzberg (614 2464/www.fsk-kino.de). U1, U8 Kottbusser Tor or U8 Moritzplatz. **Tickets** €4.50-€6. **No credit cards. Map** p307 G4.
Named after the state film rating board, this two-screen off-cinema is located deep in the heart of Turkish Kreuzberg, convenient for a wide range of bars and cafés. Most films are dubbed into German, but there are occasional American or British indie films and documentaries, and some Taiwanese and Hong Kong films with English subtitles.

Hackesche Höfe

Rosenthaler Strasse 40/41, Mitte (tickets from 2.30pm 283 4603/www.hackesche-hoefe.org). S3, S5, S9, S75 Hackescher Markt or U8 Weinmeisterstrasse. **Tickets** €5-€7. **No credit cards. Map** p316/p302 F3.
Being up four flights of stairs doesn't stop this place being one of the area's best-attended cinemas. Its claim to have the longest bar in Berlin probably helps. Mostly showing foreign films with German subtitles, plus feature length documentaries and occasional indie features in original English. Venue for the **Verzaubert: International Queer Film Festival** (*see p194*) and other occasional special events.

High End 54 im Kunsthaus Tacheles

Oranienburger Strasse 54-6, Mitte (2313 1371/ Tacheles office 282 6185/www.tacheles.de). S1, S2, S25, S26 Oranienburger Strasse or U6 Oranienburger Tor. **Tickets** €9-€12. **No credit cards. Map** p316/p302 F3.

Yet another part of the multipurpose Tacheles' many venues (formerly known as Camera im Tacheles), the programme here serves up a mishmash of independent and off-Hollywood films, as well as some interesting foreign movies in the two-screen cinema (once the screening room for the GDR State Film Archive). Films in English seem to be on the increase and foreign films sometimes have English subtitles.

Moviemento

Kottbusser Damm 22, Kreuzberg (692 4785/ www.moviemento.de). U7, U8 Hermannplatz or U8 Schönleinestrasse. **Tickets** €4.50-€6; €5 concessions. **No credit cards. Map** p307 G5.
This laidback and youthful upstairs cinema on the edge of Kreuzberg shows fewer films in English than one might expect. But English films do appear, and, with three small screening rooms (232 seats altogether), this might just be your lucky week.

Neues Off

Hermanstrasse 20, Neukölln (6270 9550/www.yorck-kino.de/yorck_net/yorck_kinos/neuesoff.php3). U7, U8 Hermannplatz. **Tickets** €4-€5. **No credit cards. Map** p307 G6.
Recently renovated, though a bit off the beaten track. Most, though not all, films are in English. A good place to catch up on the film you missed last week at the Odeon (*see below*).

Odeon

Hauptstrasse 116, Schöneberg (7870 4019/ www.yorck-kino.de/yorck_net/yorck_kinos/ odeon.php3). S4, U4 Innsbrucker Platz or S1, S4 Schöneberg. **Tickets** €4-€6.50. **No credit cards. Map** p305 D6.
Berlin's favourite English language cinema, deep in the heart of Schöneberg. Though the largest, the Odeon is often prone to sellouts, so it's wise to arrive a bit early. Shows a reasonably intelligent, though increasingly mainstream, selection of Hollywood and UK fare.

UFA Arthouse Die Kurbel

Giesebrechtstrasse 4, Charlottenburg (883 5325). S3, S5, S9, S75 Charlottenburg or U7 Adenauerplatz. **Tickets** €3.75-€6.75. **No credit cards. Map** p304 B4.
All the comforts of one of Berlin's first multiplexes, including the prerequisite incredibly raked theatre. All three screens show typical Hollywood hits – don't let the 'Arthouse' bit fool you – in original language. Sneak previews of English films every Monday at 11pm.

Xenon

Kolonnenstrasse 5/6, Schöneberg (782 8850/ www.xenon-kino.de). U7 Kleistpark. **Tickets** €4-€7; €2.50 concessions. **No credit cards. Map** p306 E6.
A small, cosy cinema, largely dedicated to gay and lesbian programming (with very loosely defined boundaries). Since a lot of this is indie stuff, mostly from the US and UK, much of the films are in English. Brought to you by the guys at Eiszeit (*see p196*).

Arts & Entertainment

Berlin International Film Festival

Berlin's image as home of one of the world's three biggest international film festivals has had less to do with glitz and glamour as with the sense of drama inherent in its position as a meeting place – some would say collision point – of East and West during the post-war, Cold War and post-Cold War periods.

Whether it was the French boycott in '59 of *Paths of Glory*, Stanley Kubrick's controversial indictment of war, the Jury revolt of 1970 over the pro-Vietnamese film *OK* or the walkout of the Eastern Bloc delegation in 1976 over the presentation of Vietnamese people in *The Deer Hunter*, the drama of the festival has never been confined to the screens.

The years immediately following the fall of the Wall were particularly exciting, as the mood of the festival reflected the transitional climate of the whole city, as it moved from joy to chaos. As the Cold War faded into the past, so did the ingredients that gave the event its political edge, and the festival found itself increasingly in search of a new identity and fresh energy. The first response was a structural one, with the relocation in 2000 to the newly built commercial centre Potsdamer Platz. While some missed being able to watch the films in the landmark cinemas scattered around the former centre of West Berlin, the concentration of events into two large neighbouring multiplexes has not only made getting around much easier, but has also generated a greater sense of festival atmosphere. In addition, last year's opening of the nearby **Filmmuseum Berlin** (*see p103*) has increased the profile of the **Retrospective** section (*see p199*) and added opportunities for interrelated events and special exhibitions.

In 2001, the festival appointed a new director, Dieter Kosslick, previously the head of Germany's biggest regional film subsidy board, and it is expected that his energetic style will engender a major change in the overall ambience of the event. And for those who miss the old movie theatres, the '50s designed Zoo Palast, a former pre-war dance palace, and the International, one of the former East Berlin's première theatres, are still part of the programme as venues for repeat performances.

What remains consistent, however, is the chance to see what is arguably the widest and most eclectic mix of any film festival in the world. Unlike its two sister festivals (Cannes and Venice), it is as much about the audiences as it is about the attendant members of the industry. Every February, the city turns out to see hundreds of films presented in eight sections, of which the most important are listed below.

THE INTERNATIONAL COMPETITION

If this is the most visible section in terms of glamour and publicity, it's also by nature the most conservative in selection. Concentrating on big budget major productions from all over the world, with a heavy (and heavily criticised) accent on America, the most appealing of these films usually make it to general release afterwards. The International Competition provides the glitz and guest stars, both from the films and in the international jury, at its nightly gala presentations. Films compete for the Gold and Silver Bears and there is often a furore accompanying the announcement of the winners. Since the evening shows are the most expensive, and most likely to sell out,

the more prudent audiences either go for the afternoon shows or the repeats in the neighbourhood cinemas.

THE INTERNATIONAL FORUM OF YOUNG CINEMA

Born out of the Jury revolt over the screening of the pro-Vietnamese film *OK* that dissolved the Competition in 1970 (*see p198*), the Forum has established a tradition of healthy opposition by providing a vital selection of the challenging and eclectic. The Forum's more rigorous selection process attracts a strong and loyal audience, and it is here – and in the **Panorama** (*see below*) – where the real discoveries are to be made. And they can be anything from the latest American indie film to African cinema to midnight shows of Hong Kong action films – and dialogues between audience and filmmaker are *de rigueur*.

KINDERFILMFEST

The Children's Film Festival. *See p191.*

PANORAMA

Originally intended to showcase films that, for whatever reason, fell outside the strict guidelines of the Competition, Panorama has broadened its horizons to give the Forum a run for its money in terms of innovative programming. Panorama is, however, less consciously serious than the Forum, and is a good place to start for the less vigorous cineastes. It focuses its spotlights on world independent cinema, has a more flexible take on the mainstream, and an accent on gay and lesbian films. Panorama films show at CinemaxX and Zoo Palast with repeats at CinemaxX, CineStar and International.

PERSPEKTIVE DEUTSCHES KINO

Newly created in 2002, 'Perspective' reflects the new regime's increased focus on German cinema, giving the international lay audience a chance to sample a stimulating selection of films seen on the home festival circuit and movie screens during the rest of the year. German cinema always seems to have a rough ride outside its borders; Perspektive offers a chance to reassess. All films shown with English subtitles.

RETROSPECTIVE

The Retro section is one of the surest bets of the festival for sheer movie-going pleasure and, although it concentrates on the established mainstream, it's always an opportunity to see films that you might never otherwise have had a chance to see on the big screen, if at all. Themes have included Cinemascope, the Cold War and even Nazi entertainment films and the work of great directors such as Erich von Stroheim, William Wyler or Fritz Lang. There is also a Homage section, which celebrates the work of film personalities, complete with personal appearances and a gala screening in the Berlinale Palast. These are usually accompanied by an exhibition and special events at the nearby **Filmmuseum Berlin** (*see p103*). Films show in the CinemaxX.

TICKETS

Tickets can be bought up to three days in advance (four days for Competition repeats) at either the main ticket office in the **Arkaden am Potsdamer Platz** (Alte Potsdamer Strasse, Tiergarten; 259 2000), or at the **Europa Center** (1st floor, Breitscheidplatz 5, Charlottenburg; 348 0088) or **Kino International** (Karl-Marx-Allee 33, corner of Schillingstrasse, Mitte; 242 5826). Cinema box offices only sell tickets for that day's shows; last minute tickets are often available. Queues for advance tickets can be insanely long, so it pays to come early and buy as much as you can at once. Films in the Competition and Panorama are described in a catalogue, which you can pick up for a nominal price at the Potsdamer Platz, and the Forum has its own, available free at every Forum theatre. Films are usually shown three times. There is also a free daily *Festival Journal* available at all theatres, with news, articles and screening info and updates.

One important development within the festival is online ticketing. While not yet set up at the time of going to press, check the festival website (*see below*) nearer the time.

Ticket prices range from €5 to €12.50. A limited number of full festival passes (Dauerkarte) are available at the Potsdamer Platz Arkaden on the first day of the festival. The last reported price was €125 (bring two passport photos). They are valid for all sections but not all theatres or times, so familiarise yourself with the limitations to avoid disappointment. Things were still in flux at press time, so it's advisable to check the festival website (**www.berlinale.de**) for current information and programme details.

Galleries

Berlin's art scene grows up and leaves home,
but remains as excitingly delinquent as ever.

Fixing a definitive, up-to-date outline of Berlin's gallery scene in print is a difficult task. We can list the main contenders, give a few insider tips and tell you what to look out for, but the scene itself, especially its more alternative aspects, is as slippery as a greased ferret when it comes to pinning down styles and venues. Nevertheless, listed in this chapter are the galleries that are either big or established enough not to evaporate overnight, small but with considerable international reputations and a good stable of artists or just downright interesting and you'll have to forgive us if they've moved, changed name or just disappeared since going to print.

While the only ripples among the Charlottenburg and established old 'west' galleries, with their pretty much unchanged stable of artists and clientele, are the odd defection to Mitte, the Mitte gallery scene took an interesting turn in 2001. During the past decade, Berlin's galleries have settled down into the following pattern: first, there are the established west Berlin private galleries with big name artists that radiate an affluent and tasteful calm, then there are the big museums and galleries full of classical treasures and modern titans that span the city. And then there is Mitte, a mad, wild, scaffolding-clad hubbub hovering in the balance between yuppie wonderland and underground frisson.

Conscious that this underground edge was beginning to fray a little under the weight of coach-loads of voyeuristic tourists (and non-buying tourists at that), a fair number of Mitte's more important (in terms of international, avant-garde yet commercially viable) gallerists decided the time was ripe to risk a move. Medhi Chouakri, carlier | gebauer, Büro Friedrich and Max Hetzler have all upped sticks and relocated to a row of renovated S-Bahn arches under S-Bahnhof Jannowitz Brücke two train stops away from Hackescher Markt and light years away in ambience. The nearest thing to a yuppie restaurant within walking distance is the local Aral petrol station.

The galleries Nordenhake, Klosterfelde, Volker Diehl, Max Hetzler and Barbara Weiss have chosen for themselves a turn of the 20th-century building on the border between Mitte and Kreuzberg that is at least close enough to Checkpoint Charlie not to be isolated.

These brave few commercial heavyweights are following the typical metropolitan gentrification phenomenon. Just as gallerists in New York left SoHo in their droves for Chelsea in the early '90s, so too are the Berlin Mitte galleries fleeing the success of their own, partially self-generated, environments for pastures new. It is no longer important to them that as many people as possible see the art they have to offer but that the 'right' people do. Not to mention that the rents are more agreeable and the spaces huge in comparison to their old rooms.

That's not to say that Auguststrasse, Berlin's famous 'Art Mile', is no longer worth visiting. There are still a great number of very interesting galleries there: EIGEN + ART, Weisser Elefant, Kunst-Werke and neugerriem-schneider to name but a few. Together with the growing success of the Art Forum art fair, after a wobbly start, it just means that Berlin is maturing as an International Art Capital so well that it can afford to have several gallery concentrations and be relatively safe in the knowledge that their reputations are good enough for people to make the effort to go to visit them.

There are two major events in the Berlin art calendar: **Art Forum Berlin** (*see p205* **Art mart**) and the **Berlin Biennale**. The former, an international art fair, takes place late October at the Messehallen unter dem Funkturm (for details contact European Galleries, Projektgesellschaft GmbH; 8855 1643). The Biennale is an erratic affair – the second event took place in 2001 three years after the first. All being well the next is planned for early 2003 sometime, but check local art press for confirmation.

LISTINGS & INFORMATION

Most galleries provide free copies of the *Mitte Gallery Guide* and/or *Berliner Galerien* (which covers all Berlin). Both have maps but neither list all galleries. Also look out for other written material in galleries, cafés and bars, as invitations to forthcoming exhibitions are often there for the taking.

Buying a copy of the *Berlin Artery* from a gallery is a far better bet. Published every two months, it contains comprehensive gallery listings with maps to pinpoint their locations,

Arndt & Partner.

reviews in both English and German, and a calendar of openings and special events, including the *Mitte Rundgang* (walkabout). On a *Rundgang* evening the Mitte galleries all open at the same time, allowing visitors to stroll from one to another. They tend to be on the evening of the first Saturday of every other month, but have become somewhat irregular of late and some of the galleries at the hipper end of the scale have opted out. You will need to check listings for dates.

Mitte

Until the summer of 2001, the **Scheunen-viertel** district of Mitte was the undoubted heart of Berlin's contemporary art scene, with the **Auguststrasse** 'Art Mile' as its main street. We have listed below the principal galleries as of early 2002, but these spaces come and go and there are many others in this neighbourhood mostly within easy walking distance. Since 2001 there are also the **Zimmerstrasse** galleries and the **Holz-marktstrasse** group to take in, both of which are only a short U- or S-Bahn ride away, and a couple of notable Kreuzberg galleries that should not be left out.

See also p84 **Sammlung Hoffman**.

aktionsgalerie

Auguststrasse 20 (2859 9650/www.aktionsgalerie.de). U8 Weinmeisterstrasse or Rosenthaler Platz or S1, S2, S25, S26 Oranienburger Strasse. **Open** 2-7pm Tue-Sat. **Credit** MC, V. **Map** p302 F2.
Originally at Grosse Präsidentenstrasse 10, this anarchic mainstay of young Berlin unknowns has tried, unsuccessfully, to move upmarket to Auguststrasse while retaining its alternative look. The grubby make-do style of its previous incarnation doesn't quite fit in the freshly renovated new premises and the artists who made their name here have long moved on to more professional pastures. The aktionsgalerie opened a dance/performance club – DNA Club – in January 2002.

Arndt & Partner

Zimmerstrasse 90-91 (280 8123/www.arndt-partner.de). U6 Kochstrasse or U2 Stadtmitte. **Open** 11am-6pm Tue-Sat. **No credit cards**. **Map** p302 F2.
Established in 1994 by Matthias Arndt to show experimental positions in international contemporary art. Recently moved to Zimmerstrasse, this is a high quality, contemporary establishment. Exhibited artists include Slater Bradley, Olaf Breuning, Sophie Calle, Via Lewandowsk and Max Mohr.

Asian Fine Arts Gallery Berlin/ Galerie Prüss & Ochs

1st Hof, Sophienstrasse 18 (2839 1387/1389/ www.asianfinearts.de). U8 Weinmeisterstrasse or S3, S5, S7, S9, S75 Hackescher Markt. **Open** 2-7pm Tue-Fri; 11am-5pm Sat. **Credit** AmEx, DC, MC, V. **Map** p316/p302 F3.
Founded by Jaana Prüss and Alexander Ochs with the aim of correcting West-centric bias in the contemporary arts scene, this is now the leading European gallery for South-East Asian contemporary art. Showing artists from China, Hong Kong, Korea, Japan, Vietnam, India and Indonesia, it has, since 1997, opened up a rich source of often breathtaking (and not at all ethnic) new Asian art. Of particular note are Ling Jian, Chiharu Shiota, Yang Shaobin, Young Hay and Yue Minjun.

Büro Friedrich

Holzmarktstrasse 15-18, S-Bahn arches 53/54 (2016 5115/www.buerofriedrich.org). S3, S5, S7, S9, S75, U8 Jannowitzbrücke. **Open** 1-7pm Tue-Fri; 2-6pm Sat, Sun. **No credit cards**. **Map** p303 G3.
Founded by Waling Boers and heavily funded by the open-minded Dutch government, this institution calls itself 'a project space for contemporary art in Berlin-Mitte'. It left the words 'experimental' and 'obscure' out of the description, though. This is fairly inaccessible art loosely organised into long-running projects. If you are prepared to make the effort to find out what the hell it's all about, you should find it pretty interesting.

carlier I gebauer

Holzmarktstrasse 15-18, S-Bahn arches 51/52 (280 8110/www.carliergebauer.com). S3, S5, S7, S9, S75, U8 Jannowitzbrücke. **Open** noon-6pm Tue-Sat. **Credit** V. **Map** p303 G3.
Once working with Barbara Thumm, Ulrich Gebauer has now gone his separate way and teamed up with ice-queen Anne-Marie Carlier, although the two stables of artists remain pretty comparable. The work of Tracey Emin, Jan van Imschoot, Aernout Mik, Luc Tymans and Fred Tomaselli is represented here. The new premises at last mean not having to hunt for the old place in obscure rooms in Torstrasse.

Chouakri Brahms Berlin

Holzmarktstrasse 15-18, S-Bahn arch 47 (2839 1153/www.chouakri-brahms-berlin.com). S3, S5, S7, S9, S75, U8 Jannowitzbrücke. **Open** 11am-6pm Tue-Sat. **No credit cards**. **Map** p303 G3.

Arts & Entertainment

Freshly relocated along with carlier | gebauer and others under the railway arches, Mehdi Chouakri (formerly of Paris) has a slick you-can-eat-off-the-floor type of space and a pan-European/North American programme. Exhibitions are heavy on conceptual photography and hip-looking furniture-as-art by the likes of Sylvie Fleury. Also represented are John M Armleder, Claude Closky and local Monica Bonvicini.

Contemporary Fine Arts (CFA)

*Sophienstrasse 21 (288 7870/www.cfa-berlin.com).
U8 Weinmeisterstrasse or S3, S5, S7, S9, S75
Hackescher Markt.* **Open** 11am-6pm Tue-Sat.
No credit cards. Map p316/p302 F3.
Established by the partnership of Bruno Brunnet and Nicole Hackert, this is one of Berlin's more upmarket galleries that made the move from Charlottenburg. It's in Sophien-Gips Höfe, the same building as the Sammlung Hoffman (*see p84*). This is where to see expensive British imports such as Damien Hirst, Sara Lucas and Chris Ofili.

Galerie Barbara Weiss

*Zimmerstrasse 88/89 (262 4284/
www.galeriebarbaraweiss.de). U6 Kochstrasse.*
Open 11am-6pm Tue-Sat. **No credit cards.
Map** p306 F4.
A beautiful and well-established conceptual art-oriented gallery, recently moved from Potsdamer Strasse in Tiergarten. Gallerist Barbara Weiss represents, among others, Maria Eichorn, Roaul de Keyser, John Miller and Janet Cardiff.

Galerie EIGEN + ART

*Auguststrasse 26 (280 6605/www.eigen-art.com).
S1, S2, S25, S26 Oranienburger Strasse or U6
Oranienburger Tor.* **Open** 11am-6pm Tue-Sat.
No credit cards. Map p316/p302 F3.
The success of the Auguststrasse phenomenon can be contributed in a large part to charismatic gallerist Gerd Harry 'Judy' Lybke. Originally from Leipzig, he ran an independent gallery there for many years and still does. Shortly after the collapse of the Wall, he started his second venture in Auguststrasse. Since then he's tirelessly promoted artists from the former East Germany and emerging international artists. A tribute to his effectiveness was the inclusion of five of them in Documenta X. Among those exhibited here was Dresden painter Neo Rauch, 1997 Turner prize nominee Christine Borland and Carsten and Olaf Nicolai.

Galerie Giti Nourbakhsch

*Rosenthaler Strasse 72 (440 6781). U8 Rosenthaler
Platz.* **Open** 11am-6pm Tue-Sat. **No credit cards.
Map** p316/p302 F3.
Located in a former empty shop premises wedged between a launderette and an abandoned Burger King, but nevertheless within spitting distance of Auguststrasse, this new gallery has all the trappings of being cool. Most of the artists you won't have heard of, some of it is rubbish, but the critics can't get enough of it – such is the art world.

Galerie Jette Rudolph

Joachimstrasse 3-4 (6130 3887/www.jette-rudolph.de). U8 Weinmeisterstrasse. **Open** 1-7pm
Tue-Fri; 11am-4pm Sat. **No credit cards.
Map** p316/p302 F3.
A new gallery featuring largely young unknowns. The gallerists have a good eye and their shows are usually worthwhile – and the space is nice too. Take a moment when you are here to look at the building next door at No.6 by architects Abcarius + Burns, which represents some of the best of the new architecture in this district.

Galerie Max Hetzler

*Zimmerstrasse 90-91 (229 2437/
www.maxhetzler.com). U6 Kochstrasse or
U2 Stadtmitte.* **Open** 11am-6pm Tue-Sat.
No credit cards. Map p306 F4.
Another newish upmarket gallery, relocated from Cologne this time, with a proclivity towards monumental and iconic photography from the likes of Rineke Dijkstra, Axel Hütte and Thomas Struth. The gallery is obviously doing well since it can afford a branch at Mitte's other new hotspot: Holzmarktstrasse 15-18, S-Bahn arch 48.

Galerie neugerriemschneider

*Linienstrasse 155 (2887 7277). U6 Oranienburger
Tor or U8 Rosenthaler Platz.* **Open** 11am-6pm Tue-Sat. **No credit cards. Map** p302 F2.
Another arriviste from Charlottenburg, exhibiting the latest and hippest from the USA, Europe and more recently even some local talent. Among the artists represented at Galerie neugerriemschneider are Olafur Eliasson, Antje Majewski, Tobias Rehberger and Rirkrit Tiravanija.

Galerie Nordenhake

*Zimmerstrasse 88-91 (206 1483/
www.nordenhake.com). U6 Kochstrasse or
U2 Stadtmitte.* **Open** 11am-6pm Tue-Sat.
No credit cards. Map p306 F4.
A sure sign that Berlin has 'made it' as an international art location is that galleries from elsewhere are opening branches here. Nordenhake is a Swedish contender with a refreshingly mature contemporary agenda. Artists include John Coplans, Antony Gormley and Mona Hatoum.

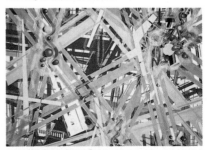

Galerie Jette Rudolph.

Galerie Paula Böttcher

*Kleine Hamburger Strasse 15 (281 1236/
www.galeriepaulaboettcher.de). U6 Oranienburger
Tor or U8 Weinmeisterstrasse or S1, S2, S25,
S26 Oranienburgstrasse.* **Open** 1-6pm Tue-Sat.
No credit cards. Map p316/p302 F3.
Opened by 25-year-old Paula Böttcher in June 1997,
this gallery works with young local and interna-
tional artists. One of her first shows was entitled
How To Make A Good Group Show If You've Only
Got One Room. Thirteen artists answered using
models of the gallery.

Galerie Schipper und Krome

*Linienstrasse 85 (2839 0139/www.schipper-
krome.com). S1, S2, S25, S26 Oranienburger
Strasse or U8 Rosenthaler Platz.* **Open** 11am-6pm
Tue-Sat. **No credit cards. Map** p316/p302 F3.
An arrival from Cologne in 1997 that settled at first
in Auguststrasse, then here. This is the place to see
work by the kind of artists currently featured in the
important art magazines. Among others, Vanessa
Beecroft, Matti Braun, Angela Bulloch, Liam Gillick
and Raymond Pettibon are represented.

Galerie Volker Diehl

*Zimmerstrasse 88-91 (2248 7922/www.dv-art.com).
U6 Kochstrasse or U2 Stadtmitte.* **Open** 11am-6pm
Tue-Sat. **No credit cards. Map** p306 F4.
Volker Diehl, a prominent and established figure
in the Berlin art world, is one of the main organisers of the Berlin Art Forum (*see p205* **Art mart**).
His new gallery space on Zimmerstrasse is dedicated to a younger stable of artists than he used to
have in West Berlin but still on the user-friendly
side of contemporary.

Galerie Weisser Elefant

*Kulturamt Mitte, Auguststrasse 21 (front house,
2nd floor) (2888 4454). U6 Oranienburger Tor
or U8 Rosenthaler Platz or S1, S2, S25, S26
Oranienburger Strasse.* **Open** 2-7pm Tue-Fri;
1-5pm Sat. **No credit cards. Map** p316/p302 F3.
Hidden away on the second floor of the red-brick
Kulturamt Mitte building on Auguststrasse, the
selection of work on show here is very interesting
if you want to have a look at what Berlin's new
young talent is up to, and it is for sale too. The gallerist Ralf Bartolomäus has been quietly observing
and showing interesting, exciting and sometimes
difficult work in Berlin since well before reunification and, unlike most of the other sharks in this
business, is not at all in it for the money: he has a
great eye and loves art.

Galerie Wohnmaschine

*Tucholskystrasse 35 (3087 2015/
www.wohnmaschine.de). S1, S2 Oranienburger
Strasse or U6 Oranienburger Tor.* **Open** 11am-6pm
Tue-Sat. **No credit cards. Map** p316/p302 F3.
The owner of this important experimental gallery,
Friedrich Loock, was born on Auguststrasse and
can quite literally claim to have been there from the
beginning. He set up the gallery in his flat in

Auguststrasse in 1988 and gave it the German name
for Le Courbusier's *machine à habiter*: living with
art and in art. It moved across the street in 1998 into
the rooms of his old local butcher's shop.

Griedervonputtkamer

*Sophienstrasse 25 (2887 9380). U8
Weinmeisterstrasse or S3, S5, S7, S9, S75
Hackescher Markt.* **Open** 11am-6pm Tue-Sat.
No credit cards. Map p316/p302 F3.
Tucked away in a quiet courtyard in Sophienstrasse,
this has to be one of Berlin's nicest small gallery
spaces. It also has a superb track record of
exhibitions despite being a relative newcomer.
Installations come from the likes of Brit-Art darling
Richard Woods.

Kicken Berlin

*Linienstrasse 155 (2887 7882/www.kicken-
gallery.com). U6 Oranienburger Tor or S1, S2,
S25, S26 Oranienburger Strasse.* **Open** 11am-6pm
Tue-Fri; noon-6pm Sat. **No credit cards.**
Map p316/p302 F3.
A new photography gallery that is not afraid of
showing the classics like Diane Arbus and Roger
Ballen. It has a large variety of German photogra-
phy from the last hundred years or so on its lists as
well as that of contemporary snappers.

Klosterfelde

*Zimmerstrasse 90-91 (283 5305/www.klosterfelde.de).
U6 Kochstrasse.* **Open** 11am-6pm Tue-Sat.
No credit cards. Map p306 F4.
Another of the new Zimmerstrasse gallery crowd,
Klosterfelde (there's also a branch in Hamburg)
concentrates almost exclusively on German and
European artists born in the 1960s. No other restric-
tions seem to apply here. The art ranges from pho-
tography to installation to painting from the likes
of Peter Land (born 1966), John Bock (1965) and
Nader (1964) et al.

Kuckei + Kuckei

*Linienstrasse 158 (883 4354/www.kuckei-
kuckei.de). U6 Oranienburger Tor or S1, S2, S25,
S26 Oranienburger Strasse.* **Open** 11am-6pm Tue-
Fri; 11am-5pm Sat. **No credit cards.**
Map p316/p302 F3.
Once a gallery called Vierte Etage in Wilmersdorf
founded by Ben and Hannes Kuckei, it's been open
in Mitte under this name since summer 1998. The
gallery deals solely with contemporary, young
relative unknowns. The location is one of the more
tastefully renovated courtyards in Linienstrasse,
directly behind the Kunst-Werke. Artists represented include Ingmar Alge, Hlynur Hallsson, Michael
Laube and Gerhard Winkler.

Kunst-Werke

*Auguststrasse 69 (243 4590/www.kw-berlin.de).
U6 Oranienburger Tor or S1, S2, S25, S26
Oranienburger Strasse or U8 Weinmeisterstrasse,
Rosenthaler Platz.* **Open** 10am-6pm Tue-Sun.
Admission €4; €1.50 concessions. **No credit
cards. Map** p316/p302 F3.

A good starting point for a gallery walk in Mitte. Originally a pioneering but modest undertaking, Kunst-Werke is now the funding-fattened HQ of artistic director Klaus Biesenbach. This is the most high-profile venue in Berlin for young and emerging contemporary art. It has been fully refurbished with a 'café pavilion' designed by Dan Graham and a new exhibition room from architect Hans Düttmann. Two perspex and zinc tube-like slides snake down the outside of the building from the upper floors serving as fire escapes that just happen to be art too. A great diversion for the young and young-at-heart if all that art gets too intense. Featured artists include Marina Abramovic, Gary Hill, Carsten Höller and Sol Le Witt.

Murata & Friends

Rosenthaler Strasse 39 (2809 9071/
www.murataandfriends.de). S3, S5, S7, S9, S75
Hackescher Markt. **Open** 2-7pm Wed-Fri; 1-6pm Sat.
No credit cards. Map p316/p302 F3.
In 1998 Murata and friends took over an utter ruin of a space in Mitte and lived the dream of many a young Berlin bohemian. The result is an interesting space specialising in the presentation of contemporary Japanese art in Berlin with a distinctly uncommercial feel.

NBK

Chausseestrasse 128-9 (280 7020/www.nbk.org).
U6 Oranienburger Tor. **Open** noon-6pm Tue-Fri;
noon-4pm Sat, Sun. **Map** p302 F2.
In a newish building that could just as easily have housed an insurance office, the Neuer Berliner Kunstverein is a well-funded society that hosts mainly curated group exhibitions by contemporary artists chosen from proposals submitted to a jury of the NBK's members. Choices and results are somewhat variable.

Galerie Barbara Thumm

Dircksenstrasse 41 (2839 0347/www.bthumm.de).
S3, S5, S7, S9 Hackescher Markt or S3, S5,
S7, S9, S75, U2, U5, U8 Alexanderplatz.
Open 1-7pm Tue-Fri; 1-6pm Sat.
No credit cards. Map p316/p303 G3.
One of Berlin's best, best-known and internationally respected private galleries. Barbara Thumm is a frequent exhibitor at international art fairs as well as showing a packed and interesting programme at home. The gallery has excellent rooms tucked away in a renovated courtyard that complement the high standard of the works shown. Artists represented include Fiona Banner, Bigert + Bergström, (e.) Twin Gabriel, Julian Opie and Bridget Smith.

Zwinger Galerie

Gipsstrasse 3, Hinterhof (2859 8907). U8
Weinmeisterstrasse or S3, S5, S7, S9, S75
Hackescher Markt. **Open** 2-7pm Tue-Fri; 11am-5pm
Sat. **No credit cards. Map** p316/p302 F3.
A long-established and reputable commercial gallery that in 1997 moved with the crowd from Kreuzberg to an atmospheric courtyard space near

Hackesche Höfe. Gallerist Werner Müller didn't want to miss out on the international visitors that the Mitte galleries now attract. Artists represented include Bettina Allamoda and Tobias Hauser.

Kreuzberg

Künstlerhaus Bethanien

Mariannenplatz 2 (616 9030/www.bethanien.de).
U1, U8, U12 Kottbusser Tor or U1 Görlitzer
Bahnhof. **Open** 2-7pm Wed-Sun.
Map p307 G4.
Located in a huge 19th-century complex of former hospital buildings, this Berlin institution was originally squatted in the 1970s, and back then hosted alternative art and theatre. These days it offers studio residencies to foreign artists; the USA, Europe, Russia and Japan are often represented (Bruce McLean was one of numerous artists-in-residence to work here) and both Sweden and Australia have permanent studio programmes. There are three main galleries almost permanently running exhibitions by the resident artists (who often sit their own shows too), along with talks, screenings and symposia. In the same building on the ground floor is the Kunstamt Kreuzberg – Kreuzberg's local government art office – which often mounts large thematic exhibitions of contemporary art. Government funding cuts have taken their toll of late but the art house battles on.

NGBK

Oranienstrasse 25 (615 3031/www.ngbk.de).
U1, U8 U12 Kottbusser Tor. **Open** noon-6.30pm
daily. **Map** p307 G4.
An offshoot of the late 1960s student movement, the NGBK (Neue Gesellschaft für bildende Kunst) has for more than 20 years produced a highly diversified and ambitious programme featuring photography, ethnic art, Berlin art and documentary shows. Exhibitions are consistent and to a high standard. Enter via the groundfloor bookshop or the courtyard to the left of the bookshop.

Tiergarten

daadgalerie

Kurfürstenstrasse 58, 1st floor (261 3640/
www.berliner-kuenstlerprogramm.de). U1,
U2, U4 Nollendorfplatz or U1, U2, U4, U15
Wittenbergplatz. **Open** 12.30-7pm daily.
Map p305 D4.
Above Café Einstein (*see p155*), this is the gallery for the German Academic Exchange Service (DAAD) that initiated an 'Artists-in-Residence' programme in West Berlin in 1965. The list of DAAD-sponsored artists reads like a 'Who's Who' of the international art world: John Armleder, Daniel Buren, Edward Kienholz, Mario Merz and Nam June Paik have all partaken. More recent recipients of this grant include Andrea Zittel, Steven Pippin and Johan Grimonprez.

Galerie Eva Poll

Lützowplatz 7 (261 7091/www.poll-berlin.de). U1, U2, U4, U12 Nollendorfplatz. **Open** 10am-1pm Mon; 11am-6.30pm Tue-Fri; 11am-3pm Sat. **No credit cards.** **Map** p305 D4.

When Eva Poll established her gallery in 1968, it was with the intention of supporting a local group of young 'critical' realists who had emerged in the mid 1960s. She currently represents Harald Duwe, GL Gabriel, Maxim Kantor, Ralf Kerbach, Volker Stelzmann, Hans Schieb and Sabine Grzimek.

Branch: Kunststiftung Poll, Gipsstrasse 3, Mitte (2649 6250).

Haus am Lützowplatz

Lützowplatz 9 (261 3805). U1, U2, U4, U12 Nollendorfplatz. **Open** 11am-6pm Tue-Sun. **Map** p305 D4.

One of the first non-commercial, private galleries to reopen in West Berlin after World War II, the Haus am Lützowplatz shows mostly figurative work of Berlin neo-realists like Elvira Bach. There are also paintings, sculpture and photography from Hungary,

Art mart

It has been acknowledged for some time now, among the international artistic community at least, that Berlin is one of the most exciting cities in the world to be in if you are a young contemporary artist. The range and breadth of experimental and creative activity permeate whole areas of the city, especially in the former East. From tiny gatherings in private apartments and performances or shows in small shops, literature salons, lounges, bars and the plethora of independent gallery spaces to exhibitions in huge regional and national establishments, Berlin is alive with the art of the moment.

This, then, is the reason why after only six years of existence, the **Berlin Art Forum** is now a major fixture of the calendars of the international art world. Anyone who has anything to do with contemporary art dealing can now ill afford missing out on the latest developments at this huge, comprehensive art fair. It professes to bring the buyers and dealers the best of what's new from a scene that changes with bewildering rapidity as it seeks to outrun (or titillate) those very individuals.

The organisers Berlin gallerist Volker Diehl and Sabrina van der Ley their European Galleries company had to overcome considerable obstacles to get their project off the ground. The resistance of galleries and buyers to yet another German art fair for one. They felt themselves already well represented with the likes of Art Cologne and the Munich Art Messe and stayed away in their droves at the beginning. Then there was the problem of sponsors: the well-publicised bankruptcy of Berlin that came to light in 2001 is apparently due, to a considerable extent, to the miserable performance of its own bank, which unfortunately also happened to be the Art Forum's main sponsor.

Nevertheless, over the last three years the attendance and participation figures ave risen progressively by a third each year (European Galleries' own figures). In 2001 the Art Forum featured 172 galleries from 28 countries chosen by their own panel of gallerists and art experts. Apart from the large number of German establishments represented, there were 19 galleries from Scandinavia, 12 from the USA, 12 from the UK, three from China for the first time, aswell as new contributions from Cuba, Iceland, Israel and various eastern European countries. Works on show ranged from painting and sculpture to video, environments, lounges, installations and large amounts of photography. The fair was visited by nearly 24,000 people over three days and was generally pronounced a hit from all sides.

While the pre-selected, paid-up, participating gallerists at the Art Forum are delighted at the presence of a willing buying public prepared to shell out tens of thousands of euros or dollars for relative unknowns and shooting stars alike, it's worth remembering that this is the top-end, the commercial icing on the cake as it were, of what was/is, essentially, a no-budget alternative and underground scene. If you happen to be in Berlin in late September/ early October, then the Art Forum is most definitely worthy of a visit. If you want to buy art and support the scene that produced it, then don't forget to explore some of those little out-of-the-way places and talk to the people who are part of it too. You may or may not end up buying something, but you'll certainly have a hell of a lot more fun making up your mind.

For more information, see www.art-forum-berlin.de or contact European Galleries (8855 1643). *See also p187.*

Bulgaria, Russia and Poland. Run under the iron hand of curator Karin Pott the gallery has a reputation of some standing. The Studiogalerie at the back is given over to young curators and artists annually to produce their own programme of events and shows. Don't forget to take a look when you are here.

Charlottenburg

The Charlottenburg galleries are mostly within walking distance of one another and are nestled between the district's designer stores and restaurants. These days they rarely receive much attention from the press and at the Berlin Art Forum many are most conspicuous by their absence. They do, however, remain reliable in their fields of interest, particularly for canvases by German artists of the pre-1990s generation – something you'd rarely find in Mitte. Here too you will find the Tiergarten galleries centring around Potsdamer Strasse and Lutzowplatz. It might be worth combining a visit here with Potsdamer Platz or, perhaps, the new embassy buildings in the Tiergarten. See p102 **Embassy row**.

Fine Art Rafael Vostell

Knesebeckstrasse 30 (885 2280/www.vostell.de). *S3, S5, S7, S9, S75 Savignyplatz.* **Open** 11am-7pm Mon-Fri; 11am-4pm Sat. **No credit cards**. **Map** p305 C4.
An upmarket gallery representing established artists such as Francis Bacon, Nam June Paik and Yoko Ono, along with younger Berlin types such as Axel Lischke, Dead Chickens and MK Kähne, and not forgetting daddy of course: Mr Fluxus – Wolf Vostell.

Galerie Anselm Dreher

Pfalzburger Strasse 80, Wilmersdorf *(883 5249/www.galerie-anselm-dreher.com).* *U1 Hohenzollernplatz or U1, U9 Spichernstrasse* *or U15 Uhlandstrasse.* **Open** 2-6.30pm Tue-Fri; 11am-2pm Sat. **No credit cards**. **Map** p305 C5.
Anselm Dreher's unique gallery on the Charlottenburg/Wilmersdorf borders has been around for more than 30 years now, uncompromisingly promoting the concrete, minimal and conceptual tendencies in contemporary art. Dreher was the first in Berlin – and for quite some time the only one – to show the work of Carl André, Joseph Kosuth, Jochen Gerz, and Ange Leccia. Recommended.

Galerie Georg Nothelfer

Uhlandstrasse 184 (881 4405/ *www.galerie.de/nothelfer).* *U15 Uhlandstrasse.* **Open** 11am-6.30pm Tue-Fri; 10am-4pm Sat. **Credit** V. **Map** p305 C4.
Georg Nothelfer, a longtime doyen of the Berlin art world, tends to concentrate on German Informel, Tachism and Lyrical Abstraction, with a sprinkling of gestural, scriptural and narrative

painting by more established artists from Europe such as Pierre Alechinsky, Arnulf Rainer and Antoni Tàpies.
Branch: Corneliusstrasse 3, Tiergarten (2575 9806).

Galerie Mönch/sic!projects

Reichstrasse 52 (3081 9454). U2, U12 Theodor-Heuss-Platz, Neu-Westend. **Open** 3-7pm Wed-Fri; 11am-3pm Sat. **No credit cards**.
Situated on the outer limits geographically, as far as galleries go, Galerie Mönch is nevertheless often worth the trek when sic!projects is hosting a show here. Eberhard Mönch tends to be more on the traditional modern art side, concentrating mainly on abstract expressionist painting and sculpture. His partner, the art critic Michaela Nolte, on the other hand, has an good eye for interesting young newcomers to the scene.

Galerie Springer & Winckler

Fasanenstrasse 13 (315 7220/www.springer-winckler.de). S3, S5, S7, S9, S75, U2, U9, *U12 Zoologischer Garten or U15 Uhlandstrasse.* **Open** 10am-1pm, 2.30-7pm Tue-Fri; 11am-3pm Sat. **No credit cards**. **Map** p305 C4.
Until the end of 1997 this was the gallery of Rudolf Springer, one of the grand old men of Berlin's art world, who opened his first gallery in 1948. Now his son and partner run it, having moved up together from their gallery in Frankfurt-am-Main to take over. Among the greats Springer has presented are Alexander Calder, Joan Miró, André Masson, Max Ernst and Henri Laurens. But he's also had a continuous passion for German post-war artists (Wols, Ernst Wilhelm Nay, AR Penck, Jörg Immendorf and Markus Lüpertz).

Galerie Thomas Schulte

Mommsenstrasse 56 (3240 0440/ *www.galeriethomasschulte.de). S3, S5, S7, S9, S75* *Charlottenburg, U7 Adenauerplatz or Wilmersdorfer* *Strasse.* **Open** 11am-6pm Mon-Fri; 11am-3pm Sat. **No credit cards**. **Map** p304 B4.
Eric Franck came from Geneva and Thomas Schulte from New York to challenge the Berlin market with fresh ideas in 1991. Now this is one of Berlin's main blue-chip upmarket galleries. The gallery represents the likes of Rebecca Horn, Sol Le Witt, Gordon Matta-Clark, Pipilotti Rist, Tony Oursler and Robert Mapplethorpe.

Raab Galerie

Kant Dreieck, Kantstrasse 155/Fasanenstrasse 81 *(261 9217/18/www.raab-galerie.de). S3, S5,* *S7, S9, S75, U2, U9, U12 Zoologischer Garten.* **Open** 10am-7pm Mon-Fri; 10am-4pm Sat. **Credit** V. **Map** p305 C4.
Ingrid Raab's established gallery moved to this location in early 2002, and is known for the expressive and figurative painting with which Berlin was once identified. Exhibited artists include Markus Lüpertz, Elvira Bach, Luciano Castelli, Adolph Gottlieb and Rainer Fetting. Keep an eye out for work by local artist Alke Brinkmann too.

Gay & Lesbian

Whatever you want, whatever you like, whatever you say,
no need to pay, you take your choice – and what a choice.

In 1897 the first institution in the world with an emancipatory homosexual agenda was founded in Berlin – the Scientific-Humanitarian Committee (Wissenschaftlich-humanitäres Komitee). Its main aims were legal reform, scientific research into the 'Third Gender' and the publication of emancipatory literature for the gay community. Its founder, Magnus Hirschfeld, helped sponsor the World League of Sexual Reform.

In the 1920s Berlin became the first city in the world to have what we might recognise as a large-scale gay and lesbian community. The club Eldorado in Motzstrasse, still Schöneberg's most lively gay street, attracted Marlene Dietrich, Ernst Röhm and Christopher Isherwood, who lived in nearby Nollendorfstrasse 17. Hitler's rise to power in 1933 resulted in the persecution of gays and lesbians, and the Scientific-Humanitarian Committee's HQ was ransacked, its library burned. Gays were forced to wear the Pink Triangle in the concentration camps. (They are commemorated on a plaque outside U-Bahnhof Nollendorfplatz.)

Since the late 1960s Berlin has resumed its role as one of the world's homosexual meccas. The Berlin gay and lesbian scenes are big and bold, and are mostly concentrated in Schöneberg, Kreuzberg and Prenzlauer Berg. There are still some differences between east and west, but contrasts are disappearing fast as *Wessis* move east and vice versa. Most outdated eastern institutions are being or have been renovated or replaced, leading to increasingly homogenous venue styles and clientele.

Summer is the most exciting time, when all contingents of the sometimes fractious gay and lesbian scenes come together and much drinking and frolicking takes place outside bars on the street. The **Schwul-Lesbisches Strassenfest** on Motzstrasse in mid June is followed by **Christopher Street Day Parade** (for both, *see p185*), a flamboyant annual event during which up to 300,000 gays and lesbians unite to commemorate the Stonewall riots.

The scene includes much more than the venues listed here, especially as regards cultural and subcultural events, such as plays, trashy drag performances or the awarding of the Gay Teddy to the best gay-lesbian film during the

annual FilmFest. 'MonGay' at **International** cinema (Karl-Marx-Allee 33; 2475 6011) shows gay-lesbian films on Mondays and the stage company Teufelsberg produces hilariously vulgar comedy shows. Gay art and history is documented at the **Schwules Museum** (*see p96*), which also has an archive. If you wish, you can live an exclusively gay or lesbian life in Berlin, working at a gay company, working out at a gay gym, using a gay internet provider, buying clothes at a gay shop, eating in a gay or lesbian restaurant... and when it's time to go, a gay undertaker can fulfil your last wish, be it a pink coffin or one with leather lining.

In June 2001, before being nominated by his party to be the new mayor of Berlin, Klaus Wowereit told the press, 'I am gay, and that's OK' ('Ich bin schwul, und das ist auch gut so!'). The tabloids blustered – he had taken the wind out of their sails – and gays had a field day. His epigram became the catchphrase of the year.

Lo and behold, a century after the first cautious attempts to view gay sexuality in an open-minded way, Berlin is now governed by a gay man.

PUBLICATIONS

Sergej (www.sergej.de) and *Siegessäule* (www.siegessäule.de) are monthly listings freebies that can be picked up at most venues. Apart from a what's-on calendar, *Siegessäule* also lists all gay and lesbian venues and pinpoints them on a city map. Also look out for *Gay Info*, *Box* and various other free magazines, and flyers. For lesbians, *Blattgold* (blattgold.berlin@snafu.de) gives information and listings on the women's scene.

A free *Berlin Fun Map* (www.gaymap.ws/berlin-english), pinpointing all places of interest, can be picked up at venues, as well as the free *Siegessäule Kompass* (www.siegessäule-kompass.de), a classified directory of everything gay or lesbian.

Mixed

In west Berlin gays and lesbians had been treading separate paths for decades, but the situation was different in the east. Making common cause under the Communists, homosexuals of both sexes shared bars, clubs and other spaces, a tradition maintained despite the powerful emergence of male-only cruise bars in Prenzlauer Berg.

That said, the western half of the city is changing. The late 1990s saw a proliferation of mixed gay and lesbian venues, and lesbians also made their voices felt in once gay-only organisations and political institutions. The formerly gay-only *Siegessäule* has become a gay and lesbian magazine, dealing with topics for both equally.

This spirit of growing together also makes itself felt in an ever-greater mix in cafés, bars and clubs such as Schall und Rauch in the east and the unique dyke/queer bar that is Roses in the west. Café Melitta Sundström and Anderes Ufer are cafés where gays and lesbians mingle.

Here we list a selection of genuinely mixed cafés, bars and clubs.

Bar & cafés

Prenzlauer Berg

Café Amsterdam
Gleimstrasse 24 (448 0792/www.pension-amsterdam.de). S4, S8, S10, U2 Schönhauser Allee. **Open** 9am-3am Mon-Thur; 9am-5am Fri, Sat; 9am-3am Sun. **No credit cards. Map** p303 G1.
Nice café in the daytime. At night, a good bar to get wrecked in, with resounding house and techno. Snacks and salads. Mixed crowd. Popular.

Schall und Rauch
Gleimstrasse 23 (443 3970/www.schall-und-rauch-berlin.de). S4, S8, S10, U2 Schönhauser Allee. **Open** 10am-3am daily. **No credit cards. Map** p303 G1.
Relaxed and friendly atmosphere, good selection of food, central location – an ideal place to spend the afternoon or kick off an evening in Prenzlauer Berg.

Kreuzberg

Café Melitta Sundström
Mehringdamm 61 (692 4414). U6, U7 Mehringdamm. **Open** 10am-late daily. **No credit cards. Map** p306 F5.
During the daytime this place serves as a café where students discuss relationships, film festivals and why they have a problem getting up in the morning over coffee. Come the evening, it's a Kreuzberg bar full of gays too lazy to go to Schöneberg. At weekends the café becomes the entrance to **SchwuZ** disco (*see p212*) and the place is hectic and fun. It's best in spring and summer, when the big terrace opens until late and gays from all over Kreuzberg flock to loiter on the pavement. A small bookshop is attached.

Roses
Oranienstrasse 187 (615 6570). U1, U8, U12 Kottbusser Tor. **Open** 10pm-5am daily. **No credit cards. Map** p307 G4.
Whoever you are, you'll fit in just fine at this boisterous den of glitter, plush and kitsch, more or less next to **SO 36** (*see p209*). It draws customers from right across the sexual spectrum – just about everybody who is gay or lesbian meets and mingles here. No place for uptights. Always full.

Anderes Ufer. *See p209.*

Schöneberg

Anderes Ufer
Hauptstrasse 157 (784 1578). U7 Kleistpark. **Open**
9am-2am Mon-Fri. **No credit cards. Map** p306 E5.
Established over 20 years ago, this is the city's
oldest gay café, now run by a gay-lesbian team and
frequented by a mixed clientele. Exhibitions of gay
art and photography.

Clubs & one-nighters

Mitte

Ackerkeller
*Ackerstrasse 12 hinterhof (280 7216). S1, S2
Nordbahnhof.* **Open** 10pm-3am Tue; 10pm-late Fri.
Admission €2. **No credit cards. Map** p302 F2.
Grungy hole for gay punks and indie queens. Cheap
drinks, hard music and rough decor. Sounds different?
It is. Sounds exhilarating? Sorry. But it is one of the
few venues where the more 'alternative' side of Berlin
reveals itself to the gay visitor. 'Female Jungle' – a
women's party – takes place one Saturday a month.

Friedrichshain

Die Busche
*Mühlenstrasse 11-12 (296 0800). S3, S5, S6, S7,
S9, S75, U1, U12 Warschauer Strasse.* **Open**
9.30pm-5am Wed, Sun; 9.30pm-6am Fri; 10pm-6am
Sat. **Admission** €3-€4.50. **No credit cards.**
Map p307 H4.
This east German relic is loud, tacky, resolutely
mixed and always full. One of east Berlin's oldest
discos for stylish lesbians and gays escorted by their
best (girl)friend, Die Busche has been in its current
location since the early 1990s. A must for kitsch
addicts and Abba fans.

Dance with the Aliens
*OstGut, Mühlenstrasse 26-30, entrance
Rummelsburger Platz (www.ostgut.de). S3, S5,
S6, S7, S9, S75, U1, U12 Warschauer Strasse.*
Open 11pm-late 3rd Fri of month. **Admission** €10.
No credit cards. Map p307 H4.
Every third Friday of the month, the one and only
house party for both gays and lesbians, boasting
three darkrooms (for gays, lesbians and undecided).
Located in the huge OstGut, it never really packs
out, but the mainly nonconformist clubbers create
an easygoing atmosphere. Don't hesitate to undress
on the dancefloor if you feel like it. Check press or
website for details.

Kreuzberg

SO 36
*Oranienstrasse 190 (6140 1306/www.so36.de). U1,
U8, U12 Kottbusser Tor.* **Open** 10pm-late Mon, Wed.
Admission €5. **No credit cards. Map** p307 G4.

A key venue for both gays and lesbians. Wednesday
('Hungry Hearts') at SO is a fixed date for every gay
man, and a lot of lesbians too – it's a fun-packed,
very mixed, sociable evening and the dancefloor
heaves. Monday ('Electric Ballroom') is not completely gay, but the hard techno sound draws a
largely male following. The last Saturday of the
month sees Gay Oriental Night ('Gayhane'), with
belly-dancing transvestites and Turkish hits.
Monthly 'm.appeal' parties bring together every
imaginable manifestation of womanhood (plus gay
friends) to dance to house and disco. Sunday is Café
Fatal, where gays and lesbians get into ballroom
dancing. Check gay press or website for other
sporadic one-nighters.

Gay

You don't need to look for the gay scene
in Berlin. It'll find you in about ten minutes.
Some areas, however, are gayer than others,
especially Schöneberg's Motzstrasse and
Fuggerstrasse, and the area around subway
station Schönhauser Allee in Prenzlauer
Berg. Bars, clubs, shops and saunas are so
many and various it's impossible to take
them all in on one visit.
  The age of consent is 16 – same as for
everyone else. Gays making contact in public
is rarely of interest to passers-by. Nevertheless,
bigots do exist and so does anti-gay violence.
In the west it tends to be by gangs of Turkish
teenagers, in the east by right-wing skinhead
Germans. But compared to other cities,
Berlin is an laid-back, innocuous place with
very little violence.
  The scene is always shifting, so the
places listed here may have changed or
new ones might have sprung up by the time
you read this. **Mann-O-Meter** (*see p275*),
Siegessäule and *Sergej* are the best sources
of current information.

Accommodation

Most hotels know gays are important to
the tourist industry and are courteous and
efficient. Here are some options catering
specifically for gay men.

Art Hotel – Connection Berlin
*Fuggerstrasse 33, Schöneberg, 10777
(2102 1880/fax 2102 18830/www.arthotel-
connection.berlin). U1, U2, U12, U15
Wittenbergplatz.* **Rates** €57-€82 single; €82-€107
double. **Credit** AmEx, MC, V. **Map** p305 D5.
Comfortable and spacious rooms (mostly en-suite),
sumptuous breakfast included and prime location
right in the middle of Schöneberg's gay area. The
SM-room is fitted with a sling, stocks and a cage.

Eastside – gayllery & guesthouse

Schönhauser Allee 41, Prenzlauer Berg, 10435 (4373 5484/www.eastside-gayllery.de). U2 Eberswalder Strasse. **Rates** €39 single; €73 double. **Credit** AmEx, MC, V. **Map** p303 G1.

Quiet guesthouse in the centre of Prenzlauer Berg, near to the gay scene. All rooms are fitted with TV/VCR and private bath. Shop selling books, articles, videos, posters and art.

Enjoy Bed & Breakfast

c/o Mann-O-Meter, Bülowstrasse 106, Schöneberg, 10783 (2362 3610/fax 2362 3619/www.ebab.de). U1, U2, U4, U12, U15 Nollendorfplatz. **Rates** €20 single; €45 double. **No credit cards. Map** p305 D5.

Excellent accommodation service for gays and lesbians. Enjoy B&B can fix you up with a room with gays or lesbians in their private apartment from as little as €20. Rooms can be viewed and booked on its website (in English). Reservations are taken by phone and at the office from 4.30pm to 9pm daily.

Pension Le Moustache

Gartenstrasse 4, Mitte, 10115 (281 7277/ www.lemoustache.de). U6 Oranienburger Tor. **Rates** €25 single; €35-€60 double. **No credit cards. Map** p302 F2.

Good value guesthouse in the centre of Berlin.

Schall und Rauch

Gleimstrasse 23, Prenzlauer Berg, 10437 (448 0770/www.schall-und-rauch-berlin.de). S4, S8, S10, U2 Schönhauser Allee. **Rates** €35 single; €65 double. **No credit cards. Map** p303 G1.

Clean, modern rooms next door to the café of the same name (*see p208*). All rooms are en-suite, and are equipped with TV and telephone. The rates include breakfast.

Tom's House

Eisenacher Strasse 10, Schöneberg, 10777 (218 5544). U1, U2, U4, U12, U15 Nollendorfplatz. **Rates** €67 single; €87 double. **Credit** AmEx, DC, MC, V. **Map** p305 D5.

An eccentric and unpredictable establishment deep in the heart of gay Schöneberg, with seven double rooms, one single room and first-rate buffet brunches from 10am to 1pm.

Bars, cafés & restaurants

Prenzlauer Berg

Darkroom

Rodenbergstrasse 23 (444 9321/www.darkroom-berlin.de). S4, S8, U2 Schönhauser Allee. **Open** 10pm-5am daily. **No credit cards. Map** p303 G1.

Yes, there is a darkroom in this small bar. Actually, there's more darkroom than bar. And with the help of camouflage netting and urinals (in the actual darkroom) it often succeeds in pulling a slightly 'harder' clientele, though on less busy nights things can feel

a bit desperate. The Naked Sex Party on Friday and the Golden Shower Party on Saturday are a big success; after disposing of your clothes in a dustbin liner, feel free to roam about like a piece of trash.

Flax

Chodowieckistrasse 41 (4404 6988). U2 Eberswalder Strasse or S4, S8, U2 Schönhauser Allee. **Open** 5pm-3am Mon-Fri; 3pm-3am Sat; 10am-3am Sun. **No credit cards. Map** p303 H2.

It may be on the edge of the Prenzlauer Berg gay scene but the Flax has developed into one of the most popular café-bars in east Berlin, drawing in a youthful crowd.

Greifbar

Wichertstrasse 10 (444 0828). S4, S8, S10, U2 Schönhauser Allee. **Open** 10pm-6am daily. **No credit cards. Map** p303 G1.

Often called the Tom's Bar (*see p211*) of the east, this cruisy bar pulls a younger Prenzl'berg crowd looking for adventure and pleasure, either by picking someone up or by roaming about in the large darkrooms. Greifbar also has a good atmosphere for just drinking.

Pick Ab!

Greifenhagener Strasse 16 (445 8523). S4, S8, U2 Schönhauser Allee. **Open** 10pm-6am daily. **No credit cards. Map** p303 G1.

Late-night cruise bar for eastern action-seekers and insomniacs, decorated in camp taste. Like most such bars it tends to fill up best during winter, when cruising heated backrooms is more comfortable than roaming freezing parks.

Stiller Don

Erich-Weinert-Strasse 67 (445 5957/ www.stillerdon.de). S4, S8, U2 Schönhauser Allee. **Open** 8pm-4am daily. **No credit cards. Map** p303 G1.

Formerly home to the local avant-garde but now attracting a more diverse crowd from all over Berlin. The set-up is like a cosy café, but it gets high-spirited at weekends and on Mondays.

Kreuzberg

Barbie Bar

Mehringdamm 77 (6956 8610). U7 Mehringdamm. **Open** 4pm-late daily. **No credit cards. Map** p306 F5.

Barbie Bar is the newest addition to the Kreuzberg scene. Tacky and camp.

bargelb

Mehringdamm 62 (7889 9299/www.bargelb.de). U7 Mehringdamm. **Open** 8pm-late daily. **No credit cards. Map** p306 F5.

A plush new bar, right across the street from SchwuZ (*see p212*), bargelb is for those who feel like prolonging their already long night into late morning. A late-opening boozer – just what this area needed.

Cruise on over to **Pick Ab!** *See p210.*

Bierhimmel

Oranienstrasse 183 (615 3122). U1, U8,
U12 Kottbusser Tor. **Open** 1pm-3am daily.
No credit cards. Map p307 G4.
When Roses (*see p208*) is too full you can always move
to this nearby bar, where gays and heteros mix in a
cooler atmosphere. Kitsch cocktail bar at the back,
open at weekends. Popular with local drag queens.

Ficken 3000

Urbanstrasse 70 (6950 7335). U7, U8
Hermannplatz. **Open** 10pm-late daily.
No credit cards. Map p307 G5.
Big basement darkroom and a mix ranging from
blue- and white-collar workers to students and night
owls. Two drinks for the price of one on Tuesdays.

Schöneberg

Café Berio

Maassenstrasse 7 (216 1946/www.berio.de).
U1, U2, U4, U12, U15 Nollendorfplatz.
Open 8am-1am daily. **No credit cards.**
Map p305 D5.
One of the best daytime cafés in Berlin, full of
good-looking, trendy young men (including the
waiters), with a good-size terrace for spring and
summer. Ideal location.

Café PositHIV

Alvenslebenstrasse 26 (216 8654/http://berlin.gay-
web.de/posithiv). U2 Bülowstrasse. **Open** 3-11pm
Tue-Fri, Sun; 6pm-late Sat. **No credit cards.**
Map p306 E5.
Managed by voluntary staff for people affected
by HIV and AIDS. Communal cooking and eating,
lectures and discussion.

Crisco

Nollendorfstrasse 27 (2101 4020). U1, U2, U4,
U12, U15 Nollendorfplatz. **Open** 9-4pm Mon-Thur;
9pm-late Fri-Sat; 6pm-late Sun. **No credit cards.**
Map p305 D5.

Bar catering for friends of fetish, with an array of
young leather and uniform guys. Sunday's 'After-
Hour-Party' concentrates on fisters.

Hafen

Motzstrasse 19 (211 4118). U1, U2, U4, U12,
U15 Nollendorfplatz. **Open** 8pm-late daily.
No credit cards. Map p305 D5.
A red plush and vaguely psychedelic bar in the
centre of Schöneberg's gay triangle. Popular with
the fashion- and body-conscious, especially at weekends, when it provides a safe haven from nearby
heavy cruising dens. Usually very crowded.

Lukiluki

Motzstrasse 28 (2362 2079/www.lukiluki.de). U1,
U2, U4, U12, U15 Nollendorfplatz. **Open** 6pm-2am
daily. **No credit cards. Map** p305 D5.
The main attraction of this restaurant isn't the
food (served until 1am) – it's the waiters, who serve
topless. Popular.

Omnes

Motzstrasse 8 (2363 83000/www.cafe-omnes.de).
Open 24hrs daily (hot meals 4pm-midnight).
No credit cards. Map p305 D5.
Round the clock café/restaurant/bar with a small
terrace, best for watching the numerous gays walk-
ing along Motzstrasse.

Prinzknecht

Fuggerstrasse 33 (2362 7444). U1, U2, U12,
U15 Wittenbergplatz or U1, U2, U4, U12,
U15 Nollendorfplatz. **Open** 3pm-3am daily.
No credit cards. Map p305 D5.
With a large but underused darkroom out back, this
huge, open bar draws in neighbourhood gays.
Somewhat provincial, but nice for a chat and a beer.
Free coffee and cake for bikers on Sunday afternoons.

Tom's Bar

Motzstrasse 19 (213 4570/www.tomsbar.de). U1,
U2, U4, U12, U15 Nollendorfplatz. **Open** 10pm-6am
Mon-Thur, Sun; 10pm-late Fri, Sat. **No credit**
cards. Map p305 D5.
Once described by *Der Spiegel* as the climax, or crash-
landing, of the night. The front bar is fairly chatty,
but the closer you get to the steps down to the darkroom, the more intense things become. Men only, but
they are of all ages and styles. Very popular, especially on Monday, when drinks are two-for-one.

Charlottenburg

Art

Fasanenstrasse 81A (313 2625/www.art-restaurant.
com). S3, S5, S7, S9, S75, U2, U9, U12 Zoologischer
Garten. **Open** noon-2am Mon-Fri; 10.30am-2am Sat,
Sun. **No credit cards. Map** p305 C4.
Underneath the S-Bahn arches, the Arc has rustic
chic, exposed brickwork, wood interior, and both
light snacks and an à la carte menu. From 8pm you
can drop into the Banana Bar next door (staffed by
the same team) and sample their fine cocktails.

Arts & Entertainment

Clubs & one-nighters

With only a few real clubs (Die Busche, SchwuZ, Connection, OstGut), one-nighters are all the rage. Some quickly come and go; others run and run. Check *Siegessäule* or flyers for details.

GMF

Check press or website for venue (www.bodyoung.de). **Open** 10pm-late Sun. **Admission** €8. **No credit cards**.

GMF was changing venue at the time this guide went to press, but this event will continue to have an unbeatable line-up of DJs, including Divinity and Westbam. The dancefloor is intense and the cocktail lounge (complete with original GDR sofas) is sociable and buzzy. Attracts a stylish and energetic crowd. Check press or website for information.

Mitte

Club 69 & GaymeBoys

Kalkscheune, Johannisstrasse 2 (2839 0065/ www.dissentertainment.de). U6 Oranienburger Tor or S1, S2, S25, S26 Oranienburger Strasse. **Open** *Club 69* 11pm-late, *GaymeBoys* 9.30pm-late, one Sat a month; phone for details. **Admission** €5-€9. **No credit cards**. **Map** p316/p302 F3.

One Saturday each month Kalkscheune hosts these two parties for the price of one (if you're under 26). Club 69 offers a wicked mix of music from the '60s, '70s and '80s for a shrieking young crowd. All kinds of activities included. GaymeBoys in the basement only lets you through its doors if you're under 26 (or look it), so shy boys are not overwhelmed by dispassionate and consciously cool nightlife. Once a month on Saturday.

House Boys

Kalkscheune, Johannisstrasse 2 (2839 0065/ www.dissentertainment.de). U6 Oranienburger Tor or S1, S2, S25, S26 Oranienburger Strasse. **Open** 11pm-late; no fixed dates, phone for details. **Admission** €5-€9. **No credit cards**. **Map** p316/p302 F3.

Excellent music and decoration make this a must for every house-loving gay. Don your baggiest trousers or ruffle your hair before coming and be careful not to look much older than 30. No fixed dates; watch the gay press or flyers.

Klub International

c/o Kino International, Karl-Marx-Allee 33 (2475 6011). U5 Schillingstrasse. **Open** 11pm-late 1st Sat of month. **Admission** €8. **No credit cards**. **Map** p303 G3.

Taking place in a cinema built by the GDR in the '50s, whose interior alone is worth the visit. Currently the biggest gay party event in Berlin, attracting up to 1,500 youngish guests. Two dance-floors with house and mainstream music.

Friedrichshain

OstGut

Mühlenstrasse 26-30, entrance Rummelsburger Platz (www.ostgut.de). S3, S5, S6, S9, S75, U1, U12 Warschauer Strasse or S3, S5, S7, S9, S75 Ostbahnhof. **Open** 11pm-late. **Admission** €5-€10. **No credit cards**. **Map** p307 H4.

OstGut is the biggest and and possibly the best techno club in the city. It hosts a huge range of events, including the deeply pervy SNAX-Club (*see p213*) and nonconformist, easygoing Dance with the Aliens (*see p209*). The 'normal' Saturday night is also well frequented by gays and lesbians of the more nonconformist kind. Inspiring. A must for techno lovers. *See also p230.*

Kreuzberg

SchwuZ

Mehringdamm 61 (693 7025/www.schwuz.de). U6, U7 Mehringdamm. **Open** 11pm-late Fri, Sat. **Admission** €4-€7.50. **No credit cards**. **Map** p306 F5.

Sip and stare outside **Café Berio**. See p211.

Saturday is the main disco night at the Schwulen Zentrum ('Gay Centre'), Berlin's longest-running dance institution. Mixed crowd, but basically a politically correct scene covering all ages and styles. There are two, sometimes three, dancefloors (one of them house music) and much mingling between the three bars and Café Melitta Sundström (*see p208*) at the front. Friday hosts various one-nighters: Popstarrz on the first Friday of the month, with independent and pop music; the much frequented Subterra on the second Friday; and Subworxx on the third Friday, with an emphasis on rock music. Events also include trashy drag shows in the small theatre and the Safer-Sex-Party (*see p213*) and various theme clubnights.

Schöneberg

Connection
Fuggerstrasse 33 (218 1432/www.connection-berlin.com/connection.php4). U1, U2, U12, U15 Wittenbergplatz. **Open** 10pm-7am Fri, Sat. **Admission** €6 (includes one free drink). **No credit cards. Map** p305 D5.
Although never quite up-to-date, Connection is especially popular on men-only Saturdays when there are no one-nighters on offer. A mixture of esoteric and Top 40 sounds ensure a packed dancefloor. Bored with dancing? Cruise through into the vast dungeons of Connection Garage, where many guests spend their time.

Leather, sex & fetish venues
See p214 **Nice 'n' sleazy.**

Prenzlauer Berg

Stahlrohr
Greifenhagener Strasse 54 (4473 2747). S4, S8, S10, U2 Schönhauser Allee. **Open** 10am-6am daily. **Admission** €7. **No credit cards. Map** p303 G1.
Small hardcore pub in the front and a huge darkroom in the back. Sex parties for every taste, including one on Sunday afternoon called Coffee-Cake-Sex. Check the gay press or websites for details.

Friedrichshain

Lab.oratory
OstGut, Mühlenstrasse 26-30, entrance Rummelsburger Platz (290 0579/www.lab-oratory.de). S3, S5, S6, S7, S9, S75, U1, U12 Warschauer Strasse. **Open** varies. **Admission** €4-€5. **No credit cards. Map** p307 H4.
Gay hardcore discotheque for more perverse tastes. More darkroom than dancefloor. Fetish parties on Fridays, Saturdays and Sunday afternoon, including mud, scat, oil and grease, fist, watersports, sneaker, rubber and sewer outfits. Watch out for flyers or check the website. Men only.

SNAX-Club
OstGut, Mühlenstrasse 26-30, entrance Rummelsburger Platz (290 0597/www.snax-club.de). S3, S5, S6, S7, S9, S75, U1, U12 Warschauer Strasse. **Open** varies. **Admission** €9. **No credit cards. Map** p307 H4.
The pervy party in Europe – the biggest hardcore event of its kind. Trance-techno and sex in a huge former factory with darkrooms catering for every perverse need. The crowd of up to 1,000, all dressed in their best leather, rubber or uniform attire, look masculine and dangerous but mostly don't take themselves too seriously. Lots of sex, fun, dancing and communication. First-comers can be distinguished by their blue jeans and amazed expressions. Held irregularly four to six times a year. Watch out for flyers or posters or check the gay press and websites. Men only.

Kreuzberg

Bodies in Emotion @ AHA
Mehringdamm 61 (692 3600/www.aha-berlin.de). U6, U7 Mehringdamm. **Open** 9pm-5am every 2nd Fri. **Admission** €6. **No credit cards. Map** p306 D5.
Every second Friday, this sex party is popular with guys under the age of 30 (or who look like it – no hairy chests here). What you wear is your business, but most put on some sexy shorts, which they then take off in the sex area, where mattresses invite you to have fun – if you can find an empty one, that is.

Club Culture Houze
Görlitzer Strasse 71 (6170 9669). U1 Görlitzer Bahnhof. **Open** 7pm-late Mon, Wed, Sun; 8pm-late Tue, Thur, Fri; 10pm-late Sat. **Admission** €5. **No credit cards. Map** p307 H5.
Diverse sex parties (some of them mixed), ranging from 'naked' to 'SM and Fetish'. Exclusive gay nights feature on Monday (Naked Sex) and Friday (Fist & Fuck Factory) and Saturdays (Gay Sex Party). Mostly body-conscious night owls visit the double-storey kitsch rooms, where mattresses invite them to lie down. But actually they do it everywhere.

Quälgeist
Körtestrasse 15-17, 2nd hinterhof (quaelgeistberlin@aol.com). U7 Südstern. **Open** 10pm-late Fri, Sat. **Admission** €8-€15. **No credit cards. Map** p306 D5.
The first institution established solely to organise SM parties. Parties include SM for beginners, bondage, slave-market and fist nights. Pick up their flyers at any leather bar or Mann-O-Meter (*see p275*). Usually a dress code.

Safer-Sex-Party @ SchwuZ
Mehringdamm 61 (693 7025/www.schwuz.de). U6, U7 Mehringdamm. **Open** varies. **Admission** €8. **No credit cards. Map** p306 F5.
The classic. A luxuriant orgy of food, draperies, cushions, kitsch and mattresses, inspired by fantasies of ancient Rome. It takes place at Christmas,

Arts & Entertainment

at Easter and on the eve of other holidays, drawing an unconventional and youngish crowd and leaving behind hundreds of used condoms. Check out posters, flyers or the gay press or website.

Triebwerk
Urbanstrasse 64 (6950 5203). U7, U8 Hermannplatz. **Open** 10pm-late Mon, Fri; 9pm-late Tue-Thur, Sat, Sun. **Admission** €5. **No credit cards. Map** p306 G5.
Small comfortable bar with a darkroom maze in the basement. Mainly Kreuzberg gays of every denomination. Monday is two-for-one drinks; Tuesday is Naked & Underwear Party; Thursday is Sportmen-Sex-Party; on Fridays Naked or Underwear Parties alternate.

Schöneberg

Ajpnia
Eisenacher Strasse 23 (2191 8881/www.ajpnia.de). U1, U2, U4, U12, U15 Nollendorfplatz. **Open** 9pm-late Sat. **Admission** €5-€6. **No credit cards. Map** p306 D5.
Every second and fourth Saturday of the month, sex party Nachtverkehr (Night Traffic); every first and third Saturday Nachtverkehr positHIV, a sex party by and for HIV-positives. Location exclusively for sex, frequented by men of all ages, who don't hesitate.

KitKatClub
Bessemerstrasse 2 (www.beepworld.de/members3/ gayinfo). S2, S4 Papestrasse or U6 Alt-Tempelhof. **Open** 9pm-late 1st Mon of month. **Admission** €5-€10. **No credit cards.**
The infamous KitKat is essentially a mixed/ straight sex club with a monthly 'special gay night – erotic dance' on the first Monday of each month. Saturday parties are also frequented by gays. *See also p231.*

New Action
Kleiststrasse 35 (211 8256). U1, U2, U4, U12, U15 Nollendorfplatz. **Open** 8pm-late Mon-Sat; 1pm-late Sun. **Admission** €8. **No credit cards. Map** p305 D5.
An atmospheric and custom-designed hardcore bar with small darkroom. In early morning, when the atmosphere is at its most bizarre, it can become quite an *omnium gatherum* of eccentric weirdos, who either don't yet want to go to bed or else just got up. Leather, rubber, uniform, jeans – but also the odd woollen pullover creates a casual atmosphere.

Nice 'n' sleazy

The hardcore and fetish scene in Berlin is huge, with the leather gays nowadays being outnumbered by the younger hardcore crowd and skinhead-type gays, who prefer rubber and uniforms. Places to obtain your preferred garb are plentiful, as are opportunities to show it off, including the eternally crowded **Leather Meeting** over the Easter holidays, the annual **Gay Skinhead Meeting** and fetish parties and events such as **SNAX-Club** (*see p213*).

Wanna have some sex? Or a lot of it? No problem, you are in the gay sex party capital of the world. Next to the usual darkrooms, gay cinemas and outdoor cruising sites, Berlin has over the last decade developed an enormous sex party scene.

It started in 1989, when **SchwuZ** (*see p212*), wanting to countermeasure the angst and anxiety caused by AIDS, staged the first of its legendary **Safer-Sex-Parties** (*see p213*). But not without a degree of uncertainty about whether it would go down well. It did.

Soon afterwards, the **AHA** (*see p213*) gave its first 'Erotik Party' for younger guys and **Quälgeist** started organising SM and fetish parties. The boom began with the fall of the Berlin Wall and the subsequent exponential enlargement of the gay scene. Sex party venues opened in rundown east Berlin buildings, naked parties started on Sunday afternoons and even the time-honoured eastern advice centre had a monthly party.

Today you can choose between around a hundred sex parties a month, serving every need and desire on a daily basis. The listings magazines (*see p207*) will give you some idea about the overwhelming variety of options.

Broadly speaking, sex parties can be divided into four groups: naked parties, sex orgies, dance-and-fuck parties and fetish parties. A naked party is more or less a standard evening in a darkroom-bar, except for the fact that everyone is naked and activity is not confined to conversation and drinking (eg at Scheune and Stahlrohr). Sex orgies are exactly that. Guests wear jockstraps, their sexiest hot pants or nothing and either lounge away time in the bar and chill-out areas or fall about in the areas of activity, which are laid out with mattresses and slings (eg at SchwuZ). The same attire is worn at dance-and-fuck parties. No designated areas here for either dancing or copulation; it's done everywhere (eg at KitKatClub, SNAX-Club). Fetish parties usually have a dress code (but naked always passes)

Scheune

Motzstrasse 25 (213 8580). U1, U2, U4, U12, U15
Nollendorfplatz. **Open** 9pm-7am Mon-Thur; non-stop
9pm Fri-7am Mon. **Admission** varies. **No credit**
cards. Map p306 D5.
Small and popular leather hardcore bar. Action in
the cellar is late and heavy. Naked Sex Party on
Sunday afternoons and rubber night every second
Friday. Very popular.

Westside Club

c/o Metropol, Nollendorfplatz (2173 6841/
www.beepworld.de/members3/gayinfo). U1, U2, U4,
U12, U15 Nollendorfplatz. **Open** varies. **Admission**
t7.50. **No credit cards. Map** p306 D5.
The KitKatClub (*see p214*) organises two nights
here: Thursday (10pm-midnight) Naked Party followed after midnight by sexual gay dance (Sodom
und Gomorrah) and on Sunday (9pm-2am) Naked
Party. Hardcore crowd of night owls in scanty dress.

Neukölln

Böse Buben

Lichtenrader Strasse 32, 2nd hinterhof
(6270 5610/www.boesebubenberlin.de).
U8 Leinestrasse/bus 104, 144, 194.

Open 8-10pm Wed; 9pm-midnight Fri, Sat.
Admission t5. **No credit cards. Map** p307 G6.
Fetish sex party location with imaginatively furnished and decorated rooms. Tiled piss room, sling
room, bondage cross and cheap drinks make this
quite a grotto of hedonism. Wednesday is SM for
softies, but weekend parties are for those who like
hard SM, fist or spanking.

Saunas

Saunas are popular and you may have to
queue, especially on cheaper days. In-house
bills are run up on your locker or cabin
number and settled on leaving. Unlike other
European saunas there are only personal
cabins. Rumour has it that the largest
European gay sauna (Aquarius) is due to
open some time in 2002.

Apollo City Sauna

Kurfürstenstrasse 101, Tiergarten
(213 2424). U1, U2, U12, U15 Wittenbergplatz.
Open 1pm-7am daily. **Admission** t13 a day
(t10 Mon) locker; t17 cabin. Short-term cabin
reservation (except Mon). **No credit cards.**
Map p306 D5.

related to the theme of the night. Action is
plentiful and hardcore (eg at Lab.oratory).
  All of them are organised in much the same
way. After entering the venue you undress
or change, have a number written on your
body for settling your in-house bills on
leaving, and are then free to roam about.

Many places offer free condoms and
lubricant, some even have showers. From
time to time Lab.oratory comes up with fist
parties lasting for two days; then they even
provide bed and breakfast.
  Tourists are universally welcome. But
always be careful to practise safe sex.

A sprawling labyrinth of sin – with 130 lockers and 60 cabins. Dry and steam saunas, porn video den, TV lounge, weights room, sun beds and a well-stocked bar. If you don't end up in one of the cabins, there's plenty of action in the dark, cruisy steam bath downstairs.

Gate Sauna
Wilhelmstrasse 81, Mitte (229 9430/www.gate-sauna.de). S1, S2 Unter den Linden or U2 Mohrenstrasse. **Open** 11am-7am Mon-Thur; non-stop 11am Fri-7am Mon. **Admission** €12 locker; €17-€20 cabin. **No credit cards**. **Map** p316/p306 F4.
Berlin's smallest sauna appeals to all ages, with an emphasis on adults. Houses all the usual facilities. The sling in the basement is a prop most welcomed by the 'Heavy Teddies' who meet here every second Sunday afternoon of the month.

Steam Sauna
Kurfürstenstrasse 113, Tiergarten (218 4060/ www.steam-sauna.de). U1, U2, U12, U15 Wittenbergplatz. **Open** 11am-7am Mon-Thur; non-stop 11am Fri-7am Mon. **Admission** €14. **No credit cards**. **Map** p305 D4.
After Apollo, this is west Berlin's other classic sauna with 180 lockers, 38 cabins and plenty of sex. Clientele of all ages, plus sauna and steam rooms, whirlpool, bar and TV room showing porn. Saturday is slightly cheaper and packed; clubbers come early on Sunday morning and stay for the day.

Treibhaus Sauna
Schönhauser Allee 132, Prenzlauer Berg (448 4503/449 3494/www.treibhaussauna.de). U2 Eberswalder Strasse. **Open** 1pm-7am Mon-Thur; non-stop 11am Fri-7am Mon. **Admission** €14.50; €20 (including drink ticket) cabin. **No credit cards**. **Map** p303 G2.
Tucked in the first courtyard (buzz for entry), this is a big favourite, especially with students and youngsters. Facilities include dry sauna, steam room, whirlpool, cycle jet and solarium. Cabins equipped with TV and VCR go on a first-come, first-served basis.

Cruising

Cruising is a popular and legal pursuit in Berlin. Most action takes place in the parks. Don't panic or jump into a bush when encountering the police – they are actually there to protect you from gay bashers and they never hassle cruisers. Summer seems to bring out all of Berlin's finery. There is no taboo attached to nudity in large parks.

Grunewald
S7 Grunewald.
The woods behind the car park at Pappelplatz. This popular daytime spot is also well frequented at night, when bikers and harder guys mingle among the trees.

Tiergarten
S3, S5, S7, S9, S75 Tiergarten. **Map** p305 D4.
The Löwenbrücke (where the Grosser Weg crosses the Neuer See) is the cruising focal point – but the whole corner south-west of the Siegessäule becomes a bit of a gay theme park in summer, including daytime, when hundreds of gays sun themselves on the 'Tuntenwiese' ('faggot meadow').

Volkspark Friedrichshain
S3, S5, S7, S9, S75, U2, U5, U8 Alexanderplatz. **Map** p303 H3.
After sundown, the area around and behind the Märchenbrunnen monument fills with horny lads. Very active at night. Some activity by day, but it involves searching the nearby slopes for it.

Lesbian

Few cities can compete with Berlin's impressive network of lesbian bars, clubs and institutions. Recent years have seen a shift in emphasis as (mostly unprofitable) women-only cafés make way for a revitalised scene populated by largely apolitical, fashion-conscious twenty-somethings. But Berlin caters for lesbians of all shapes and sizes. There are a few regular haunts but lesbian nightlife is mostly made up of one-nighters.

Yet, for all its vibrancy, Berlin's lesbian community can be difficult to penetrate. Like many Berliners, dykes can initially seem a little stand-offish, although that seems to be changing, and young lesbians can be seen having fun on Saturdays in the SchwuZ (*see p212*). In east Berlin, lesbians tend to be more open and friendly, but that can still be said of most easterners.

Cafés & bars

Mitte

Café Seidenfaden
Dircksenstrasse 47 (283 2783). S3, S5, S7, S9, S75 Hackescher Markt. **Open** 11am-9pm Mon-Fri; 1-7pm Sun. **No credit cards**. **Map** p303 G3.
Café Seidenfaden is run by women from a rehabilitation and therapy group of former addicts. Packed at lunchtime and quiet in the evenings. There are cultural events, readings and exhibitions. Strictly no drugs or alcohol.

Kreuzberg

Schoko Café
Mariannenstrasse 6 (615 1561). U1, U8, U12 Kottbusser Tor. **Open** 5pm-late daily. **No credit cards**. **Map** p307 G5.

Part of the Schoko-Fabrik women's centre, this beautiful café is mostly frequented by lesbians (and other straight women). Cakes, soups, hot snacks and occasional dance parties.

Schöneberg

Begine

Potsdamer Strasse 139 (215 1414/www.begine-kultur.w4w.net). U2 Bülowstrasse. **Open** 5pm-1am Mon-Sat. **No credit cards. Map** p306 E5.
Women-only café frequented by lesbians. Part of the 'Meeting Point and Culture for Women' centre, which organises groups and events. Party on the fourth Saturday of each month.

pe

Kalckreuthstrasse 10 (218 7533). U1, U2, U4, U12, U15 Nollendorfplatz. **Open** 8pm-late daily. **No credit cards. Map** p305 D5.
This – Berlin's oldest lesbian bar/club – is now run by a Berlin popstar as a mixed venue, except for Saturday, when it's 'Women Night'.

Charlottenburg

Neue Bar Zitrone

Knesebeckstrasse 16 (3150 3062). S3, S5, S7, S9, S75 Savignyplatz. **Open** 5pm-1am. **No credit cards. Map** p305 C4.
A small pub for women and lesbians. Friendly, talkative atmosphere.

Stonewall

Otto-Suhr-Allee 125 (3470 5530). U7 Richard-Wagner-Platz. **Open** 8pm-late daily. **No credit cards. Map** p300 B3.
Bar/bistro with the interior of a typical Berlin corner pub. Frequented mainly by lesbians.

Clubs & one-nighters

Mitte

Coco Salon

c/o Bar Lounge 808, Oranienburger Strasse 42/43 (2804 6727/www.barlounge808.com). S1, S2, S25, S26 Oranienburger Strasse. **Open** 9pm-1am 1st Wed of month. **Admission** free. **Credit** AmEx, MC, V. **Map** p302 F3.
A monthly 'Jour Fixe Cocktail Party for Ladies', just opened at the time this guide went to press.

Prenzlauer Berg

Frauenparty im EWA e.V. Frauenzentrum

Prenzlauer Allee 6 (442 5542). U2 Rosa-Luxemburg-Platz. **Open** 10pm-3am Sat. **No credit cards. Map** p303 G3.
Dance party for women every Saturday. Check the press for other events at this venue.

Friedrichshain

It's a Woman's World

Frieda Women's Centre, Proskauer Strasse 7 (422 4276). U5 Samariterstrasse. **Open** 8pm-late 3rd Fri of month. **Admission** €1.50. **No credit cards. Map** p89.
Dance party for women at the Frieda Women's Centre, which also organises breakfasts and other women-only meetings. Check the press for other events at this venue.

Kreuzberg

m.appeal @ SO 36

Oranienstrasse 190 (6140 1306). U1, U8, U12 Kottbusser Tor. **Open** 10pm-late 3rd Sat of month. **Admission** €5. **No credit cards. Map** p307 G4.
Every third Saturday of the month, young progressive lesbians gather to dance and party in a slightly trashy and comic atmosphere. Women only; drags welcome. Go-go dancers. Wild.

Schoko-Dance-Night

Schoko Café, Mariannenstrasse 6 (615 1561). U1, U8, U12 Kottbusser Tor. **Open** 9pm-late 2nd Sat of month. **Admission** €3-€4. **No credit cards. Map** p307 G5.
Women's dance party every second Saturday of the month at Schoko Café (*see p216*).

subterra @ SchwuZ

Mehringdamm 61 (693 7025/www.schwuz.de). U6, U7 Mehringdamm. **Open** 10pm-late every 2nd Fri. **Admission** €7.50. **No credit cards. Map** p306 F5.
Mixed party with distinctly more lesbians than gays, downstairs in SchwuZ (*see p212*), organised by Megadyke Productions. Two dancefloors and a massage corner in the candlelit lounge, where a professional masseuse will knead anyone's flesh. Often full to capacity.

Charlottenburg & Wilmersdorf

Die 2

Wasserturm, Spandauer Damm 168 (302 5260). Bus 145. **Open** 7pm-late Wed, Thur; 10pm-late Fri, Sat. **No credit cards. Map** p300 B3.
A romantic garden promises wonderful summer nights. Inside they play oldies like *La Vie En Rose* and *Sex Machine*. Easygoing atmosphere. A true phenomenon, largely unchanged since the 1980s. Wednesday and Thursday: After-Work-Party; Friday and Saturday: disco.

Schatulle

Fasanenstrasse 40 (8827 7912). U1, U9 Spichernstrasse. **Open** 9pm-6am daily. **Admission** free. **No credit cards. Map** p305 C5.
Disco with a 1980s atmosphere for women who want to dance but don't like techno. Men admitted.

Arts & Entertainment

Music: Rock, World & Jazz

Maybe believe the hype – Berlin's diverse music scene starts to live up to its illustrious heritage and overheated marketing.

Berlin's music scene has always reflected the tension permeating city life. Cold War division infused the music with a sense of alienation, intrigue and even impending apocalypse. Post-1989, a spirit of improvisation and experimentation midwived techno culture and fashioned new club and performance spaces out of abandoned industrial and commercial buildings or the cellars of houses still riddled with World War II bullet holes – creative reactions to the dizzying and often disorienting changes of the last decade. Berlin became a hub of club culture, and everyone from major record labels (Sony Music and V2 have head offices here, Universal Music will as of 2002) to the city government (giving at least lip service in support of the music industry, commissioning reports and organising roundtables) jumped on the bandwagon. The post-war West German music industry shunned Berlin. Left to their own devices, musicians helped themselves, with indie labels and alternative distribution. To compensate for the city's insular location, the West Berlin government offered generous subsidies for rock music, while the GDR entirely bankrolled music output. While this shielded Berlin bands from commercial pressure to an extent, the music was in danger of degenerating into state-sponsored mediocrity, or, in the East, an instrument of state control.

A NEW CAREER IN A NEW TOWN

Under Allied rule, residents of West Berlin were exempt from the draft. This attracted many young West Germans who helped to forge the alternative and avant-garde scenes in the city. But Berlin has also captured the imaginations of artists and musicians from abroad.

In the 1920s the likes of Arnold Schönberg, Kurt Weill, Bertolt Brecht, George Grosz and Max Ernst founded Berlin's reputation for artistic experimentation. It was this cutting-edge legacy, along with the thrill and peril of life in the Walled City, that lured David Bowie and Iggy Pop to Berlin in 1976. In the early 1980s Nick Cave was a fixture at the Risiko bar in Schöneberg, recruiting bartender and

Neubauten member Blixa Bargeld to the Bad Seeds. Martin Gore moved in with his Berlin girlfriend around the same time, and Depeche Mode added a Neubauten-influenced industrial flavour to their pristine synthpop. To this day, Berlin lures creative spirits from foreign lands. Françoise Cactus added the chanson tradition from her native France to Brezel Göring's tinkertoy instrumentation in Stereo Total. Two internationally acclaimed acts on Mitte-based label Kitty-yo, Peaches (see p224 **Looking at the Peaches**) and (Chili) Gonzales, finally broke out in Berlin after paying dues in the Toronto independent scene.

WALL CITY ROCK

In the Western half of the city, Allied forces radio spread the myth of rock 'n' roll. Ted Herold was promoted as a rough-hewn Elvis; the Lords tried to transplant Merseybeat to the Spree. By the early 1970s purveyors of pop music parted ways with the artificial heritage of Anglo-American rock, moving off into experimental avenues led by bands like Ash Ra Tempel and Tangerine Dream, or the radical politics of squatter patron saints Ton Stein Scherben.

The late 1970s and early 1980s witnessed an explosion of new music from Berlin, inspired by punk and postpunk. On the more commercial end of the spectrum, bands like Ideal and Nena, part of the 'Neue deutsche Welle', played tight new wave-ish powerpop with German lyrics, more playful and ironic than those of the singer-songwriters, but not necessarily less critical. On the more avant-garde side, one 1981 festival essentially spawned an entire underground, including the whimsically experimental Die tödliche Doris, radical girl group Malaria and proto-industrialists Einstürzende Neubauten whose noise was heard far beyond the Wall.

BORN IN THE GDR

'Ostrock' came into its own around the same time as its Western counterpart. After the government dissolved the Beat scene in the mid 1960s because it didn't fit the state's vision of youth, the early 1970s succession of hardliner GDR-founder Walther Ulbricht by alleged liberal

Erich Honecker saw a thaw in cultural policy. An indigenous rock culture, with German lyrics, was fostered to project an image of openness. Groups such as hard rockers the Puhdys, pomp-rockers Karat, folkish City and blues-rockers Klaus-Renft-Combo were signed by the state-run label Amiga and toured extensively; some even played West gigs. But by mid decade, things refrosted. Renft were banned in 1975 after a song all but advocating flight to the West. A year later, controversial singer-songwriter Wolf Biermann was expelled, and his stepdaughter, quirky ingenue Nina Hagen, left shortly after, launching her international career from the West Berlin punk scene. A new generation of bands emerged who accurately captured youth's growing disillusionment: Neue Deutsche Welle inspired Pankow or Silly's melodic rock with a lyrical edge.

Beyond the officially endorsed groups, a vital indie scene emerged in the early '80s. Bands such as Planlos, Ornament und Verbrechen (later to regroup as Tarwater and To Rococo Rot) and Freygang found their audiences via home recordings and concerts, often under the auspices of the oppositional Protestant Church. The government cracked down on punks, jailing or drafting them. Some indie bands went official, like Feeling B (members later formed Rammstein), Die Skeptiker or Herbst in Peking thanks to late '80s record company and radio tolerance towards *schräge Musik* ('offbeat music'). But it was too little, too late. The country was rapidly losing its youth, both spiritually and physically. In September 1989 members of Silly, Pankow, City and other rock artists signed a resolution in support of the New Forum movement, hoping to reform Socialism from within. But the avalanche was already in motion.

ELEKTROPOLIS

In the mid 1980s, the seeds of Detroit techno and Chicago house fell upon fertile ground in West Berlin clubs. DJs like Westbam and Love Parade founder Dr Motte, originally punks, embraced the pounding new beats, in turn inspired by the Teutonic synthpop of Kraftwerk, DAF (who relocated from Düsseldorf to Berlin) and its offshoot les Liaisons Dangereuses. Techno, as the danceable electronica would be called, became the soundtrack to the political changes and sense of new possibilities at decade's end. Releases on labels such as Chain Reaction, MFS, Elektro Music Dept and Tresor found international acclaim. Paul van Dyk's trance entrances audiences worldwide. Atari Teenage Riot and the other artists on frontman Alec Empire's Digital Hardcore imprint addressed techno's perceived apoliticalness with

incendiary lyrics. As the '90s progressed, artists as diverse as Rechenzentrum, Monolake and Pole have taken electronica beyond the exigencies of techno's dancefloor and dragged experimental electronic music out of the avant-garde ghetto.

BERLIN LIEBT DICH

The mid 1990s saw the pendulum swing away from high-tech beats. The lo-fi 'living room' scene bore acts such as Barbara Morgenstern and nurtured the *art brut* of Klaus Beyer's German Beatles covers. Le Hammond Inferno and their label Bungalow inaugurated an easy listening craze still evident in the laid-back sounds of Jazzanova and leg-pulling lounge lizards Fuzzy Love. Chicks on Speed update riot grrl with cheesy electronics and fashion sense. Long overshadowed by techno and postrock, guitar-driven bands made a comeback towards the end of the decade, notably Surrogat with their anthem *Berlin liebt dich* (Berlin loves you). Punk ironists die Ärzte are still going strong after nearly two decades. Berlin hip hop, long overshadowed by Hamburg and Stuttgart within the only recently credible German rap scene, has some promising purveyors in Das Department and the Turkish Islamic Force. Crossover band Beatsteaks have been signed to the Offspring's label Epitaph and are being groomed for an international career.

Diversity is perhaps the only common denominator of the 'Berlin school' label the industry is trying to hype. At the beginning of the 21st century, Berlin acts are making international headway, and the scene's output is prolific, eclectic, eccentric and sometimes even inspired.

As the distinction between live music and DJ sets becomes increasingly blurred, most clubs offer some live events several times a week. This selection includes venues devoted mainly to live performances or with an especially noteworthy booking policy.

Zitty and *tip* list gigs, as does the free, pocket-sized *Guide*. Radio Eins (95.8FM) and Radio Fritz (102.6FM) also inform about upcoming events. The bilingual site www.dorfdisco.de covers local and international acts.

Rock venues

The primarily sports venues **Max-Schmeling-Halle** (*see p247*) and **Velodrom** (*see p247*) also host occasional music events.

Arena

Eichenstrasse 4, Treptow (533 7333/www.arena-berlin.de). S4, S6, S8, S9 Treptower Park/bus 265, N65. **Open** *Tickets* 10am-6pm Mon-Fri. *Concert* varies. **No credit cards.**

Bastard!

This former bus garage is now hosting big concerts by Prodigy, Chemical Brothers and Pet Shop Boys, as well as other events needing space, notably the German adaptations of hit plays *Caveman* and *The Vagina Monologues*.

Bastard @ Prater

Kastanienallee 7-9, Prenzlauer Berg (4404 9669/ www.bastard-club.de). U2 Eberswalder Strasse/ bus N52. **Open** *Office noon-4pm Tue-Thur. Concert varies.* **Admission** *varies.* **Credit** phone for details. **Map** p303 G2.

Concert and club space with living-room charm, that is if your livingroom is four metres high and covered wall-to-wall with pictures torn from fashion or news magazines. Local avant-rock and electronica acts perform several times a week in addition to club nights and multimedia happenings.

ColumbiaFritz

Columbiadamm 9-11, Tempelhof (6981 2828/www.columbiafritz.de). U6 Platz der Luftbrücke. **Open** *Concerts varies. Disco 11pm-6am Sat.* **Admission** *Concerts €10.30. Disco €5.50.* **No credit cards. Map** p306 F6.

Former US Forces cinema now showcasing alternative rock acts ranging from Waterboys to Calexico. Namesake youth radio station Fritz regularly hosts club nights and the 'Berlin macht Schule' local talent concert series.

Columbiahalle

Columbiadamm 13-21, Tempelhof (698 0980). U6 Platz der Luftbrücke. **Open** *Concerts varies. Box office 11am-6pm Mon-Fri.* **Admission** *varies.* **No credit cards. Map** p306 F6.

New Order, Weezer, Faithless and UB40 have all recently played this spacious indoor venue. Next door to ColumbiaFritz.

Knaack Club

Greifswalder Strasse 224, Prenzlauer Berg (442 7061/www.knaack-berlin.de). Tram 2, 3, 4/bus N54. **Open** *Bar 6pm-late daily. Disco 9pm-late Wed, Fri, Sat.* **Admission** *Concerts €6-€15. Disco €2.50 Wed, before 11pm Fri, Sat; €5 after 11pm Fri, Sat.* **No credit cards. Map** p303 H2.

Knaack Club's booking policy covers the full spectrum of alternative rock. Both dancefloors and performance spaces lurk within this multi-level complex, meaning sometimes as many as three different events on any given night – a concert ticket also gets you into the club events, but not vice versa.

Maria

www.clubmaria.de. Address unknown at time of going to press.

Maria's booking policy has become a bit more commercial since its first opening in an old post office building at Ostbahnhof. That means fewer Japanese noise festivals and more crowd-pleasing appearances by acts like Le Tigre, Shellac and the Fall. Nevertheless, the cramped performance space with its generous lounge is the venue of choice for alternative/indie/popular avant-garde artists and their followings. At the time of going to press, the Maria crew had to vacate the Ostbahnhof location for a yet undisclosed new home. Check the website.

Neues Tempodrom

Möckernstrasse 10, Kreuzberg (administration 263 9980/tickets 6953 3885/www.tempodrom.de). S1, S2, S25, S26 Anhalter Bahnhof/bus N29. **Open** *Events varies. Box office noon-6.30pm Mon-Sat.* **No credit cards. Map** p306 F4.

The Tempodrom, two circus tents originally located at Potsdamer Platz, then across the street from the Reichstag, hosted some seminal '80s and '90s events: the 1981 Geniale Dilettanten festival that put the Einstürzende Neubauten on the map, performance art by la Fura dels Baus, the Heimatklänge world music concerts (*see p223*). In 1998 construction of the Federal Chancellery forced the Tempodrom out; after an interim space at Ostbahnhof, it's moved to a new location at Anhalter Bahnhof near Potsdamer Platz. The new Tempodrom encompasses a 3,400 capacity venue and smaller arena for 500, the 'Liquidrom', a saline thermal bath with soothing music and the regular E-drom virtual reality symposium. Programme highlights include Holiday on Ice, concerts by Vanessa Mae and Melissa Etheridge, and a spoken word festival. While its location has almost come full circle, the Tempodrom's vibe is a far cry from the alternative days of old. *See p94* **The time machine.**

Parkbühne Wuhlheide

An der Wuhlheide 8, Köpenick. S3 Wuhlheide.

Radiohead and REM have graced this open-air stage, smaller than the Waldbühne but also more intimate.

Podewil

Klosterstrasse 68-70, Mitte (247 496/tickets 2474 9777/www.podewil.de). U2 Klosterstrasse/bus N52. **Open** varies. **Admission** €5-€18; €5-€15 concessions. **Open** Box office 8am-10pm Mon-Fri. *Concert* varies. **Credit** MC, V. **Map** p316/p303 G3.
The former HQ of the GDR youth organisation FDJ and music-vetting centre has become Berlin's premier venue for avant-rock, improv and experimental music. Podewil artists-in-residence in music, dance, performance and media arts present their latest works. Also hosts theatre, performance art, video installations and the Total Music Meeting *(see p223).*

Razzle Dazzle

Mühlenstrasse 12, Friedrichshain (no phone/ www.razzledazzle.de). S3, S5, S6, S7, S9, S75, U1, U12 Warschauer Strasse. **Open** varies. **No credit cards. Map** p307 H4.
Sweaty and dank hall specialising in local rock, goth and punk, with occasional visits by foreign dignitaries such as rockabilly veteran Robert Gordon and Therapy?. Thursday rockabilly night.

Roter Salon an der Volksbühne

Rosa-Luxemburg-Platz, Mitte (4401 7400/ www.roter-salon.de). U2 Rosa-Luxemburg-Platz. **Open** Box office noon-6pm daily. **Admission** €5-€8. **No credit cards. Map** p316/p303 G3 & p89.
One of Berlin's most popular and controversial theatres, the Volksbühne also turns over its stage to acts such as Stereolab or Billy Bragg. The smaller Roter Salon, with its own side entrance, stucco moulding and glass chandeliers, is a venue for club nights and more marginal concerts; tangeros and swing kids shake a leg at the Grüner Salon on the other side of the building. *See also p234.*

Wabe

Danziger Strasse 101, Prenzlauer Berg (4240 2525/ www.wabe-berlin.de). S4, S8, S85 Greifswalder Strasse/bus N54. **Open** varies. **No credit cards. Map** p303 H3.
Located in a former East Berlin cultural centre (still municipally run) in Ernst-Thälmann-Park, this octagonal (thus the name 'Wabe' or 'honeycomb') multipurpose performance space is a good place to trace the legacy of 'Ostrock'. Both mainstream and underground acts from the GDR play here, such as Engerling and Iron Hennig, as well as the ska-punk outfit Blascore with its rousing skank-a-long covers of standards by Nina Hagen or the GDR's answer to Elvis, Frank Schöbel.

Waldbühne

Waldbühne, Glockenturmstrasse/Passenheimer Strasse, Charlottenburg (office 810 750/tickets 01805 332 433). U2 Olympia-Stadion (Ost) or S5, S75 Pichelsberg. **Open** Box office 10am-6pm. **Admission** €30-€70 **No credit cards.**
In summer this 22,000-seat amphitheatre in the woods near Olympiastadion hosts the likes of Neil Young, Sting and Depeche Mode.

World, folk & Latino

Hybrids like the Afro Celt Sound System or cross-continental all-star collaborations question the continued validity of the concept of 'world music'. Jazz, rock and avant-garde have absorbed non-European elements, while indigenous music has been 'watered down' to make it more palatable for Western ears. Berlin's worldbeat scene reflects this trend, its most notable acts not necessarily purist purveyors, but cutting and mixing ethnic influences as electronica artists sample records: Di Grine Kuzine's Italian-Balkan-Klezmer fusion, Genetic Drugs' Subcontinental digital travelogues, 17 Hippies playing just as many styles. Berlin also offers a broad selection of traditional music, with Klezmer, Irish pub folk and anything vaguely 'Latino' (encompassing everything from Afro-Cuban son to Brazilian forró, tango Argentino to salsa) the most popular. Trend to watch: music from the Balkans, Russia and the former Central Asian Soviet Republics.
For info tune to SFB4 MultiKulti radio on 106.8FM, or scan music listings in *tip* and *Zitty*.

El Barrio

Potsdamer Strasse 84, Tiergarten (262 1853/ www.el-barrio.de). U1 Kurfürstenstrasse/bus N5, N52. **Open** varies. **Admission** €5. **No credit cards. Map** p306 E4.
Salsa dancing with instruction, tango on Tuesday from 9pm, live music Friday and Saturday from 9pm.

Dom Kultury Berlin

Torstrasse 60, Mitte (no phone/ http://welcome.to/dkb). U2 Rosa-Luxemburg-Platz/ bus N52. **Open** 6pm-midnight Tue-Sat. **Admission** Cinema €2.50. Concerts €4-€10. **No credit cards. Map** p316/p303 G3.
This Russian record store and cultural meeting point also offers stylistically diverse live music by Russian, eastern European and Central Asian musicians.

Hackesches Hof Theater

Rosenthaler Strasse 40-1, Mitte (283 2587). S3, S5, S7, S9, S75 Hackescher Markt or U8 Weinmeisterstrasse. **Open** Box office 11am-3pm Mon-Fri. **Admission** *Theatre* €14; €8 concessions. *Concerts* €11; €8 concessions. **No credit cards. Map** p316/p302 F3.
Intimate seated space offers daily concerts of Klezmer, Yiddish and east European folk music.

Haus der Kulturen der Welt

John-Foster-Dulles Allee 10, Tiergarten (office 397870/tickets 3978 7175/www.hkw.de). S3, S5, S7, S9 Bellevue/bus 100. **Open** box office/info 10am-9pm Tue-Sun. **Credit** DC, MC, V. **Map** p302 E3.
Berlin's largest world music venue. The Café Global, which overlooks the river Spree, occasionally also features live bands.

Havanna Club

Hauptstrasse 30, Schöneberg (784 8565/
www.havanna-berlin.de). U7 Eisenacher Strasse.
Open varies. **Admission** €2.50 Wed; €6.50 Fri;
€7 Sat. **No credit cards. Map** p305 D6.
Three dancefloors with salsa, merengue and R&B.
Enormously popular both with South American and
Cuban communities as well as natives.

Never Never Land

Cranachstrasse 55, Schöneberg (855 0099/
www.never-never.de). S1 Friedenau. **Open** 5pm-2am
Sun-Fri; 3pm-2am Sat. **No credit cards.**
Australian restaurant with didgeridoo jam sessions
every Monday at 8pm.

Werkstatt der Kulturen

Wissmannstrasse 31-42, Neukölln (622 2024/
*609 7700/www.werkstatt-der-kulturen.de). U7, U8
Hermannplatz.* **Open** varies. **No credit cards.**
Map p307 G6.
Small, community centre-style venue for more
traditional, grass roots music from around the world
as well as ethno-jazz performances and club nights.

Jazz

Berlin's jazz scene is large and encompasses
everything from pub jam sessions to major
international festivals. The city also boasts
Germany's only 24-hour jazz radio station,
JazzRadio, which favours polite, melodic
sounds. The scene in general leans towards the
more traditional, and even that is being passed
up by the media in favour of rock or electronica.
A dedicated following sustains the 38 venues
around town, and initiatives such as the Berlin
Jazz and Blues Awards (with clubs choosing
the finalists competing blow-by-blow before a
jury) and the JazzRadio sponsored Fringe Jazz
Festival hope to bring the city's diverse scene
to wider attention. Despite the slant towards

Cool jazz at the **Bebop Bar**.

pre-free jazz, events such as the Total Music
Meeting (*see p223*) showcase more entropic
forms. The Berlin FMP (Free Music Production)
label's concerts often feature some of the world's
best improvisers, especially if they involve FMP
founder Peter Brötzmann, an extremely physical
baritone sax player, or pianist Alexander von
Schlippenbach. Other fixtures on Berlin's jazz
circuit are US-born singer Jocelyn B Smith and
bebop trombonist Tony Hurdle.

For current concert info, check Jazz Radio
101.9 (bilingual website www.jazzradio.net) or
the online magazine www.jazzdimensions.de.

ABC-Jazzbar

*Schiffbauerdamm 11, Mitte (281 4190). U6
Oranienburger Tor.* **Open** from 8pm Mon-Sat.
Concerts 9.30pm. **Admission** €5. **No credit cards.**
Map p316/p302 F3.
Tiny walk-up bar under the S-Bahn arches. Not a
place to discover groundbreaking talent, but a pleas-
ant stop after a play at the nearby Berliner Ensemble.

A-Trane

Pestalozzistrasse 105, Charlottenburg (313 2550/
www.a-trane.de). S3, S5, S7, S9, S75 Savignyplatz.
Open 9pm-2am Sun-Thur; 9pm-late Fri, Sat.
Concerts from 10pm daily. **Admission** varies.
Credit AmEx, DC, MC, V. **Map** p305 C4.
A swanky attempt at a New York-style jazz bar
where events are occasionally interesting enough to
be heard over the yuppie trimmings.

Badenscher Hof

Badensche Strasse 29, Wilmersdorf (861 0080/
www.badenscher-hof.de). U7, U9 Berliner Strasse.
Open 3pm-1am daily. **Admission** €10-€12.
No credit cards. Map p305 D6.
Small, friendly club offers semi-avant jazz with a
mostly African-American cast. Summer garden.

Bebop Bar

*Willibald-Alexis-Strasse 40, Kreuzberg (6950
8526/www.bebop-bar.de). U7 Gneisenaustrasse
or U6 Platz der Luftbrücke* **Open** varies. *Concerts*
from 10pm Tue, Fri-Sun. **Admission** €2.50-€5.70.
No credit cards. Map p306 F5.
Tiny bar with warm, subdued light and wood furnishings. In the back, live mainstream jazz, blues and
folk are performed nearly every night of the week.

B-Flat

*Rosenthaler Strasse 13, Mitte (280 6349). U8
Rosenthaler Platz/bus N8, N52.* **Open** from 9pm
daily. **Admission** phone for details. **No credit
cards. Map** p302 F3.
Cavernous bar fills up on weekend nights for
mostly local, mostly mainstream jazz acts and DJ sets.

Black Bar Jazz Café

Krossener Strasse 34, Friedrichshain (694 6603/
*www.blackbar.de). S3, S4, S5, S6, S8 Ostkreuz or U5
Samariter Strasse/tram 21, 23.* **Open** 7pm-3am Sun-
Thur; 7pm-5am Fri, Sat. **Admission** €1.60-€6.
No credit cards. Map p89.

Jazz poet and impresario Corbett Santana fled the bad mojo of the Black Bar's previous location next to the Junction Bar for a grittier but also chilled 'hood near Simon-Dach-Strasse's bustling nightlife. The long café isn't an ideal location for a jazz club, but the varied, adventurous programme and friendly vibe still attract the faithful.

Junction Bar

Gneisenaustrasse 18, Kreuzberg (694 6602/ www.junction-bar.de). U7 Gneisenaustrasse. **Open** *Café* 11-2am daily. *Club* 8pm-5am daily. *Concerts* 9pm Thur-Sun; 10pm Fri, Sat. **Admission** €5.50-€6.50. **No credit cards. Map** p306 F5.
Jazz in all varieties – swing, Latin, contemporary, jazz poetry – but not all on the same night. Occasionally some blues and rock too. After-show DJs spin soul, funk and R&B.

ParKHaus

Puschkinallee 5, Treptow (533 7952). S4, S6, S8, S9, S10 Treptower Park/bus 265. **Open** *Box office* from 7.30pm Wed-Sat. *Concerts* from 10pm Wed-Sat. **Admission** €2.50 Wed; varies Fri; €5 Sat. **No credit cards.**
A club that, with financial support from the Senate, puts on a jazz programme every Friday and Saturday night in the cellar of an old villa, although the booking also acknowledges local rock newcomers as well. The oldest jazz venue in Berlin.

Pfandleihe

Linienstrasse 98, Mitte (2809 7159/ www.pfandleihe.com). U8 Rosenthaler Platz or U6 Orianienburger Tor/bus N8. **Open** from 7pm Mon-Sat. **Admission** €5. **No credit cards. Map** p316/p302 F3.
Recently opened club in a renovated courtyard complex. The name is German for 'pawnshop', belying the rather gentrified exterior. A venue of the Berlin Fringe Jazz Festival.

Quasimodo

Kantstrasse 12A, Charlottenburg (312 8086/ www.quasimodo.de). S3, S5, S7, S9, U2, U9 Zoologischer Garten. **Open** *Box office* from 5pm daily. *Concerts* from 10pm daily. **Admission** €3-€30. **No credit cards. Map** p305 C4.
Small, cramped and a stopping-off point for many US bands touring Europe. Quasimodo's booking policy has expanded to include 1970s rock, blues, roots and R&B. Notoriously, the smokiest venue on Europe's jazz circuit, a fact that performers often bemoan.

Kunstfabrik Schlot

Chausseestrasse 18 (entrance Schlegelstrasse 26), Mitte (448 2160/www.kunstfabrik-schlot.de). U6 Zinnowitzer Strasse. **Open** phone for details. **Admission** phone for details. **No credit cards. Map** p302 E2.
The Prenzlauer Berg jazz club now moved to a refunctioned industrial complex in Mitte. The programme, including Polish and Czech jazz as well as cabaret and improv theatre, is intriguing, but the location is a tad sterile.

Tränenpalast

Reichstagsufer 17, Mitte (office 206 1000/tickets 2061 0011/www.traenenpalast.de). S1, S2, S3, S5, S7, S9, U6 Friedrichstrasse. **Open** *Box office* from 7pm daily. *Concerts* phone for details. **Admission** varies. **Credit** phone for details. **Map** p316/p302 F3.
This former checkpoint is now a cosy mid-sized venue not only for jazz notables such as Pharoah Sanders, but also jam sessions, cabaret, laid-back rock acts and stand-up comedians.

Festivals

Fête de la Musique

Various venues (019 058 1058/www. lafetedelamusique.de). **Tickets** free. **Date** 21 June.
For summer solstice, the city is transformed into one grooving, vibing stage. In past years, acts such as Khaled, Fun Lovin' Criminals, Stella Chiweshe and the New York Ska-Jazz Ensemble have performed. *See also p185.*

Heimatklänge

Various venues (6128 4235). **Tickets** free. **Date** 2wks in July/Aug.
Berlin's biggest world music event with a yearly regional focus. *See also p185.*

Jazz Across the Border

Haus der Kulturen der Welt, John-Foster-Dulles Allee 10, Tiergarten (office 397 870/tickets 3978 7175/www.hkw.de). S3, S5, S7, S9 Bellevue/bus 100. **Date** phone for details. **Map** p302 E3.
Programme featuring jazz interfacing with various world musics or the likes of drum 'n' bass.

JazzFest Berlin

Various venues. Organisers: Berliner Festspiele, Schaperstrasse 24, Tiergarten (2548 9100/ www.berlinerfestspiele.de). **Tickets** varies. **Credit** varies. **Date** 4 days late Oct/early Nov.
The major event in the jazz calendar, the JazzFest has a new artistic director, Swedish trombonist Nils Landgren, and is in the process of reinventing itself. The Total Music Meeting, a free jazz and improvised music event, runs concurrently, with concerts mostly taking place at Podewil (*see p221*). *See also p188.*

Karneval der Kulturen

Kreuzberg (6097 7022/www.karneval-berlin.de). **Tickets** free. **Date** 4 days in May/June.
A world music version of the Love Parade. Floats, plus gigs all over town offering everything from drumming to drum 'n' bass. *See also p184.*

Wie es ihr gefällt

Kulturbrauerei, Prenzlauer Berg (615 3708/ www.kulturbrauerei.de). U2 Eberwalder Strasse or S8, S10 Schönhauser Allee. **Date** Nov.
A forum for female musicians, 'As She Likes It' has presented avant-garde doyenne Pauline Oliveros, video artist Pippilotti Rist's combo Les Reines Prochaines, violinist Iva Bittova and Finnish riot grrls Thee Ultra Bimboos, among others.

Looking at the Peaches

Named after the most rebellious of the 'Four Women' whose plight Nina Simone mournfully describes, **Peaches** has been lionised as a post-feminist libidinal liberator and dissed as smut-peddling and gimmicky. Every track on her 2000 release *The Teaches of Peaches* oozes sex – lyrics along the lines of 'you like it when we play hardcore, the panty war, then you get pussy galore' and the bumping and grinding electronic beats (courtesy of a Roland MC505 groovebox and searing synth-guitar) that accompany them. As does the tough Peaches stage persona, clad in red leather hotpants and pink top that could seemingly fly off its wearer at any time. But her civilian incarnation Merrill Nisker – frailer, more soft-spoken and self-effacing than her alter ego – reveals that there wasn't any masterplan.

'I didn't think it was going to be such a big deal. Look at TV and everything, always alluding to sex. Look at a lot of hip hop lyrics. I like singing about sex. Instead of "beating around the bush" [pun inevitably intended], was just saying it directly. But I guess people aren't used to women doing that.'

Before her Berlin breakthrough, Nisker was a fixture of the Toronto indie scene. After some experience as a music and drama teacher, her first professional performing came with folk rock formation Mermaid Café. In the mid 1990s, she dirtied up her act.

She recorded a collection of no-wave covers (among them compatriots Rough Trade's *High School Confidential*) and wacky originals with Fancypants Hoodlum for the Barenaked Ladies' label. Next she joined the Shit, as Peaches, where she met Jason Beck, the future Chili Gonzales, who would become her (erstwhile) lover and frequent collaborator, whom she followed out of conservative career dead end Canada to promising Berlin.

Peaches' and Gonzales' electro busking quickly caught the attention of Berlin indie label Kitty-yo, which signed them both. The label released a collaboration LP *Red Leather*, but it was Peaches' solo debut and singles *Fuck the Pain Away*, *Lovertits* and *Set It Off* that really generated buzz. Peaches toured abroad, often with Gonzales. Ironically, a Canadian expat was breaking the current Berlin scene internationally.

While she probably would have done her 'shtick', as she calls it, anywhere, Berlin has proven an especially nurturing environment.

'It seems you can make a life of making music here. In Canada, you have to feel guilty for doing something like this,' she explains. 'What I like about Berlin as opposed to New York or London is that somehow it's a big place, and lots goes on, but somehow it's really easy to be quiet, to hide away. I don't think you'll be able to live like this in Berlin in ten years. I just feel really lucky that there's a time and place for me.'

Nightlife

Berlin's clubs still kick, though nightlife isn't quite the cabaret it used to be (old chum).

No closing times, a savage drinking culture, cocktails for any budget, scenes to suit every sexual proclivity, stylistic bent or musical mutation. You want nightlife? Welcome to Berlin. In this chapter we pick out the best clubs, cabaret venues and places to head for late-night snack nosh.

Clubs

Rumour has it that when the mayor sent a statistician out to count the number of bars and nightclubs in Berlin, he never returned. First-time surveyors of Berliner nightlife may find themselves alternately mystified and daunted by the variety, intensity, stamina and tolerance that characterises nightlife in this shadowy city.

Berlin has always had a reputation for the extreme. Until the end of the 1980s, the walled city attracted radicals with its military service-exemption and subsidised dissidence. Geopolitical circumstances also made it hard to get out of town at weekends, so drinking and nightclubbing became the central form of leisure. After the Wall fell many scenes moved east, converting abandoned warehouses, industrial buildings and former state-run youth clubs into techno and house dancefloors that opened for days at a time. As the Love Parade (see p186 **Slaves to love**) grew and the underground scene spilled out on to the streets and into the mainstream, at times it seemed like the whole city was a club that wouldn't close. Liberal licensing laws still do not specify any closing hours, and evenings out follow the classic continental time-frame, with restaurants serving until 11pm or midnight and clubs peaking between 2am and 4am.

Much of the variety of Berlin after dark is due to the fact that it's still a city of independent bar and club owners over a decade after the fall of the Wall opened a temporary autonomous zone. Nevertheless, the closing down of legendary squat club Im Eimer, venue Maria having to vacate its Ostbahnhof location, the uncertain future of the Tacheles cultural complex and WMF, as well as the opening of such gargantuan, upmarket nightlife ventures as Adagio and

plans for the Majorca Pacha club to spawn a Berlin branch are indicators that the last days of disco are dawning in the capital city.

While a comprehensive survey of Berlin clubland would require a whole book, musically oriented stylistic indicators can give rough impressions of particular Berlin scenes. Techno, house, trance, drum 'n' bass, hip hop, kitschy electronica, African, R&B/ soul, blaxploitation, biker, neo-rockabilly, headbanger, gothic, neo-grunge, industrial, neo-wave, post punk, lounge-core and Latin scenes all make their presence felt in regular and one-off venues around Berlin.

Clubs and bars appear and disappear like pimples on the city's changing face. The listings here were as current as we could get them at the time this guide went to press, but who knows what will have happened in a year's time. Particularly for clubs, we recommend you cross-check against local listings. To this end, clubbers and party-goers of all persuasions will be happy to find Berlin has a very developed information infrastructure. Pamphlets and party flyers can be found on bartops and in postcard and newspaper racks in cafés across the city. The pocket-sized weekly freebie *Flyer* (www.flyer.de) is very in-the-know, and anyone without a local guide should make it their bible. *Guide* (also online at www.guide.berlin.de), *Uncle Sally's* and *[030]* also carry nightlife listings, information and adverts for the larger parties. The clubradio website (www.klubradio.de) features streams from performances at OstGut and Tresor, and many bars and clubs have web presences.

The distinction between bars and nightclubs is often blurred, with many bars offering DJs and dancefloors and nightly changes of theme and atmosphere, and some putting on bands. And recurring parties without home venues may be thrown in several places over the course of a season. We've organised our listings by area partly because the different areas have different characters of nightlife, but also because any system of categorisation squelches particularities of scene and venue.

▶ For more on places for late-night drinking, *see chapter* **Cafés, Bars & Pubs**.

Boogie to the Beasties in a basement at **Bergwerk**.

Mitte

For an overview of the café, pub and bar scene in Mitte, *see p143*. For bars that also have DJs/club nights, *see p144* **Bar Lounge 808**, *p144* **Mitte Bar**, *p146* **Roberta**, *p234* **Roter Salon** *and p146* **Schokoladen**.

Bergwerk

Bergstrasse 68 (280 8876). U8 Rosenthaler Platz/bus N8. **Open** 5pm-late Mon-Fri; noon-late Sat; 10am-late Sun. **Admission** free (€3.50 for special events). **No credit cards**. Map p302 F2.
Dependable basement club for folk eager to avoid trendy clubs and pricey beer. Despite the many DJs named in listings, there is in fact only one guy who changes his repertoire depending on the night – just the sort of idiosyncrasy that makes a place worthwhile for a night of slumming and slamming to the Beastie Boys, whose various incarnations seem to be the starting points for all the various club nights here.

Cookies

Charlottenstrasse 44 (no phone). S1, S2, S3, S5, S7, S9, S25, S26, S75, U6 Friedrichstrasse/bus N5, N84. **Open** varies. **Admission** varies. **No credit cards**. Map p316/p302 F3.
The relocation from the old baked goods factory in Prenzlauer Berg to posh Unter den Linden hasn't fazed Cookies' fashion-conscious crowd, as the ballroom-like venue is packed even midweek with dancers writhing to minimal house. The slickly designed, unisex, flimsily walled toilets resemble an art installation; not recommended for the introverted or faint-hearted.

Delicious Doughnuts

Rosenthaler Strasse 9 (2809 9274/www.doughnuts.de). U8 Weinmeisterstrasse or S3, S5, S7, S9, S75 Hackescher Markt/bus N8. **Open** 9pm-late daily. **Admission** free Mon-Thur, Sun; €5 Fri, Sat. **No credit cards**. Map p316/p302 F3.

This legendary Berlin rare groove and acid jazz club no longer sells doughnuts at the bar, so far has it wandered from the old, smokin' turntable daze of the early 1990s. Several changes of ownership and a slicker-than-thou renovation – black leather booths and everything else lounge red – have cost it some regulars, but Delicious Doughnuts appears to be making a comeback of late. The cocktail menu is extensive, the staff cool and it is still a DJ-oriented venue.

Hafenbar

Chausseestrasse 20 (282 8593). U6 Zinnowitzer Strasse. **Open** 9pm-late Fri; 10pm-late Sat. **Admission** phone for details. **No credit cards**. Map p302 F2.
Somewhat past its 1990s prime, when it was the home to lounge lizards Le Hammond Inferno. Hafenbar still serves up easy listening, 1970s disco and *Schlager*, but other places have since encroached on its turf. Still, it remains a good place for mindless fun off the rather too well beaten path of Oranienburger Strasse.

Kaffee Burger

Torstrasse 60 (2804 6495/www.kaffeeburger.de). U2 Rosa-Luxemburg-Platz/bus N52. **Open** 7pm-late daily. **Admission** free-€6 (depends on event). **No credit cards**. Map p303 G2.
Former haunt of the pre-1989 Prenzlauer Berg underground literary scene, reopened in 1999. Poet Bert Papenfuss is a co-owner, thus the written and spoken word still figure strongly, with regular readings of poetry, prose and subversive non-fiction; Russian expat cult author Vladimir Kaminer DJs twice a month. That's part of an eclectic, ever-astonishing and enjoyable programme, also including film screenings, live music by local and east European acts and *Schallplattenunterhalter* (record entertainers, East German term for disc jockey) spinning anything from dub to 'thrillbient', crime-jazz to East Berlin punk.

From Prenzlauer Berg factory to chic Mitte, **Cookies** still packs 'em in. *See p226.*

Kalkscheune

Johannisstrasse 2 (5900 4340/www.kalkscheune.de).
S1, S2, S3, S5, S7, S9, S25, S26, S75, U6
Friedrichstrasse or U6 Oranienburger Tor.
Open varies. **Admission** free-€15.
No credit cards. Map p316/p302 F3.

The 'chalk stable' can be great in the summer when the courtyard bar is open, but in winter everyone has to cram into one big, smoky, poorly lit, low-ceilinged room where, if you don't want to dance (or can't find the space), you also can't talk over the music. Nice wooden bar at one end, though. There's no real defined scene here, but a variety of events and parties ranging from cabaret to house music, so check local listings for what's on. Recommended: regular bashes thrown by local station Radio Eins with various DJs spinning the records you want to dance to but were afraid to request.

Kurvenstar

Kleine Präsidentenstrasse 3 (2859 9710/
www.kurvenstar.de). S3, S5, S7, S9, S75 Hackescher
Markt/bus N5, N8, N52, N84. **Open** 5pm-late Tue-
Sat. **Admission** €5 Sat; €7 Sun. **Credit** AmEx, DC,
MC, V. **Map** p316/p302 F3.

Stylishly decorated ('70s futurist kitsch before other clubs did it to death) club-cum-bar struggling to overcome bad rep (mostly thanks to underwhelming hip hop DJs and poseur crowd) by courting media and installation artists. Time will tell if K-Star can regain ground lost to the plethora of like-minded places that have since opened.

Lime Club

Dircksenstrasse 105 (2472 1397). S3, S5, S7,
S9, S75, U2, U5, U8 Alexanderplatz/bus N8, N65.
Open 10pm-late Wed-Sat. **Admission** varies.
No credit cards. Map p303 G3.

Noteworthy for its Friday- and Saturday-nighters, when goths crawl out from under their rocks and congregate here in droves. Dress in black to feel at home. Also house, techno and hip hop events.

Mudd Club

Grosse Hamburger Strasse 17 (2759 4999). S3, S5,
S7, S9, S75 Hackescher Markt/bus N5, N8, N52,
N84. **Open** 10pm-late daily. **Admission** €2.50-€6.
No credit cards. Map p316/p302 F3.

Ever heard of the Mudd Club, the hub of early 1980s downtown New York new wave-postmodern night-clubbing? From that scene emerged talents as disparate as Madonna and Jean-Michel-Basquiat. Now Mudd Club impresario Steve Maas has set up shop in a courtyard complex off Oranienburger Strasse. It's anyone's guess if live act Wild Sammy and the Royaltones will become the new James Chance and the Contortions or if the wildly eclectic music policy will find takers in the oversaturated Berlin clubscape.

Oxymoron

Hof 1, Hackesche Höfe, Rosenthaler Strasse 40-1
(2839 1886/www.oxymoron-berlin.de). S3, S5, S7,
S9, S75 Hackescher Markt or U8 Weinmeister-
strasse/bus N5, N8, N52, N84. **Open** *Club* 8pm-1am
Wed; 11pm-late Sat. *Restaurant/café* 11am-late daily.
Admission *Club* €5-€10. **Credit** AmEx, V.
Map p316/p302 F3.

A salon-à-club with elegantly recessed booths in the heart of Hackescher Markt leisure mall, Oxymoron is a book begging to be judged by its expensive cover charges. In the restaurant/café, tourists and ad execs vie with couples from Charlottenburg for the attention of demi-mondettes modelling waitress aprons. The club (in the rear) is small but efficient, catering to guests who would be very hip in Munich. DJs play anything from house to acid jazz to package-tour dance.

Pavillion am Weinbergsweg

Veteranenstrasse 9 (449 5973). U8 Rosenthaler
Platz/bus N8, N52. **Open** varies. **Admission** free.
No credit cards. Map p302 F2.

Located on a hilltop in the Volkspark am Weinbergs-weg (called Veteranenpark by some), this GDR holdover has been remodelled to host a variety of club nights and sundry events. A broad musical spectrum encompasses blaxploitation funk, big beat, drum 'n' bass, house, disco and more. Events, such as staged readings of stories by Polish sci-fi author Stanislav Lem with lounge/electronic music accompaniment, turn on club-goers to the pleasures of other reading matter besides style 'zines. Terrace seating in summer.

Sage-Club

Köpenicker Strasse 78 (no phone). U8 Heinrich-Heine-Strasse. **Open** 10pm-late Thur-Sun. **Admission** €5-€15. **No credit cards.** **Map** p307 G4.
Upmarket and self-consciously fashionable club with an emphasis on house. There's a bit of a see-and-be-seen kind of vibe, coupled with a lot of looking down noses, so dress to feel your best. 'Funky Friday' and Sunday's Niteclub, featuring funk and old school or garage and techno respectively, are the least intimidating evenings.

Sophienclub

Sophienstrasse 6 (282 4552/www.sophienclub.de). S3, S5, S7, S9, S75 Hackescher Markt or U8 Weinmeisterstrasse/bus N8. **Open** 10pm-late Tue, Fri, Sat; 9pm-late Wed. **Admission** €3 Tue, Wed; €6 Fri, Sat. **No credit cards.** **Map** p316/p302 F3.
One of a handful of youth-oriented clubs that existed in East Berlin prior to reunification, Sophien went from jazz roots to accessible acid jazz and funk. Its legendary status in the east made it a favourite destination for west Berliners and visiting celebs after the Wall fell, but the club resolutely ignored musical trends and still does, attracting people looking to party and not terribly concerned about the music. Happy hour (cocktails only) is 9pm to 11pm.

Sternradio

Alexanderplatz 5 (246 259 320/www.sternradio-berlin.de). S3, S5, S7, S9, S75, U2, U5, U8 Alexanderplatz/bus N5, N8. **Open** 11pm-late Fri, Sat. **Admission** €8 Fri; €10 Sat. **No credit cards.** **Map** p316/p303 G3.
Named in tribute to the GDR-manufactured radio brand and located in a typical late '60s edifice, Sternradio has become a popular old-school house and techno venue, thanks in no small part to residencies by Woody, Clé and Phonique and co-operation with the No UFOs party collective.

T34

Torstrasse 134 (283 5506/www.t34-berlin.de). U8 Rosenthaler Platz/bus N8, N52. **Open** 9pm-late Thur; 10pm-late Fri, Sat. **Admission** €5-€10. **No credit cards.** **Map** p302 F2.
The name is both shorthand for the address and the type of Soviet tank used to crush the workers' uprising of 17 June 1953. This converted soap factory purports to uphold the cutting edge legacy of Mitte nightlife while courting more moneyed club-goers. That means house, disco and polite techno behind a slick pink façade with black leather and chrome interior design.

Tresor/Globus

Leipziger Strasse 126A (office 229 0414/club 609 3702/www.tresor-berlin.de). S1, S2, S25, S26, U2 Potsdamer Platz/bus N52, N84. **Open** 11pm-late Wed-Fri, Sun. **Admission** €3 Wed; varies Thur; €7.50 Fri; €7-€10 Sat. **No credit cards.** **Map** p306 E4.
Pioneering no-man's-land club, partly in the subterranean safe-deposit box room of the otherwise vanished pre-war Wertheim department store, partly in the old Globus bank building at ground level. This was *the* place in techno's good old days, and the legend just about lingers. Still good for catching Juan Atkins, Derrick May, Blake Baxter and other Detroit greats, as well as Sven Väth, when they're in town. The summer Trancegarden out back, with tables and fairy lights among the shrubbery, is the club's finest feature, complementing two internal dancefloors and a bar. But often there's no longer much happening and it's unlikely to survive much longer in its current form. There's talk of constructing a 'techno tower' on the site, full of shops and studios.

Delicious Doughnuts. *See p226.*

WMF

Ziegelstrasse 23 (2887 88910/www.wmfclub.de).
S1, S2, S3, S5, S7, S9, S25, S26, S75, U6
Friedrichstrasse or U6 Oranienburger Tor/bus N6.
Open 11pm-late Thur-Sat. **Admission** €5-€10.
No credit cards. Map p316/p302 F3.
Now in its fifth incarnation and status as uncertain
as ever, WMF remains among the forefront of the
city's electronic dance music venues, attracting a
consistent stream of top local and international acts
and experimenting with DJ/VJ combinations. The
labyrinthine layout unites a dancefloor, lounges
and an outdoor courtyard for open-air drinking
and dancing in summer. Beats Tresor (*see p227*) by
running not one but three record labels.

Zosch

Tucholskystrasse 30 (no phone/www.zosch.com). S1,
S2, S25, S26 Oranienburger Strasse. **Open** 4pm-late
Mon-Sat; 10pm-late Sun. **Admission** varies.
No credit cards. Map p316/p302 F3.
Expect the unexpected at this versatile hangout still
proudly displaying the squatter spirit. By day a
popular meeting place for *Milchcafé*, the night-time
programme in the cellar can include open readings
(every Monday), performances, or DJ sets running the
gamut from indie to disco, or live music – every
Wednesday, La Foot Creole rips through over half
a century of danceable brass-based music, from
ragtime to ska.

Prenzlauer Berg

For an overview of the café, pub and bar scene
in Prenzlauer Berg, *see p147*. For bars that
also have DJs/club nights, *see p147* **Akba**
and *p220* **Bastard@Prater**.

H2O

Kastanienallee 16 (no phone). U2 Eberswalder
Strasse/bus N52. **Open** 10pm-late daily. **Admission**
varies. **No credit cards. Map** p303 G2.
The abstract patterns on the wall evoke grafitti
without actually using spray pieces, echoing this
place's general vibe of paying respect to hip hop
while also embracing other forms of dance music.
DJs are at the turntables on weekends and on occasional weekday nights, and you may catch young
local MC hopefuls rapping live so well that you end
up mistaking it for the record of some big-name
German hip hop crew.

Icon

Cantianstrasse 15 (6128 7545/www.iconberlin.de).
U2 Eberswalder Strasse or S4, S8, U2 Schönhauser
Allee/bus N52, N55. **Open** 11.30pm-late Fri, Sat
(sometimes additional weekdays). **Admission** €6;
special events €11. **No credit cards. Map** p303 G1.
A tricky-to-locate entrance in the courtyard just
north of the junction with Milastrasse leads to an
interesting space cascading down several levels
into a long stone cellar. It's a well-ventilated little
labyrinth, with an intense dancefloor space,

imaginative lighting, good sound and a separate
bar insulated enough for conversation to remain
possible. Sometimes techno events, sometimes drum
'n' bass. At its best when the core crowd of young
locals is augmented by a wider audience for some
special event, but a cool place on any night.

Knaack

Greifswalder Strasse 224 (442 7060/www.knaack-
berlin.de). S4, S8, S10 Greifswalder Strasse/
tram N54. **Open** *Bar* 6pm-late daily. **Admission** *Club* €2.50 Wed; €2.50-
€5 Fri, Sat. *Concerts* €6-€15. **No credit cards.**
Map p303 H2.
Multi-level club that hangs on from eastern begin-
nings by attracting a very young audience with a
changing programme of hard, aggressive music in
the basement, and generic party music upstairs. The
concert hall books a steady stream of interesting
international acts. *See also p220.*

Magnet Club

Greifswalder Strasse 212-13 (4285 1335/
www.magnet-club.de). S4, S8, S10 Greifswalder
Strasse/tram N54. **Open** 11pm-late Fri, Sat;
8pm-late Sun. **Admission** €5-€8. **No credit cards.**
Map p303 H2.
Jazz venue Miles the Club went bust and reopened
under new ownership. The front lounge/dancefloor
and live space in the back are holdovers from Miles,
spruced up with Carnaby Street lighting and decor.
During the week, Magnet showcases a wide array
of local talent, while weekends are usually devoted
to funk, R&B, disco and indie club nights, attracting a surprisingly young and unpretentious crowd.

Soda-Club

Knaackstrasse 97 (4405 8707/www.soda-berlin.de).
U2 Eberswalder Strasse or S4, S8, U2 Schönhause
Allee/bus N52. **Open** varies-6am Thur-Sun.
Admission *Club* €2.50-€5. **Credit** V (restaurant
only). **Map** p303 G2.
The bar in the renovated Kulturbrauerei urban
entertainment complex is serviceable as a meeting
point, but the upstairs club-by-numbers and its
unimaginative Latin and 'black music' policy are
highly avoidable.

Friedrichshain

Mühlenstrasse is a litany of crumbling
industrial architecture – mecca, in other words,
for aspiring club owners with limited budgets,
and, thus, still host to some of the best techno
and industrial clubs, but – having pointed
potential investors' attention to the area –
some of them will have to look for a new place
soon, the first and most popular victim being
Maria am Ostbahnhof.
For an overview of the café, pub and bar
scene in Friedrichshain, *see p148*. For bars that
also have DJs/club nights, *see p149* **Cueva**
Buena Vista and *p150* **Tagung**.

For agreeable doorstaff

Be drawn to the **Magnet Club** for funk, R&B, disco and indie and the least arrogant door staff in town. *See p229.*

For cheap drinks

All the young punks, spiky electronica and bargain-priced booze: **Deli**. *See p230.*

For fashion-free fun

Sophienclub blithely ploughs its own furrow, oblivious to musical trends. *See p228.*

For fashion-oriented fun

Now on Unter den Linden, **Cookies**' cool crowd packs the place out week-long. *See p226.*

For most BPM

It's forever techno at **Sternradio**. *See p228.*

For most wah-wah pedal

Enjoy the eclectic hilltop offerings at the **Pavillion am Weinbergsweg**. *See p227.*

For pain-free queuing

The warm vibe of **Lola** extends to its sheltered entrance, making for queuing without tears in cold weather. *See p231.*

For shagging

Leave your inhibitions at the door at the legendary **KitKatClub**. *See p231.*

Astro Bar

Simon-Dach-Strasse 40 (no phone). U5 Frankfurter Tor/bus N5, N29. **Open** 9pm-late daily.
Admission free. **No credit cards.**
This is a charming dusk-till-dawn venue to see the locals at their favourite pastime: drinking and listening to funny music. The control panel in the back room could have come from a *Thunderbirds* set, and the DJs play anything from Slim Galliard to Atari Teenage Riot.

Casino

Mühlenstrasse 26-30 (no phone/www.casino-bln.de). S3, S5, S7, S9, S75 Ostbahnhof/bus N29, N44.
Open 11pm-late Fri, Sat. **Admission** varies.
No credit cards. Map p89.
With the sale of the abandoned Prenzlauer Berg baked goods factory to developers, the clubbing double threat Casino and Cookies (*see p226*) was forcibly split up. The former is now co-habiting with OstGut (*see below*). House and techno are still writ large, and big names such as Dr Motte, Clé, Paul van Dyk and even a live set by Tricky continue to pack 'em in.

Deli

An der Schillingbrücke (no phone). S3, S5, S7, S9, S75 Ostbahnhof/bus N44. **Open** varies.
Admission varies. **No credit cards. Map** p89.
Located in an old warehouse on the Spree, Deli caters to a young, almost punk-like crowd into no-nonsense electronica. Warm yourself on one of the sofas grouped around a small furnace before letting dancing and alcohol do the rest.

Geburtstagsklub

Am Friedrichshain 33 (4285 1335/ www.geburtstagsklub.de). Tram 2, 3, 4, N54/ bus 200, 257. **Open** 11pm-late Mon, Fri, Sat.
Admission €5-€8. **No credit cards.**
Map p303 H2.
Most nights this newcomer offers the standard fare of house, breakbeats, electro, funk and disco. Mondays are a different story, when the club hosts the wandering Escobar reggae/ragga/dancehall set.

Matrix

Warschauer Strasse 18 (2949 1047/www.matrix-berlin.de). S3, S5, S6, S7, S9, S75, U1, U12 Warschauer Strasse/bus N29. **Open** midnight-late Fri, Sat. **Admission** varies. **No credit cards.**
Map p307 H4.
A real hole, under the U-Bahn arches and notable for its absurd computerised drinks system, stringent door policy and what is possibly the best sound system in Berlin. The atmosphere depends mostly on the DJ and the event – traditionally, the music at Matrix is mostly house, techno and wet&hard, but nu metal, ragga and even mainstream events have been added.

Non-Tox

Mühlenstrasse 12, Friedrichshain (2966 7206). S3, S5, S6, S7, S9, S75, U1, U12 Warschauer Strasse/bus N29. **Open** varies. **Admission** varies.
No credit cards. Map p307 H4.
Grungy club in the cellar of an abandoned commercial building on Mühlenstrasse, Friedrichshain's new clubbing mile. Non-Tox's diverse musical programme encompasses everything from hardcore techno to punk. Not suitable for headbangers, as you might knock your noggin on the pipes hanging from the ceiling.

OstGut

Mühlenstrasse 26-30, access from Rummelsburger Platz (no phone/www.ostgut.de). S3, S5, S7, S9, S75 Ostbahnhof/bus N29, N44. **Open** 11pm-late Thur, Fri; midnight-late Fri, Sat. **Admission** €6 Thur; €6-€8 Fri; €10 Sat. **No credit cards. Map** p307 H4.
Warehouse-type venue hosting occasional big events with internationally renowned DJs such as Westbam or George Morel – pulsating and not too pretentious. The vibe is more commercial than relaxed and friendly, however, but OstGut is worth a visit if you can fight your way through the crowds and survive the stifling atmosphere. In case you prefer a more experimental sound, check the Panorama Bar upstairs. *See also p212.*

Arts & Entertainment

Kurvenstar. *See p227.*

Kreuzberg

For an overview of the café, pub and bar scene in Kreuzberg, *see p150*. For bars that also have club nights, *see p151* **Konrad Tönz** and *p152* **Schnabelbar**.

Lola

Schöneberger Strasse 2 (no phone). S1, S2, S26 Anhalter Bahnhof/bus N29. **Open** varies (usually 11pm-late Fri, Sat). **Admission** €8-15. **No credit cards. Map** p306 F4.

Forget the unimaginative Dietrich-inspired name that has been abused for everything from the German Film Award to overpriced cocktails – Lola is the only viable nightlife option in the environs of Potsdamer Platz. Hidden behind a cast-iron door in the bowels of an otherwise abandoned commercial building, the red-lit club evokes happy memories of early 1990s eastern clubs, where sparse, seemingly improvised yet effective decor didn't overshadow the music. At Lola, the music is also given top priority, with floating party collectives, such as the ever popular King's Club, providing a wealth of warm, soulful and irresistible electronic grooves.

Mandingo

Mehringdamm 107 (6950 6800). U6, U7 Mehringdamm/bus N4, N19. **Open** 10pm-late Fri, Sat. **Admission** varies. **No credit cards. Map** p306 F5.

Mandingo is a friendly and unpretentious Kreuzberg meeting place for Berlin's African community and other lovers of zouk, highlife, rai, reggae, ragga, funk, R&B and hip hop – the full spectrum of African, Afro-Caribbean and African-American musical styles.

Privat Club

Pücklerstrasse 34 (611 3302/www.privatclub-berlin.de). U1, U12 Görlitzer Bahnhof/bus N29, N44. **Open** 10pm-late Fri, Sat. **Admission** varies. **No credit cards. Map** p307 H4.

This long, low space in the basement of the Markthalle hosts a variety of events, from ambient performances and occasional live acts to retro parties and dance music of all stripes. Occasionally worth a look, though it's hard to predict what you'll find at Privat Club.

SO36

Oranienstrasse 190 (6140 1306/www.so36.de). U1, U8, U12 Kottbusser Tor/bus N8, N29. **Open** 9pm-late daily. **Admission** varies. **No credit cards. Map** p307 G4.

Predominantly a gay and lesbian venue, though Monday house and techno nights attract a mixed cross-section (though mostly male) less defined by sexuality than the desire to dance. The phoneline is open for enquiries between noon and 4pm. *See also p209.*

Schöneberg

For an overview of the café, pub and bar scene in Schöneberg, *see p153*. For bars that also have DJs/club nights, *see p153* **Caracas**, *p154* **Pinguin Club** and *p155* **Zoulou Bar**.

KitKatClub

Bessemerstrasse 2-14, Tempelhof (no phone/ www.kitkatclub.de). Bus 204. **Open** 9pm-late Mon, Thur-Sun. **Admission** varies. **No credit cards.**

You thought the days of true Berlin decadence were way in the past? Think again. Here it is, turn-of-the-century style – sex and drugs and uplifting, positive dance music. It's not in the least bit seedy, but no place for the narrow-minded, with half the crowd in fetish gear, the other half in no gear at all, and every kind of sexual activity taking place in full view. In its way Kit Kat is the most relaxing club night in Berlin. No one has anything to prove and everyone knows why they're there – and will almost certainly get it – but if you're not dressed up (or down) enough, you probably won't get in. Rigorous door policy.

90°

Dennewitzstrasse 37 (2300 5954/www.90grad.com). U1, U12 Kurfürstenstrasse/bus N5, N19. **Open** 10pm-late Wed; 11pm-late Fri, Sat. **Admission** varies Wed; €10 Fri, Sat. **Credit** AmEx, V. **Map** p306 E5.

Arts & Entertainment

A case of misleading labelling – same name, but precious little else to do with the overheated, oversexed early '90s haunt, where top-notch house and techno DJs as well as uproarious drag shows attracted straight and gay crowds in equal measure. Famous for being famous (and regular on 'Berlin's most embarrassing people' lists) Ariane Sommer recently was the club's 'publicist', so enough said.

Tiergarten

Adagio

Marlene-Dietrich-Platz 1 (2592 9550/www.adagio-nightlife.de). S1, S2, S25, S26, U2 Potsdamer Platz/bus N5, N19, N52. **Open** 7pm-2am Tue-Thur, Sun; 7pm-4am Fri, Sat (occasionally closed for private events). **Admission** €5-€10. **Credit** AmEx, V. **Map** p306 E4.

After the thoroughly odious Blu, this spinoff of a successful chi-chi Zurich disco is the second nightclub to open on Potsdamer Platz. Its 'medieval' decor with Renaissance frescos is jarringly at odds with the modern, Renzo Piano-designed Stella Musical Theatre whose basement Adagio occupies. Pricey drinks, abundant members-only areas and music policy encompassing classical music and classic rock cater to 40-something tourists and locals willing to shell out for a semblance of exclusivity. Dress code (no jeans or sports shoes).

Trompete

Lützowplatz 9 (2300 4794/www.trompete-berlin.de). U1, U2, U4, U12 Nollendorfplatz/bus N5, N19. **Open** 9pm-late Wed, Fri-Sun; 7pm-late Thur. **Admission** free; dance events €5. **Credit** AmEx, DC, MC, V. **Map** p305 D4.

Actor, song stylist and self-proclaimed Renaissance Man Ben Becker is the not-so-silent partner of Tresor (*see p227*) and Schwarzenraben impresario Dimitri Hegemann in this heavily publicised nightlife joint venture. Despite often intriguing DJ sets and live performances by credible acts such as the lounge parodists Fuzzy Love, this *souterrain* club usually attracts a crowd that unpleasantly parades its (imagined) wealth and generally comes on too strong.

Charlottenburg

For an overview of the café, pub and bar scene in Charlottenburg, *see p155.*

Abraxas

Kantstrasse 134 (312 9493). U7 Wilmersdorfer Strasse or S3, S5, S7, S9, S75 Savignyplatz/bus N49. **Open** 10pm-late Tue-Sun. **Admission** €3 Tue-Thur; €7 Fri, Sat. **Credit** V. **Map** p304 B4.

A dusky, relaxed disco where you don't have to dress up to get in and where academics, social workers, bank clerks and midwives populate the floor. Flirtation rules. Dance to funk, soul, latino and jazz – like techno never happened. Live events on Wednesdays.

Sleazy listening

After such prefab labels as Brazilectro, Nova Soul or Asian Lounge and more retro waves crashing than in *The Perfect Storm*, is there any musical terrain left to stripmine for a fresh clubgoing experience? You may have to cross the boundary of good taste to get there.

The so-called 'trash aesthetic' is a blanket term for anything you would have never owned up to in your late teens or early 20s, but now openly embrace under the guise of 'so bad it's good'. More polite forms of trash such as *Schlager* (German MOR) and easy listening have been flogged to death in clubland, making room for sleazier variants. Splatter filmmaker and author Jörg Buttgereit almost inadvertently let the trash ooze in when he spun bad disco records, chop socky, horror and porno soundtracks after screening his old Super 8 films at Kreuzberg's Privat Club three years ago. Since then, he has taken his collection of Super 8 flicks (edited down versions of '70s blockbusters, home movies screened on old, clattering projectors) and record collection (one gem being a 20-minute disco version of Ennio Morricone's theme from *Once Upon a Time in the West*) to various clubs around town, as well as establishing a monthly residency at Privat Club. Look out also for the Pop Labor club, opening in mid 2002 in Schöneberg, where Buttgereit will be a regular at the turntables.

Not only media-weaned and irony-drenched 30-somethings flock to trash club nights; younger punters are also curious. The Mudd Club (*see p227*), Konrad Tönz (*see p151*) and Z-Bar (Bergstrasse 2, Mitte; www.z-bar.de) are other places to wallow in the trash.

Other districts

Insel

Alt-Treptow 6, Treptow (5360 8020/www.insel-berlin.com/real_go.htm). S6, S8, S10 Plänterwald/bus N65. **Open** 7pm-late Wed; 10pm-late Fri, Sat. **Admission** free Wed; €5-€10 Fri, Sat. **No credit cards.**

Out of the way, but a brilliant place – like a miniature castle on a tiny Spree island, with several levels including a top-floor balcony. Once a Communist youth club (the 'Island of Youth'), these days it doubles as live venue and colourful club – lots of neon and ultra-violet, Goa and gabber, crusties and neo-hippies, techno and hip hop, punk and metal. Great in summer.

Cabaret

If you're longing to see real Berlin cabaret à la 1920s, you are, alas, 75 or so years too late. Several venues have invested big money into recreating the look of old Berlin cabaret, but it's mostly wishful thinking and the shows are tourist fluff. The exception is the Wintergarten. Expect the type of show known as *varieté*, with clowns, magicians, acrobats and the like. Table service in these places does not come cheap.

The other type of cabaret is more modern and less pretentious. At venues like Chamäleon Varieté, Bar Jeder Vernunft, Kalkscheune and Roter and Grüner Salon you can see anything from burlesque talkshows to poetic jesters. The latter venue in particular can't be shoehorned into one category. It's the performers who make the evening. A few to watch for: Teufelsberg Productions (clever drag cabaret), Popette Betancor (stand up comedy with fun musical numbers) and the anglophone entertainer Gayle Tufts ('denglish' stand-up comedy with pop).

But this is not what the Germans call *Kabarett*, which has a strong following in Berlin and little in common with *varieté*. *Kabarett* is political satire sprinkled with original songs, and happens at venues such as Kartoon or Distel (watch out for press listings). But if you don't speak perfect German and have a good understanding of local politics such shows will be above your head.

Traditional

Chez Nous

Marburger Strasse 14, Charlottenburg (213 1810) S3, S5, S7, S9, S75, U2, U9, U12 Zoologischer Garten. **Open** *Box office* 10am-1pm, 1.30-6.30pm Mon-Sat. *Showtimes* 8.30pm, 11pm daily. **Admission** €35. **No credit cards. Map** p305 D4.
Revue with classic drag queen numbers. Tons of glitter and feathers, and celeb lookalike lip-synching.

Friedrichstadtpalast

Friedrichstrasse 107, Mitte (2326 2474). S1, S2, S3, S5, S7, S9, S25, S26, S75, U6 Friedrichstrasse. **Open** 6pm-1am daily. *Box office* 10am-6pm Mon, Sun; 10am-7pm Tue-Sat. *Showtimes* 8pm Tue-Fri; 4pm, 8pm Sat; 4pm Sun. **Tickets** €13-€49 Tue-Fri; €17-€57 Sat, Sun. **No credit cards. Map** p316/p302 F3.
Big, Las Vegas-style musical revues at big prices. Mostly packed with coachloads of German tourists.

Kleine Nachtrevue

Kurfürstenstrasse 16, Schöneberg (2188950), U1, U2, U12, U15 Wittenbergplatz. **Open** 9pm-4am Mon-Sat. *Showtimes* 40-min shows throughout evening Mon-Fri; 10.30pm, 12.30am Sat. **Admission** from €15. **Credit** AmEx, DC, V. **Map** p305 D4.
Intimate club with the appeal of old Berlin.

Pomp, Duck and Circumstance

Gleisdreieck/Möckrenstrasse 26, Kreuzberg (2694 9200/www.pompduck.de). U1, U7, U12 Möckernbrücke. **Open** *Box office* 6pm-midnight Tue-Sat; 5-11pm Sun. *Showtimes* 8pm Mon-Sat; 7pm Sun. **Tickets** €100 Tue-Thur, Sun; €110 Fri, Sat. **Credit** MC. **Map** p306 F4.
This highly publicised *varieté* extravaganza in an old-fashioned tent supplements the show with a four-course meal. Main courses are – surprise – always something with duck. The performers work the audience constantly and are first-rate; the food is not. If you don't want to be the centre on attention take a seat at the back. Though it is very expensive, the venue is always packed.

Wintergarten Varieté

Potsdamer Strasse 96, Tiergarten (250 0880/hotline 2500 8888). U1, U12 Kurfürstenstrasse. **Open** *Box office* 10am-showtime daily. *Showtimes* 8pm Mon-Tue, Thur, Fri; 4pm, 8pm Wed; 6pm, 10pm Sat; 6pm Sun. **Tickets** €18-€43 Mon-Thur, Sun; €29-€53 Fri, Sat. **Credit** AmEx, MC, V. **Map** p306 E4.
A classy place, run by astute impresario Andre Heller. The shows are slick and professional, though sometimes of mixed quality – excellent acrobats and magicians, but often terrible clowns.

Modern

Bar Jeder Vernunft

Spiegelzelt, Schaperstrasse 24, Wilmersdorf (883 1582/www.bar-jeder-vernunft.de). U1, U9 Spichernstrasse. **Open** *Box office* noon-7pm daily. *Showtime* 8.30pm daily. **Tickets** €15-€30. **Credit** MC, V. **Map** p305 C5.
In this circus tent you can see some of Berlin's most celebrated entertainers. Friday and Saturday late-night shows are generally free and well attended.

Chamäleon Varieté

Hackesche Höfe, Rosenthaler Strasse 40-41, Mitte (282 7118/www.chamaeleonberlin.de). S3, S5, S7, S9, S75 Hackescher Markt. **Open** *Box office* noon-9pm Mon-Thur; noon-midnight Fri, Sat; 4-9pm Sun. *Showtimes* 8.30pmTue-Sat; 7pm Sun. **Tickets** €15-€27. **No credit cards. Map** p302 F3.
This beautiful old theatre with classy, comfortable table seating lies at the centre of what has become the tourist magnet of the Hackesche Höfe. As the area becomes increasingly commercialised there is the danger that the Chamäleon may become a sort of Wintergarten-Ost. Until then it still attracts a very diverse audience.

Kalkscheune

Johannisstrasse 2, Mitte (5900 4340/www.kalkscheune. de). S1, S2, S25, S26 Oranienburger Strasse or U6 Oranienburger Tor. **Open** *Box office* noon-6pm daily. *Showtimes* vary. **Tickets** varies. **No credit cards. Map** p316/p302 F3.
Not far from Friedrichstadtpalast, this listed building from the 1840s contains a cabaret, a lounge and party room. Very popular.

Arts & Entertainment

La Vie en Rose
Flughafen Tempelhof, Tempelhof (6951 3000/ www.lavieenrose-berlin.de). U6 Platz der Luftbrücke. **Open** *Box office* 10am-9pm daily. *Showtimes* 9pm Wed-Sun. **Admission** €18-€28. **Credit** AmEx, DC, V.
This revue theatre and restaurant/piano bar is situated to the left of Tempelhof Airport's main entrance. Glitter, dancing girls, soft porn, pricey drinks, German tourists and maximum cheese.

Alternative

Café Theater Schalotte
Behaimstrasse 22, Charlottenburg (341 1485). U7 Richard-Wagner-Platz. **Open** *Box office* varies. *Showtimes* 8pm variabledays. **Tickets** €10-€15. **No credit cards**. **Map** p300 B3.
A friendly, comfy café with a nice-sized theatre where a well-chosen assortment of acts can be seen.

Roter Salon/Grüner Salon
Volksbühne, Rosa-Luxemburg-Platz, Mitte (247 6772/247 7694/2406 5662). U2 Rosa-Luxemburg-Platz. **Open** varies. *Showtimes* variable. **Tickets** €5-€6. **No credit cards**. **Map** p316/p303 G3.
Sometimes the atmosphere in these two separate paces really does take you back to the secret cabarets of the 1920s – you can get the feeling that you are doing something deliciously illegal. Expect anything from drag talk shows to tango parties.

Scheinbar
Monumentenstrasse 9, Schöneberg (784 5539). U7 Kleistpark. **Open** 8.30pm Tue-Sun. **Admission** €6. **No credit cards**. **Map** p306 E4.
This intimate, hip storefront club is exploding with fresh talent. The 'Open Stage' stand up performances are very popular and can be pretty wild. One of the most experimental and fun-loving cabarets in town.

Late eating

Most restaurants in Berlin will feed you up to midnight and many *Imbisse* stay open much later. *See also chapter* **Restaurants**.

Mitte

See also p127 **Astor** *and p141* **XII Apostoli**.

Bagels & Bialys
Rosenthaler Strasse 46-8 (283 6546). U8 Weinmeisterstrasse or S3, S5, S7, S9, S75 Hackescher Markt/bus N5, N6, N8, N52, N58, N65. **Open** 24hrs daily. **Main courses** €3-€6. **No credit cards**. **Map** p316/p302 F3.
Sandwiches, kebabs, bagels – a selection of snacks from various cultures, all of it good and fresh.

City Imbiss
Oranienburger Strasse/corner Linienstrasse (no phone). U6 Oranienburger Tor/bus N6, N84. **Open** 10am-5am daily. **Main courses** €3-€5. **No credit cards**. **Map** p316/p302 F3.

The usual range of German snacks – *Currywurst, Bouletten, Kartoffelsalat* – available deeper into the night than at most places around here.

Gambrinus
Linienstrasse 133 (282 6043). U6 Oranienburger Tor/ bus N6. **Open** noon-4am Mon-Sat; 3pm-4am Sun. **Main courses** €6-€16. **No credit cards**. **Map** p303 G3.
Traditional Berlin local restaurant serving variations on the meat, potato and cabbage theme.

Meilenstein
Oranienburger Strasse 7 (282 8995). S3, S5, S7, S9, S75 Hackescher Markt/bus N5, N6, N8, N52, N84. **Open** 11am-5am daily. **Main courses** €3.50-€10. **No credit cards**. **Map** p316/p302 F3.
After 1am, the full menu is no longer available, but the friendly waiting staff will find something warm and nourishing (usually a soup or stew) to satiate any late-night hunger.

Prenzlauer Berg & Friedrichshain

See also p130 **Safran** *and p141* **XII Apostoli**.

Traube
Danziger Strasse 24, Prenzlauer Berg (441 7447). U2 Eberswalder Strasse/bus N52. **Open** 9am-5am daily. **Main courses** €3-€8. **No credit cards**. **Map** p303 G2.
Excellent Turkish *Imbiss* off Kollwitzplatz; salads and veggie snacks as well as kebabs and chicken.

Kreuzberg & Schöneberg

See p133 **Fish & Chips**, *p136* **Habibi** *and p133* **Kulinarische Delikatessen**.

Charlottenburg & Wilmersdorf

See also p139 **Fleischerei Bachhuber's bei Witty's**, *p139* **Jimmy's Diner** *and p141* **XII Apostoli**.

El Burriquito
Wielandstrasse 6 (312 9929). S3, S5, S7, S9, S75 Savignyplatz/bus N49. **Open** 7pm-5am daily. **Main courses** €10-€14. **No credit cards**. **Map** p305 C4.
Lively Spanish bar/restaurant where you can stuff yourself with tapas at a ridiculous hour in the morning, or perch at the bar and give yourself some serious hangover material. Live music daily.

Schwarzes Café
Kantstrasse 148, Charlottenburg (313 8038). S3, S5, S7, S9, S75 Savignyplatz or S3, S5, S7, S9, S75, U2, U9, U12 Zoologischer Garten. **Open** 24hrs daily (closed 3-10am Tue). **Main courses** €6-€9. **No credit cards**. **Map** p305 C4.
Young and friendly if occasionally overstretched service. Mixed clientèle. Good coffee and cheesecake is available round the clock.

Arts & Entertainment

Performing Arts

Despite continuing funding crises, Berlin still offers
theatre, classical music, opera and dance of world calibre.

Music: Classical & Opera

If music be the food of love, music lovers
can gorge themselves in this city. There are
no fewer than seven orchestras, and three
fully fledged opera houses, plus a handful of
independent companies – a legacy not only of
the city's long artistic heritage, but also of its
Cold War division. But the duplication means
financial and creative resources are sometimes
stretched, and can result in repetitive seasons.

For now, government subsidies for the
major classical venues and opera houses are
secure; politicians regularly back down on belt-
tightening moves in the face of prima donna-
like threats from temperamental artists. How
long the nearly bankrupt city can afford to
maintain its rich cultural budget remains to
be seen, though powerful voices argue that
maintaining Berlin's unparalleled cultural
offerings is key to the city's economic future.

Fresh blood at the heads of the best-known
Berlin orchestras is bringing new innovation
to once dusty repertoires (*see p236* **In with
the new**). The same is true of the opera scene,
though it's had a rough couple of years, with
more than the usual number of dramatic temper
tantrums, and continued tension over the long-
term survival of three separate houses, more
than many larger cities support.

The west Berlin-based **Deutsche Oper**, still
smarting from an ugly musicians' strike that left
the house dark for weeks in 1999, was shaken
by the sudden death of its long-time intendant
Götz Friedrich in December 2000, months before
his planned retirement. Friedrich's successor,
Udo Zimmermann, has a reputation for being
an artistic maverick, and traditionalist musical
director Christian Thielemann threatened to
exercise an 'artistic differences' escape clause
in his contract. The two eventually patched
things up, but the house's 40th anniversary
season got off to a shaky start.

Meanwhile, the stately **Staatsoper Unter
den Linden** has suffered some sour notes
of its own, including a spat between musical
director Daniel Barenboim and politicians
over a plan – since dropped – to merge the

chronically underfunded house with the
Deutsche Oper. Barenboim threatened to
quit, and managed to squeeze more money
for the opera's highly regarded orchestra,
the **Berliner Staatskapelle**, founded in 1570
by royal order. Of course, now the Deutsche
Oper is pitching a fit of its own over the
preferential treatment. And so it goes on…

With Thielemann and Barenboim, Berlin
has Germany's two best Wagner directors,
both with Bayreuth credentials, and is the
only city with two complete Ring cycles; during
the Staatsoper's Wagner festival in March
and April 2002, all ten of the ultimate Teutonic
master's major operas were staged.

Even the city's 'third' opera company, the
Komische Oper, is getting a head conductor
who has made a reputation doing Wagner.
The young Russian Kyrill Petrenko is set
to take over for the 2002-03 season.

For more avant-garde operatic fare, don't
neglect the little **Neuköllner Oper**, which
puts on witty and imaginative productions
in its unassuming, cave-like hall; the **Neue
Opernbühne**, which works magic with
small ensembles and no state funding; or
the **Zeitgenössische Oper** (Contemporary
Opera), which has no house of its own, though
its ambitious young artistic director Andreas
Rochholl has unveiled plans for one.

FESTIVALS

Music festivals pepper Berlin's calendar.
**MaerzMusik – Festival für aktuelle
Musik** (*see p188*) takes place annually over
one to two weeks in March at various venues,
and showcases trends in contemporary music.
The biennial **Zeitfenster – Biennale für
alte Musik** (*see p184*) at the Konzerthaus
on Gendarmenmarkt focuses on 17th-century
baroque music for one week in April (2002,
2004). Major-name orchestras and soloists often
open the **Classic Open Air** concert series (*see
p185*) on Gendarmenmarkt over several days
in early July. Youth orchestras from across
Europe take part in the **Young Euro Classic**
festival (*see p186*) over a couple of weeks
in August. From September to November
Berliner Festwochen (*see p187*) includes a
large number of classical music performances
at various venues.

TICKETS

Getting seats at the **Philharmonie** (*see p238*) is notoriously difficult, especially for big-name stars or when the Berlin Phil itself is in residence; tickets for concerts by visiting performers can be easier to come by. If you can plan at least eight weeks ahead, you can order tickets by post or online with a credit card, but not by phone. Likewise, if you are coming to town for the annual Berliner Festwochen festival (*see p187*), which brings some of the world's best performers to town, it's best to book well in advance (www.berlin-philharmonic.com).

Otherwise it's worth scanning the listings in daily papers or one of the two local arts-and-entertainment magazines *tip* and *Zitty*, and phoning venues to see what's available.

If all else fails, try positioning yourself outside the venue with a sign reading '*Suche eine Karte*' ('seeking a ticket'), or chatting up arriving concert-goers ('*Haben Sie vielleicht eine Karte übrig?*' means 'Got a spare ticket?'). You may also see people with extras for sale ('*Karte(n) zu verkaufen*'), but beware of ticket sharks.

Some of the former East Berlin venues – especially the Konzerthaus and the Komische Oper – are still more affordable than their western counterparts, but the days of socialist subsidies and dirt-cheap tickets are long gone. Standing-room at the top of the Konzerthaus actually gives a decent view, but before buying cheap seats for the Staatsoper ask how much of the stage you can see.

At the Komische Oper, all unsold tickets for that evening's performance are available from the box office half-price after 11am. You can see an opera for the price of a cinema seat, a commendably wise financial policy courtesy of the house's aptly named intendant, Albert Kost.

Most venues offer sizeable student discounts, and students can save even more by queuing 30 minutes before performance time at the Staatsoper, when leftover balcony seats are sold for €10.

In with the new

Berlin's batons have been changing hands at an unprecedented pace of late, with most of the city's orchestras and operas under new artistic direction. The shake-ups, while sometimes marring quality in the short term, have opened the way for a much-needed era of experimentation in a city whose classical offerings, though vast, have long been skewed toward the safely traditional.

The grande dame of the city's orchestras, the **Berlin Philharmonic**, is without question one of the world's finest, but its restive musicians have chafed under a stale, mostly 19th-century repertoire. That looks set to change, as the self-governing 'free orchestral republic' has chosen innovative British conductor **Sir Simon Rattle** to take to the podium in autumn 2002, promising to bring more adventurous music to the programme and attract a younger audience.

It took the Liverpudlian some time to win the hearts of the notoriously independent-minded Berlin Phil members. It's said that the first time he conducted the BPO, in November 1987, the players got bolshie and garrulous during rehearsal. Rattle's response: 'Ladies and gentlemen, I've always known about the legendary sound this orchestra makes, but this is not the kind of sound I had in mind.'

Rattle had better luck during his later visits as guest conductor, and recently led the orchestra to two UK Gramophone Awards and a US Grammy for an outstanding live recording of Mahler's 10th Symphony. Not afraid of controversy, he refused to sign a contract until the city government coughed up more money for the musicians' salaries, which had been lower than elsewhere in Germany, and agreed to make the BPO an independent foundation in charge of its own finances. He's even promised to learn German, foreseeing a long stint in Berlin.

A similarly fresh wind is ruffling the scores at the **Deutsches Symphonie-Orchester**, which has gained a reputation as the best place in town to hear avant-garde compositions. The flamboyant **Kent Nagano** in his first two seasons as musical director challenged audiences and pleased critics by spicing the DSO's solid romantic fare with 20th-century works. But the orchestra's artistic future remains uncertain. At press time, Nagano was threatening to leave, refusing to work under an intendant and demanding more independent control of the DSO, which had been grouped for management purposes with several other orchestras and choruses in an attempt to

Arts & Entertainment

If you're under 27 and plan to attend several events, it's worth investing in the **ClassicCard**, which costs €25 for the season and gives you the right to the best available tickets on the night of a performance for between €5 and €10. So far it works at the Berlin Phil, the Deutsche Oper and the Konzerthaus, but other venues may join the scheme too. You can buy the card at the box offices of any of the three houses, or order online at www.staatsoper-berlin.org.

TICKET AGENCIES

Tickets are sold at concert hall box offices or through ticket agencies, called *Theaterkassen*. At box offices, seats are generally sold up to one hour before the performance. You can also make a reservation by phone, except, as noted above, for concerts of the Berlin Phil. *Theaterkassen* provide the easiest means of buying a ticket, but you must be prepared to pay for the convenience as commissions can run as high as 17 per cent. Below are details of some of the major *Theaterkassen* in central Berlin. For details of the 50 or so other agencies

around the city, look in the *Gelbe Seiten* (*Yellow Pages*) under *Theaterkassen*. Beware that many places may not accept credit cards.

Hekticket

Hardenbergstrasse 29D, Charlottenburg (230 9930/www.berlinonline.de/kultur/hekticket). S3, S5, S7, S9, S75, U2, U9, U12 Zoologischer Garten. **Open** 10am-8pm Mon-Fri; 3-7pm Sun. **No credit cards**. **Map** p305 C4.
Hekticket offers discounts of up to 50% on theatre and concert tickets, so it should be your first choice if using a ticket agency. For a small commission, its staff will sell you tickets for the same evening's performance. Tickets for Sunday matinées are available on Saturday. You can check ticket availability online, though not everything is listed. The branch below is open noon-8pm Mon-Sat.
Branch: Karl-Liebknecht-Strasse 12, Mitte (2431 2431).

Kant-Kasse

Krumme Strasse 55, Charlottenburg (313 4554/booking 834 4073/www.telecard.de). U7 Wilmersdorfer Strasse. **Open** 10am-6.30pm Mon-Fri; 10am-2pm Sat. **No credit cards**. **Map** p304 B4.

save money. He might yet get his way: he pulled a similar stunt in late 1999, demanding more city funding, and won.

Groundbreaking 20th-century composers, from Hindemith to Prokofiev and Schönberg to Penderecki, have conducted their own work with the **Rundfunk-Sinfonieorchester Berlin**. The orchestra, founded in 1923 to provide programming for the new medium of radio, looks set to continue its tradition of drawing attention to contemporary works under the competent hand of musical director **Marek Janowski**, who debuts in the 2002-03 season.

Not to be outdone, the highly regarded **MaerzMusik – Festival für aktuelle Musik** (*see p188*; formerly the Musik-Biennale Berlin) is also under new leadership, which is determined to put the city on the map as Germany's capital of contemporary music.

Innovation notwithstanding, fans of the old masters are still well served in town by the likes of the solid **Berliner Sinfonie-Orchester**, which plays at the splendid Konzerthaus, under its ambitious new conductor **Eliahu Inbal**. The feisty group – founded after the building of the Wall as the East's answer to the Philharmonic – has a loyal following of its own, but one that prefers more familiar works.

The mighty **Berlin Phil**.

The Deutsche Oper.

Major venues

Deutsche Oper

*Bismarckstrasse 35, Charlottenburg (343 8401/
freephone 0800 248 9842/www.deutsche-
oper.berlin.de). U2 Deutsche Oper.* **Open** *Box office*
11am-7pm Mon-Fri; 10am-2pm Sat. **Tickets**
€1-€110. **Credit** AmEx, DC, V. **Map** p304 B4.
With roots dating back to 1912, the Deutsche Oper
built its present boxy hall (nicknamed 'Sing-Sing' by
the ever-irreverent Berliners) in 1961, just in time to
carry the operatic torch for West Berlin during the
Wall years. It has lost out in profile to the more
elegant and centrally located Staatsoper since reunification, but still has a reputation for blockbuster
productions of the great 19th-century operas. New
intendant Udo Zimmermann is promising to make
room on the programme for more contemporary
works – a welcome development, though it's
questionable whether such pieces will fill the 1,900-
seat hall. Unsold tickets are available at a discount
half an hour before performances.

Komische Oper

*Behrenstrasse 55-7, Mitte (202 600/tickets 4799
7400/www.komische-oper-berlin.de). S1, S2, S25,
S26 Unter den Linden or U6 Französische Strasse.*
Open *Box office* 11am-7pm Mon-Sat; 1pm-1hr before
performance Sun. **Tickets** €8-€87. **Credit** AmEx,
DC, MC, V. **Map** p316/p302 F3.
Despite its name, the Komische Oper puts on a
broader range than just comic works, and, after its
founding in 1947, made its name by breaking with
the old operatic tradition of 'costumed concerts' –
singers standing around on stage – instead putting
an emphasis on 'opera as theatre', with real acting
skill demanded of its young ensemble. Outgoing
artistic director Harry Kupfer strove for intelligent
opera that speaks to the public – one reason why the
Komische sings all of its productions in German.
With both Kupfer and dynamic musical director

Yakov Kreizberg leaving, the future is somewhat up
in the air for this *'klein aber fein'* ('small but fine')
house, but it should be in good musical hands with
the arriving Kyrill Petrenko. Telephone bookings
can be made 9am-8pm Mon-Sat and 2-8pm Sun.
Discounts available for tickets sold immediately
before performances.

Konzerthaus

*Gendarmenmarkt 2, Mitte (2030 92101/
www.konzerthaus.de). U6 Französische Strasse.*
Open *Box office* noon-7pm Mon-Sat; noon-4pm Sun.
Tickets €7-€99; some half-price concessions.
Credit AmEx, MC, V. **Map** p316/p306 F4.
Formerly the Schauspielhaus am Gendarmenmarkt,
this 1821 architectural gem by Schinkel (*see p12* **Ich
bin Berliner: KF Schinkel**) was all but destroyed
in the war. Lovingly restored, it was reopened in 1984
under the confusing name 'Schauspielhaus', imply-
ing a theatre for plays, not concerts (which it
originally was). There are no longer plays to be seen
here, but there are two main spaces for concerts, the
Grosser Konzertsaal for orchestras, and the Kleiner
Saal for chamber music. Organ recitals in the large
concert hall are a treat, played on the massive
Jehmlich organ at the back of the stage. The Berliner
Sinfonie-Orchester is based here, and is involved in
some of the most imaginative programming in
Berlin; a healthy mixture of the classic, the new and
the rediscovered. There are also occasional informal
concerts in the cosy little Musik Club in the depths
of the building. The Deutsches Sinfonie-Orchester,
one of the finest in the land, also often plays here, and
is particularly noteworthy for its performances of
contemporary music (*see p236* **In with the new**).

Philharmonie

*Herbert-von-Karajan Strasse 1, Tiergarten (2548
8126/www.berlin-philharmonic.com). S1, S2, S25,
S26, U2 Potsdamer Platz.* **Open** *Box office* 3-6pm
Mon-Fri; 11am-2pm Sat, Sun. **Tickets** €7-€109.
Credit AmEx, MC, V. **Map** p306 E4.

Berlin's most famous concert hall, home to the world-renowned Berlin Philharmonic Orchestra, is also its most architecturally daring; a marvellous, puckish piece of organic modernism. The hall, with a golden, reconstructionist vaulting roof, was designed by Hans Scharoun and opened in 1963. The sad news is that it's now dwarfed by new monstrosities at Potsdamer Platz. The Philharmonie's reputation for superb acoustics is accurate, but it depends very much on where you sit within the hall. Behind the orchestra the acoustics leave plenty to be desired, but in front (where it is much more expensive) the sound is heavenly. The structure also incorporates a smaller hall, the Kammermusiksaal, about which the same acoustical notes apply.

The unique **Berlin Philharmonic Orchestra** was founded in 1882 by 54 musicians keen to break away from the penurious Benjamin Bilse, in whose orchestra they played. Over the last 120 years it has been led by some of the world's greatest conductors, as well as composers like Peter Tchaikovsky, Edvard Grieg, Richard Strauss and Gustav Mahler. Its greatest fame came under the baton of the late Herbert von Karajan, who led the orchestra between 1955 and 1989, and, in 2002, it has come under the leadership of the prestigious Liverpudlian conductor Sir Simon Rattle (*see p236* **In with the** (*see p236*) new). The Berlin Phil gives about 100 performances in Berlin during its August to June season, with another 20 to 30 concerts around the world. Some tickets are available at a discount immediately before performances.

Staatsoper Unter den Linden

Unter den Linden 5-7, Mitte (203 540/tickets 2035 4555/www.staatsoper-berlin.org). U2 Hausvogteiplatz. **Open** *Box office* 10am-8pm Mon-Fri; 2-8pm Sat, Sun. **Tickets** €5-€120.
Credit AmEx, MC, V. **Map** p316/p305 F3.
The Staatsoper has a longer and grander history than the Deutsche Oper. It was founded as Prussia's Royal Court Opera for Frederick the Great in 1742, and designed along the lines of a Greek temple. Although the present building dates from 1955, the façade faithfully copies that of Knobelsdorff's original, twice destroyed in World War II. The elegant interior gives an immediate sense of the house's past glory, with huge chandeliers and elaborate wall paintings. Musical director Daniel Barenboim now divides his time between this house and the Chicago Symphony Orchestra. Chamber music is performed in the small, ornate Apollo Saal, housed within the main building. Half an hour before the performance, unsold tickets are available for €10.

The **Konzerthaus**. *See p238.*

Other venues

Many churches offer regular organ recitals. It's also worth enquiring if concerts are to be staged in any of the castles or museums in the area, especially in summer or at holiday time. Telephones are often erratically staffed, so check *tip* or *Zitty* for information.

Akademie der Künste

Hanseatenweg 10, Tiergarten (390 760/ www.adk.de). S3, S5, S7, S9, S75 Bellevue or U9 Hansaplatz. **Open** *Box office* 2-8pm Mon; 11am-8pm Tue-Sun, and 1hr before performances. **Tickets** €4-€2.50; free 1st Sun of mth. **No credit cards. Map** p301 D3.
The Academy of the Arts, founded in 1696, driven out of its home by the Nazis in 1937, and later split into competing legacies in East and West, is scheduled in 2002 to move back to a new building at its historic site on Pariser Platz, in the shadow of the Brandenburger Tor. The academy, whose members have been a Who's Who of Germany's artistic elite, from Goethe to Grass, offers everything from art exhibitions to literary readings, from films to music, specialising in performances of 20th-century compositions. Until the move, concerts are still held in a 1960 building, either in the large (507-seater) or the small (195-seater) hall, both of which have reasonable acoustics.

Ballhaus Naunynstrasse

Naunynstrasse 27, Kreuzberg (2588 6644/ www.kunstamtkreuzberg.de). U1, U8, U12 Kottbusser Tor. **Open** *Box office* 10am-6pm Mon-Fri. **Tickets** €6-€12. **No credit cards. Map** p307 G4.
Don't expect to hear anything ordinary at this Kreuzberg cultural centre. A varied assortment of western and oriental music is on the menu at Ballhaus Naunynstrasse, with drinks and snacks in the café out front. The long, rectangular hall, which seats 150, plays host to the excellent Berlin Chamber Opera, among others.

Berliner Dom

Lustgarten 1, Mitte (2026 9136/www.berliner-dom.de). S3, S5, S7, S9, S75 Hackescher Markt. **Open** *Box office* 10am-5.30pm Mon-Fri. **Tickets** €7-€25. **No credit cards. Map** p316/p302 F3.
Berlin's cathedral, having been restored from its war-damaged state, went up in flames a few years ago. It's been re-restored and now hosts some recommendable concerts, usually of the organ or choral variety. *See also p77*.

Meistersaal

Köthener Strasse 38, Kreuzberg (264 9530/ www.meistersaal.de). S1, S2, S25, S26, U2 Potsdamer Platz. **Open** *Box office* 11am-8pm Mon-Fri. **Tickets** €9-€18. **Credit** MC, V. **Map** p306 E4.
The 'Maestro Hall' plays host to solo instrumentalists and chamber groups that can't afford to book the Kammermusiksaal of the Philharmonie. But don't let that fool you. Music-making of the highest

rank occurs here in this warm and welcoming little Kreuzberg salon with superb acoustics. However, the restaurant down the hallway could use some new enthusiasm.

Musikhochschule Hanns Eisler

Charlottenstrasse 55, Gendarmenmarkt, Mitte (9029 6841). U2, U6 Stadtmitte. **Tickets** varies (usually free). **No credit cards. Map** p316/p306 F4.
Opposite the Konzerthaus, this musical academy was founded in East Germany in 1950 and named after the composer of its national anthem (which, famously and ironically, included the line 'Germany, united Fatherland'). It offers students the chance to study under some of the world-class stars of Berlin's major orchestras and operas. Rehearsals and master classes are often open to the public for free, and student performances, some of them top-notch, are held in the Konzerthaus. Some other events are held in the annexe at Wilhelmstrasse 53, Mitte.

Neuköllner Oper

Karl-Marx-Strasse 131-3, Neukölln (6889 0777). U7 Karl-Marx-Strasse. **Open** *Box office* 3-7pm Tue-Fri. **Tickets** €9-€21. **Credit** AmEx, DC, MC, V. **Map** p307 H6.
There's no grand opera here, but a constantly changing programme of chamber operas and music-theatre works much-loved by the Neuköllners who come here to see lighter, bubblier (and much less expensive) works than in Berlin's big three opera houses. This is an informal alternative to the champagne-and-chandeliers atmosphere of the Deutsche, Komische or Staatsoper. Current artistic director Peter Lund is one of Berlin's most promising young theatre directors. Pity about the acoustics.

Staatsbibliothek – Otto-Braun Saal

Potsdamer Strasse 33, Tiergarten (2660). S1, S2, U2 Potsdamer Platz. **Open** *Box office* tickets sold by the performers. **Tickets** varies. **Map** p306 E4.
The Staatsbibliothek is everything to anyone looking for a bit of culture: exhibitions, historical archives and music are all on the programme. Smaller ensembles provide the lion's share of music in this chamber of the state library.

St Matthäus Kirche am Kulturforum

Matthäikirchplatz, Tiergarten (261 3676). S1, S2, S25, S26, U2 Potsdamer Platz. **Open** *Box office* noon-6pm Tue-Sun. **Tickets** varies. **No credit cards. Map** p306 E4.
Because it's next to the Philharmonie, locals have nicknamed this classical-style house of worship the 'Polka Church'. Check listings to see who's playing what, as it could be anything from a free organ recital to a heavenly chorus of Russian Orthodox monks. Exquisite acoustics.

Universität der Künste

Hardenbergstrasse 33, Tiergarten (3185 2374). U2 Ernst-Reuter-Platz. **Open** *Box office* 3-6.30pm Tue-Fri; 11am-2pm Sat. **Tickets** €15-€30; free for student concerts. **No credit cards. Map** p305 C4.

Formerly the Hochschule der Künste, it recently took the more internationally recognisable name University of the Arts. Berlin's wannabe musical luminaries study in the adjacent building. A grotesquely ugly but thoroughly functional hall plays host to both student soloists and orchestras, as well as lesser-known, underfunded professional groups. There's a great deal of variety here, and the fact that it doesn't attract the best-known artists is certainly no reason to avoid it.

Theatre

Berlin is still a major centre of the dramatic arts, but if you come looking for signs of its theatrical golden age, you will probably be disappointed. You may fancy you see the spirit of Max Reinhard watching you in the Deutsches Theater or the shade of Bertolt Brecht as you gaze at the Brecht Monument in front of the Berliner Ensemble, but times have changed.

The legacy of these theatre revolutionaries is hard to assess. The wrong way would be to attempt to compare today's theatre scene with that of the Weimar period. The city was divided for 40 years and both sides, anxious to establish their legitimacy to the rest of the world – built an outstanding cultural life on the back of hefty subsidies. After reunification, subsidies that had once gone into the coffers of drama companies and theatres were diverted for other purposes, and many theatres closed down as a result. The remaining venues and companies are now permanently engaged in a battle for publicity and the little public money that remains.

Great performances *can* still be seen at the Deutsches Theater, Maxim Gorki Theater, Volksbühne, Berliner Ensemble and Schaubühne. All feature first-rank actors, though not every production is worth seeing. The fact that no undeniably great director is currently working full-time in Berlin might go some way to explaining why the current theatrical scene is not more dynamic. There are, though, some positive signs: Frank Castorf's unique Volksbühne, for instance, or the new Schaubühne crew, which is trying to reconcile the '68 tradition with the modern theatre.

REINVENTING THEATRE

But change is afoot. The first positive move was to give the Schaubühne to a collective of four people in autumn 2000: Thomas Ostermeier (well known for his work at the late Baracke), the celebrated choreographer Sasha Waltz and playwrights Jochen Sandig and Jens Hillje. The theatre now shows almost exclusively new drama and dance.

The 2001 season opened with new intendants at the Deutsches Theater (Bernd Wilms) and the Maxim Gorki Theater (the Zurich import Volker Hesse). The good news is that both of them favour modern drama, even English-speaking works (Sarah Kane, Nicky Silver, Mark Ravenhill and Martin McDonagh's plays have all featured). Inspired by such work, German playwrights are now starting to produce contemporary works too. It's early days, but there are glimmers of hope.

FRINGE AND ENGLISH-LANGUAGE THEATRES

Fringe theatre, known to Germans as *Off-Theater*, has been growing in profile over the past few years, but remains dangerously reliant on ever-shrinking public funds.

English-language theatre is of a high standard in Berlin. Several local groups feature excellent mother-tongue actors, and top-notch visiting companies (particularly Irish and British) often perform in the city, especially at the Friends of Italian Opera.

Unless otherwise indicated, box offices open one hour before a performance and sell tickets for that performance only. Tickets are about €8-€15 for *Off-Theater* productions, and can go as high as €40 or more for a commercial show. An international student ID card should get you a discount at local and fringe theatres on the night, but don't expect such generosity from the commercial theatres.

For information on ticket agencies, *see p237*.

FESTIVALS

Theatertreffen Berlin (*see p184*) is the major annual theatre festival. A kind of pan-German theatrical trade congress, the 'Berlin Theatre Meeting' takes place during the first three weeks of May, featuring performances and theatrical talks, lectures and exhibitions. For information contact Berliner Festspiele (*see below*).

Berliner Festspiele

Schaperstrasse 24, Charlottenburg (2548 9130/ www.berlinerfestspiele.de/www.berlinale.de).
The office that oversees most of Berlin's major festivals is a reliable source of info on events it is sponsoring, in particular the Berliner Festwochen (*see p187*) each September to November, featuring some of the world's greatest theatre companies.

Civic theatres

Berliner Ensemble

Bertolt-Brecht-Platz 1, Mitte (box office 282 3160/2840 8155/www.berliner-ensemble.de). S1, S2, S3, S5, S7, S9, S25, S26, S75, U6 Friedrichstrasse. **Open** *Box office* 8am-6pm Mon-Sat; 11am-6pm Sun. **Credit** AmEx, MC, V. **Map** p316/p302 F3.

The House that Brecht built (and where *The Threepenny Opera* was first performed in 1928). Technically speaking the Berliner Ensemble as such doesn't exist any more. It's proper name is now Theater am Schiffbauerdamm. After last year's technical refurbishment the intendant Claus Peymann tried to re-establish the theatre's former pre-eminent position among the civic theatres. But, as yet, no one knows whether he can do it – including himself. There are rumours going round that he's thinking of going back to Vienna.

Deutsches Theater/Kammerspiele des Deutschen Theaters

Schumannstrasse 13A, Mitte (box office 2844 1225/info 2844 1222/www.deutsches-theater. berlin.net). S1, S2, S3, S5, S7, S9, S25, S26, S75, U6 Friedrichstrasse. **Open** *Box office* 11am-6.30pm Mon-Sat; 3-6.30pm Sun. **Credit** AmEx, MC, V. **Map** p316/p302 E3.

New brooms have been sweeping clean at the venerable Deutsches Theater, and a crowd of young directors are setting about reinventing the place. Four premières in the first week of the season proved that the DT remains one of the most reliable companies in Berlin. New productions in 2002 include a German-language version of the big London hit *Stones in his Pockets*.

Hebbel Theater

Stesemannstrasse 29, Kreuzberg (2590 0427/ www.hebbel-theater.de). U1, U6, U12 Hallesches Tor. **Open** *Box office* 4-7pm daily. **Credit** AmEx, MC, V. **Map** p306 F5.

Performances by great local and international rep companies and a varied programme make the Hebbel a haven of theatrical quality. Occasional performances in English (and other languages) further enhance this theatre's popularity, to say nothing of the annual feast of dance, Tanz im August (*see p244*).

Maxim Gorki Theater & Studiobühne

Am Festungsgraben 2, Mitte (box office 2022 1115/ info 2022 1129/www.gorki.de). S1, S2, S3, S5, S7, S9, S25, S26, S75, U6 Friedrichstrasse. **Open** *Box office* noon-6.30pm Mon-Sat; 4-6pm Sun. **No credit cards. Map** p316/p302 F3.

The Gorki – under the new intendant Volker Hesse from Zurich – is going back to its roots, putting on pieces by Russian authors such as Sorokin or Yerofeyev, but without neglecting good old Chekhov. Plenty of productions by contemporary authors too, and German speakers shouldn't miss *Neue Mitte* in the Studiobühne – very funny.

Renaissance Theater

Knesebeckstrasse 101, Charlottenburg (312 4202/www.renaissance-theater.de). U2 Ernst-Reuter-Platz. **Open** *Box office* 10.30am-7pm Mon-Fri; 10am-7pm Sat; 3-6pm Sun. **No credit cards. Map** p305 C4.

A reputable theatre that invariably plays a role in the annual Berliner Festwochen (*see p187*). Some of

Germany's most respected stage actors tread the boards at the Renaissance in a repertoire that emphasises modern drama.

Schaubühne am Lehniner Platz

Kurfürstendamm 153, Charlottenburg (890 023/ www.schaubuehne.de). S3, S5, S7, S9, S75 Charlottenburg or U7 Adenauerplatz. **Open** *Box office* 11am-8pm Mon-Sat; 3-6.30pm Sun. **Credit** AmEx, MC, V. **Map** p305 B5.

Since a new team took over the Schaubühne (*see p241*) it has became one of the places to be for the theatrical in-crowd. Mainly modern drama by young authors played by great stage actors.

Schlosspark Theater

Schlossstrasse 48, Schöneberg (793 5002/ www.schlosspark.de). S1, U9 Rathaus Steglitz. **Open** *Box office* 1-7pm Mon-Sat; 5-7pm Sun. **Credit** AmEx, MC, V.

A fairly standard but well-performed mix of classic, major modern dramas and comedies attracts a diverse audience at the Schlosspark Theater. There have been rumours, though, that the theatre might have to close.

Volksbühne/Prater

Volksbühne *Rosa-Luxemburg-Platz, Mitte (247 6772/7694/2406 5662/www.volksbuehne-berlin.de). U2 Rosa-Luxemburg-Platz.* **Open** *Box office* noon-6pm daily. **No credit cards. Map** p303 G2.

Prater *Kastanienallee 7-9, Prenzlauer Berg (as Volksbühne). U2 Eberswalder Strasse/tram 13, 20, 50, 53.* **Open** *see above.* **Map** p303 G2.

Hipsters and intellectuals mix with more conservative types at the hugely popular 'People's Stage'. The influential Frank Castorf is supreme at this theatre at which provocation and reinterpretation rule the day. There's another stage, the Prater in an old building (a so-called *Kulturhaus*) in Prenzlauer Berg, that shows extravagantly experimental stuff.

Commercial theatres

Theater am Kurfürstendamm

Kurfürstendamm 206-9, Charlottenburg (4799 7440/www.inter-tickets.com). U15 Uhlandstrasse. **Open** *Box office* 10am-8pm Mon-Sat; 3-8pm Sun. **Credit** AmEx, MC, V. **Map** p305 C4.

Coach-loads of provincial German tourists decamp to see their favourite television stars cavorting in light farce and Boulevard comedy.

Theater des Westens

Kantstrasse 12, Tiergarten (8842 08510/ www.theater-des-westens.de). S3, S5, S7, S9, S75, U2, U9, U12 Zoologischer Garten. **Open** *Box office* 11am-7pm Mon-Sat; 11am-2pm Sun. **Credit** AmEx, MC, V. **Map** p305 C4.

The last action of the former culture minister was to sell this theatre, so it's future is uncertain. The former Städtische Oper Berlin was once probably the best place to see musicals in Berlin.

The **Philharmonie**. See p238.

Off-Theater

Berlin once boasted 100 or so fringe (or *Off-Theater*) companies; only about two dozen exist today. The spaces they occupy are often rough and ready, but performances can be revelatory. Inevitably, quality does vary considerably, though prices will always be lowish and the audience unstuffy. Most theatres' answering machines will give details of what's on.

Friends of Italian Opera

Fidicinstrasse 40, Kreuzberg (box office 691 1211/ info 693 5692/www.thefriends.de). U6 Platz der Luftbrücke. **No credit cards. Map** 306 F5.
Mostly first-rate productions by local and visiting English-language groups and performers make this little courtyard theatre Berlin's premier address for the anglophone fringe. Booking advisable; tickets can only be obtained over the phone.

Sophiensæle

Sophienstrasse 18, Mitte (283 5266/ www.sophiensaele.de). S3, S5, S7, S9, S75 Hackescher Markt or U8 Weinmeisterstrasse. **No credit cards. Map** p316/p302 F3.
Located in an old artists' squat building, the former Festsaal, where weddings and other events took place 100 years ago, this is where Sasha Waltz's company (*see p245*) put on its first performances before fame came knocking. Now it's a place for exalted performances or modern plays of a high standard. You shouldn't miss the Hungarian troupe Mozgo Hasz. Watch out for press listings. Tickets can only be booked by phone.

STüKKE

Palisadenstrase 48, Friedrichshain (4202 8148/ stuekke@t-online.de). U5 Weberwiese/bus 340. **No credit cards. Map** p303 H3.
Ambitious *Off-Theater* in the new in-area-to-live Friedrichshain showing contemporary works from around the globe. Yet, at press time, subsidy worries meant that the company may have to fold.

Tacheles

Oranienburger Strasse 54-6, Mitte (2809 6123/ www.tacheles.de). U6 Oranienburger Tor. **No credit cards. Map** p316/p302 F3.
Berlin's neo-hippie squat El Dorado of the early '90s has become an alternative Disneyland for tourists trying to find some post-Wall underground romanticism. Nevertheless, many people still consider Tacheles to be a vibrant and alternative arts space. The theatre shows interesting and recommendable experimental productions, some of which are in English. Phone to book tickets. *See also p81.*

Theater am Halleschen Ufer

Hallesches Ufer 32, Kreuzberg (251 0655/0941/ www.thub.de). U1, U6, U12 Hallesches Tor or U1, U7, U12 Möckernbrücke. **Open** *Box office* 10am-6pm Mon-Fri. **Credit** V. **Map** p306 F5.
This small theatre hosts a variety of theatre groups and solo artists, some performing in English.

Theater unterm Dach

Danziger Strasse 101, Im Kulturhaus im Ernst-Thälmann-Park, Prenzlauer Berg (4240 1080). S4, S8 Greifswalder Strasse/tram 20. **No credit cards. Map** p303 G2.
This Prenzlauer Berg venue is the place to come to see interesting fringe theatre groups performing modern drama from all over Germany. The boss used to travel around the country in search of the best companies and performances to give them a chance in the capital. For some, this was the beginning of great careers. Phone bookings only.

Theater Zerbrochene Fenster

Fidicinstrasse 3, entrance Schwiebuser Strasse 16, Kreuzberg (694 2400/www.tzf-berlin.de). U6 Platz der Luftbrücke. **No credit cards. Map** p306 F6.
Another place where anglophone productions can be seen, the 'Broken Window Theatre' is in a converted factory building – hence the odd shape of the theatre area itself. Tickets can only be booked by phone (691 2932).

Arts & Entertainment

Vagantenbühne

Kantstrasse 12A, Charlottenburg (312 4529/ www.vaganten.de). S3, S5, S7, S9, S75, U2, U9, U12 Zoologischer Garten. **Open** *Box office* 10am-4pm Mon; 10am-8pm Tue-Fri; 2-8pm Sat. **No credit cards.** **Map** p305 C4.

Next door to the glitzy Theater des Westens, this is one of the few fringe theatres still to receive government subsidies. Though it has given up its experimental roots, performance standards are high.

Dance

In a city that thrives on offbeat culture, contemporary dance has taken centre stage. No other performing art has increased as much in quality as in popularity. Within the space of just a decade, Berlin has asserted itself as one of the world's leading centres for modern dance. There is hardly an international festival that doesn't feature a production from the German capital. Politicians now recognise this asset, and in the run-up to his election as mayor there were few speeches in which Klaus Wowereit didn't mention the importance of the Berlin dance scene. That scene is now hoping he'll put his money where his mouth is, because funding is a chronic problem that for years has restricted the creative room for manoeuvre of both independent groups and the ballet companies attached to the city's three opera houses.

Nevertheless, Berlin continues to attract a growing number of adventurous international choreographers, from New York to Hong Kong, inspired by the processes taking place in a city seeking to redefine itself on all levels. On a purely physical level, Berlin offers seemingly endless possibilities to stage productions in incongruous settings: in structures waiting to be torn down or revamped, or new buildings such as the Jüdisches Museum before they are opened to the public. And then there is the cross-fertilisation phenomenon. Choreographers frequently team up with leading lights in the new media, fine arts or music scenes, working with interpreters of everything from jazz to the sounds of club culture.

The influx of dancers in the independent scene has upped the competitive edge. That, in turn, has created more professional training opportunities. There are now a handful of good schools, such as Dock 11 in Prenzlauer Berg, though the city still lacks a state-funded institution such as the Folkwang School in Essen, which trained the likes of Pina Bausch. Nevertheless, standards have improved tremendously. Half the productions showcased at the biennial **Tanzplattform** held in German cities in rotation come from Berlin.

For information on current performances, check *tip* or *Zitty* or pick up a copy of *Tanz in Berlin*, a bi-monthly calendar of performances and dance-related events, available free at theatres, cafés and hotels.

Major venues & festivals

Berlin's home for the avant-garde, the 600-seat **Hebbel-Theater** in Kreuzberg (*see p242*), has been largely responsible for bringing modern dance to a wider Berlin audience. Under its long-time director Nele Hertling, the theatre has booked such international heavyweights as Mikhail Barishnikov's White Oak Dance Project, the Bathsheba Dance Company and Nederlands Dans Theater, as well as important German acts like Susanna Linke and Reinhild Hoffmann. Hertling is retiring in 2003, but it is unlikely her successor will depart from a highly successful strategy. In February the theatre hosts **Tanz im Winter**, a three-week festival highlighting current trends. The Hebbel is also one of the main venues for summer's three-week **Tanz im August** (information from Tanzwerkstatt on 2474 9758 or Hebbel-Theater on 2590 0427), which has evolved into Germany's leading annual festival, attracting experts from all over the world who seek out acts to show at home or to work together with their own troupes. Berlin's conceptual aesthetic and innovative environment mean these festivals can't be missed by anyone wishing to keep tabs on international trends.

Known to have one of Europe's best stages for contemporary dance, the **Theater am Halleschen Ufer** (*see p243*) is the home of Berlin's independent scene. Its support of the city's choreographers has been instrumental in their success. Regular features include premières by Berlin's leading companies and soloists. Audience discussions after matinée performances are a popular fixture. In March the **Solo Duo** festival here highlights new Berlin and global trends. The theatre is one of the main organisers of **Tanznacht Berlin**, a new biennial all-night event that aims to showcase the quality and spectrum of Berlin's contemporary dance scene. Held in December in various spaces at the **Akademie der Künste** (*see p240*), it presents up to 40 different acts from the afternoon to the early hours of the following morning.

In Transit is another new festival to watch out for. To be launched in 2002 by the **Haus der Kulturen der Welt** (*see p101*), it will commission a different, non-European curator every year to travel the world and book dance and performance artists to work with Berlin groups during a three-week period in early summer. The results of their co-operation will be on show to the public both while they work and as a final production presented in the evenings, to be followed by a club night featuring the artists as DJs and other performances.

While the focus at the experimental **Sophiensæle** in Mitte (*see p243*) is now more on theatre, dance still features in its own two-week **Tanztage** festival in January. It presents fresh local talent, often giving dancers from the ballet corps of the opera houses their first crack at choreography of their own.

The **Tanzwerkstatt** organisation is based at the **Podewil** cultural centre (*see p221*). It scouts out fresh, promising talent at international festivals and books young choreographers for Berlin events and Podewil's own stage. Workshops often run parallel to performances. It is worth looking out for productions by choreographers in Podewil's artist-in-residence programme.

Contemporary companies & choreographers

Jo Fabian/Department

Image wiz Fabian began his career as an actor and director in East Germany. Since founding what he calls his 'theatre of moving architecture', he has sought to break down the boundaries between drama, dance, music performance and installation. Fabian's prize-winning productions are packed with visionary power and make strong use of video and shadow-play. In recent years, he has been developing an encoded language of movement based on the rules of writing, which he calls the 'Alphasystem', whereby dancers 'write' with their movements.

Anna Huber

An internationally acclaimed solo choreographer and dancer who has only recently begun working with groups. Anna Huber's search for new forms of expression leads to collaboration with artists from different disciplines and lends her work a sense of clarity and openness. Her duo 'L'autre et moi' with Taiwanese choreographer Lin Yuan Shang has toured the world.

Xavier Le Roy/In Situ Production

Le Roy came late to dance, while finishing his studies in molecular biology at the University of Montpellier. Since moving to Berlin in 1992, he has been part of some groundbreaking work with interdisciplinary groups pooling the talents of composers, photographers and lighting designers. The 2002 season sees the première of his *Saint François d'Assise*, an opera by Olivier Messiaen in co-operation with US architect Daniel Libeskind.

Tanzcompagnie Rubato

A pre-unification stalwart, Rubato was founded in 1985 by Jutta Hell and Dieter Baumann. Their work is marked by precision, reduction and an interchange between abstraction and emotion. Most often appearing as a duo, they are also much-sought-after guest choreographers for troupes such as Modern Dance Turkey and China's Guangdong Modern Dance Company.

Sasha Waltz

Germany's leading proponent of postmodern dance and Berlin's star of the independent dance scene, Sasha Waltz was appointed co-director of the prestigious and previously drama-only Schaubühne at Lehniner Platz in 1999. Her first production there, *Körper*, was a sensational success. The focus of her work now lies in reversing the roles of the house's actors and the dancers in her 13-member company, so that the actors dance and the dancers narrate. Waltz's site-specific projects have taken audiences on to the roof of the Schaubühne and inside the shell of Libeskind's Jüdisches Museum before it opened.

Ballet

It could be argued that a city struggling to finance three opera houses doesn't also need to pay for the upkeep of three separate ballet companies – particularly since they rarely perform to full houses. But city government plans to merge the three corps into one 'Berlin Ballet' have faltered due to resistance from the opera houses themselves, who saw the move as an infringement on their autonomy.

The **Staatsoper Unter den Linden** (*see p235 and p239*; tickets €5-€120) has the largest corps, with 64 members. The 2002 season brings 'dancer of the century' Vladimir Malakhov to the house as new ballet director. His roots in the Russian tradition will guarantee the Staatsoper's profile as home of the romantic classics. Malakhov will also star in some of the productions he stages.

The corps at the **Deutsche Oper** (*see p238*; €15-€62) has been cut to 30 dancers, and, as a result, its productions are more pared down, and neoclassical in direction. Director Sylviane Bayard invites acclaimed choreographers like Angelin Preljocaj and Juri Vamos to stage their productions.

The **Komische Oper** (*see p238*; €16-€99) has seen a rapid turnover of ballet directors. Britain's Richard Wherlock couldn't stand Berlin's political tug-of-war for funds and broke off his contract in 2001. The house is now pinning its hopes on the experimental talents of Spain's Blanca Li. Her arrival marks the end of the house's 'dance-theatre' tradition, established by Tom Schilling in the three decades before his retirement in 1993.

Arts & Entertainment

Sport & Fitness

The spectating isn't spectacular – but in
Berlin participation is the name of the game.

Hertha BSC's junior supporters' club: all painted up and somewhere to go... *See p248.*

After a wild enthusiasm in the late 1990s for
all things athletic that cut across class and age
boundaries, the city is in the throes of a sports
hangover. Premier league football squad Hertha
BSC, along with ice hockey teams Capitals and
Eisbären, have been delivering middling to poor
performances. Drug scandals – the banning of
chemically enhanced athletes and a tabloid
feeding frenzy surrounding the cocaine habit
of a prominent football coach – and controversy
concerning media mogul Leo Kirch's monopoly
on football broadcasting rights have spoilt the
party and tarnished the image of sportsmanship.

While Berliners seem disillusioned with the
national pastime football and their local athletic
heroes, other spectator sports, such as boxing
and motor sports, continue to enjoy devoted
followings. Berliners also continue to flex their
own muscles for relaxation and fun, be it an
impromptu football match in the park or a
workout in one of the city's countless fitness
centres. Participation in many team sports
and athletic disciplines is organised through

associations or *Verbände*, but it is also possible
to join in simply by checking notices at sports
centres or hanging out at sport shops. For
athletic gear and sportswear stores, *see p173.*

Major stadiums & arenas

Olympiastadion

*Olympischer Platz 3, Charlottenburg (300 633). U2
Olympia-Stadion (Ost) or S5, S75 Olympiastadion.*
Completed in 1934 as the centrepiece for the 1936
Olympic Games, the stadium is considered to be the
epitome of the Nazi aesthetic. Albert Speer was part
of the team that designed the Marathon Gate, clock
tower and bell as a last resort to appease Hitler, who
was so displeased with the previous plans that he
threatened to cancel the Games. Today, the stadium
hosts Hertha BSC (*see p248*) football matches, the
German Cup Final and the ISTAF international athletics meeting, as well as mega rock concerts. Until
approximately 2004, the stadium is under reconstruction, temporarily reducing its seating capacity
from 76,000 to 55,000. The Olympiastadion will host
the football World Cup Final in 2006.

Max-Schmeling-Halle

Am Falkplatz, Prenzlauer Berg (443 045/ www.velodrom.de). U2 Eberswalder Strasse or S4, S8, U2 Schönhauser Allee.

Originally conceived as a boxing venue in honour of its namesake, the 11,000-capacity arena is home to Berlin's basketball hotshots ALBA (*see below*). It also hosts a variety of international sporting events and rock shows. The venue's functional design copped a major architectural award for sport and leisure facilities in 2001.

Velodrom

Paul-Heyse-Strasse 26, Prenzlauer Berg (administration 443 045/tickets 4430 4430/ www.velodrom.de). S4, S8 Landsberger Allee.

Opened in early 1997, this multifunctional sports and entertainment venue (its cycling track hand-made from Siberian spruce) was designed by renowned architect Dominique Perrault to host the Six Day cycling race. It is also a prime location for everything from equestrian competitions and super-cross events to major rock concerts.

Spectator sports

American football

Since 1999 Berlin has had its own team in the newly created American Football League in Europe: Berlin Thunder, winner of the NFL Europe World Bowl title in 2001. The season is played throughout the summer.

Berlin Thunder

Friedrich-Jahn-Sportpark, Cantianstrasse 24, Prenzlauer Berg (tickets 3006 4444/www.berlin-thunder.de). U2 Eberswalder Strasse. **Tickets** €8-€30. **Credit** (advance booking only) AmEx, V. **Map** p303 G1.

Athletics

ISTAF Athletics Meeting

Olympischer Platz 3, Charlottenburg (243 1990). U2 Olympia-Stadion (Ost) or S5 Olympiastadion. **Date** late Aug/early Sept (next 6 Sept 2002). **Tickets** €7.50-€40. **No credit cards.**

Instigated a year after the 1936 Olympics, this international one-day tournament is now the final event in athletics' Golden Four, featuring 250 athletes from 50 nations.

Basketball

Berlin team **ALBA** dominate the German league, having won the national championship five years in a row. Crucial to their success is ALBA's uniquely professional management, the club's 10,000-seat arena and, most of all, their former coach, Sarajevo-born Svetislav Pesic, who lifted the team out of obscurity. The only

trainer ever to lead the German national team to a European championship, Pesic was recently replaced by his less charismatic countryman Emir Mutapcic. Regular sell-out crowds in the Max-Schmeling-Halle, Germany's largest basketball arena, give the team enough financial support to invest in top foreign players to complement the homegrown talent. With other major German cities emulating this recipe for success, ALBA may soon face as stiff competition at home as they do in the Euroleague, where the team have yet to score big. The season runs from September to May.

ALBA Berlin

Am Falkplatz, Prenzlauer Berg (308 785 685/ www.albaberlin.de). U2 Eberswalder Strasse. **Tickets** *Euroleague* €6-€21.50. *Federal League* €11-€52. **Credit** AmEx, MC, V.

Football

After years in the wilderness, Berlin is firmly back on the football map. The city's flagship club, **Hertha BSC**, are now regular top six finishers in the Bundesliga and enjoy reasonable progress in Europe. The rise in fortunes of **FC Union** (*see p249* **Union keep the red flag flying**), the most popular team from the east of the city, contrasts nicely with the demise of the most successful club from the other side of the Wall, Dynamo, thrown out of the lower reaches of the league at the

Andreas Schmidt of **Hertha BSC**. *See p248.*

start of the 2001-02 season due to bankruptcy. **Tennis Borussia** have plummeted, while ethnic Turkish and Croatian clubs continue to embellish the local leagues.

Hertha BSC

Olympischer Platz 3, Charlottenburg (club 300 9280/tickets 01805 437842/www.herthabsc.de). U2 Olympia-Stadion (Ost) or S5, S75 Olympiastadion. **Tickets** €5-€25. **No credit cards** (except online bookings).

Berlin's main club are now firmly established as one of the top clubs in the country, always in the top half of the league table and making steady progress in Europe. Despite the fact that a portion of their fans in Block O are a highly unattractive bunch and that the golden boy they all worship, international midfield prodigy Sebastian Deisler, signed a secret contract with the hated enemy team, Bayern Munich, Hertha look here to stay for some years to come. Hand in hand with the fifth highest average gate in Germany, supporting Hertha are media giants UFA, keen to challenge regular title winners Bayern – making the Deisler decision all the more baffling.

Tennis Borussia

Mommsenstadion, Waldschulallee 34-42, Charlottenburg (306 9610/www.tebe.de). S5 Eichkamp. **Tickets** €4-€10. **No credit cards**. All the insurance company money and all the imported men couldn't put Tennis Borussia into the top ten – in fact, the club even dropped into the amateur fourth league in 2001.

1.FC Union

Stadion An der Alten Försterei 263, Köpenick (tickets 6566 8861/www.fc-union-berlin.de). S3 Köpenick. **Tickets** €7.50-€17.50. **No credit cards**.

Who would have thought that less than a decade after this proud east Berlin club nearly went out of business they would be playing in the German Cup final and winning an early round of the UEFA Cup? 'Iron Union' have upset all the books and vindicated their loyal support. The financial problems of the team's owners, media conglomerate Kinowelt, may, however, dash any further hopes. Stadium bar Abseitsfalle ('Offside Trap') is by the main entrance. *See p250* **Union keep the red flag flying**.

Horse racing

Galopprennbahn-Hoppegarten

Goetheallee 1, Dahlwitz-Hoppegarten (033 423 8930/tickets 033 389 323/www.galopprennbahn-hoppegarten.de). S5 Hoppegarten. **Tickets** €3.70. **Credit** AmEx, MC, V.

Thoroughbred races take place between April and October. The betting is run on similar lines to the English Tote. The Oleander restaurant under the main grandstand is a meeting point for horse owners, trainers and race enthusiasts. Check website for race meeting dates.

Berliner Trabrennverein e.V.

Treskowallee 129, Karlshorst (5001 7121/ www.berlintrab.de). S3 Karlshorst. **Admission** free.

This track and Mariendorf (*see below*) host trotting events, aka harness racing. This entails riders jogging around in modern-day chariots, a kind of *Ben Hur* for beginners. Meetings are held all year round on Fridays at 6pm.

Trabrennverein Mariendorf

Mariendorfer Damm 222/298, Mariendorf (222 298/www.berlintrab.de). U6 Alt-Mariendorf, then bus X76, 176, 179. **Tickets** €2.50 Wed; free Sun. **No credit cards**.

Race meetings take place on Sundays at 1.30pm and on Wednesdays at 6pm. The Derby Week in August has become a major international racing event.

Ice hockey

Since German ice hockey clubs set up a completely private national league and broke from the governing *Verband* in 1994, the sport has become big business. Berlin's perennial powers, the eastern **Eisbären** (a Dynamo descendant) and the western **Capitals** (formerly the Prussian Devils), first prospered, then faltered under the new system. Both teams have performed erratically. The season runs from September to April.

Berlin Capitals

Deutschlandhalle, Messedamm, Charlottenburg (885 6000/0180 523 7454/www.berlin-capitals.com). S5 Eichkamp. **Tickets** *Standing* €10.50. *Seated* €12.50-€30. **No credit cards**. **Map** p304 A4.

EHC Eisbären Berlin

Wellblechpalast, Steffenstrasse, Hohenschönhausen (971 8400/tickets 9718 4040/www.eisbaeren.de). S8, S10 Landsberger Allee, then tram 5, 15. **Tickets** €20-€32.50. **No credit cards**.

Motor sports

Eurospeedway Lausitz

Lausitzallee 1, Klettwitz (general enquiries 035754 31110/info & ticket hotline 01805 880288/ www.eurospeedway.de). Train RB14 Senftenberg, then shuttle bus (racing days only). **Tickets** €7.50-€257.50. **Credit** AmEx, DC, MC, V.

Located 130km (81 miles) south-east of Berlin, the Eurospeedway opened in late summer 2000 to roaring crowds and rounds of praise from drivers and racing experts alike. Since then, not all headlines have been so positive, but the €115-million Eurospeedway remains the largest (seating capacity 120,000) and most modern racing facility on the Continent. It has the potential to become the world's first speedway to host motor racing's big four: Champ Car, NASCAR, Formula One and the Motorcycle World Championships. The

Call Mulder and Scully? No need – it's just the extraordinary **Velodrom**. *See p247.*

Eurospeedway Lausitz is accessible via highway A13 (exit Klettwitz) or by train to Senftenberg or even by plane and helicopter for true speed freaks.

Tennis

The **Eurocard Ladies' German Open**, held each May, is the world's fifth largest international women's tennis championship. *See p184.*

LTTC Rot-Weiss

Gottfried-von-Cramm-Weg 47-55, Grunewald (tickets & information 8957 5520). S3, S7 Grunewald. **Open** 8am-5pm Mon-Thur; 8am-noon Fri. **Tickets** vary, call for details. **No credit cards.**
The German Open uses this club's clay courts. The acronym stands for Lawn Tennis Tournament Club.

Active sports/fitness

Verbände ('associations') are the umbrella organisations that help with co-ordination, facilities, financing and other logistical aspects of sports of all kinds.

Landessportbund Berlin (LSB)

Jesse-Owens-Allee 2, Charlottenburg (300 020/ www.berlin.de/sport). S5 Olympiastadion or U2 Olympia-Stadion (Ost). **Open** 9am-3pm Mon-Thur; 9am-2pm Fri.
The Berlin Regional Sports Association's central office co-ordinates other sport-specific offices and provides general information. The Landesausschuss Frauensport, the Regional Committee for Women's Sport, shares the same address.

Athletics

Berlin Marathon

Glockenturm 23, Charlottenburg (3012 8810/ www.berlin-marathon.com). **Entrance fee** €40-€60. **Credit** call for details. **Date** last Sun in Sept.

Upwards of 30,000 people participate on foot, on skates or in wheelchairs in this annual event, making it the world's third largest marathon. The course winds past many historic sights. There's also the Berlin Half-Marathon on the first or second Sunday in April, and the New Year Fun Run begins every 1 January at the Soviet War Memorial on Strasse des 17.Juni near the Brandenburg Gate. Check website for details. *See also p188.*

Badminton

Most tennis facilities (*see p256*) also have badminton courts.

Turngemeinde in Berlin 1848

Columbiadamm 111, Kreuzberg (6110 1020/ www.tib1848ev.de). U7 Südstern or U8 Boddinstrasse. **Open** 9am to 11pm daily. **Prices** *Badminton* €7.50-€12.50 per hr. *Tennis* €19-€25 per hr. *Sauna* €8.50 per day. **No credit cards. Map** p307 G6.
New courts near Tempelhof Airport. There are also two tennis courts with carpet velour surface.

Bowling

American Bowl

Märkische Allee 176, Marzahn-Hellersdorf (9209 2092/www.american-bowl.tv). S7 Marzahn. **Open** 10am-late Mon-Sat; 9am-late Sun. **Prices** vary, call for details. **No credit cards.**
Modern bowling facility in an eastern outlying district. American-style sports bar, brunch bowling on Sunday and – believe it or not – his and her strip-bowling Sunday nights starting at 10pm.

Bowling Center Sport & Gastronomie

Rathausstrasse 5, Mitte (242 6657). S3, S5, S7, S9, U2, U5, U8 Alexanderplatz. **Open** 11am-midnight Mon-Sat; 10am-midnight Sun. **Prices** €12-€18 per hr. **No credit cards. Map** p316/p303 G3.

Union keep the red flag flying

East Berlin has seen nothing like it. A decade after unpopular Dynamo cheated their way to domination of the old GDR championship, little Union Berlin – a genuine team of the proletariat – have scaled footballing heights that no other Eastern club has reached since Reunification.

After ten difficult years of sporting and economic stagnation – near bankruptcy, even – Union Berlin made it to the German Cup final at Berlin's Olympiastadion in 2001. Union's ticket allocation, at 17,500 (five times their then-league average) sold out in 24 hours. All to no avail. Union lost 2-0 to top Bundesliga side Schalke 04, their opponents' impressive challenge in the league assuring qualification for the Champions League – and Union sneak into the UEFA Cup through the back door as cup runners-up. Once in Europe for 2001-02, Union made it through to the second round, losing to Bulgarians Liteks Lovech.

Back home, Union stand in line for a place in Germany's top flight, the Bundesliga. With the demise of Dynamo and Tennis Borussia, only mighty Hertha better them in Berlin. And all this from a team of workaday Albanians, Bulgarians, Yugoslavs, Slovaks, Czechs and East Germans, under unknown Bulgarian coach Georgi Vassiliev, playing at a ground comprising stone slabs of terrace cut into a side of woodland in Köpenick, way out east toward the terminus of the S3 line.

Union's history though is, if anything, even more bizarre. Formed in 1906 of three small neighbourhood clubs in the Grosskopf pub in Luisenstrasse, Union played in the local league until World War II. Thereafter, the club split, and one faction was based in the West,

in Moabit. Reaching qualification for the West German title in 1950, 85,000 Union 06 fans gathered in the Olympiastadion to watch their favourites sadly falter.

Once the Wall went up, Union's defection met with sanctions at the hands of the GDR sporting authorities. Refounded in 1966 as 1.FC Union, the club took their fan base once more from the factory floor, earning back the nickname 'Iron Union'. Two years later they won the GDR Cup, but a UEFA ban prevented them from playing in European competitions following the Soviet invasion of Prague.

Reunification saw Union in dire straits. Unable to prove financial stability, the new all-German FA in 1993 threatened to revoke the club's license. Fans collected 15,000 signatures almost overnight, and TV crews crammed into the clubhouse bar, Abseitsfalle ('Offside Trap'), to film supporters brandishing Mao-red 'Save Union' banners. Under the weight of such publicity, sponsors flooded to prop up the club. Notorious German punk star Nina Hagen even gave a free concert to open the following league season. The bar is still Berlin's best clubhouse, incongruously embellished by a huge mural of Edward Hopper's *Nighthawks at the Diner*.

Thanks to a takeover deal by media company Kinowelt, funds then became available to attract modest talent from across the old Eastern bloc, thus forming an honest, hard-working unit that created cup upsets. But for all their hard work, Union should not count their chickens just yet. With Kinowelt now going through difficult times, Union's future is once again tinged with uncertainty.

Equipped with 18 lanes, billiards, darts, pinball and a restaurant. Look for the big neon sign and head down the steps. A survivor from the Communist era.

New City Bowling Hasenheide

Hasenheide 107-9, Kreuzberg (622 2038/ 622 2039/www.bowling-hasenheide.de). U7, U8 Hermannplatz. **Open** *10am-midnight daily.* **Prices** *€1.70-€3.20 per person per game.* **No credit cards. Map** p307 G5.

This newly renovated bowling hangout boasts 28 spanking new lanes and scoring monitors with consoles. Hosts international competitions and is vying for the 2002 World Cup. Twelve lanes available for children. With bar/restaurant and new audience platforms.

Canoeing & kayaking

Der Bootsladen

Brandensteinweg 8, Spandau (362 5685/www.der-bootsladen.de). Bus 149. **Open** *Mar-Oct noon-7pm Tue-Fri; 9am-7pm Sat, Sun. Nov-Feb 1-4pm Fri; 10am-4pm Sat.* **Prices** *Kayak €5 per hr. Canadian double €6 per hr.* **Credit** V.

Good starting point for tours of the western canal system. Rental prices depend on boat size, but you can get good deals on more long-term rentals.

Kanu Connection

Köpenicker Strasse 9, Kreuzberg (612 2686/ www.kanu-connection.de). U1, U15 Schlesisches Tor/bus 265. **Open** *10am-7pm Mon-Fri; 9am-1pm*

Sat. **Prices** *Per boat* €20-€27 per day; €45-€60 per weekend; €90-€110 per wk. **No credit cards. Map** p307 H4.
Paddle through Kreuzberg's canals or take off into the waterways winding through the forests east of Berlin. Canoe and kayak rentals from four different landings. Guides available.

Climbing

T-Hall

Thiemannstrasse 1, Neukölln (6808 9864/www.t-hall.de). S4 Sonnenallee or U7 Karl-Marx-Strasse. **Open** *June-Sept* 10am-11pm Tue; 1-11pm Wed-Fri. *Oct-May* 1-11pm Mon-Fri; 10am-11pm Sat, Sun. **Prices** *Per day* €3-€14.50. **No credit cards.**
Spacious indoor climbing facility where Berliners train for expeditions. Instruction for beginners.

Cycling

Getting around by bike is easy in flat Berlin, especially on the designated bike lanes that line most major roads. Sport cycling is popular, as is touring in the countryside via the S-Bahn into Brandenburg. Taking your bike on the U-Bahn is also allowed except during rush hour (defined as 6-9am and 2-5pm). For bike rental, *see p273.*

Allgemeiner Deutscher Fahrrad-Club

Brunnenstrasse 28, Mitte (448 4724/www.adfc-berlin.de). U8 Bernauer Strasse. **Open** noon-8pm Mon-Fri; 10am-4pm Sat. **Map** p316/p302 F2.
The ADFC (German General Cycling Club) has an information and meeting point for cyclists and a self-help repair station. The ADFC recently published a new edition of a useful bike path map.

Berliner Radsport-Verband

Paul-Heyse-Strasse 29, Prenzlauer Berg (4210 5145/ www.bdr-radsport.de/ber). S4 Landsberger Allee. **Open** 9am-noon Tue, Thur.
Info on clubs, races and events. The **International Tour de Berlin** (a five-stage, 600-km/375-mile race) takes place every year at the end of May.

Disabled

The sports organisation **Behinderten-Sportverein Wilmersdorf e.V.** offers a variety of activities specifically for disabled people at various locations in town. Everyone is welcome to participate including partners. Phone Berlin headquarters (*see below*) for details or visit the website (www.behindertensport.de).

Behinderten-Sportverband Berlin

Hanns-Braun-Strasse, Friesenhaus 1, Charlottenburg, 14053 (3009 9675). U2 Olympia-Stadion (Ost). **Open** 10am-1pm Mon, Tue, Fri; 1-4pm Thur.
Branch: Behinderten-Sportverein Wilmersdorf e.V. Fridericiastrasse 10B, Wilmersdorf, 14050 (2562 0223).

Fitness

There are roughly 250 health clubs in Berlin, offering everything from sweaty basements for pumping iron to spa-like displays of luxury, and classes including spinning, pump, hot iron, body drill, body combat, dance/salsa/Latin/ party-aerobic, aquarobic, streetdance, chi hail and NIA. All the chains, such as Kieser, Swiss Training or Gold's Gym, have branches.

Aquarius Menfitness

Wilmersdorfer Strasse 82/83, Charlottenburg (324 1025/www.aquarius-berlin.de/Sport/home.htm). U7 Adenauerplatz. **Open** 10am-11pm Mon, Wed, Fri; 7am-11pm Tue, Thur; 7am-11pm Sat, Sun. **Prices** *Per day* €10; €5 concessions. *Per mth* €49.50 (€45 under 3mth contract). *10 admissions* €74.50. **Credit** AmEx, DC, V. **Map** p304 B4.
Men only, mostly gay.

Axxel City Fitness

Bülowstrasse 57, Schöneberg (2175 3000/ www.axxel24.de/fotos_inh.html). U2 Bülowstrasse or S1, S2, U7 Yorckstrasse. **Open** 24hrs daily. **Prices** €25 (2yr contract)-€140 per month. **No credit cards. Map** p304 B5.
For insomniac fitness freaks.

Budokan

Rheinstrasse 45, Steglitz (852 6763). U9 Walter-Schreiber-Platz. **Open** 2-10pm Mon-Fri; noon-5pm Sat; 11am-2pm Sun. **Prices** visit in person for details. **No credit cards.**
For martial arts enthusiasts.

Club Olympus Spa & Fitness

Marlene-Dietrich-Platz 2, Tiergarten (2553 1890/ berlin.hyatt.com/bergh/faci/fa01a.html). S1, S2, S25, U2 Potsdamer Platz. **Open** 6.30am-10.30pm Mon-Fri; 7.30am-9pm Sat, Sun. **Prices** *Per day* €61. **Credit** AmEx, DC, MC, V. **Map** p306 E4.
This roof-top fitness centre is for luxury lovers.

Hedon Berlin

Karlruher Strasse 20, Charlottenburg (8900 7130/ www.hedon-berlin.de). S45, S46 Halensee. **Open** 7am-11pm daily. **Prices** not fixed at time of going to press, call for details. **Credit** AmEx, DC, MC, V.
Due to open mid 2002, this monster complex will be the biggest in town: five floors, 25m swimming lanes, 15m high climbing, indoor and outdoor facilities... and everything else.

Jopp Frauen Fitness

Tauentzienstrasse 13A, Charlottenburg (210 111/ www.jopp.de). U9, U15 Kurfürstendamm or U1, U15, U2 Wittenbergplatz. **Open** 7am-11pm Mon-Fri; 10am-8pm Sat, Sun. *Friedrichstasse 50, Mitte (2045 8585). U2 Stadtmitte.* **Open** 7am-11pm Mon-Fri; 10am-8pm Sat, Sun. **Prices** *Per day* €23. *Per mth* €51 (1yr contract)-€71. **Sauna** €18. **No credit cards. Map** p316 F4/p306 F4.
Women only. See website for other branches.
Branches all over the city.

Sportschule Reichenbach

Von der Gablentzstrasse 3, Reinickendorf (4178 3449/www.sportschule-reichenbach.de). U6 Kurt-Schumacher-Platz. **Open** 7am-11pm Mon-Fri; 9am-7pm Sat; 9am-5pm Sun. **Prices** *Per day* €30 (1-yr contract)-€51. **No credit cards.**
For serious iron-pumpers.

Gay & lesbian sports

See www.vorspiel-berlin.de/start1.htm.

Golf

Golfclub Schloss Wilkendorf

Am Weiher 1, OT Wilkendorf, Gielsdorf (03341 330 960/www.golfpark-schloss-wilkendorf.com). S5 Strausberg Nord, then walk/taxi. **Open** *Nov-Feb* 9am-5pm daily. *Mar-Oct* 8am-7pm. **Prices** *Westside Platz (18 holes)* €28-€54 (Mon-Fri); €42 (Sat, Sun). *Sandy-Lyle-Platz (18 holes; members only)* €20-€45 (Mon-Fri); €50 (Sat, Sun). *Public course (6 holes)* €10-€15. **Credit** MC, V.
A short cab ride or fair walk away from the S5-line terminus, this is the only 18-hole course in the area open to non-members (at weekends only with

a *Platzreife*, 'German Golf Certificate', obtainable with any golf membership or by taking a test; call for details).

Öffentlichen Golf-Übungsanlage Berlin-Adlershof

Rudower Chaussee 4, Adlershof (6701 2421). S4, S6, S8, S9 Adlershof. **Open** 10am-dusk daily. **Prices** *Per day* €7.50; €5 concessions; (Sun) €5-€10; €3.75-€7.50 concessions. *Golf club rental* €0.50. **No credit cards.**
'Public golf for all' and excellent facilities for the new-comer with four par-three holes and a driving range.

Öffentliches Golf-Zentrum Berlin-Mitte

Chausseestrasse 94, Mitte. Office: Habersaathstrasse 34, Mitte (2804 7070). U6 Zinnowitzer Strasse. **Open** 7am-dusk daily. **Prices** free. *Golf club rental* €1. **Credit** V. **Map** p302 E2.
A 100,000 sq m (350,000 sq ft) facility with 64-tee driving range, chip and pitch, and a putting green, partly roofed, open all year and free to the public. A relaxed place; polo shirts are not required. There are also 12 beach volleyball courts and BMX courses. Free training for kids on Monday and Thursday (4-5.30pm) in summer and Thursday at 3pm in winter.

Local heroes

Erik Zabel

Cycling is a big sport in Germany, and Berlin-born Erik Zabel (*pictured*), ace sprinter for Team Deutsche Telekom, has more wins any given season than many pros will garner in their entire career. The year 2001 was especially splendid for Zabel. He won an unprecedented 6th consecutive Green Jersey in the Tour de France and concluded the year with what he considers his most important achievement, the number one spot in the UCI World Rankings – the first German ever to do so. He was named German Sportsman of the Year in 2001. Finishing in the top 20 of the UCI is another Berliner, **Jens Voigt**. His star rose in 2001 when he snatched the Yellow Jersey for a day in the Tour de France. Known for his fighting break-away style, Voigt got his start at the SC Dynamo, as did **Jan Ullrich**, another German cycling wonder who spent his formative years training in Berlin.

Franziska van Almsick

Only 23 and already preparing for a comeback, it's been almost ten years since Franzi made a splash at the Olympics in Barcelona. Nicknamed 'the goldfish', the record-holding (in 200m freestyle) swimmer from the Berlin

district of Treptow has had a career laced with drama in and out of the pool. She was first praised to the skies as Germany's girl-next-door athletic superstar, only to be dragged through the mud after flagging performances, accusations of boyfriend-snatching and some allegedly pro-Nazi remarks. Nowadays, the millions she earns in advertising campaigns have more to do with her attractive features than her sporting prowess. Van Almsick copped silver medals at the 1992 and 1996 Olympics, but has never won a gold medal.

Katarina Witt

Katarina Witt, born on the outskirts of Berlin (she trained in Karl-Marx-Stadt, the former and future city of Chemnitz), is the world's most

Ice skating

Berlin's cold climes have an upside – they make for good winter ice skating. The Christmas market on Alexanderplatz has a small outdoor rink and there's another rink at scenic Gendarmenmarkt.

Eisstadion Berlin Wilmersdorf

Fritz-Wildung-Strasse 9, Wilmersdorf (824 1012). S4 Hohenzollerndamm. **Open** *Oct-mid Mar* 9am-6.30pm, 7.30-10pm Mon, Wed, Fri; 9am-5.30pm, 7.30-10pm Tue, Thur; 9am-10pm Sat; 10am-6pm Sun. **Prices** *Per 2hrs* €3; €1.50 concessions. **No credit cards. Map** p304 B6.

With an outer ring for speed skating and an inner field for figure skaters and those with weak ankles who need to clutch the wall. Skate rental too.

Eisstadion Wedding

Erika-Hess-Stadion, Müllerstrasse 185, Wedding (4575 5555). U6 Wedding. **Open** 9am-noon, 3-5.30pm, 7.30-9.30pm Mon; 9am-noon, 3-5.30pm Tue-Sat; 9am-noon, 2-5pm Sun. **Prices** €3; €1.50 concessions. **No credit cards. Map** p302 E1.

Cheapest public rink in town – admission gets you up to three hours of skating pleasure.

Ice Skating Rink @ Kulturbrauerei

Knaackstraße 97, Prenzlauer Berg (4405 8707/ www.soda-berlin.de). U2 Eberswalder Strasse or S8, S10 Schönhauser Allee. **Open** 1am-10pm Mon-Thur; 10am-3am Fri, Sat. **Prices** *Per 90mins* €2.50; €1.50 concessions. *Skate rental* €2.50. **No credit cards. Map** p306 E4.

Small indoor rink in the Kulturbrauerei entertainment complex. Late-night openings on Friday and Saturday make this an interesting chill-out option for clubbers.

Karting

Formula One greats Michael and Ralf Schumacher and Hans-Harald Frenzen all got their start on the kart track. It's an expensive way to pass the afternoon, though.

Kartland

Miraustrasse 62-6, Reinickendorf (4356 6841/ www.kartland.de). S2 Eichborndamm or U8 Rathaus Reinickendorf. **Open** 3-10pm Mon-Thur; 2pm-midnight Fri; noon-midnight Sat; noon-10pm Sun. **Prices** *Per 10mins* €10; €6 concessions. **No credit cards.**

Good indoor track, suitable for beginners.

---

celebrated female figure skater. Two Olympic Gold Medals (in 1984 and 1988) made her the darling of the GDR sports and the political establishment. That association came back to haunt her in early 2001, when she tried to prevent her Stasi files, which designated her a 'beneficiary' as well as a victim of the hated secret police, from being publicly accessed. Witt's post-1989 career continued without missing a beat – successful ice pageants, an Emmy Award for 'Carmen on Ice', megabuck advertising deals and even a *Playboy* spread. As head of her own company and as a television ice skating commentator, Witt seems set to remain a player long after she decides to hang her skates up for good.

Berlin bruisers

'*Mann am Boden – jutet Jefühl'*
('Man goes down – what a feeling!').
Boxing pro and shady character **Graciano Rocchigiani** is one of the winning punchers that the rough-hewn city has produced. Rocchigiani and his brother – tough in and outside the ring, with alleged links to crime, red light and jail – rep resent the 'old school' West Berlin bruisers. In the '90s, after reunification, this boxing style clashed with the East German 'academics'. Boxers like

Henry Maske embodied the latter approach, boxing for points and using more brain than brawn. 'Sir Henry' was even invited to box as part of an art installation.

With Maske retired and Rocchigiani waning, new contenders quickly emerged. **Sven Ottke**, Berlin's only currently reigning world champion (super middle-weight), is a born and bred West Berliner from Spandau, with his main fan base in eastern Germany. He turned pro after 334 amateur fights at the age of 30 and has defended his IBF title ten times.

Cengiz Koc, raised in the Turkish immigrant community in Kreuzberg, is regarded by many as the next homegrown heavyweight hopeful. Only 24, Koc turned to boxing after netting the kickboxing world championship in 1996. Koc has also appeared as an actor in TV and film. He even landed a spot in the German boxing team for the Sydney Olympics, although his bid ended pitifully with a knockout in the first round. But like Maske, Koc represents a new breed of fighter – with the necessary versatility to branch out into more genteel areas.

Joschka Fischer

Foreign minister and born-again health fanatic Joschka Fischer, age 53, finished the 2000 Berlin Marathon in a respectable four hours.

Arts & Entertainment

Kart-World & Freizeit Park

Am Juliusturm 15-19, Spandau (3549 3100/ 3549 3113/www.kart-world-berlin.de). U7 Zitadelle or Haselhorst/bus 133. **Open** 3pm-midnight Mon-Thur; noon-midnight Fri; 10am-midnight Sat, Sun. **Prices** *Per 8mins* €9.20; €7.70 concessions. *10 admissions* €70; €52 concessions. **No credit cards.**

Indoor track with an interesting course. Bar and bistro with video projection for catching races live. If you guess the outcome of a Formula One race correctly, you can ride a kart all day for free.

Rok Kart

Grossbeerenstrasse 148-58, Mariendorf (7479 2827/www.rok-kart.de). S2 Marienfelde, then bus 127. **Open** 3-10pm Mon-Thur; 3pm-midnight Fri; 11am-midnight Sat; 11am-10pm Sun. **Prices** *Per 10mins* €10; €7.50 concessions. *Five admissions* €40; €30 concessions. *For 10 karts per hr* €470. **Credit** MC, V.

This first rate indoor track is particularly well suited to beginners.

Sailing & motor boating

Berlin contains a 200-kilometre (125-mile) long network of navigable rivers, estuaries and canals, and 50 lakes. The city is bordered on the west by the Havel river and to the south by the Dahme, while the Spree forms an east–west axis. If you plan a longer stay in Berlin, you might want to join one of the countless clubs or associations, many listed at www.wassersport-in-berlin.de. But there are also opportunities for the short-term visitor.

A licence is needed for boating and sailing. If you have a licence or certificate from your native country, it's worth bringing. Boat rental places may then issue you a charter pass for sailboats or motor boats, if you're lucky.

The Berlin-Brandenburg Water Sports Association (*Wassertourismus Förderverband*) has recently published a new hiking, waterway and tourism map with speed limits and landings as well as 20 hiking trails. Further information at www.wtb-brb.de.

Berliner Segler-Verband

Bismarckallee 2, Charlottenburg (893 8420/ www.berliner-segler-verband.de). S3, S7 Grunefeld. **Open** 9am-4pm Tue-Thur.

Contact this organisation for information on sailing in and around Berlin.

Blue Planet Sail

Elbestrasse 7, Neukölln (463 8058/ www.blueplanetsail.de). U7 Rathaus Neukölln/bus 104, 194, 241. **Prices** €350 per 5 persons (including snack). **No credit cards.**

Sailing boat charter company organising yacht trips for small groups on the Havel to Potsdam. Book at least two days in advance.

Yachtcharter Berlin

Müggelseedamm 70, Köpenick (6409 4310/ www.yachtcharter-berlin.de). Tram 61. **Prices** €99-€149 per day; €1,590-€1,790 per wk. **Open** *Apr-Oct* 9am-6pm daily. *Nov-Mar* 10am-noon Mon; 4-6pm Thur. **No credit cards.**

Motor boat charter company.

Sauna & Turkish bath

Many of Berlin's public baths have cheapish saunas. *See also p255* **Blub Badeparadies**.

Hamam Turkish Bath

Schoko-Fabrik, Naunynstrasse 72, Kreuzberg (615 1464/615 2999). U1, U8 Kottbusser Tor. **Open** *Sept-June* 3-10pm Mon; noon-10pm Tue-Sun. **Prices** call for details. **No credit cards.** **Map** p307 G4.

Daylight filters through the glass cupola of the main hall, where women sit in small alcoves, bathing in the warm water of the baths. Enjoy Turkish tea and a reviving massage afterwards. The bustle of Berlin seems miles away. Friendly and laid-back, the Hamam attracts a very mixed clientele, from mature Turkish women to teenagers. Children are not permitted on Tuesdays and Fridays but Thursday is children's day. It is women only but boys up to the age of six are permitted.

Thermen

Europa-Center, Nürnberger Strasse 7, Charlottenburg (general enquiries 257 5760). U1, U2, U15 Wittenbergplatz. **Open** 10am-midnight Mon-Sat; 10am-9pm Sun. **Prices** €17.90 per day; €18 per hr; €154 for 10 admissions. **No credit cards. Map** p305 D4.

Big, central, mixed facility offering Finnish saunas, steam baths, hot and cool pools, and a garden (open until October). There is a pool where you can swim outside on the roof, even in the depths of winter. Thermen also boasts a café, pool-side loungers where you can doze or read, table tennis, billiards and massage facilities.

Skateboarding, in-line skating & BMX

Berlin Parade

Irregular events gather the city's in-line skaters to demonstrate for equal rights in street traffic. Location varies; check www.berlinparade.de for dates and starting points.

Erlebniswerkstatt des Projektes Erlebnisräume

Sterndamm 82, Treptow (631 0911 answering machine). S4, S6, S8, S9, S10 Schöneweide.

Berlin's only trial track with jump ramps. The venue is also the best place to make contact with other keen cyclists and discover the latest information about hotspots.

Al fresco swimming is possible even in the deep midwinter at **Thermen**. *See p254.*

Liberty Park

Senftenberger Strasse/corner Kastanienallee, Hellersdorf. U5 Hellersdorf.
The largest BMX and skater complex course in Berlin, with half-pipe and mini-ramps.

Search & Destroy

Oranienstrasse 198, Kreuzberg (6128 9064). U1 Görlitzer Bahnhof or U1, U8 Kottbusser Tor. **Open** noon-7pm Mon-Wed, Fri; noon-7.30pm Thur; 11am-4pm Sat. **No credit cards. Map** p307 G4.
Small skateboard scene shop with helpful staff.

Volkspark Wilmersdorf

Hans-Rosenthal-Platz (near playground), Wilmersdorf. S4, U4 Innsbrucker Platz or U4 Rathaus Schöneberg. **Map** p305 D6.
The park has three asphalt pools for BMX, in-line skating and skateboarding.

Squash

Most tennis facilities also have squash courts.

TSB City Sports

Brandenburgische Strasse 53, Wilmersdorf (873 9097). U7 Konstanzer Strasse. **Open** 7am-midnight Mon-Fri; 8am-midnight Sat, Sun. **Prices** *Tennis* €17-€32. *Squash* €10-€18. *Badminton* €9-€15.60. *Sauna* €2.50-€7.50. **Credit** V. **Map** p305 C5.
Now under new ownership, this centre offers four tennis courts, nine squash courts and 12 new badminton courts, plus a sauna, a solarium and a restaurant. Coaching is available for all three sports, aerobics and classical dance.

Swimming (indoor)

Almost every district has at least one indoor pool. Check the phone book for your nearest. To beat the crowds, come early in the morning or later in the evening.

Blub Badepadies

Buschkrugallee 64, Neukölln (609 060/ www.blub-berlin.de). U7 Grenzallee. **Open** 10am-11pm daily. **Prices** *4 hrs* €9; €7 concessions. *All day* €10.50-€13; €8-€11 concessions. **Credit** AmEx, V.
Price includes communal sauna and all water attractions – whirlpools, slides, artificial beaches – in this gaudy aquatic entertainment complex. A four-hour ticket for €9 (all day €10.50) gets you the sauna garden with Turkish steamroom and Scandinavian-style sauna plus swimming.

Schwimm- und Sprunghalle im Europapark

Paul-Heyse-Strasse 26, Prenzlauer Berg (4218 6301/www.berlin.de/Apps/php/bbb). S4, S8, S10 Landsberger Allee. **Open** 6.30-10pm Mon-Thur; 9-10pm Fri; 1-7pm Sat; 10am-6pm Sun. **Prices** €3; €2 concessions. **No credit cards. Map** p303 H2.
This immense, newly opened swimming facility is the largest in Europe. It often hosts international swim meets.

Stadtbad Charlottenburg

Krumme Strasse 10, Charlottenburg (3438 3860/www.berlin.de/Apps/php/bbb). U2, U7 Bismarckstrasse or U7 Richard-Wagner-Platz or U2 Deutsche Oper. **Open** *Alte Halle* 6.30am-3pm, 5.30-8pm (women only), 8-9.30pm (handicapped) Mon; 8.30-10am, 10am-2pm (senior citizens), 3-6pm, 6-10pm (nudists) Tue; 8.30am-10pm Wed; 8.30am-3pm, 6-10pm Thur; 8.30am-2pm, 4-6pm, 6-10pm (nudists) Fri. *Neue Halle* 6.30-8am, 3-10pm Tue; 6.30-8am Wed; 6.30-8am, 3-10pm Thur; 6.30-8am Fri; 6.30am-4pm Sat; 8.30am-5pm Sun. **Prices** €3; €2 concessions. **No credit cards. Map** p300 B3.
These art nouveau baths are especially popular with nudists, so be aware of the times listed to either whip your kit off or scuttle for cover. Some times are given over exclusively to senior citizens, nudists and women, though not together.

Stadtbad Mitte

*Gartenstrasse 5, Mitte (3088 0910). S1, S2
Nordbahnhof/tram 8, 50.* **Open** 6.30am-10pm
Mon; 10am-8pm Tue; 6.30am-10pm Wed; 6.30-8am
Thur; 6.30-8am, 6.30-8pm Fri; 2-9pm Sat, Sun.
Prices €3; €2 concessions. **No credit cards.**
Map p316/p302 F2.

Swimming (open-air)

Phone any pool before setting out (or the Berlin
service hotline on 01803 102 020), as the city's
financial woes also affect pool openings. There
are also plenty of other places for swimming
on the western lakes; Schlachtensee and
Krumme Lanke are clean, set in attractive
woodland and easily accessible by U- or S-
Bahn. *See also p254* **Thermen.**

Olympia Schwimmstadion

*Olympischer Platz 3, Charlottenburg (3006 3440/
www.bbb.berlin.de). U2 Olympia-Stadion (Ost) or S5
Olympiastadion.* **Open** call for details. **Prices** €3;
€2 concessions. **No credit cards.**

Sommerbad Kreuzberg

*Gitschiner Strasse 18-31, Kreuzberg (616 1080/
www.bbb.berlin.de). U1 Prinzenstrasse.* **Prices** €3;
€2 concessions. **No credit cards.** **Map** p306 F5.
Known as Prinzenbad, a popular outdoor complex
for swimming and sunbathing. Nudist area.

Strandbad Müggelsee

*Fürstenwalder Damm 838, Rahnsdorf
(648 7777). S3 Rahnsdorf.* **Prices** call for details.
No credit cards.
North shore bathing beach, complete with nudist
camp, on the bank of east Berlin's biggest lake.

Strandbad Wannsee

*Wannseebadweg, Nikolassee (803 5612/
www.bbb.berlin.de). S1, S7 Nikolassee.* **Prices** call
for details. **No credit cards.**
Europe's largest inland beach, with sand, sun beds,
water slides, snack stalls and lots of Germans who
like to get there early. Nudist section.

Tennis

Tennis is an expensive habit in Berlin. The
cheapest time to hire a court is in the mornings,
and even then it can cost €15-€30 an hour for
an indoor court of reasonable quality. Many
badminton and squash establishments double
up as tennis centres.

TCW (Tennis Center Weissensee)

*Roelckestrasse 106, Weissensee (927 4594/
www.tenniscenter-weissensee.de). S4, S8, S10
Greifswalder Strasse.* **Open** 7am-midnight Mon-Fri;
8am-midnight Sat, Sun. **Prices** (per hr) *May-Aug*
€10.50-€15.50; €8.50-€14 concessions. *Sept-Apr*
€13-€19; €11.50-€17 concessions. **No credit cards.**
Map p303 H1.

This new centre has seven tennis courts, 16 badminton courts and four fun ball courts for the kids,
all indoors. The surface is meant to approximate
clay. Prices include use of the sauna (10am-10pm).

Tennis-Verband Berlin-Brandenburg

*Auerbacher Strasse 19, Charlottenburg (8972 8730/
www.tvbb.de). S7 Grunewald.* **Open** 10am-2pm
Mon-Fri.
Berlin-Brandenburg Tennis Federation can supply
information about joining leagues and clubs.

tsf

*Richard-Tauber-Damm 36, Marienfelde (742 1091).
U6 Alt-Mariendorf.* **Open** 7am-11pm daily. **Prices**
Tennis €12-€24 per hr. *Squash* €5-€13 per hr.
No credit cards.
Offers nine quality indoor tennis courts, six squash
courts, plus gymnastics, massage, sauna and restau-
rant facilities. There is no membership fee.
Branch: Galenstrasse 33-45, Spandau (333 4083).

Windsurfing, water-skiing, wakeboarding, surfing & kiteing

MBC Sportartikel

*Warschauer Platz 18, Friedrichshain (3260 1777/
www.mbc-sport.de). S3, S5, S6, S7, S9, S46, S75,
U1, U12 Warschauer Strasse.* **Open** noon-8pm Mon-
Fri; 10am-4pm Sat. **Credit** DC, V. **Map** p307 H4.
A shop offering sales, service and rentals for wind-
surfing, in-line skating and snowboarding.

360°

*Pariser Strasse 23/24, Charlottenburg (883 8596/
www.360berlin.com). U1, U9 Spichernstrasse.*
Open 11am-8pm Mon-Fri; 10am-4pm Sat.
No credit cards. **Map** p305 C5.
Fashion, hardware, kite courses, snowboards, skat-
ing, in-line, surfing, wakeboarding and windsurfing.

Wakeboard & Wasserski Grossbeeren

*Bahnhofstrasse 49, Grossbeeren (033701 90873/
www.wakeboarding-berlin.de). S25, S26 Lichterfelde
Süd, then RB32.* **Open** *Swimming area* (May-Sept)
11am-sunset May-Sept. **Prices** *Per hr* €12.50; €10
concessions. *Per day* €30; €25 concessions. *Board
rental* €5 per hr; €12.50 per day. *Wetsuit* €4 per 2hrs;
€6.50 per day. **Credit** MC, V.
One of Europe's most modern water skiing facilities.
Opened in August 2001.

Wet & Wild Wasserski-Seilbahn Berlin-Velten

*Am Bernsteinsee, Am Autobahndreieck Oranienburg,
Ausfart Velten (033 03 400 145/www.wasserski-
berlin.de).* **Open** Apr-Sept. **Prices** (Mon-Fri)
Per 2hrs €17; €11 concessions. *Per day* €27.50; €13
concessions. (Sat, Sun) *Per 2hrs* €19.50; €11. *Per day*
€32.50; €22.50 concessions. **No credit cards.**
Water-skiing without a boat. Imagine a ski lift in the
water and you get the idea. The season runs from
April to September.

Trips Out of Town

Trips Out of Town

Historic cities, pristine countryside, palaces, breweries and steel factories.

Berlin is a city in the middle of nowhere. For miles around, fields, lakes and dense woods are scarcely interrupted by a scattering of small towns and villages. In fact, water and greenery crowd into the city from all sides, providing a wealth of opportunities for walking, cycling and swimming (*see p112* **Other Districts** for nature escape within the city limits).

By far the most popular day trip from the city is to **Potsdam**, which is to Berlin what Versailles is to Paris; in fact, there's enough here to fill a couple of days. Neighbouring **Babelsberg** has the old UFA film studios, Germany's answer to Hollywood. Another worthwhile, though infinitely more sombre, trip is just north of the city to the former concentration camp **Sachsenhausen**.

If you fancy travelling a little further in search of nature, the **Spreewald**, a forest filigreed with small streams, is good for a stroll or boat ride, and can be reached in about an hour by train. If only the seaside will do, then head up north to the Baltic coast and the island of **Rügen**, but plan on staying at least overnight.

Two other excellent trips are south to historic cities of former East Germany. In terms of its compact picturesque centre, **Leipzig** is probably the most rewarding, though **Dresden**'s history, flamboyant baroque architecture and art collections are undeniably impressive. Both are around two hours from Berlin by train.

For a fascinating glimpse into the old East, make the trip towards the Polish border and the steel town of **Einsenhüttenstadt** and combine it with a visit to the monastery and brewery of **Neuzelle**.

And if one big city isn't enough for you, it's worth noting that **Hamburg** is a train journey of less than two and a half hours away, and if one country isn't sufficient, then **Prague** is only five hours from Berlin by train.

Around Berlin

Potsdam & Babelsberg

Potsdam is capital of the state of Brandenburg and Berlin's closest and most beautiful neighbour. And every visitor knows it. Summer weekend crowds can at times be overwhelming (particularly at weekends), so pick the time of your visit with care.

The main permanent attraction is the grandiose collection of palaces and outbuildings in **Park Sanssouci**. This in itself can take a whole day to see. Another afternoon can be pleasantly filled around Potsdam's baroque town centre, the Altstadt, as well as in Babelsberg (*see p260*).

Large parts of Potsdam town centre were destroyed in a single bombing raid on 14 April 1945, which claimed 4,000 lives. The vagaries of post-war reconstruction produced a ghastly 'restoration' of Schinkel's **St Nikolaikirche**, whose dome can be seen for miles, as well as acres of featureless 1960s and 1970s flat blocks that crowd out Platz der Einheit ('Unity Square') and the surrounding streets.

Nevertheless, the unusual, mid 18th century, Palladian-style **Altes Rathaus** (Old Town Hall) is worth admiring, particularly for its round tower, which until 1875 was used as a prison. It is now an arts centre.

Yorck- and Wilhelm-Raab-Strasse retain their baroque architecture: the **Kabinetthaus**, a small palace at Am neuen Markt 1, was the birthplace of Friedrich Wilhelm II (the only Hohenzollern both to have been born and to have died in the royal residence of Potsdam).

The baroque town centre, originally intended as a quarter to house people servicing the court, is bounded by Schopenhauerstrasse, Hebbelstrasse, Charlottenstrasse and Hegel Allee. The dwellings were built between 1732 and 1742; the best of them can be seen running west along the pedestrianised Brandenburger Strasse. Potsdam's Brandenburg Gate, at the Sanssouci end of Brandenburger Strasse, is a delightfully happy contrast to Berlin's morose structure of the same name.

The **Holländisches Viertel** ('Dutch Quarter') is between Gutenbergstrasse, Friedrich-Ebert-Strasse, Hebbelstrasse and Kurfürstenstrasse, and takes its name from the Dutch immigrant workers that Friedrich Wilhelm I, the inveterate builder, invited to the town. He ordered 134 gable-fronted red-brick houses to be built, most of which fell into neglect after the last war, but the survivors, particularly along Mittelstrasse at the junction with Benkerstrasse, have been scrubbed into shape. This is now the place to dine and shop.

The most enjoyable museum in town is the **Filmmuseum**, with an excellent exhibition on the history of German cinema.

But without question the main draw for visitors lies in **Schloss Sanssouci** ('Without Cares'), given a French name because this was the language of the 18th-century Prussian court. It was the Francophile Frederick the Great who originally began to build the extensive gardens here in 1740. They were intended to be in stark contrast to the style favoured by his detested father. The first palace to be built, and the one that gives the park its name, forms a semi-circle at the top of a terrace, on whose slopes symmetrical zigzag paths are interspersed with vines and orange trees. It also houses a collection of paintings.

Other attractions include the huge **Neues Palais**, built 1763-9 to celebrate the end of the Seven Years War. Also worth visiting in Sanssouci are: the gigantic **Orangerie**, in Italian Renaissance style; the **Spielfestung** ('toy fortress'), built for Wilhelm II's sons, complete with a toy cannon, which can be fired; the **Chinesisches Teehaus** ('Chinese Teahouse'), with its collection of Chinese and Meissen porcelain; the **Römischer Bäder**, an imitation Roman villa by Schinkel and Persius; **Schloss Charlottenhof**, with its extraordinary blue-glazed entrance hall and Kupferstichzimmer ('copper-plate engraving room'), adorned with reproduction Renaissance paintings; and the **Drachenhaus** ('Dragonhouse'), a pagoda-style coffee shop.

Outside Sanssouci Park is **Alexandrowka** (between Puschkinallee and Am Schragen), a fake Russian village built in 1826 by Friedrich Wilhelm III to house Russian musicians and their families who came into Prussian hands as prisoners of war during the Napoleonic campaigns. The houses were arranged in the form of a St Andrew's cross and designed to look like log cabins. They still carry the names of the original tenants, which are inscribed on their fronts, some in Cyrillic. The icon-filled **Alexander-Newski-Kapelle** was constructed three years later at the top of the densely wooded Kapellenberg hill.

In the Neuer Garten, at the end of Johannes-Dieckmann-Allee, the **Marmorpalais** ('Marble Palace'), overlooking the beautiful Heiliger See, was where Friedrich Wilhelm II died. Nearby, **Schloss Cecilienhof**, the last royal addition to Potsdam's palaces, was begun in 1913 and completed four years later. It was here that the Potsdam Conference (17 July to 2 August 1945) took place, and where Stalin, Truman and Attlee signed the Potsdamer Abkommen, the treaty that divided post-war Germany.

Schloss Sanssouci.

If film palaces rather than royal palaces are your forte, then you should head over the Havel river to the finest one Europe ever saw: **Babelsberg**. Now officially part of Potsdam, Babelsberg was the centre of the pre-war German film industry, and it's still the main reason why so many day trippers cross the Lange Brücke to visit Potsdam's otherwise prosaic east bank.

The first studio was opened here in 1912 by the Berlin production company Bioscop. But it was not until 1917, when the German General Staff decided that the war effort was suffering because of the inferior quality of their propaganda, that the Universum Film AG (UFA) was founded. By the 1920s the studio had become the largest in the world outside Hollywood, making as many as 100 films a year, including the expressionist *The Cabinet of Dr Caligari*, the futurist *Metropolis* and the decadent *The Blue Angel*. A mixture of success, the Depression and the rise of the Nazis saw most of the studio's talent leave for America, or the concentration camps.

Sections of the studio are open to the public but have been transformed into a tacky theme park where the product placement of international soft drink sponsors overshadow the exhibits on display. Avoid. A walk by the pretty Griebnitzsee can be a far more appealing prospect.

Filmmuseum

Marstall, Potsdam (0331 271 810/ www.filmmuseum-potsdam.de). **Open** 10am-6pm daily. **Admission** €5; €1-€2 concessions. **No credit cards.**
This fine museum is underpinned by classic material from the UFA studios in nearby Babelsberg. Contained in the elegant former Marstall ('royal stables'), it has rooms full of famous props, costumes,

set designs and projection screens. There's also a café and a large, comfortable cinema with an art house programme, including talks and special events.

Filmpark Babelsberg

August-Bebel-Strasse 26-53, entrance on Grossbeerenstrasse (0331 721 2717/ www.filmpark.de). Train to Medienstadt Babelsberg/S7 Babelsberg/bus 698 from Lange Brücke, direction Am Gehölz. **Open** Mid Mar-early 10am-6pm daily. **Admission** €15; €14 concessions. **No credit cards.**

Marmorpalais

Am Neuen Garten (0331 969 4200/www.spsg.de). **Open** Apr-Oct 9am-5pm Tue-Sun. *Nov-Mar* 10am-4pm Sat, Sun. **Admission** €3; €2.50 concessions. **No credit cards.**

St Nikolaikirche

Am Alten Markt (0331 291 682). **Open** 2-5pm Mon; 10am-5pm Tue-Sun. **Admission** free.

Sanssouci

Potsdam (0331 969 4202/www.spsg.de). **Open** *Palace & exhibition buildings* (Apr-Oct) 9am-5pm daily; (Nov-Mar) 9am-4pm daily. *Park* 9am-dusk daily. **Admission** *Palace & exhibition buildings* €8; €5 concessions. *Park* free. **No credit cards.**
Each of the various palaces and outbuildings has its own closing days each month, and some are only open mid May to mid Oct. Phone the number above for full information.

Schloss Cecilienhof

Am Neuen Garten (0331 969 4244/www.spsg.de). **Open** Apr-Oct 9am-5pm Tue-Sun; Nov-Mar 9am-4pm Tue-Sun. **Admission** €5; €4 concessions. **No credit cards.**

Where to eat & drink

There are a number of restaurants, cafés and snack bars within Park Sanssouci, and plenty throughout the Altstadt.

Café im Filmmuseum

Schlossstrasse 1 (270 2041). **Open** noon-midnight daily. **Main courses** €9-€15. **Credit** AmEx, MC, V.
The Filmmuseum's café is one of Potsdam's best.

Froschkasten

Kiezstrasse 4 (0331 291 315). **Open** noon-midnight daily. **Main courses** €7.20-€16. **No credit cards.**
One of the oldest and most pleasant bars in town. Serves some food.

Die Kneipe 'M18'

Mittelstrasse 18 (0331 2701 818). **Open** 6pm-2am Mon-Thur, Sun; noon-2am Fri, Sat. **No credit cards.**
A cheap, arty café in an old Dutch house with an appealing beer garden.

Restaurant Juliette

Jägerstrasse 39 (0331 270 1791/www.restaurant-juliette.com). **Open** noon-11pm daily. **Main courses** €12-€22. **Credit** DC, MC, V.
Cosy and romantic, this excellent place in the Holländisches Viertel offers classic classy cuisine.

Villa Kellerman

Mangerstrasse 34-6 (0331 291 572). **Open** call for details. **Main courses** call for details. **Credit** call for details.
This first-rate Italian restaurant in a late 19th-century villa is due to reopen in March 2002.

Getting there

By train Both Potsdam and Babelsberg can be reached via the S7 S-Bahn line, but it's a fairly long journey (around 40mins from Mitte). If you're going to Babelsberg, there's a direct regional train from Zoo to Medienstadt Babelsberg that takes just 15mins, and a number of regional trains to Potsdam Hauptbahnhof from Zoo that take 17-18mins.

Tourist information

Potsdam-Information

Friedrich-Ebert-Strasse 5 (0331 275 580/ www.potsdam.de). **Open** *Apr-Oct* 9am-8pm Mon-Fri; 9am-6pm Sat; 9am-4pm Sun. *Nov-Mar* 10am-6pm Mon-Fri; 10am-2pm Sat, Sun.

Sachsenhausen

Many Nazi concentration camps have been preserved and opened to the public as memorials to what happened and how. Sachsenhausen is the one nearest to Berlin.

Immediately upon coming to power, Hitler set about rounding up and interning his opponents. From 1933 to 1935 an old brewery on this site was used to hold them. The present camp received its first prisoners in July 1936. It was designated with cynical euphemism as a *Schutzhaftlager* ('Protective Custody Camp'). The first *Schutzhaftlagern* were political opponents of the government: Communists, social democrats, trade unionists. With time, the number and variety of prisoners widened to include anyone guilty of 'anti-social' behaviour, homosexuals and Jews.

About 6,000 Jews were forcibly brought here after Kristallnacht alone. It was here that some of the first experiments in organised mass murder were made: tens of thousands of prisoners of war from the Eastern Front were killed at 'Station Z'.

The SS evacuated the camp in 1945 and began marching 33,000 inmates to the Baltic, where they were to be packed into boats and sunk in the sea. Some 6,000 died during the march before the survivors were rescued by the Allies. A further 3,000 prisoners were found in the camp's hospital when it was captured on 22 April 1945.

But the horror did not end here. After the German capitulation, the Russian secret police, the MVD, reopened Sachsenhausen as 'Camp 7' for the detention of war criminals; in fact, it was filled with anyone suspected of opposition. Following the fall of the GDR, mass graves were discovered, containing the remains of an estimated 10,000 prisoners.

On 23 April 1961, the partially restored camp was opened to the public as a national monument and memorial. The inscription over the entrance, *Arbeit Macht Frei* ('Work Sets You Free'), could be found over the gates of all concentration camps.

The parade ground, where morning roll-call was taken, and from where inmates were required to witness executions on the gallows, stands before the two remaining barrack blocks. One is now a museum and the other a memorial hall and cinema, where a film about the history of the camp is shown. Next door stands the prison block.

There are another couple of small exhibitions in buildings in the centre of the camp (no English labelling), but perhaps the grimmest site here is the subsiding remains of Station Z, the surprisingly small extermination block. A map traces the path the condemned would follow, depending upon whether they were to be shot (the bullets

The memorial at **Sachsenhausen**.

were retrieved and reused) or gassed. All ended up in the neighbouring ovens.

The scale and the grisliness of the horror remembered here can be very disturbing, but it is worth noting that there are people even today who would like to pretend that none of it ever happened – some of them burned a couple of the buildings here in 1992.

It's a good idea to hire an audio guide (available in English) at the gate.

KZ Sachsenhausen

Strasse der Nationen 22, Oranienburg (03301 8037 1517). **Open** *Apr-Sept* 8.30am-6pm Tue-Sun. *Oct-Mar* 8.30am-4.30pm Tue-Sun. **Admission** free.

Getting there

By train Oranienburg is at the end of the S1 S-Bahn line (around 40mins from Mitte). From the station follow the signs to 'Gedenkstätte Sachsenhausen'; it's about a 20-min walk.

Further Afield

Spreewald

This filigree network of tiny rivers, streams and canals, dividing dense patches of deciduous forest interspersed with market garden farmland, is one of the loveliest excursions out of Berlin. Be warned, though, that the area gets extremely crowded in season, and particularly at weekends, giving the lie to its otherwise justified claim to be one of the most perfect areas of wilderness in Europe. Out of season, you can often have it almost to yourself.

Located about 100 kilometres (60 miles) south-east of Berlin, the Spree bisects the area into the **Unterspreewald** and **Oberspreewald**. For the former, Schepzig or **Lübben** are the best starting points; for the latter go 15 kilometres (nine miles) further on the train to **Lübbenau**.

The character of both sections is very similar. The Oberspreewald is perhaps better, for its 500 square kilometres (190 square miles) of territory contain more than 300 natural and artificial channels, called *Fliesse*. You can travel around these on hand-propelled punts – rent your own or join a larger group – and also take out kayaks. Motorised boats are forbidden. Here and there in the forest are restaurants and small hotels. The tourist information centre in Lübbenau can provide maps, many with walks marked on them.

Theodor Fontane described the Spreewald as resembling Venice more than 1,500 years ago. The local population belongs to the Sorbisch Slav minority, related to Czechs and Slovaks,

The **Spreewald**, near **Lübbenau**.

with their own language much in evidence in street names, newspapers and so on. This can be an exotic attraction, unlike the folk festivals regularly laid on for tourists in the high season.

Where to eat & drink

There are plenty of eating and drinking options in Lübben and Lübbenau, and little to choose between most of them. Follow your nose.

Getting there

By train There are direct trains every hour to Lübben and Lübbenau. The fastest is 52mins from Ostbahnhof and 1hr 16mins from Zoo to Lübben. Lübbenau is a further 17mins.

Tourist information

Tourist websites (www.spreewald-info.com or www.spreewald-online.de) sources of information about the area and they allow you to book hotel rooms online.

Haus für Mensch & Natur

Schulstrasse 9, Lübbenau (03542 89210/892130). **Open** 10am-5pm daily. **Admission** free. The 'House for Mankind & Nature' is the visitor and information centre for the Spreewald Biosphere Reservation, located within an old schoolhouse. It contains a permanent exhibition about the environmental importance of the Spreewald.

Spreewald Information

Ehm-Welk-Strasse 15, Lübbenau (03542 3668/www. spreewald-online.de). **Open** *Apr-Oct* 9am-6pm Mon-Fri; 9am-1pm Sat, Sun. *Nov-Mar* 9am-4pm Mon-Fri.

Rügen

The Baltic coast was the favoured holiday destination of the GDR citizen; post-reunification it is still the most accessible stretch of seaside for all Berliners. The coast forms the northern boundary of the modern state of Mecklenburg-Vorpommern. Bismarck said of the area: 'When the end of the world comes, I shall go to Mecklenburg, because there everything happens a hundred years later.'

The large island of **Rügen** is gradually resuming its rivalry with Sylt in the North Sea – both islands claim to be the principal north German resort. The island is undoubtedly beautiful, with its white chalk cliffs, beechwoods and beaches. Most people stay in the resorts on the east coast, such as Binz (the largest and best known), Sellin and Göhren. In July and August Rügen can get crowded (don't go without pre-booked accommodation), and the island's handful of restaurants and lack of late-night bars mean visitors are early to bed and early to rise. Go out of season and enjoy the solitude.

Where to stay & eat

Most accommodation on Rügen is in private houses. Your best bet is to contact the local tourist office (*see below*), which will be able to help you find a room. Camping is very popular on Rügen. Binz offers the best selection of places to eat.

Getting there

By train Most trains to Rügen terminate at Stralsund; it takes around 3hrs 30mins to reach Stralsund, then 30mins or so more to Rügen. There's one direct train a day from Ostbahnhof/Zoo to Bergen on Rügen, taking about 3hrs 30mins.

Tourist information

Tourismus Zentrale Rügen

Markt 4, Bergen, Rügen (03838 256093).
Open 9am-4pm Mon-Fri.
Heinrich-Heine-Strasse 7, Binz (038393 2782).
Open 9am-4pm Mon-Sat.
Schulstrasse 8, Göhren (038308 25940).
Open 9am-4pm Mon-Sat.
Wilhelmstrasse 40, Sellin (038308 1611).
Open 9am-4pm.
The Bergen head office can provide information, but cannot book rooms. Try the other offices for accommodation bookings. Try visiting www.ruegen.net for general information about the area.

Dresden

Destroyed twice and rebuilt one and a half times, the capital of Saxony – around 100 kilometres (60 miles) south of Berlin – boasts one of Germany's best art museums and many historic buildings.

Modern Dresden is built on the ruins of its past. A fire consumed Altendresden on the bank of the Elbe in 1685, provoking a wave of rebuilding throughout the city. On the night of 13 February 1945, the biggest of Sir Arthur 'Bomber' Harris's raids caused huge fire storms killing up to 100,000 people, mostly refugees from the Eastern Front. After the war, Dresden was twinned with Coventry, and Benjamin Britten's *War Requiem* was given its first performance in the Hofkirche by musicians from both towns. Under the GDR reconstruction was erratic, but a maze of cranes and scaffolding sprang up in the 1990s – Dresden is making up for lost time.

An unappealing resemblance to modern Coventry is immediately apparent walking from the station to the centre along hideous Prager Strasse. But press on through the tower blocks and 1960s-style shopping arcades (stopping at the tourist office to get a map) and the older city starts to assert itself.

Dresden's major attractions are the buildings from the reign of Augustus the Strong (1670-1733). The **Hofkirche**, the **Zwinger** complex – which includes a garden and a number of museums – all give a flavour of the city's baroque exuberance.

Dresden's main draw for art lovers is the **Gemäldegalerie Alte Meister** in the Zwinger. There are also exhibitions of porcelain from nearby Meissen, and collections of armour, weapons, clocks and scientific equipment.

There's more art to be enjoyed in the **Albertinum**, which contains both the **Gemäldegalerie Neue Meister** and the **Grünes Gewölbe**, a collection of Augustus's jewels and knick-knacks.

Building was continued by Augustus's successor, Augustus III, who then lost to Prussia in the Seven Years War (1756-63). Frederick the Great destroyed much of the city during the war, although not the spectacular riverside promenade of the **Brühlsche Terrasse** in the old part of the city. A victorious Napoleon ordered the demolition of the city's defences in 1809.

By the Zwinger stands the **Semperoper** opera house, named after its architect Gottfried Semper (1838-41), which was fully restored to its earlier elegance in 1985.

The industrialisation of Dresden heralded a new phase of construction that produced the **Rathaus** (Town Hall, 1905-10) at Dr-Külz-Ring, the **Hauptbahnhof** (1892-5) at the end of Prager Strasse, the **Yenidze cigarette factory** (1912) in Könneritzstrasse, designed to look like a mosque, and the grandiose **Landtagsgebäude** (completed to plans by Paul Wallot, designer of Berlin's Reichstag, in 1907) at Heinrich-Zille-Strasse 11. The finest example of inter-war architecture is

Trips Out of Town

Wilhelm Kreis' **Deutsches Hygienemuseum** (1929) at Lingner Platz 1, constructed to house the German Institute of Hygiene.

A brand new synagogue was dedicated in Dresden (Rathenauplatz) in November 2001, 63 years after its predecessor (built by Semper in 1838-40) was destroyed in the Nazi pogroms.

The ongoing reconstruction of the **Frauenkirche** at Neumarkt, the **Schloss**, and most prominently the **Altstadt** (Old Town), should see the city in its best light for its 800th anniversary in 2006.

The **Striezelmarkt** (named after the savoury pretzel you will see everyone eating) is held on Altstädtermarkt every December. The Christmas market is one of the most colourful events of the year. Dresden is also home to the best *Stollen*, a German variety of yuletide cake.

In the GDR days, this part of the country, behind the Saxon hills, could not receive Western television or radio broadcasts and was called 'Tal der Ahnungslosen' ('Valley of the Clueless'). In the process of catching up, a vibrant alternative scene has developed in the **Neustadt**, particularly in the bars and cafés on and around Alaunstrasse.

The Neustadt – on the north bank of the Elbe – literally means 'new town'. But don't be deceived: the Neustadt is over 300 years old, and, having escaped major damage during the wartime bombing raids, has much of its original architecture intact.

When Augustus the Strong commissioned the rebuilding of Dresden after the fire of 1685, his dream was to own a city on the water like Venice. The Neustadt doesn't quite evoke images of gondolas, but it does have charms of its own, such as the renovated 18th-century townhouses in Hauptstrasse and Königstrasse.

To avoid the tourist spillover from the Altstadt, head north and east of Albertplatz. Since reunification a wealth of boutiques, cafés and bars has sprung up in this maze of cobblestone streets.

Albertinum

Brühlsche Terrasse (0351 491 4622). **Open** 10am-6pm Mon-Wed, Fri-Sun. **Admission** €4.50; €2.50 concessions. **No credit cards.**
Houses two major collections of paintings and treasures – the Gemäldegalerie Neue Meister and the Grünes Gewölbe (Green Vault) – as well as coin and sculpture collections.

Gemäldegalerie Alte Meister

Zwinger, Theaterplatz (0351 491 4622/ www.staatl-kunstsammlungen-dresden.de). **Open** 10am-6pm Tue-Sun. **Admission** €3.60; €2.10 concessions. **No credit cards.**
A superb collection of Old Masters, particularly Italian Renaissance and Flemish.

Semperoper

Tickets: Aldstädter Wache, Theaterplatz (0351 491 4619). **Open** *Box office* 10am-6pm Mon-Fri; 10am-1pm Sat. **Tickets** €4.50-€56.50 concessions. **No credit cards.**

Where to eat & drink

Caroussel

Bülow-Residenz, Rähnitzgasse 19 (0351 80030). **Open** noon-2pm, 6.30-11pm daily. **Main courses** €30-€40. **Credit** AmEx, MC, V.
Particularly lovely in summer, when its leafy courtyard comes into its own, this contemporary German restaurant offers the finest cooking in Dresden.

Copas y Tapas

Goerlitzerstrasse 23 (0351 801 9960). **Open** call for details. **Main courses** call for details. **Credit** call for details.
This lively spot for cocktails and Spanish specialities is due to open under new ownership in April 2002. Limited information available at time of press.

Der Drachen

Bautzener Strasse 72 (0351 804 1188). **Open** noon-midnight daily. **Main courses** €15-€22. **Credit** DC, MC, V.
Fine modern German eaterie by the Elbe.

Herr Rosso und sein Hund

Luisenstrasse 47 (0351 801 1752). **Open** 2pm-1am Tue-Sun. **Main courses** €4-€8. **No credit cards.**
Classic coffee and cakes in the Neustadt.

Piccola Capri

Alaunstrasse 93 (0351 8024 774). **Open** noon-11pm. **Main courses** €8-€17. **Credit** MC, V.
One of the Neustadt's best Italians.

Nightlife

The Neustadt has the best nightlife in Dresden. Clubs with a different DJ each night include **Déjà-Vu** (Rothenburgerstrasse 37; 0351 802 3040) and **Flower Power** (Eschenstrasse 11; 0351 804 9814).

Where to stay

Arthotel Dresden

Ostra-Allee 33 (0351 49220/www.artotel.de). **Rates** €115 single; €130 double. **Credit** AmEx, MC, V.
Ultra-trendy art hotel, decorated with more than 600 works by local painter AR Penck.

Bastei/Königstein/Lilienstein

Pragerstrasse (Bastei 0351 4856 6661/Königstein 0351 4856 6662/Lilienstein 0351 4856 6663/ www.ibis-hotel.de). **Rates** €62-€66 single; €81-€85 double. **Credit** AmEx, MC, V.
Three functional Ibis tower-block hotels on Pragerstrasse between the rail station and Altstadt.

Bülow-Residenz

Rähnitzgasse 19 (0351 80030/
www.buelow-residenz.de). **Rates** €185 single;
€225 double. **Credit** AmEx, MC, V.
Five-star Relais & Chateaux luxury and a real old-
world elegance and intimacy.

Hostel Mondpalast

Katharinenstrasse 11-13 (0351 804 6061).
Rates €23 single; €34 double. **Credit** AmEx, MC, V.
A decent budget option in the Neustadt.

Hotel Smetana

Schlüterstrasse 25 (0351 256 080/
www.hotel-smetana.de). **Rates** €70 single;
€100 double. **Credit** AmEx,MC, V.
A pleasant three-star place, east of the centre.

Getting there

By train Direct trains run every 2hrs from
Berlin, and take 2hrs from Ostbahnhof and 2hrs
15mins from Zoo.

Tourist information

Dresden Tourist Information

Prager Strasse (0351 491 920/www.dresden-
tourist.de). **Open** 10am-7pm Mon-Fri; 9am-4pm Sat.
Schinkelwache, Theaterplatz (0351 491 920/
www.dresden-tourist.de). **Open** 10am-6pm Mon-Fri;
10am-4pm Sat, Sun.

Leipzig

One of Germany's most important trade
centres and former second city of the GDR,
Leipzig is Bach's city, a centre of education
and culture of long pedigree, and the place
where East Germany's mass movement for
political change began. Once one of Germany's
biggest industrial strongholds, the city has
been famed for its fairs for centuries; trade
fairs (*Messen*) are its bread and butter these
days. The influx of western businesspeople
stimulated a thorough scrubbing clean of the
city and a slew of major restoration schemes.
The largely pedestrianised centre of Leipzig
today has great charm, and more than
enough sights, bars and restaurants to fill
a visit of a day or two.

Located in Saxony, around 130 kilometres
(80 miles) south-west of Berlin, the city traces
its origins back to a settlement founded by
the Sorbs, a Slavic people who venerated the
lime tree, some time between the seventh to
ninth centuries. The Sorbs called it Lipzk,
meaning 'place of limes'.

Most visitors arrive at **Leipzig
Hauptbahnhof**, the huge, sparklingly
renovated central train station (the largest in
Europe; it incorporates a three-level shopping

mall). The station stands on the north-east
edge of the compact city centre, which is a mere
one kilometre (third of a mile) square, and is
surrounded by a ring road that follows the
course of the old city walls. Much of the ring
road is lined with parks, and most of Leipzig's
major attractions can be found within its limits.

The first place to head is the **Leipzig
Tourist Service** office, diagonally left across
tram-strewn Willy-Brand-Platz from the front of
the train station. Pick up the excellent guide to
the city in English (which includes a map) and
head for **Markt**, the old market square, to get
your bearings. The eastern side of the square
is occupied by the lovely Renaissance **Altes
Rathaus** (Old Town Hall), built in a mere nine
months (between fairs) in 1556-7. The building
now houses the **Stadtgeschichtliches
Museum** (Town Museum). On the square's
south side are the huge bay windows of
the **Könighaus**, one-time regular haunt of
Saxony's rulers when visiting the city during
fairs (the notoriously rowdy Peter the Great of
Russia also once stayed here).

The church off the south-west corner
of Markt is the **Thomaskirche**, where
Johan Sebastian Bach spent 27 years as
Kappellmeister, choirmaster of the famous St
Thomas's Boys Choir; the great man is buried
in the chancel and his statue stands outside
the church. Here too is the prefab Thomasshop,
which details on its side a Bach-themed stroll
around the city. Opposite the church in the
Bosehaus is the **Bach-Museum**.

Heading south from the Thomaskirche
towards the south-west corner of the ring road,
brings you to the **Neues Rathaus** (New Town
Hall), the origins of which go back to the 16th
century, although the current buildings are
only about 100 years old.

Immediately behind the Altes Rathaus is
the delightful little chocolate box of the **Alte
Börse** (Old Stock Exchange), built in 1687, and
fronted by a statue of Goethe, who studied at
Leipzig University. Follow his gaze towards the
entrance to **Mädler Passage**, Leipzig's finest
shopping arcade, within which is **Auerbachs
Keller**, one of the oldest and most famous
restaurants in Germany. It was in Auerbachs,
where he often used to drink, that Goethe
set a scene in *Faust*, which saw Faust and
Mephistopheles boozing with students before
riding off on a barrel.

North of the Alte Börse, back towards
the station, is Sachsenplatz, site of the city's
main outdoor market, and the new home of the
Museum der Bildenden Künste (Museum
of Arts Picture Gallery), which features a good
clutch of Old Masters. The museum was due
to open in the summer of 2002.

Leipzig: Goethe's statue by the Alte Börse, relaxing by the Swan Pond and... an elephant.

Just south-east of here is the **Nikolaikirche**, Leipzig's proud symbol of its new freedom. This medieval church, with its baroque interior featuring columns that imitate palm trees, is the place where regular free-speech meetings started in 1982. These evolved into the 'Swords to Ploughshares' peace movement, which led to the first anti-GDR demonstration on 4 September 1989 in the Nikolaikirchhof.

West of here, on the edge of the ring road, is the **Museum in der 'Runde Ecke'** (Museum in the 'Round Corner', the nickname of the building that once housed the local Stasi headquarters and that now contains an exhibition on its nefarious methods). North of here, outside of the ring road, is **Leipzig Zoo**.

In the south-east corner of the ring road rises the unappealing tower block of **Leipzig University** (built in 1970, and supposed to resemble an opened book on its side), ironically one of Europe's oldest centres of learning. Alumni, besides Goethe, include Schumann, Wagner, Leibniz and Heisenberg. The university runs the **Ägyptisches Museum**, and not far away there's the applied arts of the **Grassi Museum für Kunsthandwerk**.

The university tower stands at the south-eastern corner of Augustplatz, a project of GDR Communist Party leader Walter Ulbricht, himself a Leipziger. Next door to it are the brown glass-fronted buildings of the **Gewandhaus**, home of the Leipziger Gewandhaus Orchester, one of the world's finest orchestras. On the square's northern side stands the **Opernhaus Leipzig** (opened in 1960), which also has an excellent reputation.

Ägyptisches Museum

Schillerstrasse 6 (0341 973 7010/www.uni-leipzig.de/ ~egypt). **Open** 1-5pm Mon-Sat; 10am-1pm Sun. **Admission** €2; €1 concessions. **Credit** AmEx, MC, V.

Bach-Museum

Thomaskirchhof 16 (0341 913 7202/www.bach-leipzig.de). **Open** 10am-5pm daily. **Admission** €3; €2 concessions. *With tour* €6; €4 concessions. **No credit cards.**
Documents, instruments and furniture from Bach's time illustrate the work and influence of the great man.

Gewandhaus

Augustusplatz 8 (0341 12700/127 080/ www.gewandhaus.de). **Open** Box office 10am-6pm Mon-Fri; 10am-2pm Sat. **Tickets** varies. **No credit cards.**

Grassi Museum für Kunsthandwerk

Neumarkt 20 (0341 213 3719/ www.grassimuseum.de). **Open** 10am-6pm Tue, Thur-Sun; 10am-8pm Wed. **Admission** €4; €2 concessions. **Credit** AmEx, MC, V.
Currently in a temporary home, this museum was founded in 1874 and became an important centre for applied art in the 1920s.

Leipzig Zoo

Pfaffendorfer Strasse 29 (0341 593 3500/ www.zooleipzig.de). **Open** *May-Sept* 9am-7pm daily. *Apr, Oct* 9am-6pm Mon-Fri; 9am-7pm Sat, Sun. *Nov-Mar* 9am-5pm daily. **Admission** €7.50; €4-€6 concessions. **No credit cards.**
All the usual family favourites are here: lions, tigers, orang utans, polar bears and hippos.

Opernhaus Leipzig

Augustusplatz 12 (0341 12610/www.leipzig-online.de/oper). **Open** Box office 10am-8pm Mon-Fri; 10am-4pm Sat; 1hr before performances Sun. **Tickets** varies. **No credit cards.**
Call for information about tours of the building.

Museum der Bildenden Künste

Sachsenplatz (0341 216 990/www.leipzig.de/ museum-d-bil-kuenste.htm). **Open** 10am-6pm Tue, Thur-Sun; 1-9.30pm Wed. **Admission** €2.50; €1 concessions; free 2nd Sun of mth. *Temporary exhibitions* €4; €2 concessions. **No credit cards.**
Due to relocate to these new premises in mid 2002 (and located at Grimmaische Strasse 1-7 until then), this enjoyable art gallery has an interesting range of works, stretching from 15th- and 16th-century Dutch, Flemish and German paintings to German expressionism and GDR art.

Museum in der 'Runde Ecke'

Dittrichring 24 (0341 961 2443). **Open** 10am-6pm daily. *Tour* 3pm daily. **Admission** free. *Tour* €3; €2 concessions. **No credit cards.**
The subtitle of the museum – 'Stasi: power and banality, evidence of criminality' – gives more of a clue of what it contains, an interesting (despite the

lack of English labelling) look at the Stasi's fright-ening yet often ridiculous methods, such as the collecting of the scents of suspected people in jars, and a hilarious section on Stasi disguises.

Nikolaikirche

Nikolaikirchhof 3 (0341 960 5270/ www.nikolaikirche-leipzig.de). **Open** 10am-noon Mon, Tue, Thur, Fri; 4-6pm Wed. **Admission** free.

Stadtgeschichtliches Museum

Altes Rathaus, Markt 1 (0341 965130). **Open** 2-8pm Tue; 10am-6pm Wed-Sun. **Admission** €2.50; €2 concessions. **No credit cards.**

Thomaskirche

Thomaskirchhof 18 (0341 960 2855/ www.thomaskirche.org). **Open** 9am-6pm daily. **Admission** free.

Where to stay

Thanks to the proliferation of business folk attending trade fairs, accommodation prices in Leipzig are generally very high. The cheapest option is to find a private room via the Leipzig Tourist Service. North of the rail station you'll find all the luxury chains (Kempinski, Inter-Continental, Marriott, etc).

Adagio Minotel Leipzig

Seeburgstrasse 96 (0341 216 699/www.hotel-adagio.de). **Rates** €67-€80 single; €82-€102 double. **No credit cards.**
The Adagio Minotel has individually furnished rooms and a good central location.

Hotel Mercure Leipzig

Augustusplatz 5-6 (0341 21460/www.hotel-mercure-leipzig.de). **Rates** €66 single; €78 double. **Credit** AmEx, MC, V.
Not exactly packed with character, but the Mercure is well located, a few minutes' walk from the train station and the city centre.

Where to eat & drink

Apels Garten

Kolonnadenstrasse 2 (0341 960 7777). **Open** 10.30am-midnight Mon-Sat; 10.30am-3.30pm Sun. **Main courses** €8-€12. **Credit** AmEx, MC, V.
A pretty, refined restaurant offering imaginative German cooking. Don't miss the smoked fish soup.

Auerbachs Keller

Mädlerpassage, Grimmaische Strasse 2-4 (0341 216 100). **Open** 11.30am-midnight daily. **Set menus** from €20 3 courses. **Credit** AmEx, DC, MC, V.
Two restaurants in one – a small, pricey gourmet affair and a more affordable version. In both, the menu and the wine list are of excellent quality at Auerbachs. Specialities include *Leipziger Allerlei*, a dish of steamed mixed vegetables and mushrooms with crayfish.

Barthels Hof

Hainstrasse 1 (0341 141 310). **Open** 7am-midnight. **Main courses** €9.50-€17. **Credit** AmEx, MC, V.
A local favourite, offering hearty Saxon cooking in a cosy beamed and panelled *Gasthaus*.

El Matador

Friedrich-Ebert-Strasse 108 (0341 980 0876). **Open** 5.30pm-midnight Mon-Sat. **Main courses** €8-€15. **Credit** MC, V.
Decent Spanish cooking and a bullfighting theme.

Nightlife

With a major university in the centre of the city, it's no surprise that Leipzig is something of a party town. Wander the streets around Markt and you're sure to find somewhere appealing for late-night quaffing. If you're in the mood for dancing, try **Distillery** (Kurt-Eisner-Strasse/corner of Löszniger Strasse, 0341 963 0718).

Tourist information

Leipzig Tourist Service

Richard-Wagner-Strasse 1 (0341 710 4260/4265/ www.leipzig.de). **Open** 9am-7pm Mon-Fri; 9am-4pm Sat; 9am-2pm Sun.

Getting there

By train Direct trains from Berlin every 2hrs; the fastest takes 1hr 34mins from Ostbahnhof, 1hr 51mins from Zoo.

Eisenhüttenstadt & Neuzelle

The border with Poland is a mere 70 kilometres (40 miles) east of Berlin. The largest settlement in the area is the deeply unappealing city of **Frankfurt-am-Oder**, but it does act as a gateway to a couple of interesting sights that can be combined to form a rewarding day trip.

Around 25 kilometres (16 miles) south of Frankfurt is **Eisenhüttenstadt** (literally 'steel works town'), once the pride of GDR industry. Founded under its original name 'Stalinstadt' in the early 1950s as a housing estate for the local steel works, and renamed in 1961, it was enthusiastically labelled 'the first socialist town on German soil'. And, in a way, it was the last one too (considering the privileges they were granted during the GDR-ears, a good number of the inhabitants didn't quite see the point of capitalism).

Today, Eisenhüttenstadt is not exactly a major tourist draw, but, with its factory chimneys and restored socialist murals on Lindenallee (formally Leninallee), it retains a real GDR feel, and is a fascinating stop for 'ostalgics'. From ornamented and generously proportioned 1950s housing complexes to 1980s prefabricated multistorey buildings, it acts as a museum of socialist architecture.

Former engineers give guided tours of the impressive EKO steel factory that once gave work to 12,000. (Now, counting in outsourced branches, there are 5,000 jobs left.) Distances within the factory grounds are huge, so you may need to bring your own car. Tours are free and are sometimes available in English. Call to check and book, if possible 14 days in advance (03364 372 066/010).

After all that industrial grimness, the perfect antidote is a few minutes further down the train line at **Neuzelle**, with its monastery with two churches, cloisters and a beautiful garden being the main attraction. When the church of St Mary was built in the 13th century, it was Gothic in style, but after its destruction during the Thirty Years War in the 17th century, it was rebuilt in a baroque style. Its lavish mouldings, generous frescos and fine altars are something you might expect to see in Bavaria, but not (now) Protestant Brandenburg. Attached to the monastery is a brewery, which runs enjoyable tours and tastings.

Dokumentationszentrum Alltagskultur der DDR
Erich-Weinert-Allee 3, Eisenhüttenstadt (03364 417 355). **Open** 1-6pm Tue-Fri; 10am-6pm Sat, Sun. **Admission** €2.10; €1.10 concessions. **No credit cards.**
Rumour has it that in the early 1990s a west German business consultant had the idea of declaring the complete town of Eisenhüttenstadt an open-air GDR museum, including the inhabitants. He didn't succeed. However, for those interested in what it was like to live in the GDR, check out this museum of 'everyday life culture' in one of the historic 1950s buildings. The permanent exhibition covers the local steel factory's history, the educational system and displays of furniture and consumer products; special exhibitions change. English tours are available, but you should call in advance. To reach the museum from the train station, take any bus to Karl-Marx-Strasse/Strasse der Republik and get off at the post office.

Klosterbrauerei Neuzelle
Brauhausplatz 1, Neuzelle (033652 81012). **Open** by arrangement only for groups of 11 or more. **Admission** €6 (incl 3 beers). **Credit** AmEx, MC.
The brewery was founded as part of the monastery in 1589 and claims to be the oldest brewery in Brandenburg. The private management that runs it now is an example of efficient PR. First they launched a dark *Badebier* (bathing beer), which is supposed to be healthy for skin and circulation (and

you can drink it too). The brewery hit the news again when the Food Ministry refused to recognise one of its products a proper beer. Tours in German only, call in advance. If you take a tour of the brewery, don't miss the tasting. Kummerower Hof (*see below*) offers a patented beer bath.

Where to eat & drink

C'est la vie
Lindenallee 54, Eisenhüttenstadt (03364 418 899). **Open** 8.30am-7pm daily. **No credit cards.**
This is as stylish a café as you'll find in Eisenhüttenstadt. The window front is covered with a sort of blue plastic foil, which produces funny visual effects – as a result of your eyes getting accustomed to the blue light while having your coffee and sandwich, everything looks brownish-yellow once you leave the place (a very 'ostalgic' tone). The staff didn't believe us when we pointed this out to them, but try it yourself…

Klosterklause Neuzelle
Brauhausplatz 4, Neuzelle (033652 390). **Open** 11am-11pm daily. **Main courses** €10-€17. **Credit** AmEx, MC.
Right by the entrance of the monastery. The menu at the Klosterklause Neuzelle is quite broad, but go for the heavy stuff, like *Schweinshaxe* and venison goulash. Pick from a dozen types of beer, all made in the brewery next door.

Kummerower Hof
Kummroer Strasse 41, Neuzelle (033652 8110). **Open** 11am-10pm daily. **Rates** €42 single; €59 double. **Main courses** €7-€12. **Credit** V.
The trademark of this family-run inn, a couple of kilometres from the centre of Neuzelle, is the patented beer bath they prepare with a six-pint shot of Neuzelle *Badebier* (€39). You can also book a complete beer-bathing weekend, including the beer dip, a two-night stay, breakfast, a brewery tour and a beer meal for €106 per person.

Getting there

By train *To Eisenhüttenstadt* Direct trains run hourly; the fastest takes 1hr 27mins from Ostbahnhof and 1hr 42mins from Zoo. *To Neuzelle* Trains take 1hr 34mins from Ostbahnhof and 1hr 51mins from Zoo, with one change at Frankfurt-am-Oder. From the station in Neuzelle it's a 15-min walk to the monastery and brewery.

Tourist information

Tourist offices
Lindenallee 2A (Lindenzentrum) Eisenhüttenstadt (03364 413690/www.fvv-oder-neisse.de). **Open** 9am-6pm Mon-Fri; 9am-noon Sat. *Stiftsplatz 7, Neuzelle (033652 6102/ www.neuzelle.de).* **Open** 10am-noon, 12.30-4pm Mon-Fri; 11am-3.30pm Sat, Sun.

Directory

Features

Directory

Getting Around

Arriving & leaving

By air

Until **Berlin Brandenburg International Airport** is built (planned for 2007), Berlin is served by three airports: **Tegel**, **Schönefeld** and **Tempelhof**. Information in English on all of these airports (including live departures and arrivals) can be found at **www.berlin-airport.de**.

Note: the majority of Berlin's hotels are in **Mitte**, the revived centre of the united city (formerly in the east) or within easy reach of **Bahnhof Zoo** (Zoo Station), the pivotal point of the western city.

Tegel Airport

Airport Information (0180 5000 186/www.berlin-airport.de). **Open** 6am-10pm daily. **Map** p300 B1. Most flights to and from Berlin use compact Tegel Airport, which is a mere 8km (5 miles) north-west of Mitte. The airport contains a tourist information counter, exchange facilities, shops, restaurants, bars and car rental desks.

Buses 109 and **X9** (the express version) run via Luisenplatz and the Kurfürstendamm to Bahnhof Zoologischer Garten (known as Zoo Station, or just Zoo), the hub of western Berlin. Tickets cost **€2.10** (and can also be used on U-Bahn and S-Bahn services), and buses run every five to 15 minutes, and take 30-40 minutes to reach Zoo. From Zoo you can connect by bus, U-Bahn or S-Bahn to anywhere in the city (same tickets are valid). There are rail and tourist information offices at Zoo (*see p285*).

Alternatively, you can take **bus 109** to Jacob-Kaiser-Platz U-Bahn (U7), or **bus 128** to Kurt-Schumacher-Platz U-Bahn (U6). One ticket can be used for the combined journey (cost **€2.10**).

The only direct link from Tegel to Mitte is the **JetExpressBus TXL**, which travels via the Brandenburg Gate to Potsdamer Platz, and on to Französische Strasse U-Bahn station (U6) on Friedrichstrasse, close to Unter den Linden. A one-way ticket starts at **€4.10**, and the journey takes 25-30 minutes. The buses run from the airport from 6am to 11.10pm every ten minutes (every 20 minutes at weekends), and from the city centre to the airport between 5.20am to 9pm every ten minutes (every 20 minutes at weekends).

A **taxi** to anywhere central will cost around **€18-€22**, and takes 20-30 minutes, depending on the specific destination and the traffic.

Schönefeld Airport

Airport Information (0180 5000 186/www.berlin-airport.de). **Open** 24hrs daily. The former airport of East Berlin is 18km (11 miles) south-east of the city centre. It's small, and serves mainly eastern Europe, the Middle and Far East (though UK budget airline Buzz also uses it). The usual foreign exchange, shops, snack bars and car hire facilities can be found here.

Train is the best means of reaching the city centre. **S-Bahnhof Flughafen Schönefeld** is a five-minute walk from the terminal (a free S-Bahn shuttle bus operates every ten minutes from outside the airport). From here, the **Airport Express** train runs from platform seven to Mitte (20 minutes to Alexanderplatz) and Zoo (30 minutes) every half hour from 5.10am to 1.40am at 10 minutes (route RE5) and 40 minutes (route RE4) past the hour. Be warned that the final destination of the trains varies, so check the timetable for your stop. There are ticket machines on platforms 11 and 13. Alternatively, you can take S-Bahn line S9 from the station (around 35 minutes to Alexanderplatz, 45 minutes to Zoo), or travel one stop on **bus 171** to the U7 U-Bahn line at **Rudow** station, which also runs into the city centre.

All one-way tickets from the airport to the city centre cost **€2.40** (*Normaltarif*, covering zones A-C), and can be used on any combination of bus, U-Bahn and S-Bahn.

A **taxi** to Zoo or Mitte is pricey: **€30-€35**, and takes 45-60 minutes.

Tempelhof Airport

Airport Information (0180 5000 186/www.berlin-airport.de). Flight Information (6951 2288). **Open** 6am-10pm daily. **Map** p306 F6.

Berlin's third airport, Tempelhof is a mere 4km (2.5 miles) south of Mitte, but very few airlines now use it. The airport contains basic shops, snack bars, exchange facilities and car hire desks.

Connections to the rest of Berlin are easy. **Platz der Luftbrücke** U-Bahn station (U6 – direct to Friedrichstrasse and Mitte in around ten minutes) is a short walk from the terminal building, as are bus connections. **Bus 109** goes from the airport terminal to the Europa-Center, close to Bahnhof Zoo, and the western hub of the city (journey time: around 20 minutes).

All public transport tickets from Tempelhof to the centre cost **€2.10**, and can be used on any combination of bus, U-Bahn and S-Bahn services.

A **taxi** into Mitte or to Zoo will cost **€12-€18**, and will take about 15 minutes and 20 minutes, respectively.

AIRLINES

From outside Germany dial the international access code (usually 00), then 49 for Germany and then the number (omitting any initial zero). All operators speak English.

Air France 4101 2715/ www.airfrance.de
Alitalia 4101 2650/www.alitalia.de
British Airways 01805 26 65 22/ www.britishairways.com
buzz 069 5007 0133/www.buzz.de
Deutsche BA 01805 35 93 22/247 36 80/www.deutsche.ba.de
Iberia 4101 2698/0180 300 06 13/ www.iberia.de
KLM 4101 3844/www.klm.de
Lufthansa 01803 80 38 03/ www.lufthansa.de

By rail

Bahnhof Zoo

Deutsche Bahn Information, Zoologischer Garten (Bahnhof Zoo), Hardenbergplatz, Charlottenburg (Info in English 01805 99 66 33/ www.bahn.de). **Open** 5am-11pm daily. **Map** p304 C4.

Bahnhof Zoo is the point of arrival from most destinations to the west. Most of these trains also stop at **Ostbahnhof**. Bahnhof Zoo has excellent bus, U-Bahn and S-Bahn links with the rest of the city, as well as left luggage facilities, lockers, currency exchange, an information counter (which can book hotels) and the very helpful **EurAide** office (*see p285*) offering advice in English for travellers. It's also close to the main tourist office (*see p285*), and there are plenty of shops and restaurants with extended opening hours.

Bahnhof Lichtenberg, out in the wilds of east Berlin on U-Bahn line U5, and S-Bahn lines S5, S7 and S75, is the main station for destinations to the south and east, including Vienna, Warsaw, Prague, Budapest, Dresden and Leipzig. It's a small place, with limited lockers and an information desk.

Both of these stations will be superseded when the major new rail terminus at **Lehrter Stadtbahnhof** (north of Tiergarten) is completed (estimated to be in 2006), with direct links to airports.

By bus

Zentraler Omnibus Bahnhof (ZOB)

Masurenallee 4-6, Charlottenburg (Information 301 0380).
Open 5.30am-9.30pm Mon-Sat.
Map p304 A4.
Buses arrive in west Berlin at the Central Bus Station, opposite the radio tower (Funkturm) and the ICC (International Congress Centrum). From here, U-Bahn line U2 runs into the centre. A left luggage office is located at ZOB. There is no bus station in the eastern half of the city.

Getting around

Berlin is served by a comprehensive and interlinked network of buses, trains, trams and ferries. It's efficient and punctual, though not particularly cheap.

The respective transport systems of former East and West Berlin have mostly been sewn back together, though it can still sometimes be complicated travelling between eastern and western destinations. Even within one half of the city, journeys can involve several changes of route or mode of transport. But services are usually regular and frequent, and timetables can be trusted.

The Berlin transport authority, the **BVG**, operates the **bus**, **U-Bahn** (underground, some of which runs on the surface), **S-Bahn** (surface rail, some of which runs underground) and **tram** networks (only in the eastern half of the city). These, plus a few **ferry** services on the lakes, are all connected on the same three-zone tariff system (*see below* **Fares & tickets**).

Information

There are **BVG information centres** at **Turmstrasse** U-Bahn station (U9; open 6.30am-8.30pm Mon-Fri, 9am-3.30pm Sat) and at Zoo Pavillon, Hardenburger Strasse, outside **Bahnhof Zoo** (open 6am-10pm daily). In addition, the BVG website (**www.bvg.de**) has a wealth of information (in English) on city transport.

The **Liniennetz**, a map of all U-Bahn, S-Bahn, bus and tram routes for Berlin and Potsdam, is available free from info centres and ticket offices and includes an enlarged city centre map. A schematic map of the U- and S-Bahn can be picked up free at the same ticket offices or from the grey-uniformed *Zugabfertiger* – 'customer assistance personnel' – who can be found in some of the larger U-Bahn and S-Bahn stations.

Fares & tickets

The city's integrated bus, tram, U-Bahn, S-Bahn and ferry services operate on a **three-zone system**. Zone A covers the centre of the city, zone B extends out to the edge of the suburbs, while zone C stretches beyond the city limits. See the public transport map at the back of this guide for details of precisely what area is covered by each zone.

The basic single ticket is the **€2.10** *Normaltarif* (zones A and B). Few visitors will wish

to travel beyond the boundary of zone B, making it, in effect, a flat-fare system.

Apart from the *Zeitkarten* (longer-term tickets, *see below*), tickets for Berlin's public transport system can be bought from the yellow or orange machines at U- or S-Bahn stations, and by some bus stops. These take coins and sometimes notes, give change and have a limited explanation of the ticket system in English. Once you've purchased your ticket, validate it in the small red or yellow box next to the machine, which stamps it with the time and date. If you're caught without a valid ticket by an inspector, you will be fined **€30** on the spot. Ticket inspections are fairly frequent, particularly at weekends and at the beginning of the month.

Single ticket (Normaltarif)

Single tickets cost €2.10 for travel within two zones or €2.40 for all three zones (€1.40-€1.50 and €1.80, respectively, for children between the ages of six and 14). A ticket allows use of the BVG network for two hours, with as many changes between bus, tram, U-Bahn and S-Bahn and as many breaks as you like.

Short-distance ticket (Kurzstreckentarif)

The *Kurzstreckentarif* (ask for a *Kurzstrecke*) costs €1.20 (€1 concessions). It is valid for three U- or S-Bahn stops, or six bus stops. No transfers allowed.

Day ticket (Tageskarte)

The *Tageskarte* allows travel anywhere in two zones (€6.10; €4.10 concessions) or in all three zones (€6.30; €4.50 concessions) until 3am the day after validating.

Longer-term tickets (Zeitkarten)

If you're in Berlin for a week, it makes sense to buy a **Sieben-Tage-Karte** ('seven-day ticket'), for €22-€23 for two zones or €28 for all three (no concessions).

A stay of a month or more makes it worthwhile to buy a **Monatskarte** ('month ticket'), which costs €56-€58 for two zones and €69.50 for three zones (no concessions).

Directory

U-Bahn

The first stretch of Berlin's U-Bahn was opened in 1902 and the network now consists of nine lines and 170 stations. (A number of the most interesting old stations – such as Wittenbergplatz – have been renovated to coincide with the U-Bahn's 100th birthday in 2002.) The first trains run shortly after 4am; the last between midnight and 1am, except weekends on the U1/15 and U9 lines when trains run all night. The direction of travel is indicated by the name of the last stop on the line.

S-Bahn

Under constant renovation for over a decade, the S-Bahn system is no longer the rattly ride through the city's 'ripped backsides', as celebrated in Iggy Pop's *The Passenger*. It's especially useful in eastern Berlin, covers long distances faster than the U-Bahn and is a more efficient means for getting to outlying areas.

Renovation work on the S-Bahn system is almost complete, though there are still temporary disruptions. The final piece of the puzzle will be the northern segment of the inner Ringbahn – from Jungfernheide to Schönhauser Allee – scheduled for completion in autumn 2002.

Buses

Berlin has a dense network of 165 bus routes, of which 56 run in the early hours (*see below* **Travelling at night**). The day lines run from 4.30am to about 1am the next morning. Enter at the front of the bus and exit in the middle. The driver sells only individual tickets, but all tickets from the orange or yellow machines on the U-Bahn are valid. Most bus stops have clear timetables and route maps.

Trams

There are 28 tram lines (five of which run at night), all originating in the east, though some have now been extended a few kilometres into the western half of the city, mostly in Wedding. **Hackescher Markt** is the site of the main tram terminus. Tickets are available from machines on the trams, at the termini and in U-Bahn stations.

Other rail services

Berlin is also served by the **Regionalbahn** ('regional railway'), which in former times connected East Berlin with Potsdam via the suburbs and small towns that had been left outside the Wall. It still circumnavigates the entire city. The Regionalbahn is run by Deutsche Bahn and ticket prices vary according to the journey.

For timetable information and ticket prices (in English), check out Deutsche Bahn's excellent website: http://bahn.hafas.de/bin/query.exe/en.

Travelling at night

Berlin has a comprehensive **Nachtliniennetz** ('night-line network') that covers all parts of town via 60 bus and tram routes running every 30 minutes between 1am and 4am. Before and after these times the regular timetable for bus and tram routes applies. In addition, the U12 (Ruhleben to Warschauer Strasse) and U9 (Osloer Strasse to Rathaus Steglitz) lines run all night on Fridays and Saturdays, with trains every 15 minutes.

Night-line network maps and timetables are available from BVG information kiosks at stations. Ticket prices are the same as during the day. Buses and trams that run at night are distinguished by an 'N' in front of the number.

Note: The N16 to Potsdam runs only once an hour. S-Bahn lines 3 to 10 provide an hourly service. On lines N11 and N41 the bus will actually take you right to your front door if it's close to the official route.

The BVG also operates a **Taxi-Ruf-System** ('taxi calling service') on the U-Bahn for people with disabilities and for female passengers from 8pm every evening until the network closes. Just ask the uniformed BVG employee in the platform booth to phone, giving your destination and method of payment.

Boat trips

Getting about by water is more of a leisure activity than a practical means of getting around the city. Besides the BVG there are several private companies operating on Berlin's waterways.

Reederei Heinz Riedel

Planufer 78, Kreuzberg (691 3782). U8 Schönleinstrasse. **Open** *May-Sept (and fair-weather days in Oct)* 8am-4pm (and poor-weather days in Oct) 8am-4pm Mon-Fri. **Map** p306 F5.
Excursions are available that start in the city and pass through industrial suburbs into rural Berlin. A tour through the city's rivers and canals costs €5-€15.

Stern und Kreisschiffahrt

Puschkinallee 16-17, Treptow (536 3600/www.sternundkreis.de). S6, S8, S9, S10 Treptower Park. **Open** 7.30am-4pm daily.
Around 25 different cruises along the Spree and around lakes in the Berlin area. Departure points and times vary. A 3hr 30min city tour costs €14.

Taxis

Berlin taxis are pricey, reasonably efficient and numerous, yet sometimes hard to find when you need one.

The starting fee is €2.50 and thereafter the fare is €1.53 per kilometre (about €3.06 per mile) for the first six kilometres (four miles). The rate remains the same at night. For short journeys ask for a *Kurzstrecke*. For €3 this will allow you to travel for two kilometres. These are only available when you've hailed a cab and not from taxi ranks. Taxi stands are relatively numerous, especially in central areas, and can usually be found near stations and at major intersections.

You can phone for a cab 24 hours daily on **261 026**. Cabs ordered by phone are charged at the same rates. Most taxi firms can transport disabled people, but require advance notice. Cabs accept all credit cards, subject to a €0.50 charge.

The majority of cabs are Mercedes. If you want an estate car (station wagon), ask for a 'combi'. There's also a company called **Berlin Taxi** that operates vans capable of transporting up to seven people. Call **813 2613**.

Driving

Though the city is increasingly congested, driving in Berlin, with its wide, straight roads, presents few particular problems. Visitors from the UK and US should bear in mind that, in the absence of signals, drivers must yield to traffic from the right, except at crossings marked by a diamond-shaped yellow sign. In the east, trams always have right of way. An *Einbahnstrasse* is a one-way street.

Breakdown services

The following garages offer 24-hour assistance at a rate of about €58 an hour. But they won't take credit cards.

Abschleppdienst West
Mansfelder Strasse 58, Wilmersdorf (883 6851).

Eichmanns Autodienst
Rothenbachstrasse 55, Weissensee (471 9401).

Fuel stations

Both of the places below are open 24 hours a day.

Aral
Holzmarktstrasse 12, Mitte (2472 0748). **Credit** AmEx, MC, V. **Map** p307 G4.

BP-Oil
Kurfürstendamm 128, Wilmersdorf (8909 6972). **Credit** AmEx, MC, V. **Map** p304 B5.

Parking

Parking is free in Berlin side streets, but spaces are increasingly hard to find. If you park illegally (pedestrian crossing, loading zone, bus lane and so on), you risk getting your car clamped or towed away. Meters are appearing in some areas.

There are long-term car parks at Schönefeld and Tegel airports (*see p270*). Otherwise there are numerous *Parkgaragen* and *Parkhäuser* (multistorey and underground car parks) around the city, open 24 hours, that charge about €1-€2 an hour.

Schönefeld Airport Car Park
0180 5000 186. **Rates** *per day* €9; *per week* €25. **Credit** V.

Tegel Airport Car Park
0180 5000 186. **Rates** *per day* €17; *per week* €102. **No credit cards.**

Tempelhof Airport
0180 5000 186. **Rates** *per day* €12; *per week* €70. **No credit cards.**

Vehicle hire

Car hire in Germany is not generally expensive and all major companies are represented in Berlin. There are a range of car hire desks at all three of the city's airports, including the major international names. Look under *Autovermietung* in the *Gelbe Seiten* (*Yellow Pages*); prices vary, so be sure to shop around.

Cycling

The western half of Berlin is wonderful for cycling – flat, well equipped with cycle paths and with lots of parks to scoot through and canals to cruise alongside. East Berlin is no less flat, but has far fewer cycle paths and a lot more cobblestones, tram lines and holes in the road.

On the U-Bahn, there is a limit of two cycles at the end of carriages that have a bicycle sign on them. Bikes may not be taken on the U-Bahn during rush hour (defined as 6-9am and 2-5pm). More may be taken on to S-Bahn carriages, and at any time of day. In each case an extra ticket must be bought for each bike. The **ADFC Fahrradstadtplan**, available in bike shops for €6.40, is an excellent guide to the city's cycle routes. The companies below will rent bikes. Or look under *Fahrradverleih* in the *Yellow Pages*.

City Bike Service
Uhlandstrasse 106A, Wilmersdorf (861 5237/www.citybikeservice.de). U7 Blissestrasse. **Rates** *per day* from €7.50. **No credit cards.** **Map** p305 C5.

Fahrradstation
Bahnhof Friedrichstrasse, Mitte (2045 4500). S1, S2, S3, S5, S7, S9, S25, S26, S75, U6 Friedrichstrasse. **Rates** *per day* €8. **No credit cards.** **Map** p302 F3. **Branches**: *Bergmannstrasse 9, Kreuzberg (2045 4500)*; *Hackesche Höfe, Mitte (2045 4500)*.

Pedalpower
Grossbeerenstrasse 53, Kreuzberg (7899 1939/www.pedalpower.de) U1, U7 Möckernbrücke. **Rates** *per day* from €8. **No credit cards.** **Map** p306 F5.

Walking

Berlin is a good walking city. The only problem is that it's spread out. Getting around, say, Mitte is most pleasant on foot, but if you then want to check out Charlottenburg, you'll next need to take a bus or train.

Directory

Resources A-Z

Addresses

The house/building number always follows the street name (eg Friedrichstrasse 21), and numbers sometimes run up one side of the street and back down the other side. *Strasse* (street) is often abbreviated to *Str* and is sometimes not written separately but appended to the street name (as in the example above). With flats, *EG* means ground floor; *1 OG* is the first floor.

Age restrictions

The legal age for drinking is 16; for smoking it is 16; for driving it is 18; and the age of consent for heterosexual and homosexual sex is 16.

Business

Conferences

Messe Berlin
Messedamm 22, Charlottenburg (303 80). U2 Theodor-Heuss-Platz. **Open** 10am-6pm. **Map** p304 A4.
The city's official trade fair and conference organisation can advise on setting up small seminars and congresses, or big trade fairs.

Couriers

Prices vary considerably, but a package up to 5kg delivered within Germany will cost about €6.50; to the UK about €18.50; and to North America about €35. The post office runs a cheaper express service (*see p282*).

DHL
Kaiserin-Augusta-Allee 16-24, Tiergarten (2529 4927). U9 Turmstrasse. **Open** 8am-6pm Mon-Fri. **No credit cards. Map** p301 C3.
Delivers to 180 countries worldwide.

Federal Express
Mahlower Strasse, Neukölln (0130 7573). U8 Boddinstrasse. **Open** 8am-7pm Mon-Fri. **Credit** AmEx, MC, V. **Map** p307 H5.

UPS
Lengeder Strasse 17-19, Reinickendorf (0130 826 630). S25 Alt Reinickendorf. **Open** Mon-Fri 8am-7pm. **Credit** AmEx, MC, V.

Office hire & secretarial services

Regus Business Centre
Kurfürstendamm 11, Tiergarten (884 410/fax 8844 1520). S3, S5, S7, S9, S75, U2, U9, U12 Zoologischer Garten. **Open** 8.30am-6pm Mon-Fri. **Map** p305 C4.
Offices for short-term rent, multilingual secretarial services and conference facilities in two central locations.
Branch: Lindencorso, Unter den Linden, Mitte (0130 110 311).

Relocation services

The following can offer assistance in looking for homes and schools, and will help deal with residence and work permits.

Hardenberg Concept
Burgunder Strasse 5, Zehlendorf (8040 2646). S1, S7 Nikolassee. **Open** 9am-5pm Mon-Fri.

Translators & interpreters

See also *Übersetzungen* in the *Gelbe Seiten* (*Yellow Pages*).

Amerikanisch/Englisch Übersetzerteam
Kurfürstendamm 11, Tiergarten (881 6746). U9, U15 Kurfürstendamm. **Open** 9am-5pm Mon-Fri. **Map** p305 C4.

K Hilau Übersetzungsdienst
Innsbrucker Strasse 58, Schöneberg (781 7584). U4, U7 Bayerischer Platz. **Open** 10am-5pm Mon-Fri. **Map** p305 D6.

Useful organisations

American Chamber of Commerce
Budapester Strasse 16, Tiergarten (261 5586). S3, S5, S7, S9, S75, U2, U9, U12 Zoologischer Garten or U1, U2, U12 U15 Wittenbergplatz. **Open** 9am-5pm Mon-Fri. **Map** p305 D4.

American Embassy Commercial Dept
Neustädtische Kirchstrasse 4-5, Mitte (8305 2730). S1, S2, S3, S5, S7, S9, S25, S26, S75, U6 Friedrichstrasse. **Open** 8.30am-5.30pm Mon-Fri. **Map** p302 E3.

Berlin Chamber of Commerce
Hardenbergstrasse 16-18, Charlottenburg (315 100). S3, S5, S7, S9, S75, U2, U9, U12 Zoologischer Garten. **Open** 9am-5pm Mon-Fri. **Map** p305 C4.

British Embassy Commercial Dept
Unter den Linden 32-4, Mitte (201 840). S1, S2, S25, S26 Unter den Linden. **Open** 9am-noon, 2-4pm Mon-Fri. **Map** p302 F3.
Basic assistance and advice for British businesses.

Partner für Berlin
Charlottenstrasse 65, Mitte (2024 0100). U2, U6 Stadtmitte. **Open** 9am-5.30pm Mon-Fri. **Map** p316/p302 F3.
City marketing agency, funded by big companies with large stakes in the city, specialising in courting international investors.

Customs

EU nationals over 17 years of age can import limitless goods for personal use, if bought tax paid.

For non-EU citizens and for duty-free goods, the following limits apply:
• 200 cigarettes or 50 cigars or 250 grams of tobacco;
• 1 litre of spirits (over 22 per cent alcohol), or 2 litres of fortified wine (under 22 per cent alcohol), or 2 litres of non-sparkling and sparkling wine;
• 50 grams of perfume;
• 500 grams coffee;
• Other goods to the value of €175 for non-commercial use;
• The import of meat, meat products, fruit, plants, flowers and protected animals is restricted or forbidden.

Directory

Disabled

Only some U- and S-Bahn stations have wheelchair facilities; the map of the transport network (*see p314*; look for the wheelchair symbol) indicates which ones. The BVG is slowly improving things, adding facilities here and there, but it's still a long way from being a wheelchair-friendly system. You may prefer to take advantage of the **Telebus** (*see below*), a bus service for people with disabilities.

Berlin Tourismus Marketing (*see p285*) can give details on which of the city's hotels have disabled access, but if you require more specific information, try the **Beschäftigungswerk des BBV** or the **Touristik Union International**. Another option is **Movado**, which can provide info on public transport, and hotels and restaurants with disabled access.

Beschäftigungswerk des BBV

Bizetstrasse 51-5, Weissensee (927 0360). S4, S8, S10 Greifswalder Strasse. **Open** 8am-4pm Mon-Fri.
The Berlin Centre for the Disabled provides legal and social advice, together with a transport service and travel information.

Movado

Langhansstrasse 64, Weissensee (471 5145/www.movado.de). Tram 13, 23, 24. **Open** 9am-5pm Mon-Thur; 9am-4pm Fri. **Map** p303 H1.

Telebus-Zentrale

Esplanade 17, Pankow (410 200). U2 Vinetastrasse. **Open** *Office* 7am-5pm Mon-Fri.
The Telebus is available to tourists if they contact this organisation in advance. A pass has to be issued for each user, so give plenty of notice.

Touristik Union International (TUI)

Kurfürstendamm 119, Charlottenburg (311 0940/www.tui-reisecenter.com). S4 Halensee. **Open** 9am-6pm Mon-Fri. Call or write for appointment. **Map** p304 B5.
Provides information on accommodation and travel in Germany for disabled people.

Drugs

Berlin is relatively liberal in its attitude to drugs. Possession of hash or grass has been effectively decriminalised. Anyone caught with an amount under ten grams is liable to have the stuff confiscated, but can expect no further retribution. Joint smoking is tolerated in some of Berlin's younger bars and cafés. It's usually easy to tell whether you're in one. Anyone caught with small amounts of harder drugs will net a fine, but is unlikely to be incarcerated.

For **Drogen Notdienst** (Emergency Drug Service), *see p278*.

Electricity

Electricity in Germany runs on 220v. To use British appliances (240v), change the plug or use an adaptor (available at most UK electrical shops). US appliances (110v) need a converter.

Embassies & consulates

Australian Embassy

Friedrichstrasse 200, Mitte (880 0880). U2, U6 Stadtmitte. **Open** 8.30am-1pm, 2-5pm Mon-Thur; 8.30am-4.15pm Fri. **Map** p305 C4.

British Embassy

Unter den Linden 32, Mitte (201 840). S1, S2, S25, S26 Unter den Linden. **Open** 9am-noon, 2-4pm Mon-Fri. **Map** p302 F3.

Irish Consulate

Friedrichstrasse 200, Mitte (220 720). U2, U6 Stadtmitte. **Open** 9.30am-12.30pm, 2.30-4.45pm daily. **Map** p305 C4.

US Consulate

Clayallee 170, Zehlendorf (8305 1200). U1 Oscar-Helene-Heim. Visa enquiries 8.30-11.30am Mon-Fri. Consular enquiries 8.30am-noon Mon-Fri.

US Embassy

Neustädtische Kirchstrasse 4, Mitte (238 5174). S1, S2, S25, S26 Unter den Linden. **Open** 24hrs daily. **Map** p302 F3.

Emergencies

In the event of an emergency, call the numbers below. *See also p278* **Helplines**.

Police 110.
Ambulance/Fire Brigade 112.

Gay & lesbian

Help & information

Berliner AIDS-Hilfe e.V.

Meinekestrasse 12, Wilmersdorf (office 885 6400/phone counselling 19411/www.berlin.aidshilfe.de). U15 Uhlandstrasse. **Open** 10am-6pm Mon-Thur; 10am-3pm Fri; *phone counselling* 10am-noon daily. **Map** p305 C4.
Care, advice, information and counselling on every aspect of HIV and AIDS.

Lesbenberatung e.V.

Kulmer Strasse 20A, Schöneberg (215 2000/www.lesbenberatung-berlin.de). S1, S2, U7 Yorckstrasse. **Open** 4-7pm Mon, Tue, Thur; 2-5pm Fri. **Map** p306 E5.
The Lesbian Advice Centre offers counselling in all areas of lesbian life as well as self-help groups, courses, cultural events and an info-café.

Mann-O-Meter

Bülowstrasse 106, Schöneberg (216 8008/0700-MannOMeter/www.mann-o-meter.de). U1, U2, U4, U12 Nollendorfplatz. **Open** 5-10pm Mon-Fri; 4-10pm Sat, Sun. **Map** p305 D5.
Drop-in centre and helpline. Advice about AIDS prevention, finding jobs, apartments and gay contacts. Cheap stocks of safer sex materials are also available. English spoken.

Schwulenberatung

Mommsenstrasse 45, Charlottenburg (office 3270 3040/counselling 19446/www.schwulenberatungberlin.de). U7 Adenauerplatz. **Open** 11am-7pm Mon-Fri. **Map** p305 C4.
The Gay Advice Centre provides information and counselling about HIV and AIDS. Crisis intervention, consultation and advice on all aspects of gay life.

Health

EU countries have reciprocal medical treatment arrangements with Germany. All EU citizens will need the E111 form. UK citizens can obtain this by filling in the

Going *Bezirk*

Since 1 January 2001 Berlin has been made up of 12 *Bezirke* or boroughs. A reform of the *Bezirk* structure has been discussed since the mid 1990s, although wags say it has been up for grabs since 1920, when the original 20 districts comprising city boroughs and neighbouring villages constituted Greater Berlin. In 1998 the Berlin government decided upon the current 12 districts, each with 200,000-300,000 inhabitants. Of the then 23 districts, 20 joined one or even two of their neighbours, while only populous **Neukölln**, huge **Reinickendorf** and the practically independent town of **Spandau** have remained separate entities.

The financially beleaguered city government hopes to save up to €100 million by reducing district overheads, and still provide better services with the installation of *Bürgerämter*, or one-stop bureaus, reducing red tape. Popular sentiment, however, seemed to be 'if ain't broke, why fix it?' The administrative makeup of Greater Berlin has survived Weimar turmoil, the Nazi regime and the division of the city, the only exception being the spinning off Hohenschönhausen (from Weissensee), Hellersdorf and Marzahn (from Lichtenberg) in the late '70s to mid '80s to accommodate the new housing projects there.

Many suspected that the *Bezirk* fusion was a ploy to contain the Socialist PDS party, which has a much greater following in the east than the Christian Democrats or Social Democrats and is making inroads into the west. Actually, the Greens were the big losers, the fusion costing the party all three borough mayor seats held prior to 2001. But the new *Bezirke* could effect PDS showing in the 2002 Federal elections. The party needs five per cent of the vote and/or at least three directly elected representatives to remain in the Bundestag, but with some formerly eastern electoral districts now including western voters, the parliamentary race could become close.

As many predicted, the fusion didn't go off without a hitch. Citizens and civil servants alike were confused about everything from where to submit housing subsidy applications to the redivision of power between city and *Bezirk*. Many *Bezirke* bickered over names, most spectacularly **Pankow**, when an insurrection by identity-conscious Prenzlauer Berg and *Bezirk* representatives resurrected the old names as '3. Prenzlauer Berg, Weissensee und Pankow von Berlin', possibly permanently. Unwieldy hypenates like **Treptow-Köpenick**, **Tempelhof-Schöneberg**, **Marzahn-Hellersdorf** and **Charlottenburg-Wilmersdorf** won the day, the order being determined by alphabetical order, size, mellifluousness. **Lichtenberg** (merged with Hohenschönhausen) and **Mitte** (joining Tiergarten and Wedding) were content to let one name subsume the various districts.

In the consciousness of many Berliners, the old districts and neighbourhoods without district status remain firmly entrenched. Except for perhaps some Weddinger eager to shed that district's déclassé stigma and jump the hip 'Mitte' gravy train, one would be hard pressed to find a Dahlem villa dweller saying he or she lives in **Steglitz-Zehlendorf**; despite socio-economic similarities, the 'hoods in **Friedrichshain-Kreuzberg** retain their distinct flairs. But the new city map may make itself felt in other ways when some *Bezirke* have to cut already tight budgets to pay back the €22 million total advanced by the city to finance the fusion.

---

application form in leaflet SA30, available in all DSS offices or over any post office counter. You should get your E111 at least two weeks before you leave. It does not cover all medical costs (for example, dental treatment), so you may wish to take out private insurance.

Citizens from non-EU countries should take out private medical insurance.

German medical treatment is expensive: the minimum charge is roughly €35-€40.

The British Embassy (*see p275*) publishes a list of English-speaking doctors, dentists and other medical professionals, as well as lawyers and interpreters.

Should you fall ill in Berlin, take a completed E111 form to the **AOK** (*see p277*) and staff will exchange it for a *Krankenschein* (medical certificate), which you can present to the doctor treating you, or to the hospital in an emergency.

If you require non-emergency hospital treatment, the doctor will issue you with a *Notwendigkeitsbescheinigung* ('Essential Certificate'), which you must take to the AOK. Staff there will give you a *Kostenübernahmeschein*

('Cost Transferral Certificate'), which entitles you to hospital treatment in a public ward.

All hospitals have an emergency ward open 24 hours daily. Otherwise, it is customary in Germany for patients to be admitted to hospital via a practising physician. For a list of hospitals, consult the *Gelbe Seiten* (*Yellow Pages*) under *Krankenhäuser/Kliniken*.

AOK Auslandsschalter

Karl-Marx-Allee 3, Mitte (2531 8184/www.aokberlin.de). S3, S5, S7, S9, S75, U2, U5, U8 Alexanderplatz. **Open** 8am-2pm Mon, Wed; 8am-6pm Tue, Thur; 8am-noon Fri. **Map** p316/p303 G3.

Accident & emergency

There are hospitals all over the city. The following are some of the most central. All have 24-hour emergency wards.

Charité

Schumann Strasse 20-21, Mitte (28020/www.charite.de). S1, S2, S3, S5, S7, S9, S25, S26, S75, U6 Friedrichstrasse/bus 147. **Map** p302 F3.

Krankenhaus Am Urban

Dieffenbachstrasse 1, Kreuzberg (6970). U7 Südstern/bus 241, 248. **Map** p307 G5.

Krankenhaus Moabit

Turmstrasse 21, Tiergarten (39760/ www.krankenhaus-moabit.de). U9 Turmstrasse. **Map** p301 D3.

Krankenhaus Neukölln

Rudower Strasse 48, Neukölln (60041/www.knk.de). U7 Britz-Süd/ bus 141.

Martin-Luther-Krankenhaus

Caspar-Theyss-Strasse 27-31, Grunewald (89550/www.mlk.de). S4, S45, S46 Halensee/bus 110, 129. **Map** p304 B5.

St Hedwig Krankenhaus

Grosse Hamburger Strasse 5, Mitte (23110). S3, S5, S7, S9, S75 Hackescher Markt or S1, S2, S25, S26 Oranienburger Strasse. **Map** p302 F3.

St Joseph Krankenhaus

Bäumerplan 24, Tempelhof (78820). S45, S46 Tempelhof/bus 140, 184.

Complementary medicine

There is a long tradition of alternative medicine (*Heilpraxis*) in Germany; your medical insurance will usually cover treatment costs. For a full list of practitioners, look up *Heilpraktiker* in the *Gelbe Seiten* (*Yellow Pages*). There you'll find a complete list of chiropractors, osteopaths, acupuncturists and homoeopaths. Homoeopathic medicines are harder to get hold of and much more expensive than in the UK, and it's generally harder to find an osteopath or chiropractor.

Contraception, abortion & childbirth

Family-planning clinics are thin on the ground in Germany, and generally you have to go to a gynaecologist (*Frauenarzt*).

The abortion law was amended in 1995 to take into account the differing systems that existed in east and west. East Germany had abortion on demand; in the West, abortion was only allowed in extenuating circumstances, such as when the health of the foetus or mother was at risk. In a complicated compromise, abortion is still technically illegal, but is not punishable. Women wishing to terminate a pregnancy can do so only after receiving certification from a counsellor. Counselling is offered by state, lay and church bodies. Counsellors are not there to talk women out of having an abortion, though may seek to persuade women to think again.

Feministisches Frauengesundheit-zentrum (FFGZ)

Bamberger Strasse 51, Schöneberg (213 9597). U4, U7 Bayerischer Platz. **Open** 10am-1pm Tue; 10am-1pm, 3-6pm Thur. **Map** p305 D5.

Courses and lectures on natural contraception, pregnancy, cancer, abortion, AIDS, migraines and sexuality. Self-help and preventative medicine are stressed. Information on gynaecologists, health institutions and organisations can also be obtained.

Pro Familia

Kalkreuthstrasse 4, Schöneberg (3984 9898). U1, U2, U15 Wittenbergplatz. **Open** 3-6pm Mon-Thur. **Map** p305 D5. Free advice about sex, contraception and abortion. Call for an appointment.

Dentists

Dr Andreas Bothe

Kurfürstendamm 210, Charlottenburg (882 6767). U15 Uhlandstrasse. **Surgery hours** 8am-2pm Mon, Fri; noon-7pm Tue, Thur. **Map** p305 C4.

Mr Pankaj Mehta

Schlangenbader Strasse 25, Wilmersdorf (823 3010). U1 Rüdesheimer Platz. **Surgery hours** 9am-noon, 2-6pm Mon, Tue, Thur; 8am-1pm Wed, Fri. **Map** p304 B6.

Doctors

If you don't know of any doctors, or are too ill to leave your bed, phone the Emergency Doctor's Service (*Ärztlicher Bereitschaftdienst* 310 031), which specialises in dispatching doctors for house calls. Charges vary according to treatment.

In Germany, you choose your doctor according to his or her speciality. You don't need a referral from a GP. The British Embassy (*see p275*) can provide a list of English-speaking doctors, but many doctors can speak some English. All will be expensive, so either have your E111 at hand, or your private insurance document.

The following doctors speak good English.

Herr Dr U Beck

Bundesratufer 2, Tiergarten (391 2808). U9 Turmstrasse. **Surgery hours** 9.30am-noon, 4-6pm Mon, Tue, Thur; 9am-noon Wed, Fri. **Map** p305 D5.

Frau Dr I Dorow

Rüsternallee 14-16, Charlottenburg (302 4690). U2 Neu-Westend. **Surgery hours** 9-11.30am Mon-Fri; 5-7pm Mon, Thur; 4-6pm Tue. **Map** p300 A3.

Dr Christine Rommelspacher

Gotzkowskystrasse 19, Tiergarten, (392 2075). U9 Turmstrasse.
Surgery hours 9am-noon, 3-6pm Mon-Wed, Fri. **Map** p301 C3.

Gynaecologist

Dr Lutz Opitz

Tegeler Weg 4, Charlottenburg (344 4001). U7 Mierendorffplatz.
Surgery hours 8am-2pm Mon; 3-7pm Tue, Thur; 8am-noon Wed, Fri. **Map** p300 B3.

Pharmacies

Prescription and non-prescription drugs (including aspirin) are sold only at pharmacies (*Apotheken*). You can recognise these by a red 'A' outside the front door.
A list of pharmacies open on Sundays and in the evening should be displayed at every pharmacy. Phone **Emergency Pharmaceutical Services** on 19292 for information.

STDs, HIV & AIDS

For most STDs, see a doctor.

Berliner Aids-Hilfe (BAH)

Büro 15, Meinekestrasse 12, Wilmersdorf (885 6400/Advice line 19411). U9, U15 Kurfürstendamm.
Open noon-6pm Mon-Thur; noon-3pm Fri. *Advice line* 24hrs daily. **Map** p305 C4.
Information is given on all aspects of HIV and AIDS. Free consultations, condoms and lubricant are also provided. Staff speak English.

Helplines

Alkoholkranken-Beratung

Gierkezeile 39, Charlottenburg (348 0090). U7 Richard-Wagner-Platz.
Open *Advice* 3-6pm Mon; 2-4pm Tue, Fri; 10am-noon Thur. *Telephones manned* 9am-noon, 1-6pm Mon-Fri. **Map** p300 B3.
The Alcoholic Advice Centre offers free advice and information on self-help groups.

Drogen Notdienst

Ansbacher Strasse 11, Schöneberg (192 37). U1, U2, U12, U15 Wittenbergplatz. **Open** *Advice* 24hrs daily. **Map** p305 D4.

The Emergency Drug Service is open 24 hours daily for emergencies; overnight stays are possible. No appointment is necessary if you're coming for advice.

Frauenkrisentelefon

615 4243/7596. **Open** 10am-noon Mon, Thur; 10am-noon, 7-9pm Tue, Wed, Fri; 5-7pm Sat, Sun.
Offers advice and information for women on anything and everything.

Help & Advice Line

080 0111 0111. **Open** *Phone enquiries* 24hrs daily.
A crisis telephone line for the depressed and suicidal, where some staff speak English.

KUB

Turmstrasse 21, Tiergarten (781 8585). U9 Turmstrasse.
Open 4pm-midnight daily. **Map** p301 D3.
The Crisis and Advice Centre gives free, confidential advice for people in need of emotional counselling. This is the central office.

Notruf

251 2828. **Open** *Phone enquiries* 6-9pm Tue, Thur; noon-2pm Sun.
This rape crisis line offers advice and help on rape and sexual harassment, as well as help dealing with the police and doctors.

Psychiatrischer Notdienst

Horstweg 2, Charlottenburg (322 2020). U2 Sophie-Charlotte-Platz.
Open 4pm-midnight daily. **Map** p304 B4.
The staff here can put you in touch with your local psychiatric clinic.

ID

By law you are required to carry some form of ID, which, for UK and US citizens, means a passport. If police catch you without one, they may go with you to wherever you've left it.

Internet

For internet access on a short visit, try one of the cybercafés listed below. If staying longer, **Snafu** is reputed to be Berlin's best internet service provider. Call on 2543 1112 or check its website at www.snafu.de. For Berlin-related websites, *see p289.*

easyInternetCafé

Kurfürstendamm 224, Charlottenburg (8870 7970/ www.easyinternetcafe.com). S3, S5, S7, S9, 75, U2, U9, U12 Zoologischer Garten or U9, U15 Kurfürstendamm. **Open** 24hrs daily. **No credit cards**. **Map** p305 C4.
More than 350 PCs, perpetually open doors and a system by which you pay €1 for a certain amount of time online (more at off-peak than peak times).

Internet Café Alpha

Dunckerstrasse 72, Prenzlauer Berg (447 9067/www.alpha-icafe.de). U2 Eberswalder Strasse. **Open** 2pm-midnight daily. **No credit cards**. **Map** p303 G1.
Using one of the 12 computers costs €5 per hour. Wine, beer and assorted snacks can fuel your surfing.

Internet Café Haitaick

Brünnhildestrasse 8, Schöneberg (8596 1413/www.haitaick.de). S4, U9 Bundesplatz. **Open** Mon-Fri 11am-midnight daily; 1pm-midnight Sat, Sun. **No credit cards**. **Map** p306 E5.
Fifteen terminals here, at €5 per hour. Drinks and snacks available, plus assorted arcade games and a scanner. Also internet classes.

Left luggage

Airports

There is a left luggage office at **Tegel** (*see p270;* 0180 5000 186; open 5am-10.30pm daily) and lockers at **Schönefeld** (*see p270;* in the Multi Parking Garage P4) and at **Tempelhof** (*see p270;* in Parking Area P1).

Rail & bus stations

There are lockers and left luggage facilities at **Bahnhof Zoo** (*see p270*), and 24-hour lockers at **Friedrichstrasse** and **Alexanderplatz** stations. **Zentraler Omnibus Bahnhof** (ZOB; *see p271*) also has facilities.

Legal help

If you get into legal difficulties, the British Embassy (*see p275*) can provide a list of English-speaking lawyers in Berlin.

Libraries

Berlin has hundreds of *Bibliotheken/Büchereien* (public libraries). To borrow books, you need an *Anmeldungs-formular* ('Certificate of Registration', *see p285*) and a passport.

Amerika-Gedenkbibliothek

Blücherplatz 1, Kreuzberg (690 840/ www.zbl.de). U1, U6 Hallesches. **Open** 11am-6pm Mon, Thur; 11am-6pm Tue, Wed, Fri; 11am-2pm Sat. **Membership** *per year* €10; *students* €5. **Map** p306 F5.
Only a small collection of English and American literature, but an excellent collection of videos.

British Council

Hackescher Markt 1, Mitte (311 0990/www.britcoun.de/e/berlin). S3, S5, S7, S9, S75 Hackescher Markt. **Open** 1-8pm Mon, Thur; 11am-6pm Tue, Wed, Fri; 11am-2pm Sat. **Membership** *per year* €30; *students & teachers* €15. **Map** p302 F3.
The Information Centre holds 2,500 English-language videos, plus DVDs and CD-ROMs.

Staatsbibliothek

Potsdamer Strasse 33, Tiergarten (2660/www.sbb.spk-berlin.de). S1, S2, S25, S26, U2 Potsdamer Platz. **Open** 9am-9pm Mon-Fri; 9am-7pm Sat. **Map** p306 E4.
Books in English on every subject are available at this branch of the State Library – as featured in Wim Wenders' *Wings of Desire*.

Staatsbibliothek

Unter den Linden 8, Mitte (2660/ www.sbb.spk-berlin.de). S1, S2, S3, S5, S7, S9, S25, S75, U6 Friedrichstrasse. **Open** 9am-9pm Mon-Fri; 9am-5pm Sat. **Map** p316/p302 F3.
A smaller range of English books than the branch above, but it's still worth a visit, not least for its café.

Lost/stolen property

If your belongings are stolen, you should go to the police station nearest to where the incident occurred (listed in the *Gelbe Seiten/Yellow Pages* under *Polizei*), report the theft and fill in report forms for insurance purposes. If you can't speak German, the police will call in one of their interpreters at no cost.

For lost or stolen credit cards, *see p282*.

BVG Fundbüro

Potsdamer Strasse 180-182, Schöneberg (lost property 2562 3040/customer services 194 49). U7 Kleistpark. **Open** 9am-6pm Mon-Thur; 9am-2pm Fri. **Map** p306 E5.
Contact this office with any queries about property lost on Berlin's public transport system.

Zentrales Fundbüro

Platz der Luftbrücke 6, Tempelhof (6995). U6 Platz der Luftbrücke. **Open** 7.30am-2pm Mon; 8.30am-4pm Tue; noon-6.30pm Wed; 1-7pm Thur; 7.30am-noon Fri. **Map** p306 F6.
This is the central police lost property office.

Media

Foreign press

International publications are readily available at main stations, the **Europa-Center** (*see p105*) and various International Presse newsagents. Book retailers **Dussmann** (*see p163*) and **Hugendubel** (*see p161*) also carry a range of international titles. Berlin currently has no English-language magazine or newspaper for expatriates.

Newspapers

NATIONAL

BILD

Flagship tabloid of the Axel Springer group. Though its credibility varies from story to story, *BILD* leverages the journalistic resources of the Springer empire and its four-million circulation to land regular scoops, so even the German intelligentsia pays attention to its daily riot of polemic.

Financial Times Deutschland

Since first hitting newstands in early 2000, the *FTD* has overcome lukewarm circulation predictions, as well as shaky and hesitant reporting. Its circulation is steadily increasing, and though it's not likely to dethrone *Handelsblatt*, FTD's success proves there is room for different approaches within the business trade market.

Frankfurter Allgemeine Zeitung

Germany's *de facto* newspaper of record. Stolid, exhaustive coverage of daily events, plus lots of background and analysis, particularly on the business pages. Designers are itching to give it a facelift, but the *FAZ* is too busy being serious to bother. Its Berlin section focuses on culture and arts, and, in terms of listings, is as good as the local papers.

Handelsblatt

The closest thing to the *Wall Street Journal* Germany has to offer, *Handelsblatt* actually co-operates with that paper's European offshoot. Holtzbrinck's business trade has reasserted its market leadership despite competition from the *Financial Times Deutschland*. In fact, insiders say that the salmon-coloured upstart actually shook *Handelsblatt* out of its complacency and energised its reporting.

Süddeutsche Zeitung

Based in Munich, the *Süddeutsche* blends first-rate journalism with enlightened commentary and, not unusual in Germany, uninspired visuals. Also with a Berlin edition, but only one page of local coverage.

die tageszeitung

Set up in Berlin's rebellious Kreuzberg district in the 1970s, the *'taz'* was an attempt to balance the provincial world view offered by West German newspapers and give coverage to alternative political and social issues. Today, with many of its charter readers now making mainstream policies in the Bundestag, the *taz* is floundering. Still, the Berlin edition does a good job keeping watch on crooks in local government, and its regular appeals for funds are hilarious.

Die Welt

Die Welt moved its main editorial office to Berlin well in advance of the government's arrival, appointed a new editor-in-chief, went through a redesign, and is now being held up by its owners, the Springer Group, as a success story. Once a lacklustre mouthpiece of conservative, provincial thinking, *Die Welt* has widened its political horizons, but at a circulation of around 17,000 for its Berlin edition, it's a non-starter in the capital.

LOCAL

Berliner Morgenpost

Fat, fresh and self-conscious, this broadsheet is the favourite of the petty bourgeois and a profitable concern for the Springer empire.

Good local coverage, and gradually gaining readers in the east through the introduction of neighbourhood editions, but no depth on the national and international pages.

Berliner Zeitung

A black hole of investment since Gruner + Jahr bought it from Robert Maxwell in the early 1990s, this east Berlin newspaper sopped up the best journalistic talent and was redesigned in a bid to become the voice of Berlin. Gains through huge marketing in western strongholds only partly offset losses from its haemorrhaging core readership in the east. Running out of gimmicks just as the competition was preparing its own, the paper now lacks the spit and vigour of a few years ago, but remains a lively, though unauthoritative, read.

BZ

A classic tabloid, featuring the headline-writing talents of loose cannon editor-in-chief Franz Josef Wagner. The daily riot of polemic and pictures hasn't let up since it was demonised by the left in the 1970s – but its circulation has. Although still Berlin's largest seller with 270,000 copies daily, *BZ* sales are down by 70,000 copies since 1991.

Der Tagesspiegel

Solid but predictable, this is the staple of Wilmersdorf solicitors and Dahlem academics. Once thought vulnerable to the *Berliner Zeitung*'s advance, its circulation has emerged as Berlin's most stable, and a new, younger editor-in-chief is slowly managing to bring a fresher viewpoint. Losing money hand over fist, *Der Tagesspiegel* is a matter of prestige for owner Holzbrinck.

15 Uhr Aktuell

Wimpy afternoon freesheet distributed by folks in daft white Parkas after 3pm in U-Bahn stations. Although the news is abbreviated, people theoretically take it because it is more current than the morning papers. In practice, readership is heavy among people who don't buy other papers, such as teenagers.

WEEKLIES

Jungle World

Defiantly left, graphically switched-on and commercially undaunted, the editors of this fairly new Berlin-based weekly can be relied on to mock anything approaching the comfortable views of the mainstream press. Born of an ideological dispute with the publishers of *Junge Welt*, a former East Berlin youth title, *Jungle World* lacks sales but packs a punch.

Die Zeit

Every major post-war intellectual debate in Germany has been carried out in the pages of *Die Zeit*, the newspaper that proved to a suspicious world that a liberal tradition was alive and well in a country best known for excesses of intolerance. Even now, with a more friendly design, the wandering style of its élite authors still makes for a difficult read.

Magazines

Focus

Once, its spare, to-the-point articles, four-colour graphics and service features were a welcome innovation in Germany. But the gloss has faded, and *Focus* has established itself as a non-thinking man's *Der Spiegel*, whose answer to the upstart was simply to print more colour pages and become warm and fuzzy by adding bylines.

Der Spiegel

Few journalistic institutions in Germany possess the resources and clout to pursue a major story like *Der Spiegel*, one of the best and most aggressive news weeklies in Europe. After years of firing barbs at the ruling Christian Democrats, *Der Spiegel* was caught off guard when the Social Democrats were elected in 1999, but remains a must-read for anyone interested in Germany's power structure.

Stern

The heyday of news pictorials may have long gone, but *Stern* still manages to shift around a million copies a week of big colour spreads detailing the horrors of war, the beauties of nature and the curves of the female body. Nevertheless, its reputation has never really recovered from the Hitler diaries fiasco in the early 1980s.

Listings magazines

Berlin is awash with listings freebies, notably *[030]* (music, nightlife, film), *Flyer* (a pocket-sized club guide), *Siegessäule* and *Sergej* (both gay). These can be picked up in bars and restaurants. The two paid-for fortnightlies, *Zitty* and *tip*, come out on alternate weeks and, at least for cinema information, it pays to get the current title.

tip

A glossier version of *Zitty* in every respect, *tip* gets better marks for its overall presentation and readability, largely due to its better quality paper, full-colour pages throughout and a space-saving TV programme insert. This makes it more appealing to display advertisers – a double-edged sword depending on why you buy a listings magazine in the first place.

Zitty

Having lost some counter-cultural edge since its foundation in 1977, *Zitty* remains a vital force on the Berlin media scene, providing a fortnightly blend of close-to-the-bone civic journalism, alternative cultural coverage and comprehensive listings interspersed with wry, often arcane German comics. The *Harte Welle* ('hardcore') department of its Lonely Hearts classifieds is legendary.

Television

At its best, German TV produces solid investigative programmes and clever drama series. At its worst, there are cheesy 'erotic' shows and vapid folk-music programmes featuring rhythmically clapping studio audiences. Late-night TV is chock-a-block with imported action series and European soft porn, interspersed with nipple-pinching and finger-sucking adverts for telephone sex numbers.

A basic channel shakedown looks like this: two national public networks, **ARD** and **ZDF**, a handful of no-holds-barred commercial channels, and a load of special-interest channels.

ARD's daily *Tagesschau* at 8pm is the most authoritative news broadcast nationally. **N-tv** is Germany's all-news cable channel, owned partly by CNN, but lacking the satellite broadcaster's ability to cover a breaking story. **TVBerlin** is the city's experiment with local commercial television and, though more ambitious under new management, it's still catching up with ARD's local affilate **SFB**, which covers local news with more insight.

RTL, **Pro 7** and **SAT-1** are cable services offering a predictable mix of Hollywood re-runs and imported series, and increasingly producing its own fare, such as sensational magazine programmes.

Special interest channels run from **Kinderkanal** for kids to **Eurosport**, **MTV Europe** and its German-language competitor **Viva**, to **Arte**, an enlightened French-German cultural channel with high-quality films and documentaries.

Channels broadcasting regularly in English include **CNN**, **NBC**, **MTV Europe** and **BBC World**. British or American films on ARD or ZDF are sometimes broadcast with a simultaneous soundtrack in English for stereo-equipped TV sets.

Radio

Some 33 stations compete for audiences in Berlin, seven from outside town, so even tiny shifts in market share have huge consequences for broadcasters. The race for ratings in the greater metropolitan area is thwarted by a clear split between the urban audience in both east and west and a rural one in the hinterland. The main four stations in the region have their audiences based in either Berlin (**Berliner Rundfunk**, 91.4; **r.s.2**, 94.3) or Brandenburg (**BB Radio**, 107.5; **Antenne Brandenburg**, 99.7). No station can pull in everyone.

Commercial stations **104,6 RTL** (104.6) and **Hundert,6** (100.6) offer standard chart pop spiced with news. **Energy** (103.4) and **Fritz** (102.6), featuring English DJ Trevor Wilson as resident loon, are a bit more adventurous but still far from cutting edge. **Star FM**'s (87.9) rock format and **Voice of America** news broadcasts look back to the

days when the frequency was occupied by the US Armed Forces Network in Berlin. Jazz is round the clock on **Jazz Radio** (101.9). Information-based stations such as **Info Radio** (92.05) and **Berlin Aktuell** (93.6) are increasing in popularity. The **BBC World Service** (90.2) is available 24 hours a day.

Money

On 1 January 2002, the Mark ceased to be legal tender and Germany adopted the **euro** (€). One euro is made up of 100 cents. There are seven new banknotes, and eight coins.

The **notes** are of differing colours and sizes (€5 is the smallest, €500 the largest) and each of their designs represent a different period of European architecture. They are: €5 (grey), €10 (red), €20 (blue), €50 (orange), €100 (green), €200 (yellow-brown), €500 (purple).

The eight denominations of coins vary in colour, size and thickness. They share one common side; the other side features a country-specific design (note: all can be used in any participating state). They are: €2, €1, 50 cents, 20 cents, 10 cents, 5 cents, 2 cents, 1 cent.

For more information on the euro, see www.euro.ecb.int.

At the time of going to press, the exchange rate was £1 = €1.6 and US$1 = €1.1.

ATMs

ATMs are found throughout the centre of Berlin, and represent the most convenient way of obtaining cash. Most major credit cards are accepted, as well as debit cards that are part of the Cirrus, Plus, Star or Maestro systems. You will normally be charged a fee for withdrawing cash, but the exchange rate offered is usually a good one.

Banks & bureaux de change

Foreign currency and travellers' cheques can be exchanged in most of Berlin's many banks.

Wechselstuben (bureaux de change) are open outside normal banking hours and generally give better rates than banks, where changing money involves much queuing.

Reisebank AG

Zoo Station, Hardenbergplatz, Charlottenburg (881 7117). *S3, S5, S7, S9, S75, U2, U9, U12 Zoologischer Garten.* **Open** 7.30am-10pm daily. **Map** p305 C4.
The *Wechselstuben* of the Reisebank offer some of the best rates of exchange in the city. There are other branches at Ostbahnhof and Bahnhof Lichtenberg.

Credit cards

Many Berliners prefer to use cash for most transactions, although the larger hotels, shops and most restaurants will accept one or more of the major credit cards (American Express, Diners Club, MasterCard, Visa) and many will take Eurocheques with guarantee cards, and travellers' cheques with ID. In general, the German banking and retail systems are less enthusiastic about credit than their UK or US equivalents, though this is slowly changing.

If you want to take out cash on your credit card, banks will give an advance against Visa and MasterCard cards. But you may not be able to withdraw less than the equivalent of US$100. A better option is using an ATM machine.

American Express

Bayreuther Strasse 37, Schöneberg (214 9830). U1, U2, U12, U15 Wittenbergplatz. **Open** 9am-6pm Mon-Fri; 10am-1pm Sat. **Map** p305 C4.
Holders of an American Express card can use the company's facilities here, including the cash advance service.

Lost/stolen cards

If you've lost a credit card, or had one stolen, phone one of the emergency numbers listed below. All lines are open 24 hours daily.

American Express 0180 523 2377.
Diners Club 069 260 3050.
MasterCard/Visa 0697 933 1910.

Tax

Non-EU citizens can claim back German value-added tax (*Mehrwertsteuer* or *MwSt*) on goods purchased in the country (although it's only worth the hassle on sizeable purchases). Ask to be issued with a Tax-Free Shopping Cheque for the amount of the refund and present this, together with the receipt, at the refund office at the airport (prior to checking in your bags).

Opening hours

Most **banks** are open 9am to noon Monday to Friday, and 1pm to 3pm or 2pm to 6pm on varied weekdays.

Shops can stay open until 8.30pm on weekdays, and 4pm on Saturdays, though many close earlier. Most big stores open their doors at 8.30am, newsagents a little earlier, and smaller or independent shops tend to open around 10am or later.

Many **Turkish shops** are open on Saturday afternoons and on Sundays from 1pm to 5pm. Many **bakers** open to sell cakes on Sundays from 2pm to 4pm. Most **fuel stations** that stay open 24 hours also sell basic groceries.

The opening times of **bars** vary considerably, but many are open during the day, and most stay open until at least 1am, if not through until morning.

Most **post offices** are open 8am to 5pm Monday to Friday and 8am to 1pm on Saturdays.

Police stations

You are unlikely to come in contact with the German police, unless you commit a crime or are the victim of one. There are very few pedestrian patrols or traffic checks (and often they announce on local radio news where to look for them).

The central police HQ is at Platz der Luftbrücke 6, Tempelhof (6995), and there are stations at Jägerstrasse 48, Mitte (24055); Bismarckstrasse 111, Charlottenburg (33010); Friesenstrasse 16, Kreuzberg (6995); Hauptstrasse 44, Schönberg (76720); Schönhauser Allee 22, Prenzlauer Berg (57740).

Postal services

Most post offices (simply *Post* in German) are open from 8am to 6pm Monday to Friday, and 8am to 1pm Saturday. For non-local mail, use the *Andere Richtungen* ('other destinations') slot in post-boxes. Letters of up to 20 grams (7oz) to anywhere in Germany and the EU need €0.56 in postage. Postcards require €0.51. For anywhere outside the EU, a 20-gram airmail letter costs €1.53, a postcard €1.02.

Main Post Office

Joachimsthaler Strasse 7, Charlottenburg. S3, S5, S7, S9, S75, U2, U9, U12 Zoologischer Garten or U9, U15 Kurfürstendamm. **Open** 8am-midnight Mon-Sat. **Map** p305 C4. If your mail is urgent, send it from here and it should get to the UK in 3-4 days, and to the US in 7-8 days. Fax and telex facilities are also available.

Poste restante

Poste restante facilities are available at the main post office (*see above*). Letters should be addressed to the recipient, 'Postlagernd, Postamt Joachimsthaller Strasse 7, 10623 Berlin'. They can be collected from the counter marked *Postlagernde Sendungen*. Take your passport.

Public holidays

On public holidays (*Feiertagen*) you will find it can be very difficult to get things done, but most cafés, bars and restaurants stay open.

Public holidays are: **New Year's Day** (1 Jan); **Good Friday** (Mar/Apr); **Easter Monday** (Mar/Apr); **May/Labour Day** (1 May); **Ascension Day** (May/June; ten days before Whitsun/ Pentacost, the 7th Sun after Easter); **Whit/Pentacost Monday** (May/June); **Day of German Unity** (3 Oct); **Day of Prayer and National Repentance** (3rd Wed in Nov); **Christmas Eve** (24 Dec); **Christmas Day** (25 Dec); **Boxing Day** (26 Dec).

Religion

For lists of places of worship for the major religions, the website **www.berlinfo.com** is very useful (click on the link for 'community').

Safety & security

Though crime is increasing, Berlin remains a reasonably safe city by western standards. Even for a woman, it's pretty safe to walk around alone at night in most central areas of the city. Avoid the eastern suburbs if you look gay or non-German. Pickpockets are not unknown around major tourist areas. Use some common sense and you're unlikely to get into any trouble.

Smoking

Many Berliners smoke, and, though the habit is in decline, there is a lot less stigma attached than in the UK or US. Smoking is banned on public transport, in theatres and cinemas and in many public institutions, but is tolerated just about everywhere else.

Study

There are more than 160,000 students in Berlin, spread between three universities and 17 subject-specific colleges (*Fachhochschulen*). Studies last at least four years but most students take longer.

Since reunification the lot of students has worsened. Rents have risen, libraries and lecture halls are congested, while the official budget is eaten up by reunification programmes.

Language classes

Goethe-Institut

Friedrichstrasse 209, Mitte (259 063). U6 Kochstrasse. **Open** 9am-7pm Mon-Thur; 9am-5pm Fri. **Map** p306 F4.
The Goethe-Institut is well organised, solid and reliable. Facilities include a cultural extension programme (theatre, film and museum visits), accommodation for students, and a media centre with computers. A four-week intensive course costs €915; eight-week courses cost €1,695. Exams can be taken at the end of each course.

Tandem

Lychenerstrasse 7, Prenzlauer Berg (441 3003). U2 Eberswalder Strasse. **Open** 11am-2pm, 4-7pm Mon-Thur; 11am-2pm Fri. **Map** p303 G1.
For €15 Tandem will put you in touch with two German speakers who want to learn English, and are prepared to teach you German. Language classes available.

Universities

Freie Universität Berlin

Central administration, Kaiserswertherstrasse 16-18, Dahlem (8381/ www.FU-Berlin.de). U1 Dahlem-Dorf.
What is today Germany's biggest university was founded by a group of students in 1948 after the Humboldt was taken over by the East German authorities. It began with a few books, a Dahlem villa provided by the US military government and a constitution that gave students a vote on all decision-making bodies. It was intended to be free of government interference. But today the huge anonymous university is far from being a community of professors, tutors and students. The AStA (*Allgemeiner*

Studentenausschuss, 'General Student Committee'), elected by the student parliament, now has no decision-making powers. The financial situation is also getting worse: more students, fewer books, professors, tutors and services.

Humboldt-Universität zu Berlin (HUB)

Unter den Linden 6, Mitte (20930/ www.HU-Berlin.de). S1, S2, S3, S5, S7, S9, S25, S26, S75, U6 Friedrichstrasse. **Map** p302 F3.
Berlin's first university was founded by the humanist Wilhelm von Humboldt (*see p11* **Wir sind Berliner: the von Humboldts**) in 1810. Hegel taught here in the 1820s, making Berlin the centre of German philosophy. His pupils included Karl Marx. Other departments have boasted Nobel Prize winning chemists van t'Hoff and Otto Hahn; physicists Max Planck, Albert Einstein and Werner Heisenberg; and physicians Rudolph Virchow and Robert Koch. During the Nazi period, books were burned, students and professors expelled and murdered. When the Soviets reopened the university in 1946, there were hopes of a fresh start but these were stifled at birth. After the 1989 revolution, students briefly fought, with partial success, against plans to close some faculties. Today, jobs, not political activism, are the priority.

Technische Universität Berlin (TU)

Strasse des 17. Juni 135, Tiergarten (3140/www.TU-Berlin.de). U2 Ernst-Reuter-Platz. **Map** p305 C4.
The Technical University, or TU, started life as a mining, building and gardening academy in the 18th century. With its focus on engineering, machinery and business, the university was given financial priority by the Nazi government. It was reopened in 1946 with an expanded remit including the social sciences, philosophy, psychology, business studies, computers and analytical chemistry. With roughly 40,000 students, the TU is one of Germany's ten largest universities. It also has the highest number of foreign students (17%). There are special supplementary classes and a Language and Cultural Exchange Programme for foreigners (Sprach- und Kulturbörse, SKB; *see below*), where you can take intensive language courses, join conversational groups, attend seminars on international issues and apply for language exchange partnerships. The SKB services are open to students at any Berlin university.

Sprach- und Kulturbörse an der TU Berlin

Room 3012, Franklinstrasse 28-9, Charlottenburg (3142 2730). U2 Ernst-Reuter-Platz. **Open** 1-5pm Tue, Thur. **Map** p304 C4.

Useful organisations

Studentenwerk Berlin

Hardenbergstrasse 34, Charlottenburg (311 2313). U2 Ernst-Reuter-Platz. **Open** 9am-3pm Mon-Fri. **Map** p304 C4.
The central organisation for student affairs runs hostels, restaurants and job agencies.

Telephones

All phone numbers in this guide are local Berlin numbers (other than those in the chapter **Trips Out of Town**). To call them from outside the city, *see below*.

Dialling & codes

To phone Berlin from abroad, dial the international access code (00 from the UK, 011 from the US, 0011 from Australia), then **49** (for Germany) and **30** (for Berlin), followed by the local number.

To phone abroad from Germany dial **00**, then the appropriate country-code:
Australia 61;
Canada 1;
Ireland 353;
New Zealand 64;
United Kingdom 44;
United States 1.
And then the local area code (minus the initial zero) and the local number.

To call Berlin from elsewhere in Germany, dial **030** and then the local number.

For calls to the UK, Ireland, US and Canada, charges start at €0.35 per minute. Calls to Australia start at €0.40.

Public phones

At post offices you'll find both coin- and card-operated phones, but most pavement

Weather report

	Average max. temperature	Average min. temperature	Average daily hrs of sunshine	Average rainfall
January	2°C/36°F	-3°C/27°F	2	43mm/0.17in
February	3°C/37°F	-2°C/28°F	3	38mm/0.15in
March	8°C/46°F	0°C/32°F	5	38mm/0.15in
April	13°C/55°F	4°C/39°F	6	43mm/0.17in
May	18°C/64°F	8°C/46°F	8	56mm/0.22in
June	22°C/72°F	11°C/52°F	8	71mm/0.28in
July	23°C/73°F	13°C/55°F	8	53mm/0.21in
August	23°C/73°F	12°C/54°F	7	66mm/0.26in
September	18°C/64°F	9°C/48°F	6	46mm/0.18in
October	13°C/55°F	6°C/43°F	4	36mm/0.14in
November	7°C/45°F	2°C/36°F	2	51mm/0.20in
December	3°C/37°F	-1°C/30°F	1	56mm/0.22in

phone boxes are card-only. You can sometimes find a coin-operated phone in a bar or café. Phonecards for use in Germany can be bought for €5 or €10 (€10 or €20 for international phonecards) at post offices and newsstands. The minimum fee for a call from a phone box within Berlin is €0.31 (€0.02 after 6pm). Look for phone boxes marked international and with a ringing-bell symbol – you can be called back on them. At Bahnhof Zoo post office you can send telexes, faxes and use the metered pay-phones.

Most international calls are a lot cheaper if you simply dial a prefix number before the international code. This number varies regularly and can be obtained in every local newspaper or by visiting www.billigertekefonieren.de.

Operator services

For online directory enquiries (available in English), go to **www.teleauskunft.de**.

Alarm calls/Weckruf 01141 (automated, in German).
International directory enquiries 11834.
Operator assistance/German directory enquiries 11833 (11837 English-speaking only).
Phone repairs/Störungsannahme 080 0330 2000.

Telegram (Telegrammaufnahme) 01805 121 210.
Time (Zeitansage) 01191 (automated, in German).
Weather (Wettervorhersage) 0190 116 400 (automated, in German).

Mobile phones

German mobile phones networks operate at 900MHz (in common with those in the UK and Australia), so all UK and Australian mobiles should work in Berlin (providing roaming is activated). US and Canadian cell phones users (whose phones operate at 1900MHz) should check whether their phones can switch to 900MHz.

Time

Germany is on Central European Time – one hour ahead of Greenwich Mean Time. Daylight-saving time comes into operation on the last Sunday in March (clocks go forward one hour), and on the last Sunday in October (clocks go back one hour).

So, when daylight-saving is not in effect, London is one hour behind Berlin, New York is six hours behind, San Francisco is nine hours behind, and Sydney is nine hours ahead.

Germany uses a 24-hour system. 8am is '8 Uhr' (usually written 8h), noon is '12 Uhr Mittags' or just '12 Uhr', 5pm is '17 Uhr' and midnight is '12 Uhr Mitternachts' or just 'Mitternacht'.

8.15 is '8 Uhr 15' or 'Viertel nach 8'; 8.30 is '8 Uhr 30' or 'halb 9'; and 8.45 is '8 Uhr 45' or 'Viertel vor 9'.

Tipping

The standard tip in restaurants is around ten per cent, but tipping is not obligatory. Check for the words *Bedienung Inclusiv* (service included) on your bill. In a taxi round up the bill to the nearest euro.

Toilets

Berlin public toilets can be pretty scummy but the authorities have been trying to clean them up. Single-occupancy, coin-operated 'City Toilets' are becoming the norm. The toilets in main stations are looked after by an attendant and are relatively clean. Restaurants and cafés have to let you use their toilets by law and legally they can't refuse you a glass of water – though of course they can get stroppy about it.

Directory

Tourist information

Berlin Tourismus Marketing (BTM)

Europa-Center, Budapester Strasse, Charlottenburg (01805 754 040/ www.btm.de). S3, S5, S7, S9, S75, U2, U9, U12 Zoologischer Garten. **Open** 8am-7pm Mon-Sat; 9am-6pm Sun. **Map** p305 D4.

Berlin's official (though private) tourist organisation. Good website, but phoning within Berlin is ridiculously expensive. The branch below is open 9.30am-9pm daily. **Branch**: Brandenburg Gate.

EurAide

Main hall, Bahnhof Zoologischer Garten, Charlottenburg (www.euraide.de). S3, S5, S7, S9, S75, U2, U9, U12 Zoologischer Garten. **Open** *June-Oct* 8am-noon, 1-6pm daily. *Nov-May* 8am-noon, 1-4.45pm Mon-Fri. **Map** p305 C4.

Located behind the Reisezentrum in Bahnhof Zoo, this excellent office offers advice and info in English for travellers. Staff can advise on sights, hotels, tours and local transport.

Visas & immigration

A passport valid for at least three months beyond the length of stay is all that is required for UK, EU, US, Canadian and Australian citizens for a stay in Germany of up to three months. Citizens of EU countries with valid national ID cards need only show their ID cards.

Citizens of other countries should check with their local German embassy or consulate whether a visa is required.

As with any trip, you should confirm visa requirements well before you plan to travel with your country's embassy.

Residence permits

For stays of longer than three months, you'll need a residence permit. EU citizens, and those of Andorra, Australia, Canada, Cyprus, Israel, Japan, Malta, New Zealand and the United States can obtain this from the **Landeseinwohneramt Berlin**. It is free and can

normally be obtained on the day of application. Appointments are not required, but expect a long wait. You will need your passport, two photos and proof of an address in Germany (your *Anmeldungsbestätigung* – a form confirming you have registered at the Anmeldungs-amt, or registration office). If you have a work contract, take that along too and you may be granted a longer stay than you would otherwise.

If unsure about your status, contact the German Embassy in your country of origin, or your own embassy or consulate in Berlin. *See p275* **Embassies & consulates**.

Landeseinwohneramt Berlin

Friedrichstrasse 219, Mitte, 10958 (699 31 564). U6 Kochstrasse. **Open** 7.30am-2.30pm Mon, Wed; 8.30am-4pm Tue; 1-7pm Thur; 7.30am-noon Fri. **Map** p306 F4.

When to go

Berlin has a continental climate, hot in summer and cold in winter, especially when the wind blows in from the surrounding lowlands. At the end of October temperatures can fall below zero and in January and February Berlin often ices over. Spring begins in late March or April. For month by month weather details, *see p284* **Weather report**.

Women

See also p278 **Helplines** *and p275* **Health**.

Women's centres

EWA Frauenzentrum

Prenzlauer Allee 6, Prenzlauer Berg (442 5542/www.frauenzentrum.de). U2 Senefelderplatz. **Open** 10am-6pm Mon-Fri; (disco) 10pm-3am Sat. *Café & gallery* 6-11pm Mon-Thur. **Map** p303 G2.

The centre offers legal advice and counselling, and runs dozens of courses. It also hosts concerts, readings and discussion groups. The

media workshop is equipped with PCs, a darkroom, an editing suite, a well-stocked library and archive.

Working in Berlin

Berlin offers a decent range of working opportunities, but the price of accommodation is soaring and the jobs market is beginning to shrink.

The small ads in the magazines *Zitty*, *tip* and *Zweite Hand* (*see p280*) are good places to start the search for work, but jobs are filled quickly, so move fast. Teaching English is a popular choice: there is always a demand for native English speakers.

If you're studying in Berlin, try the **Studentische Arbeitsvermittlung** ('Student Job Service'). You'll need your passport, student card and a *Lohnsteuerkarte* ('tax card'), available from your local *Finanzamt* ('tax office' – listed in the *Yellow Pages*). Your tax is reclaimable. Students looking for summer work can contact the **Zentralstelle für Arbeitsvermittlung**.

The German equivalent of the Job Centre is the *Arbeitsamt* ('Employment Service'). There are very few private agencies. To find the address of your nearest office in Germany, look in the *Gelbe Seiten* under *Arbeitsämter*.

EU nationals have the right to live and work in Germany without a work permit.

Studentische Arbeits-vermittlung (TUZMA)

Hardenbergstrasse 9A, Charlottenburg (315 9340). U2 Ernst-Reuter-Platz. **Open** 7am-6pm Mon-Fri; 8am-1pm Sat. **Map** p305 C4.

Zentralstelle für Arbeitsvermittlung (ZAV)

Kurfürstendamm 206, Charlottenburg (885 9060). U12, U15 Uhlandstrasse. **Open** 8.15am-4pm Mon-Wed; 8.30am-6pm Thur; 8.15am-2pm Fri. **Map** p305 C4.

Directory

Vocabulary

see p. 42

Pronunciation

z – pronounced ts
w – like English v
v – like English f
s – like English z, but softer
r – like a throaty French r
a – as in father
e – as in day
i – as in seek
o – as in note
u – as in loot
ch – as in Scottish loch
ä – combination of a and e,
sometimes like ai in paid and
sometimes like e in set
ö – combination of o and e, as in
French eu
ü – combination of u and e, like true
ai – like pie
au – like house
ie – like free
ei – like fine
eu – like coil

Useful phrases

hello/good day – *guten Tag*
goodbye – *aufwiedersehen,*
goodbye (informal) – *tschüss*
good morning – *guten Morgen*
good evening – *guten Abend*
good night – *gute Nacht*
yes – *ja;* (emphatic) *jawohl*

no – *nein, nee*
maybe – *vielleicht*
please – *bitte*
thank you – *danke*
thank you very much – *danke schön*
excuse me – *entschuldigen Sie*
mir bitte
sorry! – *Verzeihung!*
I'm sorry, I don't speak German –
Entschuldigung, ich spreche kein
Deutsch
do you speak English? – *sprechen Sie*
Englisch?
can you speak more slowly, please? –
können Sie bitte langsamer sprechen?
my name is…– *ich heisse…*
do you have a light? – *haben Sie*
Feuer?
open/closed – *geöffnet/geschlossen*
with/without – *mit/ohne*
cheap/expensive – *billig/teuer*
big/small – *gross/klein*
entrance/exit – *Eingang/Ausgang*
push/pull – *drücken/ziehen*
I would like... – *ich möchte...*
how much is... ? – *wieviel kostet... ?*
could I have a receipt? – *darf ich bitte*
eine Quittung haben?
how do I get to... ? – *wie komme ich*
nach... ?
how far is it to... ? – *wie weit ist es*
nach... ?
where is... ? – *wo ist... ?*
airport – *der Flughafen*
railway station – *der Bahnhof*

bus station – *der Busbahnhof*
metro – *die U-Bahn*
petrol – *das Benzin*
lead-free – *bleifrei*
can you call me a cab? – *können Sie*
bitte mir ein Taxi rufen?
left – *links*
right – *rechts*
straight ahead – *gerade aus*
far – *weit*
near – *nah*
street – *die Strasse*
square – *der Platz*
help! – *Hilfe!*
I feel ill – *ich bin krank*
doctor – *der Arzt*
pharmacy – *die Apotheke*
hospital – *das Krankenhaus*

Numbers

0 *null*; 1 *eins*; 2 *zwei*; 3 *drei*; 4 *vier*;
5 *fünf*; 6 *sechs*; 7 *sieben*; 8 *acht*;
9 *neun*; 10 *zehn*; 11 *elf*; 12 *zwölf*;
13 *dreizehn*; 14 *vierzehn*; 15 *fünfzehn*;
16 *sechszehn*; 17 *siebzehn*;
18 *achtzehn*; 19 *neunzehn*;
20 *zwanzig*; 21 *einundzwanzig*;
22 *zweiundzwanzig*; 30 *dreissig*;
40 *vierzig*; 50 *fünfzig*; 60 *sechszig*;
70 *siebzig*; 80 *achtzig*; 90 *neunzig*;
100 *hundert*; 101 *hunderteins*;
110 *hundertzehn*; 200 *zweihundert*;
201 *zweihunderteins*; 1,000 *tausend*;
2,000 *zweitausend*.

It's all sausage to me!

Everyday German is rich in bizarre idioms and precise put-downs; Berliners deploy them with zest. Here are three crucial colloquialisms.

Arsch

Literally 'arse', *Arsch* is German's most common amplifier. Weather can be *arschkalt* (very cold), an observation might be *arschklar* (blindingly obvious), goods are often *arschteuer* (extremely expensive) and someone who talks a lot of crap and gets on your nerves is an *Arschgeige* ('arse violin'). To be the recipient of an *Arschkarte* ('arse ticket') is to draw the short straw, if you're *verarscht* (or *gearscht*) you've been tricked or made a fool of, and when everything's going wrong all at once you say there's an *Arschprogramm* going on. Be warned: *Arschloch* ('arsehole') is a way more serious insult than it is in English. Avoid using it unless you want to end up *am Arsch* (fucked up).

Wurst

Pork looms large in German culture. For 'I don't care' try *Mir ist alles Wurst!* – 'It's all sausage to me!'. When it comes to the crunch, say *Es geht um die Wurst!* – 'It goes around the sausage!' And if someone sulks, tell them: *Sei keine beleidigte Leberwurst!* – 'Don't be an insulted liver sausage.'

Schwein

Stuck at home alone, say *Kein Schwein ruft mich an!* – 'No pig telephones me!'. Had a stroke of luck, declare *Ich habe Schwein gehabt!* – 'I have had pig!' To express incredulity, try *Ich glaube mein Schwein pfeift!* – 'I believe my pig whistles!' A *Schweinepriester* ('pig priest') is a dishonest person, *Schweinarbeit* is a hell of a job, a *Schweinerei* is a real mess, and if a stranger's getting over-familiar, ask them: *Haben wir mal zusammen Schweine gehütet?* 'Have we sheltered pigs together?'

Directory

Further Reference

Books

We've chosen these books for quality and interest as much as for availability. Most are currently in print, but some will only be found in libraries or second-hand shops. The date given is that of the first publication in English.

Fiction

Deighton, Len *Berlin Game, Mexico Set, London Match* (London 1983, 1984, 1985)
Epic espionage trilogy with labyrinthine plot set against an accurate picture of 1980s Berlin. The next six books in the series aren't bad either.
Deighton, Len *Funeral In Berlin* (London 1964)
Best of Deighton's 1960s novels.
Döblin, Alfred *Berlin-Alexanderplatz* (London 1975)
Devastating expressionist portrait of the inter-war underworld in working class quarters of Alexanderplatz.
Eckhart, Gabriele *Hitchhiking* (Lincoln, Nebraska 1992)
Short stories viewing East Berlin through the eyes of street cleaners and a female construction worker.
Grass, Gunther *Local Anaesthetic* (New York 1970)
The Berlin angst of a schoolboy who threatens to burn a dog outside a Ku'damm café to protest against the Vietnam War is firmly satirised, albeit in Grass's irritating schoolmasterly way.
Harris, Robert *Fatherland* (London 1992)
Alternative history and detective novel set in a 1964 Berlin as the Nazis might have built it.
Isherwood, Christopher *Mr Norris Changes Trains, Goodbye To Berlin* (London 1935, 1939)
Isherwood's two Berlin novels, the basis of the movie *Cabaret*, offer finely drawn characters and a sharp picture of the decadent city as it tipped over into Nazism.
Johnson, Uwe *Two Views* (New York 1966)
Love story across the East-West divide, strong on the mood of Berlin in the late 1950s and early 1960s.
Kerr, Philip *Berlin Noir* (London 1994)
The Bernie Gunther trilogy now available in one volume, about a private detective in Nazi Berlin.

Le Carré, John *The Spy Who Came In From The Cold* (London 1963)
The prime shot-going-over-the-Wall thriller.
Markstein, George *Ultimate Issue* (London 1981)
Stark thriller of political expediency leading to uncomfortable conclusion about why the Wall went up.
McEwan, Ian *The Innocent* (London 1990)
Tale of naive young Englishman recruited into Cold War machinations with tragi-comic results.
Müller, Heiner *The Battle* (New York 1989)
Collection of plays and pieces strong on the grimness of the Stalinism and false temptations from the West.
Nabokov, Vladimir *The Gift* (New York 1963)
Written and set in 1920s Berlin, where impoverished Russian émigré dreams of writing a book very like this one.
Schneider, Peter *The Wall Jumper* (London 1984)
Somewhere between novel, prose poem and artful reportage, a meditation on the madhouse absurdities of the Wall.

Children

Kästner, Erich *Emil And The Detectives* (London 1931)
Classic set mostly around Bahnhof Zoo and Nollendorfplatz.

Biography & memoir

Baumann, Bommi *How It All Began* (Vancouver 1977)
Frank and often funny account of the Berlin origins of West German terrorism, by a former member of the June 2nd Movement.
Bielenberg, Christabel *The Past Is Myself* (London 1968)
Fascinating autobiography of an English woman who married a German lawyer and lived through the war in Berlin.
F, Christiane *H – Autobiography Of A Child Prostitute And Heroin Addict* (London 1980)
Stark account of life around the housing estates and heroin scene of 1970s West Berlin. Later filmed as *Christiane F.*
Friedrich, Ruth Andreas *The Berlin Underground 1938-45* (New York 1947)
A few courageous souls formed anti-Nazi resistance groups in Berlin.

The journalist-author's diaries capture the day-to-day fear.
Millar, Peter *Tomorrow Belongs To Me* (London 1992)
Memoir of a Prenzlauer Berg local pub by a former East Berlin Reuters correspondent.
Rimmer, Dave *Once Upon A Time In The East* (London 1992)
The collapse of communism seen stoned and from ground level – strange tales of games between East and West Berlin and travels through assorted East European revolutions.
Schirer, William L *Berlin Diaries* (New York 1941)
Foreign correspondent in Berlin 1931-1941 bears appalled witness to Europe's plunge into Armageddon.

History

Friedrich, Otto *Before The Deluge* (New York, 1972)
Vivid and entertaining portrait of Berlin in the 1920s, much of it based on interviews with those who survived what followed.
Garton Ash, Timothy *We The People* (London 1990)
Instant history of the 1989 revolutions.
Gelb, Norman *The Berlin Wall* (New York 1986)
Gripping narrative history of how the Wall went up.
Jelavich, Peter *Berlin Cabaret* (Harvard 1993)
Definitive history of Berlin cabaret from 1901to Nazi times.
McElvoy, Anne *The Saddled Cow* (London 1992)
Lively history of East Germany by a former Berlin *Times* correspondent.
Read, Anthony and Fisher, David *Berlin – The Biography Of A City* (London 1994)
Readable, lightweight history.
Richie, Alexandra *Faust's Metropolis* (London 1998)
The most detailed and exhaustive one-volume history of Berlin, but a little too heavy for holiday reading and with a rather too right-wing agenda.
Schirer, William L *The Rise And Fall Of The Third Reich* (New York 1960)
Still the most readable history of Nazi Germany.
Tusa, Ann & John *The Berlin Blockade* (London 1988)
Absorbing account of the 11 months when the Allied sector was fed from the air and Berlin, Germany and Europe proceeded to fall into two.

Architecture

Ladd, Brian *The Ghosts Of Berlin: Confronting German History In The Urban Landscape* (Chicago, 1997)
Erudite and insightful look into the relationship between architecture, urbanism and Berlin's violent political history.
Berlin-Brandenburg – An Architectural Guide (Berlin 1993)
Berlin by building, with quirky text in both English and German.
Berlin: Open City (Berlin 2001)
Excellent guide to both new building and extant architectural curiosities, built around city walks excellently detailed in fine fold-out maps.

Miscellaneous

Bertsch, Georg C & Hedler, Ernst *SED* (Cologne 1990)
Schöne Einheits Design: over 200 illustrations of crazy East German consumer product designs.
Friedrich, Thomas *Berlin – A Photographic Portrait Of The Weimar Years 1918-1933* (London 1991)
Superb photographs of lost Berlin, its personalities and its daily life, with a foreword by Stephen Spender.

Discography

From Brecht to Bowie, from Marlene to Malaria!, from Tangerine Dream to techno – 50 essential Berlin releases.

AG Geige *Raabe?* (Zensor)
One of the first post-1989 discs to emerge from the East Berlin underground came from a bizarre electronica outfit rooted in The Residents and Die Tödliche Doris.
Ash Ra Tempel *Join Inn* (Temple/Spalax)
The 1972 hippy freakout incarnation of guitarist Manuel Göttsching, before he was reborn as techno's most baffling muse.
Meret Becker *Noctambule* (Ego)
Actress/chanteuse Becker restages Weimar alongside Berliner Krankheit classics like Neubauten's *Schwarz*.
The Birthday Party *Mutiny/The Bad Seed EP* (4AD)
Nick Cave and cohorts escaped drab London for the fevered creativity of early 1980s Berlin to record their two most intense EPs, here compressed into one volatile CD.
David Bowie *Heroes* (EMI)
In which Bowie romanticises the Wall and captures the atmosphere of (misspelt) *Neuköln*.

David Bowie *Low* (EMI)
Begun in France, completed at Hansa Studios, the album that heralded Bowie's new career in a new town.
Brecht/Weill *Die Dreigroschenoper Berlin 1930* (Teldec)
Historic shellac transcriptions from 1930 featuring a young and shrill Lotte Lenya, who also contributes a brace of *Mahagony* songs.
Caspar Brötzmann/FM Einheit *Merry Christmas* (Blast First/Rough Trade Deutschland)
Guitarist son Caspar is no less noisy than père Brötzmann, especially on this frenzy of feedback and distortion kicked up with ex-Neubauten man-mountain FM Einheit on, er, stones.
Peter Brötzmann *No Nothing* (FMP)
Uncharacteristically introspective recording from the sax colossus of German improvisation for Berlin's vital Free Music Production label, which he co-founded 30 years ago.
Ernst Busch *Der Rote Orpheus/Der Barrikaden Tauber* (BARBArossa)
Two-CD survey of the great revolutionary tenor's 1930s recordings covers Brecht, Eisler and Weill, plus his morale boosters for the Spanish International Brigades.
Nick Cave *From Her To Eternity* (Mute)
The Australian expat in best Berlinerisch debauched and desperate mode, with a title track later featured in *Wings of Desire*.
Comedian Harmonists *Ihre grossen Erfolge* (Laserlight)
Sublime six-part harmonies from the Weimar singing sensations whose career was cut short during the Third Reich.
Crime & The City Solution *Paradise Discotheque* (Mute)
Underrated Berlin-Australian émigré group's finest disc (1990) is an oblique commentary on the heady 'neo-black market burnt-out ruins' amorality of the immediate post-1989 era.
DAF *Kebabträume* (Mute)
Exhilarating German punk satire of Berlin's Cold War neuroses, culminating in the coda 'We are the Turks of tomorrow'.
Marlene Dietrich *On Screen, Stage And Radio* (Legend)
From 'I Am The Sexy Lola' through 'Ruins Of Berlin', the sultry Schöneberg songstress embodies the mood of decadent Berlin.
Einstürzende Neubauten *Berlin Babylon Soundtrack* (Zomba)
More Neubauten 'Strategies Against Architecture' accompanying a highly watchable documentary about the headspinning changes in Berlin's urban landscape and the movers and shakers behind them.

Einstürzende Neubauten *Eclipse Of The Sun EP* (Mute/Rough Trade Germany)
Recorded in the run-up to their year 2000 celebrations of two decades spent in a state of permanent collapse, *Eclipse* shades in a more reflective side to Neubauten's destructive character.
Alec Empire *The Geist Of…* (Geist)
Wonderful triple CD compilation of ATR mainman Empire's less combative electronica explorations for Frankfurt brainiac label Force Inc/Mille Plateaux.
Manuel Göttsching *E2-E4* (Racket)
The great lost waveform guitar album by the ex-Ash Ra Tempel leader beloved by Berlin technoheads.
Gudrun Gut & Various *The Ocean Club* (Alternation)
Ex-Malaria! member Gudrun Gut's Ocean Club is a congenial cyberport for ambient song collaborations between singers, artists and programmers as disparate as Blixa Bargeld, Anita Lane, Katherine Franck, Thomas Fehlmann and Johnny Klimek.
Die Haut *Head On* (What's So Funny About)
Avantish Berlin equivalent of The Ventures lay down Morricone-meets-Loony-Tunes backdrops for guest singers like Alan Vega, Lydia Lunch, Kim Gordon and Jeffrey Lee Pierce.
Liaisons Dangereuses *Liaisons Dangereuses* (Roadrunner)
Formed by ex-DAF member Chrislo Haas, their solitary 1982 album of chipped beats and industrial atmospheres was a key influence on Detroit's techno pioneers.
Malaria! *Compiled* (Moabit Musik)
What with their tell-tale song titles – 'Passion', 'Jealousy', 'Power' and 'Death' – and suffocating swirls of synths and heavy-stepping beats, Malaria! was girl-pop, Berlin-style.
Maurizio *M* (M)
Essential CD compilation of Basic Channel mainman Moritz Von Oswald's vinyl releases, which lights up Chicago house with streaming beats diverted from the Berlin-Detroit techno grid.
Monolake *Hong Kong* (Chain Reaction)
Again more from the Basic Channel family, Monolake's debut album is an improbable fusion of cool central European electronica and sub-tropical humidity, rippling with strangely distressed pulses.
Barbara Morgenstern *Vermona ET-61* (Monika)
Morgenstern's everywoman voice, deceptively simple lyrics and clever accompaniment on a GDR home

organ really grow on you after repeated listenings, but *Vemona*'s achingly beautiful instrumentals are the album's true highlights.

Pole *CD1* (Kiff SM)
Ex-Basic Channel engineer Stefan Betke is now at the cutting edge of the digidub school of blunted beats and vinyl glitches.

Iggy Pop *The Idiot* (Virgin America)
With Bowie in the producer's chair, Iggy begins to absorb the influence of early German electronica and the city of bright, white clubbing.

Iggy Pop *Lust For Life*
(Virgin America)
Way back in West Berlin, Iggy the passenger cruises through the divided city's ripped-back sides and finds himself full of lust for life.

Lou Reed *Berlin* (RCA)
Although he'd never even been to the city, Lou somehow still got it right in this melancholy Meisterwerk.

Spacebow *Big Waves* (Noteworks)
Extraordinary set of reverberating metallic sound sculptures hewn from Berlin-based American expatriate artist Robert Rutman's steel cellos.

Stereo Total *My Melody*
(Bungalow)
Demented chansons with cheesy lounge backing – Mitte's kitsch aesthetic plus a Francophone spin.

Tangerine Dream *Zeit*
(Jive Electro)
Where cosmic consciousness and electronic minimalism first met by the Wall.

Terranova *Close The Door* (K7)
Dark and intelligent trip hop from the WMF axis, featuring guest appearance by Tricky.

Die Tödliche Doris *Die Unsichtbare 5te LP Materialisiert Als CD* (Die Tödliche Doris Schallplatten)
The 1980s Berlin dada trio's only CD is the product of the union of two separate vinyl albums played simultaneously.

Ton Steine Scherben
Keine Macht Für Niemand
(David Volksmund)
Ernst Busch reincarnated as the early 1970s rock commune which provided Kreuzberg's anarchists with their most enduring anthems.

Paul van Dyk *Seven Ways* (MFS)
Eisenhüttenstadt's prime export is trance's one-trick pony, but here shows it off at its best.

Various *alaska.de Soundtrack*
(Kitty-yo)
While CD One is a serviceable, if not surprising, sampler of recent Kitty-yo hits by Peaches, Gonzales, Surrogat et al., the second disc harbours meyermoserdöring's moody score, which evokes Berlin banlieue ennui with less clichés than the film's visuals.

Various *Assorted Stadtansichten*
(MFS)
The MFS stable circa 1999 respond to the changing cityscape and honour the innovators of Berlin techno. Selection includes Corvin Dalek, Chris Zippel, Cal-Q-Lator and Cybersecrecy.

Various *Das Beste Aus Der DDR Parts I-III* (Amiga)
Three-part DDR rock retrospective, divided into rock, pop and 'Kult', including Ostalgia stalwarts like Puhdys, Silly and Karat plus Sandow's alt anthem 'Born in the GDR' and an early Nina Hagen ditty.

Various *Berlin 1992* (Tresor)
On the first of several Tresor compilations Berlin techno is captured in its early, apocalyptic phase. Includes Love Parade anthem 'Der Klang der Familie' by 3Phase (at that time, Dr Motte & Sven Röhrig).

Various *Cabaret: Music From The Original Soundtrack* (MCA)
Life is a cabaret, old chum: the very definition of the Berlin myth.

Various *Digital Hardcore Recordings... Riot Zone* (DHR)
Atari Teenage Riot's 1997 riotbeat label compilation also showcases the anarcho-comicbook radicalism of acolytes Shizuo, Christoph De Babalon and EC8OR.

Various *Freischwimmer* (Kitty-Yo)
Sampler covering five years of work on Mitte's premier post-rock indie label. Acts include Laub, Tarwater, Raz O'Hara, Gonzalez.

Various *Hotel-Stadt-Berlin: A Showcase of New Electronic Record Labels from Berlin*
(Hausmusik/Kompakt/Indigo)
Handy overview bodes well for future developments, with local electronica musicians exploring paths off the beaten track of techno and trance.

Various *Pop 2000*
(Grönland/Spiegel Edition)
Eight-CD companion to TV chronicle of postwar German culture in East and West. 'Ostrock' is a bit underrepresented, but otherwise an engaging compilation of the obvious and the obscure.

Various *Tranceformed From Beyond* (MFS)
The compilation that defined Berlin trance. The segued selection includes Cosmic Baby, Microglobe, Effective Force and others.

Vermooste Vløten *ngongo*
(Flittchen)
Nico-like debut from most promising signing of women-orientated label run by former Lassie Singer Christiane Roesinger.

Westbam *A Practising Maniac At Work* (Low Spirit)
Album that effectively summarises the best of Berlin's best-known DJ, veering from stomping techno to twisted disco.

Time Out
www.timeout.com/berlin
Naturally, we think this is pretty good, containing general information and history and the useful International Agenda, a weekly calendar of things to do and see, written by residents.

berlinfo.com
www.berlinfo.com
Up-to-date information about many aspects of life in Berlin, designed for residents and visitors alike. It contains film and theatre listings, as well as handy lists of professionals – doctors, lawyers, tax accountants – who speak English.

Berlin Info
www.berlin-info.de/index_e.html
Fairly comprehensive source of information and links, but the English translation is often painful (and sometimes missing) and the writing undiscerning. Operated by the official tourist board BTM (*see p285*) and oriented to upmarket tourism.

berlin.de
www.berlin.de
Berlin's official site – run by the tourist board (BTM) – is inevitably not its most objective but is nonelessless well-written.

HotelGuide
berlin.hotelguide.net
A commercial site that sends you to the most expensive hotels, but then they're the ones which have online reservation services.

www.net4berlin.com
A goofy site, very Kreuzberg-oriented, with some hotel and restaurant listings.

SMPK
www.smb.spk-berlin.de
Smart bilingual site with information on more than 20 Berlin museums run by SMPK.

stadtplandienst
www.stadtplandienst.de
An interactive map that can pinpoint any address in the city; zoomable so you can figure out how to get there.

Stadtmuseum Berlin
www.stadtmuseum.de
Comprehensive information on Berlin's museums and useful links. In German only.

BVG
www.bvg.de/e_index.html
Online timetable and public transport information for Berlin/Brandenburg.

Zitty
www.zitty.de
The online sister of Berlin's main listings publication. This rather crowded site contains listing information and has search functions. In German only.

Directory

Index

Index

Advertisers' Index

Please refer to relevant sections for addresses
and telephone numbers

Place of interest and/or entertainment	▮
Railway station	▮
Park	▯
Hospital/university	▮
Pedestrian Area	▯
Church	✚
S-Bahn Station	Ⓢ
U-Bahn Station	Ⓤ
S-Bahn line	S1
U-Bahn line	U1
District boundary	▬
Course of Wall	▬
Area	MITTE

Maps

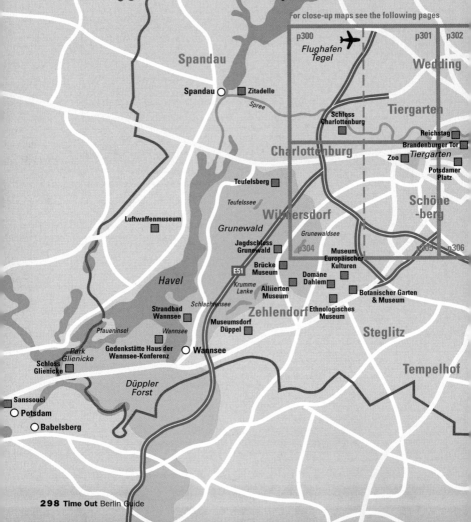

Berlin & Around

Reinickendorf

Tegeler See

For close-up maps see the following pages

p300

Flughafen Tegel

p301 p302

Wedding

Spandau

Spandau ○ ■ Zitadelle

Spree

■ Schloss Charlottenburg

Charlottenburg

Tiergarten

Reichstag ■

Brandenburger Tor ■

Zoo ■ *Tiergarten*

Potsdamer Platz ■

Teufelsberg ■

Teufelssee

Wilmersdorf

Schöne -berg

Grunewald

Grunewaldsee

Luftwaffenmuseum ■

Jagdschloss Grunewald ■

p304

p305 p306

Museum Europäischer Kulturen ■

Brücke Museum ■

Havel

E51

Krumme Lanke

Domäne Dahlem ■

Alliierten Museum ■

Botanischer Garten & Museum ■

Schlachtensee

Strandbad Wannsee ■

Zehlendorf

Ethnologisches Museum ■

Steglitz

Pfaueninsel

Museumsdorf Düppel ■

Wannsee

Gedenkstätte Haus der Wannsee-Konferenz

○ Wannsee

Park Glienicke

Schloss Glienicke ■

Tempelhof

Düppler Forst

■ Sanssouci

○ Potsdam

○ Babelsberg

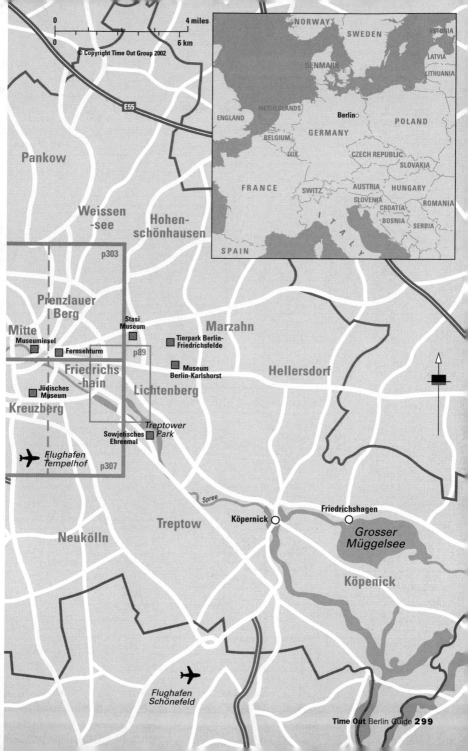

0
0
4 miles
6 km

© Copyright Time Out Group 2002

E55

NORWAY   **SWEDEN**   **ESTONIA**
LATVIA
DENMARK   **LITHUANIA**
ENGLAND   **NETHERLANDS**   Berlin○   **POLAND**
GERMANY
BELGIUM   **LUX.**   **CZECH REPUBLIC**
SLOVAKIA
FRANCE   **SWITZ**   **AUSTRIA**   **HUNGARY**
SLOVENIA   **ROMANIA**
I   **CROATIA**
T   **BOSNIA**   **SERBIA**
A
L
Y
SPAIN

Pankow

Weissen
-see   **Hohen-**
schönhausen

p303

Prenzlauer
Berg

Mitte   Stasi
Museum   **Marzahn**

Museuminsel   Tierpark Berlin-
Fernsehturm   Friedrichsfelde

p89   Museum
Berlin-Karlshorst   **Hellersdorf**

Friedrichs
-hain   **Lichtenberg**

Jüdisches
Museum

Kreuzberg   **Treptower**
Park

Sowjetisches
Ehrenmal

Flughafen
Tempelhof   p307

Spree

Treptow   Köpernick ○   Friedrichshagen ○

Neukölln   *Grosser*
Müggelsee

Köpenick

Flughafen
Schönefeld

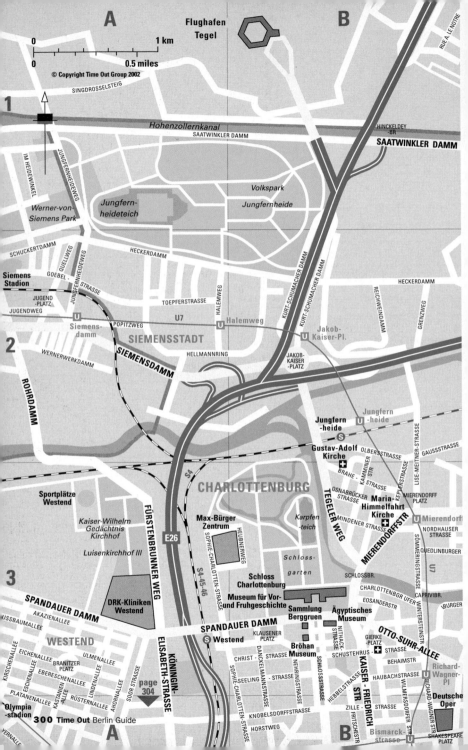

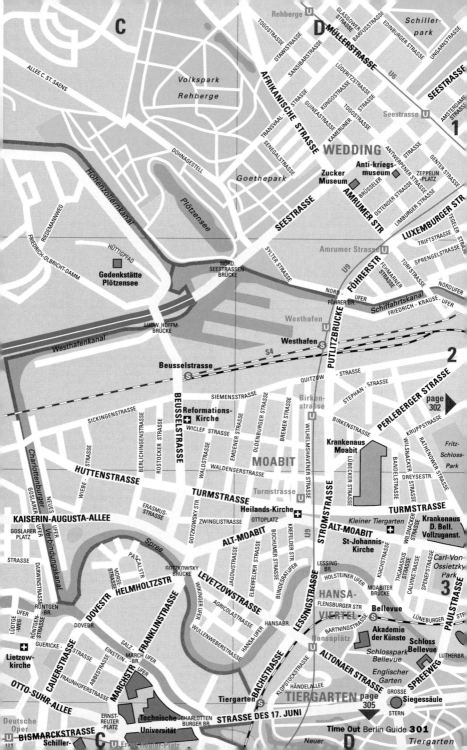

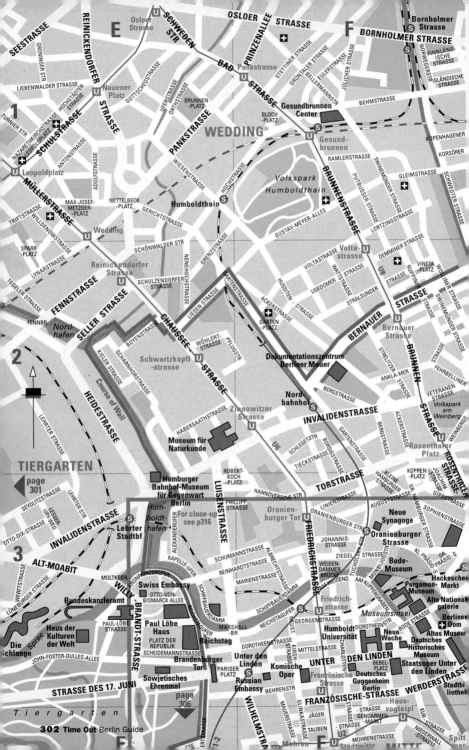

OSLOER ALLEE STRASSE

SEESTRASSE

REINICKENDORFER STRASSE

BORNHOLMER STRASSE

Osloer Strasse

SCHWEDEN STR

BAD STRASSE

Nauener Platz

PANKSTRASSE

WEDDING

Gesundbrunnen Center

Gesund- brunnen

Leopoldplatz

MÜLLERSTRASSE

Wedding

Volkspark Humboldthain

Humboldthain

BRUNNENSTRASSE

Volta- strasse

U8

FENNSTRASSE

Reinickendorfer Strasse

SELLER STRASSE

CHAUSSEE STRASSE

BERNAUER STRASSE

Bernauer Strasse

BRUNNEN-

Nord- hafen

Schwartzkopff -strasse

Dokumentations- zentrum Berliner Mauer

STRASSE

Course of Wall

HEIDESTRASSE

Zinnowitzer Strasse

Nord- bahnhof

ROSENTHALER

Museum für Naturkunde

INVALIDENSTRASSE

U6

TORSTRASSE

Rosenthaler Platz

TIERGARTEN page 301

Hamburger Bahnhof-Museum für Gegenwart Berlin

For close-up see p316

Oranien- burger Tor

Neue Synagoge

Oranienburger Strasse

INVALIDENSTRASSE

Humboldt- hafen

Lehrter Stadtbf

LUISENSTRASSE

FRIEDRICHSTRASSE

Bode- Museum

Pergamon- Museum

Alte National- galerie

ALT-MOABIT

Swiss Embassy

Friedrich- strasse

Museumsinsel

Hackescher Markt

Bundeskanzleramt

Paul Löbe Haus

WILLY-BRANDT-STRASSE

Berliner Dom

Die Schlange

Haus der Kulturen der Welt

Reichstag

Brandenburger Tor

Unter den Linden

Komische Oper

UNTER DEN LINDEN

Humboldt Universität

Neue Wache

Altes Museum

Deutsches Historisches Museum

Staatsoper Unter den Linden

WERDERSTR

Sowjetisches Ehrenmal

Russian Embassy

Französische Strasse

Deutsche Guggenheim Berlin

FRANZÖSISCHE-STRASSE

Haus- vogteipl

Stadtbi liothek

STRASSE DES 17. JUNI

page 306

Tiergarten

WILHELMSTR

GENDARMEN- MARKT

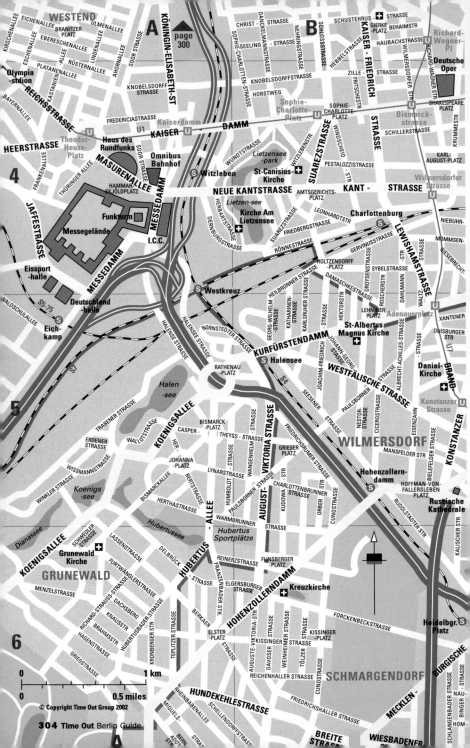

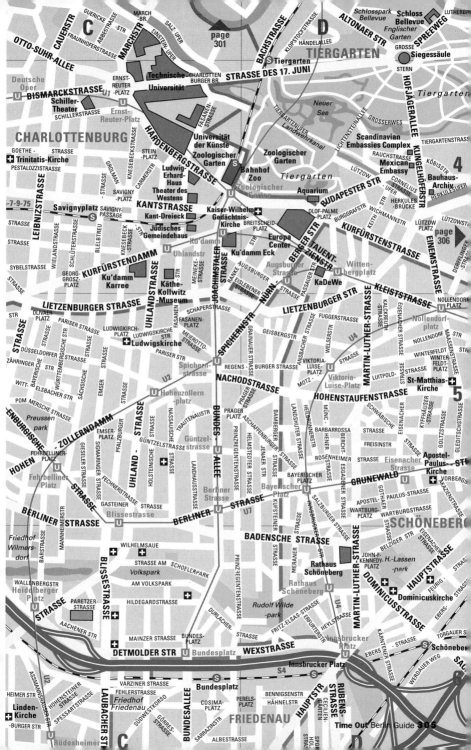

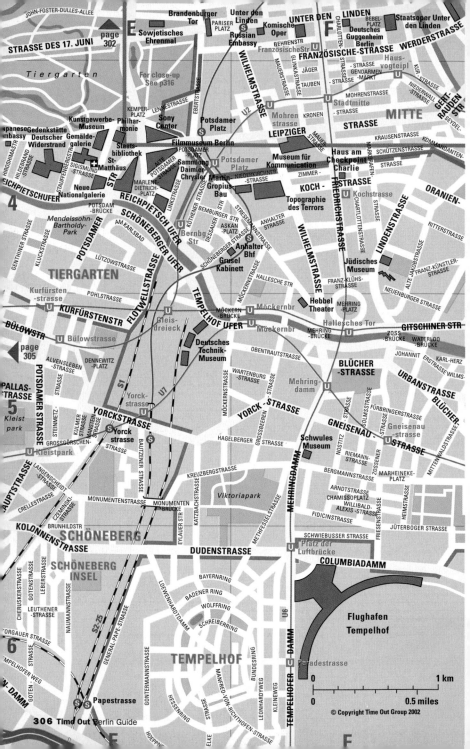

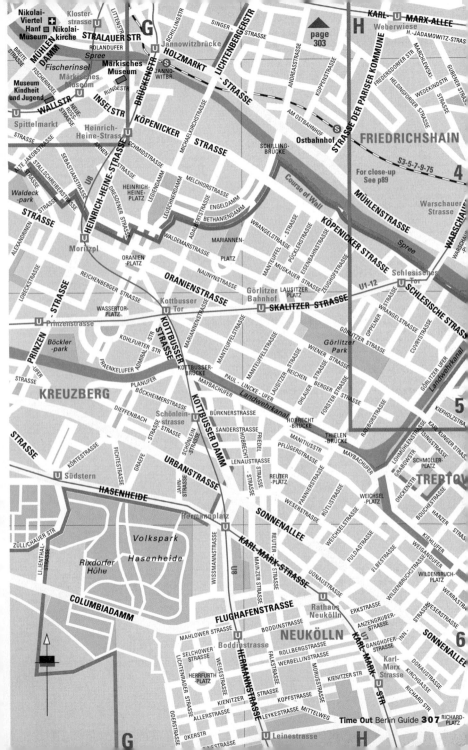

Truly Original

Time Out

LONDON'S
LIVING GUIDE
EVERY WEEK

timeout.com

PHOTO: JONATHON FOSTER/WILLIAMS

Street Index

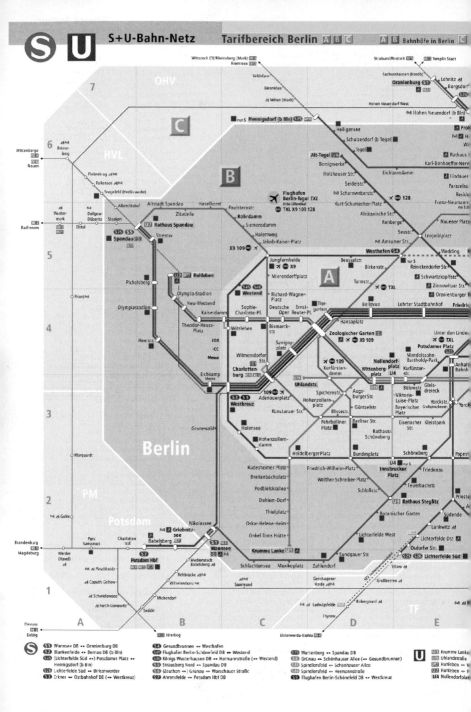

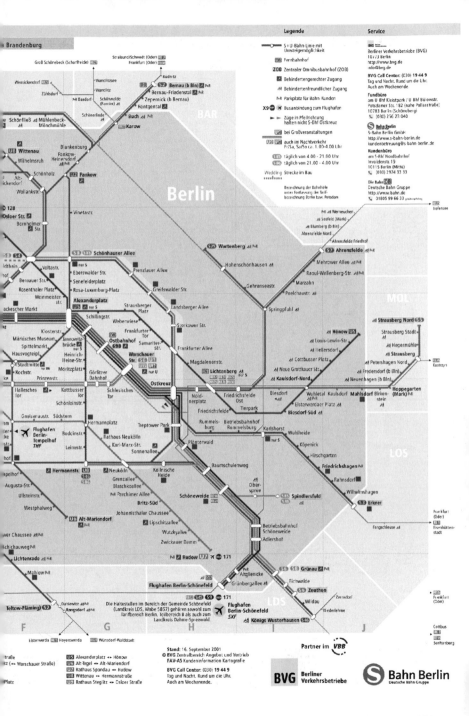

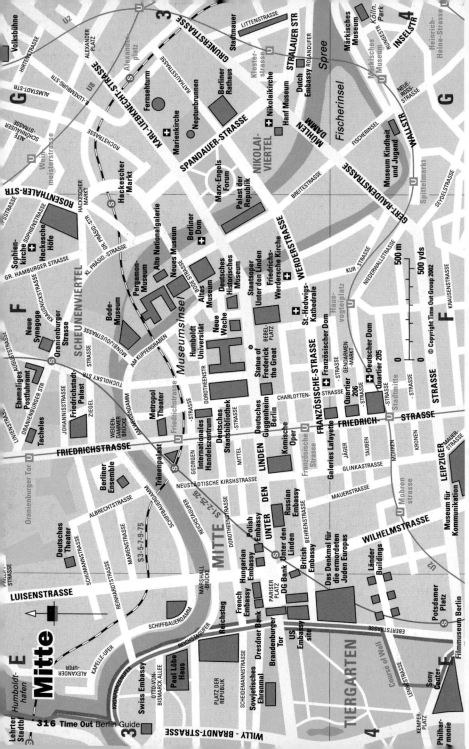

Mitte

LUISENSTRASSE